EMPIRICAL ISSUES IN RAISING EQUITY CAPITAL

ADVANCES IN FINANCE, INVESTMENT AND BANKING

SERIES EDITOR: ELROY DIMSON

VOLUME 1

Japanese Financial Institutions in Europe
D. Arora

VOLUME 2

Empirical Issues in Raising Equity Capital
M. Levis (Editor)

EMPIRICAL ISSUES
IN RAISING
EQUITY CAPITAL

Edited by
Mario Levis

1996
ELSEVIER
Amsterdam – Lausanne – New York – Oxford – Shannon – Tokyo

ELSEVIER SCIENCE B.V.
Sara Burgerhartstraat 25
P.O. Box 211, 1000 AE Amsterdam, The Netherlands

ISBN: 0 444 82469 3

Introduction to the Series

This series, presents a number of hitherto unpublished studies on a variety of financial themes.

The subjects covered by the *Advances in Finance Investment and Banking* (AFIB) book series include financial institutions and markets, corporate finance, portfolio investment, regulatory issues in banking and finance, comparative surveys, international taxation and accounting issues, and relevant macro-economics and asset pricing research studies. Books in this series include contributed volumes and edited conference proceedings, as well as single authored monographs such as this one. The attributes which bind these contributions together into a series are the focus on theoretical, empirical and applied issues within the field of finance.

Contributions stem from authors all over the world; their focus is consistently international. The editors of the AFIB series join me in hoping that the publication of these studies will help to stimulate international efforts in achieving advances within the fields covered by the series.

Elroy Dimson

Preface

The increasing reliance on capital markets as a source of business finance has gained momentum across the world over the past decade. The early success of the British privatisation programme, the liberalisation of international capital markets and the search for new investment opportunities by institutional investors helped to create a climate congenial for equity financing. In spite of such developments and the significant progress made towards a better understanding of financing decisions, our knowledge still remains incomplete.

The volume aims to help corporate financiers, investment bankers, fund managers and investors understand the factors and processes that determine the valuation of new equity issues, the methods of raising equity capital in domestic and international markets and the choice among the various funding alternatives.

The volume was motivated and compiled in the belief that new insights in this area can be gleaned from careful and consistent study of the empirical evidence. The papers have been selected to cover a wide range of issues including initial public offerings, privatisation issues, seasoned issues and international equity offerings with data from more than eight countries in Europe, the Far East and the Americas. They all represent original contributions in their specific subject areas.

There are many people who have contributed to this book. First, I wish to thank Elroy Dimson from London Business School who, as the editor for the series in *Advances in Finance, Investment and Banking,* has encouraged the development of this book.

My colleagues Meziane Lasfer and Dylan Thomas, positive as ever, have offered valuable help by providing advice on interesting papers and practical comments on earlier versions of the book. A number of people provided constructive reviews of the papers in this volume; the comments of Rajina Gibson, Shanta Hegde, Alexander Ljungqvist, Bill Rees, and Rama Seth have undoubtedly resulted in significant improvements in the overall quality of this volume. Three students at the Doctoral programme at City University Business School – Alexander Arauner, Marcus Gerbich and Chanon – have provided valuable assistance at different stages of the volume's development.

The production of the book was made possible by the determined efforts of Jome Carmichael and Kinga Gabnai while Treja van den Heuvel, the Publishing Editor has provided support and inspiration. I am indebted to them and to the City University Business School Research Fund which funded this project.

Finally, my greatest debt is to the 31 contributing authors who have entrusted me with their original and previously unpublished work. In a world increasingly dominated by research ratings and journal leagues, this is a most generous gesture. I am most grateful to them all.

Mario Levis
City University Business School

Contributors

Alexander Arauner
City University Business School

Ekkehart Böhmer
University of Berlin

Alistair Byrne
Scottish Equitable plc

Birgul Caramanolis
University of Lausanne

Chao Chen
California State University

Ali Fatemi
Kansas State University

Chenyang Feng
Georgia State University

Rajna Gibson
University of Lausanne

Costas Grammenos
City University Business School

Shanta Hedge
University of Connecticut

Christos Kazantzis
University of Piraeus

Robert Krainer
University of Wisconsin-Madison

Benoit Leleux
Babson College

Mario Levis
City University Business School

Timothy Lin
National Chung Cheng University

Alexander Ljungqvist
Oxford University

Stelios Marcoulis
City University Business School

Kojo Menyah
London Guildhall Univertsity

Robert Miller
Northern Illinois

Sudhir Nanda
Pennsylvania State University at Harrisburg

James Owers
Georgia State University

Frank Packer
Federal Reserve Bank of New York

Remy Paliard
Groupe ESC Lyon

Krishna Paudyal
Glasgow Caledonian University

William Rees
University of Glasgow

Garry Sanger
Louisiana State University

Rama Seth
Federal Reserve Bank of New York

Dylan Thomas
City University Business School

Ian Tonks
University of Bristol and London School of Economics

Nils Tuchschmid
University of Lausanne

Alireza Rad
Limburg University

Sanjay Varshney
State University of New York

Contents

Empirical Issues in Raising Equity Capital

Mario Levis
City University Business School

1. Introduction

One of the striking features of applied corporate finance is the relatively low proportion of equity used in funding new capital expenditure. Myers (1984) in his seminal paper The Capital Structure Puzzle argues that firms avoid issuing equity because they do not want to offer stock at a price they think is too low. Accordingly, they prefer internal funds as the first form of financing investment projects; issuing of equity takes place only when the firm has insufficient cash flow from internal resources and has exhausted the potential for issuing additional external debt. Given the difficulties in designing empirical tests to distinguish clearly between the pecking order theory from other alternative explanations, it is not surprising that Myers concludes that the "capital structure puzzle is tougher than the dividend one."

Although the fundamental premise of Myers' conclusion remains largely intact, the research effort of the last twelve years has proved very fruitful. We have made significant progress both in our understanding of the motivation of firms' changes in financing decisions and of the markets' response to those changes. Such gains have been achieved through meticulous and painstaking collection of relevant evidence and some innovative analysis and application. The compilation of this book is based on the fundamental belief that continuous observation and study of empirical evidence is likely to provide more immediate and valuable insights into firms' financing behaviour than a general grand theory. Thus, the objective of this volume is to shed some additional light into the main issues surrounding equity financing decisions of listed firms. Each of the 17 papers in this book offers some new empirical evidence that helps us to appreciate some of the complex issues surrounding equity financing decisions.

Our existing knowledge in the subject area can best be described by a number of stylised facts related to the three types of equity offerings most commonly used by industrial firms, i.e. Initial Public Offerings (IPOs), Seasoned Equity Offerings (SEOs) and International Equity Offerings (IEOs). The following section provides a concise review of the empirical evidence accumulated in recent years related to these three areas. It is based on the "weight of evidence" principle and focuses on what I consider to be the most important aspects of equity financing decisions. As such it does not cover a range of studies that provide interesting but rather idiosyncratic results nor does it include evidence that is deemed only peripheral to the essence of the above three types of raising equity decisions.

2. The Stylised Facts

2.1. Initial Public Offerings

Initial public offerings have been probably researched more than any of the other two types of offerings in recent years. The empirical work in this area has covered relatively long time periods with good sample sizes and, more importantly, has covered a number of national capital markets. The liberalisation of many of the world's markets in the 1980's together with rapid economic growth has also encouraged an unprecedented number of private firms to seek a public listing. These developments have brought unique opportunities to study patterns of financing behaviour across a variety of institutional settings. The collective evidence points to a number of stylised facts:

1.   IPOs exhibit significant abnormal returns at the first day of trading. Such returns are usually interpreted as evidence of deliberate underpricing at the time of the offer.[1] The average first day return in the US and the UK, the two countries with the heaviest IPO activity, is about 15%. This represents an indirect cost of raising equity and is in addition to an average 11% that represents the direct costs involved in an IPO.[2]

2.   There is not a single explanation that can account for the apparent underpricing of new issues at the time of the offer. We know, however, that first day returns are related to a number of company-specific characteristics and the reputation of the professional advisors involved in the issue.[3] The active participation of experienced venture capitalists also appears to reduce the need for underpricing.[4]

3.   Rock's winner's curse hypothesis retains its position as the academics' favourite explanation for the underpricing of IPOs. In spite of the inherent difficulties in designing unambiguous empirical tests, the available evidence is consistent with the predictions of the model.[5]

4.   First day returns are related to the method of issue and the institutional characteristics of the capital market. The choice between an offer at a fixed price (the traditional approach in the UK and in other countries) and book-building (the method favoured in the US) appears to have implications on the pricing of the issue. Other specific regulatory constraints also have a significant impact on the pricing of the new issue.[6] Their impact is probably better demonstrated in countries with unusual intervention practices in their new issue markets.

5.   There are cycles in the volume of new issues and the magnitude of first day returns. The evidence from different capital markets indicates that firms attempt to time their issues at points in time when going public is attractive. Both monthly initial returns and new issue volume are highly autocorrelated; moreover, initial returns lead volume by 6-12 months.[7] The issuing practices of closed-end fund managers also suggest some attempt to time their new issues to coincide with significant declines in the discounts of similar types of existing funds.[8]

6.   IPOs underperform similar type seasoned firms in the 3 years following their day of flotation. Although this pattern of underperformance has now been documented for a number of different countries and over different time periods,

the underlying reasons for this pattern of behaviour remain elusive.[9] The accepted wisdom in the current academic literature is that issuers take advantage of windows of opportunity to time their issues when investors are over-optimistic about the growth prospects of newly floated companies. Although this type of explanation finds support from a variety of sources, the robustness of this conclusion must still be regarded as an open issue. There is, for example, some evidence to suggest that venture capital-backed IPOs outperform nonventure capital-backed IPOs during the five years subsequent to the offering.[10]

7.   The operating performance of IPO firms deteriorates in the three years following flotation.[11] Such evidence, although consistent with the results of studies based on market performance, still runs counter to the popular belief that at least some of the newly listed firms offer exceptional earnings growth potential. Broadly similar results have been documented for Japanese investment type issuers who also appear to time their flotation around the peak of their accounting performance. In contrast to the US evidence, however, it is mainly the debt-repayment type issuers who time their offering of new shares with a hot stock market and thus underperform significantly in the aftermarket.[12] Differences in operating performance are also observed between "mature" and "younger" firms.[13]

2.2. Seasoned Equity Offerings

Equity issues take the form of either a rights issue or a general cash offer. While in Europe firms generally use rights issues, in the USA general cash offers is the dominant method. SEOs have many similarities to IPOs. They both involve the raising of equity capital, the transfer of some ownership in the company from existing to new shareholders while the distribution of shares is governed by the regulatory framework in the country of operation. Thus, it is not surprising that the empirical behaviour of SEOs shares some common characteristics with IPOs:

1.   There is a negative stock price reaction to the announcement of a new seasoned equity issue. Surveys of different studies document an average wealth loss of 3% on the announcement of equity issues by industrial firms.[14] This represents a significant drain on capital resources. The negative announcement effect is roughly equivalent to a third of the amount of capital raised.[15]

2.   Conventional academic wisdom attributes the decline in market value at the announcement of the SEO to information asymmetry problems between existing and new shareholders. Financing decisions are usually thought to reveal information about a firm's future cash flows that market participants do not have. Thus, it is argued that the sudden price decline reflects the market's belief that an equity issue conveys the signal that the assets in place are overvalued or that the level of internally generated funds is less than the market expected.[16] The presence of similar patterns of returns in the cases of rights issues, where there is no information asymmetry, continues to represent an interesting challenge.

3. The adverse selection problem is not uniform across all type of firms. A number of issue-specific characteristics such as the size of the offer, the growth of earnings and the pre-announcement price run-up appear to have a significant impact on stock offer announcement period returns.[17] The adverse selection problem is also related to the business cycle. The average negative price reaction to seasoned common stock offering announcements is significantly lower in expansionary periods and in periods with high volumes of equity financing.[18]

4. Issuing equity by a firm-commitment offer is significantly more expensive than rights issues even after adjustment for firm-specific characteristics.[19] In spite of the various possible explanations offered to account for the choice of firm-commitment offers by US firms, this preference remains a paradox.

5. There are cycles in the volume of SEO activity. The volume of SEO activity is related to the business cycle. The frequency of equity offers, relative to debt, increases in expansionary phases of the business cycle and decreases in the contractionary phases.[20]

6. There is long-run underperformance following the issuance of equity capital. The US evidence suggests that issuing firms significantly underperform similar non-issuing ones in the 3 years following the announcement of a SEO. A similar pattern of underperformance is observed for Japan and even for firms in UK and South Africa offering rights issues.[21] It is worth noting, however, that there appear to be some differences in performance depending on the intended usage of the SEO proceeds.[22]

7. There is deterioration of operating performance in the years following the SEO.[23] It appears that the improvement in operating performance usually observed in the year leading to the issue is rather short lived.[24] Performance reverses to pre-issue levels soon after the offering. A similar pattern of underperformance following a SEO has also been observed for Japanese offerings.[25] Welch and Wong (1995) argue that the apparent deterioration in operating performance may be related to the accounting practices of issuing firms. They argue that investors behave as if they naively extrapolate pre-issue earnings performance and ignore information contained in discretionary accruals to predict future stock price performance.

2.3. International Equity Offerings

International equity offerings provide companies with an enlarged ownership base, an enhanced local market for shares and the opportunity to raise new capital. Even companies in small or underdeveloped economies can raise funds from a potentially vast base of new investors. IEOs remain, the least researched of the three types of offerings. This is not surprising, however, since it is only recently that such offerings have been used widely and the data is not yet as readily as available as for domestic offerings. Most of the studies focus on American Depository Receipts (ADRs) although they are not the only form of raising capital outside the home jurisdiction. The analysis of such issues is however, often complicated by the different types of ADRs in the market. An ADR may either be sponsored or unsponsored and falls into one of four broad categories depending on the market on which the ADRs trade, whether or not new capital is raised through the programme and whether they comply with US-GAAP. The existing body of literature points to two main stylised facts about the behaviour of international equity offerings:

1.   The effect of an international listing on the value of the firm remains ambiguous. US firms listed on European or Asian stock exchanges exhibit negative or zero abnormal returns in the prelisting period.[26] On the other hand non-US firms experience positive abnormal returns around the listing in the US, or in the pre-listing period, and a decline in expected returns in the post-listing period.[27] This empirical evidence lends support to the theoretical implications that the valuation impact of international listing is determined by institutional differences across stock markets. Firms that can reduce barriers to investment by listing on a foreign stock exchange experience higher benefits from going international.

2.   The inclusion of a foreign tranche in an equity offering reduces the direct cost of the issue even after controlling for possible confounding effects. A global issue also appears to alleviate the problem of the negative stock price reaction usually associated with a seasoned equity offering.[28]

3. The Issuing Mechanism

Loughran et al. (1994), in their review of different mechanisms for distributing shares in an initial public offering, clearly demonstrate that such differences are neither cosmetic nor do they just reflect traditions in different capital markets; the varying mechanisms appear to have a marked impact of the valuation of the company and the subsequent cost of capital. In chapter 2, *Kojo Menyah and Krishna Paudyal* highlight the strategic importance of the method used for distributing shares. They focus on privatisation issues in UK during the period 1981-91. Such issues provide a suitable vehicle to test the efficacy of certain distribution methods in achieving set strategic objectives. They argue that the sale of shares at different stages, the proportion of the shares sold, the shares allocated to overseas investors and the regulatory situation of a company represent the key strategic decisions made by the government prior to the sale. In line with previous evidence in UK and other countries, they show that initial returns, as well cost of underpricing to the company, are both lower under the tender method in comparison to the offer for sale. The apparent preference for large single issues rather than a number of subsequent issues which could potentially, maximise the proceeds is based on the overriding strategy to ensure that the irreversibility of the privatisation process. The choice of a fixed price as a method of privatisation to achieve the wider ownership objective is based on the assumption that individual investors are uncomfortable with tender offers. The price for achieving these objectives was significant. It is estimated that about 23% of the value of the firms was lost by the government to subscribers. This is mainly attributed to the fact that partial sales and tender offer were not extensively used in the initial public offers. The extent of the underpricing can also be illustrated by the significant positive returns in the aftermarket and the marked reduction in underpricing for secondary offers.

Benoit Leleux and Remy Paliard, in chapter 3, refer to the persistence of some countries for the fixed-price underwritten offers as the "Posted-Price Paradox". They argue that the choice of the flotation mechanism, where available, may constitute a strategic decision with important implications for the value of the issuing firm.[29] Such choice is available in France since the regulatory framework allows both auction-type and fixed-price flotation procedures. The evidence from France suggests that auction type issues are more prevalent during 'hot' markets and are usually associated with lower initial returns. However, the long-run underperformance is not related to the state of the IPO market at issue but seems to be correlated with the flotation mechanism used, i.e. auctions exhibit larger underperformance than fixed-priced procedures. In contrast to other countries where auction-type mechanisms are not available or not used, the French experience suggests that issuing firms manage to tap the sentiment of the market without being underpriced. Auction-related introductions in 'hot' markets have proved poor investments, with small price run-ups about the introduction and strong underperformances over the long-run. On the other hand, fixed-price procedures have exhibited better prospects for appreciation and resilience over time.

Probably one on the sharpest illustrations of the implications of the institutional framework on initial underpricing is provided in chapter 4 by *Christos Kazantzis and Dylan Thomas* They examine the structure of the IPO market in Greece. The Athens Stock Exchange offers an "ideal" environment to study the implications of the regulatory framework on initial underpricing. During the period 1987 to 1994, the regime determining the pricing and distribution of IPOs changed four times. The authorities, in their effort to control the market, imposed various restrictions and controls on the pricing of IPOs in the aftermarket. The evidence clearly demonstrates that first day returns are directly related to the regulatory regime as issuing firms and their advisors adjust their pricing strategies to current circumstances.

4. The Security Design

A number of studies have analysed the potential value of superior voting rights. Lease, McConnell and Mikkelson (1984) find that superior voting shares trade at an average premium of about 5% and conclude that a dual-class capital structure provides potential for incremental benefits for both managers and outside stockholders. In general, the empirical evidence supports the contention that the right to vote is of substantial value, even though superior voting shares typically have no superior dividend rights. Thus, the choice of organisational form is likely to affect expected returns to shareholders. Mikkelson and Partch (1994) examine the long-run operating performance of dual-class firms to see if firms exploit their protected position after recapitalization and allow firm performance to deteriorate. While they document reduced operating performance following the creation of two classes of stock, this decrease is not related to an increase in managerial vote ownership. In summary, previous research has found mixed evidence on the effects of the adoption of dual-class equity structures. Most firms in these samples adopt a dual-class capital structure after going public. In these cases, it is difficult to measure potential wealth transfers between different classes of shareholders when a second class of share is created.

Dual-class IPOs offer the opportunity to the original managers to retain majority control and an active role in the firms they have founded and defend better in case of a hostile takeover bid. *Ekkehart Bohmer, Gary Sanger and Sanjay Varshney*, in chapter 5, provide valuable new evidence of the effect of such dual structures on long-run performance. They examine the performance of firms that choose to issue shares with differential voting rights. In sharp contrast with the conventional long-run performance that has been documented in other studies, they find no statistically significant abnormal long-run stock price performance over the 3 years following flotation. Moreover, the sample of dual-class outperform a matched control groups of IPOs in accounting measures of performance as well. Thus, the evidence suggests that a protected management position in a dual-class equity structure of IPOs may have significant benefits for the firm. Of course the sources for such benefits remain a challenging area for future research.

Security design is also the subject of chapter 6. *Birgul Caramanolis, Rajna Gibson and Nils Tuchscmid* examine the stock price reaction to seasoned equity offerings on the Swiss stock market across different share categories. Since most firms in the Swiss market have different type of shares in their capital structure, the Swiss framework offers an opportunity to examine both the neutrality of the rights issuance process as well as the implications of agency and corporate control differences in dual-class shares characteristics. Consistent with previous evidence related to rights issues they show no significant stock price reaction across any of the three share types. However, their evidence suggests a significant positive stock price reaction of 1.5% at the announcement date for registered shares that have neither a majority shareholder nor a diffused ownership. The presence of a positive price reaction among partially controlled firms is indicative of the potential benefits accrued to registered shareholders in terms of corporate maintenance and enhancement.

5. Underpricing and Signalling

Although the informational role of debt on firm value in general and the potential effects of signalling in reducing the underpricing of IPOs have been studied independently, the possible interactions between the two strands of literature remain largely unexplored. *Shantaram Hegde and Robert Miller,* in chapter 7, examine the signalling role of debt in the pricing of IPOs. They investigate the role of debt in explaining not only the degree of IPO underpricing but also the fraction of ownership retained as well as how debt signals the value and risk of the firm. At the same time they control for other signals such as the quality of investment banker and auditor and for general market conditions. Drawing from the capital structure signalling theories, they argue that the owner of a high quality firm uses a larger amount of debt prior to going public to convey the firm's superior prospects to the market. Their results show that the market infers a higher value and lower risk of a going-public firm, the greater the level of its pre-IPO debt. They also show provide evidence to suggest that the expected degree of underpricing and the proportional ownership retained at the IPO are decreasing functions of a firm's pre-IPO debt ratio. This result is consistent with the evidence of James and Wier (1990) and Slovin and Young (1990) who find that the presence of borrowing reduces the underpricing of IPOs.

The role of the underwriter has also be shown to play a significant part in the underpricing of IPOs.[30] One of the principal concerns of the underwriting institution relates to the legal implications of apparently overpriced issues. Thus, the lawsuit avoidance hypothesis implies that underpricing may be used to prevent subsequent litigation from distraught investors. It also implies that investment banks may be inclined to avoid underwriting speculative issues. In chapter 8, *Chao Chen and Timothy Lin* use a unique dataset to shed some further light into this issue. By comparing the characteristics of self-underwritten IPOs where the lead or co-managing underwriter is also major shareholder with a similar sample of IPOs underwritten by a third party, they demonstrate that the legal liability may be a very real concern for the underwriters. In spite of the fact that self-underwritten IPOs are usually firms that are more mature, larger and generally lower risk, their initial underpricing is not lower than non-self-underwritten IPOs. The concern of investment banks in self-underwritten issues is also reflected in the post-offer trading patterns. IPOs without investment banks/shareholders as underwriters have, on average, higher turnover ratios and lower aftermarket volatility. Given that investment banks tend to prefer investors with long-run horizons, the difference in turnover ratio between the two groups is again indicative of the importance attached to underwriters' reputation.

The role of certification, albeit in different context, is also examined by *Frank Packer* in chapter 9. He looks at the implications of the institutional affiliation of venture or bank shareholding on the pricing of initial public offerings in Japan. Previous empirical studies indicate that the bank's relationships play a significant role. Packer argues that the information production role of banks in Japan is important for smaller firms not yet publicly traded and not belonging to the *keiretsu* groups. The evidence shows that bank shareholding either direct or through venture capital subsidiaries reduces new issue underpricing. On the basis of 158 firms that went public in Japan on the OTC during 1989-91, he finds large and significant differences between types of venture capital. The results suggest that direct bank investment and investment by bank-related venture capital reduces IPO underpricing. The presence of bank pre-IPO shareholding over 3 percent is associated with lower excess returns of between 9 and 13 percent after controlling for other variables. Furthermore, the evidence suggests that securities company-related venture capital investment reduces underpricing by less than that of the other forms of venture capital investment. Thus, certification and the related alleviation of the costs of asymmetric information in raising funds, appears to be limited to the pre-IPO shareholding of commercial banks.

6. The Timing of IPOs

The market timing hypothesis claims that new issues cluster near market peaks - a time of higher equity valuations - suggesting that there are probably windows of opportunity, where original owners can achieve the best valuation for their companies while still retaining a large proportion of their holdings. Advocates of the sentiment story go much further than this; they claim that new issues come to the market when investors are over-optimistic about the future prospects of new firms. In this case poor long-run performance is explained as the result of subsequent adjustment. In this case the negative long-run abnormal returns are concentrated amongst the clusters of firms floated close to market peaks.

Chapter 10 sheds valuable additional insight into the ensuing debate. Using a sample of German IPOs over a long time period *Alexander Ljungqvist* finds that the evidence is not consistent with the sentiment timing hypothesis. In contrast to US evidence, German firms that went public in periods of heavy IPO activity and when the stock market was relatively bullish performed significantly better that light-volume and bearish-market flotations. Ljungqvist uses a number of proxies to define the state of the market but the results are robust to the alternative proxies. Probably the most damaging evidence against sentiment timing stems from the negative relationship between the proportion of equity retained and long run performance. It appears that in Germany only companies whose owners retained large stakes underperformed significantly. According to the sentiment timing hypothesis one would expect the original owners to sell a large part of their holding when they believe that valuation is too high.

Alistair Byrne and William Rees examine the cyclical behaviour in the initial returns of IPOs in the UK and they are particularly interested in the occurrence of hot IPO issue markets. In chapter 11, they show that the initial returns, after controlling for size of the issue, issue method and market of issue, are positively autocorrelated. Although this pattern of apparent cyclical behaviour can be partly explained by market-wide characteristics, their evidence suggests that certain periods demonstrate excess returns which are not susceptible to modelling. Their findings are supportive of the market timing hypothesis where firms come to the market when they can maximise their market value.

The time pattern behaviour of initial returns is also examined by *Ian Tonks* in chapter 12. Using the Baron's principal-agent framework, he argues that initial underpricing results from a sequential equilibrium in the bargaining game between the issuing firm and the investment bank over the type of contract under which the new issue is sold. An interesting implication of the model is that the degree of underpricing of new issues is cyclical with higher first day returns occurring in boom periods; these are the periods when the investment bank deliberately underprices to minimise the effort put into the sale. The UK evidence for the period 1980-1993 demonstrates a positive relationship between the state of the market and first day returns. Thus, the sequential equilibrium explanation offers an alternative perspective to the existing hypotheses on the impact of state of the market at large on the valuation of the IPO.

7. The Business Cycle

Robert Krainer's study, in chapter 13, provides a closer look at the underlying dynamics determining the impact of business cycles on the company's financing behaviour. According to his model, the procyclical pattern of risky corporate investment must be matched with coutercyclical movement in financial leverage and dividend payout rates. Thus, economic expansions are financed with equity and recessions supported by debt. In other words financial leverage is systematically related to the risk structure of assets and general economic activity, rising during periods of recession when firms pursue conservative operating strategies and falling in expansions when they implement risky operating strategies. This conclusion is based on the premise that outside shocks, which are first evaluated by the market, are an important source of cyclical fluctuations. Managers respond with a new operating strategy for the firm consistent with any change in the risk aversion or perception of risk of their shareholders resulting from the outside shock. Changes in the stock prices and the required rate of return on equity reflect changes in the risk aversion and perception of risk of equity investors and thus serve as a signal to managers on which they base their post shock operating strategy. But changes in operating decisions that change the level and risk structure of the firm's assets have a direct effect on financing decisions. Thus, the financial strategy has to be matched with an operating strategy of the firm in order to align the welfare of bondholders and stockholders over the business cycle. Thus a shock that increases both the scale and riskiness of the firm's assets must be matched with a conservative financing strategy that reduces long-term financial leverage and dividend payout rate. The reverse would be the case if the shock increased the required rate of return of equity investors thereby signalling the firm to pursue conservative operating strategies must in turn, be matched with a speculative financing strategy of increasing financial leverage and the dividend payout rate.

The implications of financing decisions may be particularly dramatic for companies operating in predominantly cyclical sectors. If highly leveraged firms, for example, are also cyclical, that is, if the firms' ability to repay varies positively with the level of economic activity, a slowdown in economic activity would adversely affect these firms' output. In chapter 14, *Rama Seth* uses firm-specific data for six industrialised countries, to analyse the implications of leverage for different groups of companies separated according to estimated cyclicality coefficients. She finds that in the US firms in cyclical industries have been increasing their leverage at a more rapid pace than firms in non-cyclical industries. As a result, firms with high interest burdens have become more concentrated in cyclical industries. In other industrialised countries, the decrease in leverage has made economies more resilient than others. Japanese firms have decreased their leverage roughly uniformly across sectors. Non-cyclical Canadian and German firms, by contrast, have decreased their debt more rapidly than cyclical firms. Firms in cyclical industries in UK have had, on average, high levels of debt.

8. International Equity Offerings

Although the need to raise equity capital at competitive rates has given rise to a dramatic increase in cross-border equity trading and global issuance of equities, international equity offerings are clearly not a recent innovation. *Sudhir Nanda, James Owers and Chengyang Feng* in chapter 15, identify the first instruments termed "American Depository Receipts" which were issued in 1926 by Selfridges Ltd and it could be argued that the instruments were used even further in response to the conditions of World War I. The total capital raised via ADRs has constantly grown from US\$ 2.6 billion in 1990 to US\$ 14 billion in 1994 with an increasing trend towards a full listing on NYSE or NASDAQ. In December 1995 there were a total of 1,450 ADRs from over 40 countries and the annual trading volume in ADRs was in the order of \$300 billion. They attribute the slow growth of ADRs in the 1960s and 1970s to the continuous impediments by regulators to market integration and international financial movement. They also shed some further light into the performance of ADRs at the time of the listing and the immediate aftermarket. Although, ADRs provide positive abnormal returns over the initial 50 trading days, there are marked differences between the investment performance of NASDAQ traded-ADRs versus NYSE/AMEX listed ADRs. There are also significant differences in performance depending on the ADR's country of origin. While ADRs from developing economies have negative investment performance, ADRs from developed economies provide positive abnormal returns.

The potential benefits resulting from a cross-listing have also been discussed extensively but the empirical evidence remains inconclusive. *Ali Fatemi and Alireza Rad* explore the determinants of the cross-listing decision in chapter 16. The study, based on a survey of 40 Dutch firms with their shares listed on the Amsterdam Stock Exchange and on at least one exchange outside of the Netherlands, sheds light into two key issues. First, it shows that considerations such as the perceived need to increase the potential investor base and public recognition are regarded as issues of major significance in their decision to seek a cross-listing. Second, it builds the profile of international firms. Cross-border listed firms are more liquid and produce a better return on their assets despite their lower profit margin on sales. They also generate a higher return on their shareholders' equity and have higher market values than firms listed only on the national exchange.

The perception of an increase in liquidity is supported by a number of empirical studies. Freedman (1991), for example, suggests an increase in the total trading volume, an increase in the depth of the market and the informativeness of prices of the dually listed shares. In chapter 17, *Alexander Arauner* and *Mario Levis* extend these findings by examining the impact of the type of offering on liquidity. They argue the choice of the method has implications not only on the direct issuing costs but on the cost of capital through its effect on the liquidity. Using a sample of 231 international equity offerings, they demonstrate that internationally listed firms have a liquidity advantage, as measured by the bid-ask spread in their respective domestic markets, over firms that opt for a private placement in the US instead of a full listing on NASDAQ or NYSE. They show that the benefits generated by lower bid-ask spreads for internationally listed firms outweigh the higher costs of public offering leading to a reduction in the cost of capital.

Finally, in chapter 18 *Costas Grammenos and Stelios Marcoulis* provide an analysis of IPOs in the shipping industry. They use a unique sample covering 31 shipping IPOs across seven countries. Their evidence points to an increasing tendency of private shipping companies to seek a listing and raise equity capital in the international capital markets. The main use of the proceeds is for fleet replacement and expansion. Although there are some differences in average first day returns across countries, they are broadly consistent with the first day returns observed for other industrial IPOs. They identify, however, some marked differences in the direct costs of going public across counties. They range from 10 percent in US to only 5.5 percent in Norway.

References

Affleck-Graves, H. and M. Page, 1995, The timing and subsequent performance of seasoned offerings: The case of rights issues, Working Paper, University of Notre Dame.

Alexander, G., C. Eun and S. Janakiramanan, 1988, International listings and stock returns: some empirical evidence, Journal of Financial and Quantitative Analysis 23, 135-151.

Asquith, P. and D. Mullins, 1986, Equity issues and offering dilution, Journal of Financial Economics 15, 61-89.

Barry, C., C. Muscarella, J. Peavy and M. Vetsuypens, 1990, The role of venture capital in the creation of public companies: Evidence from the going-public process, Journal of Financial Economics 27, 447-471.

Benveniste, L. and W. Busaba, 1995, Book building versus fixed price: An analysis of competing strategies for marketing IPOs, Working Paper, Boston College.

Brav, A. and P. A. Gompers, 1995, myth or reality? The long run underperformance of IPOs: Evidence from venture and nonventure capital-backed companies, Working Paper, University of Chicago.

Cai, J., 1995, The stock return and operating performances of seasoned equity offerings in Japan, Working Paper, Hong Kong University of Science and Technology.

Cai, J. and K. C. J. Wei, 1995, Timing effects on IPO performance, Working paper, Hong Kong University of Science and Technology.

Carter, R. B., F. H. Dark and A. K. Singh, 1995, Underwriter reputation, initial returns and the long-run performance of IPO stocks, Working Paper, Iowa State University.

Chaplinsky, S. and L. Ramchard, 1995, The rationale for global equity offerings, Working Paper, The University of Virginia.

Cheng, L., 1995, Equity issue underperformance and the timing of security issues, Working Paper, Massachusetts Institute of Technology.

Choe, H., R. Masulis and V. Nanda, 1993, Common stock offerings across the business cycle, Journal of Empirical Finance 1, 3-31.

Denis, D. J., 1994, Investment opportunities and the market reaction to equity offerings, Journal of Financial and Quantitative Analysis 29, 159-177.

Doukas, J. and K. Young, 1992, ADRs, investors' information and initial public equity offerings (IPO) underpricing, Journal of International Securities Markets 7, 341-348.

Eckbo, E. and R. Masulis, 1992, Adverse selection and the rights offer paradox, Journal of Financial Economics 32, 293-332.

Eckbo, E. and R.Masulis, 1995, Seasoned equity offerings: A survey, in Finance, R. R. Jarrow and V. Maksimovic, eds. Amsterdam: North Holland, Series of Handbooks in Operations Research and Management Science.

Freedman, R., 1991 A theory of the impact of international cross-listing, Working Paper, University of British Columbia.

Friedlan, J. M., 1994, Accounting choices of issuers of initial public offerings, Contemporary Accounting Research 11, 1-32.

Foerster, S. and G. Karolyi, 1993, International listings of stocks: The case of Canada and the US, Journal of International Business Studies, 763-783.

Fry, C., I. Lee and J. Choi, 1994, The valuation effects of overseas listings: The case of the Tokyo Stock Exchange, Review of Quantitative Finance and Accounting 4, 79-88.

Grinblatt, M. and C. Hwang, 1989, Signalling and the pricing of new issues, Journal of Finance 44, 393-420.

Howe, J. S. and K. Kelm, 1987, The stock price impact of overseas listing, Financial Management 16, 51-56.

Ibbotson, R., 1975, Price performance of common stock new issues, Journal of Financial Economics 2, 37-45.

Ibbotson, R. G., J. L. Sindelar and J. R. Ritter, 1995, The market's problems with the pricing of initial public offerings, Journal of Applied Corporate Finance, 66-74.

Jain, B.A. and O. Kini, 1994, The post-issue operating performance of IPO firms, Journal of Finance 49, 1699-1726.

James, C., 1992, Relationship specific assets and the pricing of underwriter services, Journal of Finance 47, 1865-1885.

James, C. and P. Wier, 1990, Borrowing relationships, intermediation and the costs of issuing public securities, Journal of Financial Economics 28, 149-172.

Jayaraman,N., K. Shastri and K. Tandon,1993, The impact of international cross listings on risk and return: The evidence from American Depositary Receipts, Journal of Banking and Finance, 91-103.

Jegadeesh, N., M., Weinstein and I. Welch, 1993, An empirical investigation of IPO returns and subsequent equity offerings, Journal of Financial Economics 34, 153-175.

Keloharju, M., 1993, The winner's curse, legal liability and the long-run performance of initial public offerings in Finland, Journal of Financial Economics 34, 251-277.

Koh, F. and T. Walter, 1989, A direct test of Rock's model of the pricing of unseaoned issues, Journal of Financial Economics 23, 251-272.

Lau, S., D. Diltz and V. Apilado, 1994, Valuation effects of international stock exchange listings, Journal of Banking and Finance 18, 743-755.

Lease, R. C., J. J. McConnell and W. H. Mikkelson, 1984, The market value of differential voting rights in closely held companies, Journal of Business 57, 443-468.

Lee, I., 1991, The impact of overseas listings on shareholder wealth: The case of the London and Toronto Stock Exchange, Journal of Business Accounting and Finance, 18, 583-592.

Lee, I., S. Lochhead, J. Ritter and Q. Zhao, 1995, The costs of raising capital, Working Paper, University of Illinois.

Leleux, B., 1993, Venture capital and corporate monitoring: Evidence from the French initial public offerings market, Unpublished manuscript, INSEAD, France.

Lerner, J., 1994, Venture capitalists and the decision to go public, Journal of Financial Economics 35, 293-316.

Levis, M. 1990, The winner's curse problem, interest costs and the underpricing of initial public offerings, The Economic Journal 100, 76-89.

Levis, M., 1993, The long-run performance of initial public offerings: The UK evidence 1980-1988, Financial Management 22, Spring, 28-41.

Levis, M., 1995, Seasoned equity offerings and the short-and long-run performance of initial public offerings, European Financial Management 1, 125-146.

Levis, M. and D. Thomas, 1995, Investment trust IPOs: Issuing behaviour and price performance, Journal of Banking and Finance 19, 1437-1458.

Ljungqvist, A., 1995, When do firms go public? Evidence using an auto-regressive poisson model, Working Paper, Oxford University.

Loughran, T., J. Ritter and K. Rydqvist, 1994, Initial Public Offerings: International Insights, Pacific-Basin Finance Journal 2, 165-199.

Loughran, T. and J. R. Ritter, 1995, The new issues puzzle, Journal of Finance 50, 23-51.

Loughran, T. and J. R. Ritter, 1995, The operating performance of firms conducting seasoned equity offerings, Working Paper University of Illinois.

Lucas, D. and R. McDonald, 1990, Equity issues and stock price dynamics, Journal of Finance 45, 1019-1043.

Marsh, P., 1979, Equity rights issues and the efficiency of the U.K. stock market, Journal of Finance 34, 839-862.

Marsh, P., 1982, The choice between equity and debt: An empirical study, Journal of Finance 37, 121-144.

Masulis, R. and A. Korwar, 1986, Seasoned equity offerings: An empirical investigation, Journal of Financial Economics 15, 91-118.

Megginson, W. L. and K. A. Weiss, 1991, Venture capitalist certification in initial public offerings, Journal of Finance 46, 879-903.

Michaely, R. and W. Shaw, 1994, The pricing of initial public offerings: tests of the adverse selection and signalling theories, Review of Financial Studies 7, 279-313.

Mikkelson, W. H. and M. M. Partch, 1994, Valuation effects of securities offerings and the issuance process, Journal of Financial Economics 15, 31-60.

Mikkelson, W. H. and K. Shah, 1994, Performance of companies around initial public offerings, Working paper, University of Oregon.

Miller, M H. and Kevin Rock, 1985, Dividend policy and asymmetric information, Journal of Finance 40, 1031-1052.

Myers, S., 1984, The Capital Structure Puzzle, Journal of Finance 39, 575-592.

Myers, S. and N. Majluf, 1984, Corporate financing and investment decisions when firms have information that investors do not have, Journal of Financial Economics 13, 187-221.

Pilotte, E. 1992, Growth opportunities and the stock price response to new financing, Journal of Business 65, 371-394.

Rajan, R. and H. Servaes, 1994, The effect of market conditions on initial public offerings, Working Paper, University of Chicago.

Ritter, J. R., 1987, The costs of going public, Journal of Financial Economics 19, 269-281.

Ritter, J. R., 1991, The long-run performance of initial public offerings, Journal of Finance 46, 3-26.

Rock, K. 1986, Why new issues are underpriced, Journal of Financial Economics 15, 187-212.

Slovin, M. B. and J. E. Young, 1990, Bank lending and initial public offerings, Journal of Banking and Finance 14, 729-740.

Smith, C. Jr, 1977, Alternative methods of raising capital: Rights versus underwritten offerings, Journal of Financial Economics 5, 273-307.

Spiess, D. K. and J. Affleck-Graves, 1995, The long-run performance following seasoned equity offerings, Journal of Financial Economics 38, 243-268.

Taggart, R. A., 1977, A model of corporate financing decisions, Journal of Finance 32, 1467-84.

Teoh, S. H., T. J. Wong, and G. Rao, 1994, Earnings management in initial public offerings, Working Paper, University of Maryland.

Teoh, S. H., I. Welch and T. J. Wong, 1995, Earnings management and the post-issue underperformance of seasoned equity offerings, Working Paper, The University of Michigan.

Weiss Hanley, K. and W. J. Wilhem, 1995, Evidence on the strategic allocation of initial public offerings, Journal of Financial Economics 37, 239-257.

Welch, I., 1989, Seasoned offerings, imitation costs and underpricing of initial public offerings, Journal of Finance 44, 421-449.

Endnotes

[1] For a review of the evidence on first day returns in a large number of countries see Loughran, Ritter and Rydqvist (1994).

[2] See Ritter (1987) and Lee, Lochhead, Ritter and Zhao (1995) for details of direct issuing costs in US.

[3] For a review of potential explanations see Ibbotson and Ritter (1995).

[4] See, for example, Barry, Muscarella, Peavy and Vetsuypens (1990) and Megginson and Weiss (1991).

[5] For some empirical evidence consistent with the winner's curse see Koh and Walter (1989), Levis (1990) and Keloharju (1993).

[6] Loughran, Ritter and Rydqvist (1994) provide a comprehensive review of the different issuing methods used in different capital markets. For a theoretical analysis of the differences between fixed pricing and bookbuilding, see Benveniste and Busaba (1995).

[7] Ibbotson Sindelar and Ritter (1995) document an autocorrelation coefficient of 0.66 for initial returns of US IPOs during the period 1960-92; they also report an even stronger (0.89) autocorrelation for monthly volumes of IPOs. Similar results are reported by Ljungqvist (1995) for Germany.

[8] See, for example, Levis and Thomas (1995)

[9] See, for example, Loughran, Ritter and Rydqvist (1994) for a review of international evidence on post-issue performance.

[10] See, for example, Brav and Gompers (1995)

[11] See, for example, Jain and Kini (1994)

[12] See, for example, Cai and Wei (1995)

[13] Mikkelson and Shah (1994) find that the overall decline in post-IPO operating performance is mainly associated with young, start-up firms.

[14] See for example, the surveys of Smith (1986) and Eckbo and Masulis (1992)

[15] See Asquith and Mullins (1986)

[16] See Myers and Majluf (1984) for a theoretical exposition of the former explanation and Miller and Rock (1985) for the latter.

[17] See Pilotte (1992), Denis (1994), Lucas and McDonald (1989).

[18] See, for example, Choe, Masulis and Nanda (1993)

[19] The differences in costs were first highlighted by Smith (1977) and were, more recently, confirmed by Eckbo and Masulis (1992)

[20] See for example Marsh (1982) and Taggart (1977)

[21] See Spiess and Affleck-Graves (1995) and Loughran and Ritter (1995) for the US evidence on general cash offerings and Levis (1995) and Affleck-Graves and Page (1995) for rights issues in the UK and South Africa respectively.

[22] Cheng (1995), for example, argues that this underperformance is concentrated among firms that do not use the proceeds of the issue for capital investments.

[23] See Loughran and Ritter (1995)

[24] Teoh, Welch and Wong (1995) argue that part of the increase in profits before issuing equity is due to accounting choices that increase profit growth rates. Similar arguments were made by Teoh, Wong and Rao (1994) and Friedlan (1994) for IPO firms before going public.

[25] See, for example, Cai (1995)

[26] See for example Howe and Kelm (1987) for negative price reactions and Lee (1991) and Fry, Lee and Choi (1994) for evidence of insignificant value effects. While these studies take the listing date as event date, Lau, Diltz and Apilado (1994) finf positive abnormal returns around the time of acceptance of US firms' listings on ten different foreign stock exchanges.

[27] See, for example, Alexander, Eun ans Janakiramanan (1988), Foerster and Karolyi (1993) and Jayaraman, Shastri and Tandon (1993).

[28] See, for example, Chaplinsky and Ramchard (1995) who, on the basis of this evidence, argue that the segmentation of international markets offers certain issuers an opportunity to raise equity capital at advantageous terms.

[29] Weiss Hanley and Wilhelm (1995) also find that US underwriters behave strategically in their use of the freedom to discriminate among institutional and private investors in the allocation of IPOs.

[30] Carter, Dark and Singh (1995) argue that the reputation of the underwriter is also related to the long run performance. They find that the underperformance of IPO stocks is less severe for issues handled by more prestigious underwriters.

Share Issue Privatisations:
The UK Experience

Kojo Menyah
London Guildhall University

Krishna Paudyal
Glasgow Caledonian University

Abstract

This paper investigates how the aims and objectives of privatisation influenced the methods, procedures and incentives used in the sale of state-owned shares on the London and other Stock Exchanges by the U.K. government. It concludes that the objective of ensuring the irreversibility of the privatisation process pursued through the policy of employee and wider share ownership restricted the use of partial sales and tender offers which could have maximised sales proceeds. The end result is that share issue privatisations are characterised by: higher first day returns to subscribers relative to private sector issues; significant costs of underpricing to the government; and long-term returns to investors which exceed benchmark portfolios for up to four years after initial issue. In particular, we find that it is the regulated companies which account for the largest fraction of the observed high initial and long-term returns.

1. Introduction

The policy of privatising state-owned enterprises which gained worldwide momentum with the initiation of the UK programme in the 1980s derive from similar concerns of governments around the world. For some developed economies like the UK and France, the primary aim is to reduce the role of the state in productive activities[1]; for eastern European and former communist countries, it represents the mechanism for replacing communism with capitalism (Wiseman (1991), and Ash et al. (1994)) in order to improve upon overall economic performance; while the improvement in economic performance of divested state-owned enterprises as the vehicle of economic development underlies its application in many developing countries (see, for instance, Zank (1990) and Price (1993)). These different emphases on the rationale for privatisation are rooted in the belief that competitive markets and free enterprise are superior forms of economic organisation to centralised planning, bureaucratic controls or political directions.

Divestiture methods in privatisations differ within and between countries. Generally they include sales to other private companies, management buy-outs, introduction of private ownership and share issues on stock exchanges (Vuylsteke (1988)) The divestiture methods used in part reflect the economic state of the enterprises sold and the specific objectives which different governments seek in their privatisation programmes. Some companies, for instance, may be restructured and floated on the stock market while others may be sold to private companies which are judged better able to introduce new technology and management to ensure their survival. Specific objectives of privatisations also differ between countries. In New Zealand, for instance, the main objective is to maximise sale proceeds (Browne, 1993) whilst in Japan it appears to be the extension of the role of private management in public enterprises to make the state prosperous (Strzyzewska-Kaminska, 1993). In the case of UK and France, multiplicity of objectives dominate (Vickers and Yarrow, 1988 and Giarraputo, 1994). Therefore, a study of the implementation of privatisation in specific countries will enhance our understanding of the relative importance of factors which coalesce to produce the outcomes of such programmes. Such an analytical framework is similar to that used by Boycko et. al. (1994) to reach the conclusion that voucher privatisation in former eastern European countries, though dictated by politics, has been designed to achieve some economic objectives.

This study focuses on the objectives, implementation and outcomes of share issue privatisations (SIPs) in the UK. Its justification lies in the fact that existing evaluations of UK privatisations tend to focus on management buy-outs (Wright et. al. (1989), Thompson et. al. (1990)), the efficiency of public versus private enterprises (Hutchinson (1991), Parker and Hartley (1991), Hartley et. al. (1991), Dunsire et. al. (1991)), or the appropriateness of regulatory regimes for utility companies (Thomas and Kay (1986), Helm and Yarrow (1988), Beesley and Littlechild (1989), Veljanovski (1991) and Bishop and Thompson (1992)). Specific studies of share issue privatisations are either based on small samples over short periods of time (Jenkinson and Mayer (1986)) or focus on the determinants of initial new issue returns and privatisation portfolio performance over relatively short post-issue periods (Menyah et. al. (1995)). All of them, however, document first day returns to subscribers which significantly exceed that observed in private sector issues. In this context, this paper differs from others by using a larger sample of companies over a longer period to investigate several issues in SIPs. Firstly, we undertake a comparative analysis of primary and secondary offerings to determine whether partial sales could have reduced the cost of underpricing to the government as advocated by Vickers and Yarrow (1988). The findings will be evaluated in the context of other objectives which may have dominated the conceptually optimal decision of using partial sales and tender offers. Secondly we investigate the long-term performance of UK privatisation initial public offers (PIPOs) for up to 4 years and compare with those of private sector IPOs which Ritter (1991) and Levis (1993), among others, show to be overpriced. We then analyse some of the factors which may explain our findings. Thirdly, we evaluate the extent to which the objectives of share issue privatisations have been achieved.

The rest of the paper is organised as follows: In section 2, we discuss the objectives of share issue privatisations and show how such objectives affected the procedures and methods used in making privatisation initial and secondary public offers. We also compare the methods and procedures used by the government with those used by private sector companies making initial and secondary public offers. In section 3, we estimate the first day market valuation of initial and secondary sale of shares, the returns to subscribers and the costs to the issuer (government). Cross-sectional regression analysis is also used to identify the major factors which may explain initial returns to investors. In section 4, we investigate whether UK share issue privatisations have been good long-term investments compared with their private sector counterparts. In this context, we explore the extent to which the results of the long-term gains are driven by the performance of regulated monopolies. Section 5 pulls together available evidence to evaluate the extent to which the objectives of share issue privatisations discussed in section 2 have been achieved. The final section summarises the paper and highlights the main conclusions.

2. Objectives of Share Issue Privatisations

2.1 Evolutionary nature of objectives

The U.K. privatisation programme started without a coherent official statement of its objectives. Wiltshire (1987) illustrates this point by indicating that there was no green paper, white paper or definite piece of legislation and the Tory party election manifesto of 1979 did not highlight it as party policy. Kay and Thompson (1986) reinforce this impression by characterising privatisations as a policy in search of a rationale. According to Veljanovski(1987), the goals of privatisation evolved gradually and the emphasis given to each of the goals differs between the various privatisations. John Moore, a member of the British government in the 1980s is credited with equipping the de facto policy, after the event, with a more or less consistent philosophy (Abromeit, 1988). A Department of Environment paper (1986) on the privatisation of water authorities in England and Wales appears to be one of the earliest government documents to have set out the objectives of privatisation. Vickers and Yarrow (1988 p. 157), evidently drawing on several sources list seven objectives of privatisation: (1) reducing government involvement in industry; (2) improving efficiency in the industries privatised; (3) reducing the Public Sector Borrowing Requirements; (4) weakening public sector unions and thereby easing the problems of public sector pay determination; (5) widening share ownership; (6) encouraging employee share ownership and (7) gaining political advantage. The first four objectives apply with different degrees of emphasis to all divestiture methods used in various types of privatisations. The fifth and sixth objectives relate mainly to share issue privatisations and the seventh according to McAllister and Studlar (1989) is mainly associated with the sale of local government residential properties.

In addition to the wider and employee share ownership objectives, it is clear from a perusal of National Audit Office Value for Money reports that share issue privatisations have additional objectives of: ensuring successful transfer to the private sector; maximisation of sale proceeds; and the achievement of satisfactory secondary market price performance to maintain interest in privatisations. From the foregoing, it is clear that the specific objectives of share issue privatisations either have an impact on the methods of their sale or on their pricing. A successful transfer of a company to private investors and the achievement of a satisfactory secondary market performance are more likely to be achieved if issues are so priced, as cited in Ibbotson (1975), to leave *'a good taste in investors' mouths'*. Achieving wider and employee share ownership requires investor education and some simplification of the procedures for buying and selling shares and may also be aided by underpricing. Maximising sales proceeds, on the other hand, implies minimising the magnitude of underpricing possibly through partial sales and tender offers. It is, therefore, obvious that there are contradictions in the objectives sought in share issue privatisations which ought to be carefully delineated in evaluating the outcome of the programme. In the remainder of this section, we analyze how the objectives outlined above influenced the preparation of companies for sale, the methods of sale used, pricing of the issues, allotment and payment for shares and underwriting.

2.2 Preparation of companies for flotation

Preparing companies for flotation is a major aspect of SIPs which in cases like the water and electricity companies took several years to complete. It usually covered the business, managerial, and financial aspects of companies. Usually the parts of the public enterprise which were to be sold had to be delineated, its assets and liabilities identified and a public limited company created out of it. Measures which would ensure profitability of the companies were introduced. These included appointing new board members and restructuring operations which in some cases involved labour retrenchment (Curwen, 1986). In the case of utilities in non-competitive markets, an economic regulatory structure was also devised to encourage productive efficiency. Regulatory bodies have been established for privatised electricity (Office of Electricity Regulation), water (Office of Water Services), gas (Office of Gas Supply), airports (Civil Aviation Authority) and telecommunication companies (Office of Telecommunications). The primary functions of the regulators are the implementation of price control and the encouragement of competition.

The financial aspects of the preparation usually involved preparing financial reports on the basis of historical cost conventions rather than current cost accounting used in most nationalised industries. Government ownership interest in the companies was usually converted into ordinary shares even though in some cases like the regional electricity companies, the government received a combination of debt and equity instruments in the course of designing 'appropriate' capital structures for such companies. Debt write-offs also occurred for companies such as Associated British Ports, Scottish Power, PowerGen and the water companies which were heavily indebted (Price Waterhouse (1989, 1990))[2]. The process of making companies ready for flotation though not peculiar to privatisations, (see Sabine (1993) for an outline of the structural and other changes private companies undertake before flotations) is evidently motivated by the objective of ensuring a successful transfer of state-owned enterprises to the private sector. The associated costs of making companies viable for privatisations, have however, not been completely set out in official documents. Beauchamp (1990), the National Audit Office director in-charge of privatisation audits has pointed out that *'in a number of instances considerable sums of taxpayers' money have gone into revitalising industries which have not previously been profitable' and 'in a number of instances, the Office (National Audit) has noted that considerable effort, time and money have been invested in strengthening a company financially, with no measured consideration given to whether the cost of the(se) changes will increase the value of the company in the market.'*

2.3 Methods used to pursue the objective of wider and employee share ownership

The sale of fifty-one percent of the equity of British Telecom in 1984 represents a turning point in the crystallisation of the government's objective of promoting wider share ownership through privatisations. This objective and its sibling of employee share ownership have been promoted through a variety of mechanisms designed to make it appealing to retail and employee investors to buy, pay for and retain shares. The specific methods used are: extensive advertising to create awareness about share purchases; the establishment of share information offices before flotations so that potential investors could register their interest and be given priority in the allocation of shares; loyalty bonuses for retention of shares; discriminatory allocation in favour of small quantity applicants and employees; the use of banks and share shops for the purchase of shares; clawback of shares from institutions to be sold to retail investors in the event of oversubscription; and the payment for shares in instalments. In some cases employees were also given free shares. Apart from basic advertising, distribution of shares through banks and in a few cases, preferential allocation of shares to employees, these features of SIPs are not generally associated with private sector share issues. Appendices A and B summarise the incentives given to employees and retail investors to acquire shares in various privatisations. The question which remains and has been raised by the Public Accounts Committee of the House of Commons is whether such incentives have been necessary to achieve a successful sale or the objectives of wider and employee share ownership. Beauchamp (1990) notes again that *'in all too many instances the 'added value of these incentives has not been measured'.*

Grout (1987) argues that wider share ownership may have been used to pre-commit the government not to repurchase the shares below their market value after privatisation. In this context it represents an insurance policy against re-nationalisations[3] which the parliamentary Opposition Party threatened to implement for British Telecom, British Gas, and electricity companies privatisations[4]. Remolona (1989) also argues that wider share ownership increases the number of people who bear the risks in such companies previously borne by all taxpayers as state-owned companies. It, therefore, has the effect of reducing the amount of risk borne by individual investors in the equity market. Diffused ownership of shares in a company, however, makes monitoring of managers difficult. Since the government also reduced monitoring through the market for corporate control by retaining 'golden shares'[5] in most of the companies, it may be argued that pursuing wider share ownership, *ceteris paribus*, weakened the market mechanism for encouraging mangers to act in the interest of shareholders.

Vickers and Yarrow (1988) argue for alternative ways of encouraging employee and wider share ownership. This would involve either removing tax privileges afforded to individual housing and pension investments or extending them to direct share ownership as in the case of employee share ownership and profit related pay (Estrin et al.(1987)). The fact that these alternative methods were not used coupled with the weak market mechanism for corporate control due to the government's retention of golden shares, it may be argued that the objective of making re-nationalisations difficult may have been the prime motivation behind the objective of wider and employee share ownership.

2.4 Issues relating to the pricing of shares

The pricing of shares before flotation takes into account, among other things, the quality of the firm being sold and the demand for the shares in the primary market. The practice in privatisations has been to provide information about the companies through pathfinder prospectuses, road shows and final prospectuses to reduce the asymmetry of information between issuers and investors. Demand for shares are assessed via indications of interest by the general public through share information offices, market research and informal assessment of interest by lead underwriters and brokers from their regular investors, their advisers and potential sub-underwriters. For sixteen electricity companies, the technique of book-building (common in the US but not normally applied in the UK private sector new issues) was used to assess the level of demand at certain prices by institutional and overseas investors before fixing the price of the issues. The scope and depth of information provision to investors and the extent to which demand is assessed before pricing has usually been more extensive and elaborate than that associated with private sector initial public offers.

The pricing process involved the main adviser, who is also the lead underwriter, estimating a range of prices usually based on either the dividend yield or the price earnings ratio of 'comparable' companies. Due to criticisms of a conflict of interest between the price advisory and the underwriting roles of the main adviser made by the Public Accounts Committee, independent pricing advisers have been used since the initial sale of British Telecom shares in 1984. The final offer price is agreed by the department making the sale, treasury officials, lead adviser and the independent pricing adviser after taking into account all relevant factors[6]. These procedures for determining the price of issues are relevant for sales at a fixed price, tender offers (because investors are usually given a minimum tender price) and placements.

For most privatisations a fraction of the equity sold was firmly placed with some institutions at the offer price. The remainder was sold to retail, institutional and overseas investors who were successful in their application for shares in fixed price or tender offers. In the case of the initial British Airport Authority offer and that of secondary issues of companies which were partly privatised, a fixed price offer was made to UK public applicants and a tender sale was made to international investors as well as UK retail applicants. This practice is consistent with the government's objective of maximising sale proceeds. Another method used to increase sale proceeds is the back-end tender which was applied during the sale of National Power, PowerGen, Scottish Power and Scottish Hydro. The back-end tender involved withdrawing a proportion of the shares provisionally earmarked for sale to institutional and overseas investors if UK retail demand (measured by the level of oversubscription) exceeded a predetermined level after the close of the offer. Institutional and overseas investors were then invited to bid for the shares with reference to the partly paid price. The technique raised an extra £41.5 million for National Power and PowerGen and £42.25 million for Scottish Power and Scottish Hydro.

Underwriting of share issues is basically an insurance policy taken by the issuer to ensure that the proceeds are received whether or not all the shares are sold to investors. In the UK the risk is borne by the primary underwriters who reduce it significantly by taking on a large number of sub-underwriters. In various reports on share issue privatisations, the Public Accounts Committee of the House of Commons has questioned the wisdom and cost of underwriting. They have noted the conflict of interest which the main adviser faces in the dual roles of pricing and underwriting as modelled by Baron (1982) and called on departments to either do away with underwriting or take steps to reduce its costs. The government took action to reduce primary underwriting costs by opening it to competitive bidding beginning with the sale of British Gas in 1986 and doing away with it in the cases of National Power, PowerGen, Scottish Hydro and Scottish Power. Sub-underwriting, mainly by institutions, has never been dispensed with. This involves: (1) firmly placed shares with institutions; (2) commitment shares which sub-underwriting institutions promise to purchase if not sold in the public offer (firm commitment sub-underwriting); and (3) provisionally placed shares subject to clawback in the event of oversubscription in the public offer. As noted by Chown (1993) offer for sale flotations should not have included firmly placed shares. He goes on to argue that *'issuing houses ... invented a new technique, and it was not for the benefit of the Government or the taxpayer*[7]. It evidently benefited institutions with firmly placed shares especially when there was significant underpricing. The government may have accepted firmly placed shares to ensure that the sales were successful since failed flotations would have dented the reputation of a government which believed in the effectiveness of markets but woefully unable to use markets to achieve its own objectives. Secondly underwriting certifies the quality of an IPO as modelled by Carter and Manaster (1990) and provides support for the government's view that its use helps to maximise sale proceeds.

In the light of the above analysis of the major features of SIPs, it is clear that they were influenced by the objectives sought by the government in various share sales. Whilst one objective within a single sale may have dictated the use of firm placing and underwriting to maximise sale proceeds, an opposing objective of wider share ownership may have discouraged the use of tender offers which might have actually increased proceeds. Thus it can be argued that the pricing and other outcomes of SIPs derive from the difficulty of balancing the conflicting objectives rather than a conscious attempt to obtain poor outcomes.

3. First Day Price Performance of Initial and Secondary Public Offers

3.1 The Sample

The study of initial public offers and their long-term performance is based on forty companies floated by the British government between 1981 and 1991. The analysis of secondary issues - the sale of equity retained by the government after the initial public offer, is based on eighteen offers made by eight companies which were initially sold in tranches over the period 1977 to 1995. A sample of private sector IPOs is used to make comparisons where necessary. Share prices and market index data were obtained from Datastream -a financial database. Share prices have been adjusted for partial payment wherever appropriate. Other necessary information were collected from the Stock Exchange Fact Books and Supplements, the Extel Book of Prospectus, the Stock Exchange Year Book, the Quality of Markets Review, National Audit Office Reports and Extel Weekly Financial News Summary. The forty privatized issues covered in this sample comprise sixteen electricity generators and distributors, ten water companies and the remaining fourteen belong to various industry groups including communications, petroleum and natural gas and aviation. The data for the secondary issues includes British Petroleum whose shares have been sold in secondary offerings since 1977. The gross proceeds from the sale of individual companies in the first tranche range from £22 million (Associated British Ports) to £5,434 million (British Gas). The total amount raised over the eleven year period from the first tranche of PIPOs was £33,888 million while from the secondary issues, the government raised £23,670 million[8]. Thus, over a period of eleven years the government raised over £57 billion from the sale of public corporations to the private sector.

The private sector sample covers companies which were floated on the market during the period 1981 to 1991. The initial sample frame was made up of all U.K. initial public offers which were admitted to the Official List of the London Stock Exchange. We excluded companies which were floated on other segments of the market- the Unlisted Securities Market and the Third Market since all PIPOs and secondary offers have been admitted to the Official List. The sample was further restricted to those which adopted the offer for sale method used (mainly) in PIPOs. Owing to lack of data on some issues, the final sample was mode up of 75 companies. Of these, 43 had positive first day returns, 25 had negative returns and 7 were sold at the offer price. The average size of private sector IPOs is £38.89 million, the largest issue worth £975 million raised by Abbey National in 1989.

3.2 Initial Offer Price Performance

Previous studies such as Jenkinson and Mayer (1986), Buckland (1987), Peroti and Guney (1993) and Menyah et al.(1990, 1995) provide estimates of first day returns of privatisation initial public offers using equation (1)

$$\text{Ri} = \frac{P_1 - P_0}{P_0} - \frac{M_1 - M_0}{M_0} \tag{1}$$

Where:

P_0	= Initial offer price
P_1	= Price of stock on first day of trading[9]
M_0	= Market index on the day of offer price determination
M_1	= Market index on the first day of trading

Menyah et. al. (1995) point out that estimates based on equation (1) are only available to initial subscribers who were allocated all the shares they applied for - usually the minimum number of shares, as well as institutions which received firmly placed shares[10]. They also argue that the cost of underpricing to the issuer should be estimated by taking into account the proportion of equity sold, interest earned on deposits made by IPO applicants and the market value of the firm on the first day of trading as defined by equation (2).

$$U_i = [\frac{(P_1 N_A) - (P_0 N_A) - I_{0P}}{(P_1 N_A)} - \frac{(M_1 - M_0)}{M_1}] \Psi \tag{2}$$

where

U_i	= the cost of underpricing expressed as a proportion of the value of firm i,
Ψ	= the proportion of shares sold,
M_0 and M_1	= the level of the market index at the offer date and the first day of trading respectively, and
P_0 and P_1	= offer price to be deposited on application and first day trading price.
I_{OP}	= interest earned on deposits made by IPO applicants between the close of offer date and first day of trading.
N_A	= total number of shares sold

Table 1

Initial Returns from portfolios of Primary Issues

		Returns in Percent	
Private Issues	Raw Return	Market Adjusted Returns	Underpricing
Private Sector (75 firms)	3.50	3.48	NA[2]
All Privatized stocks (40 firms)	40.37*	38.70*	23.62*
Regulated PIPOs (29 firms)	45.78*	44.27*	27.30*
Unregulated PIPOs (11 firms)	26.13*	24.00*	13.92*
Regulated vs Unregulated (T-Statistics)[1]	2.02**	2.09**	2.58*
Portfolio Classification: B			
Electricity Companies (16 firms)	45.16*	44.40*	27.33*
Water Companies (10 firms)	43.95*	41.87*	27.83*
Water vs Electricity (T-Statistic)[1]	-0.28	-0.50	0.21
Other PIPOs (14 firms)	32.35*	30.37*	16.37*

Notes:

1. Examines the significance of the difference in the mean return/underpricing of regulated vs unregulated companies.

2. Owing to lack of data such as proportion of shares sold, number of applicants, demand multiple etc. we were unable to estimate the underpricing cost of private sector IPOs.

* Indicates statistically significant at 5 percent or better

** Indicates statistically significant at 7 percent or better

We extend the analysis of Menyah et. al. (1995) by estimating subscriber returns and issuer underpricing for two utility group portfolios (water and electricity) and for regulated versus unregulated companies. The results reported in Table 1 show that the full PIPO portfolio offers an initial market adjusted excess returns of about 39 percent but the regulated companies contribute a statistically significant larger fraction of subscriber returns and issuer underpricing than the unregulated companies. Specifically, the market adjusted return of over 44 percent for regulated companies is almost twice that of the figure of 24 percent for unregulated companies[11]. The major factors which may explain the magnitude of initial returns to investors are examined empirically in the next section.

3.3 Empirical analysis of factors explaining the magnitude of initial investor returns

In the light of the institutional factors affecting PIPO pricing discussed in earlier sections and the possible reasons for underpricing of IPOs documented in the literature, we propose an empirical model which may explain the magnitude of initial investor returns. The explanatory variables included in the model are the underwriting commission, proportion of shares sold, the extent of (under) oversubscription, the regulatory situation of the company, market volatility measured as the daily variance of returns during two months prior to the sale and the proportion of shares allocated to the foreign investors.

Underwriters' reputation and their perception of the possible market demand for an issue affect the level of their commission charges. A high commission rate should, ceteris paribus, reduce the need for underwriters to use underpricing to reduce the probability of being left with a large number of unsold shares. A reputable underwriter may also charge a high commission and use its reputation to certify the quality of an issue and hence reduce the size of the underpricing as pointed out by Carter and Manaster (1990). In either scenario, we expect underwriting commission to vary inversely with subscribers' returns.

The proportion of the shares sold, the shares allocated to overseas investors and the regulatory situation of a company represent some of the key decisions made by the government before the sale of shares. Such decisions may in part be influenced by the capacity of the market to absorb an issue. Partial sales may be used by the government to determine the market valuation of a company before other tranches of shares are sold. In such a context, we expect higher underpricing as the proportion of shares sold decreases. Such a pricing scenario may still produce higher overall proceeds as subsequent tranches are sold at their market clearing prices because the initial underpricing cost will be limited to a small proportion of the value of the firm. We, therefore, expect an inverse relationship between the proportion of shares sold and initial excess returns. The capacity of the U.K. market to absorb an issue is measured by the demand multiple, which may be gauged during the pre-selling period. If the U.K. demand is high, the discriminatory allocation policy of the government in favour of retail investors is invoked and this leads to a reduction in the allocations to U.K. institutional and overseas investors. Reduced allocations may encourage such investors to acquire shares in the market. Other things being equal, we expect the demand multiple to be positively related to initial returns to investors.

The impact of the regulatory situation on initial returns is mainly due to the differences in the expectations of the issuer and investors about the economic impact of the initial regulatory framework on the value of the firm. The issuer (the government in this case) may for instance assume that the initial regulatory framework will not allow a company to earn monopolistic rents. It may therefore, 'take lower proceeds in return for, say, lower prices to customers' (Beesley and Littlechild (1989))[12]. On the other hand investors may consider what the government interprets as tight regulation to be sufficiently lenient to generate monopoly rents to the company. Such a difference in the expected impact of regulation between the issuer and investors would cause a difference in the initial valuation of the company by the two parties. Using dummy variables (one for regulated and zero for unregulated) we expect to identify the impact of the regulatory environment on the perceived initial value of the firm.

Jones et. al. (1994) argued that '... if underpricing is a deliberate wealth transfer to investors so as to build political support, governments will tend to underprice in cases where domestic investors (and thus constituents) can reap the benefits of underpricing.' Thus, a negative relationship between the proportion of shares allocated to foreign investors and initial returns to the subscribers would indicate political interest of the government in underpricing.

U.K. PIPO advisers often cite market volatility as one of the reasons for downward revision of offer prices from those initially proposed. Following Menyah et. al. (1995), this variable is measured by the daily variance of market returns during two months prior to the issue. Since higher volatility encourages the issuer to set a lower offer price (hence the possibility of higher underpricing) this variable is expected to be positively associated with excess returns.

In the light of the above, we use the regression format of expressions (3) to explain the magnitudes of subscribers' return:

$$R_i = f(Comm, PS, DMlp, R\&U, Mvol, Fgn) \tag{3}$$

Where:

R_i	= subscriber return for company i measured with equation (1);
Comm	= underwriting commission expressed as a percentage of the proceeds;
DMlp	= demand multiple or the extent of over(under) subscription;
R&U	= the regulatory status of the company;
Mvol	= market volatility;
PS	= proportion of shares sold and
Fgn	= Percentage of shares allocated to foreign investors

The above relationship is estimated with OLS method and the test statistics are adjusted for heteroscedasticity. The results are reported as equation (4).

$$R_i = \begin{array}{l} 0.371 + 0.017\ DMlp^* - 0.367\ PS^* + 0.254\ R\&U^* \\ (1.79) \quad (6.68) \qquad\qquad (-2.34) \qquad (3.71) \end{array} \tag{4}$$

$$\begin{array}{l} + 0.207\ MVol^* - 0.215\ Comm^* + 0.003\ Fgn \\ \quad (4.08) \qquad\qquad (-2.99) \qquad\qquad (0.92) \end{array}$$

Notes:
Adjusted R-Squared is 71 percent.
T-Statistics are given in parentheses.
* Indicates significant at 5 percent or better.

All significant coefficients have the expected signs. As anticipated, the demand multiple and the size of subscribers' returns are positively related. Higher demand multiple, which triggers a clawback of shares from institutional and overseas investors, encourages such investors to bid for the shares when trading begins. Similarly, the volatility of the market immediately prior to an issue has a significant positive impact on subscribers' return. This finding confirms our prior expectation that issuers would be inclined to agree to a lower offer price in the face of a volatile market. The significant negative sign for the proportion of shares sold is consistent with the view that the government expected the issues to obtain the best possible price. The extensive pre-issue marketing of PIPOs and the global nature of most issues represent specific actions which are consistent with this viewpoint. The significant negative relationship between subscriber return and underwriting commission is consistent with the argument that a lower commission rate encourages underwriters to set a lower offer price so as to reduce the probability of buying unsold shares. Such a result is consistent with the agency cost model of Baron (1982). It is also consistent with the alternative explanation that prestigious underwriters may charge a higher commission rate and use their reputation to sell the issue at a higher price and therefore reduce underpricing as suggested by Carter and Manaster (1990).

Consistent with the descriptive statistics reported in Table 1, the regulatory situation exerts a significant positive impact on subscribers' return. The significant impact supports our proposition of differences in expectations between the Government and investors regarding the economic impact of regulation. The positive sign indicates that the economic cost assigned by investors to regulation is lower than that perceived by the issuer.

Contrary to the findings of Jones et. al. (1994) the proportion of shares allocated to the foreign investors does not exert any significant impact on subscribers' return. It therefore does not support their hypothesis of deliberate underpricing by the government in favour of domestic (constituents) investors to build political support for privatisation. The excess returns appear to be independent of the nationality of subscribers.

In summary, it is clear that the demand multiple, proportion of shares sold, regulatory situation of a company, market volatility immediately prior to the issue of shares and the rate of underwriting commission taken together can explain about 71 percent of variation in initial subscribers' return. However, subscribers' return remains independent of the proportion of shares allocated to foreign investors[13].

3.4 Secondary Issues

3.4.1 First Day Price Performance

Compared with initial public offers, there are relatively few studies on the pricing of secondary equity offers. Smith (1977) using New York Stock Exchange (NYSE) and American Stock Exchange (AMEX) data reports an average return of 0.82 percent from the offer price to the close of the offer day for the period 1971-75. Bhagat and Frost (1986) on the other hand, report a significant average overpricing of -0.25 percent for negotiated offerings and -0.65 percent for competitive underwritten offers using NYSE and AMEX stocks for the period 1973-1980. Parson and Raviv (1985) develop a model which attempts to provide a rational explanation for seasoned equity pricing. In their model, there are two classes of investors with different reservation prices: high value investors (with high reservation prices) to which a firm wants to sell but cannot identify and low-value investors. This situation results in a finite price elasticity for the demand curve for the stock. Hence, high value investors concerned about the likelihood of oversubscription drive the pre-issue (and, by implication) the post-issue price above the offer price to produce underpricing. Loderer et. al. (1991) using firm commitment offerings on NYSE, AMEX and NASDAQ exchanges for the period 1980-84 report that returns based on the offer price and the close of first day trading do not suggest that prices are systematically set below the market as implied by Parsons and Raviv (1985). Even though they find the average underpricing to be positive (0.35 percent) and significant, the median is zero and only 30 percent of the returns are positive. A separate analysis of NASDAQ stocks however, shows that most secondary offers have an issue day price which is above the offer price. After considering the plausibility of several explanations in the IPO literature, they suggest that the underpricing is possibly due to asymmetric information between issuing companies and investors. The lower magnitude of the underpricing is attributed to the fact that seasoning reduces the degree of information asymmetry and hence the level of underpricing.

Table 2

Secondary Issues: Some Facts

Private company	Method of sale	Dealing date	Gross proceeds £M	Demand multiple	Offer price in pence	Sec.Day-1[a] return in %	Primary[b] initial return in %
BP	OS	24/06/77	564.00	4.7	845	22.67	N/A
	OS	9/11/79	290.00	1.5	363	2.67	-
	T	23/09/83	566.00	1.3	435	6.00	-
	T	30/10/87	724.00[1]	0.0048	330-	-29.17	-
	OS	30/10/87		0.0129	330	-29.17	-
Cab	IT	02/12/83	275.00	0.7	275	-3.00	20.83
	OS	13/12/85	933.00	2.0	587	-1.67	-
ABP	T	18/04/84	52.00	1.6	270	31.00	16.96
BAe	OS	14/05/85	551.00	12.0	375	30.50	14.00
Britoil	OS	12/08/85	449.00	10.0	185	22.00	-15.00
BT	OS	09/12/91	5350.00[c]	1.7	335	14.09	82.00
	T	09/12/91		2.0	350	0.40	-
	OS	19/07/93	5000.00[c]	1.4	410	12.00	-
	T	19/07/93		6.0	420	5.00	-
NPower	OS	06/03/95	619.14	1.6	476	9.71	37.00
	T	06/03/95	1301.00	6.5	486	3.61	-
PWGen	OS	06/03/95	428.09	1.6	512	7.30	37.00
	T	06/03/95	905.54	9.1	522	1.79	-

Notes:
a. These are the first day returns on secondary issues.
b. The first day returns when the companies were initially privatised.
c. Indicates that the gross proceeds represent the total money raised from both offer for sale and tender.

Initial Returns from Secondary Issues: A Summary

Returns in Percent

Private Issues	Day-1 Return	Excess Return	Underpricing
All PIPOs	5.87	8.99	2.22
Fixed price offer	9.01	12.15	2.97
Tender	1.95	5.04	1.27

Notes:
Excess return is Day-1 Return minus Market return
Underpricing refers to the cost of underpricing relative to the value of the firm.

Using equations (1) and (2), we estimate first day subscriber return and the cost of issuer underpricing relative to the value of the firm of privatisation secondary issues. The results reported in Table 2 show that the average gross returns available to subscribers of secondary issues is only 5.87 percent (8.99 percent after making adjustment for market). When we excluded the secondary sale of B.P. in 1987, which occurred in the middle of 1987 October crash, the average returns to subscribers stood at over 10 percent. The results presented in the final column of the table show an average issuer underpricing cost of about 2.22 percent (2.70 percent if BP 1987 is excluded) of the value of the firm14. These secondary issue results are very low compared with subscriber returns of 38.70 percent and issuer underpricing cost of 23.62 percent for privatisation initial public offers. The findings are consistent with previous studies which document lower underpricing for secondary issues.

3.4.2 Methods of Issue: Fixed Price Vs Tender Offers

Though only two PIPOs were sold by tender method, most secondary offerings included a tender component15. Since offer for sale and tender have been used simultaneously in secondary offerings, we also undertake a comparative analysis of subscribers' returns and cost of underpricing under the two methods to identify the most cost effective way of selling subsequent issues. The results presented in Table 2 show that subscribers' returns as well as cost of underpricing to the company are both lower under the tender method. This clearly justifies the use of the tender method in secondary sales where the excess returns to subscribers is about 5 percent (6 percent if B.P. is excluded) and the cost of underpricing is about 1 percent of the value of the firm, while comparable average subscribers' returns under offer for sale are over 12 percent (14 percent excluding B.P.). Therefore, the excess return in secondary issues is mainly available to investors subscribing at the fixed price (Offer for sale) and not those acquiring the shares through the tender method.

3.5 Deciding on the sale method and the proportion sold in initial and secondary offers

The preceding analyses show that partial sales and the extensive use of tender in both initial and secondary offerings could have reduced the level of subscriber returns and issuer underpricing. Why then were partial sales and tenders not extensively used? Analyses of National Audit Office reports on privatisation suggest that the British government considered the issue of full or partial sale on a case by case basis. The major issues considered before reaching the final decision included: the absorbtion capacity of the market especially in the cases of large issues (the block trade effect); whether sale in more than one tranche would create doubts about the intention to transfer the control of company to the private sector; possible financial benefits expected through sale in tranches; and the degree of confidence that the sale could be properly priced. Of the 40 PIPOs 7 were sold in tranches. All the shares in the remaining 33 companies were sold in one transaction. This suggests that the priority of the government was more focused on the objective of signalling its intention of transferring control into private hands which would reduce the possibility of re-nationalization as discussed in section 2. In relation to the other question of why tenders were not extensively used, we argue that the objective of wider share ownership may have played a part in such decisions.

The choice of a fixed price as the method of privatization to achieve the wider ownership objective is based on the argument that individual investors feel more comfortable to participate in fixed price sales than in tenders. This could be due to the scale of investment and cost of gathering information required to estimate the price of the share which is important under the tender method. On the other hand, for large institutional investors, the information gathering cost would be a small fraction of investible funds. The government opted for the method of fixed price sale to help achieve the objective of wider share ownership despite its associated higher cost of underpricing. The relatively high subscriber return in fixed price secondary issues (12 percent on average) is consistent with the conjecture of the government offering a *sweetener* to individual subscribers in pursuance of its objective of wider share ownership. However, the frequent use of tenders which produced lower initial returns in the secondary offers suggests that the government was also inclined to reduce the cost of underpricing where possible, without significantly affecting the pursuance of the objective of wider share ownership.

The above arguments about the transfer of companies to the private sector and the achievement of the objective of wider share ownership are summed up in the view expressed by John Moore, then minister in charge of privatisation.

The momentum (for privatisation) *is very strong and the process is irreversible .... Possession means power, the kind of power that matters to ordinary people - power to make choices, power to control their own lives. Our aim is to extend this power to as many people as we can. We are doing this because we believe, it is the best, indeed the only way to achieve the prosperity we seek and to protect the freedoms we value"* (J. Moore, The Value of Ownership. Conservative Political Centre, London 1986).

This is reinforced by the following extract from Margaret Thatcher (1993), British Prime Minister from 1979-1990.

..through privatization -particularly the kind of privatization which leads to the widest possible share ownership by members of the public- the state's power is reduced and the power of the people enhanced. ... Whatever arguments there may - and should - be about the means of sale, the competitive structures or the regulatory frameworks adopted in different cases, this fundamental purpose of privatization must not be overlooked. That consideration is of practical relevance. For it meant that in some cases if it was a choice between having the ideal circumstances for privatization, which might take years to achieve, and going for a sale within a politically determined timescale, the second was the preferable option.

Similar views have been expressed by Norman Lamont (1988) who was then the Financial Secretary to the Treasury. In the light of the above, it can be argued that the government was generally inclined to use privatization to pursue its populist objective of giving power to the people.

4. Long Term Performance of Initial Public Offers

Menyah et al.(1995) report that U.K PIPO portfolios offer significantly high initial returns and excess long-term returns to investors over 80 weeks after issue. Their findings contrast with the growing body of literature on private sector IPOs by Ritter

(1991) and Loughran and Ritter (1995) for the US, Levis (1993) for U.K, Uhlir (1989) for Germany and Aggrawal, Leal and Hernandez (1993) for Latin American countries among others which provide evidence of short-run price over-reaction and high initial returns but long-term price under-performance relative to appropriate benchmarks. We extend the analysis of Menyah et al. (1995) by estimating long-term returns to initial subscribers and those who acquired shares in the after-market and held for 4 years. We investigate the long-term performance for the full sample as well as several sub-samples. In particular, we distinguish between regulated and unregulated industries and also analyze electricity and water companies separately[16]. Such sub-sample analyses enable us to determine whether or not long-term returns are dominated by any category of PIPOs. The FT-All Share Index has been used as the benchmark (market) return since all PIPOs are included in the index. We estimated the holding period returns, $R_{i,t}$ with equation (3):

$$R_{it} = \prod_{t=1}^{N} (1 + r_{it}) - 1 \qquad (3)$$

Where r_{it} is the unadjusted arithmetic return for company i on day t and N takes on several values up to four years[17]. The holding period return on the market index is estimated in a similar manner. In order to evaluate the significance of long-term returns, we subtract the market return from the company return and test whether the net portfolio return is significantly different from zero using the standard t-test of mean equal to zero Vs not equal to zero. We then compare the long-term performance of PIPOs with a sample private sector IPOs. With the reported initial underpricing of PIPOs, we expect that subscribers who hold on to their shares are likely to obtain long-term holding period gains. On the other hand, if IPOs attain their equilibrium values on the first day of trading, then the returns available to investors buying on the first day of trading should not be significantly different from the returns on the market portfolio.[18]

Table 3 provides a summary of the long-term performance of all U.K. PIPOs and of a sample of private sector IPOs. Columns 2 and 3 of the table document the cumulative average raw returns and market adjusted returns on all PIPOs available to those who acquired shares on subscription and held for N periods[19]. The portfolio of all 40 PIPOs, which offered an initial raw return of about 40 percent, was more attractive in the long-term as the holding period return reaches 70 percent (62 percent market adjusted) in one year; 141 percent (105 percent market adjusted) in two years and 228 percent (177 percent market adjusted) if held for four years[20].

The next two columns show the returns from all PIPOs to an investor who bought from the market on the first day of trading and held for up to four years. The results show that PIPO investments offer statistically significant cumulative returns of 134 percent (85 percent on market adjusted basis) if the stocks are held for four years. The remaining 4 columns of the table show the raw and market adjusted holding period returns available to subscribers and secondary market investors in private sector IPOs. The numbers indicate that from investors' point of view, private sector IPOs are not as good investments as PIPOs. Unlike PIPOs, private sector IPOs generate significantly positive excess returns during the first two weeks of trading; however, in the long-run they fail to out-perform the market. This finding is consistent with previous U.K. results reported by Levis (1993).

Table 3

Holding Period Returns from New issues

	Privatization IPOs				Private Sector IPOS			
	Subscription		Market		Subscription		Market	
Holding Period	Raw	Net	Raw	Net	Raw	Net	Raw	Net
1 Day	40.37*	38.70*	NA	NA	3.50	3.48	NA	NA
2 Days	39.92*	38.15*	-0.35	-0.44	4.95*	4.82*	1.43*	1.32*
3 Days	38.63*	36.78*	-1.33	-1.50	5.26*	5.19*	1.81*	1.77*
4 Days	40.34*	38.71*	-0.10	-0.05	5.07*	4.93*	1.68*	1.56*
5 Days	42.49*	40.89*	1.41	1.49	5.03*	4.72*	1.69*	1.42*
6 Days	41.07*	39.72*	0.30	0.62	5.63*	5.31*	2.32*	2.04*
7 Days	41.67*	40.11*	0.68	0.79	6.15*	5.83*	2.82*	2.53*
8 Days	42.09*	40.71*	0.95	1.24	6.04*	5.67*	2.68*	2.34*
9 Days	41.01*	39.70*	0.19	0.56	6.17*	5.68*	2.79*	2.33*
10 Days	39.62*	38.42*	-0.86	-0.38	6.38*	5.73*	3.00*	2.38*
4 weeks	42.59*	40.05*	1.29	0.47	5.87*	4.28	2.58	0.01
3 Months	62.40*	55.22*	15.06*	9.62*	10.57*	5.38	6.87*	1.67
6 Months	74.41*	64.10*	23.93*	15.39*	13.96*	4.97	10.96*	1.97
1 Year	70.09*	62.39*	21.51*	15.54	26.40*	8.70	24.06*	6.33
2 Years	105.28*	82.95*	46.62*	26.28	41.12*	8.48	37.45*	4.74
3 Years	186.34*	141.30*	103.61*	60.97*	56.24*	8.94	52.31*	4.91
4 Years	227.88*	176.60*	133.53*	84.73*	73.34*	7.63	68.90*	3.01

Subscription = Investors subscribe during the offer
Market = Investors buy on the first day of trading from the market
Raw = Gross Returns
Net = Gross returns less market return.
* = statistically significant at 5 percent or better

In order to evaluate how competitive product market forces and regulation affect company performance and by implication returns to investors, we split the sample into regulated and unregulated portfolios. The results presented in Table 4 reveal that the stocks of regulated utilities are not only good in the short-term but also offer significantly positive higher returns in long-run. For instance, the regulated utilities offer statistically significant cumulative excess returns of 112 percent to secondary market buyers in 4 years while the unregulated firms offer only 11.82 percent (statistically not different from zero) during the same period. Therefore, the excess returns from unregulated PIPOs is mainly available to initial subscribers and not those who acquire shares in the secondary market.

We also classified the 40 PIPOs into three portfolios; electricity companies, water companies and other PIPOs. The results presented in Table 5 indicate that the major groups of utilities (electricity and water) offer higher holding period returns. The initial subscriber return offered by electricity companies (over 45 percent) is the highest of all three portfolios. The subscribers of the shares of electricity companies holding them for a year received a gross return of 76 percent (66 percent after making adjustment for market) which increased to 267 percent in three years and 319 percent in four years. After making adjustment for market returns, the holding period excess returns from this portfolio stood at 276 percent in four years. The significant high excess returns were available not only to the initial subscribers but also to the investors buying from the market on first day of trading. Consistent with the hypothesis of over-reaction, the share prices of electricity companies decline significantly from their first day price during the first month of trading. However, from three months onwards, they start to offer statistically significant positive returns which cumulated to 20 percent (11 percent after making adjustment for market returns) in one year and 184 percent (143 percent after making adjustment for market) in four years.

Table 4

Holding Period Returns for Regulated and Unregulated PIPOs

| | Regulated PIPOs | | | | Unregulated PIPOs | | | |
| | Subscription | | Market | | Subscription | | Market | |
Holding Period	Raw	Net	Raw	Net	Raw	Net	Raw	Net
1 Day	45.78*	44.27*	NA	NA	26.13*	24.00*	NA	NA
2 Days	45.17*	43.58*	-0.42	-0.51	26.09*	23.86*	-0.15	-0.25
3 Days	43.72*	42.02*	-1.43*	-1.62*	25.21*	22.96*	-1.08	-1.19
4 Days	45.60*	44.28*	-0.16	0.02	26.46*	24.04*	0.05	-0.24
5 Days	48.35*	47.14*	1.72	2.02*	27.06*	24.44*	0.61	0.11
6 Days	46.84*	45.90*	0.60	1.15	25.84*	23.42*	-0.47	-0.77
7 Days	47.95*	46.60*	1.31	1.46*	25.13*	23.01*	-0.98	-0.99
8 Days	48.62*	47.68*	1.78*	2.34*	24.89*	22.33*	-1.22	-1.65
9 Days	46.81*	45.90*	0.55	1.15	25.70*	23.34*	-0.77	-0.99
10 Days	45.29*	44.43*	-0.52	0.12	24.67*	22.59*	-1.77	-1.70
4 weeks	49.05*	47.19*	2.12	1.78	25.54*	21.24	-0.90	-3.00
3 Months	71.35*	65.40*	16.87*	12.45*	38.82*	28.39*	10.30	2.15
6 Months	85.35*	76.72*	26.06*	19.03*	45.59*	30.83*	18.31	5.80
1 Year	84.37*	81.64*	25.67*	24.44*	32.43	11.65	10.54	-7.91
2 Years	127.10*	111.03*	55.13*	40.75*	47.75	8.91	24.18	-11.88
3 Years	225.37*	190.42*	122.16*	89.17*	83.45*	11.80	54.68	-13.38
4 Years	266.95*	227.31*	149.97*	112.39*	124.86*	42.90	90.18	11.82

t-test of differences in market adjusted returns for various portfolios of secondary market buyers

| | Holding Period | | | |
Portfolios	1 Year	2 Years	3 Years	4 Years
Regulated vs Unregulated	2.86*	3.26*	4.77*	3.58*
Water vs Electricity	7.41*	-1.77	0.46	-1.68

Subscription = Investors subscribe during the offer
Market = Investors buy on the first day of trading from the market
Raw = Gross Returns
Net = Gross returns less market return.
* =statistically significant at 5 percent or better.

The cumulative holding period return from the portfolio of water companies, which offered 44 percent returns to initial subscribers, reached 89 percent (98 percent market adjusted) in one year which galloped to 240 percent (202 percent after making adjustment for market) in four years. Unlike the electricity companies' stocks, these stocks did not display any symptom of initial over-reaction. Rather, significant positive excess returns to secondary market buyers started to arise from day 5 of trading. By the end of one year, the holding period return to secondary investors had reached 32 percent and increased to 136 percent (101 percent after making adjustment for market) by the end of year four. Thus, the portfolio of water companies' stock turned out to be highly profitable to both initial subscribers and secondary market buyers.

Unlike the portfolios of electricity and water companies, the performance of the portfolio of other PIPOs tells a different story. The initial returns to subscribers of other PIPOs is much lower (32 percent) than that offered by electricity and water companies. Though the four year holding period gross returns to the initial subscribers is statistically significant (136 percent), it ceases to be significant after making adjustment for the market return, after the end of one year trading. No statistically significant excess return is available to initial subscribers for a period of four years. Hence despite the high excess return observed in the early days of trading, the portfolio of PIPOs other than electricity and water companies does not out-perform the market in the long-run. We investigated the extent to which the high initial returns on water and electricity companies could be due to the impact of a hot-issue period. We find that the average market return of 13 percent during the water and electricity privatisations (1989-1991) is lower than the average of 19.1 percent for the preceding 1981-1988 period. Secondly, the average number of new issues of 101 companies (excluding privatisations) over the 1989-91 period is not statistically different from the average of 96 companies over the period 1981-1988. Hence, both stock market performance and the volume of issues do not support the conjecture that the initial returns to water and electricity companies could be attributed to a hot-issue period.

The evidence discussed above suggests that in general PIPOs are good investments in the short-run as well as the long-run for most investors. The above-market long-term performance of PIPOs is generated by the regulated utilities rather than the unregulated. A number of reasons may explain this finding. It could be due the unwillingness or inability of regulators to introduce competition in industries where this is feasible or the absence of appropriate regulatory action to curb the excess profits of such monopolistic utilities. If this is the case, then it implies that regulators have not been successful in pursing their other objective of ensuring that consumers are not over-charged by the utility companies. Alternatively, the higher returns for the monopolistic utilities could be due to the absence of down-side risk in their cash flows. This arises from the notion that whilst regulators may be inclined to reduce tariffs for profitable companies, they are also likely to allow increases in tariffs for inefficiently managed companies if they face potential bankruptcy. Such possible regulatory behaviour, combined with monopoly power in the markets, puts a lower bound on the cash flows of companies and reduces their down-side risk.

Table 5

Long-term Buy-and-Hold of Major Utilities and Other PIPOs

Holding Period	Electricity Companies				Water Companies				Other PIPOs			
	Subscription		Market		Subscription		Market		Subscription		Market	
	Raw	Net	Raw	Net	Raw	Net	Raw	Net	Raw	Net	Raw	Net
1 Day	45.16*	44.00*	NA	NA	43.95*	41.87*	NA	NA	32.35*	30.37*	NA	NA
2 Days	43.75*	43.02*	-1.03	-0.60	45.30*	42.37*	0.97*	0.14	31.71*	29.58*	-0.52	-0.67
3 Days	41.72*	40.36*	-2.46*	-2.65*	44.95*	42.65*	0.70	0.49	30.59*	28.49*	-1.49	-1.61
4 Days	44.47*	43.21*	-0.60	-0.70	45.30*	43.85*	0.91	1.53	32.08*	29.90*	-0.24	-0.44
5 Days	44.06*	43.33*	-0.94	-0.50	53.60*	51.61*	6.80*	6.89*	32.76*	30.46*	0.25	-0.08
6 Days	45.25*	44.58*	-0.17	0.32	46.95*	45.59*	2.13*	2.84*	32.09*	29.97*	-0.46	-0.60
7 Days	45.44*	44.47*	-0.12	0.07	49.45*	47.44*	3.87*	3.94*	31.82*	29.89*	-0.68	-0.65
8 Days	46.28*	45.74*	0.45	1.07	50.55*	48.78*	4.62*	4.92*	31.27*	29.19*	-1.09	-1.19
9 Days	43.56*	43.18*	-1.31	-0.54	49.65*	47.56*	3.99*	3.98*	31.19*	30.10*	-0.80	-0.62
10 Days	40.63*	40.40*	-3.33*	-2.41*	49.65*	47.56*	3.99*	3.98*	31.31*	29.64*	-1.50	-1.18
4 weeks	38.91*	39.25*	-4.49*	-3.00*	62.00*	56.55*	12.64*	9.34*	32.92*	29.18*	-0.21	-1.91
3 Months	80.66*	67.60*	23.43*	11.64*	56.55*	60.67*	8.75*	14.83*	45.71*	37.18*	10.01	3.58
6 Months	95.81*	82.17*	33.36*	21.02*	54.30*	53.85*	7.24*	8.84*	64.32*	50.76*	25.08*	13.62
1 Year	75.90*	65.65*	20.26*	11.26*	89.22*	98.15*	31.66*	42.45*	49.78*	33.13	15.69	1.22
2 Years	156.49*	131.16*	75.35*	51.45*	86.59*	86.28*	29.72*	31.45*	60.10*	25.48	25.85	-6.19
3 Years	267.50*	218.20*	150.42*	102.83*	179.36*	165.89*	93.98*	82.82*	98.57*	35.86	56.99*	-2.49
4 Years	319.00*	276.47*	184.44*	143.50*	239.96*	201.97*	136.14*	100.97*	135.73*	64.13	87.62*	19.31

* = statistically significant at 5 percent or better
Subscription = Investors subscribe during the offer
Market = Investors buy on the first day of trading from the market
Raw = Gross Returns
Net = Gross returns less market return.

5. The Objectives and Outcomes of SIPS an Evaluation

In the light of the discussions in sections 2 and 3, it has been demonstrated that the objectives of successful transfer of firms to the private sector and ensuring the irreversibility of the process through the pursuance of the policy of wider and employee share ownership dominated the decision making process in share issue privatisations. These two objectives interacted to produce the major features of the process: sale of hundred percent of equity; the extensive use of offer for sale; elaborate promotion and marketing; the use of placing in offer for sale; clawback and discriminatory allocation to employees and small investors, instalment payments and underpricing. While some of the features have been criticised as costly and unnecessary, it can be argued, with the benefit of hindsight that successful transfer of enterprises to the private sector has been achieved. This is evidenced by the long-term price performance documented in this paper and the post privatisation operating performance outlined in Megginson et. al. (1994). The fear of re-nationalisation has also abated since the major Parliamentary Opposition Party has backed away from that policy and at worst may tighten regulation of monopolies or impose an excess profit tax on some companies. What is unclear is the extent to which privatisation has helped achieve the objective of wider share ownership.

Table 6

Initial number of shareholders and percentage retained after one year of privatisation

Company		Initial Number of shareholders[a]	% of original number of shareholders after one year
British Aerospace	1981	155,000	17.5
Amersham Int'l	1982	65,000	13.2
Britoil	1982	40,000	99.0
Ass. Brit. Ports	1983	45,000	16.6
Enterprise Oil	1984	14,000	103.3
Jaguar	1984	120,000	43.3
British Telecom	1984	2.4 million	73.6
British Gas	1986	4.5 million	70.6
British Airways	1987	1.1 million	38.2
Rolls Royce	1987	2.0 million	46.2
BAA	1987	2.18 million	48.7
British Steel	1988	650,000	64.4
10 Water Companies	1989	2.7 million	50.0[b]
12 Elec. Companies	1990	9 million	40.0
Nat. Power/PowerGen	1991	3.25 million	45.5
Scottish Power/Hydro.	1991	N/A	67.0[c]

Sources: Privatisation: The Facts, National Audit Office Reports (various), Bishop and Kay (1988).
Notes
a. The initial number of shareholders refers to the total number of shareholders after flotation.
b. Relates to 7 months after the sale
c. Relates to 6 months after the sale

Table 6 shows the number of initial shareholders and the percentage still holding shares after one year. It reveals that whilst initial enthusiasm for subscription was high, on average about one half of the shareholders sold their holdings within a year[21]. This is further borne out in Table: 7 which shows that the total number of individual shareholders increased with major privatisations but declined thereafter.

Even though the proportion of the adult population owning shares has increased from 9 percent in 1979 to 22 percent in 1993 as indicated in Table 7, the majority of individuals hold shares in only one company as shown in Table 8. This lack of diversification indicates that even though ownership may have been broadened through privatisation issues, it has not deepened or extended in any significant way to private sector shares. It is therefore not surprising that personal ownership of shares continues to decline as shown in Table 9. However, this is puzzling since the long-term performance of PIPOs (especially those of utility companies) is far better than the market in general. This casts some doubt on the rationality of expectation of small investors regarding the long-term prospects of such investments. However, small investors may have their own reason (possibly liquidity or long-term uncertainty about regulation) for being unable or unwilling to hold such shares for a long period. In the light of the above evidence, it can be argued that privatisation created new 'stags' willing to make a quick profit but unwilling (or possibly unable) to invest their funds in equities on a medium to long-term basis.

Table 7

Number of individual shareholders in the UK, 1979-1993

Year End	No. of shareholders	Main reasons for change
1979	3 million (approx.)	
1983	4 million (approx.)	profit sharing and main privatisations (B.P.; Br. Aerospace, Amersham Int'l; Britoil; Cable and Wireless; Ass. British Ports)
1984	5 million	British Telecom flotation.
1985	5.5-6 million	Further growth in profit sharing.
Year Beginning		
1987	8.4 million	British Gas and TSB
1988	9 million	British Airways, BAA, Rolls-Royce, BP
1989	9 million	British Steel
1990	10.8 million	Abbey National and Water companies
1991	11 million	Electricity generating and distributing companies
1992	9.8 million	British Telecom second tranche
Year End		
1992	9.2 million	
1993	10 million	British Telecom third tranche

Proportion of the adult population estimated to be owning shares is 9 percent in 1979 and 22 percent at the end of 1993. Source: ProShare (UK) Ltd. December 1994.

As pointed out in section 3, sale proceeds could have been maximised if partial sales and tender offers had been used. Column 2 of Table 10 provides estimates of the potential sale proceeds if all the shares in the seven companies had been sold in the first instance. The estimates assume no change in the elasticity of demand for the sale of a larger number of shares and may overestimate the proceeds. Columns 3 and 4 of

Table 10 provide the nominal and discounted proceeds of the actual total proceeds realised from partial sales. Apart from Britoil, which traded at a discount after the initial public offer, the total proceeds from partial sales exceed what could have been obtained from 100 percent sale for the other companies. The fact that partial sales and tenders which could have increased proceeds were not extensively used is largely due to the populist political philosophy of encouraging ownership (see references and quotations in section 3.5 as well as Moore (1992)) which dominated decision making and led to privatisations without adequate regard to the optimum methods of divesture. The end result is the high underpricing cost (especially for water and electricity companies) documented in section 3 and substantial out-of-pockets expenses which arose in preparing companies for sale (Beauchamp, 1990).

Table 8

Diversification of individual shareholding as at the end of 1993

No. of companies in which shares are held	Percentage of shareholders
1	51
2	18
3	9
4-10	17
11 or more	4

Source: ProShare (UK) Ltd. which extracted it from the 1993 Survey of Share Ownership by National Opinion Polls for the U.K. Treasury.

Table 9

Percentage of U.K. quoted equities owned by various sectors

Shareholders\ Year End:	1957	1963	1969	1975	1981	1989	1990	1991	1992	1993
Personal	65.8	54.0	47.4	37.5	28.2	20.6	20.3	19.9	20.4	17.7
Pension Funds	3.4	6.4	9.0	16.8	26.7	30.6	31.6	31.3	35.1	34.2
Insurance Companies	8.8	10.0	12.2	15.9	20.5	18.6	20.4	20.8	16.7	17.3
Investment Trusts	5.2	11.3	10.1	10.5	5.4	1.6	1.6	1.5	2.1	2.5
Other financial institutions	-	-	-	-	1.4	1.1	0.7	0.8	0.4	0.6
Unit Trusts	0.5	1.3	2.9	4.1	3.6	5.9	6.1	5.7	6.2	6.6
Charities		2.1	2.1	2.3	2.2	2.3	1.9	2.4	1.8	1.6
Banks		1.3	1.7	0.7	0.3	0.7	0.7	0.2	0.5	0.6
Industrial and Commercial Cos.	16.3	5.1	5.4	3.0	5.1	3.8	2.8	3.3	1.8	1.5
Public Sector		1.5	2.6	3.6	3.0	2.0	2.0	1.3	1.8	1.3
Overseas holders		7.0	6.6	5.6	3.6	12.8	11.8	12.8	13.1	16.3
TOTAL	100	100	100	100	100	100	100	100	100	100

Source: Compiled from various sources by ProShare (UK) Ltd. December 1994.

Note: The percentages of the various sectors are based on the market values of the shares owned.

6. Conclusion

This paper identifies the various objectives of UK share issue privatisation, contrasts them and demonstrates how the primary aim of reducing state involvement in economic activities influenced the design of public share sales. In particular, it argues that the wider share ownership objective may not be an end in itself, but a convenient mechanism for ensuring the development of popular support for the programme and reducing the probability of re-nationalisation by a future government. Achieving such an objective has meant that substantial restructuring, issuing[22] (underwriting, marketing and distribution) and underpricing costs have been incurred. In the case of underpricing, we estimate that about 23 percent of the value of the firms was lost by the government to subscribers. This is mainly attributed to the fact that partial sales and tender offers were not extensively used in the initial public offers. Our analysis of the results of secondary offers reinforces this by showing that in such issues, underpricing cost was reduced to 2.97 percent in offer for sale and 1.27 percent in tender offers. We therefore infer that selling all the equity in a single transaction has not been consistent with the objective of maximising sale proceeds to the exchequer.

Table 10

Total proceeds from shares sold in tranches compared with what could have been realised if all shares had been sold in one transaction.

Company	Estimated total proceeds from 100% sale (£M)	Nominal total proceeds from partial sales (£M)	Discounted total proceeds from partial sales (£M)
British Telecom	7800	14200	8816.7
British Aerospace	280	691	473.6
Cable and Wireless	457	1432	1052.6
Britoil	1076	998	884.8
Associated British Ports	43	74	67.8
National Power	2230	3258	2715.5
PowerGen	1336	2154	1776.7
TOTAL	13222	22807	15787.7

Notes:
Estimated proceeds from 100 percent sales have been calculated by grossing up the partial sale proceeds to their 100 percent equivalent. The partial sale proceeds represent the total amount raised from initial and all secondary issues. The gross redemption yields for medium-term U.K. government bonds for relevant years have been used to arrive at the discounted total partial sales proceeds.

The study also documents that over a four year period, the average holding period returns to subscribers and those who buy in the after-market exceeds the return on the FT-All Share Index. The findings are however, driven by the returns accruing to regulated monopolies, especially electricity and water companies. For unregulated companies, the long-term performance of the new issues is not qualitatively different from that observed in private sector issues. We therefore argue that the existence of a mild regulatory regime and the absence of effective competition in regulated monopolies accounts for the observed high long-term holding period returns. Whether or not the costs incurred as a result of the dominance of populist political philosophy over economic analysis can be justified, depends in part upon whether the structural economic changes introduced by privatisation can demonstrate the superiority of markets over other forms of economic organisation so that privatised firms which may fail in the future are not bailed out by taxpayers.

Appendix A

Summary of Special Arrangements for Eligible Employees

Company	Year	Free	Matching	Priority	Priority	Employee
British Petroleum	1977	-	-	No Limit	-	-
	1979	-	-	137	-	-
	1983	-	-	250	-	-
	1987	-	-	1000	-	-
British Aerospace	1981	33	600	No Limit	2.5	74
	1985	-	-	10,000	2.0	30
Cable and Wireless	1981	285,833	-	No Limit	5.0	99
	1983	-	-	1000	0	2
	1985	-	-	5000	1.0	-
Amarsham International	1982	35	350 max	No Limit	5.0	99
Britoil	1982	28	186	11,500	-	72
	1985	-	-	10,000	3.0	-
Associated British Ports	1983	53	225	No Limit	2.5	-
Enterprise Oil	1984	-	-	3500	-	71
Jaguar	1984	-	-	10,000	7.5	19
British Tel	1984	54	77	No Limit	10.0	95
	1991	-	-	1000	10.0	96
	1993	-	-	2500 min	-	-
TSB	1984	-	-	1000	-	-
British Gas	1986	52	111	20,000	5.0	99
British Airways	1987	76	120	No Limit	95	90
Rolls Royce	1987	44	88	5882	5.0	-
BAA	1987	41	82	4082	5.0	60
British Steel	1988	56 max	132	8000	10.0	95
Water	1989	29-46	83	5980	10.0	96
Electricity	1990	58 min	92	6771	4.0	98
National Power	1991	80 min	114	9280	10.0	95
	1995	-	-	2176	-	-
PowerGen	1991	80 min	114	9280	10.0	95
Scottish Power	1991	58 min	96	6917	10.0	-
Scottish Hydro	1991	58 min	96	6917	10.0	95

Sources: Privatisation: The Facts, 1989,1990. Extel Weekly Financial News Summary

Appendix B

Arrangements for Individual Investors[1,2]

Company	Year of Issue	No. of Instalments	Months to 2nd and 3rd Inst	Max Loyalty Bonus Share	Basis	Alternative in form of
BP	1977	2	6	-	-	-
	1979	2	3	-	-	-
	1983	2	4	-	-	-
	1987	3	10/18	-	-	-
BAE	1981	-	-	-	-	-
	1985	2	4	-	-	-
CABL	1981	-	-	-	-	-
	1985	2	3	-	-	-
BTOL	1982	2	5	200	1 in 10	-
	1985	2	3	-	-	-
ABP	1983	-	-	-	-	
	1984	2	3	-	-	-
ENTO	1984	2	2	-	-	-
BT	1984	3	6/16	500	1 in 10	bill vouchers[3]
	1991	3	7/15	150	1 in 10	discount[4]
	1993	3	7/15		1 in 15	discount[5]
BGAS	1986	3	6/16	500	1 in 10	bill vouchers[6]
BAIR	1987	2	6	400	1 in 10	-
RLRC	1987	2	4	-	-	-
BAA	1987	2	10	200	1 in 10	-
BS	1988	2	9	-	-	-
WATER		3	7/19	300[7]	1 in 10	dicount[8]
ELEC	1990	3	10/21	300	1 in 10	bill vouchers[9]
NPR	1991	2	11	248	1 in 10	discount[10]
PWG	1991	2	11	152	1 in 10	discount[10]
	1995	3	11/18			
SPW	1991	3	11/22	300[11]	1 in 10	bill vouchers[12]
SHY	1991	3	11/22	300[11]	1 in 10	bill vouchers[12]

Notes:

1. There were no special arrangements in respect of Jaguar and Amersham International.

2. Existing shareholders were generally given preferential treatment when applying for second and third tranche issues.

3. worth up to £216 for customers

4. 15p per share off the second and third instalments.

5. 14p per share off the second and third instalments.

6. up to £250 over a three year period on the basis of £10 per 100 shares held continuously.

7. applicable to customers. For non-customers, the maximum was 150 shares on a 1 in 20 basis

8. 10p discount per share on second and third instalments up to a maximum of £300.

9. up to a maximum of £270.

10. 14p discount per share on the second instalment.

11. applicable to customers- for non-customers, the bonus was a maximum of 150 shares on the basis of 1 in 20.

12. maximum of £270 for customers only.

Sources: Privatisation: The Facts, 1989, 1990. Extel Weekly Financial News Summary.

Acknowledgement

We are very grateful to Mario Levis for his encouragement and support in writing this paper. We also thank the anonymous referee for his constructive suggestions. Remaining errors are ours.

References

Abromeit, H., 1988, British Privatisation policy, Parliamentary Affairs, 41 1, pp 68-85.

Aggarwal, R., R. Leal, and L. Hernandez, 1993, The aftermarket performance of initial public offerings in Latin America, Financial Management, 22, pp. 42-53.

Ash, T., P. Hare, and A. Cunning, 1994, Privatisation in former centrally planned economies in Jackson, P. M. and C. M. Price (eds.) Privatisation and Regulation: A review of the issues, Harow, Longman Group Ltd.

Baron, D. P., 1982, A model of the demand for investment banking advising and distribution services for new issues, Journal of Finance, 37, pp. 955-976.

Barry, C. and R. H. Jennings, 1993, The opening price performance of initial public offerings of common stock, Financial Management, 22, Spring, pp. 54-63.

Beauchamp, C., 1990, National Audit Office: Its role in privatisation, Public Money and Management, Summer, pp. 55-58.

Beesley, M. and S. Littlechild, 1989, The regulation of privatised monopolies in the United Kingdom, Rand Journal of Economics, 20, pp. 454-472.

Bhagat, S. and P. A. Frost, 1986, Issuing costs to existing shareholders in competitive and negotiated underwritten public utility equity offerings, Journal of Financial Economics, 2, pp. 233-259.

Bishop, M. and D. Thompson, 1992, Regulatory reform and productivity growth in the UK public utilities, Applied Economics, 24, pp. 1181-1190.

Boycko, M., A. Shleifer, and R. W. Vishny, 1994, Voucher privatization, Journal of Financial Economics, 35, pp. 249-266.

Browne, A., 1993, Privatisation in Australasia, in Ramanadham V. (ed) Privatisation: A global perspective, Routledge, London.

Buckland, R., 1987, The costs and returns of the privatization of nationalised industries, Public Administration, 65, pp. 241-257.

Carter, R. and S. Manaster, 1990, Initial public offering and underwriter reputation, Journal of Finance, 45, pp. 1045-1067.

Chown, J. F., 1993, The costs of privatisation, Economic Affairs, April, pp. 22-24.

Curwen, P., 1986, Public Enterprise, Wheatsheaf Books, Brighton.

Department of the Environment, 1986, Privatisation of the Water Authorities in England and Wales, Cmnd. 9734, HMSO, London.

Develle, M., 1986, Privatisation in France: Status and Outlook, World of Banking, 7(5), pp. 13-16.

Draper, P. and K. Paudyal, 1995, Empirical irregularities in the estimation of beta: the impact of alternative estimation, assumptions and procedures, Journal of Business Finance and Accounting, January, pp. 157-177.

Dunsire, A., K. Hartley and D. Parker, 1991, Organisational status and performance: a summary of the findings, Public Administration, 69, pp. 21-40.

Estrin, S., P. A. Grout, and S. Wadhwani, 1987, Profit sharing and employee share ownership, Economic Policy, 4, pp. 14-62.

Giarraputo, J. D., 1994, Vive la privatisation, Global Finance, 8, pp. 31-33.

Great Britain: National Audit Office, (1985-1992), Value for Money Reports on the sale of government shareholding in various Nationalised Industries, HMSO.

Grimstone, G., 1988, The financial process of privatisation, in V Ramanadham (ed) Privatisation in the UK, Routledge, London.

Grout, P. A., 1987, The wider share ownership programme, Fiscal Studies, 8, pp. 59-74.

Hartley, K., D. Parker, and S. Martin, 1991, Organisational status, ownership and productivity, Fiscal Studies, 12, pp. 46-60.

Helm, D. and G. Yarrow, 1988, Assessment: the regulation of utilities, Oxford Review of Economic Policy, 4, pp i-xxxi.

Hutchinson, G., 1991, Efficiency gains through privatisation of UK industries in A. F. Ott and K. Hartley (eds) Privatisation and Economic Efficiency, Edward Elgar, Aldershot.

Ibbotson, R. G., 1975, Price performance of common stock new issues, Journal of financial Economics, 2, pp. 235-272.

Jenkinson, T. and C. Mayer, 1988, The privatization process in France and the UK, Economic Review, 32, pp. 482-490.

Jones, S. L., W. L. Megginson, R. C. Nash, and J. M. Netter, 1994, Share Issue Privatizations as Financial Means to Political and Economic Ends, Department of Banking and Finance, Terry College of Business, Manuscript.

Kay, J. A. and D. J. Thompson, 1986, Privatisation: A policy in search of a rationale, The Economic Journal, 96, pp. 18-38.

Lamont, N., 1988, The benefits of privatisation: an overview in E. Butler (ed) The mechanics of privatisation. pp. 1-9, Adam Smith Institute, London.

Levis, M., 1993, The long-run performance of initial public offers: the UK experience, 1980-1988, Financial Management, 22, pp. 28-41.

Loderer, C. F., P. Sheehan and G. B. Kadlec, 1991, The pricing of equity offerings, Journal of Financial Economics, 29, pp. 35-57.

Loughran, T. and J. R. Ritter, 1995, The new issues puzzle, Journal of Finance, 50, pp. 23-51.

McAllister, I. and D. Studlar, 1989, Popular versus elite views of privatisation: the case of Britain, Journal of Public Policy, 9, pp. 157-178.

Megginson, W. L., R. C. Nash, and M. V. Randenborgh, 1994, The financial and operating performance of newly privatized firms: An international empirical analysis, Journal of Finance, 49, pp. 403-452.

Menyah, K., K. Paudyal and C. G. Inyangete, 1990, The pricing of initial offerings of privatised companies on the London Stock Exchange, Accounting and Business Research, 21, pp. 50-56.

Menyah, K., K. Paudyal and C. G. Inyangete, 1995, Subscriber return, underpricing and long-term performance of privatisation initial public offers, Journal of Economic and Business, forthcoming.

Moore, J., 1986, The value of ownership, Conservative Political Centre, mimeo, London.

Moore, J., 1992, British privatisation: taking capitalism to the people, Harvard Business Review, January-February, pp. 115-124.

Mount, F., 1986, The practice of liberty, mimeo.

Parker, D. and K. Hartley, 1991, Status change and performance: economic policy and evidence, in: A. F. Ott and K. Hartley (eds) Privatisation and Economic Efficiency, Aldershot: Edward Elgar.

Parsons, J. and A. Raviv, 1985, Underpricing of seasoned issues, Journal of Financial Economics, 14, pp. 377-397.

Perotti, E. C. and S. E. Guney, 1993, The structure of privatization plans, Financial Management, Spring, 22, pp. 84-98

Price, C. M., 1994, Privatisation in less developed countries, in P. M. Jackson and C. M. Price (eds) Privatisation and Regulation: A review of the issues, Harlow, Longmans Group Ltd.

Price Waterhouse, 1989, Privatisation: the facts

Price Waterhouse, 1990, Privatisation: the facts

Remolona, E. I., 1989, Risk, capital markets and the large public enterprise, Federal Reserve Bank of New York, Research Paper No. 8912.

Ritter, J., 1991, The long-run performance of initial public offerings, Journal of Finance, 46, pp. 3-27.

Sabine, M., 1993, Corporate finance- flotations, equity issues and acquisitions, Butterworths, London.

Smith, C. W., 1977, Alternative methods for raising capital: rights versus underwritten offerings, Journal of Financial Economics, 5, pp. 273-307.

Strzyzewska-Kaminska, 1993, The privatisation process in Japan in the 1980s, in V. Ramanadham (ed) Privatisation: A global perspective, Routledge, London.

Thatcher, M., 1993, The Downing Street Years, Harper Collins Publishers, London.

Thomas, D., J. Kay, 1986, Privatisation and regulation: the UK experience, Clarendon, Oxford.

Thompson, S., M. Wright and K. Robbie, 1990, Management buy-outs from the public sector: Ownership form and incentive issues, Fiscal Studies, 11, pp 71-88.

Uhlir, H., 1989, Going Public in F.R.G., in R. M. Guimaraes, B. Kingsman and S. Taylor (eds) A Reappraisal of the Efficiency of Financial Markets, Springer-Verlang, New York.

Veljanovski, C., 1987, Selling the State: Privatisation in Britain, Weidenfeld and Nicolson, London.

Veljanovski, C., 1991, Regulators and the Market, Institute of Economic Affairs, London.

Vickers, J. S. and G. Yarrow, 1988, Privatization: An Economic Analysis, Cambridge, MIT Press.

Vuylsteke, C., 1988, Techniques of privatisation in state-owned enterprises Vol 1, World Bank Technical Papers No 88, World Bank, Washington DC.

Walters, Sir Alan, 1989, Comment in P. W. MacAvoy, W. T. Stanbury, G. Yarrow and R. J. Zeckhauser (eds) Privatisation of state-owned enterprises: lessons from the United States, Great Britain and Canada, pp. 247-257. Kluwer Academic Publishers, Boston.

Wiltshire, K., 1987, Privatisation, the British experience: An Australian perspective, Longmans, Melbourne.

Wiseman, J., 1991, Privatisation in the Command Economy in A. F. Ott and K. Hartley (eds) Privatisation and Economic Efficiency, Aldershot, Edward Elgar Publishing Ltd.

Wright, M., S. Thompson and K. Robbie, 1989, Privatisation via management and employee buy-outs: analysis and UK evidence, Annals of Public and Cooperative Economy, 60, pp. 399-430.

Zank, N., 1990, Privatisation and Deregulation in the LDC Financial Sector: An AID perspective, in D. J. Gayle and J. W. Goodrich (eds) Privatisation and Deregulation in Global Perspective, Pinter Publishers, London.

Endnotes

[1] Such an aim for the U.K was expressed by F Mount who was formerly head of the British Prime Minister's policy unit in the document The practice of Liberty (1986). Similar views had been expressed in a Conservative party document of 1977 The Right Approach to the Economy but was not included in the election manifesto of 1979. According to Michele Develle (1986), the French privatisations initiated in 1986 marked the end of an era of government intervention in the economy so that it could concentrate on traditional functions such as education and defence.

2 The reported debts written off for these companies amounted to £5.5 billion.

3 Sir Alan Walters (1989) who was an economic adviser to the British Prime Minister from 1981-84 also argues that the objective of wider share ownership was pursued to reduce the probability of re-nationalisation.

4 The current policy of the Labour Party is not to re-nationalise privatised enterprises but to introduce tougher regulation for monopoly companies.

5 A golden share held by the government, among others, enables it to determine whether or not a company could be dissolved or taken-over.

6 The factors which advisers took into account in making the final price recommendations included: volatility of the market index during the price fixing period; the potential difficulty of sub-underwriting at a higher price, the market's expectation of the dividend yield on a particular issue; the need to include a premium of ten percent in the offer price so as to ensure a healthy after-market in the shares and the need to price in multiples of 5 pence rather than a penny so as not to give the impression that the government is 'squeezing the last drop out of the price' or anxious about the pricing. These reasons were extracted from various issues of National Audit Office Reports on privatisations.

7 Following the report of the Ross Russell Committee on Initial Public Offers, the Stock Exchange changed its rules on 1 January 1991 to allow offer for sale to include up to 50% of firmly placed shares.

8 This amount includes the secondary sales of British Petroleum which were floated during the sample period but excludes two earlier secondary sales worth £854 million..

9 Theoretically, the most appropriate price for this purpose would be the opening price at which the investors can sell. Due to the ready availability the closing price has been used in most studies. Barry and Jennings (1993) reported no material difference between the opening price and subsequent trading price during the first day of trading. Therefore, closing price could be taken as a good proxy of opening price.

10 They also report that returns to subscribers which take account of shares received relative to the number applied for, interest forgone on application money deposited and the cost of application reduce average subscriber return to 10.23 percent.

11 The excess return of 24 percent from the unregulated companies is mainly due to very large excess returns from the issues of Rolls-Royce and TSB.

12 The initial regulatory framework may, alternatively be designed to offer good prospects and high profitability to the company. This has the advantage of ensuring the success of the sale and generating higher proceeds to the government. Nevertheless, differential expectations about the impact of regulation in such a scenario could still arise.

[13] In order to examine the determinants of issuer underpricing we reformulated equation (3) to replace the dependent variable by issuer underpricing and removed the explanatory variable 'proportion of shares sold' (the effect of this variable has already been incorporated in the calculation of issuer underpricing). The results (available on request from the authors) are broadly consistent with the estimates for subscriber return and show that issuer underpricing is positively affected by the demand multiple, regulatory situation and market volatility immediately prior to the issue of shares. On the other hand high underwriting commission reduces underpricing. The proportion of shares allocated to foreign investors variable remains insignificant at conventional level of significance (5 percent). The overall explanatory power of the equation is 69 percent.

[14] Menyah, Paudyal and Inyangete (1995) included the interest earned on the application money received from the subscribers' in their equation. Due to the lack of data, we could not include this in this estimation of the cost of underpricing. Therefore, the true cost of underpricing after taking the interest earned into account would be lower than 2.22 percent reported here.

[15] Britoil and Enterprise Oil were initially sold through tender offers. Both generated losses to the initial subscribers.

[16] The portfolio of companies other than water and electricity companies comprises of a diversified group of industries such as communications (BT and CABL), petroleum and natural gas (BTOL, ENTO, BGAS), aviation (BAIR, BAA, BA.) etc.

[17] The choice of a maximum period of four years is guided by the availability of data for the most recently privatized companies.

[18] For the purpose of market return adjustment we use 0,1 market model. Ideally, we should have used the parameters of the empirical market model. However, in the light of the problems associated with the estimation of market model parameters for new as well as seasoned stocks (see Draper and Paudyal, 1995), the use of the simple market return adjustment model appears appropriate.

[19] Number of days in column 1 excludes week ends. Therefore 10 days, for example, refers to 2 weeks and so on.

[20] These returns are adjusted for partial payments. The holder is obliged to pay the second and subsequent instalments if the stocks are held up to the instalment payment date.

[21] The proportion of shareholders retaining their shares after one year of privatisation is higher (average of 56%) for regulated companies than for those which are not regulated with an average of 49%. The higher average first day and long-run returns for regulated companies reported in Tables 1 and 4 may in part explain the higher retention rate for such companies.

[22] Appendix 6 of National Audit Office Report on the privatisation of water companies shows that issuing costs for twenty-two companies privatised between 1981 and 1989 amounted to £988 million.

The Posted-Price Paradox: Evidence on the Flotation Mechanism Selection Process in France

Benoît Leleux
Babson College

and

Rémy Paliard
Groupe ESC Lyon

Abstract

In an initial public offering (IPO) environment characterized by the prohibition of both price and allocation discriminations, high oversubscription ratios, and a choice of flotation mechanism that includes various forms of auctions, the survival of the fixed-price mechanism is paradoxical. This paper argues that the combination of technical constraints on rationing with auctions and a concern among issuers about monitoring by external shareholders justifies the recourse to this apparently less informationally efficient sales mechanism. On a sample of 108 French IPOs, the evidence indicates (1) that the choice of issue mechanism affects the magnitude of the initial price reaction, (2) that auctions are preferred by issuers, but imbalances between demand and supply for the shares, and the absence of effective ex ante demand limiting devices, may force the recourse to a fixed-price flotation, (3) that venture capitalists in the ownership structure are associated with higher quality underwriters and investment bankers and the preferred selection of auction-based flotations, and (4) that the auctions are associated with small underpricings but large negative corrections in the long term, whereas fixed-price procedures involve large underpricings and non-significantly negative long-term buy-and-hold returns. These results, combined with the correlation between IPO volume and the level of an inflation-adjusted stock index previously outlined in the literature, are consistent with issuers strategically selecting both their flotation mechanism and the timing of their issuing effort to maximize issue proceeds.

1. Introduction

Going-public involves a set of decisions that go well beyond the choice between a private and public status for a company. The type of underwriting arrangement (best-effort versus underwritten offer), the choice of underwriters, investment bankers, and auditors, the number of shares to be sold and their origin (primary versus secondary shares), the best offer price, and the timing of the issue have to be addressed as part of the flotation effort. The whole flotation process is time consuming and demanding in terms of management's efforts, involving a number of decisions and procedures the interaction of which are not fully understood.

The empirical literature on initial public offerings has highlighted a number of phenomena which have proven difficult to reconcile with standard rationality assumptions. These phenomena include the abnormally high returns accruing to initial investors between the offer price and the early prices on the market [Ibbotson, Sindelar and Ritter (1988)], the apparent underperformance of the shares in the long-run [Ritter (1991)], and the existence of significant cycles in IPO volumes and underpricings [Ibbotson and Jaffe (1975), Ritter (1984)]. Various rational expectation models have been presented to account for the evidence[1], as well as arguments assuming deviations from rationality[2].

Most of the models focus on a single anomaly, with few attempts at reconciling the overall evidence and providing a 'unifying' theory of the IPO process. One exception is the stream of research looking at 'strategic' timing and pricing by IPO issuers. The argument made there is that issuers take advantage of temporary `windows of opportunity' in IPO markets, characterized by high levels of investor optimism and/or particularly 'receptive' equity markets, to float their shares. By timing their offerings close to market 'peaks', issuers use that optimism to increase proceeds or reduce their overall cost of capital[3]. When the true prospects for the shares become public knowledge, significant corrections in prices are anticipated, translating into lower-than-expected returns. This view is said to be supported by studies documenting the abnormally low performance of IPO shares in the long-run [Ritter (1991)] and the high level of correlation between the volume of IPOs brought to market and the level of an inflation-adjusted market index [Loughran, Ritter and Rydqvist (1994)].

Strategic behavior is also apparent in papers investigating the relationship between IPOs and subsequent equity offerings [Allen and Faulhaber (1989), Grinblatt and Hwang (1989), and Welch (1989)]. Issuers are hypothesized to optimize the proceeds of their capital raising efforts not only over the initial public offering but also over all subsequent calls to the capital markets[4]. High-quality issuers credibly signal their otherwise unobservable value by underpricing (Note that the terms "initial price reaction" and "underpricing" are used interchangeably throughout this paper) in the primary market, hoping to recoup these signaling costs by obtaining better conditions on seasoned offerings when their quality will be public knowledge. Low-quality issuers are not able to replicate the signal because of their inability to recover the costs if their low quality is revealed in seasoned trade with some positive probability.

The selection of an investment bank(s), underwriter(s), and auditor(s), the decision about the fraction of equity to be sold to the public and its origin, the inclusion of venture capitalists in the ownership structure, the nature and extent of bank relationships, and the choice between best-effort and underwritten agreements are decisions that issuers attempt to optimize as well. They have all been investigated as means to reduce the information asymmetries inherent in the issuing process[5].

The *choice of flotation* mechanism is an area that has received little attention so far. In the United States, fixed-price, fixed-quantity offerings (also referred to as posted-price methods) have been the norm since World War I [Chalk and Peavy (1990)], a norm carefully maintained by both the NASD and the SEC[6]. The issuer's choice is limited to the degree of support provided by the underwriter(s) for the issuing effort (underwritten versus best-efforts)[7]. The European IPO markets offer to the prospective issuer a broader choice of flotation mechanisms, including both auctions and fixed-price procedures [Loughran, Ritter and Rydqvist (1994), table 2]. France, for example, offers at least three distinct routes for gaining a listing, including sealed-bid uniform-price auctions and repeated auctions. In general, three institutional arrangements are most frequently encountered: the offer for sale at a fixed price, the offer for sale with tender (or a form of auction), and the direct placement[8]. The choice of flotation mechanism is important because of the significant effect it has been shown to have on the magnitude of the initial price reaction[9]. If these initial price reactions correspond to voluntary underpricing by issuers (and thus qualify as direct costs of the IPO), it is crucial to understand the relationship between flotation mechanism and underpricing.

Clearly, it is not possible to isolate the effect of any one particular decision by issuers. If issuers behave strategically so as to maximize issue proceeds, they will simultaneously select not only the most appropriate time to go public but also the mechanism that will generate the highest valuation for their shares or minimize their overall cost of capital. They will also contract with the underwriter(s) and investment banker(s) best able to carry out the flotation, using the most cost-effective contractual arrangement. So it is important to consider the decisions as a group when analyzing the empirical evidence. It is also fundamental to understand the institutional constraints on the choice of flotations mechanism, such as imposed limits on rationing, the existence and effect of demand-limiting devices, and private benefits to control which may favor the selection of an apparently inefficient mechanism.

This paper examines the choice of flotation mechanism in the context of French IPOs. IPO regulations in France prohibit price and allocation discriminations, impose preset limits on rationing for auction-type sales, and provide issuers with a number of demand-limiting devices, such as prepaid and maximum-size bids. These institutional settings favor the use of auction-type procedures (also referred to as 'price-driven' because they determine not only the allocation of shares but also their price) over fixed-price mechanisms because issuers are not able to induce potential investors to reveal their private information in the pre-market process. The survival of the fixed-price procedures is referred to as the "Posted-Price Paradox", in direct reference to the "Rights Offer Paradox" of Eckbo and Masulis (1992). Two factors seem to explain the phenomenon: (1) regulatory limits on share rationing in auctions *force* the use of fixed-price introductions as mechanism of last resort. This takes place essentially during 'cold' issue markets, characterized by limited share offerings and strong imbalances between demand and supply, imbalances which do not appear to be controllable with the current demand-limiting devices. (2) a concern among issuers about possible losses of control resulting from increased public monitoring favoring dispersion-enhancing procedures, such as the nominative fixed-price offering. The presence of active insiders, such as venture capitalists, appears to control that tendency.

The paper is structured as follows. Section 2 summarizes the important features of the French IPO regulations, focusing in particular on the various going-public procedures. Section 3 surveys the sales literature to support the existence, within the French context, of a preference ordering over the choice of flotation mechanism. Formal research hypotheses are formulated in section 4, followed by a description of the database and methodology used. The results are presented in section 6, followed by a comprehensive discussion of the implications for both issuers, regulators, and investors, especially the questions of desirability of preset rationing limits, demand-limiting devices, and the arbitrary truncation of the revealed demand curve. Avenues for future research are also highlighted.

2. An Introduction to French IPO Mechanisms

The going-public process is controlled in France by three regulatory authorities:

(1) the *"Conseil des Bourses de Valeurs"* (CBV), through its *"Règlement Général"* has authority over the general functioning of the market and, accordingly, over initial public offerings. It is the true 'market authority'. (2) the *"Commission des Opérations de Bourse"* (COB) is responsible for the proper information of all investors. (3) the *"Sociétés des Bourses Françaises"* (SBF), is the executive organ of the CBV overlooking the proper functioning of the markets.

To obtain a listing, a company must first select its *"Sociétés des Bourses"* and investment banker(s), then goes through a well-defined process leading to the listing, process which involves frequent interactions with the different market regulators[10]. Most flotations do not involve the sale of primary shares *"Augmentation de Capital"*, so that raising capital is not a main concern. French firms are also characterized by concentrated ownership, with a significant fraction of the shares in the hands of the founder's family and a limited number of institutions (Ownership structure is analyzed in detail in a later section).

Flotations can take a number of forms in France, many of which are not available to the American issuer. The *"Mise en Vente"* (MV), or modified competitive auction, is related to the competitive auction used, *e.g.*, in the Treasury bill primary market in the United States. Whereas the offer for sale by tender run by the Treasury is discriminatory, the *"Mise en Vente"* is a uniform-price auction, where all bidders end up paying the uniquely determined sales price. A minimum price is specified prior to the price-and-quantity sealed-bid auction. The expressed demand curve is then arbitrarily censored by the *"Sociétés des Bourses Françaises"* (SBF) of its portion reflecting 'disguised market orders' rather than 'true' limit orders. From that truncated demand curve, and the issuer-defined offer curve, the SBF announces the final sales price and distributes the shares according to a detailed allocation schedule. In some instances, the auction is said to fail due to large discrepancies between the number of shares demanded and supplied. This happens in general when less than 6% of the demand can be met [Monnier (1993)], in which case the equilibrium price is assumed not to be representative of the whole demand curve and a second introduction is attempted using a fixed-price, fixed quantity procedure. It has been argued [Jacquillat (1989)] that the first flotation effort potentially releases information about the market demand, information that is transmitted to uninformed investors, reducing the winner's curse problem [Rock (1986)] when the final fixed-price procedure is conducted.

The *"Procédure Ordinaire"* (PO), or repeated auction, is entirely controlled by the underwriting syndicate, which is in charge of all flotation operations (allocations, reductions, determination of the first price), under the supervision of the SBF. A minimum price is specified as well as the maximum increase in price allowed through the auctions. The offer prices are successively raised, with bidders re-submitting their respective orders, until a satisfactory equilibrium is reached[11]. Strong imbalances between supply and demand can also force the underwriting syndicate to opt out of the procedure if no equilibrium can be reached within the specified price range and/or the required reduction falls below a minimum acceptable level [stated as 5 % in Pilverdier-Latreyte (1991)], and to switch to the fixed-price procedure. In that case, the offering is referred to as an "OPV-recours", or a fixed-price procedure "of last resort", since no other procedure is available for flotation if the OPV itself fails.

The *"Offre Publique de Vente"* (OPV) is a fixed-price, fixed-quantity procedure introduced in France on March 3rd 1983 which mirrors the American IPO procedure, except for the pro-rata allocation of the shares. An initial private price-and-quantity bidding is often conducted to generate indications of interest, then a definitive offering price is set and published about a week in advance of the introduction. The reductions applied have been shown to go below 1 % of the shares demanded in some cases. In such circumstances, the size distribution of orders may be truncated, with small orders receiving no allocations. To counter that possibility, a special procedure, called the *"Offre Publique de Vente Nominative"*, or nominative procedure, can be used: each bid is then accompanied by a document specifying the full identity of the bidder. The SBF allocates the shares according to a schedule that guarantees priority allocation to smaller bidders. The privatizations in 1987 and 1993 similarly involved a convoluted system of tiers in the biddings to guarantee as broad a shareholder base as possible. These mechanisms share a requirement for pro-rata allocations[12], nondiscriminatory pricing[13], and the possibility to abandon an auction *en cours* to switch to a fixed-price introduction.

3. Going Public: Underwriting, Sales Mechanism and Timing

3.1 Firm-Commitment versus Best-Effort Offerings

Ritter (1985,1988) analyzes the choice between firm-commitment and best-effort underwriting contracts. With a best-effort offering, the completion of the issue is contingent on the offer being fully subscribed. The precommitment to withdraw reduces the adverse selection problem of potential investors, so less underpricing is expected[14]. Ritter formally demonstrates that firms whose value is more certain tend to use firm commitment offers and those whose value is highly uncertain use best efforts. Ritter (1987) extends one of the implications of Rock's (1986) model, namely that firm commitment offers will be more underpriced the greater the *ex ante* uncertainty about an issuing firm's value. This implication is also developed and tested by Beatty and Ritter (1986). Bower (1989) stresses the fact that the choice of offering method can affect both the firm's cost of capital and the investors' perceptions about the value of the offering itself. Her model results in a partially separating, partially pooling equilibrium in which some firms find it profitable to incur the underwriting costs in order to have their quality revealed while others elect not to do so. Comparative statics show that increases in underwriting costs induce more firms to select best-effort offerings over firm-commitment offerings. Increases in investments costs tend to have an opposite effect.

Underwritten offerings (called *"Prises Fermes"* are rare in France [Jacquillat (1989), Pilverdier-Latreyte (1991)]. None of the firms in the sample used the procedure. This observation may be related to a number of factors, such as the choice of procedures used to float the shares, the relative scarcity of initial public offerings in France (an average of 30 companies a year obtained listings over the last 10 years), and the oversubscription levels observed. New issues are often subscribed more than 100 times, so that the *ex ante* risk of not fully placing the issue is likely small, and may not justify the expenses associated with securing the payoffs through an underwriting contract.

3.2 Auctions versus Posted-Price Mechanisms

The efficiency of auctions as sales mechanism for goods of uncertain quality as been analyzed in the game and decision theory literature[15]. In general, auctions are found to provide the proper incentives for bidders to reveal their private valuations, so that they represent optimal sales mechanisms in situations of asymmetric information.

A number of papers also investigate the settings under which fixed-price mechanisms can duplicate the efficiency of auctions. Benveniste and Spindt (1989) model the pre- market process of a fixed-price offering as an auction, conducted by the underwriter, in which investors understand how their indications of interest affect the offer price and the allocations they ultimately receive. Underpricing arises naturally as the cost of compensating investors with positive information about the value of the stock for truthfully reporting their private information. Selective and repeated allocation of shares to informed investors can be used as a lever to reduce the required underpricing and thus increase the efficiency of the capital acquisition process. Benveniste and Wilhelm (1990) extend the previous findings by investigating the consequences of various institutional restrictions on the underwriters' marketing efforts. These restrictions include the requirement that the securities be sold to all investors at a uniform price[16] and that shares be allocated in an even-handed fashion[17]. Given the opportunity, underwriters would optimize proceeds by using a combination of price and allocation discrimination. The intuition is that, in order to induce regular investors to report truthfully, a form of endogenous incentive compatibility constraint has to be imposed, whereby revelation of positive information generates more profits than negative information. Uniform pricing increases the cost of information revelation (through higher underpricing), whereas the combination of constraints on *both* pricing and allocations can lead to the impossibility for the underwriter to infer any information from the regular investors' indications of interest.

Spatt and Srivastava (1991) show that a posted-price mechanism, in conjunction with nonbinding preplay communication and participation restrictions, can maximize the seller's expected revenue by replicating the characteristics of a second-price auction. Even in situations where the second-price auction is not the optimal form of sales procedure, the posted-price mechanism, combined with those two constraints, can achieve an optimal allocation and pricing of the shares.

These arguments are used to explain why a seemingly inefficient mechanism (the fixed-price sales) can still, in practice, be optimal. But the conditions under which this can happen are fairly restrictive, especially the participation restrictions, and do not correspond to the institutional framework in effect in new issue markets outside of the United States.

The evidence indicates that fixed-price mechanisms can only duplicate the efficiency of auctions as selling instruments under quite restrictive conditions on preplay communication and price and/or participation restrictions. In other words, incentives must be present in the pre-market process to generate truthful revelation of information and allow proper evaluation of the otherwise unobservable demand curve.

3.3 'Hot' and 'Cold' Issue Markets

The clustering of new and seasoned equity issues in time, as examined initially by Ibbotson and Jaffe (1975) and Ritter (1984), is a long-standing puzzle to financial economists [Bayless and Chaplinsky (1993)]. If one takes the equity issue decision as at least partly endogenous, then hot issue markets should correspond to periods particularly 'favorable' for issuers, i.e., by the investment opportunities they offer, the reduced cost of equity relative to other sources of financing, reduced informational asymmetries, or the particularly optimistic 'sentiment' of the market[18]. As highlighted by Shleifer and Vishny (1992) and Bayless and Chaplinsky (1993), financial theory still cannot provide a fully consistent model of the equity issue decision but a set of stylized facts slowly emerges.

Bayless and Chaplinsky (1993) compare the characteristics of firms that issue seasoned equity during high volume ('hot') periods with those issuing in low volume ('cold') spells and a control sample of non-issuers. If no differences can be outlined in terms of investment opportunities or debt constraints, a logit analysis shows that 'hot' market issuers have characteristics that suggest higher costs of asymmetric information than 'cold' market issuers. Carter and Dark (1991) stress the same point when they talk of intertemporal changes in the cross-sectional magnitude of the information asymmetries between primary market investors. They relate this to the existence of periods when the number and quality of offerings is such that sufficient information gathering for all IPOs would be very difficult. They hypothesize that valuation errors are more likely to occur during 'hot' IPO markets and for firms characterized by low levels of information. Loughran, Ritter and Rydqvist (1994) show that, in 14 out of 15 countries examined, IPO volume is positively correlated with an inflation-adjusted stock market index, with some tendency for high volume periods to be associated with long-term underperformance.

3.4 Issuing Mechanisms and Informational Efficiency

Under French IPO regulations, price discrimination and participation and allocation restrictions are prohibited: pro-rata is the rule for both fixed-price and auction-related procedures. Under these settings, the ability of preplay communication to force truthful revelation of investors' private information is compromised. Even without taking into consideration the possible legal liability implications of an 'inappropriate' due-diligence process leading to the determination of the offer price [Tinic (1988), Simon (1989),

Keloharju (1993)], the fixed-price procedure does not appear, in the French context, to be as informationally efficient, from the issuer's standpoint, as an auction. As a consequence of the preference ordering, one would expect to see all issuers elect to go public through the price-driven procedures. This is not the case: as shown later in table 1, fixed-price procedures represent more than half of all introductions over the period 1983-1991. This phenomenon is referred to as the "Posted-Price Paradox", to reflect the selection of a seemingly non-optimal flotation mechanism.

4. Propositions and Research Hypotheses

The objective of this paper is to extend the previous findings [Ritter (1991), Loughran and Ritter (1993), Rajan and Servaes (1993), Loughran, Ritter and Rydqvist (1994)] regarding opportunistic behavior by issuers, in terms of issue timing and pricing, by adding to their choice domain the selection of flotation mechanism[19]. The objectives are formally stated in the following propositions:

Proposition 1 *Issuers strategically select not only the timing but also the flotation mechanism to maximize the issue proceeds or minimize their costs of capital, taking into consideration the overall state of the new issues markets and their private benefits from control.*

Proposition 2 *Under the French institutional arrangements, auction-type flotations are more informationally efficient than fixed-price mechanisms. The state of the IPO market ('cold' or 'hot') and the resulting level of demand for the shares, as well as the existence of adequate management monitoring devices, ultimately determine the choice between auctions and fixed-price procedures. The large demand for IPO shares also explains the prevalence of best-effort issuings.*

Proposition 1 and 2 translate into a set of more specific research hypotheses.

Hypothesis 1 *Successful auctions result in lower underpricing on average than direct, fixed-price sales.*

Hypothesis 1 is a direct consequence of the conclusion in section~\ref{pecking} that auction-related flotations reduce the winner's curse problem and provide better incentives for informed bidders to truthfully reveal their private information.

Hypothesis 2 *Indirect fixed-price flotations result in significantly lower initial price reactions than direct fixed-price mechanisms.*

Hypothesis 2 tests the information-conveying value of the failed auction procedures. Rational uninformed investors should be able to update their prior beliefs on the basis of the realized demand for the first issuing effort [Jacquillat (1989)], reducing the winner's curse problem [Rock (1986)]. On the other hand, auctions usually fail because of imbalances between supply and demand. If oversubscription is attributed to informed demand (assuming uninformed demand is relatively invariant), then the winner's curse problem may actually be worse in indirect fixed-price offers than in the direct procedures, requiring larger underpricings.

Hypothesis 3 *Auctions are informationally more efficient than fixed-price mechanisms. Strong imbalances between supply and demand for shares, prevalent during 'cold' issue periods, may force the cancellation of the first-choice auction and the recourse to fixed-price introductions as a procedure of last resort.*

Hypothesis 3 departs from the static nature of hypotheses 1 and 2 to introduce the notion of a preference ordering in the choice of flotation mechanism. As shown by Barry and Jennings (1993), while testing the cascade argument proposed by Welch (1992) , the initial price reaction is embedded in the first transaction prices, so that the benefits from the price increase incur only to the original investors. Consequently, underpricing comes as a direct cost to issuers[20]. If the issuers are not able to properly determine ex ante the level of demand for their shares and an appropriate minimum price to be posted for the auctions, the existing regulatory 'triggers' on rationing levels may force the cancellation of the procedure and the recourse to a fixed-price IPO. This can be tested by comparing the ratio of shares demanded and supplied in the first attempt at flotation between successful and failed auctions. It is expected that the observed rationings in failed auctions fall within the range deemed unacceptable by the SBF. Furthermore, significant modifications to the choice of procedures are expected between 'hot' and 'cold' issue markets, with fixed-price procedures (direct and indirect) more commonly used in 'cold' issue periods (when imbalances between supply and demand are more likely) and auctions prevailing in 'hot' issue periods.

To test the opportunism of IPO issuers, the long-term performance of the shares is investigated. If issuers time their flotations and select the most appropriate mechanism to maximize their issue proceeds, and both the existence of market-wide phenomena leading to temporary 'windows of opportunities' in the new issue market and the long-run efficiency of the market[21] are taken as given, then larger long-term corrections (more underperformance) are expected for firms going public during 'hot' issue using a form of auction than for those issued using fixed-price mechanisms. Similarly, firms able to use auctions during 'cold' issue period are also expected to show stronger price reversals in the long-term than those using fixed-price mechanisms. This is summarized in hypothesis 4.

Hypothesis 4 *Auctions are prevalent during 'hot' issue markets and are associated with both small underpricings and long-term underperformance. Fixed-price procedures are dominant in 'cold' markets and are associated with both large underpricings and no abnormal returns in the long-run.*

If investors are temporarily over-enthusiastic about the prospects for a particular industry or the market as a whole, then auctions may be better able to capture the 'fad' component than a fixed-price flotation. Assuming that the demand for new shares is not infinite, the clustering of issues facilitates the use of auctions by distributing the overall demand into more offerings. The auctions actually replicate the price formation mechanism in the aftermarket, leading to an offer price very close to the equilibrium price in secondary market trade. On the other hand, this ability to 'cream' the demand curve results in stronger underperformance in the long-run if the unrealistic expectations are not met.

Hypothesis 5 *The presence of venture capitalists in the ownership structure controls for the adverse selection problem inherent in the existence of private benefits to control and insufficient corporate monitoring.*

The second argument to explain the posted-price paradox is similar to one used by Eckbo and Masulis (1992). If managers value the absence of supervision, they may be willing to sacrifice the informational efficiency of auctions for the shareholding dispersion benefits of fixed-price introductions. This point is further supported by the frequent recourse to 'nominative' schemes in fixed-price offerings that guarantee maximum dispersion of the shareholding. Furthermore, a very limited fraction of the outstanding equity, barely superior to the market-imposed 10%, gets listed in the initial effort, again indicating a certain wariness on the original shareholders' part to lose control or expose their management to external monitoring.

5. Database and Methodologies

All initial public offerings of equity shares over the period 1984-1991 inclusive are identified through the *"Décisions at Avis de la Bourse"* (DAB), the annual reports of the *"Sociétés des Bourses Françaises"* (SBF), and the *"Commission des Opérations Boursières"* (COB). The relevant population of events is detailed in table 1 by method of flotation used. The table highlights significant temporal shifts in the number of firms going public and their choice of introduction mechanism. From a peak of 53 introductions in 1987, the number consistently decreases to only 11 in 1991. Also, indirect posted-price mechanisms (following failed attempts at auctions) are quite numerous, representing a quarter of the total population and about the same number as direct, fixed-price introductions.

Table 1

Initial Public Offerings in France, 1983-1991

Husson and Jacquillat (1989), Jacquillat (1989), and various COB and SBF annual reports. The "Procédure Ordinaire" is a competitive repeated auction controlled by the underwriters. The "Mise en Vente" is a best-effort, two-stage uniform-price auction with a minimum price. Finally, the "Offre Publique de Vente" (OPV) is a fixed-price, fixed-quantity offer made directly by shareholders to the investing public. Shares are allocated on a pro-rata basis.

Flotation Method Used	83	84	85	86	87	88	89	90	91	83-91
Procédure Ordinaire	9	2	1	2	4	17	4	3	3	45
Mise en Vente	1	7	23	16	12	1	6	0	4	70
Direct OPV	3	6	6	9	29	8	8	12	4	85
Indirect OPV	2	10	15	19	8	1	12	0	0	67
Total	15	25	45	46	53	27	30	15	11	267

Combining the resources from Datastream and the AFFI/SBF tapes, monthly returns[22] are obtained from issue date to July 1993 on a sample of 108 firms[23]. Specific characteristics of the issues, such as the successive offer prices, the flotation method selected, the value of the shares when issued and on the first trade day, the distribution of ownership prior to and after the IPO, etc. are collected from published sources and prospectus information. Descriptive statistics are provided in table 2.

Table 2

Characteristics of French IPO Sample

The total sample size is N=108. The offer price is the last offer price in multiple auction procedures. The value at introduction is the value of all outstanding shares at the first market price. Age at introduction refers to the number of years of existence of the firm with respect to the initial founding date, as reported in the issue prospectus. The ratios of shares demanded to shares offered for sale are measured respectively on the first and last offers.}

Sample Characteristic	Mean	Std Deviation
Value at Introduction (in ff)	373,500,000	617,230,000
Offer Price (ff per share)	237.4	132.25
Equity Offered (as % of total equity)	10.9%	0.035
Age at Introduction (in years)	28.8	23.7
Shares Demanded / Offered at 1st offer	98.87	117.89
Shares Demanded / Offered at last offer	57.42	45.36

The average age at flotation (28.8 years) is significantly higher than the figures reported for the United States by Ritter (1991), where 83.4% of the sample of 1,526 IPOs is less than 19 years old at flotation and 62.9% less than 9 years old (median age = 6 years). The French figure is also smaller than the European median reported by Loughran, Ritter and Rydqvist (1994) to stand at close to 50 years. The percentage of equity offered in the initial offering (10.9% on average) is very close to the minimum statutory limit imposed for flotation on the secondary market (10%). This indicates that a large fraction of the equity is retained for later issuing. Finally, the ratios of shares demanded to shares offered in the first and last rounds of the offerings are high, with the shares offered oversubscribed on average 98 and 57 times respectively, with a maximum of 786 times.

Returns series, adjusted for capital structure changes and including all dividend payments, are calculated for all shares in the sample. Stock market indices are also collected from Datastream.[24] A traditional event study performance analysis is conducted over the post-IPO (seasoning) period. A standard market adjustment is used to reflect conservatively the assumed high risk of IPO shares, with:

$$AR_{i,t} = R_{i,t} - R_{m,t} \qquad (1)$$

where $AR_{i,t}$ is the adjusted or abnormal return on share i in post-IPO month t, $R_{i,t}$ is the raw return on share i in event month t, and $RM_{m,t}$ is the corresponding return on the market during the same time period. An average abnormal return is calculated for each event month following the IPO, using the formula:

$$AR_t = \frac{1}{n_t} \sum_{i=1}^{n_t} AR_{i,t} \qquad (2)$$

where n_t is the number of shares present in the cross-section in post-IPO month t. The Cumulative Abnormal Returns (CAR_t) can be obtained by summing up over time the AR_t. This procedure in effect assumes monthly portfolio rebalancing of equal-amount investments in each IPO share at the same stage of seasoning. This method suffers from two drawbacks. First, it does not represent a typical investor's behavior because it implies selling stocks that have performed well in the past to purchase more of past underperformers. Second, monthly cumulations cumulate the estimation errors, as pointed out by Conrad and Kaul (1993).   Buy-and-hold returns are recommended by Loughran, Ritter and Rydqvist (1994) and used here.

The adjustment procedure for the returns assumes that IPO shares have a beta risk of 1.0 with respect to the market index used. The literature in this respect is not totally conclusive but tends to indicate that on average the beta risk of IPO shares in the immediate secondary market is greater than 1.0 [Balvers *et al.* (1988), Clarkson and Thomson (1990), and Chan and Lakonishok (1992)], with a later decline detected by some [Cotter (1992), Keloharju (1992)], so that the market adjustment is conservative for performance studies.

6. Issue Mechanism, Underpricing, and Long-Run Performance

Three alternative means of defining 'hot' versus 'cold' issue periods[25] are used, based on the total number of IPOs (HOTMKT1)[26], the number of IPOs in the 3 months prior to a firm's own flotation (HOTMKT2), and over the 6 months prior to the IPO (HOTMKT3). In the last two instances, the top quartile of the distribution is considered as a 'hot' market and the lowest quartile as a 'cold' market. These two time horizons (3 and 6 months) are used to reflect the time needed to arrange a flotation.

To control for the possibility of the state of the IPO market being associated with significant shifts in the types of firms going public, the characteristics of the firms in each subsample are compared on the basis of variables previously shown to be related to information uncertainty, such as the average age at flotation, market value, percentage of equity floated, etc. Whether using parametric or non-parametric tests, no significant differences can be outlined between 'hot' and 'cold' periods. The only exception is the number of days to equilibrium, a variable reflecting the length of time during which the SBF actively 'manages' the market in a new stock and the listed price does not correspond to the actual crossing of supply and demand[27].

6.1 Mechanism Selection, State of the Market, and Underpricing

Under the general propositions, issuers are assumed to time their offerings to take advantage of temporary 'windows of opportunity' in the new issue market.   This should be reflected in a high correlation between the overall IPO volume and proxies for market 'peaks'. Loughran, Ritter and Rydqvist (1994)[28] show that, over the period 1971-1991, the correlation between IPO volume and the market index stands at 0.5 for France, with a highly significant p-value of 0.02. Further regressions, with the inflation-adjusted GNP growth rate added as explanatory variable (proxying for changes in growth opportunities), do not alter the conclusions. These results are interpreted as supporting the notion of timing by IPO issuers.

This section investigates the relationship between the state of the IPO market, the choice of flotation mechanism, and the level of initial price reactions. The main proposition is that auctions are usually favored by issuers because they induce a more complete revelation of the demand curve and reduce the winner's curse. Unfortunately, strong imbalances between supply and demand may trigger regulatory limits on rationing and force the cancellation of the auctions and the recourse to fixed-price flotations. These imbalances are more likely to occur in 'cold' issue markets because of the limited number of issues among which the total demand can be allocated. The empirical implications of the proposition are threefold: (1) auctions are associated with smaller underpricings than fixed-price mechanisms [hypothesis 1] (2) indirect fixed-price procedures exhibit smaller underpricings than direct procedures if the failed auctions reveal information about the state of demand for the shares, resolving in part the adverse selection problem [hypothesis 2], or larger underpricings if they revealed a strong informed demand, and (3) indirect fixed-price procedures cluster in 'cold' issue periods [hypothesis 3].

Table 3 analyzes the relationship between the choice of flotation mechanism and the mean initial price[29] reaction (or underpricing), measured as the difference between the equilibrium price and the first quoted price divided by the latter. All initial price reactions are statistically different from 0 and range from 3.2% for repeated auctions to 21.2% for indirect fixed-price flotations. These figures are in line with those reported in the U.S. by Ibbotson, Sindelar and Ritter (1988) and Ritter (1991). To formally investigate hypothesis 1, the various mechanisms are aggregated into auctions and fixed-price procedures, with results synthesized in table 4.

Table 3

Flotation Mechanisms and Initial Underpricing

The *"Procédure Ordinaire"* is a repeated auction controlled by the underwriters. The *"Mise en Vente"* is a best-effort, two-stage uniform-price auction with a minimum price. Finally, the *"Offre Publique de Vente"* (OPV) is a fixed-price, fixed-quantity offer made directly by shareholders to the investing public. *Prob* > |t| indicates the confidence limit for the rejection of the null hypothesis on the mean initial price reaction being equal to 0.

Flotation Mechanism Selected	Sample Size	Mean Initial Reaction	Standard Deviation	Median Initial Reaction	t-stat	Prob>|t|
Offre Publique de Vente	31	15.5 %	0.138	10.0 %	6.256	0.0001
Offre Publique de Vente Indirecte	28	21.2 %	0.194	16.7 %	5.781	0.0001
Mise en Vente	24	15.8 %	0.238	4.6 %	3.247	0.0036
Procédure Ordinaire	24	3.2 %	0.041	3.4 %	3.877	0.0008

Table 4

Initial Underpricing: Price Driven vs Posted-Price Mechanisms

Price-driven procedures (auction-related) include the "Mise en Vente" and the "Procédure Ordinaire", whereas posted-price mechanisms include both the direct and indirect "Offre Publique de Vente". F-test is for the existence of a statistical difference in initial price reaction between price-driven and posted-price mechanisms. Prob>F indicates the confidence limit for the rejection of the null hypothesis of no difference in the initial price reactions. The significance levels are coded as (*) for 10%, (**) for 5%, and (***) for the 1% level.

Flotation Mechanism Selected	Sample Size	Mean Initial Reaction	σ	t-stat	F-test	Prob>F
Price-Driven Procedures (MV/PO)	48	9.53%	0.180	3.657	6.36	0.013
Posted-Price Procedures (OPV/OPVI)	60	18.05%	0.167	8.328		**

Auctions are associated with statistically (*F*-test = 6.36) smaller underpricings (9.53 % on average, with a *t*-test = 3.657) than fixed-price procedures (18.05 % on average, with a *t*-test = 8.328), supporting hypothesis 1. The figures for auctions are a bit surprising. Since the mechanism for setting the offer price is similar to the price-setting process in the market, the average underpricing should be close to 0. This would be the case if the issue price was set at the equilibrium level, where demand equals supply. However, in France, beside the truncation of the demand curve, the offer price is usually set at a level where some oversubscription remains[30], which explains the small abnormal price reaction at introduction. Repeated auctions (*"Procédures Ordinaire"*) are associated with even smaller price reactions. This cannot be explained by the regulation imposing the procedure by default to all firms previously publicly traded (over-the-counter or on a foreign stock exchange) since these firms have been removed from the sample because such IPOs do not correspond to true 'initial' public offerings but rather to listing transfers. An alternative explanation is that the management of the auction by the syndicate of investment bankers instead of by the SBF provides ways to control participation to the auction (reducing the asymmetric information problem) or that the syndicate would tend to set the issue price closer to the true equilibrium level. The indirect fixed-price procedures are characterized by larger underpricings [21.2% underpricing for indirect fixed-price offerings (*t*-test = 5.781) versus 15.5% (*t*-test = 6.256) for direct offerings] and larger standard deviations compared to the direct procedures. The failure of the initial auction is often due to the impossibility to balance demand and supply for the shares, which could indicate strong informed demand [in the sense of Rock (1986)] if one takes uninformed demand as relatively invariant to the quality of the stock offered. To support that explanation, table 5 examines the evolution of the oversubscription ratios between the first and the final offers made. Note that in the case of indirect fixed-price procedures, the first offer is made through an auction, the last one through a posted-price mechanism.

Auctions that ultimately failed are on average 195 times oversubscribed in the initial offer, compared to 63 times (MV) and 10 times (PO) for the auctions that succeeded.

Furthermore, the fixed-price offer ultimately conducted to sell the shares is still oversubscribed 81 times, indicating strong overall interest for the shares. The reduction in oversubscription observed between the first and the last offer for direct fixed-price procedures stems from additional constraints imposed on bids during the offers, such as prepayments and limits on bid sizes. The F-tests support the existence of significant differences across procedures. This is consistent with the results presented by Dufour and Kervern (1985), who show that, for the first 58 introductions on the second market in France, the average service rate over all procedures was 4.57%, with fixed-price offers falling as low as 0.8%. The low oversubscription in repeated auctions (PO) also supports the previous interpretation that the private management of the auction process by the underwriting syndicate provides means to control the demand for the shares, for example by limiting the number of potential bidders approached.

Table 5

Oversubscription Levels by Flotation Procedure

The oversubscription ratio are expressed as the number of times the demand exceeded the total supply of shares. The F-test investigates the existence of significant differences in oversubscription ratios between the different flotation mechanisms.

Part A: At First Offer

Introduction Mechanism	Sample Size	Mean Over - Subscription	σ	F-test	Prob > F
Direct Fixed-Price(OPV)	31	106.1	80.9	17.06	0.0001
Indirect Fixed-Price (OPVI)	29	194.8	163.5		
Single Auction (MV)	24	62.6	46.3		
Repeated Auction (PO)	24	9.8	8.7		

Part B: At Final Offer

Introduction Mechanism	Sample Size	Mean Over - Subscription	σ	F-test	Prob > F
Direct Fixed-Price (OPV)	31	69.5	47.9	18.12	0.0001
Indirect Fixed-Price (OPVI)	29	81.3	35.4		
Single Auction (MV)	24	62.6	46.3		
Repeated Auction (PO)	24	9.8	8.7		

The existence of opportunities for 'strategic' behavior by issuers depends critically on deviations from rationality in the market. If markets are efficient and rational, then shares prices at all times reflect the true prospects of the firms, and there is no room for issuer maneuvering to reduce its cost of capital. Irrational market components, such as 'fads' and periods of overoptimism, are required for strategic behavior. A number of authors, such as Ibbotson and Jaffe (1975), have hypothesized that the level of overoptimism could be reflected in high oversubscription ratios. In that interpretation, 'fads' episodes are associated with high oversubscriptions (as a proxy for investor 'frenzy') and large underpricings[31], irrespective of the procedure used for the flotation. The strength of this relationship is analyzed in a regression with the initial price reaction as dependent variable and the level of oversubscription as explanatory variable. Oversubscription is noted as ($\gamma_{i,z}$ where i stands for company i and z =1,2 is the stage of the offering, with z =1 corresponding to the first round of the offer and z =2 to the last round. The model can be described as:

$$AR_i = \alpha_z + \beta_z \, \gamma_{i,z} + \varepsilon_i \tag{3}$$

where α_z are the intercepts and β_z the coefficients of the oversubscription ratios, and the dependent variables are the abnormal initial price reactions. The results of the regressions are summarized in table 6. The issue clustering observed before can possibly generate problems of autocorrelation in the dependent variable, biasing the statistical inferences, and forcing the use of procedures like estimated generalized least squares or computer-intensive methods such as bootstrapping. Autocorrelation does not appear to be a problem though, so that OLS procedures are used with confidence throughout.

The coefficients (and their t-tests) indicate a strong relationship between initial price reaction and oversubscription. Although not reported here, this relationship does not hold within flotation procedures. The only exception is for indirect fixed-price procedures, where oversubscription is significant at the 1 % level. A multinomial logit model, with the choice of flotation mechanism as dependent variable, also supports the existence of a relationship between oversubscription level and mechanism selection. The results are not reported here. The evidence is apparently supportive of the interpretation of high oversubscription ratios as evidence of 'fads' in the market for IPOs.

Table 6

Oversubscription Levels and Initial Price Reactions

Oversubscription is the ratio of shares demanded to shares supplied in the first public offer (1) and the last offer (2). Oversupscription is noted as $\gamma_{i,z}$ where i stands for company and i and z = 1,2 is the stage of the offering. The coefficients estimated above are for the regressons $AR_i = \alpha_z + \beta_z \, \gamma_{i,z} + \varepsilon i$ where the dependent variables are the abnormal initial price reactions.

Part A: Oversubscription at First Offer

Explanatory Variables	Estimated dfCoefficient		σ	t-test Coeff=0	Prob>|t|
Intercept	1	0.09642	0.02146	4.585	0.0001
Shares Demanded/ Offered	1	0.02421	0.00014	3.181	0.0019

Part B : Oversubscription at Final Offer

Explanatory Variables	Estimated dfCoefficient		σ	t-test Coeff=0	Prob>|t|
Intercept	1	0.03077	0.02421	1.271	0.2065
Shares Demanded/ Offered	1	0.00197	0.00197	5.937	0.0001

Oversubscriptions may not necessarily correspond to periods of 'overoptimism' but simply to periods characterized by a shortage of IPO offers. To test for that possibility, the long-term performance of the shares is examined. If high oversubscription ratios proxy for 'fads', then, assuming that the market is efficient at least in the long run [Ritter (1991), Loughran and Ritter (1993)], they should also be associated with underperformance over the long-term when the market corrects its valuation errors. Accordingly, a direct relationship should also be observed between the magnitude of the initial price reaction and the long-term performance of the shares and the same relationship should hold, indirectly, between the oversubscription ratio and long-run performance. To test for that possibility, regressions using long-run buy-and-hold returns as independent variables (with horizons between 6 and 36 months) and initial price reaction as explanatory variable are tested. None of the regression coefficients have any significance, so the results are not presented here. Ritter (1991) and Belden (1992) obtain similar results on U.S. samples.

Table 7

Distribution of Issue Methods in Hot and Cold Market

MV stands for the "Mise en Vente" procedure, OPV for the "Offre Publique de Vente", OPVI for the "Offre Publique de Vente Indirecte" and PO for the "Procédure Ordinaire". *Real.* is the number of realizations in the category and *Exp* is the expected number under no association between line and column variables. *Group or Quartile* refers to either the group or the quartile considered: Q_1 refers to the top quartile (hot IPO period) and Q_4 to the bottom quartile (cold IPO period). χ^2 is the Pearson chi-square statistics on the difference between the observed and expected frequencies under the null hypothesis of no association. G^2 is the value of the likelihood-ratio chi-square statistics on the ratios between the observed and expected frequencies under the null hypothesis. *Prob* indicates the confidence limit for the rejection of the null hypothesis.)

Market Status Proxy	Group or Quartile	MV Real (Exp)	OPV Real (Exp)	OPVI Real (Exp)	PO Real (Exp)	χ^2 (G^2)	Prob
HOTMKT1	hot	11	9	7	13	6.99	0.136
		(9)	(11)	(10)	(9)	(7.32)	0.120
	cold	13	22	21	11		
		(15)	(20)	(18)	(15)		
HOTMKT3	Q_1 (Hot)	5	6	4	12	21.08	0.049
		(6)	(8)	(7)	(6)	(20.26)	0.062
	Q_4 (Cold)	7	7	10	7		
		(7)	(9)	(8)	(7)		

On the other hand, under strategic behavior by issuers, oversubscription ratios are only the consequence of issue timing, not a symptom of overoptimism in the market. Under this interpretation, issuers cluster during 'fads' periods, using the sales mechanism best able to capture the overenthusiasm of investors. As argued before, under the conditions prevailing in France, auctions will likely be used preferentially during these 'fad' periods, leading to small underpricings but large corrections in the long-run. Some firms may also be forced to go public during 'cold' issue periods, for example when the liquidity needs of the entrepreneur/investors outweigh their patience.   Again, efficiency considerations favor the use of auctions, but strong imbalances between supply and demand reduce the availability of such mechanisms because of the limits on rationing.   The long-run performance, on the other hand, should be normal since no 'fad' component is likely to be present in these 'cold' periods.   The long-term performance implications are analyzed in section 6.2.

Under strategic behavior by issuers, shifts in the choice of issue mechanisms are also anticipated between 'hot' and 'cold' IPO markets. This implication is investigated in table 7 reporting the results of χ^2 and likelihood-ratio χ^2 (referred to as G^2) tests for the existence of an association between the choice of mechanism and the state of the market.

Table 7 indicates the kind of patterns[32] expected under the main proposition. Auctions seem to prevail in hot issue quartiles, whereas fixed-price procedures, and especially the indirect version, appear to cluster in cold issue periods. The hypothesis of an absence of relationship between status of the market at issue and choice of flotation mechanism is rejected at the 5% level with the HOTMKT3 proxy, at the 14% level for HOTMKT1 and cannot be rejected with HOTMKT2.

If indeed shifts can be observed during 'hot' issue periods toward auctions, and the latter generate smaller initial price reactions, then a correlation should exist as well between the state of the IPO market (as defined previously) and the levels of underpricing. Table 8 indicates that the state of the new issue market significantly affects the average level of initial price reaction. Periods of high IPO activity are associated with lower underpricings (11.6% on average using the HOTMKT2 top quartile) than periods of low activity (21.12% on average for HOTMKT2 bottom quartile). The F-tests are significant at the 1% level for the HOTMKT2 and HOTMKT3 proxies, but not significant for the HOTMKT1 proxy.

Table 8

Hot & Cold Markets and Initial Price Reactions

HOTMKT1 is the proxy for hot issue market based on the total number of issues during the issue month, whereas HOTMKT2 is based on the number of firms that went public in the 3-month period prior to the firm's own issuing, with the distribution broken down into quartiles *Group or Quartile* refers to either the group or the quartile considered: Q_1 refers to the top quartile ('hot' IPO period) and Q_4 to the bottom quartile ('cold' IPO period). *t-test* is the value of the *t*-statistics for the significance of the mean initial price reaction. *F-test* is the value of the *F*-statistics for the effect of hot/cold issue markets on the level of initial price reactions. *Prob > F* indicates the confidence limit for the rejection of the null hypothesis of no relationship. The results are not affected by the choice of quartiles instead of quintiles.

Market Status Proxy	Group or Quartile	Mean Price Reaction	σ	t-test	F-test	Prob > F
HOTMKT1	Hot	12.71%	0.199	4.035	0.42	0.486
	Cold	15.14%	0.164	7.583		
HOTMKT3	Q_1 (Hot)	11.60%	0.143	4.164	4.62	0.004
	Q_4 (Cold)	21.12%	0.233	5.197		

Table 9

IPO Market-Adjusted Holding-Period Returns

Holding periods are expressed in full calendar months from the issue date and only include stocks for which the full seasoning period was available. Accordingly, stocks which were suspended are not represented in the long holding period subsamples. T-test values are for the two-tailed distribution and the hypothesis that the mean abnormal return is equal to zero. All abnormal returns are market-adjusted to the Datastream Paris Total Market Index. The significance levels are coded as (*) for 10%, (**) for 5%, and (***) for the 1% level.)

Holding Period	Sample Size	Mean Return	Median Return	σ^2	t-test	Pr>|t|	Signif
6 months	108	0.66%	-5.85%	0.222	0.144	0.885	
12 months	108	4.51%	-5.97%	0.789	0.525	0.601	
24 months	104	7.34%	-1.03%	0.515	1.043	0.299	
36 months	100	-9.42%	-11.17%	0566	-1.245	-0.216	

6.2 Relationship with Long Term Performance of IPO Shares

The key to understanding issuer behavior is the analysis of the long-term performance of IPO shares. If issuers time their offerings to take advantage of temporary 'fads' in the market, then significant clustering is expected to be observed in these periods. Furthermore, under the preference ordering presented above, auctions are more likely to be used to take advantage of the overoptimistic segment of the demand curve. In these circumstances, significant corrections are expected to take place when the market assimilates the more adequate discount rates or projected cash flows for the projects, resulting in low realized rates of return. Alternatively, during 'cold' markets, auctions are still preferred by issuers but may not be available as flotation mechanism because of possible imbalances between supply and demand for the shares and the existence of rationing limits.

Table 9 provides evidence on the relationship between market status at issuance and long-term performance of IPO shares, using the market-adjusted buy-and-hold abnormal returns. Although not reported here, the wealth relatives defined in Levis (1993) are also calculated and provide results similar to those obtained using buy-and-hold returns. On average, IPO shares exhibit a -9.42% market-adjusted return over the 36-month following the flotation t-test = -1.245). The results are in line with those reported in the U.S. by Aggarwal and Rivoli (1990), Ritter (1991) and Loughran and Ritter (1993), where IPO shares are shown to perform poorly in secondary trade over a period extending up to 6 years after the IPO.

The evidence can be broken down by status of the initial IPO market. As mentioned above, if hot issue markets correspond to periods of intense IPO interest and incorporate a component of overenthusiasm, then corrections should be more important for the shares issued during those periods. The availability of a flotation mechanisms to exploit that optimism may hinder the strength of the relationship. The evidence collected is ambiguous: no clear relationship can be outlined between long-term performance and the initial market status. On the other hand, the flotation mechanism selected to go public does appear to be related to the later performance of the shares. This is summarized in table 10 comparing auctions with fixed-price mechanisms.

Table 10

Price Driven vs Posted-Price Mechanisms and Long-Term Performance

Auctions include both the *"Mise en Vente"* and the *"Procédure Ordinaire"*, whereas fixed-price mechanisms include both the direct and indirect *"Offre Publique de Vente"*. *AR* stands for abnormal return over the holding period, where the adjustment is made with respect to the stock market index. *t-test* is the value of the *t*-statistics for the significance of the holding period return. *F-test* is the value of the *F*-statistics for the effect of the flotation procedure on the holding period abnormal returns. Holding periods are expressed in full calendar months from the issue date and only include stocks for which the full seasoning period was available. The significance levels are coded as (*) for 10%, (**) for 5%, and (***) for the 1% level.

Holding Period	Flotation Mechanism Used	N	Mean Period AR	σ	t-test	Prob>(t	F-test
12 months	Auctions	47	11.9%	1.29	0.64	0.53	0.59
	Fixed-Price	60	-1.3%	0.34	-0.31	0.76	
24 months	Auctions	44	12.8%	0.93	0.92	0.36	0.45
	Fixed-Price	60	3.3%	0.52	0.49	0.62	
36 months	Auctions	41	-17.7%	0.91	-1.25	0.22	0.85
	Fixed-Price	58	-3.6%	0.62	-0.44	0.66	

Over the 36-month holding period, the introductions through auction procedures achieved on average a -17.7 % market adjusted return (Competitive auctions average -17.1 %, while repeated auctions average -18.2 %), compared to -3.6 % for posted-price introductions (5.1 % for direct fixed-price procedures and -12.2 % for the indirect version). Both the *t*-tests for the existence of underperformance and the *F*-tests for differences between auctions and fixed-price procedures are not statistically significant at the usual levels of confidence. The results in this section can best be described as statistically inconclusive, even though most of the figures exhibit the signs and magnitudes anticipated.

6.3 Ownership Structure, Corporate Control, Mechanism Selection

In the preceding sections, evidence was gathered supporting one of the factors possibly explaining the posted-price paradox: the existence of temporary imbalances between supply and demand for the shares, related to the overall state of the IPO market, and the technical constraints on share rationing, combine to force the use of fixed-price mechanisms as procedure of last resort. An alternative explanation, ventured in hypothesis 5, focuses on the private benefits to control. If current owner-managers enjoy significant private benefits from the exercise of control, they may be willing to trade the efficiency benefits of auctions for the ownership dispersion properties of fixed-price procedures. As mentioned above, and a similar piece of evidence can be found in Jacquillat (1989), table V, p. 62), fixed-price flotations are usually associated with larger oversubscriptions. Assuming that the average order size is not significantly different between procedures, then fixed-price procedures, under pro-rata allocation, result in a broader dispersion of the shares. Alternatively, without this assumption, the frequent recourse to nominative fixed-price procedures, specifically designed to guarantee such broad-based allocations, is also supportive of the private benefits argument[33]. The resulting dispersion reduces the individual incentives to monitor the managers and thus enhances the managers' welfare.

Table 11

Ownership Distribution, Certification and Flotation Method

Owner/Managers refer to the founder's family and the company managers, *ST Banks* to banks having invested in the firm going public less than one year before the IPO, *LT Banks* to banks having invested more than a year before the IPO, *Venture Capital* to venture capitalists, *Public* to shares distributed in the public at large and *Others* to undefined shareholders. Auctions include both *"Mise en Vente"* and *"Procédure Ordinaire"*, Fixed-Price include both direct and indirect *"Offre Publique de Vente"*. The rankings of both lead underwriter and lead investment banker are with reference to the SBF rankings: a higher score indicates a lower average ranking. A General Linear Model (GLM) procedure is used in the analysis of variance tests for differences between the means of the equity ownerships of the different introduction mechanisms. The value for the *F*-test is reported. (is the standard deviation of the ownership positions or rankings. The significance levels are coded as (*) for 10%, (**) for 5%, and (***) for the 1% level.).

Ownership (All figures in %)	Fixed-Priced Procedures (σ)	Auction Procedures (σ)	F-test	Prob>F
Owner/Managers	68.4 (34.8)	63.3 (33.2)	0.59	0.44
Employees	2.6 (5.7)	3.7 (8.2)	0.60	0.44
Companies	15.4 (29.5)	13.3 (28.7)	0.14	0.71
ST Banks	1.6 (3.8)	1.9 (4.3)	0.12	0.73
LT Banks	4.5 (14.9)	6.9 (15.9)	0.68	0.41
Venture Capital	3.4 (6.3)	6.5 (11.2)	3.39	0.07 *
Public	0.3 (1.6)	0.1 (0.2)	1.68	0.19
Others	3.8 (8.0)	4.3 (13.2)	0.07	0.78
Total	100%	100%		
Ranking of Lead Underwriter	7.7 (4.5)	5.0 (3.8)	10.52	0.001 ***
Ranking of Lead Investment Bank	25.8 (10.9)	21.9 (10.5)	3.23	0.07 *

To test for the effect of corporate control on the choice of flotation mechanism, the distribution of ownership at the time of the IPOs is summarized in table 11. In the sample of 108 flotations, an average of 66.1 % of the shares are controlled by the owner-managers, 3.1 % by the employees, 7.3 % by banks, 14.5 % by other companies, 4.8 % by venture capitalists, and another 4.2 % by the public at large and others. The only statistically significant difference in ownership is with respect to venture capitalists: auctions are associated with a level of venture capital involvement (6.5 %) almost double the level of fixed-price procedures (3.4 %, with an F-test = 3.39). Furthermore, auctions are associated with statistically better underwriter rankings (F-test = 10.52) and investment banker prestige (F-test = 3.23).

These results are consistent with the second explanation: the presence of venture capitalists in the ownership structure may control the owner-managers incentives to dilute external monitoring through the selection of fixed-price flotations. Venture capitalists also seem to facilitate the selection of high reputation underwriters and investment bankers. This can be related to the role posited for venture capitalists in Megginson and Weiss (1991) and Barry, Muscarella, Peavy and Vetsuypens (1990). Furthermore, the results seem to highlight another important role, beside the evaluation of the demand for the issuer's shares, for investment bankers and underwriters in the French context: the management of such demand in the context of the selection of the most efficient flotation mechanism.

7. Conclusions and Implications

The objective of this paper is to extend the notion of strategic timing by IPO issuers to include the possibility of strategic behavior in the selection of flotation mechanism. This possibility arises from the simultaneous availability in France of both auction-type and fixed-price flotation procedures. Theoretical arguments from the auction literature and detailed investigation of the institutional framework in France are used to support the existence of a form of preference ordering over the selection of introduction mechanism: auction-type sales appear to be informationally more efficient than fixed-price procedures. The continued use of the seemingly inefficient fixed-price procedures constitutes the "posted-price paradox". The paradox appears to be explained in part by the combination of two factors: (1) imbalances between the level of demand and supply for the new shares leads to the inability to meet technical constraints imposed on maximum allowable rationing, forcing the use of a second-best procedure, the fixed-price approach. (2) owner-managers may trade the efficiency gains of auctions for the private welfare gains from reduced supervision by an atomistic external ownership.

The empirical evidence, on a sample of 108 IPOs over the period 1984-1991, shows that: (1) IPO issuers seem to time their offerings to be close to market peaks, (2) the level of the initial price reaction is strongly associated with both the flotation mechanism selected for going-public (auctions require smaller underpricings than fixed-price procedures) and the state of the IPO market at the time of issuance ('hot' issue markets are characterized by lower underpricings), (3) a significant shift in the choice of mechanisms occurs between 'hot' and 'cold' issue markets, with auctions prevalent during 'hot' markets and failing often in 'cold' issue markets because of strong imbalances between demand and supply for the shares, (4) long-term underperformance is apparent in the shares, although with limited statistical significance, with a magnitude comparable to figures reported in other countries, (5) the long-term underperformance is not related to the state of the IPO market at issuance but seems to be correlated with the flotation mechanism used (auctions exhibit larger underperformance than fixed-price procedures), (6) the presence of venture capitalists in the issuer ownership seems to be associated with the use of high reputation underwriters and investment bankers, and the recourse to auction-type flotations.

The results support the original proposition that issuers appear to choose their issue mechanism to maximize their proceeds. These findings complement the prior evidence regarding strategic timing and pricing by issuers. On the other hand, the existence of private benefits to control and limitations on corporate monitoring by atomistic shareholders may affect the objective function of the managers. If companies are successfully timing their offerings, then low returns will be earned by investors [Loughran, Ritter and Rydqvist (1994)]. An optimal issue mechanism, under proceed maximization, should then be characterized by low underpricings (meaning the price is appropriately set) and long-term underperformance (indicating that the overoptimism of the market was tapped). The evidence collected shows that shifts are observed during 'hot' issue periods toward auction-type mechanisms which exhibit the desirable properties. Fixed-price mechanisms are resorted to only when (1) the demand for the shares overwhelms the offer and forces rationing of an extent not considered acceptable by the authorities, or (2) when the possible losses of private benefits enjoyed by insider/managers outweigh the efficiency gains from using auctions. Fixed-price procedures are associated with large initial price reactions and non-significant underperformance in the long-term.

An alternative interpretation of the results holds that risk averse issuers may be willing to underprice their offers to be guaranteed a safe amount of capital. Three points need to be made in this regard. First, few IPOs in France involve new capital. Second, the cost of underpricing is quite prohibitive and would imply a high level of risk aversion from the issuers. Finally, most of the flotation efforts are of a best-effort type. If the ex ante expected costs of not fully placing the offerings were high, then underwritten offerings would be selected on a more regular basis.

The evidence presented here extends the space of strategic behavior by issuers. Unfortunately, it does not explain everything. There is still little explanation for the seemingly non-optimal behavior of investors. If indeed issuers select their mechanisms to maximize proceeds and benefit from temporary overoptimism in the IPO markets, individually rational investors should also be expected to update their prior beliefs on the basis of these realized outcomes. This does not seem to happen, for a number of reasons. First of all, IPOs are relatively rare events in France, so that investors may actually lack the opportunity to revise their beliefs in a Bayesian fashion. Second, underwriter support in the early seasoning market [Ruud (1993)] may add an option component to the intrinsic value of the shares. Changing volatility in the post-issue period may influence the value of the implicit put option so that trend in the total value (share and put) may actually camouflage the actual movement on the underlying share price. Third, the limited size of most introductions and the multiple lock-up agreements severely limit the number of shares which could potentially be borrowed for shorting purposes, thus restricting the impounding of negative information into the prices.

There is also no indication of causality in the reasoning above. Although the paper took as given the existence of exogenous factors creating 'hot' issue markets, the results are also compatible with a world of issuers deliberately clustering their issues in the absence of any other external factors, splitting the overall demand for shares among a larger number of offerings and extracting a larger share of the informational rents. This "impresario" approach[34] [Shiller (1990)] does not affect the 'strategic' interpretation of issuer behavior but requires its restatement. The evidence collected here, such as the linkage between 'hot' issue periods and long-term underperformance, seems hard to reconcile with this interpretation.

If the indications above have any predictive value, then investors should incorporate indications about the type of flotation mechanism used and the number of contemporaneous IPOs in their bidding rules. Auction-related introductions in 'hot' markets have proved poor investments, with small price run-ups after the introduction and strong underperformances over the long-run. On the other hand, fixed-price procedures have exhibited better prospects for appreciation and resilience over time. The implications for issuers and market regulators are equally important. First of all, it appears that the special procedures available during flotations to control the level of demand for the shares, such as prepayment and maximum receivable orders, have a fundamental role to play in facilitating the use of auctions. The other side of the argument is of course that preset limits on rationing impose real or opportunity costs on the issuers, in the sense that the inability to control demand and meet the rationing standards for an auction-type flotation may drive some issuers away from the public market altogether. If the existence of dynamic IPO markets is a prime policy objective, then it may be well advised to provide measures to facilitate the use of the most desirable procedures. The concomitant reduction in the diversity of mechanisms used may facilitate the investors' inferences about the future prospects for the firm, leading in the long-run to a more appropriate pricing and the disappearance of the long-run underperformance. The venture capitalists seem to be performing a useful monitoring role in the IPO process, keeping under control the owner-managers incentives to trade in the private benefits from control for a less efficient flotation mechanism.

The arguments presented above provide also an interesting explanation for the clustering of issuers and the apparent conflict between 'hot' issue markets and low initial price reactions. So far, the leading explanation focused on informational spillovers, a firm going public at a high P/E ratio signaling the receptivity of the market for a certain type of new issues. In this model, clustering may also reduce the imbalance between supply and demand for IPO shares, facilitating the use of the more efficient auction-type flotations. This paper obviously only scratches the surface of the problem of mechanism selection under asymmetric information. Extensions are desirable in a number of ways. First of all, France offers only a limited population of IPOs to analyze, limiting the power of statistical inferences. Britain, on the other hand, offers both the diversity of mechanisms and sample sizes sufficient to test most hypotheses. Second, and related to the point above, it is probably important to gain an industrial and company-specific knowledge of the situations. This is probably the single most promising stream of research: where the large cross-sectional investigations predominant in the literature focus on a limited number of explanatory factors, plenty is left to be learned from the individual experiences and the stakeholder relationships and behavior.

The problem of endogeneity in the variables considered is clearly to be kept in mind when interpreting the results. This is probably one of the biggest challenges still left to be tackled in IPO research. All decisions relating to the IPO itself, such as the very decision to go public, the pricing of the shares, the timing of the issue, the selection of the market on which to float the shares, the type and number of shares to be sold, the sales' mechanism, or the choice of underwriters and investment bankers are all endogenously determined. Integrating these factors in one model is obviously difficult, if not impossible, but this will be required to capture all the interactions between the relevant factors. This paper is a first step in that direction. Even though still very descriptive in nature, it represents a first attempt at reconciling the various empirical evidences collected to date on IPO pricing and performance with the set of decision variables handled by issuers.

Acknowledgement

Financial support for this project was received from both the INSEAD R&D department and the College Interuniversitaire pur les Etudes Doctorals en Sciences du Management (CIM) in Brussels, Belgium. Financial and Administrative support was also received from the Societe des Bourses Francaises (SBF) for gathering the data used in this study. We want to thank Theo Vermaelen, Gabriel Hawawini, Kevin Kaiser, Bruno Biasis, Chester Spatt, Tim Loughran, Manju Puri, Kristian Rydqvist, Maro Levis, Joel Shulman, Bill Petty, Erix Sirri and participants in the 1994 Western Finance Association Meetings, the 1994 Eastern Finance Association Conference, the 1994 Conference on European Financial Management and the 1994 Babson Entrepreneurial Research Conference for their comments and suggestions. The authors take credit for all errors and omissions.

References

Aggarwal, R., and P. Rivoli, 1990, Fads in the initial public offering market ? Financial Management, 19(4):45 - 57.

Allen, F., and G. Faulhaber, 1989, Signaling by underpricing in the IPO market, Journal of Financial Economics, 23(2):303 - 323.

Balvers, R., B. McDonald and R. Miller, 1988, Underpricing of new issues and the choice of auditor as signal of investment banker reputation, The Accounting Review, 63(4):605 - 622.

Baron, D. P., 1982, A model of the demand for investment banking advising and distribution, The Journal of Finance, 37(4):955 - 976.

Barry, C.B., and R.H. Jennings, 1993, The opening price performance of initial public offerings of common stocks, Financial Management, Spring:54 - 63.

Barry, C.B., C.J. Muscarella, J. Peavy and M.R. Vetsuypens, 1990, The role of venture capital in the creation of public companies: Evidence from the going-public process, Journal of Financial Economics, 27(2):447 - 471.

Bayless, M., and S. Chaplinsky, 1991, Expectations of security type and the informational content of debt and equity offers, Journal of Financial Intermediation, 1(3):195 - 214.

Bayless, M., and S. Chaplinsky, 1993, Seasoned Equity Issuance in Hot and Cold Markets, Working paper, Northwestern University.

Beatty, R.P., and J.R. Ritter, 1986, Investment banking, reputation, and the underpricing of initial public offers, Journal of Financial Economics, 15(1):213 - 232.

Belden, S., 1992, An Initial Inquiry into the Impact of Venture Capital Financing on the Underpricing and Aftermarket Performance of Initial Public Offerings, Working paper, University of Colorado.

Belletante, B., and R. Paliard, 1993, Does knowing who sells matter in IPO pricing: The french second market evidence, Cahiers Lyonnais de Recherche en Gestion, 14(Avril):42 - 74.

Benveniste, L.M., and P.A. Spindt, 1989, How investment bankers determine the offer price and allocation of new issues, Journal of Financial Economics, 24:343 - 361.

Benveniste, L.M., and W.J. Wilhelm, 1990, A comparative analysis of IPO proceeds under alternative regulatory environments, Journal of Financial Economics, 28:173 - 207.

Bikhchandani, S., and C.F. Huang, 1989, Auctions with resale markets: An exploratory model of treasury bill markets, The Review of Financial Studies, 2:311 - 340.

Booth, J.R., and R.L. Smith, 1986, Capital raising, underwriting, and the certification hypothesis, Journal of Financial Economics, 15(January):261 - 281.

Bower, N.L., 1989, Firm value and the choice of offering method in initial public offerings, The Journal of Finance, 44(3):647 - 662.

Byrd, J., Hensler, D., and S. Lee, 1992, The Long-Run Performance of IPOs, Underwriter Reputation, and the Timing of IPO Offerings, Working paper, University of Texas.

Carter, R.B., and S. Manaster, 1990, Initial public offerings and underwriter reputation, The Journal of Finance, 45(4):1045 - 1067.

Carter, R.B., 1992, Underwriter reputation and repetitive public offerings, The Journal of Financial Research, 15(4):341 - 354.

Carter, R.B., and F.H. Dark, 1990, Effects of Differential Information on the Aftermarket Valuation of Initial Public Offerings, Mimeo, Iowa State University.

Chalk, A.J., and J.W. PeavyIII, 1990, Understanding the pricing of initial public offerings, in: A.H. Chen, editor, Research in Finance, JAI Press, Inc., Greenwich, CT.

Chan, L.K.C., and J. Lakonishok, 1992, Institutional Trades and Intra-Day Stock Price Behavior, Working paper, University of Illinois.

Choe, H., R. Masulis and V. Nanda, 1990, On the Timing of New Equity Issues: Theory and Evidence, Working paper, Vanderbilt University.

Clarkson, P. and R. Thompson, 1990, Empirical estimates of beta when investors face estimation risk, The Journal of Finance, 45(2):431 - 453.

Conrad, J. and G. Kaul, 1993, Long-term market overreaction or biases in computed returns, The Journal of Finance, 48(1):39 - 63.

Cotter, J.F., 1992, The Long-Run Efficiency of IPO Pricing, Working paper, University of North Carolina at Chapel Hill.

Dufour, J.F., and J.L. Kervern, 1985, Analyse critique des 58 premières introduction au second marché, Etude Technique, Mai.

Eckbo, D.B., and R.W. Masulis, 1992, Adverse selection and the rights offer paradox, Journal of Financial Economics, 32:293 - 332.

Gale, I., and J.E. Stiglitz, 1989, The informational content of initial public offerings, The Journal of Finance, 44(2):469 - 477.

Grinblatt, M., and C.Y. Hwang, 1989, Signalling and the pricing of new issues, The Journal of Finance, 44(2):393 - 420.

Harris, M., and A. Raviv, 1981, \newblock Allocation mechanisms and the design of auctions, Econometrica, 49(6):1477 - 1499.

Hausch, D.B., 1986, Multi-object auctions: Sequential versus simultaneous sales, Management Science, 32(12):1599 - 1612.

Husson, B., and B. Jacquillat, 1989, French new issues, underpricing, and alternative methods of distribution, in: Guimaraes et al., editor, A Reappraisal of the Efficiency of Financial Markets, Springer-Verlag, Berlin.

Ibbotson, R.G., and J.F. Jaffe, 1975, Hot issue markets, The Journal of Finance, 30(4):1027 - 1042.

Ibbotson, R.G., J.L. Sindelar and J.R. Ritter, 1988, Initial public offerings, Journal of Applied Corporate Finance, 1(4):37 - 45.

Jacquillat, B.C., J.G. McDonald and J. Rolfo, 1978, French auctions of common stock: New issues, 1966-1974, Journal of Business Finance, 2:305 - 322.

Jacquillat, B.C., 1989, L'Introduction en Bourse, Presses Universitaires de France, Paris.

Jaffeux, C., 1990, Essai d'explication de la sous-évaluation des titres à leur introduction sur le second marché, La Revue Banque, 509:952 - 958.

Jegadeesh, N., M. Weinstein and I. Welch, 1993, An empirical investigation of IPO returns and subsequent equity offerings, Journal of Financial Economics, 34:153 - 175.

Jenkinson, T., and C. Mayer, 1988, The privatization process in France and the United Kingdom, European Economic Review, 32:482 - 490.

Johnson, J.M., and R.E. Miller, 1988, Investment banker prestige and the underpricing of initial public offerings, Financial Management, 17(2):19 - 29.

Keloharju, M., 1991, Winner's curse and optimal underpricing in initial public offerings, Working Paper, Helsinki School of Economics.

Keloharju, M., 1992, IPO Returns and the Characteristics of Subsequent Seasoned Offerings, Unpublished Doctoral Dissertation, Helsinki School of Economics and Business Administration.

Keloharju, M., 1993, The winner's curse, legal liability, and the long-run price performance of initial public offerings in Finland, Journal of Financial Economics, 34:251 - 277.

Keloharju, M., and K. Kulp, 1993, Market-To-Book Ratios, Equity Retention, and Management Ownership in Finnish Initial Public Offerings, Working paper, Helsinki School of Economics and Business Administration.

Koh, F., and T. Walter, 1989, A direct test of Rock's model of the pricing of unseasoned issues, Journal of Financial Economics, 23(3):251 - 272.

Korajczyk, R., D. Lucas and R. McDonald, 1991, The effect of information releases on the pricing and timing of equity issues, The Review of Financial Studies, 4(4):685 - 708.

Levis, M., 1990, The winner's curse problem, interest costs and the underpricing of initial public offerings, Economic Journal, 100(399):76 - 89.

Levis, M., 1993, Initial public offerings, subsequent rights issues and long-run performance, Working paper, City University Business School.

Levis, M., 1993, The long-run performance of initial public offerings: The U.K. experience 1980-1988 Financial Management, Spring:28 - 41.

Loughran, T., and J.R. Ritter, 1993, The timing and subsequent performance of IPOs: The US and International Evidence, Working paper, University of Illinois.

Loughran, T., J.R. Ritter and K. Rydqvist, 1994, Initial public offerings: International insights, Pacific-Basin Finance Journal), 2(2):165 - 199.

Lucas, D., and R. McDonald, 1990, Equity issues and stock price dynamics, The Journal of Finance, 45:1019 - 1043.

McAfee, P.R., and J. McMillan, 1987, Auction and bidding, Journal of Economic Literature, 25(June):699 - 738.

McDonald, J.G., and B.C. Jacquillat, 1974, Pricing of initial equity issues: The French sealed bid auction, Journal of Business, 33 (January):37 - 47.

Megginson, W.L., and K.A. Weiss, 1991, Venture capitalist certification in initial public offerings, The Journal of Finance, 46(3):879 - 903.

Miller, E.M., 1977, Risk, uncertainty, and divergence of opinion, The Journal of Finance, 32(4):1151 - 1168.

Monnier, P., 1993, Second marché: Marché à part entière ou entièrement à part ? Gestion de Fortune, 20:43 - 45.

Payne, J.D., 1992, Firm Quality, Underpricing at IPO and subsequent equity financing decisions, Working paper, University of Southwestern Louisiana.

Pilverdier-Latreyte, J., 1991, Le marché financier français, Economica, Paris.

Rajan, R., and H. Servaes, 1993, The effect of market conditions on initial public offerings, Working paper, University of Chicago.

Ritter, J.R., 1984, The 'hot issue' market of 1980, Journal of Business, 57(2):215 - 240.

Ritter, J.R., 1985, The choice between firm commitment and best effort contracts, Working paper, University of Michigan.

Ritter, J.R., 1987, The costs of going public, Journal of Financial Economics, 19(December):269 - 282.

Ritter, J.R., 1988, A Theory of Investment Banking Contract Choice, Working Paper, University of Michigan.

Ritter, J.R., 1991, The long-run performance of initial public offerings, The Journal of Finance, 46(1):3 - 28.

Rock, K., 1986, Why new issues are underpriced, Journal of Financial Economics, 15:187 - 212.

Ruud, J.S., 1993, Underwriter price support and the IPO underpricing puzzle, Journal of Financial Economics, 34:135 - 151.

Shiller, R.J., 1989, Initial public offerings: underpricing and investor behavior, Working paper, National Bureau of Economic Research, N. 2806.

Shiller, R.J., 1990, Speculative prices and popular models, Journal of Economic Perspectives, 4(2):55 - 65.

Shleifer, A., and R.W. Vishny, 1992, Liquidation values and debt capacity: A market equilibrium approach, The Journal of Finance, 47(3):1343 - 1366.

Simon, C.J., 1989, The effect of the 1933 securities act on investor information and the performance of new issues, American Economic Review, 79(3):295 - 318.

Simunic, D.A., and M. Stein, 1987, Product differentiation in auditing: auditor choice in the market for unseasoned new issues, Working paper, Canadian Certified General Accountants' Research Foundation.

Slovin, M.B., and J.E. Young, 1990, Bank lending and initial public offerings, Journal of Banking and Finance, 14(4):729 - 740.

Spatt, C., and S. Srivastava, 1991, Preplay communication, participation restrictions, and efficiency in initial public offerings, The Review of Financial Studies, 4(4):709 - 726.

T. Sternberg, 1989, Bilateral monopoly and the dynamic properties of initial public offerings, Working Paper, Owen Graduate School of Management, Vanderbilt University.

Tinic, S.M., 1988, Anatomy of initial public offerings of common stock, The Journal of Finance, 43(4):789 - 822.

Titman, S., and B. Trueman, 1986, Information quality and the valuation of new issues, Journal of Accounting and Economics, 8(8):159 - 172.

VanHulle, C., M. Casselman and M.O. Imam, 1993, Initial public offerings in Belgium: Theory and evidence, Tijdschrift voor Economie en Management, 38(4):385 - 423.

Weber, R.J., 1983, Multiple-object auctions, in: R. Englebrecht-Wiggans, M. Shubik, and R.M. Stark, editors, Auctions, Bidding, and Contracting: Uses and Theory, New York University Press, New York.

Welch, I., 1989, Seasoned offerings, imitation costs, and underpricing of initial public offerings, The Journal of Finance, 44(2):421 - 449.

Welch, I., 1992, Sequential sales, learning, and cascades, The Journal of Finance, 47(2):695 - 732.

Wilson, R., 1992, Strategic analysis of auctions, in: R.J. Aumann and S. Hart, editors, Handbook of Game Theory, Elsevier Science Publishers B.V.

Zeckhauser, R., J. Patel and D. Hendricks, 1991, Nonrational actors in financial markets behavior, Theory and Decision, 31:257 - 287.

Endnotes

[1] See, for example, Rock (1986) and the winner's curse hypothesis, Tinic (1988) and the legal liability model, Baron (1982) and the moral hazard problem, Welch (1989) and the signaling-by-underpricing argument, Booth and Smith (1986) and the certification rationale, to mention just a representative few.

[2] See e.g. Ritter (1991) for the 'fads' model, Shiller (1990) for the impresario hypothesis, or Miller (1977) for an heterogeneous beliefs model.

[3] Ritter (1991), Zeckhauser, Patel and Hendricks (1991), Carter and Dark (1991), Keloharju (1991), Loughran and Ritter (1993), Levis (1993), Bayless and Chaplinsky (1993), Rajan and Servaes (1993), and Loughran, Ritter and Rydqvist (1994).

[4] See Gale and Stiglitz (1989), Payne (1992), Carter (1992), Keloharju (1992), Welch (1992), Jegadeesh, Weinstein and Welch (1993), Keloharju (1993), and Levis (1993) for variations of the model and empirical tests.

[5] Booth and Smith (1986), Johnson and Miller (1988), Carter and Manaster (1990), or Byrd, Hensler and Lee (1992) for the certification effect of investment bankers and underwriters, Titman and Trueman (1986) or Simunic and Stein (1987) for the effect of auditors, Barry, Muscarella, Peavy and Vetsuypens (1990) or Megginson and Weiss (1991) for the impact of venture capital on the performance of IPOs, and Slovin and Young (1990) for the importance of bank relationships.

6 The procedure was challenged on a number of occasions. For example, in 1953, the Department of Justice attacked the fixed-price system as a violation of antitrust laws before the District Court of New York. In that case, United States vs Morgan et al., the Court reaffirmed the legality of fixed-price arrangements.

7 In underwritten offerings, underwriters pre-purchase the shares from the issuer at a mutually-agreed price [Sternberg (1989)] and carry the risk inherent in the resale process to the public at large or to a select group of institutions. In best effort offerings, the underwriter only acts as the marketing and sales agent of the issuer and does not guarantee full placement of the shares.

8 For more details on the procedures available in Britain, see Harris and Raviv (1981) and Levis (1993).

9 McDonald and Jacquillat (1974), Jacquillat et al. (1978), Jenkinson and Mayer (1988), Husson and Jacquillat (1989), Jaffeux (1990), Belletante and Paliard (1993), Loughran, Ritter and Rydqvist (1994).

10 See McDonald and Jacquillat (1974), Jacquillat (1989), Pilverdier-Latreyte (1991), Belletante and Paliard (1993), Monnier (1993), and the proceedings of the InterConference seminar on Second market IPOs held in Paris in November 1993 for further details on the procedural arrangements.

11 The PO mechanism resembles in practice the Dutch variant to the English auction described in Wilson (1992, p.230). The procedure is the default mechanism for companies already traded, for example, over the counter ("Hors Cote") or on a foreign stock exchange.

12 The possibility of blocks in the allocation schedules is not ruled out, so that pro-rata is only applied conditionally.

13 As mentioned by Loughran, Ritter and Rydqvist (1994), it is relatively rare to see different offer prices for different investors. Exceptions include Portugal, Singapore (after 1992), and Japan (after 1989), where different prices are paid by different categories of investors for the same shares offered for sale.

14 Adverse selection underlies many models of IPO pricing. Baron (1982) interprets underpricing as a form of compensation for the superior information possessed by investment bankers. In Rock (1986), underpricing serves as compensation for the biased rationing of the shares (the "winner's curse").

15 See McAfee and McMillan (1987) and Wilson (1992) for surveys, Bikhchandani and Huang (1989) and Spatt and Srivastava (1991) for analyses in financial settings, and Weber (1983), Hausch (1986) or Wilson (1992) for more general game theoretic approaches.

16 This restriction is explicitly embedded in the NASD "Rules of Fair Practice" and the French "Règlement Général" (RG) from the "Société des Bourses Françaises" (SBF).

17 As is the case in the United Kingdom [Levis (1990,1993)], Singapore [Koh and Walter (1989)], and France.

18 These arguments can be found in Shiller (1989), Lucas and McDonald (1990), Choe, Masulis and Nanda (1990), Bayless and Chaplinsky (1991), Korajczyk, Lucas and McDonald (1991), Ritter (1991), Rajan and Servaes (1993), and Loughran, Ritter and Rydqvist (1994).

[19] Loughran and Ritter (1993), in particular, attempt to disaggregate the long-run underperformance of stocks issued over the period 1968-1993. The average annual return to investing in seasoned stocks with the same size distribution as the IPOs (15% per year on average) is decomposed into 5% due to the ability of issuers to time their flotations and take advantage of market 'peaks' (because investing in seasoned stocks at the time of the IPOs generates average annual returns of only 10%) and another 8% due to the underperformance effect (because investing in IPO shares at the time of the offerings creates average annual returns of only 2%, or 8% below similar timed investments in seasoned stocks). It is that 'fad' component in IPO initial pricing that opens up the possibility of strategic plays by issuers, which are extended to include the choice of flotation mechanism here.

[20] The argument made by Welch (1989), Grinblatt and Hwang (1989), Allen and Faulhaber (1989) and tested, among others, by Payne (1992), Keloharju (1992,1993), and Jegadeesh, Weinstein and Welch (1993), that issuers actually optimize not only the proceeds from the initial equity issue but also later rounds of financing, is not addressed here.

[21] In the sense that all excesses are eventually corrected when sufficient information accumulates over the newly public firm, in the form of repeated regulatory filings, accounting and auditing reports, specialized agency ratings and investment reports, etc.

[22] Simple arithmetic returns are used because they better reflect actual trading portfolios than continuously compounded returns, as suggested by Jay Ritter and Michael Brennan.

[23] The censoring leaves out most of the early IPOs (1983 to 1985), for which returns information is not available, and firms introduced on regional exchanges.

[24] The market indices collected include the Datastream Paris Total Market, a comprehensive value-weighted index adjusted for all capital structure changes, the CAC General, and the AGEFI Second Market Indices.

[25] The very concept of 'hot' issue market lacks a clear definition and is loosely associated with periods of high issuing activity. Ritter (1984) defines it with respect to the number of IPOs and their value.

[26] The indicator variable takes on a value of 1 for issues taking place in a month where the total number of issues is larger than the median number of issues per month in the population, 0 otherwise. Two distinct periods of 'hot' markets are highlighted, from July 1985 to April 1986 and from June 1987 to May 1988 [Belletante and Paliard (1993)].

[27] The figure is significantly smaller during 'hot' issue periods, a finding that will be related later to the fact that oversubscription for the new shares is also much lower during such periods, warranting shorter intervention by the SBF.

[28] The authors conduct the analysis on IPO samples in some 15 countries, including this French database, using inflation-adjusted stock market indices as proxies for market peaks. Among all the countries analyzed, the correlations are always positive, significant at the 1% level in more than half.

[29] The equilibirum price is defined by the SBF as the first market price obtained without interference in the interaction of supply and demand. As mentioned previously, the early aftermarket for IPO shares is managed by the SBF to ensure an 'orderly' process, leading to a 'managed' equilibrium price which would not clear the market.

[30] A similar situation prevails in Belgium, as described by Van Hulle, Casserman and Imam (1993). They refer to this price-setting process as a 'dirty' auction.

[31] Ritter (1991) posits that investors not able to obtain shares in the initial offering bid up the prices in the secondary market to satisfy their desire to own the stock.

[32] Small samples create a number of problems beside the definition of quartiles of similar size. The chi-square statistics are distributed approximately as χ^2 when the null hypothesis is true but also when the sample size is large. The size and distribution of the observations here seem sufficient for running the tests but the limitations caused by the asymptotic nature of the χ^2 distribution should be kept in mind.

[33] It should be said that this concern for broad dispersion of the shares is usually publicly justified by equity and fairness motives: small shareholders deserve to receive some shares as well as larger bidders. It is of course impossible to reject this alternative explanation outright.

[34] The original impresario hypothesis by Shiller (1990) assumes that underwriters purposefully create high initial returns in IPOs to create hot markets and somehow 'cream' unsuspecting issuers and investors. Reminiscent of racketeering theories, this explanation has not received much empirical support.

The IPO Puzzle and Institutional Constraints:
Evidence from the Athens Stock Market

Christos Kazantzis
Piraeus University

Dylan C Thomas
City University Business School

Abstract

During the period 1987-1994, IPOs launched on the Athens Stock Exchange were subject to a number of varying institutional interventions, ranging from post-launch price support, a subscription support mechanism and a cap on the daily price movement. In this paper we examine the impact of the institutional interventions in force at the time on the level of subscription and on the level of first day returns for 129 IPO securities. We document significant differences in the level of first day returns between the various institutional sub-periods. Both institutional intervention variables and established factors from the underpricing literature are significant in explaining the cross-sectional variability in first day returns.

1. Introduction

Although the underpricing of initial public offerings (IPOs) has been a feature common to virtually all major capital markets, its magnitude appears to be particularly pronounced in some emerging capital markets. The average initial return, for example, for IPOs in Malaysia is 166.6 percent (Dawson, 1987) and 78.5 percent for Brazilian IPOs (Aggarwal, Leal & Hernandez, 1993).

Loughran, Ritter and Rydqvist (1994) have recently argued that at least a part of the differences in IPO initial returns across countries is due to the various contractual mechanisms used for issuing, pricing and distributing the shares in newly floated firms. Exceptionally high returns have been noted in those countries where there are binding institutional constraints on the setting of the offer price and on the mechanism which determines the movement of the stock price. Such constraints have, to date, been introduced primarily in emerging markets. In Korea, for example, the offer prices of new issues prior to June 1988 were set equal to the book value per share while even in Japan, issuing firms are required to set their offer prices based upon the multiples (e.g. price-to-earnings, market-to-book value) of three comparable companies, the Japanese government, in a number of cases, obliging the issuers to choose comparable firms with low multiples.

The Athens Stock Market over the period 1987-1994 provides a particularly rich setting for investigating the impact of the regulatory framework on the pricing of IPOs. During the eight years, the institutional interventions have included compulsory price support provided by underwriters for the immediate 6 month post-launch period, subscription support (in the form of letters of credit provided by banks) to credit-worthy prospective investors to allow them to bid for new issues and an 8 percent cap on the daily return. These changes, in addition to some features unique to Greek IPOs, create an environment in which a number of the hypotheses relating to litigation, information asymmetry, ex-ante uncertainty and equity retention have a particular relevance.

Deliberate underpricing (and subsequent support in the aftermarket) is seen, for example, as a mean of avoiding legal actions brought by investors who might otherwise suffer financial loss by investing in new issues. The supportive empirical evidence put forward by Tinic (1988) has, however, been subsequently challenged by Drake and Vetsuypens (1993). Deliberate underpricing is also seen as a mechanism whereby underwriters can build up their reputation (Booth and Smith (1986)).

Much of the information asymmetry literature has focussed on the differential information held by the issuing firm, prospective investors and sponsoring institutions. In this context, underpricing has been variously interpreted as a method by which uninformed investors are persuaded to take part in new issue activity (Rock 1986), and as a method by which the parties involved in the flotation are rewarded (Baron (1982)). Other studies have suggested the level of underpricing to be a function of the degree of involvement of the underwriter in both the share allocation method and in the collation of information from informed investors (Barry & Jennings (1993), Benveniste & Wilhelm (1990), Weiss-Hanley (1993), Welch (1991)). In general, the greater the ability of the underwriter to elicit informed judgments as to the value of the offering and the greater the underwriter's influence to direct the share allocation procedure toward informed investors, the lower the level of underpricing. Subsequent work by Benveniste, Busaba & Wilhelm (1995) and Chowdry and Nanda (1994) suggests the commitment to stabilise as an alternative strategy to underpricing and thus new issues with a credible stabilisation commitment attached to them are expected to be fairly priced. Such a commitment, however, also carries with it the risk of financial distress for the party providing that commitment. As such, the party providing the commitment would wish for the issue to be underpriced in order to minimise the incidence and cost of having to intervene in the market to support the price.

The purpose of this paper is to investigate the impact of the different types of institutional intervention on the investor response to, and the initial pricing of, new issues launched on the Athens Stock Market in the period 1987-1994. The analysis has policy implications for the Athens Stock Exchange and other capital markets where direct measures of regulatory intervention are in operation.

2. The Greek Institutional Framework

2.1 General Arrangements

The Athens Stock Exchange is a public entity supervised by the Ministry of National Economy and has been in operation since the second half of the last century but it has only been in the last decade that the Exchange has assumed a central role in the country's economic activity. Protection of investors and the enforcement of domestic laws is ensured by the Government Commissioner, the Capital Market Committee and the Council of the Athens Stock Exchange. Securities are traded on either the "Main" or on the "Parallel" Market. At the end of 1994, 174 companies were traded on the Main Market of the Athens Exchange with a total market capitalisation of 3.6 trillion Greek Drachma[1]; the capitalisation of the 15 companies traded on the Parallel Market totalled 84 billion Greek Drachma.

Under the Greek institutional framework a company applying for listing to the Athens Stock Market must comply with the relevant listing rules of the Exchange. The rules specify that:

> The company must increase its share capital by at least 25 percent to obtain a listing on the Main Market or by at least 15 percent for Parallel Market listing. Of the shares issued, 70% must be distributed to individual investors and public entities while the remaining 30% must be allocated to institutional investors[2].
>
> The minimum book equity for a listing in the Main Market is about 600 million Greek Drachma while the equivalent amount for the Parallel Market is about 120 million Greek Drachma for at least the two fiscal years prior to the application for listing.
>
> Companies applying for a listing must have a trading record of at least five years for the Main Market and three years for the Parallel Market. The accounts of the applying companies must also accord with the national accounting standards.
>
> Of the new shares issued, 60 percent of the shares must be distributed in the hands of at least 100 different shareholders. This regulation applies to listings on both Main and Parallel Markets.

New shares are sold through the intermediation of a bank and/or through a securities company with a share capital exceeding 1 billion Greek Drachma or through a syndicate of two or more banks. The name of the bank is stated in the prospectus. The price of issue is set by the underwriter who usually also acts as the sponsor. In some cases, this price setting is carried out in consultation with the group of syndicated sub-underwriters. Once the price of the issue is fixed, it can neither be changed in response to emerging investor demand prior to the first day of trading nor can the issue then be withdrawn. The issuing company usually receives the cash proceeds from the offer immediately after the allocation of the shares, typically 2 or 3 days after the closing date of the offer. Offers for sale are always underwritten. The underwriting is organised by the sponsor of the issue and may involve either a single financial institution or a syndicate comprising a group of commercial and investment banks The underwriter does, however, have absolute discretion in the decision on the timing of the first day of trading of the issue which may be delayed as a result of unforeseen circumstances or adverse market conditions. Thus, the time lapse from the announcement of the offer price to the first day of trading may range from a few days to a few months. Typically, the period during which the shares are on offer averages five trading days. Prospective investors are required to remit the appropriate amount of funds at the same time as they apply for the shares[3]. The allocation procedure in the event of oversubscription is stated in the prospectus and cannot subsequently be amended. When oversubscription occurs, shares are allocated either by a proportional lottery procedure or by a combination of rationing and a lottery procedure. Proportional lottery involves the scaling down of all applications by the same factor. No shares are allotted to those applicants whose scaled down application amounts to less than 10 shares. The rationing and lottery procedure involves awarding the minimum of number of shares (usually 10) to all applicants and then scaling down the balance of the applications by a standard factor. It is important to note that the underwriter does not have any discretion in the operation of the terms of the allocation procedure in the event of oversubscription.

There are, in addition, three factors which are specific to IPOs launched on the Athens market and which were in place throughout the period under study. Each of these factors is likely to play a role in the setting of the offer price. First, the ability of the Athens Stock Exchange to intervene in the setting of the proposed price of a new issue provides the means by which the threat of legal action by disillusioned investors can be mitigated. Informal discussions with the Exchange indicate that such intervention in reducing the proposed issue price is commonplace. Of the 45 latest IPOs, the Exchange has exercised its prerogative in reducing the issue price in 42 of the new launches. The individual cases where interventions have taken place are, however, not disclosed nor is the scale of the issue-price reductions. Taken with the other factors discussed below, such an activity is likely to lead to higher first-day returns. The certifying role provided by the Exchange is also likely to be associated with underpricing. This, it is suggested, might be a major consideration in a capital market anxious both to establish itself and to attract new company launches. Second, the underwriters can neither elicit information as to the perceived value of the issue from informed investors prior to the setting of the issue price, nor do the underwriters have the ability to provide informed investors with preferential access to shares in the event of oversubscription. Both of these limitations are likely to be associated with underpricing and positive first day returns. Third, the right of the underwriter to delay the first day of trading adds to the risks faced by both prospective shareholders and sub-underwriters. Both parties subscribe cash to the new company at the close of the offer. Delaying the first day of trading involves interest foregone on the funds subscribed as well as the increased uncertainty as to the opening market value and the specific date when shareholders would first be able to trade their holdings in the market. Both of these factors suggest that underwriters would, on average, underprice new issues in order to compensate for these risks.

2.2 The Four Regulatory Regimes

The first sub-period, January 1987 - December 1990, is characterised by a compulsory price support regime for new equity issues when underwriters were required, by law, to support an IPO at the offer price for a period of six months in the aftermarket. The explicit purpose of the price support mechanism was to boost investors' confidence and encourage participation in the new issues market. Given that, in Greece, the underwriter was not directly rewarded for providing the 6 month put option which forms the stabilisation commitment and the fact that the underwriter plays a major part in setting the price, it would therefore be expected that this facility would increase the level of underpricing in this period. Such underpricing would obviously reduce the likelihood of the underwriters having to intervene in the market to support the price and the associated cost of the capital resources involved in such an activity.

The second sub-period from 16 December 1990 to June 1992 is characterised by the total absence of any institutional intervention although the method of price setting, the underwriter's right of delay with respect to the first day of trading and the monitoring role of the Athens Stock Exchange with respect to the issue price all remain in place during the period. The third sub-period, from June 1992 to February 1994, involved the introduction of a daily 8 percent limit on the movement of share prices as well as a subscription support mechanism. More specifically, trading in a stock is suspended when the price of the stock rises or drops by 8 percent compared with the closing price of the previous day of trading. The operation of this mechanism was not subject to any time limit in the after-market but was usually triggered in the days immediately following launch. The subscription support mechanism involved guarantees given by banks to those individual customers whom they considered credit worthy. The guarantees allowed these favoured customers to subscribe for new issues using the guarantees rather than paying cash at the time of the offer. The subscription support mechanism was withdrawn in early 1994. The period between February 1994 to December 1994, where only the daily price cap was in effect, constitutes the fourth sub-period. From February 1994 onwards, prospective investors were required to put up the full amount of cash when applying for IPO shares.

3. Data and Methodology

The sample used in this study comprises the population of 96 firms offered on the Main and Parallel Markets during the period from January 1987 through November 1994. Closed-end fund IPOs, which are known to behave differently from industrial IPOs, are excluded from the sample. Of the total of 96 IPO firms, 63 of the offering firms issued only ordinary shares while the remainder issued both ordinary and preference shares. The sample therefore comprises 129 securities. All data related to the individual characteristics of an offering are taken from the prospectuses of the individual companies. Closing mid-prices on the first day of trading were collected from the financial press.

Table 1 provides data on the number of IPOs launched in each of the eight years classified by the type of share issued. The annual distribution of IPOs clearly demonstrates the presence of 'hot issue' periods. The number of offerings increased from an average of 3 issues per year in the period 1987-89 to 46 issues in 1990, 23 in 1991 and 43 in 1994.

Table 1

Number of Issues by Year and by Type of Security*

Year	Ordinary Shares	Preference	All Issues Shares
1987	2	2	4
1988	2	1	3
1989	1	1	2
1990	25	21	46
1991	16	7	23
1992	0	0	0
1993	8	0	8
1994**	42	1	43
All	96	33	129

* On both Main and Parallel Markets (investment trust IPOs are excluded).

** Up to November 1994

The majority of IPO firms issued before 1991 issued both preference and ordinary shares while almost all of the firms which went public after 1992 issued only ordinary shares.

For each offering, the returns are calculated as:

(i) The first day adjusted return for issue i is defined as the percentage change in price from the offering date to the close at the first day of trading (r_i) less the corresponding market return on the appropriate industrial sector index (r_m):

$$ar_i = r_i - r_m$$

(ii) The first day returns for the period when the price cap intervention was in operation are calculated on the assumption that the existence of such a constraint does not allow the law of supply and demand to set the price of the share to its fair value on any one particular day. In these cases we calculate the first day return to be the accumulated return over the number of consecutive days, starting at launch day, when the price cap was triggered. For example, if the share price movements trigger the price cap on the 4 consecutive days after listing and do not trigger the price cap on day 5 in the aftermarket, the first day raw return (r) is calculated as follows:

$$r = \frac{\text{Closing mid-price on day 5 - Offer price}}{\text{Offer price}}$$

4. Institutional Intervention and First Day Returns

Table 2 shows descriptive statistics for the raw and adjusted first day returns during the entire period 1987-94 and for each of the four sub-periods. The average raw first day return for the entire period is 50.89 percent and the adjusted return 51.73 percent. Both average returns are statistically significant.

Table 2

First Day Returns for Initial Public Offerings January 1987 - November 1994

Panel A: Raw Returns

	Price Stabilisation	No Intervention	Subscription Support and 8% Return Cap	8% Return Cap Only	All
Mean %	66.21	8.08	187.18	25.06	50.89
t-statistic	7.68	1.90	4.45	5.02	8.11
Median %	43.48	1.56	150.00	14.51	24.00
Standard deviation %	63.90	20.40	126.25	32.33	71.27
Kurtosis	-0.92	-0.65	-0.69	2.11	6.10
Skewness	0.64	0.57	0.72	1.59	2.15
Minimum return %	0.00	-19.05	45.42	-8.33	-19.05
Maximum return %	200.00	50.00	400.00	128.18	400.00
No. of issues with negative first day returns	0	6	0	6	12
Number of issues	55	23	9	42	129

Panel B: Adjusted Returns

	Price Stabilisation	No Intervention	Subscription Support and 8% Return Cap	8% Return Cap Only	All
Mean %	69.29	16.68	159.92	24.74	51.73
t-statistic	8.84	4.62	4.56	4.87	9.37
Median %	43.28	12.99	123.99	12.38	27.54
Standard deviation	58.15	17.30	105.15	32.90	62.70
Kurtosis	-1.24	-0.95	-0.55	2.65	4.01
Skewness	0.39	0.42	0.67	1.57	1.77
Minimum %	-15.53	-5.43	26.57	-20.72	-20.72
Maximum %	192.04	47.73	338.96	138.59	338.96
Issues with negative first day returns	4	5	0	9	18
Number of issues	55	23	9	42	129

The large difference between the mean and median values of 24 percent indicates a large positive skewness in the distribution; the skewness coefficient of 2.15 is statistically significant. However, the kurtosis coefficient of 6.1 indicates no significant deviation from normality. This general evidence provides further support for the notion of excessive underpricing for IPOs in emerging capital markets and is comparable to results found in other studies; for example: 58 percent in Thailand by Wethyavivorn and Koo-smith (1991), 45 percent in Taiwan by Chen (1992), 54 percent in Portugal by Alpalhao (1992) and 78 percent in Korea by Dhatt, Kim and Lim (1993). There are, however, significant differences in average initial returns between each of the sub-periods and these differences are discussed in the following sections:

4.1 The First Sub-period: Price Stabilisation

The average raw return for the 55 issues during the price support period is 66.21 percent with an adjusted initial return of 69.29 percent. Given the award of the free 6 month put option (to the shareholders) written by the underwriters, with their associated contingent capital commitments to maintain the issue price, it is perhaps not too surprising that the underwriters pitched the issue price on the low side. The inability of the underwriters to gauge the level of prospective demand from informed investors would have also contributed to higher level of underpricing. The price support mechanism ensured that there were no overpriced issues in this period. Although the average underpricing is high, these results are not, of themselves, sufficient to provide an indication of the magnitude of additional underpricing resulting directly from the compulsory price support mechanism. To obtain such an estimate, Kazantzis and Levis (1995) decompose the first day return into two parts: traditional underpricing and underpricing due to the price support mechanism. Underpricing due to the compulsory price support ranges from 6.87 percent to 11.93 percent depending upon the assumptions about volatility in valuing the put option. Assuming perfect foresight, for example, underwriters would increase the underpricing of IPOs by 11.51 percent to protect themselves against potential losses due to the price support mechanism. Decomposing the initial returns suggests that around 10 of the 56 IPOs during this period were overpriced. The evidence clearly shows, however, that while the price support mechanism played a part in the underpricing, accounting for perhaps between 7 and 12 percentage points, it cannot be considered as the prime determinant of the unusually high first day returns during this period. The subsequent significant under-performance of these issues in the year following launch, reported in Kazantis and Levis (1995)[4], is suggestive of some type of fad in investor reponse to the new issues launched in this period. It is also worth noting that this sub-period also saw a marked bunching in the number of IPOs; only 9 were launched in 1987-1989 followed by 46 in 1990, a year in which the General Index of the Athens Stock Exchange increased by over 100 percent.

4.2. The Second Sub-period: No Institutional Intervention

Table 2 shows the average raw and adjusted first day returns of 8.08 and 16.68 percent respectively. In accord with the findings reported in Loughran et al (1994), the first day returns are lower in those regimes not subject to regulatory intervention. However, in contrast to the empirical evidence from other IPO markets, our results document marked differences between raw and market adjusted initial returns. The average adjusted first day return for the 23 issues in this period is twice the magnitude of the equivalent unadjusted return in Panel A. This reflects partly the poor state of the market in 1992 but, more importantly, the lengthening of the time period between the announcement of an issue and the first day of trading. The average time lapse between the closing of the application and first day of trading increased in this period to 72 days compared to 37 days when the price support mechanism was in place. The delay in first day trading also means that the distribution costs to be borne by the underwriters and their distribution agents increase together with the uncertainty facing prospective shareholders. Although it is not possible to affirm whether the average initial level of returns rewarded these risks, ᵗʰᵉ long-term adjusted returns for the 23 issues made in this sub-period, as reported in Kazantzis and Levis (1995), suggest that these issues were not seriously mis-priced at issue. Similar average levels of (raw) initial returns have been reported for Canada (9.3 percent) by Jog and Riding (1987) and for the Netherlands (7.2 percent) by Wessels (1989).

4.3 The Third & Fourth Sub-periods: Price Caps with/out Subscription Support

As can be seen from Table 2, Panels A and B, the first day raw and adjusted returns for these two periods of institutional interventions, taken together, are 53.67 and 48.59 percent respectively. The average raw initial return for the 9 issues launched during sub-period three is 187.18 percent. This result is clearly driven by the weight of money applying for the shares on offer, motivated by the subscription support mechanism. Of the 9 issues, the oversubscription ratios ranged form a minimum of 5 times to a maximum of nearly 1900 times. Disaffection with the subscription support mechanism, voiced principally by small investors unable to obtain bank guarantees large enough to secure an allotment of IPO shares led to the subscription support mechanism being withdrawn in February 1994. Table 3 sets out the number of days on which the price cap was triggered by the IPOs launched during sub-periods three and four. For example, during sub-period three, the daily price movements of all 9 IPOs launched in the period hit the daily upper limit of 8% an average of 12.44 times each.

Table 3

Number of Days When the Daily 8% Price Return Cap was Triggered January 1993 - November 1994

	Sub-period 3	Sub-period 4
Mean	12.44	2.52
Median	13.00	2.00
Standard deviation	5.46	2.84
Kurtosis	-1.06	1.02
Skewness	-0.09	1.28
Minimum no. of limit-ups*	4	0
Maximum no. of limit-ups*	20	11
Minimum no. of limit-downs*	0	0
Maximum no. of limit-downs*	0	1
Number of issues	9	42

* These measures refer to the individual IPOs in each of the samples. Of the 9 IPOs in Sub-period 3, the minimum limit-ups data refers to the individual IPO which recorded the minimum number of days (4) when its share price rose by 8% on each of those days.

In other words, trading in the new issues in this period was halted, on average, on each of the 12 days immediately subsequent to launch. When the subscription support was withdrawn, the markedly lower number of daily instances where the price cap was triggered (2.52 rather than 12.44) suggests that of the difference in the average initial adjusted return between sub-periods three and four of 135 percent, an initial average return of 80 percent points is attributable to investor demand generated by the subscription support guarantees offered during sub-period three. When the subscription support guarantees were withdrawn in the following sub-period, the average initial adjusted return fell markedly to just below 25 percent. Such a large drop adds support for the notion that the very high returns noted in sub-period three were exceptional and are probably inexplicable within the current framework of theories of IPO pricing.

One of the interesting features of the adjusted returns in sub-period four is the fact that the median return for the period is close to the same measure for sub-period two, when there were no institutional interventions in place. In sub-period four, the cap and floor is equivalent to the shareholders buying a string of put options and selling a string of call options both with an exercise price set at an 8 percent band around the current share price. Such an arrangement would, under certain conditions, be roughly self-financing. Thus, although sub-periods two and four are institutionally very different, the operation of the intervention in sub-period four has the effect of making the two sub-periods very similar in economic terms. It is tempting to suggest, therefore, that an average adjusted first day return of around 12-14 percent is the appropriate level of underpricing taking into account the 'permanent' features of the Greek IPO market.

5. Further Insights to IPO Performance

Details of the total applications received for the shares on issue are given for each of the four sub-periods are set out in Table 4. During the first sub-period of price support, the demand for IPO shares was 23 times the number of shares offered. During second sub-period, with no regulatory intervention, the demand dropped to just under 9 times the number of shares issued.

Table 4

Average Times Subscribed for Initial Public Offerings January 1987 - November 1994

	Price Support Intervention	No Intervention	Subscription Support and 8% Return Cap	8% Return Cap Only	All
Mean	23.02	8.88	369.29	92.94	60.63
Median	20.00	5.70	120.00	73.00	20.00
Standard Deviation	18.77	10.64	668.35	94.42	180.34
Kurtosis	0.99	1.68	6.68	-0.96	88.17
Skewness	1.03	1.57	2.57	0.65	8.83
Minimum	1.00	1.00	5.00	1.00	1.00
Maximum	76.00	38.39	1874.00	290.20	1874.00
Number of issues	55	23	9	42	129

As expected, when the subscription support was in place in the third sub-period, investor demand was stimulated to a record level of over 369 times the number of shares on offer. Even after the withdrawal of the subscription support in sub-period four, the demand for IPOs shares remained extremely high with the demand ratio being 92 times the number of shares offered.

The subscription rates presented in Table 4 and the allocation mechanisms in the case of oversubscription clearly suggest that the average 53.3 percent market adjusted initial return computed over the complete period was unlikely to have been achieved by an investor applying for every single issue offered in the market. The allocation procedures[6] suggest that the average investor would, depending on the level of the investor's application, have been 'crowded out' of those issues that attracted high levels of subscription and therefore subject to the same type of winner's curse problems as those observed by Koh and Walter (1989) for Singapore, Levis (1990) for UK and Keloharju (1993) for Finland. In both sub-periods one and two where there was, on average, oversubscription, there were a number of IPOs (4 from 5 IPOs in sub-period one and 5 from 23 IPOs in sub-period two) which recorded negative adjusted initial returns and which were not oversubscribed. In these cases, the underpricing was, with hindsight, insufficient to attract less-informed investors to the IPO market. In the only sub-period where the the minimum adjusted return was positive (26.57 percent in sub-period three), the average level of oversubscription of nearly 370 times would, in all probability, result in most of the smaller, less-informed investors failing to secure an allotment of shares.

6. Initial Returns and Uncertainty

Although the evidence documented above indicates significant differences in initial returns across the four regulatory frameworks over the period 1987-1994, the varying levels of underpricing are not necessarily entirely attributable to the intervention mechanisms. The level of underpricing is known to be associated with other factors. A number of studies, have, for example, documented a relation between initial returns and various proxies for ex-ante uncertainty. Other studies have related initial returns to the percentage of the firm's equity sold off in the IPO. In this section, first day adjusted returns for the 129 IPOs launched on the Athens Stock Market are regressed against factors which have a pedigree within the IPO literature and other factors which are specific to the Athens market.

Leland and Pyle (1977) first introduced the notion of a signalling hypothesis within an IPO valuation framework, arguing a positive relation between fractional ownership retained and firm value. In the current study, the equity introduced into the business by the original shareholders in the four years immediately prior to listing, measured as a percentage of the new funds to be raised by the public offer, proxies as a signal of the original shareholder's private knowledge as to the future prospects of the firm. Thus, the higher the amount of equity funds contributed pre-IPO launch, the higher the confidence in the firm's future and the lower the need for underpricing. Ex-ante uncertainty is proxied by two factors; following Beattie and Ritter (1986), one measure of ex-ante uncertainty is proxied by the standard deviation of the daily stock price returns during the first 20 trading days. A size variable, proxied by the market value of the firm immediately after the IPO, is included as the alternative measure of uncertainty. Given that smaller firms tend, on average, to be more risky, first day returns are expected to be negatively related to firm size. Dummy variables are included for both the price support and subscription support periods. Although there is, to our knowledge, no prior research which has investigated the impact of oversubscription on the level of first day returns, we include such a variable. Since oversubscription is a direct result of excess demand, we expect high levels of oversubscription to be associated with underpriced shares.

The regression results are shown in Table 5. The t-statistics shown in parentheses are heteroscedasticity-adjusted. The coefficients on both dummy variables are significant, confirming the results of previous studies that report a positive association between regulatory intervention and underpricing.

Table 5

Determinants of adjusted first day returns: regression results.

The co-efficients from regressing adjusted first day returns for the 129 IPOs against the five explanatory variables are set out below. The oversubscription variable is measured as the log (the number of shares applied for / total number of shares available under the IPO). The equity subscribed variable is measured by the total equity contributed by the former owners in the four years prior to the IPO date as a percentage of total funds raised by the IPO. The volatility variable is computed as the standard deviation of the share price returns measured over the first 20 days in the aftermarket. The size variable measures the market value of the firm including the proceeds from the IPO. Two dummy variables represent the subscription support period and the price stabilisation period. The t-statistics are heteroscedasticity-adjusted.

Oversubscription	Price Stabilisation Dummy	Subscription Support Dummy	Equity Subscribed	Volatility	Size	Adj R^2
0.164	0.401	1.479	-0.298	7.49	-0.04	55.8%
(2.79)	(4.59)	(8.13)	(-2.63)	(3.33)	(-2.04)	

In particular, the positive coeffecent on the price stabilisation dummy probably reflects the deliberate underpricing to avoid the necessity of having to tie up resources in price support operations. It is not, however, possible to attribute the positive coefficient on the subscription support dummy to deliberate underpricing. The high levels of first day returns recorded in sub-period three were, as noted above, probably driven by the particularly heavy level of oversubcription which was markedly above levels in any of the other sub-periods. However, over the eight years, the level of oversubscription does have a positive impact on first day returns. Rather than being a product of deliberate underpricing, the positive coefficient probably reflects the institutional arrangement whereby the underwriters are, in the setting of the price, unable to gauge prospective investor demand and thus tend to underprice the offer. The sign on the coefficient of the ratio of equity subscribed/IPO proceeds is negative and significant. Deliberate underpricing is thus not a feature of those issues there the former owners have signalled their confidence in the future prospects of the firm by subscribing additional equity in the four years prior to the IPO launch. The results also confirm a relation between initial underpricing and both measures of ex-ante uncertainty. Larger IPO firms record, on average, lower levels of first day returns and thus suggest that less underpricing is required in such cases in order to attract investor support. The positive cdoefficient accord with the findings of a number of other studies and confirms that those issues with higher levels of ex-ante uncertainty as to their market value tend to be underpriced at launch.

7. Conclusions

Recent empirical evidence indicates that average initial returns tend to be higher, the greater the degree of government interference. In Greece, the three different institutional interventions introduced in the period 1987-1994 provide the grounds for investigating the implications of intervention on the pricing of new issues.

The obligation to support a new issue for a period of six months in the aftermarket encouraged underwriters to set offer prices at a level that minimised the need for expensive capital support operations. During the period when the compulsory price support mechanism was in operation, the average level of underpricing was one of the highest ever recorded in international IPO markets. The price support mechanism accounted for about 18 percent of the actual level of first day returns. The subsequent decision to provide subscription support stimulated investor demand resulting in very high levels of oversubscription. The differential first day returns across the sub-periods are not entirely the result of the varying regulatory framework. The regression results suggest that the underpricing noted here also reflected traditional underpricing considerations such as the pricing of ex-ante uncertainty.

Overall, the results accord with Loughran et al's (1994) conclusion that "Average initial returns tend to be higher, the greater is the degree of government interference" and thus have an important policy implication for the Athens Stock Exchange. The findings presented here clearly show that institutional interventions work against the interests of the issuing firms. The high level of underpricing noted in the periods subject to such intervention deprives young, growing firms from realising the full value of the equity capital issued in the market.

References

Aggarwal, R., R. Leal and L. Hernandez, 1993, The aftermarket performance of initial public offerings in Latin America, Financial Management 22, 42-53.

Alpalhao, R.M., 1992, Opertas publicas iniciais: O caso Portugues, working paper, Univesidade Nova de Lisboa.

Baron, D., 1982, A model of the demand of investment banking, advising and distribution services for new issues, Journal of Finance 37, 955-976.

Barry, C. B. and R.H. Jennings, 1993, The opening price performance of initial public offerings of common stock, Financial Management 22, 54-63.

Beatty, R.P. and J.R. Ritter, 1986, Investment banking, reputation, and the underpricing of initial public offerings, Journal of Financial Economics 15, 213-232.

Benveniste, L., W. Busaba and W. Wilhelm, 1995, Price stabilization as a bonding mechanism in new equity issues, working paper, Boston College.

Benveniste, L. and W. Wilhelm, 1990, A comparative analysis of IPO proceeds under alternative regulatory environments, Journal of Financial Economics 28, 173-208.

Booth, J.R. and R.L. Smith, 1986, Capital raising, underwriting and certification hypothesis, Journal of Financial Economics 15, 261-281.

Chen, H-L., 1992, The price behavior of IPOs in Taiwan, working paper, University of Illinois.

Chowdry, B. and V. Nanda, 1994, Stabilization, syndication, and pricing of IPOs, working paper, UCLA.

Dawson, S.M., 1987, Secondary stock market performance of initial public offers, Hong Kong, Singapore and Malaysia:1978-1984, Journal of Business Finance and Accounting 14, 65-76.

Dhatt, M.S., Y.H. Kim and U. Lim, 1993, The short-run and long-run performance of Korean IPOs: 1980-90, working paper, University of Cincinnati and Yonsei University.

Drake, P.D. and M.R. Vetsuypens, 1993, IPO underpricing and insurance against legal liability, Financial Management 22, 64-73.

Jog, V.M., and A.L. Riding, 1987, Underpricing in Canadian IPOs, Financial Analysts Journal, 48-55.

Kazantis, C. and M. Levis, 1995, Price support and initial public offerings: evidence from the Athens Stock Exchange in: Doukas and Lang (eds), Research in International Business and Finance, Vol 12, JAI Press.

Keloharju, M., 1993, The winner's curse, legal liability, and the long-run price performance of initial public offerings in Finland, Journal of Financial Economics 34, 251-277.

Koh, F. and T. Walter, 1989, A direct test of Rock's model of the pricing of unseasoned issues, Journal of Financial Economics 23, 251-272.

Leland, H.E. and D.H. Pyle, 1977, Informational asymmetries, financial structure and financial intermediation, Journal of Finance 32, 371-388.

Levis, M., 1990, The winner's curse problem, interest costs and the underwriting of initial public offerings, The Economic Journal 100, 76-89.

Loughran, T., J. Ritter and K. Rydqvist, 1994, Initial public offerings: international insights, Pacific-Basin Finance Journal 2, 165-199.

Rock, K., 1986, Why new issues are underpriced, Journal of Financial Economics 15, 187-212.

Tinic, S., 1988, Anatomy of initial public offerings of common stock, Journal of Finance 43, 789-822.

Weiss-Hanley, K., 1993, The underpricing of initial public offerings and the partial adjustment phenomenon, Journal of Financial Economics 34, 231-250.

Welch, I., 1991, Sequential sales, learning, and cascades, Journal of Finance 47, 695-732.

Wessels, R., 1989, The market for initial public offerings: an analysis of the Amsterdam Stock Exchange. Published in A Reappraisal of the Efficiency of Financial Markets, edited by Guimaraes et al. Berlin: Springer-Verlag.

Wethyavivorn, K. and Y. Koo-Smith, 1991, Initial public offerings in Thailand 1988-89: price and return patterns in: Rhee and Chang (eds), Pacific-Basin Capital Markets Research Volume II, Amsterdam: North-Holland.

Endnotes

[1] The exchange rate at January 1995 was 365 Drachma = £1 Sterling.

[2] Institutional investors typically include open-end and closed-end funds. Pension funds and insurance companies are not allowed to invest in the stock market.

[3] This arrangement was varied during the period June 1992 to February 1994.

[4] The average cumulative market-adjusted return 12 months after launch is -13.37 percent, excluding the first day return.

[5] On average, the sample of IPOs in this period recorded insignificant positive adjusted returns over the 12 months following launch.

[6] The proportional lottery method was employed in all but 8 of the IPOs where oversubscription occurred. These 8 cases occurred in the period 1988-1990.

The Effect of Consolidated Control on Firm Performance: The Case of Dual-class IPOs

Ekkehart Böhmer
Humboldt-Universität zu Berlin

Gary C Sanger
Louisiana State University

and

Sanjay B Varshney
University of New York

Abstract

We analyze short-term and long-term performance of firms that go public with more than one class of common stock. To assess performance differences that are due to the firm's ownership structure, we create a control sample of single-class IPOs that is matched to the dual-class firms by exchange, offer date, industry, and size. For a comprehensive sample of 98 dual-class IPOs, we document that dual-class firms outperform their matched single-class counterparts in terms of stock-market returns as well as accounting measures of firm performance. Moreover, we find no statistically significant abnormal long-run performance over a three year horizon for dual-class firms. This contrasts with Ritter's (1991) result that IPOs significantly underperform in the three years after going public. We conclude that going public with a dual-class equity structure has net benefits for investors in those firms that choose this specific organizational structure, as evidenced by better operating performance and larger equity returns relative to other IPOs.

1. Introduction

In this study, we analyze the consequences of choosing a corporate governance structure that consolidates voting control in the hands of management. Specifically, we focus on firms that choose to go public by issuing shares with disparate voting rights (henceforth, dual-class shares). We analyze how choosing a dual-class equity structure and the distribution of voting power affects characteristics of the initial public offering (IPO) and long-term firm performance by contrasting operating performance and stock-market returns of dual-class firms to those of a matched control sample of single-class IPOs.

An important difference between our paper and earlier studies on dual-class firms is that we analyze dual-class initial public offerings (IPOs), while earlier studies deal with dual-class recapitalisations. Our IPO-approach to studying the consequences of choosing to issue two classes of equity has a distinct advantage over analyzing established firms. In a dual-class IPO, the firm's owners design a governance structure for the firm prior to taking it public without potentially coercing some shareholders into holding inferior-voting stock (as argued by Ruback (1988)). In our sample, all potential wealth effects of the change to the new control structure occur prior to the IPO and the inferior-voting stock receives its fair market value at the time of going public. In contrast to analyses of recapitalisations, our results are not sensitive to potential wealth expropriations from holders of inferior-voting shares to holders of superior-voting shares.

This study of dual-class IPOs between 1984 and 1988 covers a time period with a great deal of controversy about dual-class equity structures. In 1986, the NYSE imposed a moratorium on its 60-year-old prohibition to listing non-voting stock and common stock of firms with disparate voting rights. Due to the rising popularity of dual-class recapitalisations as a takeover defense, this step was most likely a competitive reaction to the more lenient AMEX and especially NASDAQ attitudes towards shares with differential voting rights. In 1988, the SEC adopted Rule 19c-4 which permitted firms to recapitalise with a dual-class equity structure as long as it did not diminish the voting power of existing shareholders, and thus banned 'traditional' dual-class exchange offers. Rule 19c-4 was, however, invalidated by the Federal Court of Appeals in 1990 on grounds that the SEC lacked the authority to regulate on this issue. This episode re-started a lively search for an optimal public policy towards dual-class shares among the SEC, the exchanges, and NASDAQ (see Gilson (1993). This study contributes to this discussion by providing evidence on the long-term performance of those firms that chose to issue shares with differential voting rights without reacting to takeover pressure. By assessing the consequences of choosing a dual-class share structure net of potential wealth transfers, our results may help in judging the effect of recapitalisations on shareholder wealth as well.

We document below that dual-class firms substantially outperform a matched sample of similar risk, single-class firms during the three years following the IPO, both in terms of stock returns and operating performance. Moreover, dual-class stock returns are not significantly below market returns. This contrasts to Ritter's (1991) finding of significant IPO long-run underperformance during the three post-offering years for a sample of single-class IPOs.[1] This basic result is not sensitive to the method used to adjust for market movements or to the return measure we employ.

To supplement our study, we have polled executives of the dual-class firms in our sample (excerpts of responses are in the appendix). The most frequently stated reasons for the choice of this equity structure are: it allows owners to *simultaneously* raise additional capital for new projects; effectively diversify personal wealth; retain majority control and an active role in the firms they have founded, even after subsequent offerings; pursue long-term interests rather than short-term profits; and ward off any unsolicited external interference to enable the firm to stabilize itself in a new operating and legal environment after going public. In our sample, superior-voting shares are always closely held and typically give majority control to pre-IPO owners of the firm. Even though the pre-IPO owners of dual-class firms retain, on average, 70% of the cash-flow claim on the post-IPO firm, they also retain the option to substantially dilute their cash-flow claim in subsequent equity offerings without losing majority control.

Achievement of these goals has the potential to increase some of the agency costs that must be born by the owners of the firm going public while decreasing others. For example, owners of superior-voting shares may use their protected position to exploit minority shareholders. On the other hand, one can argue that holding superior-voting shares actually serves to align the interest of management and other shareholders. Bhide (1993) argues that stock-market liquidity provides easy exit opportunities for stockholders who do not agree with the firm's management. As a consequence, liquidity discourages internal monitoring. In all but two firms in our sample (out of 98), there is no public market for the superior-voting shares and hence no 'easy' exit opportunity. If holders wish to cash out, they must (1) convert their shares to low-voting stock and bear the wealth consequences of their prior decisions, and (2) give up majority control over the company. Thus, to the extent that holding this illiquid investment imposes a cost, it should reduce the divergence of interest between management and outside shareholders. The effect of choosing a dual-class structure on firm performance appears to be an empirical question which we address in the analysis below.

The remainder of this paper is organized as follows. In section 2, we relate our study to previous research and develop the implications of a dual-class equity structure. We describe the data in section 3. In section 4, we present the design and results of our empirical tests. Concluding remarks appear in section 5.

2. Relation to previous research

2.1. Related literature on IPOs

Previous IPO research has primarily focused on underpricing and long-run performance of IPOs.[2] For example, Ibbotson (1975), Ibbotson and Jaffe (1975), Ritter (1984) and others document that IPOs experience an average underpricing of 15%, and that the amount of underpricing varies substantially over time and across industries.[3] With the exception of Buser and Chan (1987), all studies that examine the long-run performance of IPOs (Stoll and Curley (1970), Ibbotson (1975), Aggarwal and Rivoli (1990), and Ritter(1991)) find evidence of negative stock-price performance. Jain and Kini (1994) document significant declines in operating performance during the three years following the IPO (relative to an industry-matched sample of seasoned firms). Moreover, Loughran et al. (1994) summarize studies of IPOs in several countries other than the U.S. where a similar phenomenon can generally be observed. While both Aggarwal and Rivoli (1990) and Ritter (1991) hypothesize that the IPO market may be subject to mean-reverting fads, there is a need for further analysis of these results. Our study extends this literature by showing that the distribution of voting power among shareholders is an important cross-sectional determinant of long-run stock-price performance.

2.2. Related theoretical work on corporate governance

Previous studies document both benefits and costs of a dual-class structure. According to Alchian and Demsetz (1972), benefits arise if there is substantial cost involved in communicating information about managerial performance or investment opportunities to outsiders. In this situation, insider-managers hold voting rights to prevent relatively uninformed outside stockholders (and outside directors) from mistakenly replacing the incumbent management team with a less productive group. Alternatively, vote ownership may be used by managers to more firmly define their property rights to returns on their investments in organization-specific human capital.[4] Focusing on the efficiency of organizational forms, Fama and Jensen (1983) argue that when only a few firm insiders have specific knowledge, the efficient governance structure consolidates control and decision power in the hands of these individuals. DeAngelo and DeAngelo (1985) argue that in these situations the returns on managers' investment in organization-specific capital are potentially expropriable if the firm is taken over. While evidence in Mikkelson and Partch (1989) does not support the claim that greater managerial vote ownership results in fewer changes in control, the empirical results in DeAngelo and DeAngelo (1985) and Lehn et al. (1990) suggest that a dual-class equity arrangement is an affordable way to protect management.

There also exist potential costs to the majority control generally associated with dual-class contractual arrangements. Managers' interests may diverge from shareholders' interests to a greater extent than under a one share-one vote arrangement and thus increase agency costs and reduce firm value (see, for example, Jensen and Meckling (1976)). Additionally, non-controlling shareholders may lose their share of a future takeover premium. Grossman and Hart (1988) and Zingales (1992a) develop models that try to capture this situation by assuming that the owner and a rival both reap quantifiable private benefits from controlling the firm, while small shareholders cause a free-rider problem. Zingales (1992a) shows that consolidation of voting control and its separation from cash-flow claims can be valuable to the firm if private benefits are sufficiently large. On the other hand, it can be harmful if private benefits are small. Shleifer and Vishny's (1986) analysis suggests, however, that a large minority shareholder is sufficient to reduce the adverse effects due to the free-rider problem. Using a different approach, Stulz (1988) shows that majority control is inferior to more dispersed control because it precludes hostile takeovers. Harris and Raviv (1988) argue that differential voting rights may be beneficial to shareholders. In their model, however, such a share structure is not socially optimal because it may allow an inferior management team to achieve control.

In sum, the theory implies that a dual-class structure may have positive or negative effects on firm value. In this paper, we analyze the performance of dual-class IPOs relative to a set of otherwise similar single-class IPOs to shed light on the conflicting predictions outlined above.

2.3. Related empirical evidence on dual-class firms

Several studies analyze the potential value of superior voting rights. Lease et al. (1983, 1984) find that the superior voting shares trade at an average premium of about 5% and conclude that a dual-class capital structure provides potential for incremental benefits for both managers and outside stockholders.[5] Zingales (1992b) analyzes the determinants of the voting premium, and finds that the structure of share ownership and takeover activity in the firm's industry are important factors affecting the premium. In general, empirical evidence supports the contention that the right to vote is of substantial value, even though superior-voting shares typically have no superior dividend rights. Thus, the choice of organizational form is likely to affect expected returns to shareholders.

Several studies analyze dual-class recapitalisations. For example, Dann and DeAngelo (1988) provide evidence that defensive dual-class restructurings are detrimental to shareholders. Jarrell and Poulsen (1988) obtain similar results, but show that wealth losses are concentrated during the period of time following the NYSE moratorium on the delisting of dual-class stocks. Results in Chang and Mayers (1992) are negative for firms with high managerial vote ownership before the recapitalisation, but positive for firms with initially low managerial vote ownership. Also Partch (1987) and Cornett and Vetsuypens (1989) find non-negative average abnormal stock-price returns on the announcement of dual-class recapitalisations with disparate voting structures, and conclude that they do not harm shareholders. Lehn et al. (1990) show that recapitalising firms tend to be high growth, low agency cost firms that subsequently issue equity more frequently than other firms. Their results imply that dual-class recapitalisations are beneficial to shareholders.

Thus, as DeAngelo and DeAngelo (1985) point out, the presence of vote ownership, anti-takeover provisions, golden parachutes, or other mechanisms that reduce the threat of a hostile takeover does not necessarily imply that managerial decisions go undisciplined. Alternatively, benefits from contracts that reduce the probability of a hostile takeover may exceed the agency costs these contracts engender. In a similar vein, Holderness and Sheehan (1988) provide evidence that majority shareholders do not use their voting power to expropriate wealth from minority shareholders and conclude that wealth expropriation is not the primary motive for concentrating ownership. Moreover, several implicit or explicit contracts could serve to align managerial incentives with the welfare of outside stockholders. For example, Holderness and Sheehan (1991) show how closely-held Turner Broadcasting uses specially designed preferred stock to shield other stakeholders from poor managerial performance.

Mikkelson and Partch (1994) examine the long-run operating performance of dual-class firms to see if managers exploit their protected position after recapitalisation and allow firm performance to deteriorate. While they document reduced operating performance following the creation of two classes of stock, this decrease is not related to the increase in managerial vote ownership. In contrast, over the three years following a dual-class recapitalisation Lehn et al. (1990) find greater growth rates of operating income for dual-class firms than for a sample of control firms. Finally, Denis and Denis (1992) show that the performance of majority-controlled firms is not inferior to that of other firms, even though there is no evidence that these firms employ additional governance structures to constrain management. They further show that choosing majority control is primarily related to owner-specific as opposed to firm-specific characteristics.

In summary, previous research has found mixed evidence on the effects of the adoption of dual-class equity structures. Most firms in these samples, however, adopt a dual-class capital structure *after* going public. In these cases, it is difficult to measure potential wealth transfers between different classes of shareholders when a second class is created. In our study, we attempt to remedy these problems by examining small, privately held firms that decide to go public and at the same time create a dual-class equity structure. This sample is not sensitive to a potential wealth expropriation from holders of inferior-voting shares.[6] The popularity of dual-class stocks among managers arises to a large extent due to their ability to control a majority of votes without having substantial claims on cash flow (and being exposed to the attendant risk). As the managers' cash-flow claim falls, their interests become less closely aligned with those of outside shareholders. This may result in sacrificing firm performance for personal benefits. On the other hand, there are certain benefits to concentrated control. If dual-class firms optimally chose their equity structure, we expect them to perform at least as well as single-class IPOs in the long run. It is our objective to provide empirical answers to these issues.

3. Data

We obtain basic information on exhaustive samples of 1270 single-class IPOs and 98 dual-class IPOs from *Investment Dealers Digest* from 1984 to 1988. From the set of 1270 IPOs, we create a control group of 98 single-class IPOs between 1984 and 1988. In order of priority, firms are matched by (1) the matching firm trades on the same exchange on which its dual-class contemporary trades,(2) the offer date for the matching firm is within 60 days of the offer date of the dual-class firm, (3) the matching firm belongs to the same industry (4-digit SIC code or at least 3-digit SIC code) as the dual-class firm, and (4) the market value of equity for the matching firm at the close of the first trading day is close to that of the dual-class firm (both classes combined, assuming they trade at the same market price). This approach yields two sets of nearly identical firms that primarily differ in their control structure. As a robustness check to our results below, we repeat our analysis using the full sample of 1270 IPOs as a control group. Since we do not obtain qualitatively different results, we report only the more appropriate results for the pairwise-matched set of 98 single-class IPOs.

We exclude all firms that are not included in the 1991 daily CRSP files immediately after their offering, as well as all best efforts offerings, unit offerings, limited partnerships, REITs, closed-end funds, ADR's and certificates. To compare the long-run stock-market performance, we compute monthly returns over successive 21-trading-day intervals for three years following the IPO, accounting for any changes in trading location. During those three years, four dual-class firms originating on NASDAQ became listed on either AMEX or NYSE (no control firms switched trading location). While two out of the 98 dual-class firms have both classes of shares trading (all four issues trade on NASDAQ), we only use returns on the inferior-voting shares in our analysis. We obtain additional information on the 98 IPO pairs, including data on offering and firm characteristics, and their voting structures from one or more of the following sources: (1) *Investment Dealers Digest,* (2) *S&P Corporation Records,* (3) *Compact Disclosure,* (4) *SEC Q-File,* (5) *Moody's Industrials, Financials, Utilities, and Transportation,* (6) 1991 COMPUSTAT, and (7) *Spectrum 3.*

3.1. Description of dual-class firms

The dual-class firms in our sample have one out of four different voting arrangements with respect to the two classes of stock. In ten (out of 98) firms, the inferior-voting shares have no voting rights at all except in matters of special interest. Thirty firms have pooled voting, where the superior-voting shares are entitled to a higher number of votes per share. The ratio of fractional voting rights ranges from 1:2 to 1:500, with a median value of 1:10. Sixteen firms have class voting, where both classes have equal per-share voting rights, but holders of inferior-voting shares are entitled to elect 25% of the directors (holders of superior-voting shares elect the remaining 75%). Finally, 42 firms have a combination of class and pooled voting. In those firms, directors are elected as in the class-voting firms, while shareholders have fractional voting rights in all other matters. Superior-voting stock is typically held by very few individuals and allows them to achieve majority control. For the median firm, considering both classes of stock, only two shareholders effectively control 70% of the votes.

In 67 dual-class firms both classes of shares have identical cash-dividend rights (a dividend on superior-voting shares requires that one be paid on inferior-voting shares). In the remaining cases inferior-voting shares have slightly higher dividend claims. Stock dividends are usually payable on the same basis and at the same time on the respective classes. In 76 firms both classes of stockholders share ratably in liquidation, while holders of inferior-voting shares receive preferential treatment for a specified amount and thereafter share ratably with other shareholders in the remaining 22 firms.

While inferior-voting shares are freely transferable at all times, the transferability of superior-voting shares is highly restricted. All superior-voting shares are convertible into inferior-voting shares, but the reverse is never allowed. In 91 firms, superior-voting shares may be converted freely at any time share-per-share. Six firms provide for automatic conversion on a pre-specified date or at the end of a preference period. In the remaining firm, each superior-voting share may be converted into one tenth of an inferior-voting share at the option of the holder.

Additionally, we checked the frequency of reverse leveraged buyouts (RLBOs) in our samples. If RLBOs were dominating the sample of dual-class IPOs, our performance results may reflect substantial organizational changes that should be attributed to the LBO, not to the IPO. Since our sample includes only nine previous LBO firms that choose a dual-class IPO and three that choose a single-class IPO (out of 98), we do not believe that our results are primarily caused by RLBOs.

3.2. Comparison of dual-class and control-group IPOs

Table 1 shows the distribution of IPOs over time and by exchange. While 83 % of all 1270 single-class IPOs list on NASDAQ (not reported in Table 1), only 67% of dual-class IPOs list on NASDAQ. For the firms included in our sample, offerings on NASDAQ are somewhat more frequent during the early part of the sample period, while those on the AMEX or NYSE are more frequent in the later part of the period. This is possibly due to the relaxation of NYSE standards regarding voting structure in 1986. In Table 2, we provide descriptive statistics pertaining to dual-class and control-group IPOs. To test for differences across groups, we analyze the null hypothesis that the mean of the pairwise differences across groups equals zero.

Table 1

Distribution of IPOs by exchange and year

The sample includes 98 dual-class IPOs between 1984 and 1988, and a sample of control IPO firms, matched by exchange, IPO date, industry, and size. Neither sample contains unit offers, American Depository Receipts, REITs, closed-end funds, or certificates.

	1984	1985	1986	1987	1988	All
Dual-class, control-group IPOs on NASDAQ	9	13	19	20	5	66
Dual-class, control-group IPOs on NYSE and Amex	2	2	12	8	8	32

The first row of Table 2 shows the fractional cash-flow claim retained by the pre-IPO owners of the firm. For dual-class firms, this figure represents the cash-flow claims from both classes of shares. Exchange-listed dual-class firms are characterized by a significantly larger retention than the control group: they retain on average 70% of the cash-flow claim versus 54% for control firms. Dual-class IPOs on NASDAQ also have a higher average retention, but the different from zero. While not reported in the Table we find that for dual-class firms about two thirds of the cash-flow claim results from holdings of superior-voting shares.[7]

Table 2

Descriptive statistics on the IPO by market: Dual-class IPOs vs. a matched control sample

The basic sample includes 98 dual-class IPOs between 1984 and 1988, and a sample of control IPO firms, matched by exchange, IPO date, industry, and size. 32 IPOs list on NYSE or Amex, while 66 trade on NASDAQ. Neither sample contains unit offers, American Depository Receipts, REITs, closed-end funds, or certificates. For dual-class IPOs, the market value represents both classes of stock assuming that the closely-held superior-voting shares trade at the same price as the inferior-voting shares. We test the hypothesis that the mean of the pairwise differences between dual-class and control-group values equals zero using a standard t-test and the hypothesis that the median equals zero using a sign test.

Variable		NYSE/Amex		NASDAQ	
	Sample	Mean	Median	Mean	Median
Proportion of cash-flow claim not sold in the IPO	Dual	70%[a]	74%[b]	66%	70%
	Control	54%	64%	63%	70%
Market value of equity ($ million)	Dual	218	117	173[b]	48[c]
	Control	249	93	51	35
Firm age at IPO	Dual	23	9	25[a]	10[b]
	Control	18	5	8	4
Offer price	Dual	12.65	13.38	11.76[a]	11.13
	Control	11.98	10.00	9.18	9.00
Offer amount in $mn	Dual	49.7[c]	29.7	29.9[b]	11.7[b,d]
	Control	128.8	27.9	15.5	12.0

Table 2 (continued)

Variable	Sample	NYSE/Amex		NASDAQ	
		Mean	Median	Mean	Median
Proportion of secondary shares sold	Dual	22%[c]	6%[a]	21%	0%
	Control	9%	0%	11%	0%
Book/price ratio	Dual	39%	34%	47%	43%
	Control	52%	32%	41%	36%
Change midfile-to-offer: share price	Dual	-8%	-8%c	-6%	-2%
	Control	-7%	-1%	-6%	-2%
Change midfile-to-offer: number of shares	Dual-	8%	0%	0%	0%
	Control	2%	0%	3%	0%
Shares outstanding after the IPO (in millions)	Dual	17.7	9.2	11.2[c]	5.2
	Control	16.6	7.2	6.8	4.0
First-day trading volume (in thousands)	Dual	757	394	745	311
	Control	1753	409	746	450

a Significantly different from the control group at the one-percent level. For the means column, the significance refers to a t-test, for the medians column, it refers to a sign test.
b Significantly different from the control group at the five-percent level. For the means column, the significance refers to a t-test, for the medians column, it refers to a sign test.
c Significantly different from the control group at the ten-percent level. For the means column, the significance refers to a t-test, for the medians column, it refers to a sign test.
d The median pairwise difference is larger than zero.

This result does not support the contention that dual-class IPOs are used by owners to rid themselves of exposure to changes in firm value while retaining majority control at the time they go public. Thus, it is unlikely that at the time of the IPO dual-class offers impose greater agency problems on the firm than single-class offers. On the other hand, owners retain the option to reduce their cash-flow claim later on (especially through subsequent equity offerings) while keeping majority control. To the extent that such behavior is anticipated at the time of the IPO, firm value may still be affected by choosing a dual-class share structure. This is not likely to be of practical importance, however, since during the three years following the IPO we did not find changes in the ratio of superior-vote to low-vote shares outstanding. Neither does the number or magnitude of seasoned equity issues during that time period differ between dual-class and control-group firms, and we find no evidence of differences in insider sales as reported to the Securities and Exchange Commission.

In Table 2, we document further differences between dual-class and control firms. On NASDAQ, the median dual-class firm is somewhat larger in terms of the market value of equity, and offers more equity in the IPO. On the exchanges, the market value of equity and the offer amount are not statistically different. The median dual-class firm is also five years older (significant for NASDAQ IPOs), and has a slightly higher book-to-market ratio immediately after the IPO. We also document that the average fraction of secondary shares offered is above 20% for dual-class firms, but only around 10% for control firms. The difference in secondary sales is a likely effect of owners substituting high-voting shares for low-voting shares at the time of the IPO. Finally, there are no significant differences in the first-day trading volume and in how the offer price and the number of shares offered differ from the initial IPO prospectus.[8]

4. The performance of dual-class IPOs

4.1. Methodology

We analyze underpricing at the time of the IPO, long-run stock-price performance, and changes in operating data. Our basic strategy is to make pairwise comparisons between dual-class performance and the performance of the matched control group, which adjusts for differences in trading location, offering date, industry, and firm size. To account for differences in size and other characteristics across trading locations, we perform separate analyses for NASDAQ firms (66 IPOs) and exchange-listed firms (AMEX or NYSE, 32 IPOs). We calculate initial returns from the offer price to the first closing price listed in the daily CRSP files, and aftermarket returns for months 1 through 36 following the IPO (excluding the initial period). Months comprise successive 21 trading days relative to the IPO, over which we compound daily returns.

Since higher systematic risk could explain higher returns of dual-class IPOs, it is important to make appropriate risk adjustments. We perform several tests for risk differences between the two groups.[9] First, we use Ibbotson's (1975) RATS (returns across time and securities) procedure to estimate the systematic risk for each group. Second, we estimate market-model betas using monthly data for the 36 months following the IPO. Neither of the risk measures reported in Table 3 results in statistically or economically different risk approximates for dual-class and control firms.[10] Finally, we also estimate unsystematic risk by (1) the mean squared error from the market-model regressions and (2) the standard deviation of monthly abnormal (market-adjusted) returns. For NASDAQ firms, unsystematic risk is even lower for dual-class IPOs. Thus, our matching procedure has largely eliminated risk differences between the two groups of firms, making the returns directly comparable after adjusting for time-specific market movements.

Table 3

Risk measures for dual-class and control-group IPOs

The basic sample includes 98 dual-class IPOs between 1984 and 1988, and a sample of control IPO firms, matched by exchange, IPO date, industry, and size. Neither sample contains unit offers, American Depository Receipts, REITs, closed-end funds, or certificates. For each of the four risk measures, we report the mean and the median in parentheses. Test statistics refer to the hypothesis that the dual-class mean (median) is different from the control-group mean.

	RATSβ^d	Time-Seriesβ^e	Market Model RMSE^f	Standard deviation of market-adjusted returns^g
Panel A: NYSE/Amex IPOs (32 firms)				
Dual	1.16	1.19	0.12	0.13
	(0.19)	(1.34)	(0.11)	(0.11)
Control	1.08	0.95	0.13	0.13
	(1.13)	(1.13)	(0.12)	(0.12)
Panel B: NASDAQ IPOs (66 firms)				
Dual	1.17	1.05	0.13^c	0.13^c
	(1.24)	(1.04)	(0.11)^b	(0.11)^b
Control	1.12	1.15	0.15	0.16
	(1.12)	(1.19)	(0.13)	(0.13)

Table 3 (continued)

a Significantly different from the control group at the one-percent level. Based on a t-test for means and a sign test for medians.

b Significantly different from the control group at the five-percent level. Based on a t-test for means and a sign test for medians.

c Significantly different from the control group at the ten-percent level. Based on a t-test for means and a sign test for medians.

d Estimates based on Ibbotson's (1975) returns-across-time-and-securities procedure and equally-weightedmarket indices for the respective trading locations.

e Estimates based on time-series (market-model) regressions based on 36 monthly observations each and equally-weighted market indices for the respective trading locations..

f Root mean squared error of market-model regressions.

g Based on 36 monthly market-adjusted abnormal returns.

For evaluating long-run stock performance, we employ a methodology similar to that used by Ritter (1991). To compute market-adjusted abnormal returns for three years following the offering date, we subtract the monthly benchmark return from the monthly raw return on each stock. Our benchmark returns are the equally and value-weighted AMEX/NYSE and NASDAQ CRSP indices, respectively. (Since our primary focus is on contrasting dual-class IPOs to control-group IPOs, the choice of the market benchmark has little effect on our results. Our results below are qualitatively identical for both benchmark choices, and we report only abnormal returns based on value-weighted indices in the aper.) Then we compute average cumulative (monthly) abnormal returns with monthly portfolio rebalancing. Additionally, we compute wealth relatives based on holding-period returns as an alternative performance measure.[11]

4.2. Results on underpricing

In panel A of Table 4, we report returns for the initial period (from the offer price to the first available closing price). On average, dual-class shares are underpriced by 3.69%, which is not significantly different from the control-group underpricing of 5.86%. While dual-class firms are underpriced to a similar extent across exchanges, single-class firms are underpriced more on NASDAQ than on NYSE or Amex. For NASDAQ IPOs, initial returns for dual-class firms are about five percent smaller than those for control firms (significant at the 10% level).

In addition to the results reported in Table 4, we performed several regression tests to analyze initial returns. While Table 4 indicates lower underpricing for dual-class firms in the aggregate, this may be related to the fact that these firms are somewhat larger than control firms (see Table 2). When we regress initial returns on a dummy variable representing dual-class firms and a set of variables that are known to affect underpricing, we cannot reject the hypothesis that the coefficient on the dummy variable equals zero (regardless of specification). Thus, we find no evidence that initial returns are affected by the share structure of the company going public.

Table 4

First-day and three-year cumulative returns.

The basic sample includes 98 dual-class IPOs between 1984 and 1988, and a sample of control IPO firms, matched by exchange, IPO date, industry, and size. Neither sample contains unit offers, American Depository Receipts, REITs, closed-end funds, or certificates. First-day returns are measured from the offering price to the first closing price. Three-year cumulative returns exclude the first-day returns. We report means, medians in parentheses, and the fraction positive in brackets. To adjust for market movements, we subtract the return on the CRSP value-weighted market index for the respective market. For hypothesis testing, we use a cross-sectional t-test for means in panel A, a t-test based on returns standardized by their time-series standard deviation in panel B, a signed-rank test for medians, and a sign test for the percentage positive.

Panel A: First-day returns (in %)	N	Amex-NYSE	N	NASDAQ	N	Total
Dual-class raw returns	32	4.18^c	66	3.45^b	98	3.69^a
		(0.91^b)		(1.59^a)		(1.34^a)
		$[59\%^b]$		$[62\%^a]$		$[61\%^a]$
Control-group raw returns	32	1.27^c	66	8.08^a	98	5.86^a
		(0.00)		(1.79^a)		(1.19^a)
		[38%]		$[67\%^a]$		$[57\%^a]$
Dual-class return minus control-group return	32	2.92	66	-4.63^c	98	-2.16
		(0.63)		$-0.06c$		(0.27)
		[59%]		[50%]		[53%]
Panel B: Three-year returns (excluding first-day returns, in %)						
Dual-class raw returns	30	-0.64	53	28.43^b	83	17.92^c
		(-15.71)		(39.22^a)		(20.45^b)
		[43%]		$[70\%^a]$		$[60\%^c]$
Control-group raw returns	30	-7.73	65	1.57	95	-1.37
		(13.74)		(3.96)		(7.47)
		[57%]		[57%]		[57%]
Dual-class market-adjusted returns	30	-44.43^b	53	-0.22	83	-16.20
		(-60.77^b)		(10.54)		(-10.89)
		$[30\%^b]$		[53%]		[45%]
Control-group market-adjusted returns	30	-51.67^a	65	-27.47^a	95	-35.11^a
		(-32.81^a)		(-22.64^a)		(-28.58^a)
		$[13\%^a]$		$[35\%^b]$		$[28\%^a]$
Adj. Dual-class minus adj. control-group returns	28	15.11	52	22.70	80	20.04^c
		(23.69)		(15.28^c)		(22.89^c)
		[64%]		[54%]		[58%]

[a] Significant at the one-percent level.
[b] Significant at the five-percent level.
[c] Significant at the ten-percent level.

4.3 Results on long-run stock-price performance

4.3.1 Three-year cumulative abnormal returns by exchange

In panel B of Table 4 we provide summary information on stock-price performance over the three years after the IPO. In Tables 5 and 6, we present holding-period returns and month-by-month abnormal returns for dual-class firms. None of our long-run measures includes the initial returns discussed in the previous section. In each table, we report means, medians, the fraction positive, and the number of firm (pairs) remaining in the portfolio after each period.[12]

Two basic observations emerge from Table 4: (1) both types of IPOs perform better on NASDAQ than on the exchanges, and (2) dual-class returns are higher in both trading locations. Similar to Ritter (1991), we also find that after three years of trading all IPO samples underperform the market index. The control-group abnormal returns are significantly negative (at the one-percent level), average -35% and range from -27% on NASDAQ to -52% on the exchanges. In contrast, dual-class abnormal returns average an insignificant -16%, and range from 0% on NASDAQ to -44% on the exchanges.

The last row of Table 4 presents summary statistics on the pairwise differences between dual-class and control-group abnormal returns. Both means and medians are positive for both trading locations and range from 15% to 24%. The median difference on NASDAQ and both the mean and the median differences for the total sample are marginally significant. Thus, dual-class IPOs significantly outperform the matched firms over the three post-IPO years of trading.[13] To check the sensitivity of our results above to the procedure used to form portfolios, we now turn to a year-by-year analysis of wealth relatives based on holding-period returns, and then to a monthly examination of control-group adjusted dual-class returns.

4.3.2 Wealth relatives based on holding-period returns

Dual-class market-adjusted wealth relatives are computed individually for each firm by dividing one plus the dual-class firm's holding-period return by one plus the contemporaneous holding-period return on the market index (the other wealth relatives are calculated accordingly). In Table 5, we present summary statistics for these measures for a one-year, a two-year, and a three-year period following the IPO for both trading locations. For each sub-period, we report the mean, the median, and the fraction of wealth relatives greater than one. Significance levels refer to tests of the hypothesis that the mean (median) equals one.

The wealth relatives for months 1 through 36 reported in the third panel of Table 5 further substantiate the superior performance of dual-class IPOs. The wealth relative based on dual-class abnormal returns has a mean of 0.95 and a median of 0.74. This indicates that an investor who invests an equal amount in each dual-class IPO and holds the investment for three years nets five percent less than he could have earned by investing in the market portfolio,[14] and that the median dual-class IPO underperforms the market by 26%. In the aggregate, only 34% of all dual-class IPOs outperform the market portfolio over the three-year holding period. In contrast, investment in a control firm averages 36% below market, with the median IPO underperforming by 41% (only 16% positive). While for dual-class firms only the median is significantly different from one (at the five-percent level), for control firms

Table 5

Wealth relatives for dual-class and control-group firms

The basic sample includes 98 dual-class IPOs between 1984 and 1988, and a sample of control IPO firms, matched by exchange, IPO date, industry, and size. Neither sample contains unit offers, American Depository Receipts, REITs, closed-end funds, or certificates. Wealth relatives are calculated as the sample holding-period return divided by the benchmark holding-period return. Months refer to successive 21-trading-day intervals. To adjust for market movements, we use the value-weighted CRSP NYSE/Amex and NASDAQ indices, respectively. Market-adjusted wealth relatives are defined as one plus the holding-period return for the sample firms divided by one plus the holding-period return for investing in an equally-weighted market portfolio. In each cell, we report the mean, the median in parentheses, the fraction greater than one in brackets, and the number of wealth relatives. For hypothesis testing, we use a cross-sectional t-test for means, a signed-rank test for medians, and a sign test for the percentage positive. For means and medians, we test the null that they are equal to one.

All returns in percent	Post-IPO months 1-12			Post-IPO months 1-24			Post-IPO months 1-36		
	Dual-class market adjusted	Control-group market-adjusted	Adjusted dual-class/adjusted control-group	Dual-class market adjusted	Control-group market-adjusted	Adjusted dual-class/adjusted control-group	Dual-class market adjusted	Control-group market-adjusted	Adjusted dual-class/adjusted control-group
Total	0.93[b]	0.86[a]	1.37[a]	0.93	0.69[a]	1.93[a]	0.95	0.64[a]	3.42[c,d]
	(0.89[b])	(0.79[a])	(1.07[b])	(0.79[c])	(0.61[a])	(1.32[a])	(0.74[b])	(0.59[a])	(1.29[a])
	[37%[b]]	[29%[a]]	[55%]	[38%[b]]	[21%[a]]	[61%[b]]	[34%[a]]	[16%[a]]	[60%[c]]
	N=97	N=97	N=96	N=92	N=96	N=90	N=83	N=95	N=80
NYSE/Amex	0.79[a]	0.92	0.95	0.80	0.67[a]	1.34[c]	0.84	0.56[a]	1.98[b]
	(0.67[a])	(0.87[c])	(0.80)	(0.63[b])	(0.62[a])	(1.09)	(0.47[a])	(0.57[a])	(1.30[c])
	[25%[a]]	[29%[b]]	[35%]	[26%[b]]	[23%[a]]	[52%]	[23%[a]]	[10%[a]]	[57%]
	N=32	N=31	N=31	N=31	N=30	N=29	N=30	N=30	N=28
NASDAQ	1.01	0.84[a]	1.56[a]	1.00	0.70[a]	2.21[a]	1.02	0.67[a]	4.19[d]
	(0.94)	(0.74[a])	(1.26[a])	(0.87)	(0.60[a])	(1.49[a])	(0.84)	(0.60[a])	(1.29[a])
	[43%]	[29%[a]]	[65%[b]]	[44%]	[20%[a]]	[66%[b]]	[40%]	[18%[a]]	[62%]
	N=65	N=66	N=65	N=61	N=66	N=61	N=53	N=65	N=52

a Significant at the one-percent level.
b Significant at the five-percent level.
c Significant at the ten-percent level.
d The large magnitude of the mean is primarily caused by one extreme outlier (Applied Power Inc., 36-month holding-period return of 266%), which performed substantially better than its control-group counterpart (Alpharel Inc., 36-month holding-period return of 2.9%). Deleting the outlier reduces the mean by about one third and makes it significantly different from one at the one-percent significance level.

both the mean and the median are significant at the one-percent level. Finally, the last column indicates that an average investment in dual-class stocks performs 242% better relative to the market than an investment in the matched control firm, with the median dual-class stock performing 29% better relative to the market.[15]

The wealth relatives described above are fairly typical for each holding period and trading location that we examine in Table 5. The underperformance of dual-class IPOs relative to the market, however, is primarily due to exchange-listed firms. In contrast, control firms show an equally poor performance on both NASDAQ and on the exchanges. The pairwise comparison of the relative dual-class performance to the relative control-firm performance usually favors dual-class firms, except that the first-year relative performance of exchange-lised dual-class firms is five percent below that of the matched firms. In summary, the evidence in Table 5 corroborates our results above and shows they are not due to short-run return fluctuations or the choice of trading location.

4.3.3 Control-firm-adjusted abnormal returns

To provide further evidence on performance differences between dual-class firms and single-class firms, we calculate matching-firm adjusted dual-class abnormal returns (after first adjusting both return series for market movements). Thus, a positive abnormal return implies superior performance (relative to the market) of dual-class firms. Each month's return calculation incorporates only those firms that remain traded up to that month. The cumulative abnormal returns (CARs) in post-IPO month 36 average 20% and repeat values that were already presented in Table 4. The remaining statistics in Table 6 show that (1) monthly abnormal returns are only slightly more often significantly different from zero than we would expect, and that (2) dual-class abnormal returns are larger than control-group abnormal returns in 25 out of 36 months. Average matching-firm adjusted CARs are mostly positive (except in months 1, 3, and 4) and are significantly positive from month 17 through month 36, the end of our testing period. The non-parametric test statistics in Table 6 (signed-rank test for median CARs and sign test for the fraction of positive CARs) generally support the conclusions derived from using t-statistics on the means.

4.3.4 Interpretation and implications

While the analysis above documents superior stock-price performance of dual-class IPOs, we cannot provide direct evidence of causality between equity structure and performance. It seems worthwhile, however, to investigate potential sources of the performance differences. We have already eliminated risk as an explanation (see Table 3). Other plausible reasons are (1) lower liquidity of inferior-vote dual-class shares, or (2) more efficient management, possibly due to lower agency cost.

If the liquidity of inferior-vote dual-class shares is lower than that of otherwise identical common stock, investors would require a higher return on dual-class stock. Since Boehmer et al. (1995) show that ordinary common shares are less liquid than dual-class shares (controlling for size and industry), the liquidity hypothesis has no empirical relevance. More appealing is the efficiency hypothesis. First, it would be consistent with managerial bonding by holding illiquid superior-voting stock (Bhide's

Table 6

Control firm-adjusted long-run abnormal returns for dual-class IPOs

The basic sample includes 98 dual-class IPOs between 1984 and 1988, and a sample of control IPO firms, matched by exchange, IPO date, industry, and size. Neither sample contains unit offers, American Depository Receipts, REITs, closed-end funds, or certificates. Each row contains information on the remaining firm pairs (i.e., if a dual-class firm is delisted, its matching control firm is also dropped from the sample, and vice versa).

Post-IPO month[d]	Number of firm pairs	Mean AR[e]	Median AR[f]	Percent AR>0[g]	Mean CAR[e]	Median CAR[f]	Percent CAR>0[g]
1	98	-0.58%	-1.54%	46%	-0.58%	-1.54%	46%
2	97	1.44	1.49	56	0.43	-0.25	48
3	97	-0.72	-1.57[c]	44	-0.29	-2.41	45
4	97	-0.22	2.87	54	-0.51	-8.32	42
5	97	1.68	-0.03	48	1.17	2.11	53
6	97	3.32[c]	5.45[b]	65[a]	4.49	-0.97	49
7	97	0.69	0.28	50	5.18	1.29	53
8	97	4.52[c]	-0.18	50	9.70	4.96	55
9	97	-1.32	-0.04	48	8.38	3.76	54
10	96	-2.41	-0.74	47	4.76	1.51	52
11	96	1.17	2.52	54	5.93	1.95	54
12	96	0.15	3.00	57	6.07	6.39	54
13	96	3.21[c]	1.95	55	9.28	14.10	52
14	96	1.63	1.44	56	10.91	8.64	54
15	96	0.87	1.13	54	11.77	8.34	54
16	95	0.40	3.23	57	12.50	17.75	58
17	94	3.58[b]	4.76[b]	62[b]	15.45[c]	15.07[c]	54
18	93	4.09[b]	5.05[b]	60[c]	20.81[b]	20.72[b]	61[b]
19	92	0.04	-0.17	49	22.85[b]	13.98[b]	53
20	92	-0.66	-0.38	49	22.19[b]	15.16[b]	55
21	92	0.53	0.38	51	22.72[b]	12.97[b]	57
22	92	0.52	-1.79	47	23.24[b]	13.65[b]	57
23	91	0.34	-0.46	49	22.66[b]	14.99[b]	59[c]
24	90	2.73	1.03	52	24.31[b]	20.61[a]	59
25	90	5.39	0.90	53	29.70[a]	27.11[a]	61[b]
26	90	0.53	3.58	53	30.24[a]	24.55[a]	63[a]
27	88	2.51	2.64	59	31.12[a]	34.16[a]	64[a]
28	86	0.81	3.16	52	30.94[a]	27.53[a]	64[a]
29	86	0.11	-0.51	49	31.05[a]	22.51[a]	62[b]
30	85	-1.12	-0.08	47	27.77[b]	20.94[a]	64[b]
31	84	-0.16	-1.62	49	26.98[b]	15.83[b]	60[c]
32	83	-0.27	-0.04	49	26.96[b]	29.20[a]	63[b]
33	82	0.01	-0.25	50	27.79[b]	28.32[b]	63[b]
34	81	0.24	2.36	59	26.70[b]	27.17[b]	59
35	80	-1.60	1.00	51	24.47[b]	29.00[b]	60[c]
36	80	-4.43	-0.03	50	20.04[c]	22.89[c]	58

a Significant at the one-percent level.

b Significant at the five-percent level.

c Significant at the ten-percent level.

d Months refer to successive 21-trading-day intervals.

e AR is computed in two steps. First, we subtract the return on the market-specific value-weighted CRSP index from the returns on dual-class and control-group IPOs. Then we subtract the market-adjusted control-group return from the market-adjusted dual-class firm return. CARs are the sum of monthly ARs of only those firms remaining in the sample by the particular month.

Table 6 (continued)

The reported significance level refers to a test based on ARs or CARs that are standardized by the individual-firm standard deviation over 36 months following the IPO, and then adjusted for the number of time periods and firms. A t-test based on cross-sectional standard deviations leads to virtually unchanged results (and with one exception to higher significance levels than those reported above).

f   The reported significance level refers to a signed rank test.
g   The reported significance level refers to a sign test.

(1993) argument). Second, it would lend empirical support to Alchian and Demsetz (1972), Fama and Jensen (1983), and DeAngelo and DeAngelo (1985), who argue that a dual-class structure decreases agency cost if firm-specific human capital is important. Third, it would lend credibility to the statements by company executives that a dual-class structure promotes stronger long-term incentives (see the appendix). In an attempt to analyze these issues in more detail, we now examine operating data for our sample firms.

4.4 Analysis of operating characteristics

We have discussed earlier the implications of bundling voting control while retaining the option to sell most of the cash-flow claim on the firm. First, creating two classes of stock may increase agency cost if managers take advantage of their protected position. This is not much of an empirical issue at the time of the IPO, however, because owners typically retain about two thirds of the cash-flow claim, directly exposing themselves to the wealth consequences of their decisions on the value of the firm. On the other hand, subsequent equity offerings, especially secondary offerings, can substantially dilute the managers' cash-flow claim without diluting their control. Second, creating two classes of stock can alleviate agency problems if firm-specific human capital is important. In this section we investigate (1) whether dual-class firms decide to employ financing strategies that are likely reduce agency problems already at the time of the IPO and (2) whether dual-class and single-class firms differ in their ability to generate cash flow.

In Table 7, we present information on several operating characteristics and various measures of operating performance for dual-class and control-group firms. For each variable, we present median levels for the first and third completed post-IPO fiscal year, and the median percentage growth over those two years. (Thus, the figures reported for year +3 approximately correspond to month 36 in our analysis of stock returns.) The last column shows the median pairwise difference between dual-class growth and control-firm growth for each variable. We were able to identify 68 firm pairs on COMPUSTAT (29 are exchange listed, 39 trade on NASDAQ) where both types of IPOs were included. Since many variables have missing values, we report the number of available observations for each cell. While not reported here, we have performed the following analysis separately for each trading location. Since we did not find any statistically significant differences between NASDAQ firms and exchange-listed firms, we report only the aggregate values in Table 7 to conserve space.[16]

Table 7

Post-IPO operating data for dual-class and matching control-group firms

The basic sample includes 98 dual-class IPOs between 1984 and 1988, and a sample of control IPO firms, matched by exchange, IPO date, industry, and size. Neither sample contains unit offers, American Depository Receipts, REITs, closed-end funds, or certificates. We can identify post-IPO operating data for 68 out of 98 matched pairs on COMPUSTAT (29 on AMEX or NYSE and 39 on NASDAQ). The table lists medians and for some columns the fraction positive in parentheses. "N" refers to the number of observations with non-missing values. For the "difference" columns, we report statistical significance based on a rank-sum test for the medians and a sign test for the fraction positive for the null hypothesis that the statistic is equal to zero.

Variable	Dual-class medians			Control-group medians			Median growth difference
	Year + 1	Year + 3	Growth (Pct. > 0)	Year + 1	Year + 3	Growth (Pct. > 0)	Dual-class growth - control-group growth (Pct. > 0)
Assets ($mn)	107.31 N=65	135.26 N=64	37.5%[a] (85.5%)[a] N=62	57.28 N=68	78.65 N=64	38.8%[a] (82.8%)[a] N=64	4.1% (53.4%) N=58
Sales ($mn)	108.43 N=62	174.27 N=64	52.5[a] (91.5%)[a] N=59	50.56 N=68	88.34 N=63	75.1[a] (93.4%)[a] N=61	5.9 (51.0%) N=53
Net operating income ($mn)	15.70 N=61	21.59 N=63	30.8[a] (72.4%)[a] N=58	5.22 N=66	3.67 N=61	-10.8 (45.9%) N=61	35.4[b] (66.0%)[b] N=53
Market value of equity ($mn)	88.68 N=62	74.32 N=63	34.4[a] (57.6%) N=59	59.14 N=68	33.21 N=64	-20.8[c] (37.5%)[c] N=64	61.0[a] (72.7%)[a] N=55
Tobin's Qd	1.42 N=61	1.44 N=63	-2.8 (48.3%) N=58	1.58 N=68	1.13 N=64	-21.5[a] (23.4%)[a] N=64	20.8[a] (75.9%)[a] N=54
Market value of equity / Assets	0.77 N=62	0.77 N=63	-16.7 (35.6%)[b] N=59	1.02 N=68	0.43 N=64	-47.5[a] (15.6%)[a] N=64	36.7[a] (78.2%)[a] N=55
Market value/ Book value of equity	2.04 N=62	1.64 N=63	-21.1 (39.0%) N=59	2.36 N=68	1.32 N=64	-32.9[b] (29.7%)[a] N=64	24.3[c] (63.6%)[c] N=55

Table 7 (continued)

Variable	Dual-class medians			Control-group medians			Median growth difference
	Year + 1	Year +3	Growth (Pct. > 0)	Year + 1	Year +3	Growth (Pct. > 0)	Dual-class growth - control-group growth (Pct. > 0)
NOI / Assets	0.15 N=61	0.12 N=63	-8.2[c] (39.7%) N=58	0.13 N=66	0.07 N=61	-45.9[a] (26.2%)[a] N=61	39.5[b] (62.3%)[c] N=53
NOI / Sales	0.14 N=61	0.13 N=61	-12.4[a] (31.0%)[a] N=58	0.12 N=64	0.06 N=61	-28.9[a] (27.1%)[a] N=59	7.3 (52.9%) N=51
NOI / Stockholders' equity[e]	0.41 N=55	0.34 N=60	-19.7[b] (34.6%)[b] N=52	0.29 N=62	0.21 N=60	-18.0 (46.6%) N=58	-5.8 (46.7%) N=45
Sales / Assets	1.11 N=62	1.01 N=64	1.3[c] (50.8%) N=59	1.18 N=68	1.20 N=63	12.9[a] (63.9%)[b] N=61	-4.4 (47.2%) N=53
Total long-term debt/Assets	0.22 N=64	0.26 N=64	3.3 (52.7%) N=55	0.16 N=68	0.21 N=64	36.8[a] (67.9%)[a] N=56	-66.9[c] (34.8%)[b] N=46
Dividends / Earnings	0.00 N=61	0.00 N=64	208.4[a] (81.3%)[b] N=12	0.00 N=62	0.00 N=62	89.3 (60.0%) N=5	393. (100.0%) N=2

a Significant at the one-percent level.
b Significant at the five-percent level.
c Significant at the ten-percent level.
d To approximate Tobin's Q, we follow Mikkelson and Partch (1994) and compute the ratio of the market value of common stock, the carrying value of preferred stock, and the book value of all liabilities, divided by total assets.
e Stockholders' equity is calculated as the sum of the book value of common stock, common stock issued, and retained earnings, minus adjustments.

4.4.1 Leverage

A higher debt level reduces free cash flow and thus increases the frequency with which the firm has to obtain external financing, reducing agency cost and increasing monitoring through capital markets (although IPO firms are typically growth firms, and hence do not generate substantial free cash flows).[17] There is some evidence that dual-class firms initially use debt as a disciplinary mechanism: they are considerably more leveraged than control firms one year after the IPO. There are 9 non-levered control firms but only 6 non-levered dual-class firms in year +1. The median ratios of total long-term debt to total assets change from 22% (dual class) and 16% (control) in year +1 to 26% and 21%, respectively, in year +3. For the median matched pair, however, dual-class leverage growth is 67% less than control-firm leverage growth. Thus, while dual-class debt may initially reduce agency cost, we find evidence that the gap between dual-class leverage and control-group leverage narrows substantially during the two years following the IPO.

4.4.2 Dividend payout

Similar to high leverage, a high payout ratio can alleviate some potential agency problems. Casual observation of the IPO market, however, suggests that high dividends (like high leverage) are uncommon for firms going public. In our sample, twelve dual-class firms and five control firms pay dividends in both year +1 and year +3, and we find only two matched pairs where both IPO types do so. While this small sample size severely reduces the reliability of inferences, we make three observations. First, while 12 (out of 68) dual-class firms pay dividends in year +1 and 25 pay dividends in year +3, only 7 (10) control firms do so. Second, the fraction of dual-class firms that consistently pay dividends over the first three years of trading is more than twice as large than that of control firms. Finally, the increase in the payout of dividend-paying firms is more than twice as large. It is not apparent, however, that dual-class firms systematically chose a higher payout ratio than control firms.

4.4.3 Assets, sales, and net operating income

One year after the IPO, dual-class firms have about twice the assets of control firms, twice the sales, and three times the net operating income (NOI) and preserve these relations through year +3. While dual-class asset and sales growth rates are only slightly larger than the respective control-firm growth, dual-class NOI increases by a significant 35% more than matched-firm NOI. Thus, with similar growth of assets and sales, dual-class firms achieve better operating results.

Consequently, the change in the ratio of NOI and Assets (ROA) also reflects the relative superior operating efficiency of dual-class firms. ROA increases a significant 40% more for dual-class firms. The levels of ROA, however, decline significantly for both groups of firms by year +3. The ratios NOI/Sales (ROS) and NOI/Stockholders Equity (ROE) also decline significantly for both groups, but the difference in the rates of decline are not statistically different across groups. Thus, the operating performance of both groups declines over the first three years of public trading, but that of dual-class firms declines at a substantially lower rate (this observation is similar to Mikkelson and Partch's (1994) results). In sum, consistent with Lehn et al. (1990) and Denis and Denis (1992), there is no evidence that dual-class firms make poorer investments than single-class firms and these results are not consistent with dual-class management expropriating holders of inferior-vote shares.

4.4.4 Measures based on the market value of equity

We have already documented above that both groups' equity loses value after adjusting for market movements, but that dual-class firms substantially outperform their matched counterparts. The firms included on COMPUSTAT behave similarly. The median market value of equity declines for both groups, but the median dual-class equity grows by a highly significant 34%, while control firms lose 21%.[18] The median pairwise difference of growth rates is a highly significant 61% in favor of the dual-class firms.[19]

Similar conclusions emerge from analyzing a proxy for Tobin's Q, the ratio of market value of equity to assets, and the market-to-book ratio of equity. Each of these measures declines for both groups to varying extents, but always more for the control firms. The median pairwise differences of these growth rates are highly significant for each measure and amount to 21%, 37%, and 24%, respectively, in favor of dual-class firms.

In summary, our analysis of these alternative market-based performance measures leads to qualitatively similar conclusions as our analysis of stock-market returns. Both dual-class firms and control firms show declining operating and stock-price performance over the three years following the IPO, but dual-class firms significantly outperform the matched single-class IPOs. Moreover, we find no evidence of different degrees of leverage or different payout ratios that would reduce free cash flow or, alternatively, could provide a substitute monitoring device for dual-class firms. More importantly, during the first three years after going public dual-class firms generate substantially higher NOI growth rates than single-class firms.

5. Conclusions

We analyze performance differences between dual-class IPOs and single-class IPOs. For a sample of all dual-class IPOs from 1984 to 1988, we find no statistically significant abnormal long-run stock-price performance over a three-year horizon. This contrasts with Ritter's (1991) result that (predominantly single-class) IPOs significantly underperform the market in the three years after going public. We establish the distribution of voting rights as an important cross-sectional determinant of post-IPO stock-market performance, indicating a clear need for further cross-sectional analysis of post-IPO performance in future research.

We find that dual-class firms significantly outperform a matched control group of firms both in terms of stock-market returns and various accounting measures of performance. While we cannot establish cause and effect, the evidence leads us to conclude that a dual-class equity structure for IPOs has net benefits resulting, ceteris paribus, in improved operating performance, and increased value of the firm's stock. Although closely-held voting control lessens the constraints on managerial decision making, benefits appear to outweigh the costs for those firms that chose to go public with two classes of stock. In particular, even though dual-class firms apparently do not substitute higher leverage or a higher dividend payout as a monitoring device (although we find marginal evidence of different degrees of leverage), our results are consistent with the arguments of Alchian and Demsetz (1972) or Fama and Jensen (1983) that firm-specific investments require a protected position of management.

This statement is, of course, not meant to imply that a dual-class structure is optimal for all firms. Investigating the factors that in fact make it optimal seems to be a fertile area for future research. Additionally, the relation between the control structure and performance is likely to depend on other variables as well. For example, the proportion of intangible assets, management compensation schemes, investment policies, and other aspects could affect the value of a protected management position. Furthermore, future research should analyze how insiders' cash-flow claim changes in relation to their voting power over a longer period of time. While we find no differences between dual-class and control-group firms during the first three years of trading, it is possible that the frequency of equity issues and/or insider sales changes as the firm seasons further.

Appendix

To get first-hand information on some reasons that motivated the founders of the sample firms in this paper to adopt a dual-class equity structure at the time of going public, we contacted the CEOs/CFOs of our sample firms. The following excerpts represent typical responses.

"The reason for creating two classes of stock is fairy simple. You will note from the proxy statement that holders of Class A common are entitled to one vote per share, while Class B has greater voting power - five per share. Mr. X, who founded the Company, retains all of the Class B common stock. Two classes of stock enabled the Company to put a substantial amount of stock into the original float - 27 million shares -but still retain 80% of the voting control through the ownership of Class B. You will note from our annual report that last year we earned approximately $282 million. That is more than four-and-a half times the earnings of our nearest competitor which earned approximately $60 million in 1992."

"At the time we went public our licensor owned 25% of the Company. My family and I owned approximately 45% of the Company. Under the then current estate tax structure, my family's interest would reduce to approximately 20% after my death, whereas our licensor, being a corporation, would never have to pay an estate tax and would never reduce its holding. Therefore, in order to protect against an ultimate change of control to our licensor the dual-class stock structure was enacted, all of which was known to the public purchasing our stock."

"The primary reason for the different classes of stock is to insure that Mr. X controls the Company. Mr. X put together the capital structure in 1987 to purchase the Company. Even though Mr. X controls the Company, his super voting rights end with the sale of his shares. Thus, all shares, whether A, B, or C have equal economic rights."

"For many years until the mid-1980's, the Company had been a family owned Company whose chief executive officer was a member of the controlling family. In 1985, the Company hired an outside executive to be chief operating officer, which was the first step away from family management. At the time of the IPO, the family was not yet ready to turn over complete control to this new management. In 1988, in a follow-up step, a nominating committee arrangement coupled with a trust management with a four-year life, which provided for the conversion of all stock into one class at the end of the four year period was finalized."

"The major reason for dual-class voting on the initial offering was to assure the founders of the Company a significant input in the future of the Company as a public entity. The founders had significant background in our industry and a clear long term strategy for the Company. Raising capital in the public markets enabled the Company to advance toward those goals at a faster pace. As the Company develops and reaches those initial goals, it was anticipated that additional capital would be required to reach new long term goals. The initial class voting difference guaranteed the ability of the founders to carry out the original plans without fear of a take over threat. Basically, the only holders of three-vote stock were the original founders of the Company with virtually the majority of their individual net worth invested in the Company. We were long term investors, not short term profit takers. Since the initial offering, several original long term goals have been achieved and we successfully completed an offering in August of 1992. That offering effectively diluted the effect of the high vote stock by about 20%. In conclusion, the high vote stock provided a mechanism to guarantee the "entrepreneurs" that started the Company the ability to reach initial long term goals without undue outside influence."

"To maintain voting control of the corporation. The Company has been family owned and the family is still active in Company operations. Dual-class was appropriate in maintaining control and providing a diversity of public holders who all purchased the IPO with an understanding of the voting situation and control issues."

"The chairman wished to retain control of the Company. In the early 1980s, we had seen the disastrous consequences of one of our largest competitors being taken over and badly managed. Our Company's roots go back almost 100 years, and I believe the chairman felt it was in the best interests of both the employees and our customers if control remained with Class B shareholders. You should note that people who own B stock cannot profit at the expense of A shareholders by selling it at a "premium." In order for B stock to be sold, it must be transferred to A stock prior to sale. The only significant exception is transfers within a family."

"Our Company had been a privately held company from 1874 to 1986. The primary purpose of the two classes of equity with differential voting rights was to preserve the management control within the Company. It is expected that the voting rights of the Class B common stock may make the company less attractive as the potential target of a hostile tender offer or other proposal to acquire the stock or business of the Company, and merger proposals might be rendered more difficult, even if such actions would be in the best interests of the holders of the Class A common stock. Accordingly, increases in the market price of the Class A common stock, temporary or otherwise, which might result from actual or rumored hostile takeover attempts, will be inhibited."

"Our Company is an indirect wholly-owned subsidiary of X Inc. which holds approximately 83% of the outstanding shares of Class A common stock, and all of the outstanding shares of Class B common stock, and through its ability to elect all directors of the company, indirectly controls all matters relating to the management of our Company. X Inc. recently formed our Company in connection with a reorganization of its oil and gas business. The reorganization and financial restructuring (including the offerings) were undertaken (i) to enable X Inc. to realize a return of a portion of its investment in our Company through the elimination of intercompany accounts and the distribution to X Inc. of a special $140 million dividend, (ii) to enable our Company to have direct access to capital markets, (iii) to establish a market value for X Inc.'s equity interest in our Company, and (iv) to create a structure in which our company would be better able to compete and expand."

"The recapitalisation through the charter amendment, combined with the results of the exchange offer, have the effect of permitting the "X" Family to elect the entire board of directors, and to determine the outcome of any other matters submitted to the stockholders for approval, including a merger or sale of substantially all of the assets of the Company. The aggregate voting power of the "X" Family is also likely to discourage any proposed takeover of the Company pursuant to a tender offer unless the terms thereof are approved by the "X" Family. The Company presently believes the "X" Family would vote together on any significant corporate matters effecting the management or ownership of the Company. The Company is unable to predict what effect, if any, the voting control of the "X" Family will have on the market price of the Class A common stock."

"We created a dual-class equity structure to provide preferential rights to the public shareholders with regard to the payment of dividends, and liquidation rights. This was to enhance the marketability of the shares being offered to the public in the IPO. Please note that since May 1, 1993 (marking the end of the preference period), the Class A and Class B common stock are identical in all respects."

"The principal purpose of the Reclassification was to provide the Company with a more flexible financial structure to facilitate raising additional equity or to make acquisitions without significantly diluting the voting power of existing stockholders, particularly members of the family of "X". One effect will be to enable the "X" family to maintain practical control over the Company's affairs as long as family members do not dispose of significant amounts of their Class B common stock. With the sale of the 1,300,000 shares of Class A common offered through the IPO, the outstanding common stock of the Company (both classes) was increased by approximately 53% while the voting power of the Class B common holders was diminished by 7.6%."

"The Company's voting structure, which is similar to voting structures adopted by a number of other media companies, was designed to promote the continued independence and integrity of the Company's media operations under the control of the holders of the Class B Voting Stock while at the same time providing for equity ownership in the Company by a broader group of stockholders through the means of a class of publicly-traded common stock. This structure renders more difficult certain unsolicited or hostile attempts to take over the Company which would disrupt the Company, divert the attention of its Directors, officers and employees and adversely affect the independence and quality of its media operations. The holders of Class B Voting Stock have the power to defeat any attempt to acquire control of the Company with a view to effecting a merger, sale of assets or similar transaction even though such a change in control may be favored by stockholders holding substantially more than a majority of the Company's outstanding equity. This may have the effect of precluding holders of shares in the Company from receiving any premium above market price for their shares in connection with any such attempt to acquire control."

"The Reclassification was implemented principally to facilitate, in the event the Company were to be sold, the negotiation of the best sale price for all stockholders. Because shares of Class B common stock are not transferable except to permitted transferees, holders of Class B common stock, in connection with any sale of the Company, will be able to sell only the Class A common stock into which such shares of Class B common stock are convertible and, thus, will not be able to obtain consideration for the Class B common stock greater than that paid to holders of Class A common stock."

Acknowledgement

We appreciate the helpful comments from Uwe Küchler, Marc Lipson, Bill Megginson, Jeffry Netter, Annette Poulsen, Raghuram Rajan, Paul Spindt, Richard Stehle, Bill Wilhelm, two anonymous referees, and participants at the 1993 Financial Management Association meeting, the Atlanta Finance Workshop, the CEPR-ESSFM Symposium in Gerzensee, and finance seminars at Humboldt Universität, Louisiana State University, the University of Georgia, Universität Gießen, and Tilburg University. The first author acknowledges partial financial support from the Schmalenbach Gesellschaft-Deutsche Gesellschaft für Betriebsirtschafslehre. The first author's research for this paper was carried our within SFB 373 of the Deutsche Forshungsgemeinschaft at Humboldt-Universität zu Berlin.

References

Aggarwal, R. and P. Rivoli, 1990, Fads in the initial public offering market, Financial Management, 45-57.

Alchian, A. and H. Demsetz, 1972, Production, Information costs, and economic organization, American Economic Review 62, 777-795.

Allen, F. and G. Faulhaber, 1989, Signaling by underpricing in the IPO market, Journal of Financial Economics 23, 303-323.

Baron, D. P., 1982, A model for the demand for investment banking advising and distribution services for new issues, Journal of Finance 37, 955-976.

Beatty, R. P. and J. R. Ritter, 1986, Investment banking, reputation, and the underpricing of initial public offerings, Journal of Financial Economics 15, 213-232.

Benveniste, L. and P. Spindt, 1989, How investment bankers determine the offer price and allocation of new issues, Journal of Financial Economics 24, 343-361.

Bhide, A., 1993, The hidden cost of stock market liquidity, Journal of Financial Economics 34, 31-51.

Blair, D. H., D. L. Golbe, and J. M. Gerard, 1989, Unbundling the voting rights and profit claims of common shares, Journal of Political Economy 97, 420-443.

Boehmer, E., G. Sanger, and S. Varshney, 1995, Managerial bonding and stock liquidity: An analysis of dual-class firms, Working Paper, Louisiana State University.

Booth, J. R. and R. L. Smith, 1986, Capital raising, underwriting, and the certification hypothesis, Journal of Financial Economics 15, 261-281.

Buser, Stephen A. and K. C. Chan, 1987, NASDAQ/NMS qualification standards, Ohio registration experience and the price performance of initial public offerings, Columbus: Ohio Department of Commerce and National Association of Securities Dealers, Inc.

Chalk, A. J. and J. W. Peavy, 1987, Why you'll never get a 'hot' new issue, AAII Journal 9, 16-20.

Chang, S. and D. Mayers, 1992, Managerial vote ownership and shareholder wealth, Journal of Financial Economics 32, 103-131.

Cornett, M. and M. Vetsuypens, 1989, Voting rights and shareholder wealth, Managerial and Decision Economics 10, 175-188.

Dann, L. Y. and H. DeAngelo, 1988, Corporate financial policy and corporate control: A study of defensive adjustments in asset and ownership structure, Journal of Financial Economics 20, 87-127.

DeAngelo, H. and L. DeAngelo, 1985, Managerial ownership of voting rights, Journal of Financial Economics, 33-69.

Denis, D. J. and D. K. Denis, 1992, Majority owner-managers and organizational efficiency, Working Paper, Virginia Polytechnic Institute and State University.

Fama, G. and M. Jensen, 1983, Separation of ownership and control, Journal of Law and Economics 26, 301-326.

Gilson, Ronald, 1993, Regulating the equity component of capital structure: The SEC's response to the one-share, one-vote controversy, Journal of Applied Corporate Finance 5, 37-43.

Grinblatt, M. and C. Y. Hwang, 1989, Signalling and the pricing of new issues, Journal of Finance 44, 393-420.

Grossman, S. J. and O. D. Hart, 1988, One share-one vote and the market for corporate control, Journal of Financial Economics 20, 175-202.

Hanley, K. W., 1993, Underpricing of initial public offerings and the partial adjustment phenomenon, Journal of Financial Economics 34, 231-250.

Hanley, K. W. and J. R. Ritter, 1992, Going public, in: P. Newman, M. Milgate, and J. Eatwell (eds.), The new Palgrave dictionary of money and finance (Stockton Press, London).

Harris, M. and A. Raviv, 1988, Corporate governance: Voting rights and majority rules, Journal of Financial Economics 20, 203-235.

Hartmann-Wendels, T. and P. von Hinten, 1989, Marktwert von Vorzugsaktien, Zeitschrift für betriebswirtschaftliche Forschung 41, 263-293.

Holderness, C. G. and D. P. Sheehan, 1988, The role of majority shareholders in publicly held corporations, Journal of Financial Economics 20, 317-346.

Holderness, C. G. and D. P. Sheehan, 1991, Monitoring an owner: The case of Turner Broadcasting, Journal of Financial Economics 30, 325-346.

Horner, M. R., 1988, The value of the corporate voting right, Journal of Banking and Finance 12, 69-83.

Ibbotson, R. G. and J. F. Jaffe, 1975, 'Hot issue' markets, Journal of Finance 30, 1027-1042.

Ibbotson, R. G., 1975, Price Performance of common stock new issues, Journal of Financial Economics 3, 235-272.

Jain, B. and O. Kini, 1994, The post-issue operating performance of IPO firms, Journal of Finance 49, 1699-1726.

Jarrell, G. A. and A. B. Poulsen, 1988, Dual-class recapitalizations as antitakeover mechanisms: the recent evidence, Journal of Financial Economics 20, 129-152.

Jegadeesh, N., M. Weinstein, and I. Welch, 1993, An empirical investigation of IPO returns and subsequent equity offerings, Journal of Financial Economics 34, 153-175.

Jensen, M. and W. Meckling, 1976, Theory of the firm: managerial behavior, agency costs and ownership structure, Journal of Financial Economics 3, 305-360.

Jensen, M., 1989, The eclipse of the public corporation, Harvard Business Review 5, 61-74.

Lease, R., J. J. McConnell and W. H. Mikkelson, 1983, The market value of control in publicly traded corporations, Journal of Financial Economics 11, 439-471.

Lease, R., J. J. McConnell and W. H. Mikkelson, 1984, The market value of differential voting rights in closely held corporations, Journal of Business 57, 443-467.

Lehn, K., J. Netter and A. Poulsen, 1990, Consolidating corporate control: Dual-class recapitalization versus leveraged buyouts, Journal of Financial Economics 27, 557-580.

Levy, H., 1982, Economic evaluation of voting power of common stock, Journal of Finance 38, 79-93.

Loughran, T., J. R. Ritter, and K. Rydqvist, 1994, Initial public offerings: International insights, Pacific Basin Finance Journal 2, 165-199.

Megginson, W. L., 1990, Restricted voting stock, acquisition premiums, and the market value of control, The Financial Review, 175-198.

Mikkelson, W. and M. Partch, 1989, Managers' voting rights and corporate control, Journal of Financial Economics 25, 263-290.

Mikkelson, W. and M. Partch, 1994, The consequences of unbundling managers' voting rights and equity claims, Journal of Corporate Finance, forthcoming.

Moyer, C. and P. Sisneros, 1991, Initial public offerings by dual class firms: Pricing and firm characteristics, Working Paper, University of Houston.

Moyer, R., R. Rao, and P. Sisneros, 1992, Substitutes for voting rights: Evidence from dual class recapitalization, Financial Management 21, 35-47.

Partch, M., 1987, The creation of a class of limited voting stock and shareholder wealth, Journal of Financial Economics 18, 313-339.

Ritter, J., 1984, The 'hot issue' market of 1980, Journal of Business 32, 215-240.

Ritter, J., 1991, The long-run performance of initial public offerings, Journal of Finance 46, 3-27.

Robinson, C. and A. White, 1990, The value of a vote in the market for corporate control, Working Paper, York University.

Rock, K., 1986, Why new issues are underpriced, Journal of Financial Economics 15, 187-212.

Ruback, R. S., 1988, Coercive exchange offers, Journal of Financial Economics 20, 153-173.

Ruud, J. S., 1993, Underwriter price support and the IPO underpricing puzzle, Journal of Financial Economics 34, 135-151.

Rydqvist, K., 1987, The pricing of shares with different voting power and the theory of oceanic games, EFI Stockholm.

Shleifer, A. and R. W. Vishny, 1986, Large shareholders and corporate control, Journal of Political Economy 94, 461-488.

Sisneros, P., 1989, Dual class common stock: an analysis of the agency costs of differential voting rights, 1989, Unpublished Dissertation, Texas Tech University.

Smith, C. W., 1986, Investment banking and the capital acquisition process, Journal of Financial Economics 15, 3-29.

Stoll, Hans R. and A. J. Curley, 1970, Small business and the new issues market for equities, Journal of Financial and Quantitative Analysis 5, 309-322.

Stulz, R. M., 1988, Managerial control of voting rights, Journal of Financial Economics 20, 25-54.

Tinic, S., 1988, Anatomy of initial public offerings of common stock, Journal of Finance 43, 789-822.

Weber, M., E. Berg and H. Kruse, 1992, Kurs- und Renditevergleich von Stamm- und Vorzugsaktien - eine empirische Analyse, Zeitschrift für betriebswirtschaftliche Forschung 44, 548-565.

Welch, I, 1989, Seasoned offerings, imitation costs and the underpricing of initial public offerings, Journal of Finance 44, 421-449.

Zingales, Luigi, 1992a, Insider ownership and the decision to go public, CRSP Working Paper 367, University of Chicago.

Zingales, Luigi, 1992b, The value of voting rights in the U.S., CRSP Working Paper 368, University of Chicago.

Zingales, Luigi, 1994, The value of the voting right: A study of the Milan stock exchange experience, Review of Financial Studies 7, 125-148.

Endnotes

[1] Consistent with Ritter's results, we document substantial underperformance for the control sample of single class IPOs.

[2] See Smith (1986) and Hanley and Ritter (1992) for a review of the literature on IPOs.

[3] Several studies attempt to describe underpricing as an endogenous decision. Some theories have focused on informational asymmetries at the time of the IPO (for example, Allen and Faulhaber (1989), Welch (1989), and Grinblatt and Hwang (1989)), although Jegadeesh et al. (1993) argue that their evidence does not support the signalling theories.

Other studies analyze the reputational capital of underwriters as a disciplinary mechanism (Booth and Smith (1986)), the monopsony power of investment banks (Ritter (1984), Chalk and Peavy (1987)), the informational advantage of investment banks over issuers (Baron (1982)), and the existence of uninformed investors (Rock (1986)). Beatty and Ritter (1986) extend Rock's model and show that expected

4 Blair et al. (1989) develop a model to analyze the benefits of a separate market for votes. They find that such a market is eneficial if capital-gains taxation is introduced into the model.

5 Similar results are obtained in studies by Levy (1982) for Israel, Hartmann-Wendels and von Hinten (1989) and Weber et al. (1992) for Germany, Rydqvist (1987) for Sweden, Horner (1988) for Switzerland, Megginson (1990) for the UK, Robinson and White (1990) for Canada, and Zingales (1994) for Italy. Several of these studies measure even larger premia for the stock markets they examine.

6 Moyers and Sisneros (1991) and Sisneros (1989) also study dual-class IPOs. Their focus is on IPO underpricing and IPO-specific differences between dual-class firms and other IPOs, while ur focus is on the long-run stock-market and operating performance of these firms.

7 In this paper, we do not discuss the relation between cash-flow retention and voting control in more detail. For such an analysis, see Moyer and Sisneros (1991), Sisneros (1989), or Mikkelson and Partch (1994).

8 Benveniste and Spindt (1989) develop a model where information is revealed during the pre-selling phase of the IPO, affecting changes in the price and quantity of shares from the initial to the final prospectus. Hanley (1993) examines their model empirically.

9 We can only estimate market value and risk measures for the dual-class firms based on inferior-voting shares, because only two firms list both classes.

10 Assuming that returns behave according to the CAPM, a 0.1 difference in β would imply a 1% difference in annual returns for a market-risk premium of 10%.

11 The average monthly market-adjusted return for event month t is

$$AR_t = \frac{1}{N} \sum_i (r_{it} - r_{mt})$$

for the N firms still trading in month t, where r_{it} is the 21-trading-day return for firm i, and r_{mt} is the return on CRSP's value-weighted market index for the respective trading location.

The cumulative market adjusted returns for event months 1 through 36 are given by

$$CAR_t = \sum_{s=1}^{1} ARs$$

To reduce problems due to non-surviving firms, we first average across firms and then sum across time.

We compute holding-period returns as

$$HPR_t^i = \prod_{s=1}^{t} (1 + rs), \text{ where } i \in (\text{dual - class, control, market})$$

and define benchmark-adjusted wealth relatives as

$$WR^{dual}_t = HPR_t^{dual}/HPR_t^{market}$$

and similarly for control group firms. Taking into account different offering dates for dual-class IPOs and the matched control firms, we compute the control-firm adjusted wealth relatives as

$$WR_t = WR_t^{dual}/WR_t^{control}$$

[12] Our sample includes 15 dual-class IPOs and 3 control-group IPOs that stop trading during the three years following the IPO. Among the control firms, two delisted due to financial difficulties and one due to a merger. Among the dual-class IPOs, four delisted due to financial difficulties, seven due to mergers, and four due to other reasons.

[13] Since the performance differences are most pronounced on NASDAQ, it should be noted, however, that the differences in size and age are larger on NASDAQ than on the exchanges (see Table 2). Since Ritter (1991) documents more favorable returns for large and old firms, these results may be partially driven by the matching procedure. On the other hand, since significant returns differences also exist when we use all 1270 IPOs as a control sample it is unlikely that the size and age divergence is primarily causing our results.

[14] We assume that all proceeds due to stocks that stop trading are reinvested proportionally in the remaining firms of each portfolio.

[15] The large mean reported in table 5 is partilaly due to an outlier. See footnore (d) in table 5.

[16] Consistent with the stock-price performance, however, dual-class firms have better operating performance on both trading locations, and both groups perform better when trading on NASDAQ.

[17] Moreover, dual-class firms may have more intangible assets and hence issue more debt to reduce their tax liability.

[18] It may seem peculiar that the median market value of dual-class firms declines and at the same time the median growth rate is significantly positive. One can construct a simple numerical example to show that one scenario that would cause such a result is the following: (1) most firms that lie below the median in year +1 gain value, but not enough to go above the median; (2) most firms that lie above the median in year +1 also gain; and (3) some firms that are above the median in year +1 lose value and drop below. Here (1) and (2) guarantee a significantly positive median growth, while (1) and (3) reduce the level of the median.

[19] At the time of the IPO, the median market value of equity for the 68 matched pairs included on COMPUSTAT is $84.65 mn for the dual-class firms and $65.65 mn for control firms.

Dual Class Shares Firms and Seasoned Equity Offerings: Empirical Evidence from the Swiss Stock Market

Birgul Caramanolis
Rajina Gibson
and
Nils S. Tuchschmid

Lausanne University

Abstract

In this paper, we examine the seasoned equity issuance process on the Swiss stock market. We first investigate whether the neutrality of the preemptive right issuance process is corroborated and, secondly, whether differences in the stock price reaction of dual class shares can be detected. On the aggregate level, we do not detect any significant stock price reaction for the bearer, the registered and the non-voting shares. However, when the analysis of the event's impact on each share category is refined, we observe a positive significant announcement date stock price reaction on the registered shares of partially controlled firms. The latter result emphasises the importance of corporate control valuation and agency cost reduction in the seasoned equity issuance process of dual class shares firms.

1. Introduction

Empirical studies have systematically shown that seasoned equity offerings affect the prices of common stocks, thus questioning the capital structure irrelevance assumption. Abnormal stock price reactions are often detected and can be related to inefficiencies in capital markets, to informational asymmetries, to agency costs, etc... Considering security offerings without preemptive rights (PR's hereafter)[1], three theoretical explanations are generally invoked to explain these positive or negative stock price reactions: the agency cost theory, the signalling or information asymmetry theory and the control and ownership structure based theory of seasoned equity issues.

According to the first theory, seasoned equity issues should have a positive impact on the firm's value since they reduce the agency costs of debt stemming from conflicts of interests between shareholders and debt holders, as has been pointed out by Jensen and Meckling [1976][2]. As far as the signalling theory is concerned, it has been argued (see Myers and Majluf [1984]) that equity issues are costly to the firm due to the fact that the managers' decision to increase firms' equity is perceived by the market as a signal suggesting that the share price is overvalued. This negative market reaction, resulting from asymmetric information, dilutes old shareholders' wealth. According to Myers and Majluf [1984], the stock price decline should be greater the more asymmetric the information between insiders and outsiders. Lucas and McDonald [1990] claim that firms tend to raise new equity when their stock prices are high enough. In a debt and equity financed firm, the signalling theory suggests that good firms will prefer to issue debt rather than equity to finance their new projects. Thus, a seasoned equity issue is perceived as a "negative" signal. Finally, the literature focusing on control and ownership structure considerations argues that modifications of the capital structure, i.e. an increase in leverage, can be used as an antitakeover device among others such as voting trusts, share repurchase agreements, stock pyramids or dual classes shares (see Harris and Raviv [1988]). Debt issues (without carrying voting rights as opposed to equity) enable the management to keep the firm's control in existing shareholders' hands. For instance, if the shareholders are not in favour of a management change, an equity issue would have a negative impact on the stock prices of firms that are susceptible to face hostile takeovers since the issue diffuses the ownership. Moreover, the resulting impact can be different according to the fraction of equity owned by the management in place. Indeed, Stulz [1988] finds a negative impact in firms where the equity fraction owned by the management is small. In contrast, an equity issue will have a positive impact for firms displaying larger managerial ownership since it diffuses ownership concentration, thus increasing the probability of a hostile takeover if the shareholders agree with it[3]. These findings are consistent with Jensen and Meckling's [1976] and Leland and Pyle's [1977] assertion that the value of the firm increases with greater managerial equity ownership.

Several empirical studies have been conducted to test the implications predicted by the mentioned above theories. The general conclusion is that seasoned equity issues have a negative impact on the firm's share value (see, for instance, Asquith and Mullins [1986], Hess and Bhagat [1986], Masulis and Korwar [1986], Mikkelson and Partch [1986], Kalay and Shimrat [1987], Hansen and Crutchley [1990]) supporting the signalling hypothesis and the existence of downward sloping demand curves for financial securities. However, most of these studies have focused on seasoned equity offerings without PR's raised in the United States through placing[4].

In most European countries such as Finland, UK, France and Switzerland, seasoned security offerings consist of issues accompanied by PR's and they are generally issued under the firm commitment method. One can also explain stock price reactions to the right issues method for raising equity in light of the theories focusing on agency costs, on signalling and on control and ownership structure. From the shareholders' point of view, PR's provide a mechanism that allows them to protect their wealth since it prevents its redistribution to new investors. Indeed, PR's are similar to options and exercing or selling them should represent a neutral operation for the existing shareholders irrespective of the offering price. From the firms' point of view, PR's prevent, to a small degree, diversification of ownership (particularly in small firms) and the risk of failure of equity financing, due to the settlement of the offering price, is reduced. Moreover, in many European countries such as Switzerland, companies use firm commitment placement procedures undertaken by investment banks. They provide a higher probability of success. A last consideration is about the ability of firms to keep the level of their dividends constant. This is more difficult with the rights issues method since, with a lower issue price, the total number of shares to be issued is higher than with the direct financing method for the same amount of capital to be raised.

The main objective of this study is to analyse the stock price r-action to a seasoned equity issue on the Swiss stock market across different share categories and thus shareholder clienteles within the same firm. Indeed, we wish to acknowledge whether differences in corporate control rights, liquidity degree and therefore differences in information gathering across Bearer, Registered and Non Voting stocks result from shareholder clienteles different reactions to the issue announcement. Our results on the aggregate level indicate that there is no significant stock price reaction and no significant difference across share type for the equity issuance process with preemptive rights on the Swiss stock market. However, when we analyse the stock price reaction looking at firms' specific attributes such as their size or degree of corporate control concentration, we find a significant positive effect for one category of shares, namely the Registered one. This finding therefore questions the neutrality of the preemptive right protection both from a monetary and a corporate control perspective. In addition, it is consistent with Jensen and Meckling's conjecture [1976] about the existence of agency problems among various category of shareholders.

The structure of this paper is as follows: in section 2, we briefly review theoretical and empirical studies of seasoned equity issues with PR's. In section 3, we then proceed with the description of the main features of the seasoned issuance process prevailing on the Swiss stock market. In section 4, we present our sample and the event methodology used to measure share price reactions. In section 5, we analyse the stock price reaction to seasoned issues at the aggregate level. Finally, in section 6, we further investigate the stock price reaction of each share type by analysing whether firm size, ownership structure or general stock market movements (such as "hot markets") may lead to differences in their response. To conclude, we provide a possible theoretical justification for the positive stock price reaction observed in the case of Registered shares within partially controlled firms.

2. Theoretical and Empirical Findings on Seasoned Equity Issuance with PR's

Several theoretical explanations have been provided to explain why firms would issue seasoned equity through the PR's method. First, the rights issues, particularly under the investment bank's firm commitment should solve the conflicts of interest between managers and shareholders and between existing and new shareholders. Managers are no more responsible for possible failure of the issue and shareholders do not bear the monitoring costs of issuance. Secondly, Heinkel and Schwartz [1986] argue that equity financing method is perceived by the market as a signal of firm quality. More precisely, Heinkel and Schwartz [1986] provide a model in which the choice of issuing method conveys a signal about the firm's quality in a world of asymmetric information. In particular, they show that low quality firms prefer to remain indistinguishable in a pool of firms choosing firm-commitment offers and expecting to benefit from uninformed underwriters[5]. Finally, Hansen and Pinkerton [1982] find that firms preferring security offerings than rights issues are different from others in terms of their corporate control structure. They provide an explanation to the use of rights issues in terms of merchandising costs saving since direct costs such as exchange listing fees, registration fees, state taxes are common to both rights and underwritten offerings. Cost saving for rights issues results from the fact that printing and engraving expenses decline as the number of external buyers declines. Moreover, physical transfer of ownership title is simplified with the ownership density and the transfer agent fees decline at the same time. Despite of the cost advantages of rights issues, Hansen and Pinkerton [1982] observe that most US firms use investment bank underwritten offerings method to distribute their shares to the public, a paradox which they associate to the ownership structure of those firms which is very diffused[6].

Although right issues provide considerable advantages both to the firms and to the investors, the market does generally not react significantly positively to the announcement of rights issue offerings (Marsh [1979] and Hachette [1994]), and even sometimes negatively [see, Eckbo and Masulis (1992]). In Switzerland, Loderer and Zimmermann [1988] find that most companies experience, albeit insignificant, positive abnormal returns in the month of the announcement of rights issues thus confirming Marsh's [1979] and Hachette's [1994] empirical findings. Two conflicting reasons may be advanced to explain the weak insignificant positive stock price reactions observed by Loderer and Zimmermann. First, the subscription price is set below the market price and the presence of PR's should prevent wealth transfer from existing to new shareholders. Hence, the decision to raise capital does not depend on whether the firm's stock is over- or undervalued unlike to what Myers and Majluf [1984] suggest. Secondly, since the issue price is known on average forty-three days before the issuance day, it leads to shortened-life of information asymmetry which is consistent with Myers and Majluf's [1984] theory. Briefly described, Loderer and Zimmermann [1988] study rests on monthly data over the period of 1973-1983 to analyse the announcement effect of seasoned equity offerings carrying PR's on the stock prices for 76 rights issues in Switzerland. Their non-parametric test suggests that the number of companies with positive abnormal returns in the preannouncement period and on the announcement date is significant. But positive average abnormal returns during the announcement month are statistically insignificant both for the total sample and the subsamples of voting and non voting shares.[7]

Finally, Loderer and Zimmermann [1988] analyse the relation between the stock market's reaction and the equity fraction issued and the offering's volume. This relation is negative: an increase of 1% in the number of shares issued leads to a decrease of 0.1% in stock prices. Therefore, they find both weak positive returns on the preannouncement and announcement dates and a volume effect on the stock prices afterwards. They conclude that weak positive returns are probably due to the shortened-life of information asymmetries (on average shorter than two months between the announcement and realisation dates) and to the fact that Swiss stocks' demand curves are downward sloping. The latter feature explains the effect of the issue volume on stock prices subsequent to the seasoned equity issues with PR's. To summarise, their results emphasising insignificant positive returns in the month of the issue announcement[8], thus suggest that, at the aggregate firm and share type levels, existing shareholders are protected against wealth dilution.

Contrarily to Loderer and Zimmermann's empirical study [1988], we will mainly analyse price reactions to a seasoned equity issue for each category of shares in order to investigate whether the PR's market valuation fully prevents wealth as well as corporate control dilution across different shareholder clienteles. As by-products of our study, we first rely on a fairly new event study methodology and secondly we extend Loderer and Zimmermann [1988] results with respect to the time period considered, the reliance on daily data and finally the decomposition of the event study with respect to firms' specific characteristics.

3. Description of the Swiss Seasoned Equity Issuance Process

The Swiss stock market is characterised by two main features. First of all, most firms have different types of shares in their equity capital structure. Indeed, for a variety of reasons such as the fear of foreign hostile takeovers and more generally in order to maintain corporate control, Swiss firm can issue Bearer, Registered and Non Voting shares (respectively *B*-shares, *R*-shares and *NV*-shares hereafter). Notice that the *R*-shares can have a lower par value than the *B*-shares while satisfying the one-share one-vote rule. In addition, the latter share category could previously be restricted meaning that their ownership transfer could be denied to some categories of investors. Indeed, the Swiss corporate law explicitly allowed firms to issue restricted *R*-shares meaning that the company had the authority to deny ownership transfer to the buyer of such a share without any specific motivation. Since the revision of the corporate law, in July 1992, Swiss firms must justify the ownership restriction motivation associated to *R*-shares. As of today, three reasons can be invoked to deny ownership transfer[9]. Over the past, when issuing restricted *R*-shares, Swiss companies mainly targeted foreign investors and thereby could completely eliminate foreign takeovers threats. The change of legislation in 1992 has removed this politically invoked argument by Swiss firms that de facto led them to adopt discriminatory policies as far as corporate control transfer is concerned. It is also true that the issuance of *NV*-shares remains a corporate control enhancing mechanism for Swiss firms. In particular, small concentrated ownership companies which are reluctant to open their capital structure to new shareholders had over the past issued *NV*-shares to raise new capital without threatening the corporate control rights and dominant status of existing shareholders.

Another important feature that characterises the Swiss stock market is the legally imposed PR's issuance process. Before the revision of the corporate law in 1992, firms were however allowed to offer new shares without PR's either through their corporate charter amendments or if the existing shareholders accepted the PR's removal at the general shareholder assembly. This "free lunch" in the legislation allowed them to remove PR's from their charters without justification although they generally issued shares with preemptive rights[10]. In other countries such as France and the UK, the opposite tendency was adopted. PR's were legally imposed until 1973 in France and until 1975 in the UK and were abolished afterwards. However, the principle of preemption offering has been reintroduced in the UK with the aid of the Investor Protection Committees. One should also mention that, in Switzerland, like in many other European stock markets -for instance in Germany- firms' primary source of long term financing is their cash flow. For instance, in 1992, the estimated cash flows of Swiss firms accounted for 53'250 millions SFr while the net equity issued represented a net amount of 2'104 millions SFr, that is, 4% of the firms' aggregate cash flow. Moreover, we should mention that the process generally adopted on the Swiss stock market to issue equity is the firm-commitment procedure whereby an investment bank becomes the leading underwriter of the issue. In terms of costs, this procedure leads to underwriters fees and other various commissions which can add up to 3% of the aggregate issue.

Finally, for most share types, with the exception of non voting shares, the system precluded authorised equity issuance. This restriction implied that shares reserved for the purpose of a convertible or warrant linked debt instruments had to be issued at once and kept by an investment bank until the exercise or conversion policy was activated by the investors. This suggests that, in many cases, a fraction of the equity issue was de facto reserved -often without PR's- for such special purposes and not traded on the secondary market over period as long as five years or even more. Thus, we can conclude by saying that, in general, when a Swiss firm issues equity, all types of shares are increased in the same proportions as previously with equal adjusted -for par value differences- subscription prices for each type of shares. Through PR's, the pecuniary rights of existing shareholders will be protected. As far as voting rights are concerned, the same protection is not insured. Indeed, there could be conflicts of interests between the different classes of shareholders since the holders of lower par value R-shares will invest less and still acquire the same voting rights as the holders of B-shares. This argument is valid even if the proportion of each type of share is kept constant in the capital structure after the issue. As for the holders of the NV-shares, they invest in the firm without having any control on the use of the funds raised.

Only recently have Swiss firms begun to question the suitability of maintaining such "divided" capital structure, especially from the point of view of their weighted cost of capital which thereby bears additional liquidity -or segmentation- premia. Since the beginning of the nineties, many large firms, with diffused ownership, have started to simplify their capital structure, returning to a single share category. Some of the results detected in this seasoned equity issuance study may well explain why this policy has been adopted in firms which have a widely diffused ownership and thus less agency problems among their shareholder clienteles.

4. Sample Data and Methodology

In this study, we rely on a sample of 97 seasoned equity issues that took place over the period January 1980 to December 1992[11]. They represent issues stemming from 47 different Swiss companies active in various economic sectors. 55% of them belongs to the services and the remaining to the industry sector. The full description of the sample firms characteristics is reported in the appendix. Most of the seasoned equity issues are concentrated in some specific months as can be seen in Figure 1 below. It shows a clustering of the announcement dates between February and May. This is not surprising given that most companies hold their annual general assembly meeting between March and July. Indeed, according to the Swiss corporate law the decision to issue equity has to be approved by the shareholders during this meeting.

Figure 1

Monthly number of equity issue announcements during the sample period 1980-1992.

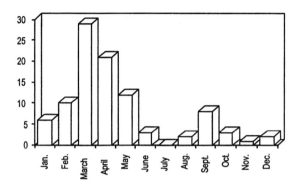

One can also see that a "hot issue" market emerges over the sample period studied as shown in Figure 2. Indeed, almost half of the sample issues (48 out of 97 issues) are clustered from January 1985 to January 1988. Once again, this is not surprising given the upward trend in the Swiss stock market that prevailed prior to the October 1987 crash. This observation is interesting in itself since it leads us to analyse whether liquidity effects could have induced price pressure on the issues concentrated over this period.

As far as the type of equity issue is concerned, three main distinctions are made in our sample. First, it contains 18 "pure" seasoned issues with PR's. Secondly, 37 issues can be called "hybrid" in the sense that a fraction of these issues is without PR's and/or a fraction of the new equity is attributed to special purposes like the exercise of convertibles or warrants as described before. In the two above mentioned cases, the fraction of the issue is homogeneous across share types. In other words, this suggests that if a company had an equity outstanding of SFr 2 millions par value of *B*-shares and SFr 5 millions of *R*-shares, an equity issue does not affect the proportion of each share types on the capital structure. It involves for instance ending up with a capital structure of SFr 7.7 millions after the issue with SFr 2.2 millions of *B*-shares and SFr 5.5 millions of R-shares respectively. Finally, 42 offerings had the property of modifying the existing proportion of each share type in the capital structure, that is, firms issued non proportional amounts of one or more share categories. A typical example is a company whose equity is composed of both *B*-shares and *R*-shares and which decides to issue only *R*-shares with PR's being given to both shareholder categories. This "restructuring" category of equity issues represents 43% of our sample.

As far as the computation of abnormal returns is concerned, we use both the market model (MM) and the mean adjusted return method (MAR)[12]. The parameters of both models have been computed using two business months prior to the beginning of the month preceding the announcement date and using daily continuously compounded returns. The market index selected as a proxy of the market portfolio is the Swiss Bank Corporation market index. It is a market weighted performance based index, the oldest available in Switzerland and it comprises all stocks listed on the three Swiss stock exchanges[13]. All price and thus return series are adjusted for dividend payments. The bearer and registered shares price and return series are adjusted for equity structure modifications such as equity issues with PR's, stock splits or stock dividends while the *NV*-shares data series are unadjusted due to the unavailable information for some of the *NV*-shares issues. As far as abnormal returns of *NV*-shares are concerned, the unadjustment only affects the first execution day returns during which one should observe an "abnormal" negative stock price decline. The theoretical price adjustment method that accounts for the technical dilution associated with PR's issues is generally used on all European stock markets. Therefore, under the null hypothesis that new equity issues with PR's fully protect against any stock price dilution, we should not observe significant abnormal returns for the bearer and registered shares given that their stock price and returns series are adjusted.

Figure 2

Number of equity issues for each year covering the sample period 1980-1992.

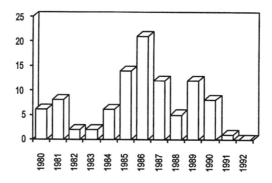

Our event study calendar time ranges from 25 business days prior to the announcement date to 25 business days after the execution date of the issue. We further decompose it into seven event windows described as follows:

- *An25* and *An1* represent two windows prior to the equity issue announcement date consisting of the cumulative abnormal returns observed respectively during the 25 preannouncement business days and during the business day prior to the announcement date[14].
- *Ann.* measures the announcement date abnormal return. More precisely, we compute the cumulative abnormal returns over a two-day interval, that is, ranging from the business day prior to the one after the announcement date.
- For the post announcement date period, we finally consider four different windows: First, we define an intermediate period window (*Int.*) which captures the total abnormal return earned from the announcement date until the day prior to the first subscription day. This intermediary period is of unequal length across firm types but it generally lasts a little bit more than one month[15]. Secondly, we measure the abnormal return from the date prior to the subscription date, i.e. from the last day the stock trades with PR's, to the first day the stock trades without PR's. This

window is denoted by *Ex1*, Third, we compute the abnormal return between the last day the stock trades with PR's to the second day the stock trades without PR's in a windows denoted by *Ex2*. Finally, we analyse the long term abnormal performance of the seasoned equity issues over a window which ranges from the last day prior to the subscription date to the twenty-fourth business day after, *Ex25*.

We use a modified event study methodology in order to account for the heterogeneous nature of the seasoned equity issue process studied. In our case, heterogeneity is associated to the events themselves as well as to the firms' attributes and shares types. Indeed, the seasoning process may itself consist of an issue with PR's and with a proportional increase in all share types or of a non proportional issue with PR's or of an hybrid issue with a fraction of shares raised without PR's. Moreover, the effect may be different given the variety of firm sizes, ownership structures and voting right concentrations observed within our sample. This means that each share abnormal return is related its specific variance as well as to its own attribute such as firm size[16]. More precisely, the methodology we apply first assumes that abnormal returns are normally distributed with zero mean and a standard deviation si measured over a prior estimation period, that is, $AR_{it} \sim N(0, \sigma_i^2)$ Formally, for each of the 97 events in our sample, we thus have the following null and alternative hypotheses:

$$H_0: AR_i \sim N(0, \sigma_i^2)$$

against

$$H_a: AR_i \sim N(\alpha F, \sigma_i^2)$$

where Fi is a weighting factor which allows us to compute our statistics by directly taking into account different attributes such as firm size or the type of the issue. For that matter, we consider the explicative factor, Fi, as a dummy or an ordinary variable[17]. We then standardise the average daily abnormal returns, AR_{it}/T, where T is the length of the window[18], by dividing the latter within each event window by its estimated standard deviation $\sigma_i/\sqrt{T}$:

$$SAR_{it} = \sqrt{T}\,\frac{\overline{AR_{it}}}{\sigma_i}$$

In order to maximise the power of the test, it can be shown that the standardised abnormal returns have to be weighted by the ratio F_i/σ_i. Then, under the null hypothesis one wishes to test, the weighted sum of the SARit is distributed with a zero mean and a unit variance since:

$$z = \frac{1}{\sqrt{T}}\frac{\sum\limits_{i=1}^{97}\frac{F_i}{\sigma_i^2}AR_i}{\sqrt{\sum\limits_{i=1}^{97}\left(\frac{F_i}{\sigma_i}\right)^2}} = \sqrt{T}\frac{\sum\limits_{i=1}^{97}\frac{F_i}{\sigma_i^2}\overline{AR_{it}}}{\sqrt{\sum\limits_{i=1}^{97}\left(\frac{F_i}{\sigma_i}\right)^2}} = \frac{\sum\limits_{i=1}^{97}\frac{F_i}{\sigma_i}SAR_{it}}{\sqrt{\sum\limits_{i=1}^{97}\left(\frac{F_i}{\sigma_i}\right)^2}}$$

such that:

$$E[z] = \frac{\sum_{i=1}^{97} \frac{F_i}{\sigma_i} E[SAR_{it}]}{\sqrt{\sum_{i=1}^{97} \left(\frac{F_i}{\sigma_i}\right)^2}} = 0$$

and

$$Var(z) = \frac{\sum_{i=1}^{97} \left(\frac{F_i}{\sigma_i}\right)^2 Var(SAR_{it})}{\sqrt{\sum_{i=1}^{97} \left(\frac{F_i}{\sigma_i}\right)^2}} = 1$$

Hence, the distribution against which the z-statistic has to be tested is a standard normal distribution and, for large sample, it can be viewed as a t-test with the main difference that it relies on out-of-sample standard deviation estimates. In other words, we standardise each mean abnormal return by its out-of-sample standard deviation estimate instead of measuring the "in-the-sample" single standard deviation in order to take into account heterogeneity across firms and share types. Notice however that we implicitly assume that the seasoned equity issue event does not modify the shares' abnormal return residual variances since we adjust each abnormal return by its historical standard deviation. Patell [1976] suggests to apply a correction factor to take into account the changes in the residuals volatility during the event period. There is also a recent trend in the event study methodology (see, for example, Boehmer, Musumeci and Poulsen [1991], De Jong, Kemna and Kloek [1992], Kryzanowski and Zhang [1993]) focusing on more elaborated econometric techniques to capture changes in the mean as well as in the variance of the abnormal returns induced by the event itself. Although at first sight restrictive, our hypothesis that seasoned equity issues do not modify the variance of the residuals should be judged with respect to its influence on the results. As far as the latter are concerned, we always observed significant statistics associated with high mean abnormal returns and this irrespective of the model chosen to compute the abnormal returns and their variance. Moreover, both abnormal mean return computation methods lead to the same significant results. This therefore suggests that the impact of possible fluctuations in the residual variance is minor[19].

5. The Effect of Seasoned Equity Issues on the Swiss Stock Market

Traditionally, the capital structure literature has mainly focused on the debt and equity holders potential conflict with the firm and its potential consequences on seasoned debt or equity issues. In this context, seasoned equity issues, by reducing agency problems should represent good news within the firm and thus lead to a positive stock price effect. However, empirical evidence from the US stock market seems to detect a negative stock price effect which is however smaller when debt is issued than when new equity is raised by the firm. This negative stock price announcement effect seems to corroborate the signalling hypothesis. According to the latter, good firms would prefer to issue debt whereas bad firms will have no other choice than to issue additional equity to finance their cash flow or investment needs. An interesting feature of the empirical literature is that it has never, since the pioneering paper of Jensen and Meckling [1976], addressed the problem of seasoned equity issuance under the hypothesis that there may as well exist conflicts of interest among different types of shareholders categories in the firm. For that matter, the Swiss stock market offers an ideal framework for studying and testing whether there exist agency problems among the owners of respectively Bearer, Registered and Non Voting shares issued by the same firm. It allows us to go a step beyond the traditional seasoned debt versus equity announcement effect by investigating whether the impact of raising additional equity is homogeneous for shares which embody different types of ownership and corporate control rights.

In this respect, it is interesting to recall that, based on a different sample period and on a different event study methodology, the study by Loderer and Zimmermann [1988] shows no significant price effect for the aggregated share categories. However, one additional and interesting aspect of Swiss corporations capital structure which has so far been left unexplored is that, even after adjusting for equal par value, Bearer, Registered and Non Voting shares may not confer the same corporate control benefits to their respective shareholders. In addition, the value of corporate control per share may not be perceived equally by potential and existing shareholders in our sample of firms. For instance, if a corporation is already owned by a majority shareholder, one may expect that the value of corporate control embodied in a single R-share traded on the stock market will be small whereas it may be highly valued within a corporation where one or several coalitions of minority shareholders play a dominant role (see, Zingales [1992]). When new equity is issued, the situation may change since we have to account for the desire or willingness of existing shareholders to maintain or increase their controlling position. In this case, one should reexamine the PR's neutrality hypothesis whenever the new issue may reduce their position in the high voting power shares. Our conjecture is that, if there is a difference in the pre or post announcement stock price reaction across share types, this could suggest that these reactions convey additional information about the corporate control privileges and the degree of liquidity associated to different share types. More precisely, the main hypothesis tested in this study is that in corporations where control is highly valued, existing shareholders will, all else being equal, at least try to maintain their dominant position when issuing new equity. This could create a positive price reaction on the R-share category since the latter generally conveys the highest corporate control privileges to its owners. Table 1 gives the mean abnormal returns for the aggregate firms' sample equity issues that occurred on the Swiss stock market between 1980 and 1992. The results and their associated z-statistics are computed for both the market model and mean adjusted abnormal returns[20].

Looking at the results per share category, that is, B-shares, R-shares and NV-shares, we observe that they corroborate the null hypothesis of a neutral stock price reaction for preemptive right seasoned equity issues. The only noticeable exception is the negative stock price reaction for the NV-shares with high z-statistics of -4.134 and -3.362 respectively. As far as the NV-share price reaction is concerned, since it is only clustered on the first execution date and since we use unadjusted price series, the negative significant z-statistics essentially captures the pure technical dilution with an abnormal negative return of 4.60%, representative of the average dilution. To further investigate if it is a pure technical dilution one should also look at the cumulative abnormal return over the window Ex2 which should not depart from the first statistics.

Table 1

Stock Price Reaction on the total sample of equity issues

The table gives the daily average abnormal returns (ARt) obtained with the market model (MM) and with the mean adjusted model (MAR) for all the 97 equity issues covering the period 1980-1992. The results are computed on the cumulative abnormal returns 25 days before the announcement date (An25), one day before the announcement date (An1) and on the announcement date (Ann.). They are also computed on the cumulative abnormal returns observed between the announcement date and the execution date (Int.), between the last preexecution date and the first execution day (Ex1), between the last preexecution date and the second execution day (Ex2) and between the last preexecution date and the twenty-fourth execution day (Ex25) respectively. The mean abnormal returns are reported for the B-Shares, the R-Shares and the Non Voting shares (NV).

97 Obs. 1980-1992 Type of Share		Method	An25	An1	Ann.	Int.	Ex1	Ex2	Ex25
B	AR_t	MM	0.0%	0.1%	0.3%	0.0%	0.5%	0.1%	0.0%
	AR_t	MAR	0.0%	0.0%	0.3%	-0.1%	0.6%	0.2%	0.0%
R	AR_t	MM	0.0%	-0.1%	0.6%	-0.1%	0.2%	-0.2%	-0.2%
	AR_t	MAR	0.0%	-0.1%	0.6%	-0.1%	0.3%	-0.1%	-0.2%
NV	AR_t	MM	0.1%	0.2%	0.4%	-0.1%	-4.6%[a]	0.0%	0.0%
	AR_t	MAR	0.0%	0.2%	0.5%	-0.1%	-4.6%[a]	0.1%	0.0%

[a] denotes significance at the level of 1%

This is not corroborated by the price increase that occurs on the second execution day of the issue and which leads the cumulative abnormal return to become insignificant. Given that we only have transaction prices and no bid and ask or volume information in the data base, the results could be interpreted as a substitute for wide bid and ask spreads prevailing just at the beginning of the subscription period, that is, the first transaction price being closer to the bid price on the first day and in the vicinity of the ask price the second day.

At this stage, the stock price reaction observed on the entire sample of voting share categories (on the Registered and the Bearer stocks adjusted price series) needs to be investigated in greater detail before asserting the neutrality of the PR's procedure. To do so, we analyse in the next section the robustness of these first results through the decomposition of the event impact per share category in light of the following attributes: firm size, calendar time, type of equity issues and finally ownership concentration.

6. Further Analysis of the Registered Share Stock Price Reaction

The objective of this section is to investigate whether the neutral stock price reaction is invariant across share types (*B*-share vs. *R*-share), across the firms' sample and across the time period analysed. For that purpose, we first check whether there is any price effect that could be related to firm size. We therefore use the same event methodology as in section 4 but with two different weighting schemes. First, the factor "F_i" is defined as the relative market value of firm "i" in order to give more weight to large capitalised firms. Secondly, "F_i" is defined as the inverse of the relative market value of firm "i" in order to place emphasis on small capitalised firms[21]. The z-statistics, reported in Table 2, show no significant effect neither for the B-share nor for the R-share both in the preannouncement and in the post announcement periods irrespective of the weighting scheme used. We observe however higher z-statistics of respectively 1.17 and 1.12 in the case of small firm R-shares which might suggest that some specific ownership structure factors related to those firms may lead to a positive announcement effect[22].

Table 2

The Effect of Firms' Size on Equity Issue Stock Price Reaction

The table gives the z-statistics of the cumulative abnormal returns obtained either with the market model (MM) or with the mean adjusted model (MAR) when the weight factor "Fi" is the firm "i" total market value and the inverse of the firm "i" total market value resepctively. The z-statistics are computed on the cumulative abnormal returns 25 days before the announcement date (An25), one day before the announcement date (An1) respectively and on the announcement date (Ann.). They are also computed on the cumulative abnormal returns observed between the announcement date and the execution date (Int.), between the last preexecution date and the first execution day (Ex1), between the last preexecution date and the second execution day (Ex2) and between the last preexecution date and the twenty-fifth execution day (Ex25) respectively. The results are reported for the B-Shares, the R-Shares and the Non Voting shares (NV).

97 Observations weighted by firms' size									
Type of Share		Method	An25	An1	Ann.	Int.	Ex1	Ex2	Ex25
B	MM	z-stat	0.122	0.383	-0.283	0.010	0.581	0.317	0.332
	MAR	z-stat	-0.288	0.274	-0.178	-0.120	0.842	0.505	0.371
R	MM	z-stat	0.102	0.402	0.185	-0.353	-0.30	-0.415	0.010
	MAR	z-stat	-0.178	0.334	0.026	-0.622	0.049	-0.098	0.095
NV	MM	z-stat	0.065	0.269	-0.06	-0.034	-2.29^b	0.441	0.118
	MAR	z-stat	-0.194	0.221	-0.11	-0.211	-1.49^d	0.727	0.200
97 Observations weigthed by the inverse of firms' size									
Type of Share		Method	An25	An1	Ann.	Int.	Ex1	Ex2	Ex25
B	MM	z-stat	0.180	0.114	0.253	-0.105	0.718	0.301	-0.032
	MAR	z-stat	0.084	0.047	0.233	-0.164	0.731	0.327	-0.072
R	MM	z-stat	0.328	-0.007	1.178	-0.221	0.529	-0.06	-0.406
	MAR	z-stat	0.222	-0.004	1.119	-0.362	0.533	-0.01	-0.434
NV	MM	z-stat	0.307	0.017	0.408	0.147	-2.33^b	0.365	-0.310
	MAR	z-stat	0.269	0.020	0.349	0.172	-2.07^b	0.421	0.062

^{b} and ^{d} denotes significance at the level of 10% and 20% respectively

We then investigate whether the null hypothesis is sustainable once we decompose the results according to the Swiss stock market trends observed over the entire 1980-1992 sample period. For that purpose, we simply assign different dummy variables to create three subsample periods, ranging from 1980 to 1984, 1985 to 1987 and 1988 to 1992 respectively, so that each of them characterises different degree of activity in terms of seasoned equity offerings (see Figure 2). To do so, the weighting factor, Fi, is simply set to one if, for instance, the seasoned equity issue occurs during the first subperiod and to zero otherwise. Obviously, this methodology is analogous to partitioning our data set across time periods when analysing the stock price reactions. Interestingly, the three subperiods lead to different results reported in Table 3 below.

Table 3

Stock Price Reaction on Equity Issues and Market Trend

The table gives the cumulative abnormal returns and the daily average abnormal returns (ARt) obtained either with the market model (MM) or with the mean adjusted model (MAR) when the weight factor "Fi" is equal to one for equity issues on the sample period 1980-1984, 1985-1987 and 1988-1992 respectively and equal to zero otherwise. The results are computed on the cumulative abnormal returns 25 days before the announcement date (An25), one day before the announcement date (An1) and on the announcement date (Ann.). They are also computed on the cumulative abnormal returns observed between the announcement date and the execution date (Int.), between the last preexecution date and the first execution day (Ex1), between the last preexecution date and the second execution day (Ex2) and between the last preexecution date and the twenty-fourth execution day (Ex25) respectively. The mean abnormal returns are reported for the B-Shares, the R-Shares and the Non Voting shares (NV).

24 Observations: 1980-1984									
Type of Share	Method		An25	An1	Ann.	Int.	Ex1	Ex2	Ex25
B	AR_t	MM	-0.1%	-0.2%	-0.3%	-0.2%	1.0%	0.5%	0.0%
	AR_t	MAR	-0.1%	-0.3%	-0.4%	-0.3%	1.0%	0.5%	0.0%
R	AR_t	MM	0.0%	0.2%	-0.2%	-0.1%	-0.1%	0.0%	-0.1%
	AR_t	MAR	0.0%	0.0%	-0.3%	-0.2%	-0.1%	0.1%	-0.1%
NV	AR_t	MM	0.1%	0.1%	0.5%	-0.1%	-3.9%[a]	0.3%	0.0%
	AR_t	MAR	0.1%	0.0%	0.3%	-0.1%	--3.9%[b]	0.5%	0.1%

47 Observations: 1985-1987									
Type of Share	Method		An25	An1	Ann.	Int.	Ex1	Ex2	Ex25
B	AR_t	MM	0.07%	0.4%	0.8%	0.0%	0.3%	-0.2%	-0.0%
	AR_t	MAR	0.06%	0.4%	0.8%	-0.0%	0.2%	-0.1%	-0.0%
R	AR_t	MM	0.09%	0.06%	1.51[c]	-0.1	0.4%	-0.2%	-0.2%
R	AR_t	MAR	0.05%	0.1%	1.51[c]	-0.1%	0.3%	-0.2%	-0.2%
NV	AR_t	MM	0.0%	0.1%	0.6%	0.01%	-4.6%[b]	0.2%	-0.0%
	AR_t	MAR	0.0%	0.2%	0.6%	-0.0%	-4.8%[b]	0.2%	-0.0%

26 Observations: 1988-1992									
Type of Share	Method		An25	An1	Ann.	Int.	Ex1	Ex2	Ex25
B	AR_t	MM	0.06%	-0.3%	0.0%	0.0%	0.6%	0.2%	-0.0%
	AR_t	MAR	0.04%	-0.4%	-0.0%	0.0%	0.9%	0.3%	0.0%
R	AR_t	MM	-0.0%	-0.5%	-0.0%	-0.2%	0.2%	-0.3%	-0.2%
	AR_t	MAR	-0.1%	-0.5%	-0.1%	-0.1%	0.6%	-0.2%	-0.1%
NV	AR_t	MM	0.1%	0.5%	0.3%	-0.2%	-4.97%[c]	-0.4%	-0.1%
	AR_t	MAR	0.0%	0.2%	0.4%	-0.1%	-4.59%[d]	-0.2%	0.0%

[a], [b], [c] and [d] denotes significance at the level of 1%, 5% ,10% and 20% respectively

Table 4

The Effect of Equity Issuance Type on the Stock Price Reaction

The table gives the z-statistics of the cumulative abnormal returns obtained either with the market model (MM) or with the mean adjusted model (MAR) when the weight factor "Fi" is respectively equal to one for pure, "hybrid" and "restructuring" equity issues and equal to zero otherwise. The z-statistics are computed on the cumulative abnormal returns 25 days before the announcement date(An25), one day before the announcement date (An1) respectively and on the announcement date (Ann.). They are also computed on the cumulative abnormal returns observed between the announcement date and the execution date (Int.), between the last preexecution date and the first execution day (Ex1), between the last preexecution date and the second execution day (Ex2) and between the last preexecution date and the twenty-fifth execution day (Ex25) respectively. The results are reported for the B-Shares, the R-Shares and the Non Voting shares (NV) on 18 observations.

18 Observations on Pure PRs									
Type of Share	Method		An25	An1	Ann.	Int.	Ex1	Ex2	Ex25
B	MM	z-stat	0.408	0.285	-0.241	-0.115	0.481	0.563	0.500
	MAR	z-stat	0.246	0.192	-0.253	-0.116	0.437	0.554	0.495
R	MM	z-stat	0.115	0.096	0.123	-0.055	0.303	0.073	0.018
	MAR	z-stat	0.232	0.063	0.026	0.041	0.357	0.162	0.235
NV	MM	z-stat	0.031	-0.009	0.294	-0.208	-2.24^b	-0.117	0.443
	MAR	z-stat	-0.059	0.105	0.224	-0.078	-1.99^b	0.000	0.517

37 Observations on "Hybrid" issues									
Type of Share	Method		An25	An1	Ann.	Int.	Ex1	Ex2	Ex25
B	MM	z-stat	-0.154	0.213	0.206	0.083	0.702	0.795	0.240
	MAR	z-stat	-0.534	0.142	0.221	-0.148	0.700	0.867	0.096
R	MM	z-stat	0.140	0.197	0.503	-0.563	-0.154	-0.255	-0.297
	MAR	z-stat	-0.196	0.105	0.278	-0.932	-0.100	-0.148	-0.261
NV	MM	z-stat	-0.199	0.415	0.053	-0.132	-3.09^a	0.583	0.007
	MAR	z-stat	-0.372	0.387	-0.042	-0.349	-2.37^b	0.738	0.009

42 Observations on Restructuring issues									
Type of Share	Method		An25	An1	Ann.	Int.	Ex1	Ex2	Ex25
B	MM	z-stat	-0.052	0.040	0.021	-0.350	-0.196	-0.440	-0.360
	MAR	z-stat	-0.158	0.017	0.109	-0.324	0.203	-0.241	-0.288
R	MM	z-stat	0.168	-0.230	1.44^d	-0.160	0.427	0.082	-0.668
	MAR	z-stat	0.055	-0.212	1.42^d	-0.200	0.578	0.198	-0.691
NV	MM	z-stat	0.634	0.094	0.466	0.106	-1.69^c	0.134	-0.255
	MAR	z-stat	0.518	0.040	0.483	0.033	-1.47^d	0.275	-0.238

^{a}, ^{b}, ^{c} and ^{d} denotes significance at the level of 1%, 5%, 10% and 20% respectively.

First of all, we observe that in the first and in the last subperiods, the neutral preemptive right hypothesis cannot be rejected for each share type. Thus, for 50 out of 97 observations, there is no significant stock price reaction to be detected. Contrarily, in the hot issue market of 1985 to 1987, we observe a positive stock price effect on the R-shares which is significant at the 10% level. These results already speak in favour of our former conjecture in that any significant stock price reaction may be attributable to the owner- ship structure of the firm since it is only detected in the *R*-share segment of the market. Moreover, since the positive stock price reaction on the *R*-shares is only observed in the intermediary time ranging from period 1985 to 1987, it contradicts a learning curve hypothesis. In light of the above results, we clearly need to refine our analysis.

Therefore, the next natural step is to analyse the effect on each share type produced by the different types of seasoned equity issues as defined in section 2. More precisely, we investigate whether the stock price reactions to a pure, a hybrid or a restructuring equity issue will be the same. The significance of the results reported in shows a positive stock price reaction for the *R*-share category when "restructuring" seasoned issues are undertaken. This positive stock price reaction effect does corroborate the previously detected significant results for *R*-shares over the period 1985-1987. Yet, its significance is fairly weak, at the 20% level with z-statistics of 1.41 and 1.44. Two reasons may be invoked to explain the latter result. First, most non proportional equity issues took place during the hot issue market of 1985-1987. Indeed, over that time period, 22 non proportional issues out of a total of 42 were launched on the Swiss stock market. Secondly, since restructuring equity issues aggregate various types of seasoned issues, it is not surprising to detect only a weak price reaction due to compensatory effect in terms of wealth and corporate control transfers across Bearer, Registered and Non Voting shareholder categories.

We finally analyse if the ownership structure and corporate control differences across firms may explain the *R*-share price reaction and therefore isolate the significance of the results across firms with different degrees of corporate control concentration. For that purpose, we run three separate event studies. In the first one, we use as the weighting factor a dummy variable which is equal to one when dominant shareholders hold strictly less than 10% of the total equity of the firm and zero otherwise. The process is then repeated for the two event studies with threshold levels set between 20% and 50% and above 50% respectively[23] We thus decompose our sample into disseminated ownership firms, dominant shareholders owned firms and majority shareholder owned firms.

The results provided in Table 5 show that, for the dominant shareholders firm category, there is a significant positive announcement effect on the *R*-share price. Moreover, one observes that the abnormal *R*-share return at the announcement date is far from being negligible. It is equal to 1.40%/1.50% according to whether the market model or the mean adjusted model are used in the event study methodology. Contrarily, there is no significant effect in the subsamples of widely diffused ownership and majority owned firms. This suggests that when corporate control does not have any additional value on the secondary market for the potential share acquirer, the issue is fairly priced. Indeed, in those two cases, because of a widely diffused ownership or because the firm is already held by a majority shareholder, it is either very difficult to acquire additional corporate control or impossible to extract any corporate control benefits through the issuance of new equity. It is also interesting to observe that in those two extreme categories of firms, it is impossible to gather any valuable information regarding the positive or negative proceeds from the cash being raised.

Table 5

Stock Price Reaction on Equity Issues and Firm Ownership Structure

The table gives the daily average abnormal returns obtained either with the market model (MM) or with the mean adjusted model (MAR. The weight factor "Fi" is equal to one for publicly held firms, for the partially controlled and for the majority controlled respectively and equal to zero otherwise. The results are computed on the cumulative abnormal returns 25 days before the announcement date (An25), one day before the announcement date (An1) and on the announcement date (Ann.). They are also computed on the cumulative abnormal returns observed between the announcement date and the execution date (Int.), between the last preexecution date and the first execution day (Ex1), between the last preexecution date and the second execution day (Ex2) and between the last preexecution date and the twenty-fourth execution day (Ex25) respectively. The mean abnormal returns are reported for the B-Shares, the R-Shares and the Non Voting shares (NV).

57 Observations / Diffused Ownership firms

Type of Share		Method	An25	An1	Ann.	Int.	Ex1	Ex2	Ex25
B	AR_t	MM	0.05%	0.15%	0.5%	-0.1%	0.0%	-0.4%	-0.1%
	AR_t	MAR	0.05%	0.1%	0.5%	-0.1%	0.1%	-0.2%	-0.1%
R	AR_t	MM	0.1%	0.3%	0.6%	-0.1%	-0.3%	-0.5%	-0.3%
	AR_t	MAR	0.0%	0.3%	0.6%	-0.2%	-0.2%	-0.4%	-0.3%
NV	AR_t	MM	0.1%	0.3%	0.5%	-0.1%	$-3.8\%^a$	0.2%	0.0%
	AR_t	MAR	0.1%	0.2%	0.5%	-0.1%	$-3.7\%^b$	0.3%	0.0%

22 Observations / Partially controlled firms

Type of Share		Method	An25	An1	Ann.	Int.	Ex1	Ex2	Ex25
B	AR_t	MM	0.0%	-0.0%	0.3%	-0.0%	1.1%	0.2%	-0.0%
	AR_t	MAR	0.0%	-0.0%	0.3%	-0.0%	1.1%	0.3%	-0.0%
R	AR_t	MM	0.0%	-0.8%	$1.4\%^c$	-0.2%	0.7%	0.2%	-0.1%
	AR_t	MAR	0.0%	-0.8%	$1.5\%^c$	-0.2%	0.7%	0.1%	0.0%
NV	AR_t	MM	0.0%	0.7%	-0.2%	-0.1%	$-9.0\%^b$	-0.5%	-0.2%
	AR_t	MAR	0.0%	0.7%	-0.1%	-0.2%	$-8.8\%^b$	-0.4%	-0.0%

17 Observations / Majority controlled firms

Type of Share		Method	An25	An1	Ann.	Int.	Ex1	Ex2	Ex25
B	AR_t	MM	0.0%	-0.1%	-0.1%	-0.1%	0.7%	0.7%	0.0%
	AR_t	MAR	-0.1%	-0.1%	0.0%	0.0%	0.8%	-0.1%	-0.2%
R	AR_t	MM	-0.2%	-0.6%	0.1%	0.0%	0.8%	-0.1%	-0.2%
	AR_t	MAR	-0.3%	-0.5%	0.0%	-0.1%	0.9%	0.0%	-0.2%
NV	AR_t	MM	-0.1%	-0.4%	0.9%	0.0%	$-4.6\%^b$	0.0%	0.0%
	ARt	MAR	-0.1%	-0.3%	0.9%	-0.1%	$-4.6\%^c$	-0.1%	0.0%

^{a}, ^{b} and ^{c} denotes significance at the level of 1%, 5% and 10% respectively

However, the results for the dominant shareholder category suggest that existing and new shareholders of these firms do not behave neutrally with respect to corporate control valuation. In this sense, the positive stock price reaction of R-shares at the announcement date is not inconsistent with the agency cost reduction theory across shareholder types. Indeed, while the focus of this study is not centred on the potential conflicts between stockholders and bondholders, it raises the conjecture that similar conflicts might also exist among different type of shareholders. This conclusion is partially supported by the fact that the positive stock price reaction is only detected in the dominant (20 to 50 percent) shareholder owned firms while it is not present in the majority owned firms as can be seen from Table 5. Indeed, there seems first to be no wealth transfer across the different shareholder types since no significant negative price reaction has been detected on the other share types. Secondly, the agency cost reduction hypothesis is supported by the fact that the *R*-share price reaction has been detected in the restructuring equity issues which consisted almost exclusively of *R*-shares or *NV*-shares issues. In both cases, they allow existing registered shareholders at least to maintain their degree of corporate control. In this respect, an additional clarification has to be made when providing this agency hypothesis explanation since the positive stock price reaction might also be due to the valuation of corporate control and of its derive perks within the firm. In this respect, it suggests that the theoretical value of the PR's underestimates the mere benefits of corporate control to *R*-shareholders in partially controlled firms. Indeed, we know that R-shares have at least equal or higher voting power than *B*-shares belonging to the same firm and that dominant shareholder firms were over the past financed mainly by registered and non-voting equity. Finally, as a possible additional explanation to this positive stock price reaction, one should mention that it is easier to detect a positive price effect in the *R*-share segment of the market than in the *B*-share one which includes more heterogeneous categories of firms and shareholders. The bearer segment of the Swiss stock market is therefore more liquid and consists also of shares issued by more disseminated ownership firms. Contrarily, *R*-shares belonging to the partially or totally controlled subsample of firms generally refer to family-owned businesses and thus suffer from infrequent trading. All these considerations led us to investigate the announcement effect on each share type and for each seasoned equity issue more closely. This investigation shows that the positive stock price reactions display a lot of variability. In particular, the significant positive *R*-share price reaction within the partially owned firms subsample is noticeably influenced by the 1985 Lindt & Sprungli seasoned equity issue which was undertaken in order to finance an (ex-post) highly profitable foreign acquisition. For that reason, there is no economic justification to remove that seasoned equity from the sample. Even more interestingly, and in accordance with our tested hypothesis, we observe for the latter issue as well a much weaker *B*-share than *R*-share price reaction.

The most interesting result stemming from this empirical study is to emphasise that corporate control and heterogeneous clientele of shareholders may affect the seasoned equity issuance process across firms and share types. In the case of Switzerland, our results do suggest that the issuance of additional equity was beneficial to the *R*-shareholders of partially dominated firms. A further theoretical explanation would be required to characterise the origin of this positive stock price reaction more precisely: is it mainly a proof of an agency cost reduction hypothesis which is sensitive to shareholder types and hierarchy or does it result from an incorrect pricing of the preemptive right of *R*-shares which abstracts from these shares additional corporate control benefits? Notice that these two hypotheses are closely related and that it seems very difficult at this stage to discriminate among them given that when the corporate control structure is not maintained after the issue, additional agency problems will arise within firms with different types of shareholder clienteles.

7. Conclusion

In this study, we examined the seasoned equity issuance process on the Swiss stock market. The objective was to test two main hypotheses: first, whether the neutrality of the preemptive right issuance process is corroborated for the aggregate equity issue sample and, secondly, whether differences in the stock price reaction of dual class shares, mainly *B*-shares vs. *R*-shares could be detected. In the latter case, we further analyse if the stock price reactions could be attributed to agency and corporate control differences in dual-class shares characteristics.

On the aggregate level, the modified event study methodology applied in this paper does corroborate the semi-strong efficient market hypothesis. Indeed, based on a sample of 97 seasoned equity issues covering the time period 1980 to 1992, we could not detect any significant stock price reaction across share types.

We furthermore refined our analysis for each stock type by looking at their price reaction according to the heterogeneity of the event studied. For that purpose, we first study the event according to the firms' size and the Swiss stock market trends. Then, we classified the event into three issue types, namely the "pure", the "hybrid" and the restructuring issues. Finally, we distinguished firms by their degree of ownership concentration. When this latter decomposition was accomplished, the neutrality for the subsample of *R*-shares issued by partially controlled corporations was clearly rejected. Indeed, the significant positive stock price reaction of 1.5% at the announcement date suggests the existence of additional corporate control benefits for registered shareholders in dominant firms. A potential explanation being that the fund raising activity did not interfere with their corporate control position within the firm. The cash raised, essentially through the issuance of *NV*-shares or *R*-shares in non proportional fractions, could be valuably "controlled" and exploited. However, the preemptive right issuance process is traditionally perceived as a mechanism that provides monetary neutrality to existing shareholders. Since it ignores the heterogeneous voting and corporate control rights of *B*-shares and *R*-shares, an alternative, albeit non conflicting hypothesis, to explain the results observed would consist in redefining the PR's presumed neutrality in light of the omitted control differentials across shareholder clienteles in dual class shares firms. In this case, the positive *R*-shares price reaction could be reinterpreted as a positive corporate control "premium" excluded from the PR's theoretical valuation. The latter hypothesis is corroborated by the fact that the positive price effect is only detected on *R*-shares in firms which have neither a majority shareholder nor a diffused ownership. Thus, the dominant firms' *R*-shareholders "collect" a premium in terms of the corporate control "value" charged to new investors at the announcement date. The positive stock price reaction detected on the Swiss stock market is thus consistent with the Jensen and Meckling's [1976] analysis of agency problems within a firm with heterogeneous claimants. Here, this hypothesis testing has been extended from the traditional bond and stockholder agency cost reduction (through the issuance of additional equity) to explicit recognition of shareholder clienteles which might have different and perhaps conflicting interest when equity is raised within dual-class shares. The positive announcement effect on R-share prices detected among partially controlled firms may therefore indicate that their registered shareholders benefit -in terms of corporate control maintenance or enhancement- from issuing additional equity to an extend which is not accounted for by the monetary definition of the PR's value.

These preliminary results on the Swiss stock market finally suggest that any capital structure decision should also be analysed and valued by shareholders' clienteles in light of its repercussion on their relative corporate control privileges within the firm. In

Switzerland, this was essentially applicable during the eighties to moderate size firms owned by dominant shareholders who placed more emphasis on the preservation of their corporate control than on the opening -and thus greater liquidity- of their firm's capital structure. Finally, it would be interesting to extend this study to other European stock markets, in order to investigate whether corporate control valuation differentials can be detected from seasoned equity issuance heterogeneous stock price reactions within dual class share firms.

Appendix: Sample Firms' Main Characteristics

The table lists the firms included in our sample with their main economic sector and their maket value in percentage of the total Swiss stock market capitalisation in June 1992[†].

Company	Sector	Market Value	No of offerings
Adia	Services	0.27%	2
Alusuisse	Aluminium	0.75%	1
Atel	Utility	0.27%	1
Baloise	Insurance	0.77%	1
BBC	Engineering	2.60%	3
Bernoise	Insurance	0.19%	2
Biber	Paper Industry	0.04%	2
BPS	Banking	0.43%	2
Bobst	Machinery	0.36%	1
BSI	Banks	0.34%	2
Crossair	Transport	0.05%	3
CS	Banks	3.27%	3
Electrowatt	Utility	0.72%	2
Feldschlosschen	Beverages	0.16%	1
Fischer	Machinery	0.23%	3
FM Laufenburg	Utility	0.11%	1
Forbo	Building Industry	0.26%	3
Globus	Dept. Store	0.16%	2
Helvetia	Insurance	0.42%	1
Hero	Food	0.28%	1
Holderbank	Cement	0.89%	2
Hurliman	Beverages	0.09%	1
Intersport	Retail trade	0.01%	1
Jacob Suchard	Food	-.-	4
Jelmoli	Dept. Store	0.17%	1
Konsumverein	Retail trade	0.09%	3
Landis & Gir	Engineering	0.33%	2
Lindt Sprungli	Food	0.16%	3
Maag	Machinery	0.02%	1
Merkur	Retail trade	0.39%	3
Mikron	Machinery	0.03%	2
Movenpick	Hotel Industry	0.13%	4
Nestl	Food	13.50%	1
Oerlikon BŸrhle	Machinery	0.33%	1
R assurances	Insurance	2.02%	2
Roche	Chemicals	11.18%	1
Sandoz	Chemicals	7.62%	1
SBS	Banking	3.48%	6
Sibra	Beverages	0.08%	1
SIG	Machinery	0.18%	1
Sika	Chemicals	0.22%	2
Sulzer	Machinery	0.71%	2
Swissair	Transport	0.58%	3
UBS	Banking	6.60%	5
Von Roll	Machinery	0.14%	2
Winthertur	Insurance	1.93%	2
Zurich	Insurance	3.01%	3

† In mid-June 1992, 401 Swiss firms were quoted on the Swiss stock Exchange for a total market value of 271 billions Swiss francs.

Acknowledgement

We are grateful to Lucien Gardiol for his helpful assistance. We also thank the editor Mario Levis, two anonymous referees and participants at the 1995 International ARRI Conference in Finance for their comments and advice. We acknowledge fanancial support from the Swiss National fund for Scientific Research.

References

Asquith, Paul and David Mullins, 1986, Equity issues and offering dilution, Journal of Fnancial Economics 15, 61-89.

Bergström, Clas and Kristian Rydqvist, 1990, Ownership of equity in dual-class firms, Journal of Banking and Finance 14, 255-269.

Bhagat, Sanjai, 1983, The effect of preemptive right amendments on shareholder wealth, Journal of Financial Economics 12, 289-310.

Bhide, Amar, 1993, The hidden costs of stock market liquidity, Journal of Financial Economics 34, 31-53.

Boehmer, Ekkehart, Jim Musumeci and Annette Poulsen, 1991, Event study methodology under conditions of event-induced variance, Journal of Financial Economics, vol 30, N0 2, 253-272.

Carter, Richard and Steven Manaster, 1990, Initial public offerings and underwriter reputation, Journal of Finance, v.45 n.4, 1045-1067.

Chattarjee, Sris and James Scott, 1989, Explaining differences in corporate capital structure, Theory and new evidence, Journal of Banking and Finance 13, 283-309.

Cooney, John and Avner Kalay, 1993, Positive information from equity issue announcements, Journal of Financial Economics 33, 149-173.

De Jong, Franck, Angelien Kemna and Teun Kloek, 1992, A Contribution to event study methodology with application to the dutch stock market, Journal of Banking and Finance, v. 16, No 1, 11-36.

Eckbo, Espen and Ronald Masulis, 1992, Adverse selection and the rights offer paradox, Journal of Financial Economics 32, 293-332.

Fama Eugene and Kenneth French, 1992, The Cross-Section of expected returns, Journal of Finance, v. 47, 427-65.

Franks, Julian and Colin Mayer, 1994, The ownership and control of German corporations, London Business School and Oxford University, unpublished manuscript.

Gabillon, Emmanuelle, 1994, Structure financière optimale et sensibilité informationnelle des titres, Cahier de recherche, Université de Droit, d'Economie et de Gestion, Tunis III, Tunisie.

Gajewski, Jean-François and Edith Ginglinger, 1994, La réaction des cours à l'annonce d'une émission d'actions ou d'ABSA, Cahier de recherche, Université Paris Val de Marne, France.

Ginglinger, Edith, 1993, Augmentations de capital en numéraire: Faut-il maintenir le droit préférentiel de souscription?, Cahier de recherche, Université Paris Val de Marne, France.

Green, Richard, 1984, Investment incentives, debt and warrants, Journal of Financial Economics 13, 115-136.

Grossman, Sanford and Oliver Hart, 1988, One share-one vote and the market for corporate control, Journal of Financial Economics 20, 175-202.

Hachette, Isabelle, 1994, Opérations financières et transfert de richesse, Presses Universitaires de France, Paris, 197 pp.

Haeberle, Rainer and Jacques Pasquier-Dorthe, 1991, La valeur relative des actions nominatives, des actions au porteur et des bons de participation, Cahier du séminaire d'économie d'entreprise et de gestion financière, no 39, Université de Fribourg, Switzerland.

Handjinicolaou, George and Avner Kalay, 1984, Wealth redistributions or changes in firm value, Journal of Financial Economics 13, 35-63.

Hansen ,Robert and Claire Crutchley, 1990, Corporate earnings and financings: an empirical analysis, Journal of Business, v. 63, n. 3, 347-371.

Hansen, Robert and John Pinkerton, 1982, Direct equity financing: A resolution of a paradox, Journal of Finance, v.37 n.3, 651-665.

Hansen, Robert and Paul Torregrosa, 1992, Underwriter compensation and corporate monitoring, Journal of Finance, v.47 n.4, 1537-1555.

Harris, Milton and Artur Raviv, 1988, Corporate governance: voting rights and majority rules, Journal of Financial Economics 20, 203-236.

Harris, Milton and Artur Raviv, 1991, The theory of capital structure, Journal of Finance, v.46 n.1, 297-355.

Haugen, Robert and Lemma Senbet, 1981, Resolving the agency problems of external capital through options, Journal of Finance, v.36 n.3, 629-647.

Heinkel, Robert and Eduardo Schwartz, 1986, Rights versus underwritten offerings: An asymmetric information approach, Journal of Finance, v.41 n.1,1-18.

Hess, Alan and Sanjai Bhagat, 1986, Size effects of seasoned stock issues: Empirical evidence, Journal of Business, 567-584.

Hietala, Pekka and Timo Lšyttyniemi, 1992, An implicit dividend increase in rights issues: Theory and evidence, INSEAD, France, unpublished mansucript.

Horner, Melchior, 1988, The value of the corporate voting right, Evidence from Switzerland, Journal of Banking and Finance 12, 69-83.

Jensen, Michael and William Meckling, 1976, Theory of the firm: Managerial behaviour, agency costs and ownership structure, Journal of Financial Economics 3, 305-360.

Jog, Vijag and Allan Riding, 1986, Price effects of dual-class shares, Financial Analysts Journal, Jan.-Feb., 58-67.

John, Teresa and Kose John, 1993, Top-management compensation and capital structure, Journal of Finance, v.48 n.3, 949-974.

Kadlec, Gregory, Claudio Loderer and Dennis Sheehan, 1991, The pricing of equity offerings, Journal of Financial Economics 29, 35-57.

Kadlec, Gregory, Claudio Loderer and Dennis Sheehan, 1993, Issue day effects for common stock offerings: Causes and consequences, Bern University, Switzerland, unpublished manuscript.

Kalay, Avner and Adam Shimrat, 1987, Firm value and seasoned equity issues, Journal of Financial Economics 19, 109-126.

Kothare, Meeta, 1992, Equity financing: an investigation of the rights offers anomaly, Partial fulfillment of PhD dissertation, University of Rochester, New York, USA.

Kothare, Meeta, 1993, The impact of equity issuance on stock liquidity: Rights versus public offers, Working paper, University of Texas, Texas, USA.

Kryzanoswki, Lawrence, and Hao Zhang, 1993, Market behaviour around stock-split ex-dates, Journal of Empirical Finance, v 1, No 1, 57-83.

Kunz, Roger and Reena Aggarwal, 1992, Why initial public offerings are underpriced: Evidence from Switzerland, Journal of Banking and Finance.

Leland, Hayne and David Pyle, 1977, Information asymmetries, financial structure, and financial intermediation, Journal of Finance, v. 32, 371-388.

Levy, Haim, 1982, Economic evaluation of voting power of common stock, Journal of Finance, v.38 n.1, 79-93.

Loderer, Claudio and Dennis Sheehan, 1993, Seasoned stock offerings and the bid-ask spread, Bern University, Switzerland, unpublished manuscript.

Loderer, Claudio and Heinz Zimmerman, 1988, Stock offerings in a different institutional setting, The Swiss case, Journal of Banking and Finance 12, 353-378.

Loughran, Tim and Jay Ritter, 1993, The timing and subsequent performance of IPOs: The US and international evidence, Working paper, University of Illinois at Urbana-Champaign, USA.

Loughran, Tim, Jay Ritter and Kristian Rydqvist, 1993, Initial public offerings: International insights, unpublished manuscript.

Lucas, Deborah and Robert McDonald, 1990, Equity issues and stock price dynamics, Journal of Finance, v. 45, 1019-1043.

Marsh, Paul, 1979, Equity rights issues and the efficiency of the UK stock market, Journal of Finance, v.34, 839-862.

Marsh, Paul, 1982, The choice between equity and debt: An empirical study, Journal of Finance, v.37 n.1, 121-144.

Masulis, Ronald and Ashok Korwar, 1986, Seasoned equity offerings, an empirical investigation, Journal of Financial Economics 15, 91-118.

Mehran, Hamid, 1992, Executive incentive plans, corporate control and capital structure, Journal of Financial and Quantitative Analysis, December, 539-560.

Mikhelson, Wayne and M. Megan Partch, 1986, Valuation effects of securities offerings and the issuance process, Journal of Financial Economics 15, 31-60.

Miller, Merton, 1977, Debt and taxes, Journal of Finance, v.32 n.2, 261-275.

Modigliani, Franco and Merton Miller, 1958, The cost of capital, corporation finance and the theory of investment, American Economic Review v.48 n.3, 261-297.

Myers, Stewart and Nicolas Majluf, 1984, Corporate financing and investment decisions when firms have information that investors do not have, Journal of Financial Economics 13, 187-221.

Myers, Stewart, 1977, Determinants of corporate borrowing, Journal of Financial Economics 5, 147-175.

Myers, Stewart, 1984, The capital structure puzzle, Journal of Finance, v.39 n.3, 575-592.

Patell, James, 1976, Corporate forecasts of earnings per share and stock price behavior: empirical tests, Journal of Accounting Research, vol 14, No 14, 246-276.

Parsons, John and Artur Raviv, 1985, Underpricing of seasoned issues, Journal of Financial Economics 14, 377-397.

Rawlinson, Mark, 1993, UK rights issues: a step by step guide, International Financial Law Review, 27-29.

Rock, Kevin, 1986, Why new issues are underpriced, Journal of Financial Economics 15, 187-212.

Rydqvist, Kristian, 1992, Takeover bids and the relative prices of shares that differ in their voting rights, Working paper, CEPR, European Science Foundation.

Stulz, René, 1988, Managerial control of voting rights: Financing policies and the market value for coporate control, Journal of Financial Economics 20, 25-54.

Stulz, René and Walter Wasserfallen, 1991, Foreign equity investment restrictions: Theory and evidence, Ohio State and Gerzensee Study Center, unpublished manuscript.

Zingales, Luigi, 1992, The value of voting right, unpublished manuscript, MIT, Boston.

Zingales, Luigi, 1994, The value of the voting right: A study of the Milan stock exchange experience, Review of Financial Studies 7, 125-48.

Endnotes

[1] A preemptive right allows existing shareholders to subscribe to new shares in proportion to their equity holdings before general public at a price below the market value.

[2] Agency costs of debt arise from the undervaluation of bonds when debt holders correctly anticipate that shareholders have incentives to invest in suboptimal projects since they capture most of the benefit if the project succeeds and debt holders bear the consequences associated with a bad project selection because of the limited liability of the shareholders. This phenomenon is less severe in reputationally constrained firms.

3 If the new management has more ability. Thus, shareholders can capture capital gains through the takeover premium.

4 The terms tender offer or direct financing are also used.

5 This means by assumption in their model that expiration market price of the stock is unobservable by neither the underwriter nor the investors.

6 Hansen and Pinkerton [1982] also compare actual issue costs of those firms with costs they would have undergone if they had used rights offerings. In fact, they would have realised an increase in their flotation costs if they had used rights offerings. They conclude that flotation costs of rights issues are significantly elastic to the degree of ownership concentration. However, this conclusion does not strictly signify that highly concentrated ownership firms must raise equity by rights issues. The reason is that those firms would incur risks of non- or undersubscription if the large blockholder is reluctant to subscribe to the new shares. This would lead us to say that if the firm knows that existing shareholders are reluctant, it will not use rights offerings to avoid losing more because of a higher underpricing.

7 However, Loderer and Zimmermann [1988] did not analyse the influence of a given share category offering on the prices of the other categories of shares.

8 See Loderer and Zimmermann [1988] Table 1, page 359.

9 First of all, firms can impose a quota on the maximum percentage of votes per shareholder such that any individual can not benefit from the corporate control rights of his/her additional R-shares. The number of shares exceeding the quota will only entitle him/her pecuniary rights. Secondly, registration can be denied to any acquirer who does not reveal his/her identity and/or the one of the person for whom he /she acts as an intermediary. Finally, in order to keep domestic control on real estate ownership, registration could be denied to foreign investors buying real estate companies' shares.

10 With the new corporate law, firms must provide valid justification for the removal of PR's.

11 Originally, over this time period, 52 companies undertook a total of 231 seasoned equity issues. However, 4 issues had to be eliminated from the sample due to the lack of relevant information about stock prices, announcement and execution dates or due to conflicting information stemming from the three main data sources used (Telekurs, Swiss Stock Guide and various press releases).

12 That is, the abnormal return (ARit) is computed according to:

$$AR_{it} = Rit - \alpha i - \beta_i R_{mt} \text{ and } AR_{it} = Ri_t - \bar{R}_i \text{ respectively.}$$

13 All price series have been provided by Datastream available at the CEDIF, Lausanne University.

14 We also measure and test the significance of the cumulative abnormal returns for windows of twelve, five and two business days prior to the announcement date. Since no substantial differences were observed, we do not report the results which are available upon request.

[15] Our methodology enable us to aggregate the abnormal return statistic even though the length of the period is unevenly spread across firms.

[16] Indeed, the traditional event study methodology which divides the cumulative abnormal mean return by its internal standard deviation clearly cannot provide a reliable t-statistic in this case.

[17] Notice that in a traditional event study methodology, the weighting factor is simply equal to one.

[18] In our case, T is the same for each observation, i = 1, ..., 97, with the exception of the intermediary window (Int.) since it depends on the length of time between the announcement date and the execution date for each company.

[19] As far as the reference model is concerned, one may also argue that using the market model may be criticable especially in light of recent empirical evidence (see, for instance, Fama and French 1992). However, this criticism is mitigated in our case since both the market model and the mean abnormal returns method lead to the same results.

[20] The reader is referred to section 4 for the explanation of the relationship between the z-statistics and the standard t-statistics.

[21] The statistics used for the market values have been collected every year in the Swiss Stock Guide.

[22] At this stage, it would have been possible to use a multiple regression methodology where the mean abnormal returns are regressed on a series of explicative variables like firms' size and ownership structure. Notice however that, compared to the latter methodology, the weighting schemes approach used in this paper leads to the same qualitative results.

[23] The ownership data is obtained from the "Who Owns Whom in Switzerland" annual guide which unfortunately does not provide the percentage of voting rights but rather the percentage of equity held by dominant shareholders (which can be viewed as a lower bound to voting power concentration). A more refined analysis of corporate control according to the identity or status of dominant shareholders could not be pursued due to the lack of information for most Swiss firms on this matter.

The Informational Role of Debt and the Pricing of Initial Public Offerings

Shantaram P. Hegde
School of Business Administration
The University of Connecticut

Robert E. Miller
College of Business
Northern Illinois University, Dekalb

Abstract

The current literature on financial signaling indicates that an entrepreneur chooses a higher level of debt to convey his/her superior information to the asymmetrically informed market. We investigate the following two pricing implications of the signaling role of debt in the context of initial public offerings (IPOs) of common stocks: (1) the expected value (risk) of a going-public firm is an increasing (decreasing) function of the level of its pre-IPO debt; and (2) the expected degree of underpricing and the proportional ownership retained at the IPO are decreasing functions of a firm's pre-IPO debt ratio. Empirical evidence drawn from a sample of 890 non-financial IPOs supports these hypotheses.

1. Introduction

When an entrepreneur knows more about the prospects for a new investment project than outsiders, asymmetric information models show that rational investors (the market) price firm's securities correctly, *on average*. However, the average price set by the market results in the securities of a high-quality firm being underpriced while those of a low-quality firm are overpriced. Consequently, a high-quality firm has an incentive to convey its private information to the market through various means such as: (a) by issuance of securities which are least sensitive to the firm's performance, like low-risk or riskless debt; (b) screening and certification by auditors and financial intermediaries; and (c) signaling by its choice of capital structure, dividend policy and investment policy.[1] The extant literature on financial signaling shows that one of the primary means used by a high-quality firm is debt financing (see, for example,

Blazenko (1987), Harris and Raviv (1990), Heinkel (1982), John (1987), Leland and Pyle (1977), Myers and Majluf (1984), Narayanan (1988), and Ross (1977)).

A widely documented puzzle in corporation finance is the underpricing of IPOs of common stocks by the issuing firms. The available evidence indicates that a firm sets the offering price of its IPO more than ten percent (on average) below the subsequent initial market price (see Smith (1986)). Rock (1986) attributes this phenomenon to informational frictions between informed and uninformed investors in the IPO market. In his model, a firm underprices the IPO to compensate uninformed investors for their expected loss on new issue subscription. The available empirical evidence in Beatty and Ritter (1986), Koh and Walter (1989), and Levis (1990) support Rock's winner's curse model. In contrast, Allen and Faulhaber (1989), Grinblatt and Hwang (1989), and Welch (1989) develop signaling models in which a high-quality firm underprices the IPO in order to distinguish itself from a low-quality firm, so that it could make subsequent stock offerings at its true value.[2]

Neither the winner's curse model nor the underpricing signal models examine the role of capital structure signaling by firms going public. Our objective is to integrate the two strands of literature on IPO underpricing and signaling by the choice of capital structure. Drawing from the capital structure signaling theory, we argue that the owner of a high-quality firm uses a larger amount of debt prior to going public to convey the firm's superior prospects to the market. A larger pre-IPO leverage ratio serves as a credible signal of firm quality because it raises the risk of his/her underdiversified stock ownership. We empirically examine the informational effects of the level of pre-IPO debt: (1) on the value and risk of a firm as assessed by the less informed market (external assessment) at the IPO; and (2) on the choice of other signals such as the degree of underpricing and fraction of ownership retained (internal assessment) by the owner at the IPO. Specifically, the two external assessment hypotheses we test are: the higher the level of pre-IPO debt chosen by a firm (a) the higher the expected value and (b) the lower the variance of returns on assets. The two internal assessment hypotheses examined are: the higher the pre-IPO debt-to-assets ratio (a) the lower the expected fraction of ownership retained and (b) the lower the expected degree of underpricing by the owner at the IPO. These two internal assessment hypotheses allow us to make a strong case that the alternative tax-based and winner's curse explanations do not provide, by themselves, a completely satisfactory account of the role of debt financing.

We use a sample of 890 non-financial IPOs drawn from 1981-85 to test these hypotheses. Consistent with the external assessment hypotheses, our cross-sectional results indicate that the aggregate market value of the firm varies directly with the amount of pre-IPO debt, while the standard deviation of its returns is negatively related to the pre-IPO debt ratio. More importantly, as predicted by the internal assessment hypotheses, both the fraction of ownership retained and the degree of underpricing vary inversely with the pre-IPO debt ratio.

We are the first to study the signaling role of debt in pricing IPOs. Perhaps closest in spirit to ours are studies by James and Wier (1990) and Slovin and Young (1990). James and Wier focus on the existence of borrowing (bank as well as non-bank) relationships, whereas Slovin and Young are concerned with the presence of bank debt and/or lines of credit in the capital structure of a firm prior to IPO. Both studies conclude that the existence of the specified debt relationship lowers the underpricing of IPOs. Our study is distinguished from these papers in several ways. Our primary motivation is capital structure signaling; that is, the firm's choice of debt level signals the expected value as well as the risk of a project. James and Wier and Slovin and Young test a related hypothesis that borrowing relations provide a signal about a firm's risk. Their empirical tests rely on a *binary variable* to represent the presence of a specific type of debt relationship, whereas we examine the role of the *amount* of total debt. They investigate the impact of the existence of borrowing relationships on IPO underpricing. We examine the role of debt in explaining not only the degree of IPO underpricing but also the fraction of ownership retained as well as how debt signals the value and risk of the firm. While doing so, we control for other signals such as the quality of investment banker and auditor and general market conditions. Finally, we use a much larger sample of 890 IPOs in contrast to 549 IPOs of James and Wier and 166 IPOs of Slovin and Young.

Furthermore, our results are consistent with the information effects of debt level changes in Cornett and Travlos (1989) and Masulis (1983), who find that the announcement of debt-for-equity exchange offers by seasoned firms leads to abnormal stock price increases. But our favorable evidence on the signaling role of debt is in sharp contrast to the findings of Eckbo (1986), James (1987) and Mikkelson and Partch (1986). These studies report that the announcement of straight debt offerings (public as well as private) has non-positive price effects on the common stocks of seasoned firms.

The rest of the paper is organized as follows. In Section 2 we discuss three hypotheses regarding the effects of pre-IPO debt on the expected value of the firm, its risk, degree of underpricing, and ownership retention. Section 3 describes the sample and measurement of variables. Empirical results are presented in Section 4. We conclude the paper with a summary of findings in Section 5.

2. Testable Hypotheses

The launching of a new business venture represents a classic case of extreme informational frictions between a firm and outsiders (the capital market). The firm's insiders—the entrepreneur, key employees and venture capitalists—possess private information about the expected value and variance of payoffs of the project. Invariably, the first external source of financing the owner-manager taps is private debt in the form of trade credit and short-term loans. Subsequently, as the firm contemplates going public with a new equity issue, the entrepreneur selects an auditor and an investment banker. Finally, at the time of going public, the insiders make at least two important decisions, the fraction of ownership retained and the offer price of the new stock issue. The current literature indicates that through these actions and decisions the owner of a high-quality firm seeks to convey his/her inside information in order to minimize the underpricing of the firm's securities by the market. In this section we examine: (a) how rational outsiders infer the value and riskiness of the firm from the observable level of its pre-IPO debt; and (b) how the owner accounts for the pre-IPO debt ratio in choosing the fraction of ownership retained and the offer price of the new stock issue (or equivalently its degree of underpricing (see Grinblatt and Hwang, 1989)).

2.1 Debt and Firm Quality

In a perfect and frictionless world, Modigliani and Miller (1958) show that the value of the firm is invariant with respect to its debt-to-assets ratio, given the investment policy of the firm. In such a world, the expected return on the firm's assets is a weighted average of expected returns on its equity and risky debt, where the weights are given by the proportional market values of equity and debt, respectively. Also, the beta of the firm's assets is a weighted average of the betas of its equity and risky debt (see Galai and Masulis (1976) and Hamada (1972)).

The current literature on capital structure identifies at least five sources of frictions that cause the expected value and risk of the firm to be related to the amount, default risk and maturity of its debt. These market imperfections are taxes and bankruptcy costs, capital raising costs, agency costs, corporate control, and asymmetric information. Several of these frictions are less important in the context of IPOs than in a seasoned firm because of the substantial ownership stake of the owner-manager in an IPO. For instance, in our sample the average ownership retention at the IPO is 69 percent. Since the degree of separation between ownership and management is quite low in an IPO firm, agency problems discussed by Grossman and Hart (1982), Harris and Raviv (1990), and Jensen and Meckling (1976) have less effect on its capital structure decision. Further, given its above-average growth prospects, a new firm has much less free cash flow and the attendant managerial entrenchment problem (Stultz (1990)).

Perhaps the more important capital market imperfections in the context of IPOs are taxes and asymmetric information. In the tax-based theories of DeAngelo and Masulis (1980) and Masulis (1980, 1983), the expected value of the firm is maximized when the marginal expected gain from debt tax shields equals the marginal expected loss from bankruptcy costs (also see Miller (1977)). Further, an increase in the variability of firm's earnings reduces the expected value of debt tax shields while raising the probability of incurring the costs of financial distress. This suggests that, as in Bradley, Jarrell, and Kim (1984) and Myers (1984), the optimal debt ratio is negatively related to the volatility of the firm's earnings if the costs of financial distress are significant.

In the face of asymmetric information, a high-quality firm uses debt for two different reasons (see Harris and Raviv (1991)). The first is to mitigate inefficiencies in its investment decisions (i.e., the under- or over-investment problem) due to the information asymmetry. In Myers and Majluf (1984), a firm will reject even positive net present value projects if it has to issue equity that is severely underpriced by the market. It prefers to issue debt because debt is more accurately priced. In their model, the firm does not use debt as a signal of value, but the market interprets the debt issue as "good news". Narayanan (1988) develops a model in which debt reduces the over-investment problem (i.e., a case where even negative net present value projects will be accepted) relative to all equity financing. Brennan and Kraus (1987), Constantinides and Grundy (1989), and Noe (1988) show that a firm does not always prefer to issue straight debt over equity and that the underinvestment problem can be resolved through signaling by a wider set of financial securities. However, in Noe's model the quality of firms issuing debt is on average higher than those issuing equity.

The second reason why a high-quality firm prefers debt to equity is to signal its private information to the market. Ross (1977) develops a financial incentive signaling model in which a manager has inside information about firm's prospects. In this model, managerial compensation is tied to firm's performance. The manager stands to gain if the firm's securities are priced higher by the market but is penalized in the event of firm's bankruptcy. The manager has an incentive to signal his/her firm's higher quality by choosing a higher level of debt. Leland and Pyle (1977) show that the entrepreneur uses a higher ownership retention and debt level to signal the value of a project.[3] In Heinkel's (1982) costless signaling equilibrium model, the amount of debt used by a firm varies directly with its intrinsic value. John (1987) considers a case in which a firm faces both information asymmetry about its quality and the agency problem. In his agency signaling equilibrium, the optimal amount of debt chosen by the firm reveals its true quality to the market. His model shows that the higher the amount of debt, the more favorable the signal.[4] Finally, Diamond (1984) and Fama (1985) suggest that debt allows a firm to share its inside information privately with financial intermediaries, whose monitoring serves to mitigate information asymmetry about the business strategy and managerial quality of the firm.

To focus on the signaling role of debt, consider a world without taxes where the owner holds private information about the expected value and standard deviation of returns on a firm's assets. Define a high-quality firm as one with a high expected return or a low standard deviation of returns on assets or both. Since the less informed market assigns an average value, a high-quality firm finds the expected return on its assets underestimated while the standard deviation of returns is overestimated, with the result that the market value is below its intrinsic value. To mitigate this problem, Leland and Pyle (1977) show that, independent of possible bankruptcy costs, a firm with a riskier return will have a lower optimal debt level.[5] James and Wier (1990) observe that low-risk firms signal their type by borrowing prior to IPO. In Grinblatt and Hwang (1989), the firm underprices its IPO to signal its low risk, whereas in Hughes (1986) the owner retains a larger fraction of the firm to reveal the low standard deviation of returns.

We argue that prior to going public the owner of a high-quality firm uses debt to signal inside information about the expected value and standard deviation of returns on assets. A larger debt ratio allows the owner of a high-quality firm to increase the expected return on equity. It is a credible signal of firm quality because the risk of undiversified stockholdings of the owner increases with leverage, which serves to deter mimicking by low-quality firms. Moreover, in the signaling models of Allen and Faulhaber (1989), Grinblatt and Hwang (1989), and Welch (1989), the probability that the true quality of the firm will be revealed by nature between the initial and subsequent offerings plays an important role. The pre-IPO debt acts as a proxy for revelation probability because the larger the debt the greater the probability that outsiders will have the opportunity to detect the firm's ability to service its debt obligations in the aftermarket.[6]

Based on the foregoing discussion, we propose the following two hypotheses on the relationship between debt and firm quality:

HYPOTHESIS 1:   *The risk of a going-public firm is a decreasing function of its pre-IPO debt ratio.*

HYPOTHESIS 2:   *The expected value of a going-public firm is an increasing function of the level of its pre-IPO debt.*

2.2. Tradeoffs Between Signals

Besides debt, a firm uses at least two more pre-IPO signals to convey its inside information to the market. These are the choice of an investment banker and of an auditor. Titman and Trueman (1986) show that an entrepreneur with favorable information about the expected value of the firm chooses a higher quality auditor and investment banker than another with less favorable information.[7] Moreover, in Allen and Faulhaber (1989), Grinblatt and Hwang (1989), Hughes (1986), Leland and Pyle (1977), and Welch (1989), the owner chooses the degree of underpricing and fraction of ownership retained to signal firm quality at the time of IPO.

Since these signals are costly to the firm, we would expect a tradeoff between the three pre-IPO and the two IPO signals. Specifically, a high-quality firm that has already issued stronger pre-IPO signals in the form of a higher debt ratio and higher quality of investment banker and auditor will find that such a strategy diminishes the expected marginal benefits of the two IPO signals—degree of underpricing and ownership retention.[8] This suggests that a firm with higher levels of the pre-IPO signals will choose lower levels of underpricing and ownership retention. This leads us to our final hypothesis:

HYPOTHESIS 3:   *The expected degree of underpricing and the fraction of ownership retained at the IPO are decreasing functions of a firm's pre-IPO debt ratio and the quality of its investment banker and auditor.*

3. The Sample and Measurements

Our sample is drawn from the five-year period of 1981-85. It consists of firm commitment equity IPOs on the over-the-counter market with a first-day closing bid price of at least a dollar per share. We exclude IPOs by financial corporations because governmental guarantees and regulation may affect their capital structure decisions.[9] Data on the amount of debt, offer price, number of shares offered, investment banker, auditor, and overallotment option are taken from *Going Public: The IPO Reporter*. The aftermarket data are taken from the CRSP NASDAQ file. These selection criteria produced a sample of 890 IPOs with complete data.

As in Downes and Heinkel (1982) and Ritter (1984), we use post-market value of equity (i.e., number of shares outstanding times the first day average of closing bid and ask prices) to represent firm value, V. The standard deviation of daily stock returns over the first 15 trading days in the aftermarket is used as a proxy for total risk, σ of a firm. The quality of investment banker, I is measured by a binary variable based on their reputation. Following Hayes (1971), we consider the "bulge" group underwriters as high quality and assign them a value of 1; others are assigned a zero value[10] Likewise, the Big Eight auditors, A, are thought of as high quality and assigned a unitary value and the rest a zero value.[11]

The aggregate amount of debt, D used by the firm prior to going public is measured by its book value.[12] The debt ratio, DR is computed as book value of debt divided by the sum of debt and post-market value of equity, V.[13] The fractional ownership retained by the entrepreneur, α is defined as the number of shares retained (after adjusting for the secondary offering) divided by the total number of shares outstanding post issue.[14] Consistent with previous studies, the degree of underpricing, U is represented by the difference between the first day closing bid and the offer price divided by the offer price.

4. Empirical Analysis

In this section we present descriptive statistics on the signals and their determinants. This is followed by tests of the three hypotheses.

Of the total sample of 890 IPOs, 53 are underwritten by high-quality (i.e., "bulge" bracket) investment bankers, while 691 are audited by high-quality (i.e., Big Eight) auditors. From panel A of Table 1, the mean post-market value of equity is $65 million with an average standard deviation of daily aftermarket stock returns of 3.12 percent. The average debt level is $15 million, which translates to an average debt ratio of 17.86 percent. On average, the owners retain 69.2 percent of the firm and offer a discount (underpricing) of 9.14 percent in our sample. The average age of firms at the IPO is 11.8 years.

Panel B presents pair-wise correlations among the variables. Notably, the estimates of simple correlations of: (a) V and the signals D, I, A, α, and U are positive; (b) σ and the signals D, I, A, and α are negative, while that of σ and U are positive; and (c) the pre-IPO signals D, I and A and the IPO signal $U(\alpha)$ are negative (positive). Since the three hypotheses are concerned with partial correlations, we now turn to multivariate analysis of the relationship among firm value, risk, and the signals.

As noted before, the firm's signals, represented by D (or DR), I and α and the market's inference of V and σ are not simultaneous events. The firm chooses first the level of debt, followed by the quality of investment banker and auditor, and finally decides on the degree of underpricing and ownership retention. The market infers the value and risk of the firm after observing these signals. Therefore, it is essential to control for other signals in evaluating the informational role of debt.

Our first hypothesis posits that the higher the pre-IPO debt-to-assets ratio (DR), the lower the firm risk inferred by the market. Lacking data on the market value of debt, we use the standard deviation of daily aftermarket returns of equity over the first 15 trading days of an IPO (σ) as a proxy for firm risk. Since leverage increases the standard deviation of stock returns, σ is an upward-biased measure of firm risk. In a cross-section of firms with similar earnings volatility (firm risk), standard deviation of stock returns will be positively related to DR. This implies that our use of σ as a proxy for the risk of disparate firms biases our test against finding the hypothesized negative relationship between firm risk and DR.

As a first step, we present in panel A of Table 2 average values of σ (with sample sizes in parentheses) for quintiles of DR cross-classified by the degree of underpricing, U. Entries in the last row show that the average values of σ fall consistently from 4.05 percent for the first quintile of DR to 2.54 percent for the last quintile. The cell averages of σ confirm that this relationship obtains with minor exceptions even after controlling for U.

Table 1

Summary Statistics

Panel A of this table reports cross-sectional means and standard deviations of several variables for a sample of 890 over-the-counter initial public offerings (IPO) of non-financial common stocks during 1981-85. The post-market value of equity, V, is based on the first day average of closing bid and ask stock prices. σ denotes standard deviation of daily stock returns over the first 15 trading days. Debt is measured as the book value of total debt, and debt ratio is the ratio of debt to assets $(=D + V)$. U represents the percentage difference between the first day closing bid price and offer price of an IPO. denotes cumulative daily returns on the NASDAQ Composite Index over 20 trading days preceding an IPO and σ^M is the standard deviation of market returns over 5 trading days prior to an IPO. Panel B presents the correlation matrix. A stands for auditor quality with value equal to one for Big Eight auditors and zero otherwise. I denotes investment banker quality with a value equal to one for "bulge" bracket underwriters and zero otherwise.

A. Means and Standard Deviations

Variables	Mean	Standard Deviation	Variables	Mean	Standard Deviation
1. Post-Market of Equity	65.00	104.00	7. Ownership Retension	69.20	11.31
2. Standard Deviation of Daily Aftermarket IPO Returns $(\sigma,\%)$	3.12	1.70	8. Degree of Underpricing $(U,\%)$	9.14	17.18
3. Primary Offering $(OF, \$ \text{ Millions})$	10.25	13.05	9. Average of First-day Closing Bid and Ask Prices	11.52	6.54
4. Debt $(D, \$ \text{ Millions})$	15.00	34.00	10. Market Runup $(MR, \%)$	0.93	4.67
5. Debt Ratio $(DR, \%)$	17.86	15.96	11. Market Uncertainty $(\sigma^M,\%)$	0.54	0.29
6. Overallotment Option $(OA, \%)$	11.07	4.21	12. Age of Firm (in years)	11.80	16.72

B. Correlation Matrix

	V	σ	OF	D	I	A	α	U	MR	M	OA
σ	0.007										
OF	0.827	0.004									
D	0.356	-0.140	0.346								
I	0.234	-0.061	0.197	0.189							
A	0.128	-0.074	0.174	0.084	0.067						
α	0.378	-0.077	0.267	0.116	0.151	0.124					
U	0.063	0.287	-0.014	-0.114	-0.078	-0.101	-0.051				
MR	0.100	0.080	0.090	-0.064	-0.032	-0.006	-0.010	0.215			
σ^M	0.080	0.139	0.063	0.042	-0.002	-0.004	0.033	0.130	-0.101		
OA	-0.067	-0.150	-0.048	0.036	0.040	0.032	0.044	-0.159	-0.098	-0.162	
AGE	0.122	-0.157	0.063	0.209	0.098	-0.003	0.052	-0.081	0.004	-0.015	-0.046

Table 2

Debt Ratio and Firm Risk

Panel A. This panel presents the average standard deviation of daily aftermarket stock returns (σ, which is used as a proxy for earnings volatility) for quintiles of debt ratio (*DR*) cross-classified by degree of underpricing (*U*). Parenthetical numbers denote sample size.

		Debt Ratio Quintiles (*DR*)					
Degree of Underpricing		Lowest				Highest	Marginal
Quintiles (U)		1	2	3	4	5	Means
Lowest	1	3.39	2.95	3.26	2.49	2.45	2.83
		(26)	(19)	(31)	(37)	(46)	(159)
	2	3.27	2.73	2.52	2.56	2.67	2.71
		(33)	(35)	(45)	(52)	(54)	(219)
	3	3.22	2.88	2.74	2.70	2.24	2.68
		(15)	(32)	(25)	(37)	(41)	(156)
	4	4.54	3.25	2.87	3.05	2.71	3.32
		(39)	(32)	(40)	(37)	(30)	(178)
Highest	5	4.61	3.84	4.01	3.26	3.13	4.08
		(65)	(54)	(37)	(15)	(7)	(178)
Marginal Means		4.05	3.22	3.07	2.73	2.54	3.12
		(178)	(178)	(178)	(178)	(178)	(890)

Panel B. This panel reports weighted least squares estimates (t-values in parentheses) for equation (1). The dependent variable is the standard deviation of daily aftermarket stock returns multiplied by the weighting factor of log of (1000 + pre-IPO annual Revenues). *I* denotes investment banker quality with a value equal to one for bulge bracket underwriters and zero otherwise. *A* stands for auditor quality with a value equal to one for Big Eight auditors and zero otherwise. *MR* denotes cumulative daily returns in the NASDAQ Composite Index over 20 trading days preceding an IPO and σ^M is the standard deviation of market returns over the preceding 5 trading days. *U* represents the percentage difference between the first day closing bid price and the offer price. α stands for the fraction of ownership retained at the IPO.

Constant	Debt Ratio (DR)	I-Banker (I)	Auditor (A)	Ownership Retention (α)	Degree of Underpricing (U)	Age	Market Runup (MR)	Market Uncertainty (σ^M)	Adj. R^2
36.77	-0.55	0.78	-0.25	0.52	0.02	-0.10	0.02	0.66	0.17
(10.51)[a]	(-1.92)[c]	(0.23)	(-0.13)	(1.62)	(5.49)[a]	(-2.17)[b]	(1.90)[c]	(3.89)[a]	

[a] Significant at the 1 percent level

[b] Significant at the 5 percent level

[c] Significant at the 10 percent level

To test the first hypothesis, we estimate the following cross-sectional linear regression equation:[15]

$$\sigma_i = a_0 + a_1 DR_i + a_2 I_i + a_4 \alpha_i + a_5 U_i + a_6 AGE_i + O_3 A_3 + a_7 MR_i + a_8 \sigma^M_i + \in_{1i} \qquad (1)$$

In this formulation, outsiders are assumed to infer firm risk from the signals issued by the firm and general market conditions. Both the first hypothesis and the tax-based theory predict that $a_1 < 0$. In Titman and Trueman (1986) and Carter and Manaster (1990), the less risky the firm, the higher the quality of auditor and investment banker chosen, which implies $a_2 < 0$ and $a_3 < 0$ Grinblatt and Hwang (1989) and Leland and Pyle (1977) show that firm risk and ownership retention are negatively related because the cost of signaling by α increases with σ. This suggests that $a_4 < 0$. In Beatty and Ritter (1986), Grinblatt and Hwang (1989), and Rock (1986), the degree of underpricing is an increasing function of earnings volatility because the latter aggravates information asymmetry. Therefore, we expect that $a_5 > 0$. Previous studies show that AGE is negatively related to firm risk, implying $a_6 < 0$ (see Beatty and Ritter (1986), Carter and Manaster (1990), and James and Wier (1990)).

In addition, prevailing market conditions influence the assessment of firm risk. We use two variables to describe the market conditions surrounding a new issue. MR_i denotes the cumulative daily returns on the NASDAQ Composite Index over 20 trading days leading to the ith issue. σ^M_i measures the standard deviation of daily market returns over 5 trading days preceding the ith IPO. Risky firms have an incentive to go public when market conditions are favorable. Further, earnings volatility of a firm is positively related to market uncertainty.[16] Therefore, we expect $a_7 > 0$ and $a_8 > 0$.

Since the error terms in equation (1) are heteroscedastic, we multiply all variables by the natural log of *[1000 + Revenue]*, where revenue denotes annual sales prior to going public. The resulting weighted least squares (WLS) estimates are presented in panel B of Table 2.[17] Consistent with our first hypothesis, the coefficient estimate for is negative and significant at the 10 percent level. Of the remaining estimates, those for *U, AGE, MR* and σ^M support our arguments and the rest are statistically insignificant.

The second hypothesis predicts that the value of a firm varies directly with the level of its pre-IPO debt. As noted before, we use the initial market value of equity, *V*, as a proxy for firm value. Panel A of Table 3 presents average values of *V* (in millions of dollars with sample size in parentheses) for quintiles of debt, *D*, cross-classified by fractional ownership retention, α. From entries in the last row, we find that the average stock value increases consistently from \$20 millions in the first quintile to \$132 millions in the fifth quintile of *D*. The cell averages indicate that this pattern persists within each quintile of ownership retention.[18]

Table 3

Debt and Firm Value

Panel A. This panel reports the average initial market value of equity (V, in millions of dollars, used as a proxy for firm value) for quintiles of dollar debt (D) cross-classified by ownership retention (α). Parenthetical numbers denote sample size.

Ownership Retention Quintiles (Q)		Lowest 1	Debt Quintiles (D) 2	3	4	Highest 5	Marginal Means
Lowest	1	8	16	22	31	65	23
		(64)	(30)	(35)	(26)	(23)	(178)
	2	19	18	31	37	90	34
		(39)	(41)	(42)	(33)	(23)	(178)
	3	17	27	54	55	99	51
		(30)	(39)	(33)	(40)	(36)	(178)
	4	28	68	71	94	105	77
		(24)	(40)	(37)	(38)	(40)	(179)
Highest	5	49	76	104	144	218	139
		(21)	(28)	(31)	(41)	(56)	(177)
Marginal Means		20	40	55	77	132	65
		(178)	(178)	(178)	(178)	(178)	(890)

Panel B. This panel reports weighted least squares estimates (t-values in parentheses) for equation (2). The dependent variable is the initial market value of equity divided by offer size (V/OF), where OF is the weighting factor. I denotes quality of investment banker with a value equal to one for bulge bracket underwriters and zero otherwise. A stands for auditor quality with a value equal to one for Big Eight auditors and zero otherwise. σ denotes standard deviation of daily stock returns over the first 15 trading days in the aftermarket. MR denotes cumulative daily returns in the NASDAQ Composite Index over 20 trading days preceding an IPO and σ^M is the standard deviation of market returns over the preceding 5 trading days. U represents the percentage difference between the first day closing bid price and the offer price. α stands for the fraction of ownership retained at the IPO.

Constant	Debt (D)	I-Banker (I)	Auditor (A)	Ownership Retention $(\alpha, \times 10^8)$	Degree of Under- $(U, \times 10^5)$	Offer Size (OF)	Firm Risk $(\sigma, \times 10^6)$	Age	Market Runup $(MR, \times 10^5)$	Market Uncertainty $(\sigma^M, \times 10^7)$	Adj. R^2
-7.53	1.52	2.11	-0.16	1.50	3.82	0.22	-4.78	0.03	-1.06	-2.21	0.51
(-9.87)[a]	(16.38)[a]	(1.65)[b]	(-0.21)	(15.25)[a]	(6.16)[a]	(0.25)	(-0.74)	(1.64)	(-0.40)	(-5.29)[a]	

[a] Significant at the 1 percent level.
[b] Significant at the 10 percent level.

To further scrutinize our second hypothesis, we estimate the following cross-sectional linear relationship:[19]

$$V_i = b_0 + b_1 D_i + b_2 I_i + b_3 A_i + b_4 \alpha_i + b_5 U_i + b_6 OF_i + b_7 \sigma_i + b_8 AGE_i + b_9 MR_i + b_{10} \sigma_i^M + \varepsilon_{2i} \quad (2)$$

where OF denotes the dollar size of primary offering and ϵ_2 the disturbance term. The second hypothesis as well as the tax-based theory predict that $b_1 > 0$. Titman and Trueman (1986) suggest that $b_2 > 0$ and $b_3 > 0$. The signaling model of Leland and Pyle (1977) and the agency theory of Jensen and Meckling (1976) predict $b_4 > 0$. In Allen and Faulhaber (1989), Grinblatt and Hwang (1989), and Welch (1989), the higher the intrinsic value of a firm, the higher the optimal degree of underpricing, which implies $b_5 > 0$. From the tax-based theory of capital structure, the lower the firm risk, the larger the expected value of debt tax shields and the higher the firm value. This suggests that $b_7 < 0$ and $b_8 < 0$. Offer size, OF, is included because it serves to reduce the effect of heterogeneity of the sample on the coefficients of interest. We expect $b_6 > 0$. Aware of the firm's incentives to time a new issue soon after a market runup, outsiders find it more difficult to distinguish a good firm from a bad one under favorable market conditions. Therefore, we expect that firm value will be negatively related to MR, $b_9 < 0$. Finally, an increase in market uncertainty σ^M lowers the tax advantage of debt and lowers firm value. This implies that $b_{10} < 0$.

As the residuals in equation (2) are heteroscedastic, we deflate all variables by the dollar size of primary offerings.[20] The WLS estimates of equation (2) are presented in panel B of Table 3.[21] Consistent with our second hypothesis and the tax-based theory, the coefficient estimate for   is positive and significant at the 1 percent level.[22] The coefficient estimates for   and   are also strongly significant.[23]

Since the evidence reported in Tables 2 and 3 is also consistent with the tax-based theory of capital structure, it casts doubts on the informational role of the level of pre-IPO debt. However, there are three reasons why we think the signaling role of debt deserves greater recognition. First, both the theoretical and empirical evidence on the tax-based theory is not without controversy. For instance, Eckbo (1986) finds no significant correlation between the announcement period abnormal stock returns and the change in the debt-related tax shield, which is inconsistent with the evidence in Masulis (1983) and Mikkelson (1985). Second, in DeAngelo and Masulis (1980) and Masulis (1983), the expected marginal tax effect of debt on firm value depends among other things upon the probability of full corporate tax shield utilization. If a firm is of high quality, its expected marginal tax effect of debt as well as the optimal debt ratio will be higher, *ceteris paribus*. Therefore, the overall tax effect of debt is indeed the sum of pure tax effect and information-related tax effect. The higher the debt ratio, the larger the information-related tax effect of debt on firm value.[24]

Third, a theory based only on the pure tax effect of debt predicts no systematic relationship between the pre-IPO debt ratio and the degree of underpricing. Under such a theory a high-quality firm will set a high offer price to correspond to the high after-tax value of equity. Therefore, we should expect no systematic variation between the degree of underpricing U and the pre-IPO debt ratio DR. Similarly, in Myers and Majluf (1984) debt does not play a signaling role. Their analysis implies that leverage increases with the extent of information asymmetry. Since the degree of underpricing is positively related to the severity of information asymmetry, their model implies that U is positively related to DR. In contrast, when the choice of debt level conveys information to the market, our third hypothesis predicts that a firm with a higher pre-IPO debt ratio chooses a lower degree of underpricing.

Table 4

Debt Ratio and Degree of Underpricing

Panel A. This panel presents the mean degree of underpricing (U, with sample sizes in parentheses) for quintiles of debt ratio (DR) cross-classified by ownership retention (α).

Ownership Retention Quintiles (α)		Debt Ratio Quintiles (DR)					Marginal Means
		Lowest 1	2	3	4	Highest 5	
Lowest	1	20.50	15.98	10.88	5.61	1.79	9.85
		(36)	(21)	(32)	(45)	(44)	(178)
	2	25.68	16.50	10.95	2.78	3.14	10.59
		(28)	(29)	(37)	(36)	(42)	(178)
	3	19.21	13.33	7.3	4.18	3.01	8.73
		(23)	(43)	(30)	(34)	(41)	(178)
	4	13.22	11.05	7.35	5.75	2.04	8.54
		(43)	(45)	(30)	(32)	(29)	(179)
Highest	5	10.92	9.44	9.47	4.37	1.04	8.01
		(48)	(40)	(38)	(31)	(20)	(177)
Marginal Means		16.81	12.71	9.27	4.57	2.36	9.14
		(178)	(178)	(178)	(178)	(178)	(890)

Panel B. This panel reports weighted least squares estimates (with t-values in parentheses) for equation (3) using $ln [1000 + Revenue]$ as the weighting factor. The dependent variable is the Degree of Underpricing divided by $ln [1000 + Revenue]$. V stands for the initial aggregate market value of equity. I denotes investment banker quality with a value equal to one for bulge bracket underwriters and zero otherwise. A stands for auditor quality with a value equal to one for Big Eight auditors and zero otherwise. σ denotes standard deviation of daily stock returns over the first 15 trading days in the aftermarket. MR denotes cumulative daily returns in the NASDAQ Composite Index over 20 trading days preceding an IPO and σ^M is the standard deviation of market returns over the preceding 5 trading days. U represents the percentage difference between the first day closing bid price and the offer price. α stands for the fraction of ownership retained at the IPO. OA stands for the percentage overallotment option issued to underwriters.

Constant	Debt Ratio (DR)	I-Banker (I)	Auditor (A)	Ownership Retention (α)	ln[Market Value of Equity] (U)	Firm Risk (σ)	Age	Market Runup (MR)	Market Uncertainty (σ^M)	Over allotment Option (OA)	Adj. R^2
12.23	-21.56	-69.85	-52.61	-15.34	1.15	1.72	-0.47	0.65	4.87	-0.23	0.17
(0.27)	(-6.74)[a]	(-2.03)[b]	(-2.75)[a]	(-2.89)[a]	(3.82)[a]	(5.11)[a]	(-0.96)	(6.04)[a]	(2.76)[a]	(-1.92)[c]	

[a] Significant at the 1 percent level
[b] Significant at the 5 percent level
[c] Significant at the 10 percent level

Panel A of Table 4 reports average values of U for quintiles of the pre-IPO DR, with α as the control variable. Marginal means in the last row indicate that the average level of underpricing falls from 16.81 percent for the first quintile of DR to 2.36 percent for the last quintile. As the cell entries reflect, this behavior is quite pervasive. Further, marginal means in the last column suggest that U tends to decrease as α increases. To formally test the predicted negative relationship between U and DR, we estimate the following cross-sectional regression:[25]

$$U_i = c_0 + c_1 DR_i + c_2 I_i + c_3 A_i + c_4 \alpha_i + c_5 ln(V_i) + c_6 \sigma_i + c_7 AGE_i + c_8 MR_i + c_9 \sigma_i{}^M + c_{10} OA_i + e_{2i} \quad (3)$$

where
DR_i = total debt-to-assets ratio
$ln(Vi)$ = natural log of post-market value of equity; our proxy for intrinsic value of a firm
OA_i = overallotment option (%)

The third hypothesis predicts that $c_1 < 0$, $c_2 < 0$, and $c_3 < 0$. In choosing U, the owner is assumed to know all the variables on the right-hand side of equation (3). The relationship between U and α is governed by several forces, some of which conflict with one another. The models of Allen and Faulhaber (1989), Grinblatt and Hwang (1989), and Welch (1989) indicate that a high-quality firm uses a lower offer price and quantity (or equivalently a higher U and α) to distinguish itself from a low-quality firm. In these models, U and α tend to vary together and constitute a pair of reinforcing signals. The higher the degree of underpricing, the more wealth loss per share the owner suffers. To minimize this loss, the owner offers to sell fewer shares initially and retains a larger fraction of the firm, with the result that U and α tend to be positively related. However, in bivariate signaling models there is a substitution effect which reflects a trade-off between the two signals depending on their relative marginal costs and benefits (see Hughes (1986)). Other things equal, the greater the α, the greater the mitigation of the adverse information problem and the lower the need to underprice a new issue. Also, for a given amount of money to be raised, if the firm issues fewer shares (i.e., retains a larger α), the offer price will be higher and U will be lower. Therefore, the sign of c_4 is an empirical question.

Given other things, as the intrinsic value increases, a high-quality firm must spend more on signaling to discourage low-quality firms from mimicking, which implies a positive sign for c_5. Since the degree of information asymmetry is an increasing function of (see Rock (1986)) and a decreasing function of AGE, we expect $c_6 > 0$ and $c_7 < 0$. The larger the MR, the more difficult it is for outsiders to gauge the quality of a firm. Therefore, as MR increases, good firms need to underprice their issues more to deter bad firms from imitating, implying $c_8 > 0$. Further, an increase in market uncertainty aggravates the adverse information problem. This implies $c_9 > 0$.

Finally, the overallotment option, OA, allows an underwriter to issue up to 15 percent additional shares of an oversubscribed issue. Ritter (1987) argues that this flexibility somewhat mitigates the winner's curse problem and thus reduces the required amount of underpricing. In Benveniste and Spindt (1989), underpricing is related directly to the amount of stock allocated to investors who indicate low interest in the issue. Firm-commitment offers give an incentive to investment bankers to presell the whole issue which leads to higher allocations to low-interest investors and thus add to underpricing. In their model, overallotment option is a means of reducing underpricing because it limits the number of shares the underwriter has an incentive to presell and gives him the option to distribute a larger amount when demand is high. These arguments suggest that $c_{10} > 0$.

Since the disturbance term ε_3 in (3) is heteroscedastic, we multiply all variables by ln [1000 + Revenue] and present the WLS estimates in panel B of Table 4.[26] The coefficient estimates for *DR, I, A, ln(V), σ, MR, σ^M*, and *OA* are consistent with our predictions. Notably, the significant negative coefficient on suggests a tendency on the part of issuers to trade-off between the two IPO signals.

These regression results indicate that firms with higher debt ratios set offer prices on IPOs close to their intrinsic values, which results in lower underpricing. This implies that the variance of underpricing for the high-debt ratio group will be lower than that for the low-debt ratio group. To verify this implication, we divide the total sample into two subsamples of IPOs. The low *DR* sample consists of 445 IPOs with pre-IPO debt ratios less than or equal to the median debt ratio for the total sample. The high *DR* sample consists of the remaining IPOs. The variances of *U* for the high and low *DR* groups, respectively, are 117.97 and 424.74 percent. The F-statistic for the difference in variance between the two groups is 3.60. Consistent with our third hypothesis, the variance of underpricing of the high-debt ratio group is significantly (at the 1 percent level) lower than that of the low-debt ratio group.

The third hypothesis also predicts a negative relationship between ownership retention and debt ratio. A larger pre-IPO debt ratio not only reduces the signaling benefit of α, but it also increases the signaling cost of α by increasing the risk of stock ownership. To verify this prediction, we present in panel A of Table 5 the average values of α for quintiles of *DR* cross-classified by *U*. As expected, the average ownership retention drops from 70 percent in the first *DR* quintile to 67 percent in the last quintile. Panel B reports the ordinary least squares estimates of the following cross-sectional regression:

$$\alpha_i = d_0 + d_1 DR + d_2 I_i + d_3 A_i + d_4 U_i + d_5 ln(V_i) + d_6 \sigma_i + d_7 AGE_i + d_8 MR_i + d_9 \sigma_i^M + d_{10} R_i + \varepsilon_{4i} \quad (4)$$

Based on the earlier discussion, we expect that $d_1 < 0, d_2 < 0, d_3 < 0$ and $d_5 > 0$ with the sign of d_4 being difficult to predict. Given the intrinsic value of the firm and other variables, an increase in renders α a more costly signal. Therefore, we predict that $d_6 < 0$ and $d_7 > 0$. As *MR* increases, a high-quality firm needs to raise α to deter low-quality firms from imitating. Likewise, an increase in σ^M worsens informational frictions, which calls for a stronger signal. These arguments suggest that $d_8 > 0$ and $d_9 > 0$. represents *ln [1000 + Revenue]*, and serves as an added control with $d_{10} > 0$.

The results indicate that of the three pre-IPO signals only the coefficient estimate for *DR* has a significant negative sign at the 1 percent level. The significantly negative sign for the coefficient of *U* seems to reinforce the substitution effect between α and *U*. As expected, the estimate for the coefficient of *ln (V)* is significantly positive, but the coefficient estimate for is inconsistent with our arguments. The remaining estimates are insignificant.

Although the tradeoffs between the pre-IPO and IPO signals strengthen the case for the hypothesized informational role of the pre-IPO debt, they do not represent irrefutable evidence in favor of the signaling function of debt. In the alternative model of Rock (1986), the higher the volatility of a firm's earnings, the greater the degree of expected underpricing required to compensate uninformed investors. If we view the

Table 5

Debt Ratio and Ownership Retention

Panel A. This panel presents the mean fraction of ownership retention (α, with sample sizes in parentheses) for quintiles of debt ratio (*DR*) cross-classified by degree of underpricing (*U*).

		Debt Ratio Quintiles (*DR*)					
	Underpricing Quintiles (*U*)	Lowest 1	2	3	Highest 4	5	Marginal Means
Lowest	1	0.71 (26)	0.70 (19)	0.69 (31)	0.70 (37)	0.67 (46)	0.69 (159)
	2	0.72 (33)	0.72 (35)	0.70 (45)	0.70 (52)	0.68 (54)	0.69 (219)
	3	0.76 (15)	0.72 (38)	0.72 (25)	0.68 (37)	0.66 (41)	0.70 (156)
	4	0.71 (39)	0.72 (32)	0.71 (40)	0.69 (37)	0.68 (30)	0.70 (178)
Highest	5	0.68 (65)	0.69 (54)	0.69 (37)	0.67 (15)	0.64 (7)	0.68 (178)
Marginal Means		0.70 (178)	0.71 (178)	0.70 (178)	0.68 (178)	0.67 (178)	0.69 (890)

Panel B. This panel reports ordinary least squares estimates (t-values in parentheses) of equation (4). The dependent variable is the fractional ownership retained by the entrepreneur (α). denotes investment banker quality with a value equal to one for bulge bracket underwriters and zero otherwise. *A* stands for auditor quality with a value equal to one for Big Eight auditors and zero otherwise. *MR* denotes cumulative daily returns in the NASDAQ Composite Index over 20 trading days preceding an IPO and σ^M is the standard deviation of market returns over the preceding 5 trading days. *U* represents the percentage difference between the first day closing bid price and the offer price. α stands for the fraction of ownership retained at the IPO. *Revenue* represents annual sales prior to IPO.

Constant	Debt Ratio (DR)	I-Banker (I)	Auditor (A)	Under Pricing (v)	ln[Market Value of Equity] (ln(V))	Firm Risk (σ)	Age	Market Runup (MP)	Market Uncertainty (σ^M)	ln[1000+ Revenue] (OA)	Adj. R²
-0.325 (0.27)	-0.093 (-6.74)[a]	-0.010 (-2.03)[b]	-0.007 (-2.75)[a]	-0.001 (-2.89)[a]	0.061 (3.82)[a]	-0.002 (5.11)[a]	-0.000 (-0.96)	-0.001 (6.04)[a]	-0.003 (2.76)[a]	-0.000 (-1.92)[c]	0.34

[a] Significant at the 1 percent level.
[b] Significant at the 10 percent level.

pre-IPO debt as a proxy that is negatively related to the *ex ante* uncertainty about firm value, then the observed negative relationship between *U* and *DR* in equation (3) is also consistent with Rock's winner's curse model. In addition, the observed negative relationship between α and *DR* in equation (4) may simply be due to risk aversion on the part of the owner. As leverage increases, the owner may reduce stockholdings because of the greater probability of bankruptcy, not necessarily for informational reasons. However, the strong statistical significance of the coefficient of *DR* even in the presence of σ (and *AGE, I* and *A*) casts some doubt that Rock's model and risk aversion provide a complete explanation of IPO underpricing.

The above evidence extends the results of James and Wier (1990) and Slovin and Young (1990) who find that the presence of borrowing relations reduces the underpricing of IPOs. Although our findings are based on the levels of leverage and firm value, risk, underpricing and ownership retention, they are consistent with the widely documented evidence that an unanticipated change in leverage causes a like change in firm value due to new information (Harris and Raviv (1991)). In particular, these results add to the informational role of debt reported by Cornett and Travlos (1989) and Masulis (1983) in their study of debt-for-equity exchange offers. However, our results are inconsistent with the non-positive stock price response to announcement of private and public straight-debt offers reported by Eckbo (1986), James (1987), Mikkelson and Partch (1986).

5. Summary and Conclusion

IPOs provide a special opportunity to scrutinize the informational role of debt because the choice of debt level is one of the first potential signals issued by a firm prior to going public. Also, given the severe degree of information asymmetry about a firm's prospects, the effects of debt on firm value and other IPO signals tend to be more pronounced and are presumably less difficult to isolate. In this study, we provide additional evidence on the informational role of debt in the context of IPOs. Our results show that the less-informed market infers a higher value and lower risk of a going-public firm, the greater the level of its pre-IPO debt. However, the positive relationship between debt and firm value by itself is not a sufficient evidence because it is also consistent with the tax-based theory of capital structure. To discriminate between this alternative theory and the signaling role of debt, we further examine the relationship between the debt ratio and two additional signals—degree of underpricing and ownership retention—chosen by the firm at the time of going public. This also allows us to test the substitution effect in multivariate signaling which posits that a firm with a large pre-IPO debt ratio and high-quality investment bankers and auditors has less incentive to choose a large fraction of ownership and a high degree of underpricing. The empirical evidence we report is largely consistent with such a trade-off between the pre-IPO and IPO signals. This leads us to conclude that the alternative theories based on debt tax shields and winner's curse do not by themselves provide a complete explanation of the association between debt level and the pricing of IPOs by owners and the asymmetrically informed market.

Acknowledgement

We would like to acknowledge useful comments from John Clapp, Don Christensen, Tom O'Brien, Mike Vetsuypens, and participants in the 1991 Financial Management Association meeting and in finance workshops at the University of Connecticut and Northern Illinois University.

References

Allen, F. and G.R. Faulhaber, 1989, Signaling by underpricing in the IPO market, Journal of Financial Economics 23, 303-323.

Balvers, R.J., B. McDonald, and R.E. Miller, 1988, Underpricing of new issues and the choice of auditor as a signal of investment banker reputation, The Accounting Review 63, 605-622.

Baron, D.P., 1982, A model of the demand for investment banking advising and distribution services for new issues, Journal of Finance 37, 955-976.

Beatty, R.P. and J.R. Ritter, 1986, Investment banking, reputation, and the underpricing of initial public offerings, Journal of Financial Economics 15, 213-232.

Benveniste, L.M. and P.A. Spindt, 1989, How investment bankers determine the offer price and allocation of new issues, Journal of Financial Economics 24, 343-361.

Bhagat, S. and P.A. Frost, 1986, Issuing costs to existing shareholders in competitive and negotiated underwritten public utility equity offerings, Journal of Financial Economics 15, 233-259.

Bhattacharya, S. and G.M. Constantinides, ed., 1989, Financial Markets and Incomplete Information Rouman & Littlefield Publishers, Inc.

Blazenko, G.W., 1987, Managerial preference, asymmetric information, and financial structure, Journal of Finance 42, 839-862.

Booth, J.R. and R.L. Smith, 1986, Capital raising, underwriting, and the certification hypothesis, Journal of Financial Economics 15, 261-280.

Bradley, M., G. Jarrell, and E.H. Kim, 1984, On the existence of an optimal capital structure: Theory and evidence, Journal of Finance 39, 857-878.

Brennan, M. and A. Kraus, 1987, Efficient financing under asymmetric information, Journal of Finance 42, 1225-1243.

Carter, R. and S. Manaster, 1990, Initial public offerings and underwriter reputation, Journal of Finance 45, 1045-1067.

Constantinides, G.M. and B.D. Grundy, 1989, Optimal investment with stock repurchase and financing as signals, Review of Financial Studies 2, 445-466.

Cornett, M.M. and N.G. Travlos, 1989, Information effects associated with debt-for-equity and equity-for-debt exchange offers, Journal of Finance 44, 451-468.

DeAngelo, H. and R.W. Masulis, 1980, Optimal capital structure under corporate and personal taxation, Journal of Financial Economics 8, 3-30.

Diamond, D., 1984, Financial intermediation and delegated monitoring, Review of Economic Studies 51, 393-414.

Downes, D. and R. Heinkel, 1982, Signaling and the valuation if unseasoned new issues, Journal of Finance 37, 1-10.

Drake, P.D. and M.R. Vetsuypens, 1993, IPO underpricing and insurance against legal liability, Financial Management 22, 64-73.

Dybvig, P.H. and J.F. Zender, 1991, Capital structure and dividend irrelevance with asymmetric information, Review of Financial Studies 4, 201-219.

Eckbo, E.B., 1986, Valuation effects of corporate debt offerings, Journal of Financial Economics 15, 119-151.

Fama, E., 1985, What's different about banks? Journal of Monetary Economics 15, 29-36.

Flannery, M.J., 1986, Asymmetric information and risky debt maturity choice, Journal of Finance 41, 19-37.

Galai, D. and R.W. Masulis, 1976, The option pricing model and the risk factor of stock, Journal of Financial Economics 3, 53-81.

Garfinkel, J.A., 1993, IPO underpricing, insider selling and subsequent equity offerings: Is underpricing a signal of quality? Financial Management 22, 74-83.

Grinblatt, M. and C.Y. Hwang, 1989, Signaling and the pricing of new issues, Journal of Finance 44, 393-420.

Grossman, S. and O. Hart, 1982, Corporate financial structure and managerial incentives, in J. McCall, ed.: The Economics of Information and Uncertainty (Chicago: University of Chicago Press.)

Hamada, R.S., 1972, The effect of the firm's capital structure on the systematic risk of common stock, Journal of Finance 27, 435-452.

Harris, M. and A. Raviv, 1990, Capital structure and the informational role of debt, Journal of Finance 45, 321-349.

————, 1991, The theory of capital structure, Journal of Finance 46, 297-355.

Hayes, S.L. III, 1971, Investment banking: Power structure influx, Harvard Business Review 49, 136-152.

Heinkel, R., 1982, A theory of capital structure relevance under imperfect information, Journal of Finance 37, 1141-1150.

Hughes, P.J., 1986, Signaling by direct disclosure under asymmetric information, Journal of Accounting and Economics 8, 119-142.

Ibbotson, R., 1975, Price performance of common stock new issues, Journal of Financial Economics 2, 235-272.

James, C., 1987, Some evidence on the uniqueness of bank loans, Journal of Financial Economics 19, 217-235.

———— and P. Wier, 1990, Borrowing relationships, intermediation, and the cost of issuing public securities, Journal of Financial Economics 28, 149-171.

Jegadesh, N., M. Weinstein, and I. Welch, 1993, An empirical investigation of IPO returns and subsequent offerings, Journal of Financial Economics 34, 153-175.

Jensen, G.R., D.P. Solberg, and T.S. Zorn, 1992, Simultaneous determination of insider ownership, debt, and dividend policies, Journal of Financial and Quantitative Analysis 27, 247-263.

Jensen, M.C. and W.H. Meckling, 1976, Theory of the firm: Managerial behavior, agency costs and ownership structure, Journal of Financial Economics 11, 305-360.

John, K., 1987, Risk-shifting incentives and signaling through corporate capital structure, Journal of Finance 42, 623-641.

Koh, F. and T. Walter, 1989, A direct test of the Rock's model of the pricing of unseasoned issues, Journal of Financial Economics 23, 251-272.

Leland, H and D. Pyle, 1977, Information asymmetries, financial structure, and financial intermediation, Journal of Finance 32, 371-387.

Levis, M., 1990, The winner's curse problem, interest costs and the underpricing of initial public offerings, The Economic Journal 100, 76-89.

Masulis, R.W., 1980, The effects of capital structure change on security prices: A study of exchange offers, Journal of Financial Economics 8, 139-178.

————, 1983, The impact of capital structure change on firm value: Some estimates, Journal of Finance 38, 107-126.

———— and A.N. Korwar, 1986, Seasoned equity offerings: An empirical investigation, Journal of Financial Economics 15, 91-118.

Michaely, R., and W.H. Shaw, 1994, The pricing of initial public offerings: Tests of the adverse selection and signaling theories, Review of Financial Studies 7, 279-320.

Mikkelson, W.H., 1985, Capital structure change and decreases in stockholder wealth: A cross-sectional study of convertible security calls, in B.M. Friedman, ed.: Corporate Capital Structures in the United States (University of Chicago Press, Chicago, IL).

———— and M.M. Partch, 1986, Valuation effects of security offerings and the issuance process, Journal of Financial Economics 15, 31-60.

Miller, M., 1977, Debt and taxes, Journal of Finance 32, 261-276.

Modigliani, F. and M. Miller, 1958, The cost of capital, corporation finance, and the theory of investment, American Economic Review 48, 261-297.

Mulford, C.W., 1985, The importance of a market value measurement of debt in leverage ratios: Replication and extensions, Journal of Accounting Research 23, 897-906.

Muscarella, C.J. and M.R. Vetsuypens, 1989, A simple test of Baron's model of IPO underpricing, Journal of Financial Economics 24, 125-135.

Myers, S.C., 1984, The capital structure puzzle, Journal of Finance 39, 575-592.

———— and N. Majluf, 1984, Corporate financing and investment decisions when firms have information investors do not have, Journal of Financial Economics 13, 187-221.

Narayanan, M.P., 1988, Debt versus equity under asymmetric information, Journal of Financial and Quantitative Analysis 23, 39-51.

Noe, T., 1988, Capital structure and signaling game equilibria, Review of Financial Studies 1, 331-356.

Ritter, J.R., 1984, Signaling and the valuation of unseasoned new issues: A comment, Journal of Finance 39, 1231-1237.

————, 1987, The costs of going public, Journal of Financial Economics 19, 269-281.

Rock, K., 1986, Why new issues are underpriced, Journal of Financial Economics 15, 187-212.

Ross, S., 1977, The determination of capital structure: The incentive signaling approach, Bell Journal of Economics 8, 23-40.

Slovin, M.B. and J.E. Young, 1990, Bank lending and initial public offerings, Journal of Banking and Finance 14, 729-740.

Smith, C.W., 1986, Investment banking and the capital acquisition process, Journal of Financial Economics 15, 3-29.

Sternberg, T., 1989, Signaling in the market for initial public offerings: New approaches and tests, Unpublished manuscript, Vanderbilt University.

Stultz, R., 1990, Managerial discretion and optimal financing policies, Journal of Financial Economics 26, 3-27.

Tinic, S.M., 1988, Anatomy of initial public offerings of common stocks, Journal of Finance 43, 789-822.

Titman, S. and B. Trueman, 1986, Information quality and the valuation of new issues, Journal of Accounting and Economics 8, 159-172.

———— and R. Wessels, 1988, The determinants of capital structure choice, Journal of Finance 43, 1-20.

Welch, I., 1989, Seasoned offerings, imitation costs and the underpricing of initial public offerings, Journal of Finance 44, 421-449.

Endnotes

[1] For recent surveys of this literature, see Bhattacharya and Constantinidis (1989) and Harris and Raviv (1991).

[2] Garfinkel (1993), Jegadeesh, Weinstein, and Welch (1993), and Michaely and Shaw (1994) present evidence on the signaling theories. In addition, there are two other explanations of IPO underpricing. In the lawsuit avoidance theory of Ibbotson (1975), Drake and Vetsuypens (1993), and Tinic (1988), a firm underprices the IPO to minimize the expected loss due to lawsuits by disgruntled stockholders. Baron (1982) develops a principal-agent model where the investment banker possesses superior information about demand for new issues, and the firm underprices the IPO to induce the banker to maximize issue proceeds. However, Muscarella and Vetsuypens (1989) find that the IPOs of investment banking firms are also underpriced, an evidence which is not completely consistent with Baron's model.

[3] Also see Blazenko (1987).

[4] Assuming that managerial compensation is chosen optimally, Dybwig and Zender (1991) show that investment is optimal and capital structure and dividend policy are irrelevant in a large class of asymmetric information models. In their model, the IPOs are priced correctly on average (see p. 209 and p. 217), which is in sharp contrast to the widely documented empirical evidence that IPOs are underpriced on average in excess of ten percent.

[5] In Leland and Pyle (1977) information asymmetry is limited to the expected return on assets. For a counter example on the relation between volatility of earnings and optimal debt ratio, see Heinkel (1982).

[6] In addition to the amount of debt, firm value is inversely related to the maturity of debt for informational reasons. As Flannery (1986) argues, when the debt market

cannot distinguish between high and low quality firms, the default premium on long-term debt will appear most unreasonable to the high-quality firm. This is because the market imputes a higher probability of credit quality deterioration than the insider does. Flannery shows that with positive transaction costs a separating equilibrium sometimes obtains in which a high-quality firm borrows short and a low-quality firm borrows long. Also, Blazenko (1987) suggests that under asymmetric information, short-term debt financing is a relatively more encouraging signal of firm quality than long-term debt financing. For lack of data, we do not pursue debt maturity as a separate signal of firm value.

7 See Booth and Smith (1986) and the references cited therein for a discussion on the role of investment bankers in certifying firm quality and on reputational signaling. For empirical evidence on this issue, see Balvers, McDonald, and Miller (1988), and Beatty and Ritter (1986).

8 Jensen, Solberg, and Zorn (1992) present evidence that in seasoned firms debt and insider ownership are inversely realted. The informational role of debt also implies that a firm that has already chosen a high level of debt has less incentive to choose stronger signals in the form of high quality investment bankers and auditors. We do not pursue this issue because we have only a dichotomous measure of the quality of investment bankers and auditors, which makes it diffIcult to detect the hypothesized substitution effect.

9 We identified 45 financial IPOs during our study period. This group had an average debt-to-assets ratio of 52 percent, roughly three times the average leverage ratio of their non-financial counterparts.

10 Investment bankers included in the "bulge" group as defined in Hayes (1971) are First Boston, Goldman Sachs, Merrill Lynch, Morgan Stanley, and Salomon Brothers.

11 This treatment is consistent with Balvers, McDonald, and Miller (1988) and other studies cited therein.

12 This is in line with previous studies by Bradley, Jarrell, and Kim (1984) and Mulford (1985). Lacking data on maturity, we are unable to use the distinction between short-term and long-term debt as an additional signal of firm value. This is unlikely to pose a serious missing variable problem in estimation because empirical studies suggest that small firms tend to use significantly more short-term debt than large firms (Titman and Wessels (1988)). Also, there are important non-signaling motivations for use of short-term debt such as lower issue and agency costs. Finally, the correlation between (the excluded) debt maturity and other signaling variables is probably small.

13 The results reported in the next section are not sensitive to whether equity is valued at the offer price or the first-day dosing market (bid) price for determining DR.

14 In computing α, no adjustment was made for the overallotment option.

15 This implicitly assumes a linear relationship between σ and DR, which may not

necessarily hold in theory. Also see footnote 19.

[16] Masulis and Korwar (1986) use a variable similar to MR in their analysis of the announcement effects of seasoned equity offerings. A variant of M is used by Bhagat and Frost (1986) in examining the issue costs associated with public utility equity offerings.

[17] The WLS estimates reported in panel B are essentially indistinguishable from their ordinary least squares counterparts.

[18] We observed essentially the same relationship when U and OF were substituted for the control variable α.

[19] Most signaling models suggest that firm value is a non-linear function of α and U. However, these studies focus only on univariate or bivariate signals assuming away the pre-IPO signals. Since the shape of the equilibrium valuation function in the presence of both the pre-IPO and IPO signals is unknown, we assume a linear relationship in (2). It should be noted that since V may not be a monotonic function of the signals, negative coefficients on the signals should not necessarily be interpreted as evidence against their signaling roles (see Sternberg (1989)).

[20] This weighting procedure is similar to that of Downes and Heinkel (1982). The results remain essentially the same when firm book values are used as weights.

[21] To raise a given amount of money, the firm needs to sell a smaller fraction of ownership (and so retain a larger α) the larger the firm value. Terming this as the "wealth effect," Ritter (1984) argues that the WLS regression in (1) is subject to simultaneous equations bias. However, Sternberg (1989) points out that in a signaling context V always influences . He contends that there is no simultaneous bias in (2) because there is only one behavioral relation between V and α (i.e., the market infers V after observing α and other signals). Consistent with this argument, we use WLS to estimate (2).

[22] Since we are using the market value of equity as the dependent variable, $\hat{a}_1$ underestimates the response coefficient of D to firm value by 1. However, the coefficient estimates of other variables in equation (2) are not affected by our choice of the proxy.

[23] In the Leland and Pyle (1977) signaling model, firm value depends on as well as the amount invested in the new project. Tests of the Leland and Pyle model have used variants of OF as a proxy for investment in the new project (see Downes and Heinkel (1982), Ritter (1984), and Sternberg (1989)). They find that the estimated coefficients of the proxies are at variance with their expected value of one. We also run into this common problem since the estimate of $a6$ reported in Table III is not significantly different from zero.

[24] Even though both Masulis (1983) and Mikkelson (1985) find a positive relationship between abnormal stock returns and proxies for debt-induced tax shield, both

authors caution that their tax variables may also be capturing information effects of debt. Also see Eckbo (1986).

[25] Again, we adopt a straightforward approach to testing this prediction. First we assume a linear functional form for convenience. Second, we estimate the U and α equations separately. In the recent signaling models of Allen and Faulhaber (1989), Grinblatt and Hwang (1989), and Welch (1989), the endogenous variables α and U are determined simultaneously. We resort to single-equation estimation of α and U because the residuals in (3) are known to be heteroscedastic, but those in (4) are not, which renders the simultaneous estimation of (3) and (4) difficult.

[26] Beatty and Ritter (1986) use *ln [1000 + Revenue]* as weights in their test for the winner's curse model. Our results remain essentially unchanged when all variables are deflated by σ.

The Information Content of Self-Underwritten IPOs

Chao Chen
School of Business Administration and Economics
California State University, Northridge

and

Timothy H. Lin
Securities and Exchange Commission, ROC
and National Chung Cheng University

Abstract

This paper studies the characteristics of self-underwritten initial public offerings (IPOs) where the lead or co-managing underwriter is also a major shareholder. We document significant underpricing for both self-underwritten and non-self-underwritten IPOs. Although the self-underwritten IPOs are by firms that are larger, more mature, and have smaller risk measures, the self-underwritten IPOs do not have lower underpricing than non-self- underwritten IPOs. This result indicates that investment banks are concerned about potential litigation or potential damage to their reputations in the cases of self-underwritten IPOs. In addition, investment banks/shareholders who underwrite the new issue tend to refrain from unwinding their shares and charge lower service fees in the self-underwritten IPOs (relative to non-self-underwritten IPOs). This evidence is consistent with the signaling hypothesis that investment banks in self-underwritten IPOs refrain from selling their position to signal that the shares are not overpriced.

1. Introduction

The pricing of initial public offerings (IPOs) is one of the most challenging issues in corporate finance and for investment bankers because there is no observable market price for a privately held firm before going public. Numerous studies, such as Ibbotson (1975), Ritter (1984), Miller and Reilly (1987), Carter and Manaster (1990), and Barry and Jennings (1993), document systematic underpricing of IPOs of common stock. Several theories have been offered to explain IPO underpricing including the asymmetric information models of Baron (1982), Rock (1986), and Chemmanur

(1993), the signaling models of Allen and Faulhaber (1989), Grinblatt and Hwang (1989), and Welch (1989), and the litigation risk or lawsuit avoidance hypothesis of Tinic (1988), Drake and Vetsuypens (1993), and Hughes and Thakor (1992)[1].

In this paper, we study the information content of self- underwritten new issues by examining venture-capital (VC)-backed IPOs. Studying self-underwritten IPOs is appealing for at least three reasons. First, it provides a direct comparison of IPO underpricing and the characteristics of issuing firms between IPOs when investment banks/venture capitalists/principal shareholders serve as the lead or co-managing underwriters, and IPOs where they don't. Second, it studies whether underwriters are concerned about the potential conflict of interest or potential litigation when they are lead or co-managing underwriters of self-underwritten IPOs. If they are concerned, they may behave differently and have a great incentive to avoid potential litigation. Third, it studies whether underwriters/shareholders refrain selling their shares in the self-underwritten IPOs relative to non-self-underwritten IPOs. They may refrain from unwinding their position to signal that the new issues are not overpriced.

The notion that underpricing reduces legal liability was initially suggested by Logue (1973) and Ibbotson (1975). Hughes and Thakor (1992) provide a formal model for the hypothesis. They argue that the underwriter makes pricing decisions to maximize his own welfare, but faces the potential risk of litigation against him for overpricing. Therefore, issuers and underwriters use underpricing to reduce the probability of a lawsuit under federal securities laws for material misstatements in the offering prospectus. Although Hughes and Thakor (1992) show that the mere existence of litigation risk does not suffice to produce underpricing when all agents are rational, IPO underpricing does emerge if the IPO price influences the probability of a future price decline and if the ex ante equilibrium pricing strategies of underwriters affect ex post belief of whether the price decline is attributable to "bad luck" or to "overpricing."

While the lawsuit avoidance hypothesis seems reasonable, empirical results of previous studies that examine this hypothesis are mixed. Tinic (1988) shows that IPOs issued after 1933 exhibit larger initial excess returns than the new issues brought to the market before the enactment of the Securities Act. Tinic (1988) also finds that prestigious investment banks started to avoid underwriting highly speculative small issues after 1933. Alexander (1991) provides direct evidence on the significance of taking precautions against the risk of litigation. Alexander shows that the potential litigation is associated with post-IPO price decline and that most of the class action suits are settled before going to trials, with the majority of the plaintiffs receiving some relief. Such results imply that issuers and underwriters are concerned about potential damage to their reputation if trial occurs. Hence, IPO underpricing can serve to avoid litigation. However, Drake and Vetsuypens (1993) examine a sample of 93 firms being sued by investors under the 1933 and 1934 Securities Acts relating to their IPOs. They show that the magnitude of monetary costs caused by lawsuits is far less than the value of underpricing. Their evidence suggests that IPO underpricing is an expensive form of insurance against lawsuits.

Our data set consists of 75 IPOs in which underwriters and/or their affiliates are the principal shareholders of the issuing firms, and 50 IPOs in which investment banks/shareholders are not the representatives of the underwriters for the offerings. The data set reveals that investment banks tend to refrain from unwinding their shares when they serve as lead or co-managing underwriters of their portfolio firms. In addition, investment banks charge lower service fees for their portfolio firms. An analysis of the initial return, defined as the percent change from offer price to the closing price of the first trading day, shows that issuing firms underwritten by investment banks/shareholders are more underpriced than those where investment banks/shareholders are not serving as underwriters. The evidence indicates that underwriters have to underprice these self-underwritten IPOs more because they have a conflict of interest and cannot creditably certify the issue. The post-IPO return, calculated from the difference between the closing price of the tenth trading day and the closing price of the first trading day of IPOs with investment banks/shareholders as underwriters, is also higher than that of the IPOs without investment banks/shareholders as underwriters. In addition, both the magnitudes of initial returns and post-IPO returns are the greatest when investment banks/shareholders serve as the lead underwriters. Finally, we use the turnover ratio and the standard deviation of daily returns over a one-year period after going public as the proxy for the risk of the issuing firm. This study finds that issuing firms with investment banks/shareholders as underwriters appear to have a lower risk than those of issuing firms without investment banks/shareholders as underwriters. This finding is consistent with the hypothesis that investment banks intend to avoid litigations by purposely underpricing their portfolio companies more when they act as the underwriters, and selectively avoid speculative issues.

The remainder of this paper is organized as follows: the next section presents our data and sample; section 3 discusses the empirical findings; and concluding remarks are presented in section 4.

2. Data

An investment bank may become a shareholder of an IPO issuing firm by providing venture capital investments or by obtaining the compensation from the issuer when a successful private placement was completed. Lim and Saunders (1990) report that many investment banks started their own venture capital funds. An investment in a new company provides the investment bank with the opportunity to manage the financing needs of the company as it grows. The investment bank hopes to earn fees from managing and underwriting public or private placements of equity as well as debt issues. In addition, Fabozzi and Modigliani (1992, p. 75) state that in raising venture capital for clients, investment bankers are frequently offered the opportunity to share in the prosperity of the company. The opportunity typically comes in the form of an option to buy a specified number of shares at a price that is set at the time the funds are raised.

To create a data base of IPOs with investment banks as issuers' principal shareholders, 497 VC-backed IPOs from 1979 through 1990 were initially identified from the annual report of *Venture Capital Journal*, which reports IPOs of VC-backed firms with offering amounts of $3 million or more and offer prices of at least $3 per share. Information about the IPOs is compiled from prospectuses on file with the Securities and Exchange Commission. The front page of the prospectus and the "Principal and Selling Shareholders" section in the prospectus allow us to identify whether a lead underwriter or a co-managing underwriter is the principal shareholder of the issuing firm. The front page reveals information about the offer price, offer size, gross spread, underwriting expenses, and overallotment option. The Principal and Selling Shareholders section discloses pre- and post-IPO shares held, and shares intended to be sold by principal shareholders, key managers and directors. The footnotes of the Principal and Selling Shareholders section indicate whether a shareholder is an affiliate of the representatives of the underwriters. The initial public offering dates are obtained from the Center for Research in Security Prices data tapes, the Securities and Exchange Commission's *Registered Offering Statistics* data tape, various Moody's *Bank and Finance Manuals*, and *Standard & Poor's Corporation Records*.

With this process, we identify 75 IPOs where the lead underwriter or co-managing underwriter held at least 3% of the issuing firm's outstanding shares before going public. Table 1 lists the investment banks that were principal shareholders of the issuing firms. There are 26 investment banks that had taken their portfolio companies public from 1979 through 1990. The column labeled 'type of involvement' in Table 1 describes the role an investment bank played in the IPO process for its portfolio companies. In 46 cases, the investment banks acted as lead underwriters. In the remaining 29 IPOs the investment banks served as co-managers and were listed on the front page of the offering prospectus. Hambrecht and Quist (H & Q hereafter) is the most active underwriter who took its portfolio companies public and served as a lead and a co-managing underwriter for 10 and 13 times, respectively. Column three of Table 1 reports the percentage of shareholdings of underwriters before their portfolio companies went public. On average, the investment banks/shareholders held 10.6% of the issuing firms. The result is similar to Barry, Muscarella, Peavy, and Vetsuypens (1990) who report that average shareholdings for a VC firm in its portfolio companies are 11.4 percent. Column four of Table 1 reveals the length of the holding period, defined as the offering date minus the initial investment date by underwriters. The initial investment date is identified from the "Certain Transactions" section of the prospectus. The longest holding period belongs to Lehman Brothers Kuhn Loeb Inc. that invested in American Management System, Inc. for 7.8 years before the firm went public. Table 1 shows that the investment banks average a holding period of 2.2 years before their portfolio companies go public.

For comparison purposes, we construct a control sample from the VC-backed IPOs that have the same 26 investment banks as issuers' shareholders, but are not the representatives of underwriters for the issuing firms. The second half of Table 1 reports 15 out of the 26 investment banks that were involved in 50 cases from 1981 to 1990. The largest shareholding belongs to Montgomery Medical Venture Limited Partnership, one of the affiliates of Morgan Stanley & Co., that holds 35.1 percent of William & Clarissa. The average percentage of shareholdings of the investment banks are 9.7 percent, which is lower but not significantly different from that of IPOs with investment banks/shareholders as underwriters. While 25 cases do not have information about the initial investment dates, the remaining 25 cases have an average holding period of 2.4 years.

Table 1

Initial public offerings (IPOs) that have investment banks as principal shareholders from 1979 to 1990.

Investment banks	IPOs with investment banks/shareholders as the underwriters				IPOs with investment banks/ shareholders when they are not the underwriters		
	Type of involvement		Average percent of share holding before IPO (%)	Average length of holding before IPO (year)[a]	Number of observ- ations	Average percent of share holding before IPO (%)	Average length of holding before IPO (year)[a]
	Lead under- writer	Coman- aging under- writer					
Alex Brown & Sons	3	1	5.4	2.3	2	7.2	2.5
Allen & Co. Inc.	3	1	7.2	1.3	2	14.5	NA
Blyth Eastman Paine Webber Inc.	1	0	7.3	3.1	0	NA	NA
Cable Howse & Ragen	2	1	18.5	2.4	6	10.9	3.4
Dillon Read & Co. Inc.	1	0	8.9	NA	1	2.8	NA
Donaldson Lufkin and Jenrette Securities Corp.	4	1	15.3	1.6	6	11.9	3.5
Drexel Burnham Lambert, Inc.	2	1	8.0	NA	1	21.4	NA
E F Hutton & Co., Inc.	2	0	16.1	2.1	1	6.2	3.4
First Analysis Securities Co.	0	1	5.8	NA	0	NA	NA
Hambrecht & Quist	10	13	10.2	2.3	13	5.7	1.7
J Henry Schroder Wagg & Co., Ltd.	0	1	5.0	1.8	0	NA	NA
Kidder Peabody & Co.	2	0	14.5	1.0	0	NA	NA
Kleinwort Benson, Inc.	0	1	13.3	2.5	0	NA	NA
L F Rochschild Unterberg & Towbin	2	0	6.7	1.8	2	4.6	1.3
Lehman Brothers Kuhn Loeb, Inc.	1	1	16.6	7.8	0	NA	NA
Merrill Lynch Capital Markets	3	0	8.2	1.2	3	10.6	1.1
Montgomery securities	0	2	8.1	2.3	3	15.8	1.8
Morgan Stanley & Co.	1	0	7.2	2.4	2	25.7	1.6
Robertson, Coleman, Stephens and Woodman	2	2	7.2	3.5	1	17.7	NA
Robinson-Humphrey Co.	1	0	6.2	NA	0	NA	NA
Rotan Mosle, Inc.	0	1	17.1	NA	0	NA	NA
Rothschild, Inc.	1	1	7.1	3.4	5	5.0	2.4
Smith Barney, Harris Upham & Co., Inc.	2	0	24.2	3.0	2	8.7	3.2
Swergold Chefitz & Sinsabangh Inc.	1	0	3.4	1.2	0	NA	NA
Vope & Covington	1	0	3.1	0.7	0	NA	NA
William Blair & Co.	1	1	17.9	1.3	0	NA	NA
All	46	29	10.6	2.2	50	9.7	2.4

NA: not available.

[a] Defined as the issuing year minus the initial investment year of investment banks/shareholders.

3. Empirical Results

Table 2 compares the different characteristics between IPOs with and without investment banks/shareholders as underwriters. When investment banks take their portfolio companies public, the mean offer price and offer size are larger than those that are underwritten by other investment banks ($13.1 dollars versus $11.1 dollars, and $30.5 million versus $21.7 million). The t-statistics are significant at the 5 percent level. In addition, IPOs with investment banks/shareholders as underwriters have lower underwriter spread, defined as gross spread divided by offer price, and underwriting expense per dollar raised than those of IPOs without investment banks/shareholders acting as underwriters (7.1% versus 7.6%, and 2.4% versus 3.4%, respectively). The results suggest that investment banks charge lower underwriting fees when they underwrite their own portfolio companies. While VC-backed firms have younger age, defined as the issuing year minus the year of incorporation, firms with investment banks/shareholders as underwriters tend to be older than firms without investment banks/shareholders as underwriters[2]. In addition, IPOs taken public by their investment banks/shareholders have significantly larger revenues and book value of assets ($65.9 million versus $17.3 million and $57.4 million versus $18 million), which may suggest that investment banks/shareholders are more likely to serve as the representatives of underwriters when the issuing firms are more mature.

The exercise of overallotment by underwriters may indicate whether the IPO is a hot or a cold issue. The information of overallotment is disclosed on the front page of the prospectus of new issues. Typically, overallotment option ranges from five to fifteen percent of the planned offer size. Information on the actual exercise of overallotment is obtained from the Registered Offering Statistics up to 1988. While 59 cases (79% of the subsample) for IPOs with investment banks/shareholders as underwriters and 30 cases (60 percent of another

Table 2

Test of differences in characteristics for initial public offerings (IPOs) with and without investment banks/shareholders as the underwriters.

Variable	IPOs with investment banks shareholders as underwriters	IPOs without investment banks shareholders as underwriters	t-statistic
Offer price	13.1	11.1	2.64**
Offer size[a]	30.5	21.7	2.57**
Underwriter spread[b]	7.1%	7.6%	2.71***
Underwriting expense[c]	2.4%	3.4%	2.38**
Year of issuing firms being incorporated before an IPO	8.5	5.5	1.76*
Preceding year's revenue[a]	65.9	17.3	2.37**
Book value of assets[a]	57.4	18.0	2.89**
Over-allotment	9.0%	8.7%	0.19

[a] in million of dollars.
[b] Define as the gross spread over offer price.
[c] Define as underwriting expense over offer size.
* Significant at the 10% level.
** Significant at the 5% level.
*** Significant at the 1% level.

subsample) for IPOs without investment banks/shareholders as underwriters exercise overallotment options, the difference in mean of the overallotment ratio, defined as overallotment over offer size, between the two groups is not significant.

Table 3 illustrates the selling decision in IPOs and the pre- IPO holding period return for investment banks/shareholders. Because potential lawsuits are more likely to occur when investment banks piggyback their shares in the offering of their self- underwritten IPOs, we consider that investment banks/shareholders are less likely to sell their shares in IPOs when they are the lead or co-managing underwriters of the issuing firms. In Panel A of Table 3, we find only in four cases (5 percent of the sample with investment banks/shareholders as underwriters) that the investment banks sell shares. For the selling underwriters, they sold, on average, 12.2 percent of their holdings. In contrast, we find that in 13 cases (26 percent of IPOs without investment banks/shareholders as underwriters) the investment banks/shareholders piggyback their shares in the secondary offerings. They sold 30.6% of their holdings. These findings suggest that investment banks/shareholders refrain from selling in IPOs to avoid potential litigation. A close examination of the selling group shows that a majority (eight out of 13 cases) of the IPO firms employ more prestigious investment banks than their investment banks/shareholders. This result indicates that insiders utilize reputable investment banks to unwind their positions in IPOs. This evidence is also consistent with the signaling hypothesis. That is, investment banks in self-underwritten IPOs refrain from unwinding their position to signal that the new issues are not overpriced.

Panel B of Table 3 reports descriptive evidence on the pre-IPO average annual holding period return, defined as Log(offer price/initial investment price) divided by the number of years in the holding period. Since the holding shares reported on the "Principal and Selling Shareholders" section represent shares that have gone through stock split or stock conversion from preferred stock, we adjust the purchasing price with the stock split and/or conversion ratio to obtain the initial investment price[3].

Table 3

The selling decision and holding period return for initial public offerings (IPOs) with investment banks as principal shareholders. (number of observations in parentheses).

Panel A. Number of investment banks/shareholders sell shares in IPOs			
	All	Do not sell shares in IPOs	Sell shares in IPOs
Investment bank/shareholder is the underwriter	75	71	4
Investment bank/shareholder is not the underwriter	50	37	1
Panel B. Pre-IPO annual holding period returns.[a]			
	All	Do not sell shares in IPOs	Sell shares in IPOs
Investment bank/shareholder is the underwriter	95.4% (49)	94.0% (47)	127.8% (2)
Investment bank/shareholder is not the underwriter	52.3% (24)	55.4% (17)	44.5% (7)
t-statistic	2.69***	2.02**	5.12***

** Significant at the 5% level. *** Significant at the 1% level.

[a] Holding period return is defined as log(offer price/initial investment price) divided by the holding period before IPO. Initial investment price is adjusted for stock split and stock conversion.

Nevertheless, because of lack of information about either initial investment date, initial purchase price, or conversion ratio for 52 issues, we are only able to calculate the holding period return for 49 cases and 24 cases for IPOs with and without investment banks as underwriters, respectively. Within the first group, only one case has negative holding period return (-16.9 percent), while the remaining 48 cases have positive returns. The highest holding period return is the case in which H & Q purchased $4.8 per share from KLA Instruments Corp. in March 1980. KLA Instruments Corp. went public in August 1980 with an offer price of $13 dollars per share. The annual holding period return for H & Q is 350 percent.

While the pre-IPO average annual holding period return for investment banks/shareholders serving as underwriters is 95.4% (much greater than those not serving as underwriters 52.3%), investment banks/shareholders sell shares only when the holding period return is extremely large (127.8%). The evidence suggests that investment banks are more likely to underwrite and sell shares of their portfolio firms when these IPOs are substantially underpriced.

Table 4 presents summary statistics on initial returns and post-IPO returns. The initial return is measured by log(the price at the end of the first trading day/offer price), while the post- IPO return is measured from the price at the end of the first trading day to the price at the end of the tenth trading day. Panel A reveals that the mean initial return for the 75 IPOs is 10.8 percent, which is significantly different from zero at the 1 percent level. Fifty-nine out of the 75 firms (or 79 percent of the whole sample) have positive initial returns.

We also partition the sample by the degree of involvement by investment banks. Table 4 shows that new issues in which the underwriters acted as lead managers are more underpriced than other issues. The average initial return for 46 issues in which the underwriters acted as the lead managers is 11.7 percent. This is significantly different from zero at the 1% level and larger than the 9.5 percent average initial return of the 29 issues where the underwriters were the co-managers. Since the underwriter acting as the lead manager is likely to have the greatest influence on the offering price, the evidence that IPOs with investment banks/shareholders as lead managers are more underpriced than others is consistent with the lawsuit avoidance hypothesis.

Although IPO investors can sue anyone who signs the prospectus, serving on the board of directors increases the liabilities of underwriters. Panel A reports that when underwriters also served on the board of directors, their IPOs have average initial returns of 11.2 percent, whereas the average initial returns when underwriters did not serve as directors is 10 percent. Both returns are statistically significant at the 1% level. This result confirms our conjecture that serving as the directorship increases the incentive for underwriters to underprice the IPOs. Panel A also shows that the average initial return of the IPOs without investment banks/shareholders acting as lead or co-managing underwriters is 9.3 percent which is less, though not significantly, than that of the IPOs with investment banks/shareholders acting as underwriters.

Panel B of in Table 4 presents the results of post-IPO returns. For the sample with investment banks/shareholders as underwriters, the mean return from the first to the tenth trading day is 1.6 percent. Further inspection of the data reveals that IPOs with investment banks/shareholders as lead underwriters experience a significantly positive price movement of 3.4 percent in the aftermarket. On average, 29 co-managing IPOs experience a negative return, but not statistically significant, of 1.4

Table 4

Summary statistics on the price performance of initial public offerings (IPOs) with and without investment banks/shareholders as representatives of underwriters.

Sample	No. of obs.	Mean return	t- statistic[a]	Number of positive	Number of zero	Number of negative
Panel A. Initial return						
(defined as from offer price to closing price at the end of the first trading day)						
IPO with shareholders as underwriters	75	10.8%	5.75***	59	4	12
IPOs partitioned by underwriter serves as						
lead manager	46	11.7%	4.18***	33	3	10
co-manager	29	9.5%	4.57***	26	1	2
IPOs partitioned by underwriter serves as						
director	53	11.2%	4.60***	44	3	6
non-director	22	10.0%	3.66***	15	1	6
IPOs without shareholders as underwriters	50	9.3%	4.00***	38	3	9
Panel B. Post-IPO returns						
(defined as from the closing price at the end of the first trading day to the closing price at the end of the tenth trading day).						
IPOs with shareholders as underwriters	75	1.6%	1.40	41	2	32
IPOs partitioned by underwriter serves as						
lead manager	46	3.4%	2.42**	29	1	16
co-manager	29	-1.4%	-0.78	12	1	16
IPOs partitioned by underwriter serves as						
director	53	2.1%	1.55	30	1	22
non-director	22	0.3%	0.16	11	1	10
IPOs without shareholders as underwriters	50	-1.9%	-1.44	21	3	26

** Significant at the 5% level.
*** Significant at the 1% level.
[a] The t-statistic is used to test whether the mean return is significantly different from zero.

percent during the after market period. Panel B further summarizes statistics on post-IPO returns for subsamples of firms partitioned by whether or not underwriters are on the board of directors. The results reveal that 53 firms with underwriters as directors produce an average post-IPO return of 2.1 percent. In contrast, IPOs without underwriters as directors have an average post-IPO return of negative 0.3 percent. The number, however, is not statistically significant. The bottom row of Panel B presents 50 IPOs without investment banks/shareholders as underwriters. It shows that the post-IPO return is negative 1.9 percent, and more than half of these 50 IPOs have negative returns.

We further investigate the nature of IPO price performance with and without investment banks/shareholders acting as underwriters based on the following cross-sectional regressions. We use the initial return (RET) as the dependent variable.

$$RET_i = \alpha + \beta_1 TYPE_i + \beta_2 RANK_i + \beta_3 RISK_i + \beta_4 ALLOT_i + e_i \qquad (1)$$

where RET_i is the initial return of IPO firm I; $TYPE_i$ = 1 if firm I has an investment bank/shareholder as the lead or co-managing underwriter, otherwise it is zero; $RANK_i$ = the proxy for IPO firm I's lead underwriter reputation, defined as the Carter and Manaster 's (1990) ranking, where 9 indicates the highest level of prestige and 0 represents the lowest level; $RISK_i$ = the standard deviation of daily stock returns for the first twenty trading days after IPO for issuer I, and finally $ALLOT_i$ is the overallotment of issue I.

Table 5 presents the results for equation (1). Column 1 contains information for using the initial return as the dependent variable. The results show that the initial return is positively, though not significantly, related to the presence of an investment bank/shareholder as the underwriter. The coefficient on underwriter ranking is significantly negative at the one percent level, which suggests that new issues underwritten by reputable underwriters are priced close to their after-market value. Consistent with Ritter's (1991) finding, the firm risk is significantly and positively related to the initial return. In their model, Benveniste and Spindt (1989) suggest that the size of overallotment reflects the popularity of an offer. They show that the higher the percentage of the overallotment, the greater the demand for issues that have good information revealed, which in turn result in higher initial return. The positive and significant coefficient on overallotment is consistent with this conjecture.

As an alternative specification, we estimated the model substituting ten-day cumulative return, (defined as the percent change from offer price to the close of the tenth trading day), with initial return as the dependent variable. Column two reports the regression results. Ten-day cumulative return is positively related to cases where an investment bank/shareholder is the underwriter. The evidence provides slight evidence for the lawsuit avoidance hypothesis that investment banks/shareholders intend to protect themselves against litigation by setting an offer price at a lower level. The lead underwriter s prestige is negatively related to post-IPO ten-day return. This result is consistent with Carter and Manaster (1990) and Booth and Smith (1986), who argue that reputable investment bankers can certify a new issue. The positive coefficient on firm risk indicates that where the volatility of an issuing firm is an important component of post-IPO returns, less risky firms have lower post-IPO returns. Consistent with Benveniste and Spindt 's (1989) information revelation argument, the coefficient on overallotment is positively and significantly associated with ten-day cumulative return. These findings suggest that IPOs incur higher underpricing when investment banks/shareholders are underwriters of the issuing firms.

The preceding analysis indicates that the price performances of IPO issues are affected by whether investment banks/shareholders are issuers' underwriters. Next, we examine the risk factor of an issue with and without investment banks/shareholders as underwriters. We use turnover ratio and post-IPO volatility as proxies for the risk of a firm.

Table 5

Cross-sectional OLS regressions with initial returns and cumulative returns as the dependent variable, respectively. The data set consists of 75 IPOs with investment banks/shareholders as underwriters and 50 IPOs without investment banks/shareholders as underwriters. (t-statistic in parentheses). The OLS regression is expressed as:

$$RET_i = \alpha + \beta_1 TYPE_i + \beta_2 RANK_i + \beta_3 RISK_i + \beta_4 ALLOT_i + e_i$$

TYPE = 1 if an investment bank/shareholder is the lead or comanaging underwriter, otherwise 0. RANK stands for underwriter quality, as defined by Carter and Manaster (1990).

RISK is measured as the standard deviation of daily return over the first twenty trading days after going public. ALLOT is the overallotment of the issue.

		Dependent variable	
Independent variable	Predicted sign	Initial return	Cumulative return (from the offer price to close of the tenth trading day)
Intercept		0.115	0.123
		(2.41**)	(2.24**)
TYPE	+	0.018	0.060
		(0.63)	(1.85*)
RANK	-	-0.018	-0.024
		(-2.91***)	(-3.35***)
RISK	+	0.087	0.086
		(3.50***)	(3.01***)
ALLOT	+	0.413	0.355
		(2.85***)	(2.12**)
Adjusted R^2		0.17	0.19
F-value		7.34***	6.78***
Number of observation		125	125

* Significant at the 10% level.   ** Significant at the 5% level.   *** Significant at the 1% level.

Table 6 reports the turnover ratios of IPOs ten days after going public. The turnover ratio is defined as the fraction of trading volume of shares offered. Table 6 shows that the average turnover ratios are 42 percent and 52.4 percent for IPOs with and without investment banks/shareholders as underwriters for the first trading date, respectively. The average turnover ratio drops substantially after the second trading date and decays gradually as the trading day is away from the first public trading date. IPOs without investment banks/shareholders as underwriters have higher turnover ratio in eight out of the 10 trading days. We reject the hypothesis of mean equality in six out of the 10 trading days. Combined with the fact that IPOs with investment banks/shareholders as underwriters produce higher initial return and after market performance, the findings are consistent with Carter and Dark's (1993) evidence that demonstrates a negative relation between the after market performance of IPO firms and early trading volume. In addition, Carter and Dark argue that a low after market trading volume reflects the presence of either unsophisticated investors or sophisticated investors with a long-term investment horizon, and find that turnover declines as underwriter reputation increases when underwriters have reputations higher than a certain critical point. Given the fact that the underwriters included in this study belong to the upper class in the Carter and Manaster 's (1990) ranking, our results are consistent with Carter and Dark's (1993) argument that investment banks prefer to confine IPO sales to investors with long-run horizons in an effort to maintain reputation[4]. The difference in turnover ratio between these two groups suggests that distribution efforts are more important when underwriters take their own portfolios companies public.

Table 6

Turnover for IPOs with and without investment banks/shareholders as the lead or comanaging underwriters. Turnover is defined as the fraction of trading volume of shares offered.

| | Average Turnover Ratio | | |
| | IPO with investment banks/shareholders as | IPOs without investment banks/shareholders as | |
Day after IPO	underwriters (%)	underwriters (%)	t-statistic
1	42.0	52.4	1.84*
2	12.5	17.8	2.62**
3	6.9	9.5	2.16**
4	4.8	5.7	1.39
5	4.2	4.3	0.22
6	3.1	4.4	1.95*
7	2.6	3.7	2.07**
8	3.0	2.8	0.43
9	2.4	2.8	0.87
10	2.5	3.8	2.17**
All	8.4	10.7	2.28**

* Significant at the 10% level.   ** Significant at the 5% level.

To provide further evidence about the relation between a firm's risk when an investment bank/shareholder is the lead or co- managing underwriter and when it is not, we conduct a cross- sectional regression by using the standard deviation (STD) of daily stock returns of one-year after going public as the dependent variable. The regressors include whether an investment bank/shareholder is the lead or co-managing underwriter (TYPE), the underwriter's reputation (RANK), the log of the offer size (PROCEED), and the age of the issuing firm (AGE). TYPE equals one if the issue is underwritten by its investment bank/shareholder, otherwise it is zero. The regression can be expressed as:

$$STD_i = \alpha + \beta_1 TYPE_i + \beta_2 RANK_i + \beta_3 PROCEED_i + \beta_4 AGE_i + e_i \qquad (2)$$

Table 7 reports the results of regression (2). The coefficient on TYPE is negative and significant at the 5% level. The result suggests lower volatility when firms have investment banks/shareholders as the representatives of underwriters. The coefficient on lead underwriter ranking is not significant. Offer size is positively associated with post-IPO stock volatility. Contrary to Ritter's (1991) findings, the results provide new evidence on the difference between VC-backing and non-VC-backing IPOs. For example, Barry, Muscarella, Peavy, and Vetsuypens (1990) find a positive relation between offer size and post-IPO volatility. Lastly, a negative relation exists between the issuing firm's age and the post-IPO stock volatility. The finding is consistent with Ritter's (1991) argument that the longer a firm is in business, the smaller the information asymmetry of the company.

Table 7

Cross-sectional OLS results with the standard deviation of daily returns for the one-year period after going public as dependent variable. (t-statistic in parentheses) The regression can be expressed as:

$$STD_i = \alpha + \beta_1 TYPE_i + \beta_2 RANK_i + \beta_3 PROCEED_i + \beta_4 AGE_i + e_i$$

TYPE = 1 if an investment bank/shareholder is the lead or co-managing underwriter, otherwise 0. RANK stands for underwriter quality, defined as Carter and Manaster (1990) ranking. PROCEED is the log of the offer size. AGE is the age of an issuer from incorporation to going public.

Independent variable[a]	Predicted sign	Coefficient
Intercept		0.010
		(0.62)
TYPE	-	-0.006
		(-2.34**)
RANK	-	-0.001
		(-0.08)
PROCEED	-	0.003
		(1.94*)
AGE	-	-0.0003
		(-2.89***)
Adjusted R^2		0.09
F-value		4.17***
Number of observation		125

188 The Information Content of Self-Underwritten IPOs

4. Conclusions

The pervasive phenomenon of IPO underpricing has attracted many explanations. While many of the explanations are based on the information asymmetry among issuers, investors, and underwriters, the lawsuit avoidance or legal liabilities hypothesis suggests that IPO underpricing is used to prevent litigation by leaving money on the table. The lawsuit avoidance hypothesis also implies that investment banks would avoid underwriting speculative issues.

We investigate these implications by analyzing the behavior of self-underwritten IPOs. We document significant underpricing for both self-underwritten and non-self-underwritten IPOs. However, the self-underwritten IPOs are by firms that are more mature, larger, and have smaller risk measures. All else equal, these characteristics would predict that self-underwritten IPOs would have lower underpricing than non-self-underwritten IPOs. The finding indicates that self-underwritten IPOs do not have lower underpricing than non-self-underwritten IPOs. This evidence supports the legal liabilities hypothesis. We also find that self- underwritten IPOs appear to have lower turnover ratios and stock price volatility than cases where investment banks/shareholders don't serving as underwriters. These results indicate that investment banks/shareholders are concerned about potential litigation when they serve as lead or co-managing underwriters of their portfolio firms and they have a greater incentive to underprice these less speculative new issues.

In addition, Investment banks/shareholders who underwrite the new issue tend to refrain from unwinding their shares and charge lower service fees in the self-underwritten IPOs (relative to non- self-underwritten IPOs). This evidence is also consistent with the signaling hypothesis that investment banks in self-underwritten IPOs refrain from selling their position to signal that the shares are not overpriced.

Acknowledgement

We are grateful for helpful comments and suggestions from David Mauer, Jay Choi, and Jean Loo on previous drafts of this paper which were presented at the 1995 Financial Management Association Annual Conference and the 1995 Global Finance Association Annual Conference. The research support from the School of Business Administration and Economics at California State University, Northridge is gratefully acknowledged.

References

Alexander, J.C. , 1991, Do the merits matter? A study of settlements in Securities Class Actions, Stanford Law Review 43, 497-588.

Allen, F. and G. Faulhaber , 1989, Signalling by underpricing in the IPO market, Journal of Financial Economics 23, 303-323.

Barry, C.B., C.J. Muscarella , J.W. Peavy III, and M.R. Vetsuypens , 1990, The role of venture capital in the creation of public companies, Journal of Financial Economics 27, 447-471.

Barry, C.B. and R.H. Jennings, 1993, The opening price performance of initial public offerings of common stock, Financial Management 22, 54-63.

Benveniste , L.M. and P.A. Spindt , 1989, How investment bankers determine the offer price and allocation of new issues, Journal of Financial Economics 24, 343-363.

Booth, J. and R. Smith, 1986, Capital raising, underwriting, and the certification hypothesis, Journal of Financial Economics 15, 261-281.

Carter, R.B. and F.H. Dark, 1993, Underwriter reputation and initial public offers: The detrimental effects of flippers, The Financial Review 28, 279-301.

Carter, R.B. and S. Manaster , 1990, Initial public offerings and underwriter reputation, Journal of Finance 45, 1045-1068.

Drake, P.D. and M.R. Vetsuypens , 1993, IPO underpricing and insurance against legal liability, Financial Management 22, 64- 73.

Fabozzi, F.J. and F. Modigliani , 1992, Capital Markets: Institutions and Instruments, Prentice-Hall, Englewood Cliffs, New Jersey.

Grinblatt, M. and C.Y. Hwang , 1989, Signalling and the pricing of new issues, Journal of Finance 44, 393-420.

Hanley, K.W. , 1993, The underpricing of initial public offerings and the partial adjustment phenomenon, Journal of Financial Economics 34, 231-250.

Hughes, P. and A. Thakor , 1992, Litigation risk, intermediation, and the underpricing of initial public offerings, Review of Financial Studies 5(4), 709-742.

Ibbotson, R., 1975, Price performance of common stock new issues, Journal of Financial Economics 2, 235-272.

Koh, F. and T. Walter, 1989, A direct test of Rock's model of the pricing of unseasoned issues, Journal of Financial Economics 23, 251-272.

Lim, J. and A. Saunders, 1990, Initial public offerings: The role of venture capitalists (The Research Foundation of The Institute of Chartered Financial Analysts, Charlottesville, Virginia).

Logue, D., 1973, On the pricing of unseasoned equity issues, Journal of Financial and Quantitative Analysis, 91-103.

Miller, R. and F. Reilly , 1987, An examination of mispricing , returns, and uncertainty of initial public offerings, Financial Management 11, 33-38.

Muscarella, C.J. and M.R. Vetsuypens , 1989, A simple test of Baron's model of IPO underpricing, Journal of Financial Economics 24, 125-135.

Ritter, J., 1984, The hot issue market of 1980, Journal of Business 57, 215-241.

Rock, K., 1986, Why new issues are underpriced, Journal of Financial Economics 15, 187-212.

Tinic, S., 1988, Anatomy of initial public offerings of common stock, Journal of Finance 43, 789-822.

Welch, I., 1989, Seasoned offerings, imitation cost and the underpricing of initial public offerings, Journal of Finance 44, 421-449.

Endnotes

[1] The theoretical models such as the winner's curse model, the dynamic information acquisition model, and the information cascades model can be classified under the asymmetric information theory. See Ibbotson, Sindelar, and Ritter (1994).

[2] Barry, Muscarella, Peavy, and Vetsuypens (1990) report the average age for non-VC-backed IPOs is 14 years, about twice the length of VC-backed IPOs.

[3] Among 84 observations which we are able to identify the investment instrument used by investment banks/shareholders, 53 cases and 31 cases use convertible preferred stocks and common stocks respectively.

[4] In the Carter and Manaster (1990) ranking scale, the average lead underwriter ranking is 6.5 and 6.3 for IPOs with and without investment banks/shareholders as underwriters, respectively. The difference between the two groups is not statistically significant.

Venture Capital, Bank Shareholding, Private and IPO Underpricing in Japan

Frank Packer
Federal Reserve Bank of New York

Abstract

This paper tests whether the institutional affiliation of venture capital or bank shareholding makes a difference in how pre-IPO investment affects the pricing of initial public offerings in Japan. We find supportive evidence in instrumental variable regressions for the hypothesis that bank shareholding either direct or through venture capital subsidiaries reduces new issue underpricing. This finding relates to a body of empirical work which suggests that U.S. venture capitalists are able to reduce information asymmetry and lower the costs of going public for the firms in which they invest.

The evidence further suggests that bank shareholding reduces new issue underpricing by the same amount whether or not the bank belongs to a major keiretsu. This is consistent with the interpretation that all major banks can alleviate the costs of asymmetric information for the firm going public in Japan, not just the major keiretsu banks.

By contrast, other forms of venture capital shareholding are not associated with a reduction in new issue underpricing. In fact, securities company-related venture capital increases new issue underpricing, which implies that the conflicts of interest inherent in the related securities companies' role as underwriter may be binding.

1. Introduction

It has been established as an empirical regularity in all of the world's stock markets that new equity issues tend to be priced at a discount relative to their subsequent trading price in the aftermarket. (Ibbotson et al, 1988; Ritter and Ibbotson, 1992; Loughran et al, 1994) One of the more well-known theories accounting for the phenomenon is that underpricing is required to compensate uninformed investors who foresee being disproportionately allocated bad issues.[1] Third party certification, by credibly assuring that the offering price reflects private information, represents one solution to the problem of asymmetric information.[2]

The institution which certifies should not only have better information about the firm than uninformed investors, but it should have sufficient capital, reputational or otherwise, at stake such that there would be no incentive to falsely certify. Mechanisms of certification can take many forms,[3] but here we focus on investment prior to the IPO in the company's stock. In this respect, this paper parallels a body of work which suggests that venture capitalists in the United States who take concentrated equity positions in the issuing firm—and contribute to the credibility of certification by retaining significant portions of their holdings subsequent to the IPO— are able to reduce problems of information asymmetry, and lower the costs of going public.[4] (Barry et al, 1990; Megginson and Weiss, 1991; Megginson and Mull; 1991).

This paper brings new data from a sample of initial public offerings to bear on the issue of how venture capital may affect the cost of going public. The evidence is from Japan, where unlike the U.S., venture capitalists are only rarely independent, but instead affiliated with local governments, securities companies, and banks. We are able to test in this context the hypothesis that venture capital can have different effects on observed underpricing depending on institutional affiliation.

Another form of shareholding which we shall examine along with that of venture capital is direct bank shareholding. Unlike the U.S., banks can own significant equity shares (up to 5 percent of any single company) in Japanese firms. Many firms in Japan have ties both to a "main bank" which owns equity in the firm, and looser ties with other banks which also hold shares in the firm. As we document in this paper, banks are often major shareholders of firms prior to their going public in Japan. Given strong priors in light of evidence on the role of Japanese banks in resolving informational problems in investment,[5] we also test the hypothesis that direct bank shareholding reduces the costs of going public in Japan.

The analysis is based principally on the published data of a sample of 158 companies which went public in Japan on the OTC in the years 1989-1991. Our principal empirical findings are as follows:

1) Among classes of venture capital and bank pre-IPO shareholding in Japan, bank shareholding is the most common, and it is the only class of shareholding to distinctly increase after the IPO.

2) Firms with a bank investor as a large shareholder tend to have less underpricing at the time of the IPO. This finding is independent of whether the shareholding is directly that of the bank or comes through a bank-affiliated venture capital company, or whether or not the bank is a member of a keiretsu group.

3) By contrast, the pre-IPO shareholding of any of the other forms of venture capital in Japan - either semi-governmental or securities firm related - is not associated with a reduction in new issue underpricing. In fact, companies with a securities firm related venture capitalist as a major shareholder tend to have new issue underpricing *larger* than average. Plausible interpretations of this result relate it to the conflicting role of lead underwriter which the related securities firm often assumes.

The remainder of this paper will proceed as follows. In the next section, we describe the environment for IPOs in Japan, giving special attention both to the rapid growth of the OTC market and the pre-issue auction system, an extremely significant reform introduced in 1989. In Section 3, we examine and quantify the types of pre-IPO investment in company stock by venture capital and banks. Differences in investor behavior after the IPO are highlighted and testable hypotheses of the effects of different sorts of shareholding stakes on new issue underpricing are proposed. In section 4, the data and methodology are introduced in detail. In section 5, we present statistical evidence concerning the hypothesized effects of venture capital on IPO underpricing. We conclude with a brief review of the principal results and their implications in section 6.

2. The IPO Environment and the OTC Market

2.1 The Rise of the OTC

The history of initial public offerings (IPOs) in Japan has been characterized by the existence of especially active periods. Three "hot" periods were commonly identified as of the early 1990s: first in the early 1960s, then in the early 1970s and finally from 1985 until the end of 1991. The latter period differed from the earlier ones in that service and high technology issues were the most common.

The increase in initial public offerings that began in 1985 was particularly encouraged by a relaxation of regulations on the over-the-counter market (OTC). In the past, the very stringent requirements for exchange listing had meant that firms less than 15 years old had little to no chance of raising funds in the public market. However, in November 1983, the Ministry of Finance relaxed regulations with a particular aim of giving younger small and medium sized companies increased access to the stock market. Previously only already issued stock could be registered on the OTC, but now the issue of new stock on the OTC was allowed. Further, requirements for OTC registration were relaxed. The time since firm establishment and per share dividend requirements were abolished, and a per-share profit requirement was relaxed from 10 yen per share after-tax to 10 yen per share before-tax.

OTC registration requirements which were less severe that exchange listing requirements[6] were particularly attractive to smaller size companies, and by the late 1980s, the OTC had become the central market for initial public offerings in Japan. Table 1 shows how new registrations on the OTC all IPOs overtook the combined number of new listings (which includes simple transfers from the OTC which were not IPOs) on Tokyo and seven other local exchanges by the late 1980s. Fully 70 percent of the OTC registered issues at the end of 1991 had gone public in the four years 1988-1991.

Another reason that the OTC became popular in relation to the exchanges was that the information rastructure for secondary market trading had improved. In the past, registration on the OTC market had been considered a stepping stone to listing on a more prestigious organized exchange, but by the late 1980s, many companies had started to register on the rket without a future listing on the Tokyo or Osaka exchange in mind. (Kato and Matsuno, 1991).

Table 1

New Registrations on the OTC Relative to New Listings on the Major Exchanges: 1983-1991

Calendar Year	New Registrations on the OTC (A)	New Listings on one of Eight Major Exchanges (B)	(A) / (A+B) (percent)
1983	4	25	13.8%
1984	10	28	26.3%
1985	15	30	33.3%
1986	22	44	33.3%
1987	19	51	27.1%
1988	53	56	48.6%
1989	73	54	57.5%
1990	86	55	61.0%
1991	95	43	68.8%

Source: Kato and Matsuno, p. 30, until 1990. 1991 data provided by the Japan Securities Dealers Assocation for OTC registrations; exchange listings taken from Kaisha Shikiho, 1991 and 1992 quarterly issues. The eight major exchanges are the Tokyo, Osaka, Nagoya, Hiroshima, Fukuoka, Niigata, Kyoto, and Sapporo Stock Exchanges.

2.2 The Introduction of the Auction System in 1989

Initial public offerings had long been greatly underpriced in Japan. In the 1980s, the price of newly listed or registered stock had on average climbed to 30-50 percent above its flotation price. Price runups had been particularly large in the late 1980s: Between 1986 and 1988, the offering prices of issues were discounted from first market price around 55 percent, with extreme discounts of nearly 75 percent on average characterizing the 1988 market (Jenkinson, 1990). These large discounts on IPOs became the target of public criticism during the Recruit scandal in which favorably treated third parties had made large capital gains and led to the introduction of a new system governing initial public offerings in 1989.[7]

Prior to reforms, initial public offering prices had been determined around 20 days prior to the IPO by the comparable company method.[8] Namely, the managing underwriter would choose as a comparable company an already registered or listed firm similar to the issuing company on the basis of major business lines or products. If none could be found, then the growth of sales and profits, size on a net worth basis, or the dividend payout ratio could be used as criteria for selection. The current share price of the comparable company was then multiplied by the weighted average of the ratio of the issuing company's per-share dividends, earnings, and book value to that of the comparable to determine an IPO offer price,

$$\frac{Price(ic)}{Price(cc)} = \frac{1}{3}\frac{DPS(ic)}{DPS(cc)} + \frac{1}{3}\frac{EPS(ic)}{EPS(cc)} + \frac{1}{3}\frac{BVPS(ic)}{BVPS(cc)} \qquad (1)$$

where: DPS, EPS, and BVPS stand for dividends, earnings, and book value per share, and (ic) and (cc) stand for issuing company and comparable company, respectively. The price determined by formula was to be approved by the issuing company at a meeting of the board of directors.

Although seemingly unbiased, the procedure gave the managing underwriter considerable degrees of freedom in choosing which data to input into the formula. In addition to choosing the comparable company, the managing underwriter could use either average per-share figures over the past three years or the last year's figure. Further, either the average stock price for the comparable company over the last month could be used, or the average stock price over three to six months prior. That the procedure resulted in many floatation prices being far lower than the initial market price suggests that securities companies, which gained from underpricing in the reduction of their underwriting risk, were able to choose comparable companies and financial data in a cartel-like fashion to their own advantage.[9]

During the stock scandals of 1988, the authorities decided to reform the IPO system, in particular the mechanism for the determination of the offering price. The procedures of the U.S., where the flotation price was negotiated on a "road show" and the final price adjusted and determined immediately prior to issue was examined but rejected. This was because the securities companies' ability to obtain a low price in Japan would not necessarily be affected by such a scheme.[10]

The Ministry of Finance decided to continue using a comparable company method with minor revisions[11], but the value which resulted would only serve as a floor on the subsequent offer price a total of about 30-40 percent of the shares would be auctioned off in a discriminatory auction fully open to the public where a maximum limit price of 30 percent above the floor price was also established. The balance would be sold at a offer price equal to the weighted average of successful bid prices. If the issue was overbid at the maximum limit price, then rationing of the bids at this level would occur according to strict lottery.[12]

Participation in the auction is prohibited to special related parties (such as directors and their relatives, the top ten shareholders), bids occur in units of a thousand, and any one party can only bid 2000 shares. (Kato and Matsuno, 1991) The auction occurs two weeks before the public offering of the balance and data such as the total amounts bid and the settlement prices are released to the public on the day of the auction.

The new IPO system began in April 1989, and the evidence is that it decreased the underpricing of IPOs on the OTC by around 15 percent on average. (Hebner and Hiraki, 1992). However, the underpricing of IPOs had by no means been eliminated: for the sample of 158 IPOs made on the OTC between 1989 and 1991 which we will be examining more closely later, the average difference between offer price and initial trading price was 14 percent.

3. Types of Venture Capital and Bank Shareholding

In the following, section we examine the types of venture capital which were invested in initial public offerings on the OTC during the sample period. Although the principal shareholders prior to the IPO are usually managers, related parties, or employee stock ownership groups, it is not uncommon for venture capital companies and banks to own shares as well.

3.1 Japanese Venture Capital: An Overview

Venture capital companies which invest in unlisted companies tend to be relatively young compared to their American counterparts. The first private venture capital firms in Japan were established in 1972-1974 by eight banks and securities houses, inspired by a boom in American venture capital. By March 1991, 109 firms had been established with an aggregate investment portfolio of 717 billion yen. (Nikkei Venture, 1991). Despite high growth and new entrants, the venture capital industry remains quite concentrated: the top 4 firms accounted for 39.6 percent of outstanding investment, while the top 10 accounted for 62.1 percent.

There are other significant differences between venture capital in Japan and the United States. The staff of venture capital companies usually have little to no technical background, and, unlike the U.S., they are prevented by the Anti-Monopoly law from taking active positions on the board of the companies they invest in.[13] But perhaps the most striking characteristic of Japanese venture capital is that only one of the top twenty-five venture capital firms is independent. The rest are, with one exception, either semi-governmental institutions (4), or the affiliates of securities companies (10) and banks (10).[14]

The presence of venture capital is clearly evident in our sample of 158 firms which went public in Japan between April 1989 and March 1991 on the over-the-counter market. (Table 2) 63 firms, or approximately 40 percent, have a venture capitalist among the top 10 shareholders prior to listing. There are also 45 cases of secondary venture capitalists among the top ten shareholders.

Table 2

PreIPO Investment by Types of Venture Capital:IPOs on the OTC, April 1989-March 1991

Type of venture capital	Cases for which this type is lead venture capitalist prior to IPO (A)	Cases for which this type is secondary venture capitalist prior to IPO (B)	(A)+(B)	Percent of IPO Sample (A)+(B)/158
SBIC	9	0	9	5.7%
Securities Firm Subsidiary	37	16	53	33.5%
(of which JAFCO)	19	4	23	14.6%
Bank Subsidiary	16	15	31	19.6%
Foreign Firms	0	12	12	7.6%
Other	0	2	2	1.3%

Note: A venture capitalist is counted as the lead if it is among the top 10 shareholders prior to the IPO and has more shares than all other venture capitalists. All other venture capitalists among the firm's top ten shareholders are secondary venture capitalists. SBIC stands for small business investment corporations, semigovernmental institutions set up in Tokyo, Nagoya, and Osaka with capital contributed by local governments and local financial institutions. JAFCO stands for Japan Affiliated Finance Company, a venture capital subsidiary of Nomura.

Source: Kaisha Shikiho, quarterly issues, 19891991; Japan Securities Dealers Association.

The average stake of the lead venture capitalist is only around 7 percent, less than one-half of the participation documented in similar studies of the United States. On average, the post-IPO equity share held by the lead venture capitalist in around one-half of the pre-IPO share. (Table 3) This implies that a substantial degree of cashing out occurs, since the increase in the number of shares outstanding following a public offering is limited to 30 percent. (Yamashita, 1989)

3.2 The Small Business Investment Corporations

There appear to be distinct patterns in the behavior of venture capital depending on institutional affiliation. The oldest venture capital firms in Japan are the semi-governmental institutions. In 1963, Small Business Investment Companies were set up in Tokyo, Nagoya, and Osaka by the enactment of the Small Business Investment Law under MITI's initiative. Capital was contributed into these SBIC's by both local government institutions and local financial institutions and companies. Regulations limit their investment to small, yet profitable dividend paying companies, and further require that the investment be at least 15 percent of the total equity. (Clark, 1988). Because of their early start, the investments outstanding of the three SBICs are still relatively large, and they are ranked 5th, 11th, and 22nd in a 1991 ranking of top venture capital firms. However, their role decreased greatly as the venture capital industry grew in Japan.[15]

The fruits of past SBIC investment decisions are evident in the 158 firm sample of IPOs. Table 2 indicates that they were the leading venture capitalist in 9 out of the 63 cases in which pre-IPO venture capital funding occurred. A distinctive feature of SBIC cases is that they are the leading venture capital shareholder in every case in which their investment appears. This phenomenon reflects the minimum shareholding requirement mentioned above. Another distinctive feature is a greater continuation of the shareholding role subsequent to the IPO. In Table 3, we see that the SBIC equity share in the company on average decreased by less than 20 percent subsequent to the IPO, a percentage decrease which is far less than that of the other classes of venture capital.

3.3 Securities-Company Affiliated Venture Capital

Another class of players in the Japanese venture capital industry are those companies which are affiliates of a Japanese securities company. Five out of the top ten, and eleven out of the top twenty-five firms are affiliated with securities companies. A striking parallel with the securities industry is the dominance of one firm in particular: Nomura's affiliated subsidiary, Japan Affiliated Finance Company (JAFCO), which controls around 24 percent of the private venture capital business, a share which showed no sign of decreasing in the early 1990s.[16]

It is widely held that venture capitalists affiliated with securities companies have as their principle investment motive the obtaining of the lead underwriter position for the parent if and when the company goes public.[17] In Table 4, it is indeed apparent that a company whose top ten shareholder is a securities company affiliated venture capitalist is far more likely to choose that securities company as its managing underwriter.[18]

Table 3

Venture Capital Investment: Pre-IPO and Post-IPO Compared

	No. of Firms	(A) Mean No. of Venture Capitalists as Major Shareholder (PreIPO)	(B) Mean No. of Venture Capitalists as Major Shareholder (PostIPO)	(B)/(A) (Percent)	(C) Mean % of Equity Held by Lead Venture Capitalist (PreIPO)	(D) Mean % of Equity Held by Lead Venture Capitalist (PostIPO)	(D)/(C) (Percent)	(E) Mean % of Equity Held by Venture Capitalists Which are Major Shareholders (PreIPO)	(F) Mean % of Equity Held by Venture Capitalists Which are Major Shareholders (PostIPO)	(F)/(E) (Percent)
Firms with Venture Capitalist as Major Shareholder Prior to IPO	63	1.68	0.98	58.2%	6.80	3.59	52.8%	8.87	4.10	46.2%
(of which Securities firm subsidiary is lead venture capitalist)	37	1.83	0.97	53.1%	6.82	2.66	39.0%	9.56	3.30	34.5%
(of which JAFCO is lead venture capitalist)	19	1.95	1.00	51.4%	7.70	3.19	41.4%	12.23	3.45	28.2%
(of which bank subsidiary is lead venture capitalist)	16	1.41	0.94	66.7%	4.59	2.69	58.7%	6.14	3.24	52.8%
of which SBIC is lead venture capitalist)	9	1.22	1.11	91.1%	11.39	9.57	84.0%	11.93	9.80	82.1%

Note: Lead venture capitalist is defined as on Table 2.   Sources: Kaisha Shikiho, quarterly issues, 1989-92.

Table 4

The Relationship Between Venture Capital Participation and the Position of Lead Underwriter: IPOs on the OTC, April 1989 March 1991

Securities Firm	Number of IPOs in Which Subsidiary was the Lead Venture Capitalist (A)	Number of (A) in Which the Securities Firm was the Lead Underwriter (B)	(B)/(A) (Percent)	Percent of Other IPOs in Which the Securities Firm was the Lead Underwriter
Nomura	23	15	65.2%	20.7%
Daiwa	5	4	80.0%	15.0%
Nikko	6	4	66.7%	12.5%
Yamaichi	2	2	100.0%	19.9%
Sanyo	6	0	0.0%	0.6%
Marusan	3	2	66.7%	0.0%
Okusan	2	1	50.0%	0.0%
Maruman	1	0	0.0%	0.0%
Kankaku	1	1	100.0%	0.0%
Daiichi	1	0	0.0%	0.6%
Universal	1	0	0.0%	0.0%
TOTAL	51	29	56.9%	— —

Note: Lead venture capitalist is defined as on Table 2.

Sources: Kaisha Shikiho, 1989/1991 quarterly issues for venture capital identification; Japan Securities Research Institute for the identification of lead underwriter.

Though in Japan, many securities firms are normally appointed to handle the underwriting of an issue, the firm usually appoints one as a lead manager one to two years before listing.[19] It is customary for the managing underwriter to take a far larger share of the underwriting risk than is the case in the U.S. - normally between 40-60 percent of the issue is underwritten by the lead manager.[20]

The concentration of underwriting risk should tend to decrease the potential for securities company-related venture capital to certify public offerings, as it exacerbates a conflict of interest. The ability of an issuer to get a high offer price can also result in a greater exposure to risk of the relevant underwriting institution, since underwriters are committed to buying up unsold issues. Further interests at odds with certification are apparent in the documented practice of distributing underpriced IPOs as a means to compensate favored clients.[21]

Securities firm-related venture capitalists are the most numerous in the pre-IPO investment ledger of the 158 firm sample. 37 of the 62 firms with venture capital funding had one as lead venture capitalist, another 16 had one as a secondary provider of venture funds. In striking contrast to the semi-public venture capital firms, the securities company-related venture capital firms appear to be quick to unload their shares upon issue (Table 3). The average pre-IPO equity share held by the lead venture capitalist in securities-affiliate led cases declines from 6.82 percent to 2.66 percent, or by more than three-fifths. These venture capitalists are relatively less long-term oriented than their U.S. counterparts.[22]

3.4 Bank Affiliated Venture Capital and Direct Bank Investment

The third major class of players in the Japanese venture capital industry are those companies which are affiliates of Japanese banks. Four out of the top ten, and ten out the top twenty-five firms in the industry are affiliated with commercial banks.

In the 158 firm IPO sample, the presence of bank venture capital subsidiaries among the top ten shareholders is about half as frequent as that of the securities firm subsidiaries.   27 percent of the companies with a venture capitalist as a top ten shareholder has a bank subsidiary as their lead venture capital investor prior to the IPO.

Bank-affiliated venture capital involvement parallels to some degree that of securities company-related funding in terms of post-IPO holdings. The proportion of the lead venture capitalist falls from 4.6 percent to 2.7 percent, or by a factor of more than two-fifths. (Table 3)

However, the importance and staying power of bank shareholding is greatly misrepresented by looking only at venture capital affiliates, for bank pre-IPO investment need not occur only through venture capital subsidiaries.   Unlike U.S. banks, which may not hold stocks of nonfinancial corporations,[23] Japanese banks are allowed to take equity positions in Japanese companies. It has been proposed by a number of scholars that shareholding is a mechanism through which Japanese banks reduce the agency costs associated with debt.[24] Direct bank shareholding may also be of relevance to the costs of information asymmetries in going public as well.

The recruitment of banks as major shareholders generally occurs in advance to going public, and is usually given high priority in "how to go public" manuals in Japan.[25] It can be seen in Table 5 that the presence of banks as major shareholders for companies going public is far more common than that of the more formal providers of venture capital.   Nearly three-quarters of all companies in our sample have at least one bank as one of their top ten shareholders prior to going public. Among these firms, the average number of banks among the top ten shareholders is more than 2.

Bank shareholding is usually associated with a lending relationship. In the 158 firm sample, the lead bank shareholder subsequent to the IPO is listed as the top transaction bank by the firm more than 85 percent of the time.

An important difference between direct bank shareholding and the behavior of most of the more formal forms of venture capital shareholding can be seen in the columns of Table 5 which document post-IPO holdings. Not only do more banks on average enter the ranks of the top ten shareholders with a larger aggregate share, but the share of the lead bank shareholder increases subsequent to the IPO to 3.24 percent on average.   Banks increase their shareholding either during or subsequent to the IPO, which suggests that direct bank shareholding may have more credibility as a mechanism of certification than that of the other formal venture capital institutions in Japan.

Table 5

Bank Investment: PreIPO and PostIPO Compared

	No. of Firms	(A) Mean No. of Banks as Major Shareholder (Pre-IPO)	(B) Mean No. of Banks as Major Shareholder (Post-IPO)	(B)/(A) (Percent)	(C) Mean % of Equity Held by Lead Bank Shareholder (Pre-IPO)	(D) Mean % of Equity Held by Lead Bank Shareholder (Post-IPO)	(D)/(C) (Percent)	(E) Mean % of Equity Held by Banks Which are Major Shareholders (Pre-IPO)	(F) Meann % of Equity Held by Banks Which are Major Shareholders (Post-IPO)	(F)/(E) (Percent)
Firms with Bank as Major Shareholder Prior to IPO	119	2.23	2.79	125.1%	2.64	3.29	124.6%	5.09	7.32	143.8%
(of which group bank is lead bank shareholder)	66	2.26	2.70	112.0%	2.55	3.01	111.8%	5.05	6.79	134.5%
Firms with Bank as Major Shareholder After IPO	147	1.80	2.70	150.0%	2.11	3.15	149.3%	4.10	6.79	165.6%
(of which group bank is lead bank shareholder)	81	1.84	2.64	143.5%	2.07	2.96	143.0%	4.08	6.52	159.8%

Note: A bank is counted as the lead if it is among the top 10 shareholders prior to the IPO and has more shares than all other banks.
Sources: Kaisha Shikiho, quarterly issues, 1989ï1992.

3.5 Hypotheses

On the basis of the above descriptive evidence, we propose the following testable hypotheses regarding the impact of various forms of venture capital on IPO underpricing in Japan.

H1:   *Investment by SBICs reduces IPO underpricing.* Since among types of venture capital, SBICs own and retain post-IPO the largest fraction of the firm, they may play a certification role by alleviating informational asymmetries and reduce equilibrium underpricing.

H2:   *Direct bank investment and investment by bank-related venture capital reduce IPO underpricing.* As banks are often seen as reducing the agency costs of debt in Japan, bank investment may also reduce the information-related costs of going public in Japan.

H3:   *Bank-related venture capital investment reduces IPO underpricing by less than direct bank investment.* Although bank-related venture capital retains a substantial fraction subsequent to the IPO, of the types of pre-IPO shareholding stakes examined in this paper, only direct bank shareholding increases subsequent to the IPO.

H4:   *Direct keiretsu bank investment and investment by keiretsu bank-related venture capital reduces IPO underpricing by more than similar investment by non-keiretsu firms.* Numerous empirical studies have associated the beneficial impact of bank relationships in Japan with memberships in a keiretsu or relationships with a keiretsu bank. (Hoshi et al, 1990; Flath, 1990)

H5:   *Venture capital investment by securities company-related firms reduces IPO underpricing by less than other forms of venture capital, or direct bank investment.* Securities company-related venture capital investment tends to be smaller and retain less subsequent to the IPO than other forms. Further, since the parent securities companies often act as the IPO's lead manager, they have more to gain from underpricing than the other forms of venture capital.

H6:   *Venture capital investment by JAFCO reduces IPO underpricing by more than that of other securities company-related venture capitalists.* JAFCO, the Nomura subsidiary, is by far the largest venture capitalist in Japan and more likely than the other securities company-related venture capitalists to be invested in issues that its parent is not the lead underwriter for.

4. Data and Methodology

4.1 Data

The sample consists of 158 firms which went public in Japan between April 1989 and March 1991 on the over-the-counter market. Firms were chosen which went public only on the over-the-counter market for the sake of preserving the homogeneity of the sample, as listing requirements are much more strict for companies on the Tokyo and regional exchanges. The period is chosen so that the entire sample postdates the reforms of March 1989, but precedes additional reforms of early 1992, and thus give a consistent set of "rules-of-the-game" over which to estimate coefficients.[26]

Shareholding data (both pre-and post-IPO), firm size and age, as well as identification of the transaction bank, have been taken from 1988-1991 quarterly, the *Kaisha Shikiho*, which has numerous data about each publicly traded company, including the number of shares held by the top ten shareholders at the latest accounting period, which was always pre-IPO data for the most recently registered companies. Price and quantity information about the auction and initial public offerings were provided by the Japan Securities Dealers Association which included the number of shares put up for sale, the allowable bid interval, and the number of bids submitted, and weighted average of bids (offering price) from the auction; and number of shares offered, and the first trading price on the day of the initial public offering.

4.2 Methodoogy

To test our hypotheses of certification, we regress the percent difference between the first trading price and the offering price on certification dummy variables. We include other explanatory variables to control for Japanese institutional features as well as other firm-specific factors. All equations we will estimate are of the following basic form :

$$R_i = \alpha A_i + \beta L_i + \gamma Y_i + \delta S_i + \theta_s C_{i_s} + \theta_b C_{i_b} + \theta_g C_{i_g} + \varepsilon_i \qquad (2)$$

where:

R_i = $([P_m - P_o]/ P_o) * 100$, or the percent change in the first trading price (P_m) relative to the offer price (P_o) for firm i;

A_i = An instrument for the ratio of the total number of bids at the pre-issue auction for firm i to the number of shares for sale at the auction;

L_i = The percent change in the OTC market index during the period between the auction and the formation of an initial trading price for firm i;

Y_i = The natural log of one plus the age of firm i, or the years that have passed since the incorporation of firm i to its initial public offering;

S_i = The natural logarithm of the gross proceeds of the initial public offering of firm i in hundreds of millions of yen;

C_{i_s} = 1 if a securities firm-related venture capitalist owns more than 3 percent of firm i;

C_{i_b} = 1 if a bank and its related venture capitalist own more than 3 percent of firm i;

C_{i_g} = 1 if a SBIC owns more than 3 percent of firm i.

The auction bid ratio is public information that should be positively related to expectations after the auction concerning the actual value of the issue.[27] However, since the auction bid ratio is endogenous, an instrument for the auction bid ratio is used which is suggested by the 2SLS procedure.[28] The lag variable (Li) is included since institutional lags of this sort have been found to be significant in regressions of IPO initial returns (Ritter, 1984).[29] Age (Yi) is included as older firms are considered less likely to have associated uncertainty, and less subject to equilibrium underpricing. Similarly, the monetary size of the issue (Si) has been shown by Beatty and Ritter (1986) to be associated with less underpricing in the U.S.

Since we only have information on the top ten shareholders, it is necessary to establish a percent shareholding cutoff when defining the certification dummies.[30] As the percent holdings of the tenth shareholder differ widely among firms, using all known shareholdings to define the dummy would lead to biased results.[31] Our cutoff of three percent means the exclusion of around one-third of the cases in which firms have venture capitalist firms among their top ten shareholders.

5. Results

5.1 Sample Summary Statistics

In Table 6, characteristics of the 158 firms which went public on the OTC between April 1989 and March 1991 are presented according to the existence and type of venture backing. The average initial return of firms which have a venture capital investor holding more than 3 percent of the shares prior to issue have moderately smaller initial returns, a somewhat larger issue size, and are slightly older on average. However, more striking differences are evident when we divide the sample by different types of venture capital.

The firms in which SBICs invest are greatly older than average (38.6 years as opposed to the average of 26.6 years) and have a much smaller issue size. Also, the initial return on SBIC-backed issues is generally much lower, a phenomenon paralleled by much less demand on average for the issue during the auction.

Venture capital issues in which securities company-affiliates were the lead tend to be much younger (5 years) than the average issue, while the size of the issues is not significantly different. However, the initial return is nearly 4 percent larger than average. Somewhat surprisingly, this return difference appears to be due to the subsample of firms for which JAFCO is the lead venture capitalist.

On the other hand, new stock issues in which bank-related venture capital or direct bank investment is the principal type of pre-IPO investment, tend to be larger and older than average, with a slightly lower initial return on the date of the IPO. Differences are again more striking when a further sub-sample is examined: this time, the firms in which group banks have the principal investment have a dramatically smaller average initial return.

Table 6

Sample Characteristics According to Type of Venture Backing

Initial return is defined as the percentage difference between the offer price and the first price reached in the secondary market. The auction bid ratio is the ratio of the total number of bids submitted for the shares at the preissue auction to the number of shares which were up for sale in the auction. An issue was identified as rationed at auction if this ratio was greater than one. Age is the number of years between the founding and registration of the firm on the OTC. SBIC's, securitiesfirmaffiliated, and bankaffiliated venture capital issues add up to more than the total of 76 due to ties.

	Number	Initial Return	Percent of Issues Rationed at Auction	Auction Bid Ratio	Age	Issue Size (¥100 mm)
All Firms	158	13.9%	53.0%	8.8	26.6	53.8
Lead Venture Capitalist Owns >3% of preIPO Shares	76	12.7%	50.0%	8.6	28.3	54.1
(SBIC)	9	7.7%	33.0%	4	38.7	35.4
(Securities Firm Affiliated)	23	17.8%	48.0%	6.5	21.5	51.7
(JAFCO)	15	23.9%	47.0%	7.2	24.7	32.4
(Bank Affiliated and Direct Bank Investment	57	12.4%	54.0%	9.7	29.1	60.9
(Group Bank)	28	5.4%	42.0%	9	31.7	45.7
(Excluding Direct Bank Investment)	12	13.9%	53.0%	8.8	26.6	53.8
Lead Venture Capitalist Owns < 3% of preIPO shares	82	15.0%	54.0%	8.9	25.1	53.2

Sources: Kaisha Shiki Ho, quarterly, 1989/1991; Japan Securities Dealer Association.

5.2 The Determinants of Initial Return

Table 7 reports the results of instrumental variable regressions (A)-(D), all adhering with minor variation to the basic formulation of (2). In equation (B), Cb is redefined to equal one only if the venture capital affiliate of a bank owned more than 3 percent of the company's stock prior to the IPO. In equation (C), Cb is redefined to equal one only if a bank and/or its venture capital affiliate which belongs to one of the six major keiretsu—Sumitomo, Mitsubishi, Mitsui, Fuyo, Sanwa, and DKB—owned more than 3 percent of the company's stock prior to the IPO. In equation (D), Cs is redefined to equal one only if the Nomura venture capital subsidiary, JAFCO, owned more than 3 percent of the company's stock prior to the IPO.

The resulting R^2 statistics round to either .11 and .12 for the four specifications. These are similar to R^2 statistics of .07 to .15 for most of the studies purporting to explain cross-sectional variation in the underpricing of IPOs in the United States.[32] Coefficients on both the instrument for the auction bid ratio and the institutional lag variable are highly significant, with the expected signs. Coefficients on age and issue size are neither of the expected sign, and the surprisingly positive coefficients for issue size are statistically significant. At least for the sample period on the OTC market, issue size is related to greater overpricing.

Estimated coefficients on the certification dummy variables in the four specifications all bear on the hypotheses proposed above. The hypothesis that SBICs reduce IPO underpricing (H1) is rejected in all specifications: the coefficients are of the wrong sign and statistically insignificant. However, the hypothesis that direct bank investment and investment by bank-related venture capital reduce IPO underpricing (H2) cannot be rejected: all the coefficients in all specifications are negative and statistically significant. The presence of bank pre-IPO shareholding over 3 percent is associated with lower excess returns of between 9 and 13 percent after controlling for other variables.

What form the bank investment takes and what type of bank makes it does not appear to be important as conjectured in (H3) and (H4). Equation B's coefficient on a dummy which only counts bank-related venture capital investment is not significantly different from the coefficient on the more inclusive dummy of equation A. Similarly, the coefficient on Equation C's keiretsu bank dummy is not significantly different from equation A's inclusive dummy, indicating that the certification effect of bank investment does not change when it takes place only through a keiretsu-related firm.

As expected from H(5), securities company-related venture capital investment reduces underpricing by less than that of the other forms of venture capital (and direct bank) investment.[33] In fact, even relative to the case of no pre-IPO investment, securities company-related investment has a significantly positive effect on IPO underpricing in all four estimations. The coefficient is not significantly changed when we look at JAFCO backing alone, which indicates that JAFCO's effect on pricing is not materially different from other venture capitalists of the same class, rejecting H(6).

That bank shareholding is the one which serves to certify issues of companies going public is consistent with the prevailing view of the post-war Japanese financial system as "bank-led." For listed companies, bank shareholding has been shown to be empirically related to a reduction in the agency problems of debt. (Flath, 1990; Prowse, 1990; Kim, 1991) The evidence presented here suggests that pre-IPO bank investment also reduces the cost of going public for the Japanese firm. It suggests that the information-production role of banks in Japan extends beyond the contingencies of the debt contract and the provision of loans.

The fact that securities company-related venture capital investment not only reduces underpricing by less than bank shareholding, but increases it is striking support for the existence of conflicts of interest in their affiliation. Securities company venture investment may increase the securities company's bargaining power vis-a-vis the issuer when it comes to setting the limit prices for the pre-issue auctions.[34] Another possible explanation is that the securities companies may have engaged in substantially more initial day price support of issues in which they were both the lead underwriter and venture capitalist.[35]

Table 7

Estimates of the Relation between Initial Returns on IPOs, Control Variables, and Types of Venture Capital Participation (t-statistics in parentheses)

The dependent variable is the initial return defined as the percentage difference between the offer price and the first price reached in the secondary market. Auction Bid Ratio is the ratio of the total number of bids submitted for the auction to the number of shares which were up for sale in the auction. Institutional Lag is the return measured in percentage points of the Nikkei OTC index during the period between the auction and the listing of the stock. Age is the natural log of one plus the number of years between the founding and listing of the issuing firm. Issue Size is the natural log of the gross proceeds from the offering in hundreds of millions of yen. SemiPublic Venture Dummy equals 1 if a semipublic venture capital institution owned more than 3% of the company's stock prior to listing, 0 otherwise. Sec. Venture Dummy equals 1 if the venture capital affiliate of a securities firm owned more than 3% of the company's stock prior to listing, 0 otherwise. Nomura Venture Dummy equals 1 if JAFCO firm owned more than 3% of the company's stock prior to listing, 0 otherwise. Bank Dummy equals 1 if a bank and/or its affiliated venture capital institution owned more than 3% of the company's stock prior to listing, 0 otherwise. Keiretsu Bank Dummy equals 1 if a keiretsu bank and/or its affiliated venture capital institution owned more than 3% of the company's stock prior to listing, 0 otherwise. Bank Venture Dummy equals 1 if the venture capital affiliate of a bank owned more than 3% of the company's stock prior to listing, 0 otherwise.

	Auction Bid Ratio	Insti- tutional Lag	Age	Issue Size	Semi- Public Venture Dummy	Sec. Venture Dummy	Nomura Venture Dummy	Bank Dummy	Keiretsu Bank Dummy	Bank Venture Dummy	R^2
(A)	4.39	2.30	8.82	7.56	9.21	17.65		12.02			0.11
	(3.41)	(3.44)	(1.39)	(2.10)	(0.94)	(2.13)		(2.40)			
(B)	4.61	2.38	9.11	7.12	7.80	18.19			9.55		0.12
	(3.34)	(3.38)	(1.42)	(1.99)	(0.80)	(2.32)			(1.75)		
(C)	5.01	2.59	8.86	8.33	11.25	22.00				13.76	0.11
	(3.52)	(3.56)	(1.39)	(2.24)	(1.13)	(2.72)				(1.83)	
(D)	4.14	2.19	6.32	7.39	8.48		19.15	10.45			0.12
	(3.39)	(3.42)	(1.08)	(2.13)	(0.89)		(2.50)	(2.11)			

Note: Due to endogeneity of auction bid variable, the instrumental variable approach is taken. The instrument is the estimated value which results from a regression of the bid ratio on preissue market, age, size, the three dummy variables, and the percentage return of the OTC index between the setting of the auction parameters and the auction itself. Constant term not reported.

6. Conclusion

Initial public offerings differ both between and within nations. The Japanese IPO environment includes a pre-issue partial auction system which was a direct result of the reforms following the securities scandals of 1989. Another major national difference lies in venture capital. Venture capital is far more likely to be affiliated with larger financial institutions than its counterparts in the United States or the United Kingdom.

Among Japanese firms, the degree of IPO underpricing, or the percentage increase from the offering price to the initial secondary market price, differs greatly. It has been the principal proposition of this essay that underpricing in Japan may be differentially related to the different types of venture capital and direct bank shareholding. Indeed, we find evidence of large and significant differences between types of venture capital. Certification, and the related alleviation of the costs of asymmetric information in raising funds, appears to be limited to the pre-IPO shareholding of commercial banks and their venture capital affiliates.

This study has broadened not only the set of firms for which bank relationships have been shown to be empirically important in Japan, but also the set of banks. While previous empirical studies have looked at major companies listed on the Tokyo Stock Exchange, this study shows that the information production role of banks in Japan is important for smaller firms not yet publicly traded, and can be played by banks that do not belong to the keiretsu groups. One implication for future empirical work is that the role of non-keiretsu banks should be given more attention when categorizing firms as bank-related.

Acknowledgement

The author wishes to thank Yasushi Hamao, Jean Helwege, R. Glenn Hubbard, Hugh Patrick, and an anonymous referee for comments on earlier drafts of this paper.

References

Akerlof, G.A. 1970. The Market for 'Lemons': Quality Uncertainty and the Market Mechanism, Quarterly Journal of Economics 84, 488-500.

Allen, F., and Faulhaber, G.R. 1989. Signalling By Underpricing in the IPO Market, Journal of Financial Economics 23, 303-323.

Aoki, M. 1988. Information, Incentives, and Bargaining in the Japanese Economy. Cambridge: Cambridge University Press.

Barry, C., Muscarella, C., Peavy J., and Vetsuypens, M.R. 1990. The Role of Venture Capital in the Creation of Public Companies: Evidence from the Going-Public Process, Journal of Financial Economics, 27, 447-471.

Beatty, R.P. 1989. Auditor Reputation and the Pricing of Initial Public Offerings, The Accounting Review 64, 693-709.

Beatty, R.P. and Ritter, J.R. 1986. Investment Banking, Reputation, and the Underpricing of Initial Public Offerings, Journal of Financial Economics 15, 213-232.

Benveniste, L.M. and Spindt, P.A. 1989. How Investment bankers Determine the Offer Price and Allocation of Initial Public Offerings, Journal of Financial Economics 24, 343-362.

Benveniste, L.M. and Wilhelm, W.J. 1990. A Comparative Analysis of IPO Proceeds Under Alternative Regulatory Environments, Journal of Financial Economics 28, 173-207.

Carter, R., and Manaster, S. 1990. Initial Public Offerings and Underwriter Reputation, Journal of Finance 45, 1045-1067.

Chemmanur, T.J. 1993. The Pricing of Initial Public Offerings: A Dynamic Model with Information Production, The Journal of Finance 48, 285-304.

Clark, R. 1988. Venture Capital in Britain, America, and Japan, Croom Helm, London.

Flath, D. Shareholding Interlocks in the Keiretsu, Japan's Financial Groups, Unpublished working paper. January 1990.

Hanley, K.W., and Wilhelm, W. J. 1995. Evidence on the Strategic Allocation of Initial Public Offerings, Journal of Financial Economics 37, 239-257.

Hebner, K.J., and Hiraki T. 1992. Japanese Initial Public Offerings, IMRI Working Paper Series, No. 1992-005.

Hoshi, T., Kashyap A., and Scharfstein, D. 1990. Bank Monitoring and Investment: Evidence from the Changing Structure of Japanese Corporate Banking Relationships, in R. Glenn Hubbard, ed., Asymmetric Information, Corporate Finance, and Investment. Chicago: University of Chicago Press.

Ibbotson, R.G. 1975. The Price Performance of Common Stock New Issues, Journal of Finance 30, 1027-1042.

Ibbotson, R. G., Sindelar, J., and Ritter J. 1988. Initial Public Offerings, Journal of Applied Corporate Finance 1, 37-45.

Ishizu, K. 1991. Shosetsu: Tento Kabu Kokai. Tokyo: Kanki Shuppan.

James, C. and Wier, P. 1990. Borrowing Relationships, Intermediation, and the Costs of Issuing Public Securities, Journl of Financial Economics 28, 149-171.

James, C. 1992. Relationship-specific Assets and Underwriter Servces Journal of Finance 47, 1865-1885.

Jenkinson, T. 1990. Initial Public Offerings in the United Kingdom, the United States, and Japan. Journal of the Japanese and International Economies 4, 428-449.

Kakitsuka, M. 1991. Oonaa Kaisha no Kabushiki Kokai 50 no Mikketsu. Tokyo: Gyosei.

Kaisha Shikiho. Quarterly. Toyo Keizai. Kato M., and Matsuno, Y. 1991. Kabushiki Kokai no Chishiki. Tokyo: Nikkei Shimbunsha.

Kim, S.B. 1991. Lender-cum-Shareholder: How Japanese Banks Financed Rapid Growth. Doctoral Dissertation, University of Toronto.

Koh F., and Walter, T. 1989. A Direct Test of Rock's Model of the Pricing of Unseasoned Issues, Journal of Financial Economics 23, 251-272.

Kunz R., and Aggarwal, R. 1994. Why Initial Public Offerings are Underpriced: Evidence from Switzerland, Journal of Banking and Finance 18, 705-723.

Lerner, J. 1995. Venture Capitalists and the Decision to Go Public, Journal of Financial Economics 35, 293-316.

Loughran, T., Ritter, J., and Rydqvist, K. 1994. Initial Public Offerings: International Insights, Pacific-Basin Finance Journal 2, 165-199.

Megginson, W. L. and Weiss K. 1991. Venture Capitalist Certification in Initial Public Offerings, Journal of Finance 46, 879-903.

Megginson, W. L. and Mull, R. Financial Characteristics and Financing Decisions of Venture Capital Backed Firms. Unpublished Working Paper, May 1991.

Ministry of Trade and Industry, Venture Enterprise Center. 1991. Promotion of Venture Businesses and the Venture Capital Industry.

Myers, S., and Majluf, J. 1984. Corporate Financing and Investment Decision When Firms Have Information that Investors Do Not Have, Journal of Financial Economics 13, 187-221.

Nikkei Venture. June 1991. Nihon Keizai Shimbunsha.

Pettway, R. and Kaneko, T. 1995. The Effects of Removing Price Limits and Introducing Auctions Upon Short-Term IPO Returns: The Case of Japanese IPOs. Unpublished working paper.

Prowse, S.D., 1990. Institutional Investment Patterns and Corporate Financial Behavior in the United States and Japan, Journal of Financial Economics, 27, 43-66.

Puri, M. Commercial Banks in Investment Banking: Conflict of Interest or Certification Role? Unpublished working paper, July 1994.

Rock, K. 1986. Why New Issues Are Underpriced, Journal of Financial Economics 15, 187-212.

Ritter, J.R. 1984. The 'Hot Issue' Market of 1980, Journal of Business 57, 215-240.

Ritter, J.R. 1987. The Costs of Going Public, Journal of Financial Economics 19, 269-281.

Ritter, J.R., and Ibbotson, R. 1992. Initial Public Offerings, draft chapter for North-Holland Handbooks of Operations Research and Management Science: Finance, R.A. Jarrow, V. Maksimovic, and W.T. Ziemba, editors.

Ruud, J.S. 1993. Underwriter Price Support and the IPO Pricing Puzzle, Journal of Financial Economics 34, 135-151.

Schultz, P. and Zaman, M.A. 1994. Aftermarket Support and Underpricing of Initial Public Offerings, Journal of Financial Economics 35, 199-219.

Shihon Shijo Kenkyukai. 1989. Kabushiki Kokai no Arikata ni Tsuite. Tokyo.

Sudo, M. 1987. Nihon no Shokengyo. Tokyo: Toyo Keizai Shinposha.

Sutton, D. P., Benedetto, M.W. 1990. Initial Public Offerings. Chicago: Probus Publishing Company.

Tokyo Stock Exchange. Shoken. Monthly.

Tomatsu (Accounting Company). 1990. Kabushiki Kokai Zen Nouhau: Q + A ni yoru Jitsumu Sodan. Tokyo: Nihon Keizai Shimbunsha.

Venture Enterprise Center, Ministry of International Trade and Industry. 1991. Promotion of Venture Businesses and the Venture Capital Industry.

Yamada, Y. 1990. Medium Standing Companies in an Era of Proliferating Stock Flotation, Capri Review, Capital Markets Research Institute.

Yamashita, T. 1989. Japan's Securities Markets: A Practitioner's Guide. Singapore: Butterworths.

Endnotes

1 The role of rationing in an IPO in the presence of asymmetrically informed investors was explicitly introduced by Rock (1986). Empirical support for the relation of rationing and underpricing was found for the Singapore market by Koh and Walter (1989). Other theory (Beneviste and Spindt, 1989; Beneviste and Wilhelm, 1990), and empirical work (Hanley and Wilhelm, 1995) emphasize the role of underwriter book-building in mitigating informational asymmetries, but are not inconsistent with another role for third-party certification by pre-IPO investment. The general application of Akerlof's lemons' market problem (1970) to equity finance was made in Myers and Majluff (1984).

2 Signalling models, in which "good" corporate insiders can distinguish themselves from others and unilaterally transmit their private information, are another context in which potential market failure can be averted. In this paper, the possibility of firms to unilaterally signal their true value is ignored. Similarly, we ignore the possibility that underpricing itself may be a signal of value to be rewarded in later equity sales (Allen and Faulhaber, 1989), or that underpricing may be a means for insiders to induce outsiders to produce information about the firm. (Chemmanur, 1989)

3 Empirical research has found evidence that the participation of certain underwriters and auditors, and the existence of outstanding loans from commercial banks, can help to reduce new issue underpricing. On the role of accounting firms as certifiers, see Beatty (1989); the role of underwriters, see Carter and Manaster (1990) and James (1992); the role of banks, see James and Weir (1990). A certification role for banks as underwriters has been found with Pre-Glass-Steagall evidence as well. (Puri, 1994)

4 In this paper, we focus on the benefits from a hypothetical reduction in underpricing, rather than the role venture capitalists may have in improving the timing of the IPO so as to occur around market peaks, as shown in Lerner (1994).

5 For example, a steady relationship with a "main bank" has been shown to be associated with greater independence of investment from cash flow constraints. (Hoshi et al, 1990) underpricing.

6 The OTC's requirements for the number of listed stocks, the number of shareholders, the amount of profits, the examination of past financial statements, and past dividends are all lower than those of the major exchanges. As a result, financial advisors generally advise firms wishing to go public that it will take 2-3 years of preparation for OTC registration, versus 3-5 years for an exchange listing. (Tomatsu, 1990, p. 21-22)

7 A thirteen member appointed committee to investigate the problem of initial stock issues was appointed in 1988 and met six times from September 1988. Its discussion of the problems along with its recommendations were issued in December of that year and were published concurrently with the introduction of new reforms in April of the following year: in Kabushiki Kokai no Arikata ni Tsuite, Shihon Shijo Kenkyukai, April 1989.

8 A more detailed account of the determination of the IPO price is to be found in Yamashita (1989), pp. 48-54.

9 Ultimately, the price was a function of bargaining power since while the managing underwriter proposed the price, the issuer could veto it. For a fictional account—accurate in procedural detail—of bargaining over the price where the president of the issuing company demanded and got a far higher initial price through a change in the choice of related companies, see Ishizu (1991), pp. 200-207. In addition to the reduction of their underwriting risk, securities companies benefitted from underpriced issues in the increased ability to compensate favored clients through the distribution of IPO shares. In the 1991 scandal concerning compensation for losses of large clients, distribution of new issues were documented as a means of compensation, and limitations on the shares that could be distributed to any one customer were introduced as a result.

10 In the words of a Ministry of Finance representative, a road show would "not go down well with existing practices in the market ... the checking mechanism outlined earlier [of a U.S. style road show] does not function as effectively as we might wish." (Yamada, 1990)

11 Managing underwriters were given a little less freedom in the determination of this price, as dividends per share were dropped from the formula determining price.

12 This had been the method which had been used for determining the flotation price of the shares during the privatization of NTT and Okinawa Electric Power.

13 Other reasons given by Clark (1988) for the relatively small scale of Japanese venture capital compared to the U.S. are (1) The power and adaptability of the large Japanese manufacturing corporations; (2) The lifetime employment system; (3) The aversion to contractual business relations; (4) The practice of shareholding as an expression of business relations.

14 A list of the top twenty-five in 1991 is to be found in Nikkei Venture, June 1991. A larger sample of 104 venture capital firms is identified in 1991 by MITI's Venture Enterprise Center. 19 are classified as independent, 22 as affiliated with securities companies, 59 with banks, and 4 with foreign venture funds. (MITI, 1991)

15 Though they now account for less than 10%, as recently as 1985, the SBIC's accounted for around one-quarter of outstanding venture capital. (Clark, 1988)

16 In addition to its market share dominance, JAFCO is also the only venture capital firm whose the shares are publicly traded. Six Nomura group members are among the top ten shareholders, holding an aggregate 35 percent of the shares.

17 The market for the underwriting of primary securities offerings is greatly concentrated in Japan. For example, between 1975-1984, 80-90% of all stock underwriting was performed by the "Big Four" securities companies: Nomura, Yamaichi, Daiwa, Nikko. (Sudo, 1987). This concentration is also reflected in the sample studied here.

18 The underwriting fee is set by regulation to be around 3.6% of the issue. The actual formula followed is 3.5% * (Offering price plus 2 yen) * (Number of Stocks Issued). See Tomatsu: 16-17. This is much less than the typical underwriting commission paid in the U.S., where there has been documented a distinct decline with the size of the issue, but the average underwriting commission was still 7.24% for the largest category (Ritter, 1987). This perhaps accounts for the far larger share taken by the lead underwriter (discussed below).

19 The responsibilities of the lead underwriter are substantial. The lead underwriter has the responsibility for preparing the application documents for listing. Furthermore, the investigation section of the securities company examines the company in sort of a mock examination in preparation for the exchange examination. In the case of an OTC company, it is also given the responsibility for the official investigation.

20 An examination of the underwriting shares of the lead manager for twelve companies listing on the Tokyo Stock Exchange in the last three months of 1990 found the share for more half the issues to be at 60% or over, over 50% for another quarter of the issues, over 40% for another 2 issues, and at 33% for 1 issue. (Tokyo Stock Exchange, 1990) In the United States, the managing underwriter is normally responsible for 25-35% of the stock. (Sutton and Benedetto, 1990)

21 See discussion in endnote 9. In the U.S. conflict of interest issues appear to be less of an issue due to competition. Beatty and Ritter have found evidence that the market "punishes those underwriters who cheat." (Beatty and Ritter, 1986) Carter and Manaster have posited that low dispersion firms will attempt to reveal their low risk characteristics to the market by selecting prestigious underwriters who only market IPO's of low dispersion firms, and found empirical evidence of significantly negative relations between underwriter prestige and the price run variance for the IPOs they market, as well as the magnitude of underpricing. (Carter and Manaster, 1990)

22 US venture capitalist holdings have been documented to decrease their holdings by less than forty percent over the year subsequent to the IPO. (Megginson and Weiss, 1991)

23 U.S. banks can still act as agents of "certification" through the provision of loans ("inside debt"). In fact, U.S. studies show that IPO's of firms with credit relationships with private lenders are less severely underpriced on average (James and Weir, 1990). In the Japanese context, the loan/no loan dichotomy is not quite as interesting, since only extremely rarely does a firm go public without having bank loans on its books. (For example, only 4 out of 158 in our sample had no bank loans, as compared to 24% in the IPO sample of James and Weir).

24 For empirical work, see Prowse (1990) and Flath (1990). For theory concerning the role of bank shareholding, see Aoki (1988), or Kim (1991).

25 For example, see Kakitsuka (1991). The emphasis is usually on the creation of stable shareholders and by extension the minimization of "floating" shareholdings which can fall into unfriendly hands. As stable shareholders, banks are not only expected to hold on to their pre-IPO shares, but also to buy up shares in the offering or after-market to preserve or increase the proportion of their holdings.

26 In March 1992, the minimum bid price for auctions of newly listed stock was dropped from 100 to 85 percent of the comparable company price, and the ceiling on the bid price was removed. In general, it has been shown in a number of papers that major structural changes in the Japanese market change underpricing significantly. (Hebner and Hiraki, 1992; Pettway and Kaneko, 1995)

27 In fact, if one assumes the cost of submitting a bid to be constant across bidders, and zero expected profits in equilibrium among all bidders, the expected return to the bidder whose bid is accepted at the time of the auction will be inversely proportional to the probability of the bid being accepted (the ratio of bids to shares for sale).

[28] Namely, the auction bid ratio will be regressed against all the other independent variables of (2) as well as an additional variable which measures market movement over the period between setting of the auction price parameters and the actual auction itself. The estimated values for the auction bid ratio which result will be then used as the instrumental variable for the auction bid ratio in the reported regressions.

[29] Ritter (1984) looked at natural resource issues alone during the "hot issue" market of 1980. Although he found the change in the Natural Resource Index (NRI) between the registration date and the offering date to be a statistically significant factor, it only explained a small percentage of observed initial returns. Kunz and Aggarwal (1994) did not find institutional lag to be a significant determinant of IPO underpricing in Switzerland.

[30] Clearly, the choice of cut-off point is arbitrary. It should be below 5% as Japanese banks are limited by statute to a maximum of 5% (though in combination with their venture capital subsidiaries, the gross share of a bank, as calculated here occasionally exceeds 5%). If the intent is to eliminate bias of the sort discussed in the previous footnote, the lowest feasible integer is 3%. When the cut-off point was changed to 4% or 4.5%, the regression results were not significantly altered.

[31] Within the sample, the holdings of the tenth shareholder range from 0.1% for extremely closely held firms to 2.7% for firms with more dispersed shareholding. If only the top ten shareholders were examined without regards to shares held, the participation of venture capital in widely held firms would be understated relative to closely held firms. It is also likely that a percentage share should be above a certain point to be viewed by third parties as certifying the value of an issue.

[32] Beatty and Ritter (1986) explain the low R^2's in the U.S. as a result to be expected since an unpredictable initial return is what gives rise to the winner's curse problem.

[33] Due to the high standard error of the coefficients on the SBIC dummies, the coefficients on securities company-related venture capital investment are significantly greater in a statistical sense (reduce underpricing less) only relative to the bank-related dummy coefficients.

[34] In the U.S., firms are more likely to switch underwriters if underpricing is greater than expected (James, 1992). Such a check on underwriter-related mispricing in Japan may be less when the securities company is perceived as having already provided support with venture capital.

[35] Aftermarket price support has been inferred from statistical return distributions to be an important factor in observed cross-sectional variation in underpricing in the U.S. (Ruud, 1994), and direct evidence for aftermarket support has been found in Schultz and Zaman (1994).

Can Firms Outwit the Market?
Timing Ability and the Long-Run
Performance of IPOs

Alexander P. Ljungqvist
Oxford School of Management Studies
and Merton College

Abstract

Recent evidence has shown IPOs to be poor investments in the long-run. Using German data, this paper tests the "sentiment timing" proposition (Ritter, 1991), which states that companies go public when investors are over-optimistic about their growth prospects, such that long-run returns will be abnormally poor as investors correct their misvaluation over time. Based on a variety of proxies, my results not only strongly refute a negative relationship between long-run performance and investor sentiment, but instead suggest the existence of a positive relationship. In particular, new issues perform significantly better when issued at times of heavy IPO volume or in a bullish stock market. Moreover, only companies whose owners retained large stakes underperform significantly, while sentiment timing would logically imply the opposite. These results are inconsistent with firms collectively exploiting their alleged ability to spot fads in investor behaviour. Furthermore, IPOs are also more underpriced when issued in a bullish market. Taken together, this gives rise to an exploitable pattern of high initial and neutral long-run returns among shares floated when investor sentiment runs high, vs. low initial and negative long-run returns when priced in pessimistic periods.

1. Introduction

There is a growing body of evidence which suggests that initial public offerings not only are underpriced, as is by now broadly accepted, but also perform poorly in the long-run. Loughran and Ritter (1995), for example, report that IPOs in the US underperformed a matching-firm index over the first five years of seasoning, resulting in a considerable and significant loss for IPO investors. Evidence from other countries, surveyed in Loughran *et al.* (1994), seems to confirm this finding, although a word of caution is in order: there is little consensus on the measurement of long-run abnormal returns and their risk adjustment.

While there is a large number of competing explanations for the stylised fact of large initial returns (for a survey, see Ibbotson and Ritter, (1995)), long-run performance has received much less theoretical attention. This is unfortunate, since a tendency of IPOs to perform badly over the long term may cast doubt on the supposition that new issues are initially underpriced: Aggarwal and Rivoli (1990) argue that if the long-run rather than the initial trading price reflects a firm's true value, IPOs might initially be overvalued rather than underpriced.

A recent paper by Rajan and Servaes (1994) has made a rare attempt to model, in a unified framework, both underperformance and the underpricing phenomenon, as well as a third empirical anomaly: in many countries, new issues seem to cluster near market peaks - a time of higher equity valuations - suggesting there are windows of opportunity during which going public is more attractive. The attraction may be a higher IPO price and thus less dilution of insiders' ownership stakes: the higher market multiples, the smaller the fraction of a firm that needs to be sold to finance a given capital requirement.

This "market timing" contrasts with a more far-reaching proposition, which claims that firms may go public not only when equity valuations are *higher,* but when they are *too* high, that is, when investors are overoptimistic about the growth prospects of newly floated companies (Aggarwal and Rivoli 1990, Ritter 1991, Seyhun 1992, Loughran and Ritter 1995, and Loughran *et al.* 1994). Poor long-run performance could then easily be explained: as more information becomes available and investors correct their initial overvaluation, prices adjust downwards and long-run underperformance ensues.[1] This "sentiment timing" hypothesis, formalised in the Rajan-Servaes model, is chiefly based on the casual observation that negative long-run abnormal returns seem concentrated amongst the clusters of firms floated close to market peaks.

This paper aims to (i) develop testable implications which help discriminate between market and sentiment timing, and (ii) investigate the empirical validity of the sentiment timing proposition in the context of one non-US market that has seen a considerable increase in IPO activity during the 1980s: Germany.

Section 2 discusses the model and existing evidence on the alleged sentiment timing ability, and presents criticisms based on methodological and theoretical considerations. Evidence on the long-run performance of German initial public offerings will be given in Section 3. Section 4 reports tests of the spirit of sentiment timing. Section 5 concludes.

2. Analysis of the Sentiment Timing Proposition

2.1 Extant Theoretical and Empirical Results

Ritter (1991) gives three possible explanations for the negative long-run performance IPOs seem prone to. (i) Risk mis-measurement: few long-run studies adjust for systematic risk, but most researchers tend to view the resulting bias as negligible; given the extent of underperformance, betas would have to be implausibly small or even negative (in rising markets) to explain away long-run losses purely as risk-adjusted returns; (ii) bad luck; and (iii) fads or overoptimism, the focus of the present paper.[2] The fact that IPOs in high-volume years seem to have the worst long-run performance - documented for Canada (Shaw 1971) and the US (Aggarwal and Rivoli 1990, Ritter 1991, Carter and Dark 1993, and Loughran 1993) - helps distinguish between the second and third explanation. Ritter (1991, p. 19) asserts:

"The negative relation between annual volume and after-market performance [...] is consistent with the following scenario: firms *choose* to go public when investors are willing to pay high multiples (price-earnings or market-to-book), reflecting optimistic assessments of the net present value of growth opportunities." (Italics added.)

Importantly, the above passage claims not only that the new issue market may be subject to fads, but also that firms may be able to spot such fads and "time" their flotations to take advantage of them. This interpretation is supported by the following quotation from Ritter (1991, p. 4):

"If the high-volume periods are associated with poor long-run performance, this would indicate that issuers are successfully *timing* new issues to take advantage of 'windows of opportunity'." (Italics added.)

Apart from the link between new issue volume and long-run performance, there is also circumstantial evidence which may indicate IPO investors are systematically overoptimistic. Jain and Kini (1994) and Mikkelson and Shah (1994) report that the rapid growth rates of earnings per share in the year prior to an IPO decline markedly after flotation, suggesting that investors mistakenly extrapolate from past growth and therefore overpay. Rajan and Servaes find that analysts systematically overestimate future earnings for newly-listed firms, but that expectations are revised downwards over time, which is consistent with the observed long-run underperformance.

Using annual time series, Loughran *et al.* (1994) document a positive (and mostly significant) correlation between the number of IPOs and the inflation-adjusted stock market level in fourteen of the fifteen countries they investigate, which - taken together with the evidence of poor long-run performance in high-volume years - they interpret thus (p. 188):

"If companies are successfully timing their offerings for periods when the cost of equity capital is relatively low, this should manifest itself in low returns subsequently being earned by investors. This could be because firms are able to ascertain when the entire market is overvalued, when investors are willing to overpay for a specific firm relative to other firms, or some combination of either absolute or relative misvaluations."

However, using Swedish data Högholm and Rydqvist (1995) throw some doubt on this interpretation: going private volume also is positively correlated with stock market levels, which by the same reasoning would indicate that managers buy back their shares when the market allegedly overvalues their true worth, a finding which is inconsistent with timing ability.

Rajan and Servaes formalise Loughran *et al.*'s intuitive insights in a model with some irrational traders, simultaneously addressing initial and subsequent performance. It predicts that both underpricing and long-run returns are negatively related to time-varying investor sentiment, the equivalent of Loughran *et al.*'s propensity to overpay for certain industries at certain times. Their evidence from the US supports the underperformance link when proxying sentiment by market-to-book ratios. Underpricing, on the other hand, is *positively* related to their proxies.

2.2 Methodological and Theoretical Criticisms

While I accept that firms may choose to market time their flotations to benefit from higher equity values, sentiment timing is more controversial in that it makes rather strong assumptions about firms' ability to predict time-varying investor sentiment. The validity of these assumptions is not directly testable, but their main empirical implication is: *ex post*, the higher investor sentiment when a firm goes public, the worse subsequent performance. The main challenge is to find reasonable proxies for overoptimism. Methodologically, these can amount to either forward-looking predictions of investor sentiment, or backward-looking assessments of the state of demand. Forward-looking variables, however, should be used sparingly to avoid crediting firms with too much forecasting ability. This paper will accordingly make use of proxies based on backward-looking event-time, thus imposing less stringent assumptions on firms' information sets.

Econometrically, the empirical evidence Loughran *et al.* and Ritter (1991) use to support the sentiment timing story suffers from two drawbacks: inefficiency and non-stationarity. Using calendar-yearly data leads to only a crude indication of firms' supposed timing ability and hence a loss of efficiency. Methodologically, it seems better to use event-time variables (as do Rajan and Servaes), to avoid the claim that windows of opportunity exactly coincide with, and have the length of, a calendar year. The second problem is more severe. Stock market prices are usually believed to follow a random walk with drift. Regressing IPO volume, a stationary variable, on such a non-stationary series results in the 'non-sense' problem (Yule 1926) of grossly misleading t-statistics. It is thus far from certain that the stock market level really has a significant effect on IPO volume.

More fundamentally, why should stock market peaks matter? Say companies do predominantly go public when the stock price index is high. While this may be an indication of successful market timing, it need not imply sentiment timing. For the latter, one would need to assume that high equity values are a sign of overoptimism, or in other words, that every major upturn in the stock market - when accompanied by higher IPO volume - is due not to fundamentals, but to overly optimistic assessments of the prospects for particular industries or firms. The missing link in the logical chain is long-run performance: only if firms perform worse when floated in a buoyant rather than bearish market can we infer sentiment timing ability. Even then the inference can be only tentative: unless we could prove (which we can't) that firms *knew* investors' expectations when timing their issue, long-run underperformance is merely consistent with, rather than conclusive proof of, the proposition. Two testable hypotheses must therefore be distinguished:

Hypothesis 1: *Sentiment timing.* If firms have sentiment timing ability, long-run performance is negative following states of excessive optimism, but neutral otherwise.

Hypothesis 2: *Market timing.* Firms predominantly go public when equity valuations are high.

In practice, proxies for investor optimism will often coincide with equity valuations variables, so the analysis of long-run performance is crucial to discriminate between the hypotheses. In modelling the time series of IPO volume in Germany, Ljungqvist (1995) tests hypothesis 2; the present paper will concentrate on hypothesis 1.

On a theoretical note, sentiment timing is hard to reconcile with underpricing. Presumably, its benefits to a firm lie in the ability to charge investors a price, P_0, exceeding true value, P_t. But to get the empirically observed initial price appreciation ($P_1 > P_0$), investors must overpay by more, in the after-market, than they are being overcharged by at subscription, that is, $P_1 > P_0 > P_t$. In other words, the empirical presence of underpricing implies that firms do not maximise the premium $P_0 - P_t$ they can extract from faddish investors. Why don't firms, despite their alleged predictive ability, fully take advantage of investor overoptimism?[3]

Of the information-based underpricing models, only signalling makes the same assumptions about the information structure as the sentiment timing story: firms have an informational advantage over investors (Allen and Faulhaber 1989, Grinblatt and Hwang 1989, and Welch 1989). But if firms really could tell when investors are overoptimistic, why should they follow the two-stage funding strategy - raise some funds in an IPO and cash in on the underpricing signal in a later seasoned equity offering - that is at the heart of signalling models? Such a strategy would entail not one but two costs: the opportunity cost of underpricing and the cost of being found out to have overcharged over-enthusiastic investors in the first place, with a likely attendant mark-down of the share price and thus lower proceeds from the second-stage sell-out. Might it then not be better to pursue a one-stage financing strategy, selling the company for more than its true worth to overoptimistic IPO subscribers, rather than giving investors time to realise their mistake? Put differently, if successful timing implies that after-market returns are going to be poor, this is inherently at odds with the signalling proposition: signalling requires share prices to go up after the IPO - how else could the firm cash in on its signal?[4]

3. The Long-Run Performance of German IPOS

3.1 Sample and Data

The data set comprises all companies floated on one or more of Germany's eight stock exchanges between January 1970 and December 1990, excluding relistings, transfers from another market, mergers and demergers of previously listed firms (but not spin-offs and equity carve-outs), offerings in the none-too-transparent telephone market (the "Ungeregelter Freiverkehr", abolished in 1988), and listings not accompanied by an offer of equity (so called introductions). One IPO was excluded as adjustment for capital changes was impossible. In total, 145 companies (identified from stock exchange statistics and reports compiled by large underwriters) satisfied these sample selection criteria.

Share price data was taken from two financial dailies, *Handelsblatt* (until 1977) and *Börsen-Zeitung* (after 1977). Observations before 1980 are averages of bid and ask prices; the remainder are daily "single quotations". Care was taken to ensure these prices represent actual trades. The data consist of event-fortnightly returns, adjusted for stock slits, capital changes, and dividend payments. As is common in long-run IPO performance studies, in which no pre-flotation data exists, abnormal returns are calculated from the market model under the assumption that beta is one and hence constant across both time and securities: $AR_{j,t} = R_{j,t} - R_{m,t}$. These abnormal returns are cumulated over time using Ball and Brown's (1968) standard cumulative abnormal return metric, the Abnormal Performance Index:

$$CAR_{1,t} = \frac{1}{n}\sum_{j=1}^{n}\left[\prod_{t=1}^{\tau}(1+AR_{j,t})\right] - 1 \qquad (1)$$

This measure gives the abnormal investment results an investor would achieve from buying equal Deutsche Mark amounts of the N new issues and holding the shares for T periods, after adjusting for general market movements. None of my 145 companies was permanently delisted during its three-year window. Event-time clustering and the attendant heteroscedasticity were not a problem.

As a proxy for the market portfolio I use Göppl and Schütz's (1993) "DAFOX" system of value-weighted total-return indices, which track top-tier companies on the Frankfurt Stock Exchange. These are, in fact, the only indices that are adjusted consistently for both capital changes and dividend receipts and that cover more than just the last few years. Dimson and Marsh (1986) show that with long windows performance measurement becomes sensitive to benchmark choice, in particular when the size composition of the index differs from that of the event securities. Since the companies in my sample are considerably smaller than those tracked by the broad-market DAFOX index, the small-firm DAFOX-SC index - which roughly corresponds to the bottom decile by market capitalisation - will also be used.

3.2 Long-Run Returns

The mean initial discount for the 145 IPOs in 1970-1990 was 11.8 per cent (*t*-value: 8.92). Figure 1 charts the cumulative abnormal returns, exclusive of the initial underpricing return, accruing to an investor who bought the issues on their respective first trading day and held them for three years. Raw cumulative returns became significantly positive after about four months and climbed to approximately sixteen per cent over the three years. This, however, represents an annual return of only about five per cent, not much higher than a risk-free return. When adjusted for movements in the broad-market index, performance looks bleaker still: the sample began to underperform significantly half-way through the second year, resulting in an average cumulative abnormal loss of 8.3 per cent (*t*-value: -2.09) on the third listing anniversary; if weighted by first trading day market capitalisation, the mean cumulative abnormal return is only slightly less negative, -7.7 per cent. The median IPO firm lost fifteen per cent, which being lower than the mean indicates that the distribution of three-year CARs is positively skewed. In fact, it is also leptokurtic, and a Jarque-Bera test rejects normality at high significance levels. This may throw doubt on the use of parametric *t*-tests in assessing the significance of my findings; however, a bootstrap with a thousand replications rejected the null of zero average cumulative abnormal returns after three years at the .05 level.

Figure 1

Three Year Cumulative Abnormal Returns

The figure charts average cumulative returns, during the first three years of trading, for the 145 IPOs seasoned between 1970 and 1990. There are three graphs: one for raw returns, and two for returns adjusted using the broad-market DAFOX Index and the small-cap DAFOX-SC Index, respectively. Returns are cumulated event-fortnightly and the initial abnormal return is excluded. Average raw cumulative returns are significantly positive at the .10 level or less as from t=90. When adjusted by the broad-market index, CARs are significantly negative at .10 or less during the latter half of the second and for most of the third year of trading, as well as on the third listing anniversary. The small-cap-adjusted CARs are also significantly negative at .10 or less during the third year of trading; at all other times, however, they are neutral. Moreover, the cumulative loss of 5.3 per cent on the third listing anniversary is not statistically significant. In general, what underperformance there is, is incurred in the third year of trading.

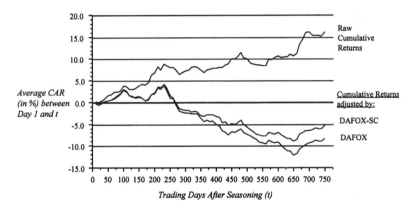

Trading Days After Seasoning (t)

Adjusting returns by the small-firm version of the DAFOX, to allow comparison with a size-equivalent investment, the sample appears not to underperform: the third-anniversary average cumulative abnormal return, -5.3 per cent (t-value: -1.3, confirmed in a bootstrap), is not reliably different from zero and thus does not allow rejection of the null of neutral performance relative to the small-firm index. Moreover, value-weighting yields an average of -1.3 per cent. On the other hand, abnormal returns were significantly negative during most of the third trading year, if not at its end, and the median firm did no better relative to the small-firm than the broad-market index: it lost 13.6 per cent. Due to the problem of benchmark choice, the conclusions that emerge are not clear-cut; but with broad-market adjusted three-year returns being negative and significant, I cannot rule out the hypothesis that German IPOs underperformed in the long term. On the whole, though, the magnitude of long-run losses seems rather smaller in Germany than in the US.

4. Tests of the Timing Story

4.1 Definition of Variables

The decision to go public is a binary choice variable, related to investment opportunities, financing needs etc. Timing proponents would augment it with a latent index, the profitability of the flotation as a function of investor overoptimism (sentiment timing) or equity valuations (market timing). The challenge is to find proxies for the unobservable, overoptimism. This paper will employ six such proxies and two control variables. As noted earlier, my assumptions about firms' timing and predictive ability will be less stringent than Loughran *et al.*'s: information sets will consist solely of past and contemporaneous data, the pricing date being the cut-off point[5]. Thus I concentrate on "weak-form" sentiment timing ability.

Loughran *et al.*'s first proxy for investor sentiment is IPO volume: under the null of sentiment timing, an increase in the number of firms going public - if associated with poor long-run returns - is seen as indirect evidence of companies taking advantage of overoptimism. Next, under the joint hypothesis that market conditions and fads are highly positively correlated and firms can predict sentiment, one may expect poor long-run performance conditional on pre-pricing bullishness. Three variants of Loughran *et al.*'s proxy for market conditions, the inflation-adjusted stock market index level, will be used: (i) observable (as opposed to predicted) index returns prior to pricing; (ii) price-earnings ratios; and (iii) market-to-book ratios[6]. As the earlier quotation from Ritter (1991, p. 19) shows, proponents of sentiment timing explicitly assert that US firms choose to go public when investors are willing to pay high PE ratios or value the market at high market-to-book ratios.

Further insight into the state of investor optimism may be gleaned from the investment behaviour of equity unit trusts (mutual funds): if these institutional investors increase the fraction of total funds allocated to domestic shares (rather than to bonds, cash, or foreign equity), one might infer greater confidence in the equity market. Conversely, greater institutional demand may just increase liquidity, thus making market timing more attractive. Again, this points to the crucial role of a long-run performance evaluation in discriminating between the two types of timing.

Lastly, if there are windows of opportunity in which it is favourable for firms to issue equity, from a market or sentiment point of view, it would be odd if only unlisted companies exploited them. Indeed, already-listed companies may well be in a better position to do so, via discretionary rights issues which are much quicker to arrange than IPOs. The high positive correlation (62.7 per cent) between the quarterly number of German flotations and the real market value of all rights issues of already-listed firms suggests that both seasoned and unseasoned firms market-time their equity issues[7]. To test for sentiment timing, one must check whether this bunching during periods of heavy rights issue activity translates into long-run underperformance. Interestingly, Loughran and Ritter (1995) report that US firms raising seasoned equity capital underperform in the long-run, just like IPOs, from which they infer that sentiment timing is prevalent in the equity market in general, rather than only among IPO firms.

4.2 Long-Run Performance Conditional on Pre-Pricing Market Conditions

In this subsection, the sample will be dichotomised by the three market conditions proxies to test the hypothesis that IPOs perform worse when issued in an "optimistic" market. The relative importance and significance of these and all other variables will later be analysed in a multiple regression framework. First, the sample is partitioned by *MARKET*, a dummy which measures whether a firm priced its shares in a relatively buoyant or sluggish market, based on whether the broad-market DAFOX return during the three months preceding the firm's pricing day was above or below the *historic* average pre-pricing return of all previous IPOs[8]. To illustrate, if the historic pre-pricing market run-up was two per cent, but a firm prices its flotation following a six per cent market appreciation, it knows it is going public in a relatively bullish market. Using historic averages provides a benchmark against which to measure a firm's pre-pricing market climate.

The second market conditions proxy, *PER_1YR*, is a measure of whether the market as a whole traded at a historically high price-earnings ratio when IPO prices were fixed. To this end, the market's average PE ratio in every pricing week (defined as the week containing the starting day of the subscription period minus two days) is divided by its 52-week moving average (from week t-51 to t), and IPOs are classified according as this variable is above or below unity[9]. *PER_1YR* is highest when the market is trading at high prices relative to its normal level. One possible objection to this proxy is its use of aggregate market rather than industry data. While industry PE ratios were not available, the force of this objection may be somewhat diminished due to the fact that German IPOs occur overwhelmingly in such established industries as machine tools and building materials, which are heavily represented in average market PE ratios. To the extent that an IPO represents a young growth industry, it is likely to be the very first listed company of its kind and thus lack peers.

The final market conditions proxy, *MTB_5YR*, measures whether the stock market as a whole traded at historically high market-to-book (MTB) ratios when IPOs were priced, and is defined as the ratio of the market value of total equity capital divided by its book value, for all firms with listed *common* shares (including firms listing both common and preference shares)[10]. This ignores untaxed reserves and other accounting entities sometimes included in book values. The variable used here is MTB_t/5-year average MTB (from month t-59 to t), with no adjustment for inflation or possible trending. A value greater than 1 indicates that the market is trading at unusually high multiples. 129 firms were priced in a month of high market multiples, versus fourteen in low-multiple months, indicating market timing.

The three proxies yield essentially the same insights. If priced in a bullish market, as measured by pre-pricing index returns or PE and MTB ratios, flotations were significantly more underpriced - by a wide margin - than otherwise.[11] This suggests that German IPOs are priced more conservatively the more upbeat the market.[12] With underpricing-type price jumps, it is difficult to tell whether the subscription price was set too low $(P_1=P_t>P_0)$ or the after-market price was bid up too high $(P_1>P_t=P_0)$, or both $(P_1>P_t>P_0)$. But if firms did use sentiment timing, it would be strange if they underestimated, or failed to anticipate altogether, after-market willingness to pay, so if anything, one would expect underpricing to be lower when investor sentiment runs high, *ceteris paribus*. This evidently is not the case. In line with my findings, Rajan and Servaes, who use a proxy very similar to *MTB_5YR*, also find a positive relationship with underpricing, which is at odds with their model.

In the long-run, bullish-market issues generally performed better (net of either the broad-market or small-firm index, and exclusive of the underpricing return) than those issued during a relatively calm market, the difference in three-year returns being significant when using PER_1YR and MARKET.[13,14.] Figures 2.a-2.c illustrate. Moreover, only when seasoned in months of low PE or MTB multiples or of low stock market returns do IPOs underperform significantly. This suggests that underperformance is concentrated amongst firms that are seasoned under relatively bearish market conditions. This result is rather striking. If I am correct to assume that a relatively bullish market signals positive investor sentiment, and this is adequately captured by my proxies, German IPOs behave in exactly the opposite way from what sentiment timing would predict.

Table 1

Initial and Long-Term Performance Conditional on Pre-Pricing Stock Market Conditions.

This table categorises the sample according to three proxies for pre-pricing market conditions. The unknown pricing date is assumed to occur two days before the starting date of the subscription period.lie proxies are: (i) stock market returns, (ii) price-eamings ratios, and (iii) market-to-book ratios; the correlation matrix in table 5 shows that these three proxies are largely independent. They are defined as follows: (i) For each IPO the broad-market DAFOX index return over the sixty trading days before pricing was compared to the historic average pre-pricing return ofall 1POs preceding the IPO in question. The flotation was then defined to have been priced in a relatively buoyant (sluggish) market if its pre-pricing market return was historically high (low). (ii) The market's average price-earnings ratio in every pricing week, divided by its 52-week moving average (from week t-51 to t), was used to partition the sample into IP0s priced when the market traded at historically high (above unity) or low (below unity) multiples. (iii) Similarly, the sample was dichoton-dsed according as the average market-to-book ratio of the market as a whole in the pricing month exceeded or fell below its 5-year moving average. For data sources, see footnotes accompanying the text. Cumulative abnormal returns exclude initial abnormal returns. Sample size: 143 or 141 in Panels A and B (subscription and thus pricing dates unknown for two private placements; two further firms preceded the price-eamings series), 141 in Panel C (two 1POs preceded the DAFOX-SC Index series). On any ofthe threeproxies, 1POs are significantly more underpriced if priced in a buoyant market. In the long-run, they perform significantly better, net of either index, if priced when index returns or price-eamings ratios were historically high; the same pattern obtains for market-to-book ratios, but there lacks significance. Moreover, only firms issued in sluggish markets, using any ofthe proxies, underperform significantly, suggesting that underperformance is concentrated amongst firms that are seasoned under relatively calm market conditions. This may be taken as evidence against the sentiment timing hypothesis and investor overoptimism, provided that my proxies adequately capture investor optimism. Ale results are robust to different classifications (above vs. below mean or median rather than above vs. below 1) and changes in the length of time over which moving averages are computed.

Table 1 (continued)

	Priced when index returns were		Priced when average price-earnings ratios were		Priced when average market-to-book ratios were	
	historically low	historically high	historically low	historically high	historically low	historically high
Panel A: Underpricing						
mean initial abnormal return (%)	8.90	15.58	7.56	14.64	1.83	12.93
t-stat.	5.96	6.77	4.29	7.90	1.30	8.95
p-value	0.00	0.00	0.00	0.00	>0.10	0.00
st.dev.	13.36	18.26	12.96	17.29	5.28	16.40
n	80	63	54	87	14	129
ANOVA	F-stat: 6.38 (p=0.01)		F-stat: 6.70 (p=0.01)		F-stat: 6.30 (p=0.01)	
Panel B: Long-Run Performance, Broad-Market adjusted						
mean CAR after three years (%)	-14.36	0.19	-19.70	-0.58	-18.90	-6.76
t-stat.	-3.07	0.03	-4.16	-0.10	-2.27	-1.56
p-value	0.00	>0.10	0.00	>0.10	0.04	>0.10
st.dev.	41.80	53.87	34.79	53.72	31.20	49.29
n750	80	63	54	87	14	129
ANOVA	F-stat: 3.31 (p=0.07)		F-stat: 5.42 (p=0.02)		F-stat: 0.79 (p>0.10)	
Panel C: Long-Run Performance, Small-Firm adjusted						
mean CAR after three years (%)	-11.85	3.57	-15.12	1.17	-20.03	-3.55
t-stat.	-2.35	0.50	-2.97	0.19	-2.52	-0.77
p-value	0.02	>0.10	0.00	>0.10	0.03	>0.10
st.dev.	44.74	56.56	37.47	56.68	28.70	52.23
n750	79	62	54	87	13	128
ANOVA	F-stat: 3.26 (p=0.07)		F-stat: 3.51 (p=0.06)		F-stat: 1.25 (p>0.10)	

Besides a refutation of sentiment timing a puzzling pattern emerges from the interaction of initial and long-term returns: firms floated in a bullish market have a high initial underpricing return, followed by neutral long-term performance. To take but one illustration, the three-year CAR *including the initial underpricing return* is large, positive and significant following a historically high index return: 15.4 per cent net of the broad-market return (*t*-value: 1.97). Thus the stock market does not seem to correct downwards the initial underpricing among bullish-market IPOs. In this sense, the initial returns on these flotations seem to capture "true" underpricing.

In contrast, the rather lower initial returns on bearish-market offerings are more than eroded over the subsequent three years of trading, and the overall performance (including the initial return) is strongly negative, whatever proxy used. For instance, the average three-year abnormal return, inclusive of the initial return, following low index returns is only -6.8 per cent (t-value: -1.26). Thus, the initial discounts on bearish-market IPOs seem to reflect transitory underpricing.

The resulting trading strategy for investors is remarkably clear: subscribe to IPOs priced in a relatively up-beat market which yield both superior short- and long-run returns. Moreover, the strategy is robust to beta adjustment and transactions costs: depending on the proxy used, buoyant-market flotations outperform bearish-market ones by up to a significant 23 per cent, adjusted for systematic risk using Ibbotson's (1975) RATS procedure, which is highly positive even if round-trip transactions costs of about 2-3 per cent are taken into account.

Figure 2.a
Three-Year CARs Conditional on Pre-Pricing Market Returns.
When priced after historically high market returns, IPOs perform neutrally throughout the three years, whereas otherwise they start underperforming the market in a significant fashion as from t=310 days. The difference in performance between the subsamples is significant at the .07 level on the third listing anniversary.

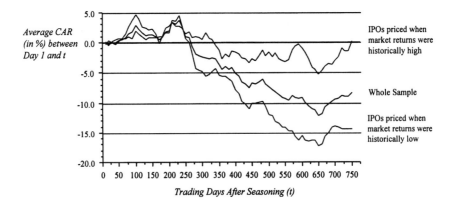

4.3 Long-Run Performance Conditional on Pre-Pricing Number of IPOs

If the number of IPOs in the three months preceding a firm's pricing date exceeded the historic median pre-pricing IPO volume for all previous flotations, a company is defined to have gone public during a hot issue period; and vice versa for a *cold issue* period.[15] To illustrate, if a firm prices its shares after a quarter that has seen six flotations, when the historic median number is only three, it knows it is going public in a high-volume period.

There is no reason a priori why IPO activity should have any bearing on initial returns, and table 2 shows that indeed there was no significant difference in underpricing (12.7 and 11.2 per cent for the cold and hot-issue samples, respectively). After three years, however, the average cumulative abnormal return on hot-issue IPOs was (weakly) significantly higher than that on firms seasoned in cold issue periods, net of either benchmark. Moreover, while hot-issue flotations performed neutrally, cold-issue offerings significantly underperformed both the broad-market (-15.9 per cent) and the small-firm index (-13.5 per cent). Figure 2.d hints at a caveat, though: the two subsamples track each other fairly closely, sharing a marked downward trend from the end of the first to the middle of the third year of trading. This notwithstanding, the evidence suggests at the least that underperformance is not clustered amongst hot-issue flotations, and may well be concentrated among cold-issue IPOs instead. This of course runs counter to sentiment timing: there is no indication of many companies taking advantage of the same window of opportunity, opened by investor over-optimism, and this in turn leading to abnormally low returns.[16]

Figure 2.b
Three-Year CARs Conditional on Pre-Pricing Market Price-Earnings Ratios.
When priced while average PE ratios were historically high, IPOs outperform the benchmark significantly between event days 50 and 270, and end their three-year spells at close to zero cumulative returns. Otherwise, they start underperforming significantly after 30 days and run up total losses of 19.7 per cent after three years. The difference in performance between the subsamples is significant at the .02 level on the third listing anniversary.

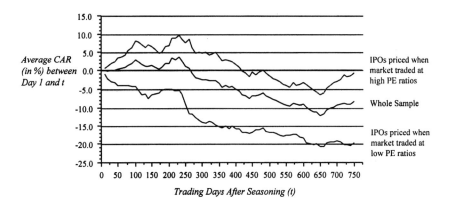

Trading Days After Seasoning (t)

Figure 2.c
Three-Year CARs Conditional on Pre-Pricing Market-to-Book Ratios.
When priced while average market-to-book ratios were historically low, IPOs start underperforming the benchmark significantly after 50 days. Otherwise, new issues do not underperform significantly until the third year of trading. While high-multiple flotations always perform better than low-multiple ones, the difference in performance is not significantly different from zero on the third listing anniversary.

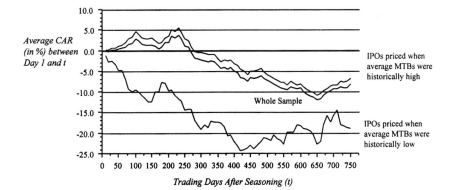

Trading Days After Seasoning (t)

Table 2.

Initial and Long-Term Performance Conditional on Pre-Pricing IPO Volume, Unit Trusts' Investment Behaviour, and Rights Issue Activity.

This table categorises the sample according to three proxies for pre-pricing investor sentiment. As before, the unknown pricing date is assumed to occur two days before the starting date of the subscription period. The proxies are: (i) IPO volume, (ii) unit trusts' equity investment behaviour, and (iii) seasoned equity issue activity; the correlation matrix in table 5 shows that these three proxies are largely independent. They are defined as follows: (i) For each IPO the number of firms going public over the sixty trading days before pricing was compared to the historic median pre-pricing number of flotations for all IPOs preceding the IPO in question. A new issue was then defined to have been priced in a hot (cold) issue market if IPO volume was historically high (low) when it priced its shares. (ii) The fraction of total funds that equity unit trusts held in domestic equity in every subscription month, divided by its 5-year moving average, was used to partition the sample into IPOs priced when unit trusts were relatively heavy (above unity) or light (below unity) investors in shares. As unit trusts are important investors in the equity market, this variable may capture the expectations of future price changes among well-informed investors. (iii) Similarly, the sample was dichotomised according as seasoned firms' equity issue activity in the pricing month exceeded or fell below its 5-year moving average. If there are windows of opportunity in which it is favourable for firms to issue equity, as the timing hypotheses claim, one would expect both unlisted and listed firms to take advantage of these windows. For data sources, see footnotes accompanying the text. CARs exclude initial abnormal returns. Sample size: 143 or 141 in Panels A and B (subscription and thus pricing dates unknown for two private placements; two further firms preceded the unit trust and rights issue series), 141 in Panel C (two IPOs preceded the DAFOX-SC Index series). IPOs are significantly more underpriced if priced when unit trusts are relatively bullish about equities or when rights issues are running at above-normal levels. In the long-run, they perform significantly better, net of either index, if priced in a hot issue market or when unit trusts are bullish. Moreover, underperformance is concentrated amongst firms priced in a cold issue market or when unit trusts were relatively bearish. With respect to rights issue activity, there is no significant difference. Provided the proxies adequately capture investor sentiment, this may be taken as evidence against the sentiment timing hypothesis. The results are robust to different classifications (above vs. below mean or median rather than above vs. below 1) and changes in the length of time over which moving averages are computed.

Table 2 (continued)

	Priced when IPO volumes was		Priced when equity unit trusts' investment in domestic shares was		Priced when rights issue activity by already-listed firms was	
	historically low	historically high	historically low	historically high	historically light	historically heavy
Panel A: Underpricing						
mean initial abnormal return (%)	12.71	11.17	9.39	16.15	8.04	14.27
t-stat.	5.89	6.58	6.92	5.89	4.64	7.64
p-value	0.00	0.00	0.00	0.00	0.00	0.00
st.dev.	16.98	15.28	12.72	19.94	12.60	17.53
n	62	81	88	53	53	88
ANOVA	F-stat: 0.32 (p>0.10)		F-stat: 6.04 (p=0.02)		F-stat: 5.11 (p=0.03)	
Panel B: Long-Run Performance, Broad-Market adjusted						
mean CAR after three years (%)	-15.91	-1.86	-18.23	9.25	-8.71	-7.41
t-stat.	-2.86	-0.33	-3.88	1.34	-1.42	-1.38
p-value	0.01	>0.10	0.00	>0.10	>0.10	>0.10
st.dev.	43.82	50.17	44.06	50.12	44.78	50.31
n750	62	81	88	53	53	88
ANOVA	F-stat: 3.07 (p=0.08)		F-stat: 11.58 (p=0.00)		F-stat: 0.02 (p>0.10)	
Panel C: Long-Run Performance, Small-Firm adjusted						
mean CAR after three years (%)	-13.50	1.18	-16.33	13.64	-8.38	-3.07
t-stat.	-2.20	0.20	-3.35	1.86	-1.37	-0.53
p-value	0.03	>0.10	0.00	0.07	>0.10	>0.10
st.dev.	47.46	52.35	45.69	53.40	44.58	54.17
n750	60	81	88	53	53	88
ANOVA	F-stat: 2.93 (p=0.09)		F-stat: 12.52 (p=0.00)		F-stat: 0.36 (p>0.10)	

Figure 2.d
Three-Year CARs Conditional on Pre-Pricing Number of IPOs.
When priced following historically high IPO volume, new issues perform significantly better than the benchmark for most of their first trading year, worse for the first half of their third trading year, and neutrally at all other times. Otherwise, IPOs start underperforming the market significantly as of the second trading year. The difference in performance between the subsamples is significant at the .08 level on the third listing anniversary.

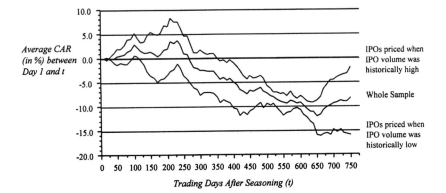

Average CAR (in %) between Day 1 and t

IPOs priced when IPO volume was historically high

Whole Sample

IPOs priced when IPO volume was historically low

Trading Days After Seasoning (t)

4.4 Long-Run Performance Conditional on Unit Trusts' Equity Holdings

UNIT_5YR is defined analogously to *MTB_5YR*: the fraction of total funds held in shares in every subscription month is divided by its 5-year moving average (from month t-59 to t), and in table 2 IPOs are classified according as this variable is above or below unity.[17] A value greater than one indicates that unit trusts are holding above-normal amounts of domestic equity. The results are similar to, but stronger than, those in the previous subsections: IPOs are significantly more underpriced, and perform significantly better in the long-run (by up to 30 percentage points), when priced while unit trusts invest heavily in equities; figure 2.e shows this quite clearly. The pattern of interaction between underpricing and long-run returns, mentioned earlier in the context of the proxies for market conditions, also is considerably stronger here: high underpricing returns amongst offerings priced when unit trust equity holdings are historically high, are followed by significantly positive returns, whilst the reverse is true for the rest of the sample. Again, this pattern is robust to risk adjustment, adding another strong dimension to the trading strategy advocated earlier.

Figure 2.e
Three-Year CARs Conditional on Pre-Pricing Unit Trusts' Holdings of Shares.
When priced while equity unit trusts invested relatively heavily in shares, IPOs outperform the broad-market index significantly between event days 70 and 400. Otherwise they start underperforming the benchmark significantly after 260 days. The difference in performance between the subsamples is significant at the .001 level on the third listing anniversary.

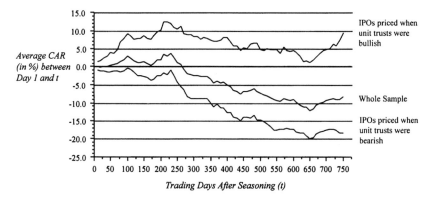

4.5 Long-Run Performance Conditional on Pre-Pricing Rights Issue Activity

Perhaps the most damning evidence against sentiment timing emerges from an analysis of the state of *listed* firms' rights issue activity around the pricing date. The variable SEO_5YR measures the strength of seasoned capital-raising, by dividing the real market value of all listed firms' rights issues in every subscription month by its 5-year moving average.[18] In table 2, the sample is partitioned in the now familiar way. To restate, the null hypothesis derived from the sentiment timing proposition is that firms should perform worse in the long-run when priced in a heavy-issuance period. The evidence in the table flatly rejects this null. However, in contrast to the previous proxies, the evidence does not favour the opposite conclusion: on the third listing anniversary, there simply is no difference in performance. Figure 2.f indicates, though, that this is not consistently the case: heavy-issuance IPOs do outperform their light-issuance brethren during the first year, in violation of the sentiment timing null, and it is not until the third year that performance converges. Thus, certainly for some time, investors would have been significantly better off - and never significantly worse off - investing in those flotations that sentiment timing would suggest are bad investments.

Figure 2.f
Three-Year CARs Conditional on Pre-Pricing Rights Issue Activity.
When priced when seasoned issue activity was historically low, IPOs underperform the benchmark significantly during the second and third years of trading. Otherwise, they outperform both the benchmark and the low-issuance group during the first year of trading, although thereafter performance deteriorates and third-year abnormal returns are significantly negative. The difference in performance between the subsamples is insignificant after three years.

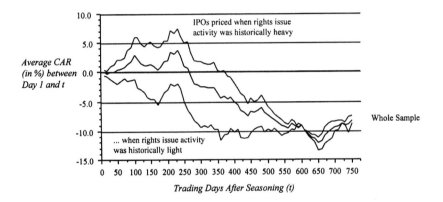

4.6 Controlling for After-Market Capital Policy

A valid question to ask at this stage is whether the results in the preceding four subsections might be distorted by the effects of after-market capital policy: one would not expect firms to use their alleged sentiment timing ability to take advantage of investors, if they planned to increase their capital in a subsequent equity offering. As was pointed out earlier, this is because timing leads to a decline in share prices (as investors realise they were overoptimistic), which is not in the interest of firms pursuing the kind of multi-stage financing strategy familiar from signalling models. Therefore, it is more likely that only firms that did not have a rights issue (within the three-year period) attempt to time investor sentiment.[19] This holds unless firms could return to the market *before* investors had marked down share prices, in practice some time during the first year of trading. However, the timing pattern of rights issues suggests otherwise: only seven companies issued rights during the first year of listing, and the median or average firm did not reissue until 480 trading days (23 months) after the IPO. By that time, performance was already significantly negative on average;

therefore, it seems reasonable not to expect any sentiment timing-induced patterns amongst firms with rights issues, implying that timing ability should only matter for companies that did not reissue, if at all.

Fifty-four firms announced one or more rights issues within three years of going public (three of these conducted their capital increase within two months after their third listing anniversaries), while 91 firms did not tap the equity market in that time frame. Companies with rights issues performed significantly better than those without (abnormal returns of 12.3 per cent vs. -20.5 per cent; figure 2.g illustrates),[20] further strengthening the case for controlling for capital increases: it could be the case that my previous proxies just happen to coincide with - and thus pick up differences in - funding policy.

Table 3 re-examines the six proxies, holding after-market capital policy constant. As expected, there is no US style sentiment timing effect within the group of firms that had rights issues: bullish-market issues did not perform significantly worse than bearish-market ones (on the contrary, for all my market conditions proxies they performed better); the same holds for *UNIT_5YR, SEO_5YR* and *HOT_ISSUE*.

More conditional on no rights issues, all my proxies reject the sentiment timing hypothesis, although unlike in the univariate cases analysed above, they do not necessarily all support its opposite. To choose but one proxy for illustration, in panel D only cold-issue flotations underperformed, with the difference in long-term abnormal returns across the two states of IPO activity being statistically significant at high levels. This is clearly inconsistent with sentiment timing. Therefore, even when controlling for capital increases there is no evidence of successful timing leading to underperformance. Moreover, the puzzling univariate finding of significantly better long-run performance following high PE ratios, hot issue periods, and heavy unit trust share purchases still holds.

Figure 2.g
Three-Year CARs Conditional on Seasoned Equity Offerings.
Firms that do reissue consistently outperform the broad-market index, frequently significantly so. By contrast, companies without seasoned equity offerings after their IPO start underperforming the benchmark significantly after 280 days. The difference in performance between the subsamples is significant at the .001 level on the third listing anniversary.

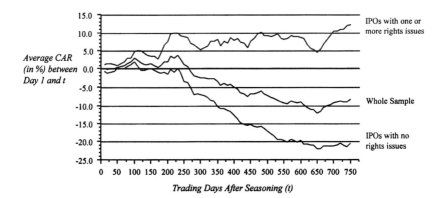

Table 3.

Contingency Tables Controlling for After-Market Capital Policy.

This table categorises all firms that had traded for three years as of 31st December 1993 and for which data is available, by the six proxies MARKET, PER_1YR, MTB_5YR, HOT_ISSUE, UNIT_5YR and SEO_5YR, controlling for after-market capital policy. 53 firms had announced one or more rights issues within three years of going public (three of these conducted their capital increase within two months after their third listing anniversaries); 90 firms did not tap the equity market in that time frame. The null hypothesis of no relationship between the state of the proxy and after-market rights policy cannot be rejected for any of the proxies. The table tries to control for the effect of multi-period capital-raising strategies on the timing story: if firms had sentiment timing ability, they should not use it if they planned to increase their capital later on. See text for further explanation and analysis.

PANEL A: MARKET

3-year CARs	Sluggish Market	Buoyant Market	t-test of Difference in Means
No Rights Issues	-25.83% -5.44/52	-12.17% -1.56/38	-1.49
	-22.90% -4.44/51	-7.88% -0.91/37	-1.49
One or More Rights Issues	6.93% 0.79/28	18.97% 1.65/25	-0.83
	8.28% 0.86/28	20.51% 1.76/25	-0.81
t-test of Difference in Means	-3.27	-2.24	broad-market t-stat/number
	-2.86	-1.95	small-cap t-stat/number

PANEL B: PER_1YR

3-year CARs	Low PE Ratio	High PE Ratio	t-test of Difference in Means
no Rights Issues	-28.80% -6.12/34	-14.87% -2.30/54	-1.74
	-23.00% -4.51/34	-12.54% -1.77/54	-1.20
one or more Rights Issues	-4.23% -0.46/20	22.81% 2.35/33	-1.88
	-1.72% -0.17/20	23.61% 2.36/33	-1.68
t-test of Difference in Means	-2.64	-3.23	broad-market t-stat/number
	-2.08	-2.95	small-cap t-stat/number

Table 3 (continued)

PANEL C: MTB_5YR

3-year CARs	Low Market-to-Book	High Market-to-Book	t-test of Difference in Means
no Rights Issues	-40.16% -6.68/ 7	-18.37% -3.98/83	-1.36
	-41.03% -7.88/ 6	-14.79% -2.92/82	-1.39
one or more Rights Issues	2.36% 0.22/ 7	14.17% 1.76/46	-0.56
	-2.03% -0.20/ 7	16.50% 1.96/46	-0.84
t-test of Difference in Means	-3.46	-3.50	broad-market t-stat/number
	--3.30	-3.18	small-cap t-stat/number

PANEL D: HOT_ISSUE

3-year CARs	Cold Issue Period	Hot Issue Period	t-test of Difference in Means
no Rights Issues	-30.82% -6.92/41	-11.06% -1.63/49	-2.43
	-29.20% -5.86/39	-6.54% -0.89/49	-2.56
one or more Rights Issues	13.20% 1.13/21	12.22% 1.34/32	0.07
	15.67% 1.24/21	12.99% 1.39/32	0.17
t-test of Difference in Means	-3.51	-2.05	broad-market t-stat/number
	-3.31	-1.65	small-cap t-stat/number

PANEL E: UNIT_5YR

3-year CARs	Low Unit Trust Equity Holdings	High Unit Trust Equity Holdings	t-test of Difference in Means
no Rights Issues	-33.52% -7.85/54	0.83% 0.10/34	-3.79
	-30.63% -6.73/54	5.72% 0.64/34	-3.64
one or more Rights Issues	6.07% 0.70/34	24.32% 1.97/19	-1.23
	6.37% 0.70/34	27.80% 2.22/19	-1.38
t-test of Difference in Means	-4.10	-1.66	broad-market t-stat/number
	-3.62	-1.46	small-cap t-stat/number

Table 3 (continued)

PANEL F:	SEO_5YR				
3-year CARs	Low Unit Trust Equity Holdings		High Market-to-Book		t-test of Difference in Means
	-24.28%		-18.17%		-0.75
no	-4.51/30		-2.98/58		
Rights Issues		-22.36%		-13.59%	-0.99
		-3.82/30		-2.06/58	
	11.60%		13.38%		-0.12
one or more	1.05/23		1.42/30		
Rights Issues		9.86%		17.26%	-0.49
		0.91/23		1.68/23	
t-test of Difference in Means	-3.13		-2.81		broad-market t-stat/number
		-2.77		-2.52	small-cap t-stat/number

More interestingly, conditional on no rights issues, all my proxies reject the sentiment timing hypothesis, although unlike in the univariate cases analysed above, they do not necessarily all support its opposite. To choose but one proxy for illustration, in panel D only cold-issue flotations underperformed, with the difference in long-term abnormal returns across the two states of IPO activity being statistically significant at high levels. This is clearly inconsistent with sentiment timing. Therefore, even when controlling for capital increases there is no evidence of successful timing leading to underperformance. Moreover, the puzzling univariate finding of significantly better long-run performance following high PE ratios, hot issue periods, and heavy unit trust share purchases still holds.

4.7 Controlling for Insider Holdings

So far, I have tested for sentiment timing using refined as well as new proxies for Loughran *et al.*'s variables. Introducing a new variable will allow an indirect test. Sentiment timing, it will be recalled, is essentially about exploiting investors by overcharging them at flotation, at the expense of poor after-market performance. But in most initial public offerings, in Germany as well as in the US, initial insiders do not sell all the shares they own, implying that they would suffer from timing-induced underperformance on the shares they retain as much as would new outside shareholders. Consequently, insiders face a trade-off between the gains from a higher subscription price by overcharging on shares that are sold, and the loss from long-run underperformance on shares that are retained.[21] *Ceteris paribus*, therefore, I would expect that the higher is the fraction of capital that insiders sell, the more profitable is sentiment timing, and consequently the worse is long-run performance.[22]

Table 4 categorises the sample according to the fraction of post-IPO equity capital sold (one minus the fraction retained) in the initial public offering. Three categories are shown: firms selling less than a blocking minority of 25 per cent; those selling at least a blocking minority but not an outright majority; and those selling a majority of their share capital. Most firms (89 out of 145) fall into the second category.[23] The results are at odds with sentiment timing: regardless of index used, long-run abnormal returns increase (decrease) monotonically with the fraction of equity sold (retained),[24] and moreover, while firms that sold majority stakes performed neutrally, the other two categories significantly underperformed the broad-market index (see figure 2.h). This suggests that underperformance is concentrated amongst firms in which insiders retain a majority stake. Conversely, whenever it would be most profitable for firms to exploit their alleged sentiment timing ability (namely when selling relatively large fractions of the firm), they evidently do not do so.[25]

Table 4.

Initial and Long-Term Performance by Fraction of Equity Sold.

This table categorises the sample according to the proportion of equity capital offered in the initial public offering. Three categories are shown: those firms selling less than a blocking minority of 25 per cent; those selling at least a blocking minority but not an outright majority; and those selling a majority of their share capital. While all three groups are significantly underpriced, initial discounts are significantly highest when less than 25 per cent is offered. Long-term abnormal returns increase monotonically with the fraction of equity sold, regardless of index used. Moreover, while issues involving majority stakes perform neutrally, the other two categories significantly underperform the broad-market index. This suggests that underperformance is concentrated amongst firms in which insiders retain a majority stake. CARs exclude initial abnormal returns. Sample size: 145.

	Fraction of Equity Capital Offered in IPO		
	less than 25 per cent	25 to 49.9 per cent	more than 50 per cent
Panel A: Underpricing			
mean initial abnormal return (in %)	20.90	9.91	6.77
t-stat.	5.83	6.45	3.73
p-value	0.00	0.00	0.00
st.dev.	20.27	14.50	8.89
n	32	89	24
ANOVA		F-statistic: 7.67 (p=0.00)	
Panel B: Long-Run Performance, Broad-Market Adj.			
mean CAR after three years (in %)	-13.48	-9.36	2.67
t-stat.	-1.95	-1.77	0.26
p-value	0.06	0.08	>0.10
st.dev.	39.04	49.97	49.74
n750	32	89	24
ANOVA		F-statistic: 0.84 (p>0.10)	
Panel C: Long-Run Performance, Small-Firm Adj.			
mean CAR after three years (in %)	-10.91	-6.26	5.95
t-stat.	-1.55	-1.10	0.54
p-value	>0.10	>0.10	>0.10
st.dev.	39.95	53.20	53.29
n750	32	88	23
ANOVA		F-statistic: 0.78 (p>0.10)	

Figure 2.h
Three-Year CARs Conditional on the Fraction of Equity Sold.
The dashed graph tracks companies which sold more than 50 per cent of equity capital at the IPO, the solid line
those that sold between 25 and 50 per cent, and the dotted graph those that offered less than 25 per cent. The
last two groups experience significant underperformance starting in the second year, while firms offering a
majority of capital perform neutrally throughout.

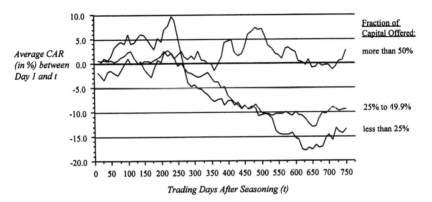

Trading Days After Seasoning (t)

4.8 Regression Results

The results outlined in the preceding subsections are confirmed in a multivariate least-
squares regression. Three-year cumulative abnormal returns were regressed on the six
proxies and two control variables whose univariate behaviour was examined above:

MARKET   a dummy coded one if the issue was priced in a relatively buoyant
market (ie, if the market return during the three months preceding the
pricing date exceeded the historic mean pre-pricing market return);

PER_1YR   the ratio of the market's PE ratio in the pricing week and its 52-week
moving average;

MTB_5YR   the ratio of the market's market-to-book ratio in the pricing month and
its five-year moving average;

HOT_ISSUE   a dummy coded one if the firm was priced following a hot issue period
(ie, if the number of IPOs during the three months preceding the pricing
date was above the historic median of all previous flotations);

UNIT_5YR   the ratio of the fraction devoted by equity unit trusts to domestic shares
in the pricing month and its five-year moving average;

SEO_5YR   the ratio of the market value of all listed firms' rights issues in the pricing
month and its five-year moving average;

RIGHTS   a dummy coded one if the firm conducted one or more rights issues
within three years of going public;

LN_CAP   the natural logarithm of one plus the fraction of share capital offered to
the public.

For simplicity, I fit a regression model only for the broad-market index; using the small-firm index yields similar insights. Table 5 summarises the results. In column I, all eight variables are included. Three of the six "investor sentiment" proxies - *PER_1YR*, *MTB_5YR* and *SEO_5YR* - are insignificant and therefore excluded in column II. Note, though, that they still reject sentiment timing, which predicts negative signs for all proxies. Only one proxy, *PER_1YR*, has such a negative coefficient but since it is not significantly different from zero, it cannot support the null of sentiment timing.

The fact that long-run performance is significantly *positively* related to the three remaining proxies strongly refutes sentiment timing and confirms the results discussed earlier: firms priced following (i) a heavy issuance period; (ii) a buoyant market; or (iii) when equity unit trusts' investment in domestic equities is above-normal, perform significantly better, even when controlling for *RIGHTS* issues. In contrast to some of the univariate analyses, these marginal effects are now all significant at the .05 level. (iv) Firms with rights issues turn in a superior performance;[27] and finally, (v) the higher (lower) the fraction of capital initially sold (retained), the better long-run performance. The adjusted R^2 of 20.1 per cent in column II is very high by the standards of long-run performance studies, and none of the diagnostics give cause for alarm.

I also regressed *initial* returns on the above variables (minus *RIGHTS*, which has no theoretical justification in this context) and a risk proxy (the inverse of real gross proceeds) to test Rajan and Servaes' prediction on underpricing and investor sentiment. Although not reported here, the results are inconsistent with their model: the only negative coefficient is on *HOT_ISSUE*, and three of the other five proxies (*MARKET*, *MTB_5YR* and *SEO_5YR*) are significantly positive. Adjusted R^2, very low in Rajan-Servaes, is a high 26.7 per cent after dropping insignificant variables. Thus my results support neither Rajan and Servaes' initial nor long-run prediction concerning the effects of investor sentiment.

Table 5.

Ordinary Least Squares Regression of Long-Run Performance

The dependent variable is the three-year cumulative abnormal return. MARKET equals one if the issue was priced in a relatively buoyant market (cf. table 1). PER_1YR is the market's price-earnings ratio in the pricing week divided by its 52-week moving average. MTB_5YR is the ratio of the market's average market-to-book ratio in the subscription month and its 60-month moving average. HOT_ISSUE equals one if the firm was priced following a hot issue period (cf. table 2). UNIT_5YR is the fraction of all equity unit trusts' total value that is held in domestic shares rather than bonds, foreign shares or cash, divided by its 60-month moving average. SEO_5YR is the average real market value (in million 1991 DEM) of all rights issues conducted during the pricing month. RIGHTS is a dummy which takes the value one if the firm conducted one or more rights issues within three years of going public, zero otherwise. LN_CAP is the natural logarithm of one plus the fraction of share capital offered to the public. t-statistics in italics under the estimated coefficient. Ramsey's RESET test uses the square of the fitted value to test for functional form. The heteroscedasticity test is based on the regression of squared residuals on squared fitted values. Sample size: 141.

Table 5 (continued)

Cumulative Abnormal Returns		
Column	I	II
Predictors		
CONSTANT	-2.144***	-2.245***
	-3.48	-3.73
MARKET	0.150	0.165*
	1.90	2.23
PER_1YR	-0.094	
	-0.24	
MTB_5YR	0.121	
	0.71	
HOT_ISSUE	0.138	0.163*
	1.76	2.21
UNIT_5YR	1.574*	1.767**
	2.12	2.85
SEO_5YR	0.020	
	0.79	
RIGHTS	0.329***	0.316***
	4.33	4.23
LN_CAP	0.562	0.546
	1.93	1.90

Diagnostics		
R^2	23.9 %	23.0 %
Adjusted R^2	19.3 %	20.1 %
Standard error (%)	43.14	42.91
F-statistic	5.21***	8.11***
RESET: c2-stat.	0.10	0.73
Heterosced.: c2	0.01	0.00

Estimated Correlation Matrix						
PER_1Yr	MTB_5yr	HOT_ISSUE	UNIT_5YR	SEO_5YR	RIGHTS	LN_CAP
0.141	0.209	-0.154	-0.068	-0.045	0.055	0.012
	0.191	0.010	0.496	0.046	0.002	0.069
		0.220	0.351	0.287	-0.062	0.079
			-0.014	0.158	0.052	-0.046
				0.130	0.001	0.149
					-0.109	-0.062
						-0.029

*** Significant at .001 or less. ** Significant at .01 or less. * Significant at .05 or less. Significant at .10 or less.

5. Conclusions

This paper has set out to analyse and test the proposition, put forward by Ritter (1991) and Loughran et al. (1994) and formalised by Rajan and Servaes (1994), that companies can successfully time their initial public offerings to take advantage of investor overoptimism, leading to abnormally poor long-run returns. This sentiment type of timing is distinct from market timing, the attempt to issue shares when equity valuations are high: sentiment timers issue equity when valuations are *too* high. The testable implication of sentiment timing posits that long-run performance is negative following states of excessive optimism, but neutral otherwise. The challenge is to find proxies for investor sentiment. Ideally, these should refrain from making too unreasonable assumptions about firms' information sets and predictive ability; the methodology advocated here, therefore, relies on backward-looking variables defined in terms of event-time, rather than forward-looking ones such as future movements in share prices.

The evidence in this paper, based on a non-US data set, a refined methodology, and a number of new proxies, finds no support for sentiment timing. German IPOs seasoned between 1970 and 1990 shared the US experience of negative long-run abnormal returns, underperforming a broad-market index over the first three years of seasoning, although the 8 per cent loss was much lower than in the US. But contrary to the US evidence, firms that went public in periods of heavy IPO activity and when the stock market was relatively bullish (as measured by, for instance, stock market returns) performed significantly *better* than light-volume and bearish-market flotations, respectively. Similar results hold for a proxy of institutional investor sentiment, the aggregate investment policy of equity unit trusts. Furthermore, IPOs seem to occur predominantly in periods of heavy equity issuance by seasoned firms, which suggests the existence of windows of opportunity. However, since empirically, there is no link to long-term performance, this is consistent only with market timing, not sentiment timing. The results are robust to allowing for possible interactions between intended capital structure changes and incentives to time: if firms plan to raise more capital shortly after the IPO, it is not in their interest to see their share prices tumble due to overcharging in the meantime.

None of these results is consistent with the predictions of the sentiment timing story. It can, of course, not be ruled out that my proxies do not, in fact, capture sentiment. They should, therefore, be understood as an attempt to investigate certain patterns of behaviour the US literature has previously documented (heavy volume and market peaks) or hypothesised (market-to-book and PE ratios). However, a final indirect test casts serious doubt on the sentiment timing proposition: whereas sentiment timing would logically suggest that firms whose insiders retained only a small fraction of equity capital should be more likely to overcharge investors and thus witness underperformance, the empirical evidence points in the exact opposite direction: only companies whose owners retained large stakes underperformed significantly. If firms really wanted to overcharge investors, this would be odd: one would expect them to sentiment-time when selling a large fraction of capital - not vice versa - for this would maximise the short-run gain from overcharging and minimise the long-run loss on their retained stakes. This strongly suggests that sentiment timing cannot explain long-run underperformance, at least not in Germany.

Although the US evidence on sentiment timing is scant and so far rather impressionistic, no claim can be made as to the applicability of my findings for the US, as many factors idiosyncratic to Germany may account for the absence of sentiment timing; for instance, the greater maturity of firms going public in Germany may result in less overoptimism, or German investors may simply be more conservative than their US counterparts.

While inconsistent with the sentiment timing hypothesis, my analysis presents two puzzles: (i) why are IPOs more underpriced when issued in a bullish market (using any of my definitions), and (ii) why is long-run performance positively related to some of my variables? The fact that IPOs perform significantly better if priced following historically high index returns, IPO volume, or unit trust investment in equities, points to a curious potential violation of the efficient markets hypothesis. Furthermore, a surprisingly strong trading strategy emerges when looking at underpricing and long-run performance in conjunction: investors should subscribe only to IPOs priced in a relatively bullish market. Such firms have high initial and neutral long-run abnormal returns (even after adjusting for differences in systematic risk), while the low initial returns on bearish-market flotations are quickly eroded and even turn negative over a three-year window.

Acknowledgement

This paper is based on Chapter VI of the author's 1995 D.Phil. Thesis at Oxford University. Previous drafts were presented at seminars at Nuffield College Oxford, the University of Illinois at Urbana-Champaign, the Oxford School of Management Studies, and Lancaster University. I wish to thank Charlie Calomiris, Narasimhan Jegadeesh, Tim Jenkinson, Inmoo Lee, Colin Mayer, John Muellbauer, and Jay Ritter for helpful discussions. Financial support from the Goodhart Fund, the George Webb Medley Fund, Citibank London, and the Royal Bank of Canada is gratefully acknowledged. Hermann Göppl and Heinrich Schütz kindly supplied me with their DAFOX Index. The usual disclaimer applies.

References

Aggarwal, R. and P. Rivoli, 1990, Fads in the initial public offering market?, Financial Management 19, 45-57.

Allen, F. and G.R. Faulhaber, 1989, Signaling by underpricing in the IPO market, Journal of Financial Economics 23, 303-323.

Ball, R. and P. Brown, 1968, An empirical evaluation of accounting income numbers, Journal of Accounting Research 6, 159-178.

Carter, R.B. and F.H. Dark, 1993, Effects of differential information on the after-market volatility of initial public offerings, journal of economics and business 45, 375-392.

Davis, E.W. and K.A. Yeomans, 1976, Market discount on new issues of equity: The influence of firm size, method of issue and market volatility, Journal of Business Finance and Accounting 3, 27-42.

Dimson, E. and P. Marsh, 1986, Event study methodologies and the size effect, Journal of Financial Economics 17, 113-142.

Göppl, H. and H. Schütz, 1993, The design and implementation of a German stock price research index (Deutscher Aktienindex-Forschungsindex DAFOX), in: W.E. Diewert, K. Spremann and F. Stehling (eds.), "Mathematical Modelling in Economics.Essays in Honour of Wolfgang Eichhorn" (Berlin: Springer-Verlag).

Grinblatt, M. and C.Y. Hwang, 1989, Signalling and the pricing of new issues, Journal of Finance 44, 393-420.

Högholm, K. and K. Rydqvist, 1995, Going public in the 1980s - evidence from Sweden., in European Financial Management 1, 287-316.

Ibbotson, R.G. and J.R. Ritter, 1995, Initial public offerings, in: R.A. Jarrow, V. Maksimovic and W.T. Ziemba (eds.), "North-Holland Handbooks of Operations Research and Management Science: Finance" (Amsterdam: North-Holland).

Ibbotson, R.G., 1975, Price performance of common stock new issues, Journal of Financial Economics 2, 235-272.

Jain, B.A. and O. Kini, 1994, The post-issue operating performance of IPO Firms, Journal of Finance 49, 1699-1726.

Jegadeesh, N., M. Weinstein and I. Welch, 1993, An empirical investigation of IPO returns and subsequent equity offerings, Journal of Financial Economics 34, 153-175.

Lee, P. J., S.L. Taylor and T.S. Walter, forthcoming, Australian IPO Pricing in the short and long run, forthcoming in Journal of Banking and Finance.

Levis, M., 1995, Seasoned equity offerings and the short and long-run performance of initial public offerings, European Funancial Management, 1, 125-146.

Ljungqvist, A.P., 1995, When do firms go public? - Poisson Evidence from Germany, mimeo, Oxford School of Management Studies.

Loughran, T., 1993, NYSE vs. NASDAQ Returns: market microstructure or the poor performance of initial public offerings?, Journal of Financial Economics 33, 241-260.

Loughran, T. and J.R. Ritter, 1995, The new issues puzzle, Journal of Finance 50, 23-51.

Loughran, T., J.R. Ritter and K. Rydqvist, 1994, Initial public offerings: international insights, Pacific Basin Finance Journal 2, 165-199.

McGuinness, P., 1992, An examination of the underpricing of initial public offerings in Hong Kong: 1980-90, Journal of Business Finance and Accounting 19, 165-186.

Michaely, R. and W.H. Shaw, 1994, The pricing of initial public offerings: tests of adverse-selection and signaling theories, Review of Financial Studies 7, 279-319.

Mikkelson, W.H. and K. Shah, 1994, Going public and operating performance, mimeo, University of Oregon.

Rajan, R. and H. Servaes, 1994, The effect of market conditions on initial public offerings, mimeo, University of Chicago.

Reilly, F.K., 1977, New issues revisited, Financial Management 6, 28-42.

Ritter, J.R., 1991, The long-run performance of initial public offerings, Journal of Finance 46, 3-27.

Rydqvist, K., 1993, Initial public offerings in Sweden, Working Paper No. 48, Stockholm School of Economics.

Seyhun, N., 1992, Information asymmetry and price performance in initial public offerings, mimeo, University of Michigan.

Shaw, D.C., 1971, The performance of primary common stock offerings: a Canadian comparison, Journal of Finance 26, 1101-1113.

Welch, I., 1989, Seasoned offerings, imitation costs, and the underpricing of initial public offerings, Journal of Finance 44, 421-449.

Yule, G.U., 1926, Why do we sometimes get non-sense correlations between time series? A study in sampling and the nature of time series, Journal of the Royal Statistical Society 89, 1-64.

Endnotes

[1] The Economist popularised this view, arguing an increase in IPO volume should be viewed as a harbinger of fads and thus of an imminent fall in stock prices ("Burnt Offerings", 29th May 1993, p. 104.)

[2] Aggarwal and Rivoli (1990) offer two reasons for why new issues should be good candidates for fads. (i) Fads are more likely to occur the harder it is to estimate firm value. (ii) Riskier shares such as IPOs are likely to have higher levels of noise trading.

[3] There are two further scenarios that would lead to underpricing-type price jumps. First, investors might overpay in the after-market even though the subscription price was set fairly (P1 > P0 = Pt). In this case firms would not take advantage of any sentiment timing ability at all. Second, investors may bid up IPO share prices to fair value when trading starts, after having subscribed at deflated prices (P1 = Pt > P0).

This is of little interest here as it entails no overoptimism. It is precisely this latter scenario that is most commonly assumed in theoretical explanations of underpricing.

4 It is theoretically possible that (i) firms return to the market or (ii) insiders sell their remaining stakes before investors mark down share prices. However, empirically this is not the case.

5 This date is the last moment at which a firm could withdraw its offering; it is hence the relevant date for evaluation of the latent profitability index and thus of proxies for investor sentiment. I will assume that IPOs are priced, at the latest, two days before the starting date of the subscription period.

6 In using pre-pricing index returns, I depart from Loughran et al.'s proxy in two ways: whereas Loughran et al. use future (or concurrent) market peaks, a levels variable, I employ past price changes. Levels are introduced instead by setting prices into relation to expected earnings (price-earnings ratios) or book values (market-to-book ratios).

7 This also seems to be the case in the US; cf. Loughran and Ritter's (1995) figure 1.

8 Note that I am using rolling quarters rather than calendar-yearly data to define this and the HOT_ISSUE proxy introduced in the following subsection.

9 Source: Datastream. The Datastream market index covers around 80-90 per cent of total market capitalisation.

10 Source: Deutsche Bundesbank, "Statistische Beihefte zu den Monatsberichten, Reihe 2: Wertpapierstatistik", various issues. Market and book values for firms not listing common but only preference shares are unavailable at the required (monthly) frequency; analysis of what data is available shows slightly lower MTBs than among firms which list their common shares. As the latter firms account for about 95-97% of total listed equity capital, exclusion of preference-only firms has little effect on estimated MTBs. Since market values for unlisted shares (either common or preference) are unavailable, such shares are assigned the same value as listed common shares. In the case of dual-class listings, the preference shares are also assigned the same value as the common shares, which somewhat overstates their true market value.

11 For ease of exposition, I use the terms "bullish" and "bearish" (and their synonyms) as generics for high and low values, respectively, of the three market conditions proxies.

12 Davis and Yeomans (1976) [UK], Reilly (1977) [US], McGuinness (1992) [Hong Kong] and Rydqvist (1993) [Sweden] also find a significantly positive relationship when regressing initial returns on market returns.

13 These and all following results are robust to changes in classification (above vs. below mean or median), definition (shorter or longer moving averages), and adjustment for systematic risk using Ibbotson's (1975) RATS procedure.

14 If a different classification (above vs. below median or mean rather than above vs. below 1) is used, the difference in long-run performance classified by MTB ratios becomes significant as well.

15 Pre-sample data for the 1960s was used to construct a meaningful historic median for firms going public early on in my sampling window.

[16] Using least-squares on annual data (not reported), there was a weak, positive relationship between IPO volume and long-run abnormal returns in Germany, in contrast to Ritter's (1991) significantly negative one for the US.

[17] Source: Deutsche Bundesbank, op. cit.

[18] Source: Deutsche Bundesbank, op. cit.

[19] Ex post realisations might, of course, not coincide with ex ante plans.

[20] This is consistent with Michaely and Shaw's (1994) evidence for the US.

[21] Although not statutory as in the US (Rule 144, Securities Act of 1933), German underwriter contracts often require insiders - at least implicitly - not to sell private stakes in the first two years of after-market trading. In the absence of such lock-in clauses, of course, insiders could avoid the loss from long-run underperformance by selling out before investors realised their mistake, which would weaken my claim.

[22] Even in the absence of sentiment timing, signalling considerations would yield the same implication, but for a different reason: firms planning to return to the market later will issue the smallest fraction possible at the IPO to minimise the amount of underpricing needed to signal their high value; if the market correctly infers from this signal true firm value, long-term performance should not be negative.

[23] Due to the presence of non-voting preference stock, equity capital is not necessarily equivalent to voting rights; the table thus does not investigate control but wealth effects.

[24] The same pattern holds in Australia (Lee et al.).

[25] Like every proxy, this one may suffer from drawbacks. For instance, it may be the case that those insiders who negotiate the IPO price have sentiment timing ability and sell out, while all other insiders retain their shares, resulting in a high insider retention rate despite successful timing. Strictly speaking, therefore, I am assuming homogeneous insiders with equal retention rates.

[26] RIGHTS is exogenous only if the rights issue is planned independently of share price performance, eg, as part of a multi-stage financing plan of the sort that signalling models assume firms to follow when going public. If, however, firms reissue because they infer from positive after-market performance favourable information about their own ventures (Jegadeesh et al.'s 1993 market-feedback hypothesis), not only are the informational assumptions of the sentiment timing proposition violated, but the RIGHTS dummy also becomes potentially endogenous and should not be used as a regressor variable. Fortunately, exclusion of RIGHTS (not reported) does not alter the results presented in this subsection.

[27] Although no claim to causality should be made here: I do not address the question when, in relation to the reissue date, the good performance occurs. (Levis (1995)).

The Time Series Behaviour of Initial Returns on UK IPOs

William Rees
University of Glasgow

and

Alistair Byrne
Scottish Equitable

Abstract

This paper investigates the time series behaviour of the first week's returns on U.K. initial public offers (EPOS) during 1984-1990. We confirm that initial returns are related to firm size, method of issue, the market in which the issue is made, and the concurrent return on the market index. Even after allowing for the impact of these variables the pattern of average monthly returns demonstrates cyclical behaviour. This behaviour can be partly modelled by market wide characteristics, most notably the price-to-earnings ratio, but tests of the residuals show that certain periods demonstrate excess returns which are not susceptible to modelling. Thus, to some extent at least, the apparent anomaly of lengthy periods of abnormally high or abnormally low returns on IPOs is susceptible to economic explanation.

Nevertheless a significant proportion of the temporal instability in initial returns remains unexplained. Perhaps surprisingly, given the emphasis in earlier studies, it is not the 'hot issue' market of 1986 and 1987 which the model but the earlier cold market. We also find that the price-to-earnings ratio has a significant positive influence on the number of issues coming to the market and the interest rate has a significant negative influence.

1. Introduction

In this paper we investigate the tiine series behaviour of the initial returns available on U.K. IPOs in recent years. This research is motivated by:

a) Persistent evidence of a cyclical element in the level of initial returns on IPOs in the U.S. market as demonstrated by Ibbotson and Jaffe (1975), Ritter (1984) and Ibbotson et al (1988 and 1994). This cyclical behaviour results in distinct periods, known as hot issue markets, when the average level of initial returns on 1POs is markedly greater than at other times.

b) Recent tentative evidence which suggests the average level of initial returns on U.K. IPOs may also follow some cyclical pattern. The Bank of England (1990) report that *'there is a systematic tendency for the size of the discount to vary over time'* and that their *'study identifies a "hot issue period " during 1987 when the discount on IPOs averaged about 25%.'* (Bank of England 1990 p246)

c) Extensive evidence from the U.S., U.K. and other countries which has been interpreted as supporting the argument that the initial return on IPOs are characterised by 'fads'. To the extent that patterns in the initial return on IPOs cannot be explained they are consistent with faddish behaviour. We attempt to explain the pattern of initial returns on 1POs using rational economic hypotheses thereby narrowing the scope of the pattern that is left to irrational explanations.

We are interested in carefully documenting the existence of hot issue markets in the U.K. and, as far as is possible, explaining them. While it is interesting to model the pattern of initial returns on IPOs, the peaks in initial returns may not in themselves be exceptional. Rather they may be the normal result of influences such as general stock market conditions. Conversely, the peaks may be unusual and show returns greater than could be expected given market conditions. We therefore investigate: a) whether there is cyclical behaviour in the initial returns of IPOs in the U.K.; b) to what extent such behaviour can be explained by the specific characteristics of the issues, or by general market conditions; and c) whether there are exceptional hot issue periods after allowing for normal cyclical behaviour. As hot issue markets are often associated with an abnormally high number of new issues we also investigate whether those factors which affect initial returns also affect the number of new issues coming to the market.

The remainder of this paper is organised as follows. The following section discusses the result of previous time series investigations of IPO initial returns and outlines some of the theories put forward to explain the existence of hot issue markets. A description of the data and methods used in our empirical investigation is then presented, followed by the results. Finally, we give our conclusions.

2. Previous Research Regarding Hot Issue Markets

Ibbotson and Jaffe (1975), Ritter (1984) and Ibbotson et al (1994) review the possible causes of hot issue markets. These include the following:

a) The initial return on IPOs is expected to be positively related to risk (Ritter 1984) and if there are periods with more risky companies going to the market then these periods should be characterised by average initial returns greater than at other times. Whilst Ibbotson et al (1994) and Ritter only refer to the 'changing risk composition' element of this hypothesis it can be presumed that any variable expected to impact on initial return could explain some of the variation in these returns[1].

b) The second hypothesis put forward by Ibbotson et al (1994) is that some investors follow 'positive feedback' strategies whereby they assume positive autocorrelation in the initial returns on IPOs bidding up the price of new issues in the after market if previous IPOs have shown increases in price. This activity may then induce the autocorrelation assumed by the investors. In other words it becomes self fulfilling. As it is difficult to sell IPOs short there is little scope for more rational investors to exploit and thence counteract this activity. Ritter (1984) referred to this as the speculative bubble hypothesis.

c) A further argument is that hot issue markets correspond to periods when new issues can be sold at high prices compared to their underlying values, or as Ibbotson et al (1994) put it, at high price-to-earnings or market-to-book multiples. This attracts an increasing volume of new issues and issuers are willing to allow generous initial returns. Ibbotson et al assume that overpricing of this sort during hot issue markets would be followed by under performance.

d) Ibbotson and Jaffe (1975) suggest an alternative explanation of hot issue markets. They argue that hot issue markets stem from sustained rises in the level of the stock market as a whole. Subsequently Ritter (1984) referred to this as the 'institutional lag hypothesis'. Substantial mispricing of IPOs is thought to occur during bull markets for equities as issuers' expectations, and those of their advisers, regarding the price for the issue are 'left behind' by rising share prices. The Bank of England (1990) have revived this explanation. They suggest that the hot issue market during 1987 was the result of the 50% rise in stock prices over the twelve months leading up to July 1987.

e) The final explanation which has been put forward in the literature is the monopsony power hypothesis where investment bankers or underwriters are able to exploit issuers by underpricing their offerings. As Ritter (1984) explains regarding the 1981 hot issue market in the U.S. *'Underwriters intentionally underpriced the issues, and earned profits by allocating these issues only to favoured customers'.* An analogy could be made with the privatisation issues in the U.K. (Kumar 1992).

Despite the lack of convincing reasons for hot issue markets the empirical evidence is strong. The first formal evidence comes from Ibbotson and Jaffe (1975). They constructed a series of issue date to month end returns for all U.S. new issues during 1960 to 1970 and deducted the equivalent market return. They then estimated the autocorrelation of this series (first order 0.744) and of the first difference of the series (first order -0.268) and also conducted runs tests which confirmed their basic results. Ritter (1984) extended Ibbotson and Jaffe's dataset from 1971 up to 1982. Ritter notes that first order autocorrelation of the returns series is 0.62 and for the number of issues in each month it is 0.88.

In an attempt to explain this 'equilibrium phenomenon' Ritter (1984) relates the individual IPO initial returns during the 1977-1982 sample to two measures of risk; pre-issue total sales and post issue stock return volatility. In both cases there is a clear link between riskier issues (lower sales or higher volatility) and initial returns but it fails to explain the 1980-81 hot issue market. What does explain this hot issue market is the high initial returns on natural resource issues. If these are removed the market performance of IPOs is quite normal. Dark and Carter (1993) present evidence which explicitly contradicts Ritter's (1984) results regarding the after market price performance of issues made during the 1980 hot issue market. They contrast the initial returns in that market with those observed in surrounding cold markets and match the initial returns with the subsequent eighteen months returns. The hot market issues earned 11.9% in the initial return and -14.8% in the following eighteen months whilst the cold market issues initial return was 7.3% with eighteen month returns of -0.9%.

Thus the evidence that 'hot issue markets' exist in the U.S. is quite convincing. The most recent data is presented by Ibbotson et al (1994) and using monthly readings from 1960 to 1992 they report autocorrelation of 0.66 for initial returns and 0.89 for the number of issues. It should perhaps be noted that simple product moment correlation statistics may be less than ideal for the initial returns which are highly skewed and the number of issues which are skewed positive integers.

For the U.K. the Bank of England (1990) report initial returns peaking at 28.7% in the second quarter of 1987 compared to a 198589 average of 12.1%. Using a larger sample of 712 firms from 1980-1988 Levis (1993) reports average returns of 14.30% with a 1987 average of 25.69%. There appears to be larger returns on placements (15.28%) than offers for sale (11.50%), and marginally higher returns on the Unlisted Securities Market (USM) (15.25%) than on the Official List market (13.08%). Both these samples include privatisations and Levis calculates the initial return on 12 privatisations to be 37.35%. With regards to risk characteristics Levis reports the relationship between gross proceeds and initial returns for both offers for sale and placements. Only in the two smallest sections of issues by placement is there any evidence of higher returns: 21.0% and 17.31% compared to the overall 14.30%. Otherwise the relationship is erratic. Nor is there much evidence of industrial variation. Over 15 industry groups excluding privatisations initial returns range from 10.00% to 20.00% baring two outliers - 4.37% for 15 office equipment issues and 24.36% for 16 health and household issues. Finally Levis presents evidence that there is no clear relationship between initial return and subsequent market performance - although in general new issues seem to under perform the market during the three years after the issue. Of five portfolios selected by initial return it is the middle portfolio which displays the best market adjusted performance over the 36 months following the issue. Thus there is little evidence from the UK that variation in initial returns over time is likely to be explained a) by monopsony power (other than for privatisations) as there is little evidence of industrial differences, b) by risk variation for if gross proceeds are a good indicator of risk the relationship to initial returns is weak, nor c) by speculative bubbles as the relationship between initial returns and subsequent market performance is weak.

3. Research Methods

The approach used is to analyse U.K. IPOs by firstly examining the relationship between individual initial returns on IPOs modelled by the characteristics of each issue. The residuals from that analysis are averaged for each month in the sample and these form the basis the time series of initial returns which are further modelled using market wide characteristics. The explanatory variables in both models are derived from prior research discussed in the preceding section.

The initial returns of the individual IPOs are modelled by the contemporaneous market return and the fundamental characteristics of the issues: market, method and capitalization. In this and subsequent models we are agnostic about using the variables in their natural log or untransformed versions. There is no a priori reason to prefer either. We finally use log transformations for all variables except dummy variables as this tends to reduce the influence of outliers and diagnostic tests of the estimated models suggest that they are better specified in log form than when the variables are not transformed.

$$LogR_i = \alpha_0 + \alpha_1 LogR_m + \alpha_2 USM_i + \alpha_3 PLA_i + \alpha_4 LogRMV_i + \varepsilon_i \tag{1}$$

Here R_i is return on the new issue over the initial five trading days defined as $[MP_{t+5}/IP_t]$ where MP is the market price and IP the issue price. R_m is the return on the market for the three weeks preceding the issue date and the five first days of trading defined as $[FTA_{t+5}/FTA_{t-15}]$ where FTA is the FT All Share Index. The definition of market return is designed to capture the return on the market from the time at which the issue price is finally decided until the end of the first five days trading. The zero-one dummy variable USM designates issues made on the USM rather than the Official List (one indicating USM) and the zero-one dummy variable PLA designates issues made by a placing rather than by offer for sale (one indicating a placing). RMV is the real market value of the issue, defined as the number of ordinary shares in issue, not necessarily only those issued in the IPO, times the issue price adjusted by the GDP deflator to 1990 prices.

A monthly time series of average adjusted returns (AAR_M) is computed as the mean of all residual returns from equation (1) for each month. One month in the series (October 1989) is not represented in our sample. For this one case we fit a reading using ARIMA processes although the fitted value is very close to the mean of all other months and we obtain very similar results if the mean is substituted for the fitted value.

Following Ibbotson and Jaffe (1975) we compute the autocorrelation coefficients for the time series and for the first difference of the series. However we are more interested to see if the variation in the initial returns can be explained by other characteristics of the market. We therefore model the AARM series using the pre-issue return on the market to capture any institutional lag effect, the dispersion of market returns prior to the issue as a measure of market risk, the interest rate at the time of the issue following Levis' (1990) evidence that interest rates affect final returns to investors, two alternative measures of the cost of the market (the inflation adjusted FT All Share Index and the FT500 price-to-earnings ratio), and the lagged dependent variable (although the model was tested both with and without this regressor).

$$AAR_M = \beta_0 + \beta_1 LogRM_M + \beta_2 Log\sigma RM_M$$

$$+ \beta_3 LogINTR_M + \beta_4 LogPE_M + \beta_5 AAR_{M-1} + \eta_M \tag{2}$$

In equation 2 the explanatory variables are RM_M the return on the FT All Share Index for the six months prior to the issue, $[FTA_M/FTA_{M-6}]$ which is deemed to approximate to the length of the IPO planning process, σRM_M the standard deviation of weekly returns to the FT All Share Index over the six months prior to the issue, $INTR_M$ the London interbank one month middle rate [expressed as one plus the interest rate as a decimal], and PE_M, the FT500 price-to-earnings ratio. Loughran et al (1994) use the inflation adjusted market index as a method of pricing the market but note that market wide market-to-book and price-to-earnings ratios are viable and possibly preferable alternatives. Consequently we examine the sensitivity of our results to replacing the price-earnings variable with $RFTA_M$, the real market index which is the FT All Share Index converted to 1990 prices using the GDP deflator, as well as to the inclusion or omission of the lagged dependant variable.

Ibbotson and Jaffe (1975) investigate the impact of average monthly initial returns on the number of subsequent issues using four months lags of the initial return. Given the length of the IPO planning process this is unlikely to be a powerful test. However the cross-correlation between the two variables does reveal some statistical relationship - most obviously contemporaneous. We therefore investigate the impact of the market characteristics on the number of issues coming to the market by replacing AAR_M as the dependent variable with TNO_M - the total number of new issues recorded in each month by KPMG[2].

$$TNO_M = \beta_0 + \beta_1 LogRM_M + \beta_2 Log\sigma RM_M + \beta_3 LogINTR_M + \beta_4 LogPE_M + v_M \qquad (3)$$

As the dependent variable is a positive integer equation 3 is estimated using poisson regression (See Greene 1990). Again the model is tested to examine its sensitivity to estimation with and without the lagged dependent variables, and with $LogPE_M$ replaced by $LogRFTA_M$.

As argued earlier it is our view that a hot issue market may be more than simply the normal highs observed in a fluctuating time series. Finding autocorrelation in the behaviour of initial returns may be interesting but does not identify any particular hot issue market, nor does it demonstrate that the hot issue market is abnormal behaviour. We use CUSUM and CUSUM squared tests to investigate abnormal behaviour. These models use recursive residuals and have the advantage that each residual is calculated from a prediction from a model estimated using the preceding cases. Therefore a month which is part of a hot issue market is assessed by a model estimated from data which doesn't include that month.

The CUSUM of recursive residual (v_j) is defined by

$$W_t = \hat{\sigma}^{-1} \sum_{j=k+1}^{t} v_j \qquad (4)$$

where

$$\hat{\sigma}^2 = \sum \frac{(v_t - \bar{v})^2}{(T - k - 1)} \qquad (5)$$

and $\bar{v}$ is the arithmetic mean of the residuals, T is the number of months in the sample, and k is the number of regressors. The significance of the computed value W_t is assessed by comparison with the boundaries

$$W = \pm[\alpha \sqrt{T\text{-}k} \quad 2\alpha (t\text{-}k) \sqrt{(T\text{-}k)}] \tag{6}$$

where t is the month in question. α is 0.948 for a significance level of 0.5%.
The CUSUM squared test is given by

$$WW_t = \sum_{t=k+1}^{t} v_t^2 / \sum_{t=k+1}^{t} v_t^2 \tag{7}$$

and the significance boundaries are given by

$$WW = \pm C_0 + \frac{(t\text{-}k)}{(T\text{-}k)} \tag{8}$$

The critical values (C_0) is given by Harvey (1990) Table C as 0.12745 for n=80 when
the confidence level is 5%.

4. Results

KPMG Peat Marwick McLintock (KPMG various issues) list a total of 987 non-introduction IPOs in the U.K. between January 1984 and December 1991. Of these issues, 513 were in the Official List and the remaining 474 on the USM. Issue price and closing price at the end of the first 5 days of trading were retrieved from Datastream for 744 issues in the above sample. (368 Official List, 376 USM) For the remaining 243 issues listed by KPMG, data was not available as Datastream no longer list the firm, possibly due to its subsequent acquisition. A further 64 issues, mainly Investment Trusts, were dropped from the sample as Datastream did not record daily price changes for these stocks and an initial return could not be calculated. The KPMG publications provide details of the issue method for the remaining 680 issues and of the total capitalization at issue price of the issuing firms.

Table 1 contains the preliminary regression of initial returns modelled by the characteristics of the individual issue - the method, market, capitalization and market return for the period from three weeks before until one week after the first day of trading.

Table 1

Initial Return on Individual IPOs.

This table contains the results of the OLS estimation of equation (1).

$$Log\ (1+R_i) = \alpha_0 + \alpha_1 Log(1+R_m) + \alpha_2 USM_i + \alpha_3 PLA_i + \alpha_4 Log(RMV_i) + \varepsilon_i$$

Ri is the initial return on the IPO, R_m is the four week return on the market ending at the conclusion of the initial return week, USM is a zero-one dummy where one indicates an issue on the USM, PLA is a zero-one dummy where one indicates an issue by placing, RMV is the inflation adjusted capitalization of the issuing firm adjusted to 1990 prices, and Log is the natural log operator.

Table 1 continued

Variable	Constant	LogRm	USM	PLA	LogRMV
Coefficient	-0.0746	1.0884	0.0439	0.0331	0.0130
p-value	0.2420	0.0000	0.0006	0.0262	0.0198
R^2 =	0.121				
$(\bar{R})^2$ =	0.115				
F[4,675] =	23.131				

The results of the OLS regression model indicate that initial returns are significantly higher for USM issues, issues made by placing and for firms with higher capitalization. The relationship with the concurrent market return is slightly higher than one, but not significantly so. The adjusted R^2 of the model is modest at 11.5% but tests show that the model is not significantly heteroscedastic and the collinearity between the explanatory variables is not problematical. All these results are as expected save for the positive relationship between initial returns and market capitalization, which is the opposite of what would be expected if smaller firms bore more risk than larger ones. It is interesting that we find negative correlation between initial returns and capitalisation but a positive relationship is found when initial returns are also modelled by information regarding the market and method of issue as well as the capitalisation.

Table 2

Descriptive Statistics

This table contains descriptive statistics regarding the variables included in the statistical tests reported in tables 3 to 7 in their natural form and as transformations as incorporated in the regression models. AAR is the monthly average of residuals from equation 1, TNO is the total number of issues made in each month, RM is the return on the market for the six months prior to the issue, sRM is the weekly standard deviation in market returns over the six months prior to the issue, RFTA is the FT All Share Index rebased to 1990 prices, INTR is the London interbank offer rate for each month, PE is the FT500 price-to-earnings ratio for each month, and Log is the natural log operator. There are 81 cases in the sample.

Descriptive Statistics				
Variable	Mean	Std. Dev.	Minimum	Maximum
AAR	-0.00873	0.0674	-0.172	0.169
TNO	14.802	6.4273	5.000	32.000
RM	1.0977	0.1381	0.738	1.406
σRM	0.0210	0.0091	0.013	0.052
RFTA	10.362	1.9421	6.610	14.740
INTR	1.1161	0.0217	1.074	1.152
PE	13.069	2.1615	9.930	20.100
LogRM	0.0849	0.1323	-0.303	0.341
LogσRM	-3.921	0.3204	-4.343	-2.960
LogRFTA	2.3200	0.1946	1.889	2.691
LogINT	0.1096	0.0194	0.072	0.141
LogPE	2.5585	0.1494	2.296	3.001

The residuals from the regression are combined to produce an average abnormal return for each month. After October 1990 we find that many months do not contain any IPOs in our sample so we drop all months after that date. We also necessarily drop the first month, January 1984, as our analysis includes lagged dependent variables in certain tests. One remaining month, October 1989, contains no IPOs in our sample and rather than drop this case we fit a value. The results are no noticeably different if we omit the case from our analysis. Table 2 contains the descriptive statistics regarding the time series of initial returns and the market characteristics, both untransformed and transformed as used in subsequent analyses. The abnormal returns are centred on zero by construction and range from -17.2% to plus 16.9%, there are on average 15 IPOs per month, including introductions. The market characteristics show that the period under review was erratic. Six monthly market returns averaged 10% but range from 40% to -26%, interest rates average 11.6% but include 7.4% and 15.2%, and price-to-earnings ratios fluctuate from 9.9 to 20.1. The cross-correlations reported are largely as would be expected with high price-to-earnings ratios being associated with high returns on the market, high inflation adjusted index, and low interest rates.

The preliminary results, which can be compared with the U.S. results of Ibbotson (1975), Ritter (1984) and Ibbotson et al (1988, 1994), are the autocorrelation in the averaged series and in its first difference. Our results in Table 3 confirm first order serial correlation which is significantly positive for the series and significantly negative for its first difference. Our results are somewhat weaker than the U.S. evidence and this may follow from the larger number of cases in each month in the U.S. studies producing a less erratic time series. US evidence also suggests that the monthly number of new issues is autocorrelated and whilst we confirm significant negative serial correlation in the first difference of the number of issues, serial correlation in the series itself is insignificantly different from zero - although positive as expected. A runs test on this data does confirm significantly fewer runs than would be expected so there is some evidence that the number of issues is positively correlated.

Table 3

Autocorrelation Function of the Monthly Series

This table records first to fifth order autocorrelations for the averaged monthly residuals from equation 1 (AAR) and the total number of issues in each month as recorded by KPMG, and for the first difference of both series. The data covers 1984 to October 1990. * indicates significantly different from zero at 5% confidence level. There are 82 observations in the series of levels and 81 in the sample of first differences.

Order of Lag	Initial Returns	Initial Returns - First Difference	Number of Issues	Number of Issues - First Difference
1st	0.381* -	0.305*	0.177	0.363*
2nd	0.178	-0.179	-0.037	-0.084
3rd	0.207	0.040	-0.116	-0.027
4th	0.134	0.027	-0.153	-0.148
5th	0.127	0.176	0.042	0.089

Tables 4 and 5 contain the correlation matrix and the results of the time series models of the behaviour of initial returns.[3] In table 5 we include the lagged dependent variable. Tests for first order autocorrelation, adjusted for the presence of a lagged dependent variable, suggest that it is insignificant. Table 5 therefore relies on unadjusted OLS estimation.

Table 4

Correlation Matrix

The following panels contains the correlation matrix for the variables included in the statistical tests reported in tables 5 to 7. AAR is the monthly average of residuals from equation 1, TNO is the total number of issues made in each month, RM is the six month return on the market for the six months prior to the issue, sRM is the weekly standard deviation in market returns over the six months prior to the issue, RFTA is the FT All Share Index rebased to 1990 prices, INTR is the London interbank offer rate for each month, PE is the FT500 price-to-earnings ratio for each month, and Log is the natural log operator. There are 81 cases in the sample.

	AAR	TNO	Log RM	Log σRM	Log RFTA	Log INTR	Log PE	AAR$_{M-1}$
TNO	0.268							
LogRM	0.266	0.166						
LogσRM	-0.050	-0.028	-0.647					
LogRFTA	0.050	0.083	0.137	-0.037				
LogINTR	-0.278	-0.300	-0.051	-0.417	0.164			
LogPE	0.564	0.307	0.347	0.097	0.551	-0.461		
AAR$_{M-1}$	0.413	0.153	0.112	0.064	-0.071	-0.280	0.366	
TNO$_{M-1}$	-0.024	0.179	0.169	-0.047	0.120	-0.336	0.234	0.201

Table 5

Time Series Models of Average Initial Returns

This table contains the OLS results from equation 2.

$$AAR_M = \beta_0 + \beta_1 LogRM_M + \beta_2 Log\sigma RM_M = \beta_3 LogINTR_M + \beta_4 LogPE_M + \beta_5 AAR_{M-1} + \eta_M$$

AAR is the monthly average of residuals from equation 1, RM is the return on the market for the six months prior to the issue, σRM is the weekly standard deviation in market returns over the six months prior to the issue, RFTA is the FT All Share Index rebased to 1990 prices, INTR is the London interbank rate for each month, PE is the FT500 price-to-earnings ratio for each month, and Log is the natural log operator.

Variable	Constant	LogRM	LogσRM	LogINTR	LogPE	AAR$_{(M-1)}$
Coefficient	-0.6597	-0.0143	-0.0322	-0.2012	0.2146	0.2239
p-value	0.0015	0.8502	0.3180	0.6278	0.0001	0.0196

R2 = 0.381   (_R) 2 =   0.340   F[5,75] = 9.250   Autocorrelation = 0.038

The model reported in table 5 includes the lagged dependent variable and the price of the market is measured using the market wide price-earnings ratio. In this model both the P/E and lagged dependent variable slope coefficients are significant and the R^2 is 34.0%. In the market index specification, not reported, only the lagged dependent variable is significant at conventional levels but the model has an R^2 of 20.2%. The models which omit the lagged dependent variable have R^2 of 9.9% when the market index is used and 29.9% when the P/E ratio replaces it. In the first model the interest has a negative coefficient which marginally fails the conventional 5% significance test, but when the market index is replaced by the P/E ratio the interest rate is no longer significant, although the P/E ratio coefficient is positive and significant at a very high level. There is some evidence that the variability of the market in the six months prior to the issue has a negative impact on initial returns. Thus the market index is dominated by the P/E ratio and in the presence of the P/E ratio the interest rate is ineffective. We presume that these results confirm that the P/E ratio is a better measure of the 'price of the market' than the relative index, and that interest rates only appear to be significant in the market index models as a surrogate for that proportion of the P/E ratio which is not captured in the market index. However in the presence of collinearity between variables, even the relatively mild collinearity reported table 4, such conclusions should be tentative.

Our interpretation of the results given in table 5 is that the monthly average abnormal returns on new issues are autocorrelated even when the data is conditioned by general market characteristics but that a considerable proportion of the variation in initial returns is related to the market wide P/E ratio at the time of the issue. At this stage we have confirmed that the typical result for the U.S. is also present in the U.K. and extended this result to show that the serial correlation in initial returns is not dependent on serial correlation in a set of market wide and issue specific characteristics.

To examine whether there are certain hot or cold markets which depart significantly from the estimated model we examine the cusum and cusum squared plots where the cusum might be thought of as cumulative signed residuals and cusum squared as cumulative unsigned residuals. Figures 1 and 2 are the cusum and cusum squared plot for a model similar to the model as specified in equation 2 save for excluding the two ineffectual regressors, LogRM and Log INTR. Thus the model includes the PE variable (LogPE), the market risk variable (LogsRM) and the lagged dependent variable. In this model the coefficients estimated for lagged dependant variable and the PE variable are both clearly significant whilst the risk measure attracts a p-value of 0.217. Early results from a CUSUM model are very sensitive to unusual readings in the first few cases and in this sample the first four average abnormal returns are all positive, three of the unusually so. The most striking pattern apparent from figure 1 is the negative slope from late 1984 until 1986. Although a brief steep upward trend is observed at the start of 1987 the model appears to cope well with the 1987 hot issue market. However the CUSUM squared results shown in figure 2 reveal that the 1987 residuals are larger in magnitude than would be expected. Taken together we interpret these results as indicating that, given the model of abnormal returns used, the 1987 hot issue market was not surprising. The model estimates average returns over this period quite well although it struggles to cope with the increased variability of these returns. It is not the hot issue market which produces a period which is difficult to model but the relatively cold market in 1985. We have tested these results to different specification of the model and over different time periods and the results mention are robust but it should be conceded that the time series is relatively short and it would be interesting to extend this model to different environments and over different, and preferably longer, time periods.

Figure 1

CUSUM Plot

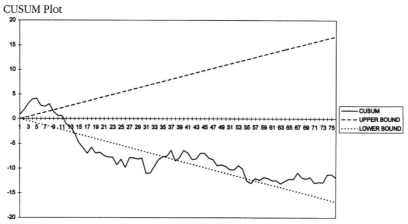

Figure 2

CUSUM SQD Plot

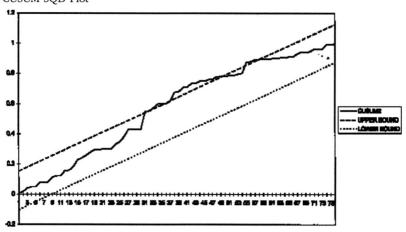

Table 6 reports the results of our investigation of the impact of market wide characteristics on the total number of new issues coming to the market in that month. Apart from the change in the dependent variable and the use of poisson regression estimation rather than OLS this model is identical to those used to explain initial returns. It should be remembered that an interval of one month is probably shorter than ideal given the low number of issues in the typical month and the long planning horizon for new issues. However in this paper we choose to retain a monthly interval to maintain comparability with our initial returns analysis and to ensure a reasonable number of readings in our seven year sample.

We do not report results of the model incorporating a lagged dependant variable as this variable is insignificant and the other variables are unchanged. Following the suggestion of a reviewer we investigated certain alternative specifications for the lagged dependent variable. If, for example, it is cumulated over the six months prior to the month in question the lagged dependent variable is positive and clearly significant but all other variables that are shown as being significant in table 6 remain so, and the significance of marginal variables is improved. Thus our basic results remain unchanged. Unfortunately this approach introduces severe autocorrelation in the residuals and would be better investigated in a time series using longer, possibly quarterly, intervals, but this would demand a larger sample.

Table 6

Time Series Models of Total Number of Issues

This table contains the poisson estimated results from equation 3.

$$TNO_M = \beta_0 + \beta_1 LogRM_M + \beta_2 Log\sigma RM_M = \beta_3 LogINTR_M + \beta_4 LogPE_M + \nu_M$$

TNO is the total number of IPOs in each month, RM is the return on the market for the six months prior to the issue, σRM is the weekly standard deviation in market returns over the six months prior to the issue, RFTA is the FT All Share Index rebased to 1990 prices, INTR is the London interbank offer rate for each month, PE is the FT500 price-to-earnings ratio for each month, and Log is the natural log operator.

Variable	Constant	Log RM	LogσRM	LogINTR	LogPE
Coefficient	0.8541	-0.2043	-0.2824	-6.7114	0.0135
p-value	0.3624	0.5610	0.0612	0.0005	0.0135
Log-likelihood =	-276.01	-274.73			
Restricted Log-L =	-291.18	-291.18			
Chi-squared =	190.05	187.33			

The model demonstrate predictive power but the return on the market is insignificant and there is only weak evidence that high standard deviation in market returns depresses the number of new issues. This may well be influenced by the 1987 crash and the subsequent decline in new issues. More convincing evidence is that a high market wide price-to-earnings ratio (or a high inflation adjusted market index) stimulates new issues whilst high interest rates depress them. However, when interpreting these results it should be remembered that the market index is reasonably highly correlated with the P/E ratio and with the interest rate (0.55 and -0.46 respectively)[4].

5. Conclusion

Our attempt to explain the time series pattern of U.K. IPO returns found that the temporal variation of returns is in part related to changes through time of the relative proportions of various characteristics of the issues. The characteristics found to have influence are firm size, market of issue, and method of issue. However, the explanatory power of these 3 variables is quite low. Variation in the average characteristics of issuing firms and their offerings may contribute to observed hot issue markets but it is not the main cause. The time series of monthly initial returns after conditioning the data by capitalization, issue method and market of issue is positively autocorrelated, and the first difference negatively autocorrelated, consistent with earlier U.S. evidence.

An examination of the relationship between market characteristics and the initial return confirms a strong relationship between the market wide price-to-earnings ratio and the initial returns but the series remains significantly autocorrelated. There is weak evidence of some relationship between the other market variables and initial returns. When a lagged dependent variable is included in the model the residuals from the model no longer display significant first order autocorrelation and the relationship between the price-to-earnings ratio and initial returns is confirmed. An examination of the recursive residuals using CUSUM techniques suggests that 1987 was an extraordinary period in that the variation of returns was higher than expected but the level of the returns was not markedly abnormal even after the model makes allowance for the autocorrelation and price-to-earnings effects. However the low returns in 1985 do, according to our results, seem to be out of line with those that the model estimates.

At this stage it is useful to highlight the contribution of this study. Firstly we have confirmed that the autocorrelation observed in U.S. IPO returns is found in the U.K.. More importantly we have presented evidence consistent with a considerable amount of the pattern in the time series of initial returns being caused by issue specific and market wide characteristics. Thus, to some extent at least, the apparent anomaly of lengthy periods of abnormally high or abnormally low returns on IPOs is susceptible to economic explanation. Nevertheless a significant proportion of the temporal instability in initial returns remains unexplained. Perhaps surprisingly, given the emphasis in earlier studies, it is not the 'hot issue' market of the mid to late 1980s which the model but the earlier cold market.

It is interesting to speculate on the possible explanations of this residual hot issue behaviour. Obviously we may have simply omitted important explanatory variables. There is a very long list of causal factors which have been shown to be related to initial returns in various empirical studies. We have used only the most obvious of these factors and refrained form including others to avoid over fitting the data. We do not believe that additional issue specific variables will make a significant difference to the explanatory power of this part of the analysis. It seems more probable that market wide variables may be decisive but there is limited theoretical or empirical evidence to justify the inclusion of any particular factor. Discussions with market practitioners suggest that the demand for new investments - possibly related to the net investment in the market by investment intermediaries such as pension and life assurance funds - might be a consideration, as might changing incentives to underwriters to support issues that are not performing well. As yet we are reluctant to test these, and other, market wide variables without more theoretical support. There does of course remain the possibility that new issue returns are largely driven by fads but testing for irrational behaviour is clearly going to be difficult. If initial returns are unusually high it might be supposed that subsequent returns would be unusually low. There is some evidence to support this from the U.S. but only weak evidence from the U.K.. We are left with an economic phenomenon which is as yet on partly susceptible to economic explanation.

The same market indicators were used to model the number of new issues coming to the market as were used to analyze average initial returns. The monthly series of the number of new issues is erratic and difficult to model effectively but there is evidence that the price-to-earnings ratio has a significant positive relationship with the number of issues and the interest rate is significantly negatively related. These results are consistent with Loughran et al (1994) who report a significant relationship between their measure of the 'price of the market', the inflation adjusted index, and the number of issues. Whilst these final results are tentative they do suggest that studies of the factors which influence the number of firms coming to the market might provide further insights into the IPO process although such studies may well be more successful if they investigate the annual or quarterly, rather than monthly, number of new issues and over a longer time period.

Acknowledgement

The authors would like to thank Johan Lohne, Tom Berglund, Mario Levis and other contributors at the 1994 European Financial Management Congress for their invaluable comments and the Chartered Association of Certified Accountants for their financial support.

References

Allen F. & Faulhaber G. A. (1989) Signalling by underpricing in the IPO market. Journal of Financial Economics 23, pp303-323.

Bank of England. (1990) New equity issues in the UK. Bank of England Quarterly Bulletin, May, pp243-252.

Barron D. & B. Holstrom (1980) The investment banking contract for new issues under asymmetric information: delegation and the incentive problem. Journal of Finance, Vol 35. pp1115-1138.

Benveniste L. M. & Spindt P. A. (1989) How investment bankers determine the offer price and allocation of new issues. Journal of Financial Economics 24, pp343-361.

Dark F. & R. Carter (1993) Effects of differential information on the after-market valuation of initial public offerings. Journal of Economics and Business, Vol. 45 pp375-392.

Drake P. & Vetsuypens M. (1994) IPO underpricing and insurance against legal liability. Financial Management, Forthcoming.

Greene W. (1990) Econometric analysis New York, MacMillan.

Harvey C. (1990) The econometric analysis of time-series New York, Allan

Ibbotson R. G. & Jaffe J. F. (1975) Hot issue markets. Journal of Finance 30, pp1027-1045.

Ibbotson R. G., Sindelar J. L. & Ritter J. R. (1988) Initial public offerings. Journal of Applied Corporate Finance 1, pp37-45.

Ibbotson R. G., Sindelar J. L. & Ritter J. R. (1994) Initial public offerings. Journal of Applied Corporate Finance, Forthcoming.

KPMG (Various) New issue statistics. KPMG Peat Marwick McLintick, London.

Kumar (1992) An empirical analysis of privatisation through public offerings Working paper the Wharton School, University of Pensylvania.

Levis, M. (1990) The winner's curse problem, interest costs and the underpricing of initial public offerings. Economic Journal 100, pp28-41.

Levis, M. (1993) The long-run performance of initial public offerings: The UK experience 1980-1988. Financial Management 22(1), pp28-41.

Loughan, T. Ritter, J. & Rydqvist, K. (1994) Initial public offerings: international insights Pacific Basin Finance Journal. March.

Ritter, J. R. (1984) The 'hot issue market' of 1980. Journal of Business 17, pp217-239.

Ritter, J. R (1991) The long-run performance of initial public offerings. Journal of Finance 46, pp3-27.

Rock, K. (1986) Why new issues are underpriced Journal of Financial Economics 15, pp187-212.

Tinic, S. M. (1988) Anatomy of initial public offerings of common stock. Journal of Finance 43, pp789-822.

Welch, I. (1989) Seasoned offerings, imitation costs, and the under-pricing of initial public offerings. Journal of Finance 44, pp421-449.

Endnotes

[1] In the same article Ibbotson et al (1994) consider seven possible causes of IPO underpricing. These are, (a) Rock's (1986) information asymmetry/winners curse model which in common with some other analyses predicts that initial returns will increase with increasing risk; (b) Benveniste and Spindt's (1989) model which predicts that investment bankers will underprice new issues so as to encourage investors to truthfully reveal price relevant information in the pre-selling period which implies that IPOs which have their issue price revised upwards will still offer higher initial returns than other IPOs; (c) the informational cascade model (Welch 1989) which predicts that investors are influenced by other investors behaviour and therefore issuers will underprice to stimulate such a cascade; (d) the litigation avoidance hypothesis of Tinic (1988) and Drake and Vetsuypens (1994) which suggests that issuers and their advisers may underprice issues to increase the chance of positive returns thereby discouraging subsequent law suits; (e) the "good taste" hypothesis of Allen and Faulhaber (1989) and others which predicts that issuers intend to follow the IPO with secondary issues thereby reducing the need to expend effort selling the stocks and allowing them to offer underpriced stocks to business   contacts; (g) although of limited relevance to Europe and America regulators in some countries specify issue prices often on the basis of conservative accounting numbers thereby underpricing the issue; and (h) when undervaluation is typical of new issues, the process may be exploited as a method of allocating value to chosen individuals and/or business contacts.

[2] In the UK new issues can include introductions where a widely held stock is admitted to the market or issues use to raise capital, either to expand the equity base or to release entrepreneurs investments. Although different in form the net effect can be identical as issuers have the choice of realising their investment before or after listing.

[3] In table 5 there is no lagged dependent variable. We find that the residuals display a significant amount of serial correlation indicating that conditioning of the data by market characteristics has not eliminated the autocorrelation discovered in the series. In order to derive reliable estimates of the coefficients and standard errors we employ the Prais-Winsten estimator and report the results for the adjusted OLS results.

[4] The reported results are estimated using poisson regression which assumes that the observations are drawn from a poisson distribution where the mean and variance are equal. This restriction is rarely encountered in practice and the model was estimated a second time using negative binomial regression techniques. There confirmed the significance of the interest rate variable but the price earnings variable is only marginally significant. A somewhat larger sample will be needed to resolve this question.

The New Issue Market
as a Sequential Equilibrium

Ian Tonks
University of Bristol and
London School of Economics

Abstract

This paper shows that a price discount in the new issue market will result from a sequential equilibrium in the bargaining game between the issuing firm and the investment bank over the type of contract under which the new issue is sold, as a solution to the moral hazard problem faced by the issuing firm with respect to the effort put into the sale by the issuing bank. An implication of this model is that the degree of underpricing of new issues is cyclical, with deeper discount occurring in boom periods. This result is consistent with the empirical findings by Ibbotson and Jaffe (1975), Ritter (1984) and Trundle et al (F1990) of hot issue periods. We also present our own evidence using a sample of IPO discounts in the UK over the period 1980-93 to show that this prediction is consistent with the data.

1. Introduction

The new issue market is a financial market that persistently displays evidence of market inefficiency. Ibbotson (1975) originally documented that US new issues were underpriced, and Loughran, et.al. (1994) have shown that the phenomenon is widespread across countries. In a number of international markets it is possible for investors who subscribe to new issues to make initial abnormal returns. In addition Ibbotson and Jaffe (1975) identify *"hot issue"* periods, when the underpricing is particularly apparent.

Ibbotson, et.al. (1994) provide a survey of a number of theories which have been advanced to explain these phenomena, and these explanations can be grouped into three categories of asymmetric information models. The first group include papers by Baron and Holmstrom (1980) and Baron (1982) which have emphasized the principal agent relationship that arises on the supply side of the market when a firm issues new securities through an investment bank. It can be shown that due to asymmetric information between the issuing firm and the investment bank, in order to induce the investment bank to supply the correct unobserved effort level, the second best solution involves a distortion of the offer price from its fair value.

The second category concentrates on a demand side explanation for the price discount. Rock (1986) shows that the existence of investors with different amounts of information means that if new issues were on average priced at their fair value uninformed investors would find their actual gains negative, since they are rationed when securities are underpriced and only receive their full bid when securities are overpriced. This *"winners curse"* paradox means that in equilibrium, securities must be underpriced to ensure participation from uninformed investors. In Rock's model there is no role for investment bankers; Beatty and Ritter (1986) argue that the equilibrium is enforced by the reputation effects of investment banks which prevents firms cheating on the uninformed. Benveniste and Spindt (1989) extend the Rock model to allow investment banks to extract information from investors in a premarket auction: informed investors are compensated for revealing information to the investment bank by receiving underpriced new issues. Koh and Walter (1989) find support for Rock's model using data from the Singapore Stock Exchange, and Levis (1990) has found that the first day abnormal returns for initial public offerings on the London Stock Exchange can be explained by a combination of the winner's curse problem and the settlement mechanism applicable to the UK new issues market.

The third explanation advanced in papers by Allen and Faulhaber (1989), Grinblatt and Hwang (1989) and Welch (1989), have explained the price discount as the result of a signalling equilibrium between the better informed firm owners and less informed investors: firms differ in the quality of projects and the high quality firms can signal their high value by offering large initial discounts.

In this paper we provide a refinement to the supply side explanation to the existence of the price discount in the new issue market, by seeing whether there is a game-theoretic structure which will *"implement"* the principal agent solution. The discount arises in the sequential equilibrium of a game played between the investment bank and the issuing firm, and an empirical implication of this equilibrium is consistent with the Ibbotson and Jaffe (1975) finding that underpricing occurs in waves. The principal agent framework adopted in this paper means that the model is most closely related to Baron (1982). Instead of focusing on contract design though, we concentrate on the type of contract offered, in particular whether the contract requires the issuing bank to bear the price risk, which in the US is called a firm commitment contract, or in the case of a best efforts contract the issuing firm bears the risk and the bank acts as the firm's agent. Evidence for the US suggests that firm commitment contracts are the predominant method of issuing new shares. Ritter (1987) finds that the direct expenses are of the same order of magnitude for both contract types, but the underpricing is greatest for best efforts contracts. Smith (1986) reports that over the period 1977-82 only 35 per cent of initial public offerings were sold by best efforts contracts with the firm bearing the underlying risk of the issue, and further these issues raised just 13 per cent of the gross proceeds.

For the UK, Jackson (1986) and Trundle et al (1990) outline the various new issue methods on the London Stock Exchange. An offer for sale is equivalent to a firm commitment contract with the bank bearing the risks, and an offer for subscription is the direct equivalent to the issuing firm bearing the risk under a best efforts contract. In the UK placings and tender offers are also used to issue new shares. Placings were traditionally used for very small new issues, and in a placing *"the issuing house* [investment bank] *also technically underwrites the entire issue for a short period but its main economic function is not to bear risk but to act as a distributor"* [Trundle et al. (1990)], which means that we will also take a placing to represent a best efforts contract. In a tender offer investors tender for the new issue, and the issue price is set such that all shares are sold. In Table 1, we document the evidence on the choice of issue method by firms obtaining an initial listing on the London Stock Exchange over the period 1983-89. It can be seen that in the UK in the late 1980s offers for subscription were overtaken by placings, as the alternative method of new issue to offers for sale, though according to the London Stock Exchange's Stock Exchange Quarterly (January-March 1992, p.60) offers for subscription are still used by some companies. Placings became popular because the issue costs associated with a placing are lower than with other methods, and after 1986 the Stock Exchange changed the size limit for placings from 3 million or less to up to 15 million. The table shows that 80 per cent by value of the amounts raised in initial public offerings on the London Stock Exchange (excluding privatization receipts) were by firm commitment contracts.

This paper will offer a new reason for the underpricing of initial public offerings which occurs because the investment bank is able to underprice to reduce the amount of marketing effort exerted in the new issue. We show that this underpricing occurs in the equilibrium of a game played between the bank and the firm. Further we claim that our results are also consistent with the empirical findings that underpricing occurs in waves and that the predominant new issue method is a firm commitment contract.

2. Order of Play

A firm has sole access to an investment opportunity with a positive net present value and wishes to finance the investment by issuing securities on the new issue market. It can do this through an investment bank which has specialist knowledge in marketing and distribution of new financial securities[1]. The investment bank has the responsibility of marketing the firm's shares to investors who subscribe to the issue on the basis of the beliefs about the returns to the project. In addition although there are many firms and many banks, each firm has developed a special relationship with one particular bank and both parties have acquired asset specificity. The firm and the bank bargain over the offer price at which the issue will be sold, the form of the contract, and the amount of effort that the bank will put into the sale. We assume that the bargaining problem can be modeled as a game with the following order of play.[2]

The investment bank observes a binary variable $x \in (\bar{x}, \underline{x})$, not observed by the issuing firm, which reflects the state of the market. The value $\bar{x}$ corresponds to a good state in which it is easy to sell shares at a fair price, because investors are optimistic about the future and consequently are willing to upgrade their beliefs about the specific project and pay a higher price for its shares. The value $\underline{x}$ reflects a bad state in which it is more difficult to sell shares. We might think that the investment bank discovers the state of the market by holding costly conversations with prospective purchasers of securities, which the issuing firm is not a party to. Having observed x, the bank states the offer price. The firm is not allowed to argue with the bank's formidable knowledge, but instead the firm responds with its choice of contract.[3] There are two types of contract, firm commitment (FC) and best efforts (BE).

Under FC, the bank acts as the principal and bears the issue risk. It buys the shares from the firm at a price q, and then issues them at the offer price p by marketing them

Table 1

Amounts raised by new issue method on the London Stock Exchange, 1983-89

year	1983		1984		1985		1986		1987		1988		1989		Total 1983-89	
	no	Amt	no	Amt	no	Amt	no	Amt	no	Amt	no	Amt	no	Amt	no	Amt
up to £10m raised																
Offers for sale	5	20.8	10	59.4	20	126.2	16	97.3	3	18.3	0	0	0	0	54	322
Tenders	10	53.3	2	10	4	22.5	2	11.5	0	0	0	0	0	0	18	97.1
Placings	0	0	7	19.0	3	8.3	16	58.7	40	192.5	29	160.9	14	67.8	109	507.2
Subscrpt	0	0	1	5.0	0	0	0	0	0	0	0	0	0	0	1	5.0
More than £10m raised																
Offers for sale	4	79.4	9	4,358.1	9	477.1	21	2,277.6	9	1,002.4	11	643.4	5	1,212.8	68	10,050.8
Tenders	5	93.2	3	625.7	2	80.4	3	246.5	0	0	0	0	0	0	13	1,045
Placings	0	0	0	0	0	0	6	11.7	10	78.4	1	314.8	1	12.1	18	237.0
Subscrpt	0	0	1	10.8	0	0	0	0	0	0	0	0	0	0	1	10.8

Source: Bank of England Quarterly Bulletin, December 1986 and 1990

to the public, putting an amount of effort into the sale. The bank responds to the choice of contract FC from the firm by choosing its optimal level of effort. We suppose this is also a binary choice a ε (ā, a̲). The value ā corresponds to a high level of effort, and a̲ to some minimum effort level that the firm can enforce. The firm is unable to observe the amount of effort expended by the bank above the minimum level; it can only observe the demand for the new issue. The public have a demand function Q(.), which depends upon the offer price, the state of the market and the effort of the bank. Under FC the payoffs to each party, assuming both the firm and the bank are risk neutral, are

$$P^B = pQ(p,x,a) - q - ga \tag{1a}$$

$$P^F = q \tag{1b}$$

where g represents the disutility of effort to the bank. We can rationalize the inclusion of the state of the market and the effort level of the bank in the investors' demand functions by appealing to the idea, not explicitly modeled here, that investors have parameterized the uncertainty about the future returns from the new issue. Investors have subjective beliefs about the value of these parameters which are influenced by the state of the market and the effort level of the bank. For example, if the economy is expected to undergo a boom, the expected returns on the new issue will be increased by macroeconomic factors. Similarly an extensive advertising campaign about the merits of the new issue, involving a great deal of effort from the bank, can convince investors that they should upgrade their expectations of the new project's mean return.

Under BE, the bank acts as the agent. The firm pays the bank a fixed sum to sell the issue s, and the firm bears the risk of the issue and keeps the receipts of the issue. Again having specified BE, the bank responds by supplying an amount of effort a ε (ā, a̲). Under BE the payoffs are

$$P^B = s - ga \tag{2a}$$

$$P^F = pQ(p,x,a) - s \tag{2b}$$

Since the effort supplied by the bank is unobservable by the firm, a moral hazard problem arises since the bank has an incentive to lie in the BE case and claim that it is a poor state of the world, in order to minimize the effort necessary to achieve a given level of sales.[4] One way to overcome this moral hazard problem is for the firm to write a contract with the bank which is incentive compatible with the bank's objectives, which is the route taken by Baron (1982). However in this paper we take a different approach, which specifies only two types of contracts: a best efforts and a firm commitment. The design of each type of contract, whether best efforts or firm commitment, is not negotiable: the contracts have packaged, standard formats. Our intention is to distinguish between the nature of a contract and its design. We justify our approach by supposing that designing a contract that specifies all contingencies is expensive, or not verifiable [see Hart and Moore (1988)]. We assume that bargaining over the nature of a standardized contract rather than the design of a specific contract is a more efficient method of inducing a given effort level. We show that in order to alleviate the moral hazard problem, the firm and bank bargain over the type of contract and in equilibrium the outcome of this bargaining process is a situation where new issues are on average underpriced. Our approach is an example of implementation theory addressed by Moore and Repullo (1988), where the outcome of a contract between parties is sustained by the equilibrium of a specified game. In this paper we specify the stages of a game that will produce an outcome of underpricing of new issues in equilibrium

In order to achieve an explicit solution to this game, we impose additional restrictions on the model with the following assumptions.

Assumption 1: The demand function is linear

$$Q = x(a - bp) \tag{3}$$

Note that this linear demand curve would be consistent with investors having a constant absolute risk averse utility function, where a has the interpretation of the mean return on the new project, and x is the inverse of the variability of returns. Assumption 1 coupled with the binary state of the market and the binary effort levels, implies that there are four possible demand curves, illustrated in Figure 1.

Figure 1: Demand function for new share

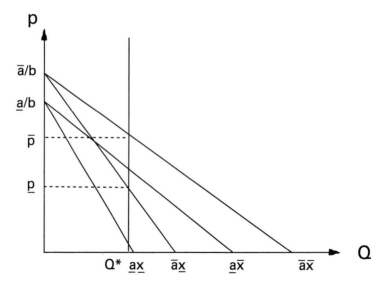

The downward sloping linear demand curve for the firm's securities represents uncertainty by risk averse investors as to the expected returns from the project.

Assumption 2: The firm has a fixed quantity of shares Q^* that it wishes to issue.

More realistically we might imagine that the firm has a fixed quantity of funds it needs to raise, and it would vary both the price and the quantity of share to achieve this. However the analysis with two choice variables p and Q, would be more complicated, and therefore we make the simplifying assumption that the supply of shares is inelastic in order to concentrate on the choice of the issue price.

Define $\underline{p}$ as the first best price when the state of the market is poor

$$\underline{p} = \frac{\bar{a}}{b} - \frac{Q^*}{b\underline{x}} \tag{4}$$

Similarly define $\bar{p}$ as the first best price when $x = \bar{x}$

$$\bar{p} = \frac{\bar{a}}{b} - \frac{Q^*}{b\bar{x}} \tag{5}$$

The bank in announcing the issue price has to choose between equation (4) and equation (5). These first best prices include the firm's requirement that the bank is expected to exert maximum effort. In the event that the bank does not supply the higher effort level, the supply Q^* will be undersold, with the result that the price in the aftermarket, not modeled here, will adjust to a new equilibrium below the first best price.

Assumption 3: The firm is able to force the bank to accept no more than its reservation payoff u in each outcome of the honest game.

The format of the contract specifies the fixed payments to be made and is not negotiable, that is s and q are specified as $\bar{s}$ and $\bar{q}$ when $p = \bar{p}$; and $\underline{s}$ and $\underline{q}$ when $p = \underline{p}$.

$$\underline{s} = \bar{s} = u + g\underline{a} \tag{6}$$

$$\bar{q} = \bar{p}.x(\bar{a}-b\bar{p}) - g\bar{a} - u \tag{7}$$

$$\underline{q} = \underline{p}.\underline{x}(\bar{a}-b\underline{p}) - g\bar{a} - u \tag{8}$$

In (6) we suppose that the firm's payment to the bank in the event of a BE contract recognizes that the bank will only supply the minimum effort, which is shown to be the case in Proposition 2 below. This results from effort being unobservable by the firm, so that the firm is unable to condition its payments to the bank on the level of effort. Equations (7) and (8) recognise that if the bank bears the risk with an FC contract, it will supply the higher effort level, and the firm exploits this by appropriating the additional revenues in the fixed payment that the bank gives the firm under an FC contract. We might guess that the assumptions in (6) to (8) means that the firm always prefers an FC contract in the honest game. This will ensure that the bank supplies the higher effort level even though the firm cannot observe this effort. Indeed we show in Propositions 1 and 2 below that this conjecture is correct.

Figure 2

First best case

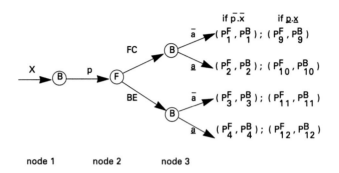

The game is represented in extensive form in Figure 2, when the bank observes x and plays the first best price (ie is honest). PF_t and PB_t denote the payoffs to the firm and the bank under each final outcome t. An expanded description of these payoffs is given in Pay-off Table A, for each outcome $t=(1,4)$ when the state of the market is good.

Pay-off Table A

Pay-off to issuing firm	Pay-off to bank
$PF_1 = \bar{q}$	$PB_1 = \bar{p} . \bar{x} (\bar{a} - b\bar{p}) - \bar{q} - g\bar{a}$
$PF_2 = \bar{q}$	$PB_2 = \bar{p} . \bar{x} (\underline{a} - b\bar{p}) - \bar{q} - g\underline{a}$
$PF_3 = \bar{p} . \bar{x} (\bar{a} - b\bar{p}) - \bar{s}$	$PB_3 = \bar{s} - g\bar{a}$
$PF_4 = \bar{p} . \bar{x} (\underline{a} - b\bar{p}) - \bar{s}$	$PB_4 = \bar{s} - g\underline{a}$

As can be seen from Figure 2 there are three sets of decision nodes in the game. At the third node the bank must decide upon its optimal effort level. At the second node the firm chooses the type of contract. At the first node the bank decides upon the offer price, which will be a sequential equilibrium with respect to the subsequent nodes.

3. Sequential Equilibrium

In order to solve the sequential equilibrium, we need to solve for Nash equilibria in the sub-games that are played after the issue price has been announced. Consider first the subgame between ($\bar{a}$, $\underline{a}$) for the bank.

3.1 Subgame at Node 3

Proposition 1   (i) Given FC, bank plays $\bar{a}$ if $\bar{p} \cdot \bar{x} > g$.

(ii) Given BE, bank plays $\underline{a}$

Proof (i) The bank plays $\bar{a}$ if (from pay-off Table A) $P^B_1 > P^B_2$, which will be the case if $\bar{p} \cdot \dot{x} > g$, ie if the net benefits of supplying the high level of effort $\bar{a}$ are positive | |

Proof (ii)   The bank plays $P^B_3 < P^B_4$ | |

Under a firm commitment contract when the bank bears the risk of the issue, the bank will supply the high effort level. With a best efforts contract, there is no incentive for the bank to supply more than the minimum effort level. Note that when the firm decides the contract it is not possible to make the payments q or s a function of the bank's effort, since effort is unobservable.

3.2 Subgame at Node 2

Now consider the firm's choice of contracts. If it offers FC and $\bar{q}$ it gets P^F_1 provided $\bar{p} \cdot \bar{x} > g$. If it offers BE and $\bar{s}$ it gets P^F_4. Hence we may state

Proposition 2 Firm plays FC if $\bar{p} \cdot \bar{x} > g$.
Proof, $P^F_1 = \bar{q}$ *and* $P^F_4 = \bar{p} \cdot \bar{x}(\underline{a} - b\bar{p}) - \bar{s}$
From Assumption 3, $\bar{s}$ is given by equation (6) and $\bar{q}$ by equation (7), so $P^F_1 > P^F_4$ | |
In Pay-off Table B we give an expanded description of the payoffs to both parties when the state of the market is poor.

Pay-off Table B

Pay-off to issuing firm	Pay-off to bank
$P^F_{\bar{9}} = \underline{q}$	$P^B_9 = \underline{p} \cdot \underline{x}(a - b\underline{p}) - \underline{q} - g\,a$
$P^F_{10} = \underline{q}$	$P^B_{10} = \underline{p} \cdot \underline{x}(\underline{a} - b\underline{p}) - \underline{q} - g\,\underline{a}$
$P^F_{11} = \underline{p} \cdot \underline{x}(a - b\underline{p}) - \underline{s}$	$P^B_{11} = \underline{s} - ga$
$P^F_{12} = \underline{p} \cdot \underline{x}(\underline{a} - b\underline{p}) - \underline{s}$	$P^B_{12} = \underline{s} - g\underline{a}$

Corollary 1: If $(\underline{x}, \underline{p})$, then firm plays FC and bank responds with $\bar{a}$, if $\bar{p} \cdot \bar{x} > g$

Dominant strategies which denote Nash equilibria in this honest game are illustrated in Figure 2 by double lines. We could think of the honest game as the symmetric information case where the firm has the same information as the bank i.e. the firm too observes x. It can be seen that in the honest game the firm will prefer the firm commitment contract, and allow the bank to take on the risk of the issue. The firm accepts the fixed payoff q. The firm choosing FC and the bank responding with $\bar{a}$ is a Nash equilibrium.

3.3 Equilibrium at Node 1

Now consider the opportunity for deception by the bank, which occurs when the firm cannot observe the state of the market. If in state $\bar{x}$ the bank suggests offer price $\underline{p}$, what are the payoffs to the bank? The extended form of the asymmetric case is illustrated in Figure 3.

Figure 3

Asymmetric information case

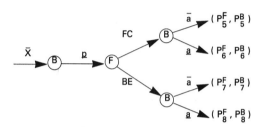

Referring back to Figure 1 it can be seen that if the bank plays $\underline{p}$ when $x = \bar{x}$ there is excess demand, and we will suppose that in this case the bank can supply minimum effort and still sell all the shares. That is, if the state of the market is good but the bank suggests an offer price of $\underline{p}$ then since investors have optimistic beliefs about the returns from the project and at price $\underline{p}$ these returns seem very attractive, the bank is able to sell the entire offer with little effort. Pay-off Table C gives an expanded description of the payoffs in the asymmetric case.

Pay-off Table C

Pay-off to issuing firm	Pay-off to bank
$pF_5 = \underline{q}$	$pB_5 = \underline{p}\, Q^* - \underline{q} - g\underline{a}$
$pF_6 = \underline{q}$	$pB_6 = \underline{p}\, Q^* - \underline{q} - g\underline{a}$
$pF_7 = \underline{p}\, Q^* - \underline{s}$	$pB_7 = \underline{s} - g\underline{a}$
$pF_{12} = \underline{p}\, Q^* - \underline{s}$	$pB_8 = \underline{s} - g\underline{a}$

Proposition 3   If $(\bar{x}, \underline{p})$ and firm plays FC, then bank plays $\underline{a}$.
Proof   Since $pB_5 < pB_6$ | |

Thus in contrast to Proposition 1, the bank is able to supply minimum effort and still sell all the issue because the state of the market is good and the issue is underpriced. The firm must now decide whether to play FC or BE, by comparing the payoffs pB and pB.   Before outlining the asymmetric information case which is left until Proposition 4, it is instructive to consider the firm's choice of contract assuming symmetric information, such that the firm as well as the bank observes the state of the market.

Lemma   With symmetric information, if $(\overline{x}, \underline{p})$ firm plays BE.
Proof, from (4) and (6), $P^F_8 = pQ^* - \underline{s} = \underline{p}.\underline{x}(\overline{a}-b\underline{p}) - g\underline{a} - u$
and from (8), $P^F_6 = q = \underline{p}.\underline{x} \, (\overline{a}-b\underline{p}) - g\overline{a} - u$, *then* $P^F_8 > P^F_6$ ∥

If the issue is underpriced, ie in state $\overline{x}$, bank plays $\underline{p}$, then the issue will be rationed irrespective of the effort put in by the bank. Proposition 3 says that in this full information case the firm would then rather take the profits than the fixed payment of q, so that the firm prefers to take a best efforts contract, employing the bank as the agent.

However under asymmetric information the firm does not know whether $x = \overline{x}$ or $\underline{x}$. If the bank is being honest when it suggests the offer price $\underline{p}$, (implying that the state of the market is $\underline{x}$) then if the firm plays BE it gets the low payment P^F_{12}. However if the state of the market is $\overline{x}$ when the firm plays BE, the firm receives P^F_8. On the other hand if the firm plays FC in response to the bank's price $\underline{p}$, the firm gets $P^F_9 = P^F_6 = q$ for certain. The firm's optimal decision in these circumstances is stated as Proposition 4.

Proposition 4   With asymmetric information, when the bank announces $\underline{p}$, the firm plays BE if $\underline{p}.\underline{x} < g/(1-\lambda)$
Proof, $E[P^F \setminus FC] = q$
$E[P^F \setminus BE] = (1-\lambda)P^F_{12} + \lambda \, P^F_8 = \underline{p}.\underline{x}[(1-\lambda) \, \underline{a} + \lambda \, \overline{a} - b\underline{p}) - g\underline{a} - u$
where λ is the firm's belief that the state is $\overline{x}$, so firm plays BE, since from equation
(8) $q < E[P^F \setminus BE]$ if $\underline{p}.\underline{x} \, (1-\lambda) < g$

The condition in Proposition 4 is more likely to hold the higher is λ, the firm's initial beliefs that $x = \overline{x}$, since this means that it is more likely that the firm will receive P^F_8. Proposition 4 implies that the bank, knowing how the firm will react, can choose a pricing strategy that will make the firm indifferent between BE and FC.

Theorem   1 There exists a probability θ that ensures $q = E[P^F \, BE]$ if $\underline{p}.\underline{x}[(1-\lambda) < g < \underline{p}.\underline{x}$
Proof, let θ be the conditional probability of $\overline{x}$ given $\underline{p}$, ie $\theta = Pr[\overline{x}|\underline{p}]$, then we require
$q = \theta P^F_8 + (1-\theta)P^F_{12}$. *Using Bayes' rule this probability solves:*

$$q = \frac{\lambda Pr[\underline{p}|x]}{(1-\lambda) + lPr[\underline{p}|\overline{x}]} \, (pQ^* - \underline{s}) + \frac{(1 - \lambda)}{(1-\lambda) + lPr[\underline{p}|\overline{x}]} \, [\underline{p}.\underline{x}(\underline{a} - b\underline{p}) - \underline{s}] \quad (9)$$

Define $\omega = Pr[\underline{p}|\overline{x}]$, then solve for ω,

$$\omega = \frac{(1 - \lambda)}{\lambda g} \, (\underline{p}.\underline{x} - 1) \quad (10)$$

The conditions under which the theorem holds derive from Corollary 1 and Proposition 4 which ensure that the parameter values are such that the equilibrium will exist ∣ ∣

The theorem states the firm will be indifferent between BE and FC when it observes $\underline{p}$. This is because the bank chooses to play $\underline{p}$ when $\overline{x}$ has been observed with probability ω, such that this probability ω ensures that the expected payoff to the firm from playing BE is equal to the sure payoff to the firm from playing FC. We must now see what the bank's optimal strategy is when it observes $\bar{x}$.

On observing $\bar{x}$ if the bank plays $\bar{p}$ it gets $P^B_1 = u$. If it plays $\underline{p}$, it either receives P^B_8 when the firm chooses BE, or the bank receives P^B_6 when the firm picks FC. Since the firm is indifferent between BE and FC we will assume that it randomly chooses between BE and FC with probability $(\rho, 1- \rho))$.

Theorem 2   On observing $\bar{x}$, the optimal strategy for the bank is to play a mixed strategy with respect to pricing policy. It should play $\underline{p}$ with probability ω.
Proof, On observing $\underline{p}$, given Theorem 1 the firm is indifferent between BE and FC. Suppose it plays BE with probability ρ. Having observed $\bar{x}$, the bank compares the expected payoff from being dishonest, and the resulting random choice by the firm of BE or FC, with the reservation utility of being honest, and playing the pure strategy $\bar{p}$. Is $\rho P^B_8 + (1-\rho)P^B_6 > P^B_1$? Using equations (6) and (8) $P^B_8 = P^B_1 = u$ and $P^B_6 = g(\bar{a}- \underline{a}) + u$; so that the left hand side of the inequality is always greater for all values of ρ. Furthermore we can show that it is not optimal for the bank to play the pure strategy $\underline{p}$, since from Proposition 4 we know that the firm will play BE if the bank always plays $\underline{p}$, so that the payoff to the bank would be $P^B_8 = P^B_{12} = u$, which is again less than the payoff to the mixed strategy. Hence it is optimal for the bank having observed $\bar{x}$, to play a mixed strategy. Using theorem 1, it should play $\underline{p}$ with probability ω | |

If the bank always played pure strategies it would only receive its reservation utility. For example if the bank always played $\bar{x}$ when it observed the good state it would receive P^B_1; if it always played $\underline{p}$ when it observed the bad state it would receive P^B_9; if it always played $\underline{p}$ whatever the state, from Proposition 4 the firm would choose the best efforts contract and again the bank would only receive its reservation utility. In this case the firm also would not be receiving a surplus since under the Best Efforts contracts the bank only supplies the minimum effort. However by playing a mixed strategy $\underline{p}$ with probability ω when it observes the good state, the bank can increase its payoff above its reservation utility by appropriating some of the firm's surplus. This is because by playing a mixed strategy the bank can induce the firm to be indifferent between a firm commitment and a best efforts contract, and under a firm commitment contract when the bank has announced $\underline{p}$ in response to observing $\bar{x}$ the bank receives more than its reservation utility.

Corollary 2:   An investor will on average buy shares below their fair value, since the proportion of time that $\underline{p}$ is observed is $(1 - \lambda + \lambda\omega)$, yet the market is only in a poor state $(1 - \lambda)$ portion of the time.

When the bank observes a bad state it always suggests $\underline{p}$ as the offer price. When the bank observes a good state which occurs with probability λ the bank will quote $\underline{p}$ with probability w. Thus assets are underpriced $\lambda\omega$ per cent of the time. Theorem 2 therefore suggests that the underpricing of new issues is more likely to occur in a good state, so that underpricing is more acute in boom periods and this is a testable proposition which we will examine in the next section of the paper. The identification of "hot issue" periods by Ibbotson and Jaffe (1975), Ritter (1984) and Trundle et al

(1990) when large initial discounts occur across different stocks, is consistent with this proposition. Note also that when the bank announces the high price the firm always replies with Firm Commitment contract, and only randomly chooses a Best Efforts contract when the bank announces the low price. This strategy by the firm is likely to result in a greater number of contracts being firm commitment in line with the findings of Ritter (1987).

4. Empirical Results

The model developed in the previous section of the paper has argued that the initial discount on IPO's can arise as the equilibrium to a game played by the issuing firm and the investment bank. Not only did we argue that the discount was an outcome of this game but a corollary of this result is that the discount is more likely to occur in good states. We now test this corollary using data on a sample of initial public offerings in the UK over the period 1980-1993.[5] The dataset consists of the first day discounts for each of a sample of 936 new issues on the London Stock Exchange from May 1980 to May 1993. The first day discount is defined as the percentage difference in the issue price of the IPO and the closing price on the first day of trading. For each month in the sample period, except for those months when there were no new issues, the average discount across new issues was computed, and this variable formed the dependent variable to be explained in the subsequent regressions. The testable hypothesis developed in this paper is that discounts are more likely to occur when the market is in a good state. The variable we use to proxy for the state of the market is the return on the FT-All Share Index, on the basis that the value of the index changes in anticipation of future states of the economy. The motivation for the information asymmetry in the paper was that the investment bank has better information about the state of the market than any issuing firm. This information assumption coupled with the assumption that the change in the FTA proxies for the state of the market, means that we are assuming that investment banks are able to predict future changes in the index better than an issuing firm.

We ran a time-series regression of the monthly average discount on the return on the market index.[6] According to Davis and Yeomans (1974) and Levis (1993) the time-lag between the offer price being set and the first day of trading will be between two to three weeks, and further the investment bank will initially advise on a price band within which the shares might be offered, which may be some months before the issue date. Hence investment banks may advise on the offer price based on their current view of the market, but market conditions may have changed by the time that the issue date arrives. For these reasons it is likely that lagged changes in the market index may also affect the size of the initial discount. The time-series regressions also included lagged changes in the market index, and the lag length was determined empirically. In addition ex ante uncertainty may also affect the size of the discount, since it may be that riskier firms go public in a boom market, with less risky firms floated in bear markets. For this reason we also included a measure of risk of the issue which was proxied for by the market capitalisation of the new firm in the year of issue [Fama and French (1992) document that firm size is a proxy for risk]. The measure of risk in each month was taken as the inverse of the average market capitalisation of the companies being floated in that month, and this measure was indexed back to

1980 by the value of the FT-All Share index to allow for inflation in asset values. We would expect a positive relationship between the measure of ex ante uncertainty and the initial discount, and since our explanatory variable is the inverse of firm size the coefficient on this variable should be positive. The final explanatory variable in the regression was the number of companies floated in a particular month, and we might expect a positive relationship between this variable and the initial discount on account of the price pressure from substitute new issues.

Table 2 provides some descriptive statistics of the data. Averaging the 936 new issues during the month of issue produced 138 monthly observations, and the average first day discount was 13.2%, though there were months when the discount was negative. The average monthly return on the FTA over the sample was 1.08%, though the period included the 1987 crash with a recorded monthly fall of 26%. Table 3 also reproduces the descriptive statistics for the data averaged over quarters which yields 50 data points.

Table 2

Descriptive statistics for Initial Public Offerings, 1980-93

The first day returns on each of the 936 IPO's are grouped by month or quarter, and the variable $IPORET_t$ is calculated as the average IPO return for each month or quarter. $FTRET_t$ is the monthly/quarterly return on the FTSE-100. The data set extended from May 1980 to May 1993, but any month or quarter without an IPO was excluded. RMV_t is the market value of the newly issued firms averaged over the month, and indexed back to market values in 1980 in £ million. NO_t is the number of new issues in month t.

Variable	Number of Observations	Mean	Standard Deviation	Median	Minimum	Maximum
Monthly						
$IPORET_t$	138	0.1328	0.1203	0.1005	-0.1296	0.5285
$FTRET_t$	138	0.0108	0.0529	0.0169	-0.2604	0.1443
RMV_t (£mn)	138	35.33	122.99	6.70	0.19	1235.0
NO_t	138	6.71	5.22	5.00	1.00	22.00
Quarterly						
$IPORET_t$	50	0.14371	0.1173	0.1150	-0.0161	0.7020
$FTRET_t$	50	0.03428	0.0863	0.0364	-0.2761	0.1896

Correlation matrix of monthly variables

	$IPORET_t$	$FTRET_t$	$FTRET_t-1$	$FTRET_t-2$
$IPORET_t$	1.0			
$FTRET_t$	0.126	1.0		
$FTRET_{t-1}$	0.242	-0.071	1.0	
$FTRET_{t-2}$	0.144	-0.111	-0.0643	1.0

Table 3

Empirical results

The first columns report the estimated coefficients and diagnostics for the monthly data estimated by OLS. The second column reports the results for maximum likelihood estimation of a first order autocorrelated model.Reported results for the quarterly data in the final column use a Newey-West heteroscedasticity consistent covariance matrix and autocorrelation consistent matrix.

	OLS: Monthly obs.	Maximum likelihood (autocorrelation adjusted) Monthly obs.	Quarterly obs.
Constant	0.104 (5.81)	0.106 (5.08)	0.105 (7.495)
$FTRET_t$	0.398 (2.18)	0.441 (2.62)	0.432 (2.89)
$FTRET_{t-1}$	0.608 (3.35)	0.613 (3.56)	0.373 (2.43)
$FTRET_{t-2}$	0.422 (2.26)	0.342 (2.05)	0.299 (1.59)
$RINVMV_t$	0.014 (1.287)	0.013 (1.08)	
NO_t	0.001 (0.529)	0.001 (0.51)	
autocorrelation parameter ρ		0.348 (4.35)	
$\bar{R}^2$	0.122	0.223	0.116
Durbin-Watson	1.297	2.052	
Breusch-Pagan with 5 d.f.	4.234		
Ramsey Reset Test using squared value of predicted dependent variable			
$IPORETHAT^2$	3.829		1.40
Jarque-Bera normality test			
χ^2_2	30.99		209.4

Dependent variable IPORETt (t-statistics in brackets)

The results of the OLS regressions for the monthly observations are presented in the first column of Table 3. We find a positive and significant effect of the FTA returns and the initial discount, and though the firm size variable was of the anticipated sign it was insignificant. Diagnostic tests reported in the lower half of this table indicated that autocorrelation was present in this regression, though not heteroscedasticity (which may be because the firm size variable is standardising the variance of the error term). We therefore corrected the model for first order autocorrelation using a maximum likelihood method and the results are given in the second column of Table 3. These results strongly support our hypothesis that underpricing is more likely to occur in boom periods. It can be seen that there is a clear statistically significant relationship between the current and lagged values of the return on the FTA index and the average IPO first day return which suggests that the initial discount on an IPO is higher when the current and lagged market returns are positive. To check whether the inclusion of the lagged market returns indicate any collinearity of the independent variables, Table 2 reports the correlation matrix of the dependent and independent variables. It can be seen that successive values of the market index appear relatively uncorrelated, so that it not simply a bull market effect that we have identified. The evidence is more suggestive of the investment bank having knowledge of future market movements. The adjusted R^2 in the monthly data set is only 22%, which suggests that there may well be other factors that can add to the explanation of the initial discounts, but we are only interested in testing the hypothesis suggested by our theory. The final column in Table 3 reports the estimation results for the quarterly data series, which can be thought of as a robustness check on our results. We estimated this model with a Newey-West correction for both autocorrelation and heteroscedasticity. A final qualification for these results is that the Jarque-Bera test indicates that the residuals are not normally distributed. This qualification aside the results of this exercise are supportive of our theory: the underpricing is more pronounced in boom periods, which according to our theory is when the investment bank deliberately underprices to minimise the effort put into the sale.

5. Conclusions

It has been shown that a price discount in the new issue market will result from a sequential equilibrium in the bargaining game between the issuing firm and the investment bank. The issuing firm knows that the bank has an incentive to claim that the state of the market is poor, when in fact it is good, so that the bank can get away with supplying little effort, and receiving the issue proceeds. The response of the firm to this moral hazard problem is to take the incentives away from the bank by insisting on a best efforts contract that leaves the firm with the issue proceeds. However if the firm always followed this strategy when the bank claimed it was a bad state, then sometimes the firm would indeed find itself in a bad state and the issue proceeds are low, since the bank when acting solely as the distributor supplies only low effort. Knowing that the firm faces this dilemma, when the bank observes a good state it will claim it is a bad state ω per cent of the time. The adoption of this strategy by the bank ensures that the firm is just indifferent between specifying a firm commitment or a best efforts contract: the strategy is a sequential equilibrium. Importantly for the phenomenon of underpricing of new issues, this sequential equilibrium results in a new issue being underpriced on average. Whenever the bank observes $\underline{x}$ which occurs $1-\lambda$ per cent of the time, the bank announces $\underline{p}$. Whenever the bank observes $\bar{x}$ it plays a mixed strategy and states $\underline{p}$ with probability ω, and $\bar{p}$ with probability $1-\omega$. This strategy by the bank means that whenever the firm observes the bank offering $\bar{p}$, it replies with FC (offer for sale). However when the firm finds the bank offering $\underline{p}$, the firm randomizes between FC (offer for sale) and BE (placing or subscription). If we suppose that the chances of the market being in a good state are as likely as it being in a bad state, and given the randomizing strategy by the firm with respect to the contract choice when the firm announces a bad state, then our results are consistent with the stylized facts of IPO's documented in Smith (1986) and Ritter (1987). The majority of initial public offerings are firm commitments, these new issues are underpriced on average and underpricing is more likely to occur in boom periods. We have shown using data on 936 IPO's on the London Stock Exchange over the period 1980-93 the 1underpricing is indeed more pronounced when the market return is high.

Acknowledgement

I should like to thank Martin Cripps, Edward Davies, Suzanne Espenlaub, Miles Gietzmann, Jim Gordon, Mario Levis and an anonymous referee for comments on an earlier draft.

References

Allen, F. and G. R. Faulhaber, 1989, Signalling by underpricing in the IPO market, Journal of Financial Economics, vol. 23, 303323.

Baron, D.P., 1982, A model of the demand for investment banking advising and distribution services for new issues, Journal of Finance, vol. 37, 95576

Baron, D.P. and B. Holmstrom, 1980, The investment banking contract for the new issues under asymmetric information: Delegation and the incentive problem, Journal of Finance, vol. 35, 11538.

Beatty, R.P. and J.R. Ritter, 1986, Investment banking, reputation, and the underpricing of initial public offerings, Journal of Financial Economics, vol. 15, 21332.

Benveniste, L.M. and P.A. Spindt, 1989, How investment bankers determine the offer price and allocation of new issues, Journal of Financial Economics, vol. 24, 343361.

Davis, E. W., and K. A. Yeomans, 1974, Company Finance and the Capital Market, (Cambridge University Press).

Fudenberg, D. and J. Tirole, 1991, Game Theory, (MIT Press).

Grinblatt, M. and Chuan Yang Hwang, 1989, Signalling and the pricing of new issues, Journal of Finance, vol. 44, 393420.

Hart, O. and J. Moore, 1988, Incomplete contracts and renegotiation, Econometrica, vol. 56, no. 4, 755786.

Ibbotson, R.G., 1975, Price performance of common stock new issues, Journal of Financial Economics, vol. 3, 23572

Ibbotson, R.G. and J. Jaffe, 1975, Hot issue markets, Journal of Finance, vol. 30, 102742.

Ibbotson, R.G., J.R. Ritter and J.L. Sindelar, 1994, Initial public offerings, Journal of Applied Corporate Finance, vol. 7, 614.

Jackson, P.D., 1986, New issue costs and methods in the UK equity market, Bank of England Quarterly Bulletin, vol. 26, 53242.

Koh, F. and T. Walter, 1989, A direct test of Rock's model of the pricing of unseasoned issues, Journal of Financial Economics, vol. 23, 251272.

Kreps, D.M. and R. Wilson, 1982, Sequential equilibria, Econometrica, vol. 50, 86394.

Levis, M., 1990, The winner's curse problem, interest costs and the underpricing of initial public offerings, Economic Journal, vol. 100, 7689.

Levis, M., 1993 Long-run performance of initial public offerings in the UK, Financial Management.

Loughran, T., J.R. Ritter and K. Rydqvist, 1994, Initial public offerings: international insights, Pacific Basin Finance Journal, vol. 2, 165199.

Moore, J. and R. Repullo, 1988, Subgame perfect implementation, Econometrica, vol. 56, 11911220.

Ritter, J.R., 1984, The hot issue market of 1980, Journal of Business, vol. 57, 21540.

Ritter, J.R., 1987, The costs of going public, Journal of Financial Economics, vol. 19, no. 2, 26981.

Rock, K., 1986, Why new issues are underpriced, Journal of Financial Economics, vol. 15, 187212.

Smith, C.W., 1986, Investment banking and the capital acquisition process, Journal of Financial Economics, vol. 15, nos. 1/2, 329.

Trundle, J.M., T.J. Jenkinson, R.S. Benzie and M.J. Dicks, 1990, New equity issues in the United Kingdom, Bank of England Quarterly Bulletin, vol. 30, 243252.

Welch, I., 1989, Seasoned offerings, imitation costs and the underpricing of initial public offerings, Journal of Finance, vol. 44, 421449.

Endnotes

1 This same assumption about information asymmetries is also made in Baron (1982). Models of the IPO process differ in the information assumptions they make. The signalling models of Allen and Faulhaber (1989), Grinblatt and Hwang (1989) and Welch (1989) assume that the owners of the firm have more information than potential investors. The demand side model of Rock (1986) assumes that some groups of potential investors have more information than other groups.

2 Of course as Fudenburg and Tirole (1992, pages 398-99) note, the outcome of a game will be sensitive to the assumptions made about the negotiation process, and game theory tends to focus on structures which generate a unique solution.

3 Fudenburg and Tirole (1992, page 422) suggest that efficiency arguments imply that the informed player should play first. So that a bank with the information about the state of the market announce the price at which he is willing to sell the issue first of all. This is partly because the reason that thefirm chooses to employ an investment bank is because the firm knows that the bank has expert knowledge.

4 Note that we do not allow the firm to have the issue fully underwritten with a Best Efforts contract, since this would remove the issue risk from the firm. A partially underwritten Best Efforts contract would not affect the intuition of the following analysis

5. I am very grateful to Mario Levis for providing this dataset.

6 We repeated the exercise averaging the data over a quarterly time period.

Financial Aspects of Business Cycles: an Analysis of Nine OECD Countries

Robert E. Krainer
**University of Wisconsin, Madison
and Templeton College, Oxford**

Abstract

This article proposes a theory of how external shocks are transmitted into pricing, production, investment, and financing decisions by managers who are required by contract to coalesce the welfare of their bondholders and stockholders over the business cycle. In this set-up managers direct operating strategy (i.e., a set of pricing, production, and investment decisions) to benefit equityholders, and financial strategy (i.e., capital structure and dividend payout decisions) to benefit bondholders. The theory predicts that changes in share prices precede changes in the risk structure of firm assets, and that procyclical movements in risky corporate investments are matched with countercyclical movements in financial leverage and dividend payout rates. These predictions are not rejected for most of the nine OECD countries studied in this article.

1. Introduction

How does the financial system coordinate real activity in a market economy? Are there systematic business cycle patterns in the way firms finance real economic activity? These are important practical questions when it comes to assessing the impact, if any, of alternative monetary, fiscal, and corporate financial policies on the real business activity of a country. While it is true that the older Keynesian and monetarist demand-oriented theories attributed importance to financial matters (particularly the stock of real money balances) in the determination of real activity, the more recent relative price misperception and real business cycle variants of the new classical theory downplay the importance of financial matters. Consequently there has not been a great deal of interest recently in detecting, much less studying, the so-called financial "stylized facts" of business cycles in countries with developed capital markets.

The objective of this paper is to analyze the investment and financing behavior of firms in nine OECD countries. Some progress has already been made in linking the financial side to the real side of an economy.[1] In two recent studies (Krainer, 1985, 1992), a model of corporate investment and the financing of that investment was presented and empirically tested with data from the nonfinancial corporate sector in the United States. In that work the hypothesis was put forward that financing decisions must be systematically linked to operating decisions in order to rationalize the continued existence of a debt and equity claim structure to the income stream and assets of the firm. One of the important empirical implications of this model is that the procyclical pattern of risky corporate investment must be matched with a countercyclical movement in financial leverage and dividend payout rates. In other words, economic expansions are financed with equity and recessions supported with debt. In the empirical part of our previous work (Krainer, 1992, Chapter 4), the countercyclical movement in financial leverage was found to be an important and a significant "stylized fact" of the post World War II business cycle in the United States. One of the major findings in this paper is that the countercyclical pattern of financing can also be observed in other OECD countries. We also find some evidence that the stock market value of firms in these countries is systematically related to the risk structure of their assets.

The order in which these issues are addressed in this paper will be as follows. Section 2 motivates the empirical investigation by presenting a hypothesis of enterprise financing based on the inherent conflict between bondholders and stockholders in the same firm, a conflict well understood in the option pricing and agency literature in finance. Since the particular model of conflict presented in Section 2 is described in great detail in Krainer (1992, Chapter 3), the discussion here will be relatively brief. Section 3 describes the data and data sources for the nine OECD countries studied in this paper, while Section 4 presents the results of the statistical experiments. Finally, Section 5 concludes the paper with a short summary of the main empirical results.

2. An Intertemporal Model of Investment and Financing

It is a simple fact from basic accounting definitions that the assets of a firm must be supported or financed with equity claims and perhaps debt claims. This truism not only applies when the enterprise is first created, but also when the firm expands or contracts its assets. It is also a fact of common observation that assets and technologies within a firm as well as across firms differ in terms of their risk characteristics. Risk in this sense refers to the unobserved but perceived variability of returns generated on the assets of the firm, and hence the value of those assets. Finally, securities or the claims on the firm's assets differ in terms of their own risk characteristics. Debt represents a fixed and legally prior claim to the income and assets of the firm, whereas equity is a variable and residual claim. For this reason the debt securities of a given firm with a given risk structure of productive assets can be considered less risky than the associated levered equity.

The question then is whether the firm should finance its mix of assets (with different risk characteristics) with a particular mix of debt and equity securities when these debt and equity securities have their own individual risk characteristics. The well-known

Modigliani-Miller analysis tells us that at a given point in time and for a given mix of assets, the debt-equity and dividend payout decisions are irrelevant. The equally well-known option pricing analysis, on the other hand, tells us that over time and with a changing mix of assets the financing decision of the firm is very relevant for both bondholders and stockholders. The reason is that over time a firm can (and often does) change the relative mix of its safe and risky assets which will then change the risk characteristics but not the promised payment on the bonds. Since the business cycle is an intertemporal phenomena, it seems reasonable to pursue the insight that financing decisions can be relevant over time.

To analyze this question further consider a private monetary economy comprised of risk averse investors, but where some investors are more risk averse than others. To simplify matters still further, suppose the relatively more risk averse investors only hold bonds (the existence of which is assumed) while the less risk averse only hold equities. Since the debt represents a fixed and prior claim to the income and assets of the firm, it is reasonable to assume a positive risk premium or

$$R(b) < R = \bar{X}/K \leq R(s) \qquad (1)$$

where
$R(b)$ = the rate of return on bonds.
$\bar{X}$ = the expected income generated on the firm's assets.
K = the value of the resources employed by the firm.
R = the rate of return on the capital employed by the firm.
$R(s)$ = the rate of return on levered equity.

A 1-firm 1-good economy of a given size (in terms of K and $\bar{X}$) characterized by the inequality in (1) is graphically displayed in the box diagram in Figure 1. The horizontal sides of the box measure the resources K invested in this firm/economy by bondholders b and stockholders s. The vertical sides of the box represent the expected income $\bar{X}$ earned on the invested resources. Thus $\bar{X}(b)$ is the expected income earned by bondholders on their investment of K(b) units of resources in the firm/economy, while $\bar{X}(s)$ is the expected income earned by stockholders for their investment of K(s) in the firm/economy. The diagonal line running from B to S describes the sharing rule for an all equity firm/economy. This line says that any investor providing α percent of the total invested resources of an all equity firm lays claim to percent of the expected and actual income generated on those resources. The point Z in the diagram describes the expected income and risky investment sharing between bondholder partners and stockholder partners in a levered economy in which the risk premium is given by (1). In other words, the fact that R(b) < R(s), implies that Z must lie somewhere below the diagonal line running from B to S. It can also be seen in the figure that the marginal and average rates of return R(b) and R(s) are assumed to be constant in and around some small neighborhood centered on Z. Finally, business cycles in this economy would be described by horizontal and vertical expansions and contractions of the box in the figure.

Figure 1

Input and Expected Output Sharing in a Debt and Equity Economy

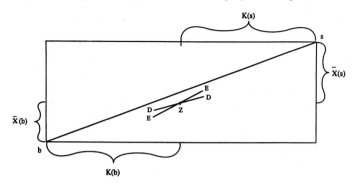

In developing this idea further, the expected income of bondholders for small variations of K(b) around Z can be written as

$$\bar{X}(b) = R(b) \ K(b) \tag{2}$$

where R(b) is a constant. The expected income generated on the total resources invested in the firm/economy is:

$$\bar{X} = R[K(b) + K(s)] \tag{3}$$

The residual income going to levered equityholders is then given by:

$$\bar{X}(s) = \bar{X} - \bar{X}(b) \tag{4}$$

Putting (3) into (4) and then dividing the result into (2) yields the following nonlinear relationship between $\bar{X}(b)/\bar{X}(s)$ and K(b)/K(s).

$$\frac{\bar{X}(b)}{\bar{X}(s)} = \frac{\dfrac{K(b)}{K(s)}}{\dfrac{R}{R(b)} + \left[\dfrac{R - R(b)}{R(b)}\right]\dfrac{K(b)}{K(s)}} \tag{5}$$

The linear approximation to (5) is given by the dd schedule in Figure 2. Everywhere along the schedule the expected rate of return on bonds equals the required rate of return of bondholders, and therefore the market value of bonds equals the book value of bonds. In other words, R(b) represents two rates of return which are equal in equilibrium: an expected rate of return, R(b, BV); and a required rate of return, R(b, MV). The price for one unit of a bond is then given by:

$$P(b) = \frac{\bar{X}(b)}{R(b, MV)} \cdot \frac{1}{N(b)} \tag{6a}$$

where
N(b) = the number of units of bonds.

Multiplying both sides of (6a) by K(b)/K(b), and defining R(b, BV) = $\bar{X}$(b)/K(b) yields

$$P(b) = \frac{R(b, BV)}{R(b, MV)} \cdot \frac{K(b)}{N(b)} \qquad (6b)$$

Thus whenever R(b, BV) differs from R(b, MV), the market price of a bond, P(b), will be different than the book value of a bond, K(b)/N(b). However, along an equilibrium dd schedule R(b, BV) = R(b, MV) and P(b) = K(b)/N(b), or, the net present value of bonds is zero. For a given K and $\bar{X}$ there are many different rates of return on debt securities that satisfy the inequality in (1), and for each one of these rates of return there will be a separate dd schedule. From (5) it can be seen that a dd schedule with a higher R(b) lies above a schedule with a lower R(b). The dd schedule presented in the figure is for a given required rate of return on bonds. Therefore, points above (or below) this schedule—indicated by the sign of + (or -) in the figure—represent combinations of K(b)/K(s) and $\bar{X}$(b)/ $\bar{X}$(s) for which the market value of bonds is greater (or less) than the book value embedded in the schedule. This is because points above the dd schedule in Figure 2 lie on schedules with higher rates of return than the rate of return along the schedule displayed in Figure 2, while points below lie on schedules with lower rates of return. If bondholders require the rate of return embedded in the dd schedule shown in the figure but actually earn a return that is lower (i.e., they are somewhere in the (-) region below the schedule), they will price the bonds at a discount from book value in the market place so that the rate of return on market value is what they require in the assumed given state of nature.

Figure 2

Financial Market and Product Market Equilibrium in a Debt and Equity Economy

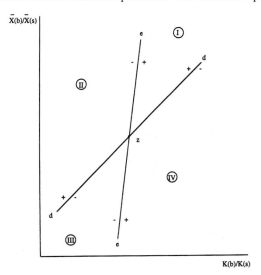

The ee schedule in Figure 2 can be derived in much the same way as the dd schedule. In this connection let $\bar{X}(s)$ be the expected income required by shareholders for an investment of $K(s)$ in the economy, and that $R(s)$ is invariant for small variations in $K(s)$ so that:

$$\bar{X}(s) = R(s)\ K(s) \tag{(7)}$$

The expected income on the total assets of the economy is as before.

$$\bar{X} = R[K(b) + K(s)] \tag{3}$$

From the perspective of shareholders, the income available for bondholders is simply equation (3) minus equation (6) or

$$\bar{X}(b) = X - \bar{X}(s) \tag{8}$$

Substituting (3) into (7) and dividing the result by (6) yields:

$$\frac{\bar{X}(b)}{X(s)} = \left[\frac{R - R(s)}{R(s)}\right] \frac{R}{R(s)} \left[\frac{K(b)}{K(s)}\right] \tag{9}$$

Equation (9) describes a particular ee schedule for a given $R(s)$ satisfying the inequality in (1). Along this schedule the market value of equity equals the book value of equity, or, stated differently, stockholders earn their required rate of return. As was the case for $R(b)$, $R(s)$ represents two rates of return which are equal in equilibrium: an expected rate of return, $R(s, BV)$; and a required rate of return, $R(s, MV)$. Ignoring growth considerations, the price of one share of stock is given by:

$$P(s) = \frac{\bar{X}(s)}{R(s, MV)} \cdot \frac{1}{N(s)} \tag{10a}$$

$N(s)$ = the number of shares of stock.

Multiplying both sides of (10a) by $K(s)/K(s)$ and defining $R(s, BV) = \bar{X}(s)/K(s)$ yields

$$P(s) = \frac{R(s, BV)}{R(s, MV)} \cdot \frac{K(s)}{N(s)} \tag{10b}$$

Here again whenever $R(s, BV)$ is different than $R(s, MV)$, the market price of stock, $P(s)$, is different than its book value, $K(s)/N(s)$. When the two yields are equal along an equilibrium ee schedule, the market price of equity is equal to the book value of equity, or, the net present value of stock is zero. It can also be seen from (9) that there are many required rates of return on equity satisfying the inequality in (1), and each one of these rates of return lie along a different ee schedule. In this case, however, higher rates of return schedules lie below lower rate schedules. Accordingly, points below (above) a *given* ee schedule represent combinations of financial leverage and distributions of income among bondholders and stockholders for which the market value of equity is greater (smaller) than book value, and these points are represented by a + (or -) in the figure.

In Figure 2 it can be seen that the ee schedule intersects the dd schedule from below at point z. This is because of the positive risk premium of stock yields over bond yields assumed in (1).[2] At point z the capital market value of the economy's assets equals the book value of assets, and the book values of debt and equity securities equals their respective market values. Bondholders and stockholders are earning their required rates of return. From the perspective of both groups of investors, there is no incentive for the firm/economy to move from z.

Note from Figure 2 that there are four non-equilibrium zones where the market values of securities are different than their respective book values. In Zone II (i.e., points in the figure that are simultaneously above the dd and ee schedules) the market value of bonds exceeds their book value, while the market value of equity is below book value. The reverse is true in Zone IV (i.e., points that are simultaneously below the dd and ee schedules) where the market price of debt is below book value, and the market value of equity is above book value. In our previous work (Krainer, 1992, Chapters 3 and 5) rational financial contracting was designed to   that are simultaneously above dd and below ee) is different in that market values on both securities are above their book values.   Points in Zone I cannot represent an equilibrium for the economy since a firm can be created in the product market at a cost represented by book value, and then sold in the capital market for a greater value. Arbitrage between the product market and capital market would eliminate this discrepancy in valuations, and in the process create a business cycle expansion. For the same reason points in Zone III cannot represent a sustainable equilibrium since in this zone (i.e., points simultaneously below dd and above ee) the book value of the firm/economy's resources is greater than the capital market prices on both debt and equity securities. In this case some firms or parts of firms are worth more "dead than alive." The optimal arbitrage strategy for the firm is then to sell productive resources back to the factor/product market at the higher book value, and buy back their securities from the capital market at the lower market price. The implementation of this arbitrage strategy is the cause of business cycle recessions in this model.

What then causes economic fluctuations in this debt and equity economy when it is at some equilibrium contract point like z in Figure 2? The answer must be anything (such as an external shock) that changes the required rates of return embedded in the dd and ee schedules will change the contract point z. When the contract point z changes, managers in this economy will respond with a coordinated set of pricing, employment, output, investment, dividend payout, and financing decisions in their competitive drive to equate the book value of firm assets and securities to the new capital market values of those securities.

Finance performs two functions in this business cycle model. The first is a signalling function for change in the operating strategies of firms when external shocks induce a discrepancy between the book and capital market values of debt and equity securities. Any change in the operating strategies of firms will change the risk structure of assets, and the risk and return sharing among bondholders and stockholders compared to what it was at z. The second function of the financial system in this model is to coalesce the welfare of bondholders and stockholders as firms change their operating strategies thereby taking the economy through different stages of the business cycle. Thus as firms implement more risky operating strategies (by accumulating risky assets and pushing the economy into the expansion phase of the business cycle) in response to a positive external shock, an optimal financial contract between bondholders and stockholders will require these firms to implement a more conservative financing strategy of reducing financial leverage and dividend payout rates. Stockholders benefit from the riskier operating strategy while bondholders benefit from the conservative financial strategy. When firms are managed in this way over the business cycle, debt and equity securities are economically viable sharing rules for long run rational investors.[3]

To *illustrate* this model in the context of the geometry in Figure 2, consider the following hypothical example. Suppose an economy initially in a contract equilibrium like z experiences a positive external shock that increases the expected wealth of shareholders and/or reduces their perception of risk in the environment. (Suppose also—and unrealistically—that this shock has no effect on bondholders.) If consumption were highly substitutable across time and if these shareholders had decreasing relative risk aversion utility functions, then they would increase their savings and reduce the required rate of return on equity securities which according to equation (9) would shift the ee schedule to the left somewhere like e'e' in Figure 3. The result of the shock is that the contract point for the economy changes from z to z where the dd schedule intersects the ee schedule. The capital market now signals a post shock equilibrium at z.   When the firm/economy is at z but the new equilibrium is at z, the market value of equity will be greater than book value. This is the case because when at z equity investors are earning a higher expected rate of return than they require in the post shock environment at z. Stock prices will therefore rise above book value at z which is the signal to firm managers to implement a riskier operating strategy. In other words, the increase in stock prices is the shareholder's way of telling managers that they should now pursue more speculative operating strategies since these wealthier shareholders perceive a less risky environment and have become less averse to risk.

Figure 3
Equilibrium Expansions in a Debt and Equity Economy

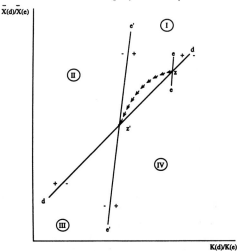

In the business cycle model of Krainer (1992), firms speculate in the product market by accumulating risky inventories (and planning for the accumulation of plant and equipment) on which they expect to earn higher profits for their shareholders sometime in the future. The mix of assets of the firm then changes, shifting towards relatively risky assets and away from safe assets. Firms accumulate these risky inventories by expanding production and possibly raising output prices. Prices, production, and investment are important "stylized facts" characterizing business cycles in market economies and have been the subject of much study in business cycle analysis. What has not been studied extensively is the additional financing that is now required to support the expansion in risky investments and general economic activity.

Of course, the decision to embark on a speculative operating strategy of expanding risky investments and production, and possibly raising output prices is not one that will please relatively risk averse bondholders. The reason is that bondholders will not be the beneficiaries of a successful speculation due to the fact that their income is bounded from above by the promised payment, and they may even suffer losses if the speculation is unsuccessful. In these circumstances, a rational contract between bondholders and stockholders would call upon the firm to offset the increased risk of the operating strategy with a conservative financing strategy of reducing financial leverage. Going one step further, a super rational financial contract between bondholders and stockholders would require firms to respond to external shocks with operating and financing strategies that enable both groups of investors to earn their required rates of return in the expansion (or recession) contract equilibrium. The case for an economic expansion is illustrated in Figure 3. In going from the pre-shock equilibrium of z to the post-shock equilibrium z' the firm accumulates risky assets, shifting expected income towards stockholders by reducing $\overline{X}(b)/\overline{X}(s)$, and at the same time financing the speculative operating strategy and expansion in economic activity with equity thereby reducing $K(b)/K(s)$. In the new equilibrium at z' bondholders and stockholders earn their required rates of return. This was achieved by firms implementing operating decisions (e.g., pricing, employment, output, and investment decisions) and financing decisions (the choice of a dividend payout rate and financial leverage) so as to equate market to book value of their debt and equity securities. A negative shock that raises the required rate of return on equity would induce the opposite operating and financing strategies and take the economy into a recession.[4]

There are at least three empirical implications that follow from this risk and return sharing theory of the business cycle for debt and equity financed economies. The first implication is that changes in equity valuations precede changes in the risk structure of firm assets and the general level of economic activity. The prediction that changes in equity valuations precede changes in economic activity is not unique to the risk and return sharing theory but is shared with all those theories of the business cycle that accord an important role to interest rates and investment spending.[5] The second empirical implication of the model is that financial leverage is systematically related to the risk structure of assets and general economic activity, rising during periods of recession when firms pursue conservative operating strategies and falling in expansions when they implement risky operating strategies. The third implication is a variant of the second, namely, the dividend payout rate follows a countercyclical path. These three empirical implications will be tested (where possible) with aggregate data from the nine OECD countries in our sample in Section 4.

3. Data and Data Sources

Before presenting the empirical findings in Section IV, it will be useful to briefly describe the data and data sources used in this study. A more complete description of the data will be presented in the appendix. The countries in the sample are Canada, Finland, France, Germany, Italy, Japan, Norway, the United Kingdom, and the United States. This sample of countries offers a wide variety of economic structures and institutions in which to study the cyclical pattern of operating and financing strategies.

At this point it will be useful to define more precisely what is meant by an operating strategy and a financing strategy. Of the two, the firm's financing strategy seems the easier to define. This study will consider two types of financial decisions, financial leverage and the dividend payout rate. The leverage variable used in this paper is the marginal change in long-term financial leverage for a given year. The dividend payout rate will be the ratio of cash dividends paid to shareholders to the sum of cash dividends plus earnings retention (net of depreciation) for a given year. An operating strategy is somewhat more difficult to precisely define and measure. It seems reasonable to think of it as a set of employment, output, pricing, and investment plans that makes the firm more or less risky in terms of the variability of its operating income. In our previous work (Krainer, 1992) an operating strategy was identified with output growth rates, and various categories of investment and investment plans such as inventory accumulation, new appropriations for capital, and new orders for machine tools. When firms accumulate these types of assets relative to total assets they are presumed to be pursuing a risky operating strategy. Unfortunately, for what follows below, new capital appropriations and new orders for machine tools were unavailable for the non-U.S. countries in our sample. On the other hand, it was also observed in our previous work that there is a high correlation between inventory accumulation, and both the appropriation stage and ordering stage of the capital accumulation process in the United States. For that reason inventory accumulation (relative to total assets, and sources and uses of funds) will be the proxy measure for a change in the operating strategy of the firms in the nine country sample. In other words, changing the rate of inventory accumulation is one *observable* operating decision (examples of other decisions not readily observable would include the planning and ordering of new plant and equipment, redirecting research and development, new product development, and designing new promotional strategies) firms implement when they change the risk of their operating strategy to match the risk aversion of their shareholders. An increase in this ratio is assumed to reflect a change toward a more risky operating strategy.

As can be seen these proxy measures for a financial strategy and operating strategy require data from various types of financial statements. The financial statements for this sample of countries are available in various issues of the *OECD Financial Statistics, Part 3, Nonfinancial Enterprises Financial Statements*. More specifically, the OECD collects data on balance sheets and sources and uses of funds statements for nonfinancial enterprises in all nine countries, and income statements for all of these countries except Canada, Germany, and Italy. Share prices and product market variables (e.g., various indices for output and prices) were obtained from the *International Financial Statistics Yearbook 1993* published by the International Monetary Fund.

4. Empirical Results

4.1 Introduction and Some Preliminary Findings

There is a potential measurement problem associated with the financial statements from various countries that should be addressed before presenting the main empirical results. The problem is that the OECD balance sheets for nonfinancial enterprises are stated in terms of historical cost book values.[6] The regression experiments in Tables 2 and 3 relate such balance sheet items as inventory investment and long-term financial leverage to the total assets of nonfinancial enterprises. It is possible that historical cost book value measures of assets could distort some of these relationships. For example, long-term financial leverage in this study is defined to be the marginal change in long-term debt relative to total assets. Two countries might have the same degree of long-term financial leverage when assets are valued at historical costs, but the country that has experienced the more rapid inflation in asset valuations will have the lower economically effective amount of financial leverage. It is often said that Japan is such a country in that financial leverage in that country is very high when assets are valued at historical costs but would be much lower if assets (particularly land) were valued at current costs. For this reason and others we will not make cross country comparisons of inventory investment and financial leverage. Instead the focus of attention in this study will be the business cycle path of long-term financial leverage and inventory accumulation in each individual country.

To partially alleviate this problem within countries, we will use two measures of inventory accumulation and financial leverage; one based on the OECD current cost sources and uses of funds statements, and the other based on the historical cost balance sheet statements. For the sources and uses of funds statements, inventory accumulation will be defined as the increase in inventories divided by the total sources and uses of funds, or (Inv/S=U). Financial leverage, in turn, will be defined as the ratio of new issues of long-term liabilities to the total sources and uses of funds, or (LT Liab/S=U). This new issue flow measure of long-term financial leverage is probably less contaminated by measurement problems than the balance sheet measures based on historical cost valuations of assets. The balance sheet measure of inventory accumulation will be defined as the year to year change in the ratio of inventories to total assets, or, $\Delta(\text{Inv}/A)$. Long-term financial leverage from the balance sheet will be defined to be the change in the ratio of long-term liabilities to total assets, or $\Delta(\text{LT Liab}/A)$.

While the criticisms against historical cost asset valuations seem plausible in principle, it remains to be seen whether they are important in practice. For example, covenants in U.S. bond contracts almost always set constraints on long-term financial leverage in terms of historical cost book values. If these covenants govern financial strategy then we would expect historical cost book value measures of long-term financial leverage to have the countercyclical path predicted by the risk and return sharing theory. In other words, if financial policy constraints are generally stated in terms of historical cost book values, then the theory should be tested with historical cost book value data. In any event it might be asked whether historical cost measures of inventory accumulation and long-term financial leverage actually have a different cyclical pattern than reproduction or current cost measures of these balance sheet variables. If they don't, then we might use either measure of asset valuations in the empirical tests of the risk and return sharing theory of the business cycle. Fortunately, there is data available for the U.S. manufacturing sector that will enable us to construct balance sheets based on both historical cost and reproduction cost valuations of assets.[7] It is therefore possible to see whether the two measures of inventory accumulation and long-term financial leverage have different business cycle paths.

Table 1 presents comparisons between the cyclical pattern of historical cost and reproduction cost measures of inventory accumulation and marginal long-term financial leverage for the manufacturing sector in the United States for the period 1965-90. As in our previous work (Krainer, 1992, Chapter 4) inventory investment, (ΔInv/ΔA), is hypothesized to be positively related to output growth rates (the percentage rate of change in the industrial production index, $\dot{IP}$), price inflation (the percentage rate of change in the producer price index, $\dot{PH}$), and the lagged value of industrial share prices, SP_{t-1} deflated by the consumer price index. The general idea is that firms receive a stock market signal to change the risk of their operating strategy which in this specification of the model takes the form of inventory accumulation. Firms then implement the new inventory investment policy by changing the rate at which they produce output and the price they charge in the market place for the output. As can be seen from Table 1 in R1 and R2 these conjectures of this particular specification of firm operating strategy are not rejected by the historical cost or reproduction cost measures of inventory accumulation. All estimated coefficients are positive as hypothesized by the theory and statistically significant. The only difference between the two regressions is that the one based on reproduction cost of assets has estimated coefficients on the three explanatory variables that are somewhat larger in absolute value than the one based on historical cost, and that the inflation rate is slightly more important than output growth rates in the reproduction cost regression whereas this is reversed in the historical cost regression. Both regressions provide strong support for one of the empirical implications of the risk and return sharing theory of the business cycle; namely, manufacturing firms in the U.S. vary their operating strategy (proxied by ΔInv/ΔA) in response to signals from the stock market. Moreover this response is roughly the same for historical cost and reproduction cost measures of inventory accumulation. These regressions also confirm another hypothesis in Krainer (1992) that firms use pricing and output decisions to influence their investments in inventories.

The next two regressions provide evidence on the cyclical pattern of marginal adjustments in long-term financial leverage. Regressions R3 and R4 relate the financial leverage measure (ΔLT Debt/ΔA) to output growth ($\dot{IP}$), inflation rates ($\dot{PP}$ I), and a dummy variable $(DV)^{85-86}$ reflecting the structural change in the tax environment associated with the Tax Reform Act of 1986).[8] The prediction from the risk and return sharing theory is that the estimated coefficients on the output growth and price inflation variables will be negative. As can be seen, the estimated coefficients on output growth and price inflation for both historical cost and reproduction cost measures of long-term financial leverage are negative, and the negative relationship is statistically significant. Here again the estimated coefficients are somewhat larger in absolute value for the reproduction cost measures of financial leverage. The two regressions indicate that over the 1965-90 period long-term financial leverage followed a countercyclical path as predicted by the theory.

Table 1

Historical Cost and Reproduction Cost Balance Sheet Measures of Investment and Financing Decisions in the Manufacturing Sector of the United States

R1.
$$\left[\frac{\Delta Inv}{\Delta A}\right]_t^{HC} = \underset{(-4.42)}{-.2400} + \underset{(7.04)}{1.7808\,(IP)_t} + \underset{(5.94)}{1.5204\,(P\dot{P}I)_t} + \underset{(4.45)}{.1910\,(SP)_{t-1}}$$

$$S = .063 \qquad \bar{R}^2 = .800 \qquad DW = 1.69$$

R2.
$$\left[\frac{\Delta Inv}{\Delta A}\right]_t^{RC} = \underset{(-4.21)}{-.3324} + \underset{(5.74)}{2.1136\,(IP)_t} + \underset{(6.76)}{2.5172\,(P\dot{P}I)_t} + \underset{(3.86)}{.2408\,(SP)_{t-1}}$$

$$S = .091 \qquad \bar{R}^2 = .774 \qquad DW = 2.27$$

R3.
$$\left[\frac{\Delta LT\ Debt}{\Delta A}\right]_t^{HC} = \underset{(9.74)}{.2564} - \underset{(-4.87)}{1.3369\,(IP)_t} - \underset{(-2.73)}{.8371\,(P\dot{P}I)_t} + \underset{(4.35)}{.2418\,(DV)_t^{85-86}}$$

$$S = .067 \qquad \bar{R}^2 = .732 \qquad DW = 1.93$$

R4.
$$\left[\frac{\Delta LT\ Debt}{\Delta A}\right]_t^{RC} = \underset{(8.31)}{.3813} - \underset{(-3.56)}{1.7014\,(IP)_t} - \underset{(-3.49)}{1.8692\,(P\dot{P}I)_t} + \underset{(3.41)}{.3305\,(DV)_t^{85-86}}$$

$$S = .118 \qquad \bar{R}^2 = .673 \qquad DW = 1.94$$

S   =   Standard error of estimate adjusted for degrees of freedom.

$\bar{R}^2$ =   Coefficient of determination adjusted for degrees of freedom.

DW   =   Durbin-Watson statistic.

The t-scores in the parentheses beneath the estimated coefficients are computed using White's Heteroskedastic consistent procedure for calculating standard errors.

The regression results in Table 1 are very encouraging for two reasons: first, they tend to support the empirical implications of the risk and return sharing theory of the business cycle presented in Section II; and second, the estimated coefficients in the historical cost and reproduction cost measures of inventory accumulation and financial leverage are fairly similar. These results indicate that marginal changes in inventory investment (as that variable proxies for a risky operating strategy) are procyclical while marginal changes in long-term financial leverage follow a countercyclical path. This is the same result we obtained in an earlier study (Krainer, 1992, Chapter 4) but for a different sample of companies and over a different time period. Even more important for what follows below, these estimated coefficients are pretty much the same when inventory investment and financial leverage variables are measured in terms of historical costs and reproduction cost valuations of total assets. With this support we now move on to analyze the historical cost based financial statements of nonfinancial enterprises in the nine OECD countries in the sample. Moreover this analysis will use essentially the same regression specification for inventory accumulation and long-term financial leverage that was used for the U.S. manufacturing sector in Table 1.[9] While there is no a priori compelling reason to believe that nonfinancial enterprises in this sample of OECD countries adjust operating and financing strategies in exactly the same way as U.S. manufacturing companies, in the absence of any other information it seems an appropriate way to begin the study.

4.2 Some Evidence on Asset Adjustments in Nine OECD Countries

The risk and return sharing theory asserts that outside shocks are an important source of cyclical fluctuations, and that these outside shocks are first evaluated in the stock market. After their evaluation in the stock market, managers respond with a new operating strategy for the firm consistent with any change in the risk aversion or perception of risk of their shareholders resulting from the outside shock. Changes in stock prices and the required rate of return on equity securities reflect changes in the risk aversion and perception of risk of equity investors and thus serve as a signal to managers on which they base their post shock operating strategy. An empirical assumption underlying this work is that changes in the rate of inventory accumulation are one way (among many) managers can change the operating strategy of their firms. Thus a negative external shock that raises the required rate of return of equity investors and depresses share prices is the signal for managers to pursue the less risky operating strategy of reducing inventory investment. In implementing this conservative strategy managers reduce the rate of production and perhaps the price charged per unit of output. In the end this new conservative operating strategy that produces an economic recession is now consistent with the shock induced increase in risk aversion and/or perception of risk of equity investors.

A regression test of this theory of asset adjustment as a change in operating strategy was presented in Table 1 for the U.S. manufacturing sector and took the following simple form.

$$
\begin{aligned}
\text{(Inventory Investment)} = \text{Constant} \\
+ a_1(\text{Output Growth}) + a_2(\text{Price Inflation}) \\
+ a_3(\text{Equity Variables}) + \text{Random Disturbances}
\end{aligned}
\tag{11}
$$

The hypotheses being tested are whether a_1, a_2, and a_3 are positive. In R1 and R2 of Table 1 the statistical estimates of a_1, a_2, and a_3 were positive and statistically significant. The U.S. manufacturing sector conforms fairly well to this general specification of inventory investment over the 1965-90 period. In what follows below this same specification for inventory investment—as that variable proxies for changes in operating strategy—will be used for the nonfinancial enterprises in the sample of nine OECD countries.

Two measures of inventory investment will be used in the regressions reported in Table 2. The first comes from the sources and uses of funds statements and is the ratio of increases in inventories to total sources and uses of funds, or (Inv/S = U). The second measure of inventory investment comes from the OECD historical cost balance sheets. This measure takes the form of the change in the ratio of inventories to total assets, or Δ(Inv/A).

The output growth and inflation rate variables in the inventory investment regressions are taken from the Prices and Production section (for each country in the sample) of the *International Financial Statistics Yearbook 1993*. The output growth variables used in the individual country regressions were either the percentage rates of change in the industrial production index, (IṖ), or the index of gross domestic product (GḊP). The price inflation variable used in each country regression was the percentage rate of change in one of the following four price indices: the wholesale price index (WṖI), the consumer price index (CṖI), the gross domestic product price deflator (GDP-I), and the producer price index (PṖI). The choice of the output growth and price inflation variables for each country depended on the availability of the data for the entire sample period. Finally, two capital market variables were used to proxy for changes in investor risk aversion in the nine OECD countries. One was simply the lagged value of real share prices, $(SP)_{t-1}$. The second was a price-earnings ratio measured in two different ways. One measure was the ratio of lagged real share prices to current dividend payments to shareholders, $SP_{t-1}/(Div)_t$. The second measure was the ratio of lagged real share prices to the sum of current dividend payments and current retained earnings, $SP_{t-1}/(Div + RE)_t$. The choice of the capital market variable used in the individual regressions was based solely on statistical significance considerations.

The inventory accumulation regressions for the nonfinancial enterprises in the nine OECD countries and the more narrow manufacturing sector in the United States are presented in Table 2. The predictions from the risk and return sharing theory presented in Section II are that the estimated coefficients on output growth, inflation rates, and lagged stock market variables are all positive. In the table there are 18 estimates for each of the three slope coefficients. For the output growth variable all 18 estimated coefficients are positive. Moreover, 17 of the 18 positive coefficients are statistically significant at the five percent (or better) level on a one-tail test of significance. The one exception occurs in R13 for Italy where the measure of inventory accumulation is taken from the sources and uses of funds statements. Turning next to the inflation rate variable, the table indicates that all 18 estimated coefficients are positive with 16 being statistically significant at the five percent level on a one-tail test. The two exceptions occur in R5 for Canada (when inventory investment is taken from the sources and uses of funds statements), and R14 for Italy (when inventory investment is taken from the balance sheets). These results indicate that for most of the countries in the sample, the data is consistent with the view that firms use output and pricing decisions to implement their inventory investment strategy. The stock market signalling hypothesis receives somewhat less support in these regressions. The results in the table indicate that 17 of the 18 estimated coefficients on the stock market variable are positive, and of the 17 only 10 are statistically significant at the five percent (or better) level on a one-tail test of significance. The one estimated coefficient that is negative occurs in Canada (in R6) when inventory investment is obtained from the OECD balance sheets. However, the t-score indicates that this estimated coefficient is not significantly different than zero. The countries in which the positive estimated coefficient on the lagged stock market variable is not significantly different than zero include Canada (R5), Finland (R7 and R8), Germany (R11 and R12) and the U.K. (R19).[10]

Table 2

Inventory Investment Decisions in Nine OECD Countries

Canada: Nonfinancial Corporations

1970-92

R5.
$$\left[\frac{\text{Inv}}{\text{S=U}}\right]_t = \begin{matrix} -.0740 \\ (-1.06) \end{matrix} + \begin{matrix} 1.2052\,(\text{IP})_t \\ (2.35) \end{matrix} + \begin{matrix} .3766\,(\text{WPI})_t \\ (1.40) \end{matrix} + \begin{matrix} .0323\,(\text{SP})_{t-1} \\ (.55) \end{matrix}$$

$$S = .061 \qquad \bar{R}^2 = .502 \qquad DW = 1.94 \qquad AR(1) = .338$$

1972-92

R6.
$$\Delta\left[\frac{\text{Inv}}{\text{A}}\right]_t = \begin{matrix} .0006 \\ (.06) \end{matrix} + \begin{matrix} .0519\,(\text{IP})_t \\ (2.52) \end{matrix} + \begin{matrix} .0381\,(\text{WPI})_t \\ (1.79) \end{matrix} - \begin{matrix} .0381\,(\text{SP})_{t-1} \\ (-.55) \end{matrix}$$

$$S = .006 \qquad \bar{R}^2 = .226 \qquad DW = 2.12$$

Finland: Nonfinancial Corporations

1968-91

R7.
$$\left[\frac{\text{Inv}}{\text{S=U}}\right]_t = \begin{matrix} -.2289 \\ (-3.27) \end{matrix} + \begin{matrix} 3.7594\,(\text{GDP})_t \\ (5.24) \end{matrix} + \begin{matrix} 2.3371\,(\text{GDP-I})_t \\ (4.26) \end{matrix} + \begin{matrix} 6.7546\Delta \\ (.39) \end{matrix}\left[\frac{\text{SP}_{t-1}}{(\text{Div})_t}\right]$$

$$S = .124 \qquad \bar{R}^2 = .608 \qquad DW = 1.78$$

1968-91

R8.
$$\Delta\left[\frac{\text{Inv}}{\text{A}}\right]_t = \begin{matrix} -.0311 \\ (-4.16) \end{matrix} + \begin{matrix} .3154\,(\text{GDP})_t \\ (2.52) \end{matrix} + \begin{matrix} .2270\,(\text{GDP-I})_t \\ (3.21) \end{matrix} + \begin{matrix} 2.3561\Delta \\ (.86) \end{matrix}\left[\frac{\text{SP}_{t-1}}{(\text{Div})_t}\right]$$

$$S = .019 \qquad \bar{R}^2 = .306 \qquad DW = 1.80$$

Table 2 (continued)

France: Industrial Enterprise

1970-92

R9. $\left[\dfrac{\text{Inv}}{S=U}\right]_t = \begin{array}{c} -.4505 \\ (-3.17) \end{array} + \begin{array}{c} 1.4348\,(\text{IP})_t \\ (2.88) \end{array} + \begin{array}{c} 5.2641\,(\text{CPI})_t \\ (5.78) \end{array} + \begin{array}{c} .1457\,(\text{SP})_{t-1} \\ (2.32) \end{array}$

$S = .083 \qquad \bar{R}^2 = .782 \qquad DW = 1.88$

1971-92

R10. $\Delta\left[\dfrac{\text{Inv}}{A}\right]_t = \begin{array}{c} -.0757 \\ (-7.73) \end{array} + \begin{array}{c} .1091\,(\text{IP})_t \\ (1.82) \end{array} + \begin{array}{c} .5002\,(\text{CPI})_t \\ (5.61) \end{array} + \begin{array}{c} .0267\,(\text{SP})_{t-1} \\ (5.21) \end{array}$

$S = .012 \qquad \bar{R}^2 = .586 \qquad DW = 2.18$

Germany: Nonfinancial Enterprises

1969-92

R11. $\left[\dfrac{\text{Inv}}{S=U}\right]_t = \begin{array}{c} -.0388 \\ (-.90) \end{array} + \begin{array}{c} 1.1914\,(\text{IP})_t \\ (8.18) \end{array} + \begin{array}{c} 2.0060\,(\text{WPI})_t \\ (9.81) \end{array} + \begin{array}{c} .0366\,(\text{SP})_{t-1} \\ (.98) \end{array} + \begin{array}{c} .1059\,(\text{DV})_t^{87} \\ (3.95) \end{array}$

$S = .034 \qquad \bar{R}^2 = .795 \qquad DW = 1.73 \qquad AR(1) = .519$

1968-92

R12. $\Delta\left[\dfrac{\text{Inv}}{A}\right]_t = \begin{array}{c} -.0105 \\ (-2.60) \end{array} + \begin{array}{c} .0770\,(\text{IP})_t \\ (6.55) \end{array} + \begin{array}{c} .1785\,(\text{WPI})_t \\ (7.88) \end{array} + \begin{array}{c} .0019\,(\text{SP})_{t-1} \\ (.48) \end{array} + \begin{array}{c} .0293\,(\text{DV})_t^{87} \\ (11.40) \end{array}$

$S = .004 \qquad \bar{R}^2 = .735 \qquad DW = 2.07 \qquad AR(1) = .388$

Italy: Nonfinancial Corporations

1969-92

R13. $\left[\dfrac{\text{Inv}}{S=U}\right]_t = \begin{array}{c} -.0503 \\ (-1.04) \end{array} + \begin{array}{c} .6744\,(\text{GDP})_t \\ (1.15) \end{array} + \begin{array}{c} 1.1621\,(\text{GDP-I})_t \\ (2.99) \end{array} + \begin{array}{c} .0297\,(\text{SP})_{t-1} \\ (2.12) \end{array}$

$S = .057 \qquad \bar{R}^2 = .453 \qquad DW = 1.98 \qquad AR(1) = .308$

1970-92

R14. $\Delta\left[\dfrac{\text{Inv}}{A}\right]_t = \begin{array}{c} -.0180 \\ (-2.09) \end{array} + \begin{array}{c} .2262\,(\text{GDP})_t \\ (2.03) \end{array} + \begin{array}{c} .0435\,(\text{GDP-I})_t \\ (.80) \end{array} + \begin{array}{c} .0041\,(\text{SP})_{t-1} \\ (1.77) \end{array}$

$S = .013 \qquad \bar{R}^2 = .203 \qquad DW = 2.00 \qquad AR(1) = -.200$

Table 2 (continued)

Japan: Manufacturing Industries

1973-92

R15. $\left[\dfrac{Inv}{S=U}\right]_t = \underset{(-1.12)}{-.0248} + \underset{(2.11)}{.5257\,(\dot{IP})_t} + \underset{(7.22)}{1.1935\,(\dot{WPI})_t} + \underset{(1.97)}{.0229\,(SP)_{t-1}}$

$S = .056 \qquad \bar{R}^2 = .769 \qquad DW = 2.02 \qquad AR(1) = -.305$

1973-92

R16. $\Delta\left[\dfrac{Inv}{A}\right]_t = \underset{(-3.74)}{-.0082} + \underset{(2.62)}{.0429\,(\dot{IP})_t} + \underset{(9.55)}{.1024\,(\dot{WPI})_t} + \underset{(1.94)}{.0034\,(SP)_{t-1}}$

$S = .006 \qquad \bar{R}^2 = .686 \qquad 2.10$

Norway: Nonfinancial Corporations

1969-91

R17. $\left[\dfrac{Inv}{S=U}\right]_t = \underset{(-6.21)}{-.4496} + \underset{(5.03)}{2.8913\,(\dot{GDP})_t} + \underset{(6.44)}{2.6524\,(GDP-I)_t} + \underset{(5.27)}{.2793\,(SP)_{t-1}}$

$S = .076 \quad \bar{R}^2 = .664 \quad DW = 1.80 \quad AR(1) = -.268$

1972-91

R18. $\Delta\left[\dfrac{Inv}{A}\right]_t = \underset{(-4.95)}{-.0673} + \underset{(2.56)}{.2461\,(\dot{GDP})_t} + \underset{(2.45)}{.2316\,(GDP-I)_t} + \underset{(4.97)}{.0377\,(SP)_{t-1}}$

$S = .019 \quad \bar{R}^2 = .289 \quad DW = 2.13 \quad AR(1) = -.527$

United Kingdom: Nonfinancial Corporations

1979-90

R19. $\left[\dfrac{Inv}{S=U}\right]_t = \underset{(1.92)}{.1425} + \underset{(7.15)}{1.5894\,(\dot{IP})_t} + \underset{(5.48)}{2.5170\,(\dot{PPI})_t} + \underset{(.28)}{.0117\,(SP)_{t-1}}$

$S = .068 \qquad \bar{R}^2 = .495 \qquad DW = 1.84 \qquad AR(1) = -1.103 \qquad AR(2) = -.578$

United States: Nonfinancial Corporations

1967-92

R20. $\left[\dfrac{Inv}{S=U}\right]_t = \underset{(-.68)}{-.0082} + \underset{(5.15)}{.6412\,(\dot{IP})_t} + \underset{(1.36)}{.2207\,(\dot{PPI})_t} + \underset{(2.43)}{1.1306\,\Delta}\left[\dfrac{SP)_{t-1}}{(Div+RE)_t}\right]$

$S = .025 \qquad \bar{R}^2 = .647 \qquad DW = 2.19 \qquad AR(1) = .333$

1967-92

R21. $\Delta\left[\dfrac{Inv}{A}\right]_t = \underset{(-2.88)}{-.0048} + \underset{(3.41)}{.0562\,(\dot{IP})_t} + \underset{(2.43)}{.0770\,(\dot{PPI})_t} + \underset{(2.77)}{.2977\,\Delta}\left[\dfrac{SP_{t-1}}{(Div+RE)_t}\right] + \underset{(-15.45)}{.0364\,(DV)_t^{81}}$

$S = .004 \qquad \bar{R}^2 = .813 \qquad DW = 1.94 \qquad AR(1) = .214$

Table 2 (continued)

United States: Manufacturing Corporation

1965-92

R22. $\quad \Delta\left[\dfrac{Inv}{A}\right]_t = \underset{(-6.50)}{-.0155} + \underset{(4.88)}{.0934\,(I\dot{P})_t} + \underset{(2.41)}{.0524\,(P\dot{P}I)_t} + \underset{(2.16)}{.0978}\left[\dfrac{SP_{t-1}}{(Div + RE)_t}\right]$

$\qquad\qquad S = .004 \qquad \bar{R}^{\,2} = .548 \qquad DW = 1.93$

$\dfrac{S}{R^2}$ = Standard error of estimate adjusted for degrees of freedom.

$\bar{R}^2$ = Coefficient of determination adjusted for degrees of freedom.

DW = Durbin-Watson statistic.

AR(1) = First-order autocorrelation coefficient used in the Cochrane-Orcutt correction for autocorrelation in the residuals.

AR(2) = Second-order autocorrelation coefficient used in the Cochrane-Orcutt correction for autocorrelation in the residuals.

The t-scores in the parentheses beneath the estimated coefficients are computed using White's Heteroskedastic-consistent procedure for calculating standard errors.

In summing up the regression results in Table 2 and endnote 10, the hypothesis that firms initiate a change in operating strategy in response to a stock market signal and then implement the strategy by changing the rate of inventory accumulation with output and pricing decisions seems to receive the most statistical support in Canada, France, Japan, Norway, and the nonfinancial and manufacturing sectors in the United States.[11] The other countries (Finland, Germany, Italy, and the United kingdom) provide varying degrees of support for the predictions of the theory.[12] Clearly, pricing and output decisions have a significant impact on inventory investments in most of these countries. The role of the stock market is less clear. The hypothesis that a stock market signal triggers a change in inventory accumulation has its strongest support in the United States (in both the manufacturing and nonfinancial corporate sectors), Norway, Italy, France, and even Japan. Mixed support for the hypothesis was observed for Canada and Finland in Table 2 and endnote 10. And finally, very little support for the hypothesis was found in Germany and the U.K. In these two countries managers do not seem to be guided in their selection of an operating strategy (at least in the form of inventory accumulation) by the stock market.

4.3 Financial Leverage and the Business Cycle in Nine OECD Countries

Changes in the operating strategies of debt and equity financed firms are not the only business decisions set in motion by an external shock filtered through an informationally efficient stock market. Financing decisions must be made whenever the operating decisions change the level and risk structure of the firm's assets. According to the risk and return sharing theory described in Section II, financial strategy must be matched with the operating strategy of the firm in order to coalesce the welfare of bondholder partners and stockholder partners over the business cycle. Thus a shock induced (via a signalling stock market) speculative operating strategy that increases both the scale and riskiness of the firm's assets—which when taken together for all firms results in the expansion phase of the business cycle—must be matched with a conservative financing strategy that reduces long-term financial leverage and the dividend payout rate. The reverse would be the case if the shock increased the required rate of return of equity investors thereby signalling the firm to pursue conservative (and recessionary) operating strategies which must, in turn, be matched with a speculative financing strategy of increasing financial leverage and the dividend payout rate. This financing hypothesis will be empirically tested in two different ways in parts C and D of this section.

Table 3 presents the first of these tests of the financing hypothesis contained in this theory of the business cycle using the OECD financial statements data. As can be seen, the regression specification of the hypothesis is the same as the one contained in R3 and R4 in Table 1 for the U.S. manufacturing sector; namely,

$$
\text{(Long-term Financial Leverage)} = \text{Constant} \qquad\qquad (12)
$$
$$
+ \; b_1 \; \text{(Output Growth)} + b_2 \; \text{(Price Inflation)}
$$
$$
+ \; b_3 \; \text{(Equity Variables)} + \text{Random Disturbances}
$$

The output growth rates and price inflation variables in the regressions are the same for each country as those used in the inventory investment regressions in Table 2. Moreover, like the inventory investment regressions in Table 2, long-term financial leverage (where possible) will be taken from the current cost sources and uses of funds statements and the historical cost balance sheets for each country.[13]   The sources and uses of funds measure of financial leverage is the ratio of new issues of long-term liabilities to total sources and uses of funds, or, (LT Liab/S=U). The balance sheet measure of long-term financial leverage is the change in the ratio of long-term liabilities to total assets, or, $\Delta \left[\frac{\text{LT Liab}}{A}\right]$. Finally, a lagged stock market variable is included in the regressions only when it improved the overall statistical results.[14]

Consider first the impact of lagged share valuations on adjustments in long-term financial leverage in the countries where it is included as an explanatory variable. The sign of the estimated coefficient on the lagged stock market variable can be positive or negative. One line of reasoning is that to the extent real stock prices determine the risk of the firm's operating strategy, they also, according to the theory, determine the matching financial strategy. Thus if stock prices signal a risky and expansionary operating strategy, they also signal a more conservative financial strategy of reduced financial leverage. The estimated coefficient on lagged share prices would be negative in this case. On the other hand, real share valuations might also reflect the true value of assets better than the historical cost measures in the OECD financial statements. In this case stock prices partly proxy for asset valuations in the denominator of the financial leverage variable which is actually measured in terms of historical cost book values. Since the value of assets partly determines the capacity to borrow, a rise in stock prices would be associated with an increase in financial leverage suggesting that the estimated coefficient is positive.

Consider next the main empirical hypothesis, namely, the relationship between adjustments in long-term financial leverage and output growth along with price inflation rates. The theory predicts that b_1 and b_2 in (12) are both negative; that is, long-term financial leverage is countercyclical to output growth rates and price inflation rates. The test of this hypothesis is presented in Table 3. In the table there are 17 estimated coefficients for the output growth and inflation rate variables in the leverage regressions. All of the 17 estimated coefficients on the output growth variable for the nine different OECD countries are negative as predicted by the theory. Using a one-tail test, 15 of the 17 estimated coefficients are statistically significant at the five percent (or better) level of significance. The results of Table 3 indicate that for a majority of the countries in this sample, there is considerable evidence that long-term financial leverage is countercyclical to output growth rates. The only exceptions are the balance sheet regression R34 for Norway, and the sources and uses of funds regression R37 for nonfinancial enterprises in the United States.[15]

Table 3
Capital Structure Adjustments and Economic Activity in Various OECD Countries

Canada: Nonfinancial Corporations

1969-92

$$\text{R23.} \quad \left[\frac{\text{LT Liab}}{\text{S=U}}\right]_t = \underset{(12.17)}{.2333} - \underset{(-3.95)}{.6705}(\text{IP})_t - \underset{(-3.58)}{.6179}(\text{WPI})_t - \underset{(-2.79)}{.1551}\Delta(\text{SP})_t$$
$$S = .039 \qquad \bar{R}^2 = .719 \qquad DW = 1.99 \qquad AR(1) = .330$$

1973-92

$$\text{R24.} \quad \Delta\left[\frac{\text{LT Liab}}{A}\right]_t = \underset{(6.54)}{.0193} - \underset{(-2.00)}{.0359}(\text{IP})_t - \underset{(-6.13)}{.2807}(\text{WPI})_t - \underset{(-2.93)}{.0512}\Delta(\text{SP})_t^{\text{U.S.}}$$
$$S = .007 \qquad \bar{R}^2 = .708 \qquad DW = 2.18 \qquad AR(1) = .616$$

Finland: Nonfinancial Corporations

1968-91

$$\text{R25.} \quad \left[\frac{\text{LT Liab}}{\text{S=U}}\right]_t = \underset{(6.11)}{.4780} - \underset{(-4.51)}{2.3697}(\text{GDP})_t - \underset{(-4.45)}{2.2010}(\text{GDP-I})_t + \underset{(2.24)}{39.7311}\left[\frac{\text{SP}_{t-1}}{(\text{Div})_t}\right]$$
$$S = .101 \qquad \bar{R}^2 = .473 \qquad DW = 2.02 \qquad AR(1) = .294$$

1968-91

$$\text{R26.} \quad \Delta\left[\frac{\text{LT Liab}}{A}\right]_t = \underset{(2.87)}{.0451} - \underset{(-1.88)}{.3291}(\text{GDP})_t - \underset{(-2.46)}{.4151}(\text{GDP-I})_t$$
$$S = .024 \qquad \bar{R}^2 = .411 \qquad DW = 1.85$$

France: Industrial Enterprise

1972-92

$$\text{R27.} \quad \left[\frac{\text{LT Liab}}{\text{S=U}}\right]_t = \underset{(3.89)}{.5022} - \underset{(-3.46)}{1.4232}(\text{IP})_t - \underset{(-2.72)}{2.2168}(\text{CPI})_t - \underset{(-3.98)}{.2120}(\text{SP})_t + \underset{(5.21)}{135.4717}\left[\frac{\text{SP}_{t-1}}{(\text{Div})_t}\right]$$
$$S = .070 \qquad \bar{R}^2 = .474 \qquad DW = 2.12 \qquad AR(1) = .238 \qquad AR(2) = -.608$$

Table 3 (continued)

1973-92

R28. $\Delta \left[\dfrac{\text{LT Liab}}{A} \right]_t = \begin{array}{l} .0610 \\ (1.83) \end{array} - \begin{array}{l} .2404\,(\dot{IP})_t \\ (-2.32) \end{array} - \begin{array}{l} .3761\,(\dot{CPI})_t \\ (-1.87) \end{array} - \begin{array}{l} .0321\,(SP)_t \\ (-2.17) \end{array} + \begin{array}{l} 15.6131 \\ (1.71) \end{array} \left[\dfrac{SP_{t-1}}{(Div)_t} \right]$

$S = .013 \qquad \overline{R}^2 = .404 \qquad DW = 1.85 \qquad AR(1) = .465 \qquad AR(2) = -.571$

Germany: Nonfinancial Enterprises

1972-92

R29. $\Delta \left[\dfrac{\text{LT Liab}}{A} \right]_t = \begin{array}{l} -.0077 \\ (-3.28) \end{array} - \begin{array}{l} .0785\,(\dot{IP})_t \\ (-3.78) \end{array} - \begin{array}{l} .0670\,(\dot{WPI})_t \\ (-4.67) \end{array} + \begin{array}{l} .6896 \\ (3.96) \end{array} \left[\dfrac{SP_{t-1}}{(Profit)_t} \right]$

$S = .003 \qquad \overline{R}^2 = .504 \qquad DW = 1.92 \qquad AR(1) = -.295$

Italy: Nonfinancial Corporations

1969-92

R30. $\left[\dfrac{\text{LT Liab}}{S=U} \right]_t = \begin{array}{l} .1169 \\ (.35) \end{array} - \begin{array}{l} 3.1022\,(G\dot{D}P)_t \\ (-11.71) \end{array} - \begin{array}{l} .4073\,(GDP-I)_t \\ (-1.17) \end{array} - \begin{array}{l} .0213\,\Delta(SP)_{t-1} \\ (-1.75) \end{array}$

$S = .056 \qquad \overline{R}^2 = .700 \qquad DW = 2.27 \qquad AR(1) = .949$

1970-92

R31. $\Delta \left[\dfrac{\text{LT Liab}}{A} \right]_t = \begin{array}{l} .0120 \\ (1.40) \end{array} - \begin{array}{l} .4919\,(G\dot{D}P)_t \\ (-3.98) \end{array} - \begin{array}{l} .0259\,(GDP-I)_t \\ (-.36) \end{array} - \begin{array}{l} .0078\,\Delta(SP)_{t-1} \\ (-1.83) \end{array} + \begin{array}{l} .0738\,(DV)_t^{82} \\ (4.04) \end{array}$

$S = .013 \qquad \overline{R}^2 = .724 \qquad DW = 1.78 \qquad AR(1) = .388$

Japan: Manufacturing Industries

1974-92

R32. $\left[\dfrac{\text{LT Liab}}{S=U} \right]_t = \begin{array}{l} -.0351 \\ (-1.15) \end{array} - \begin{array}{l} 1.5766\,(\dot{IP})_t \\ (-5.61) \end{array} - \begin{array}{l} .0363\,(\dot{WPI})_t \\ (-.29) \end{array} + \begin{array}{l} 2.6251 \\ (6.73) \end{array} \left[\dfrac{SP_{t-1}}{(Div)_t} \right]$

$S = .071 \qquad \overline{R}^2 = .579 \qquad DW = 2.01 \qquad AR(1) = -.650 \qquad AR(2) = -.355$

1973-92

R33. $\Delta \left[\dfrac{\text{LT Liab}}{A} \right]_t = \begin{array}{l} -.0104 \\ (-1.88) \end{array} - \begin{array}{l} .1484\,(\dot{IP})_t \\ (-5.08) \end{array} - \begin{array}{l} .0400\,(\dot{WPI})_t \\ (-1.79) \end{array} + \begin{array}{l} .2685 \\ (3.01) \end{array} \left[\dfrac{SP_{t-1}}{(Div)_t} \right]$

$S = .008 \qquad \overline{R}^2 = .643 \qquad DW = 1.99$

Table 3 (continued)

Norway: Nonfinancial Corporations
1970-91

R34. $\left[\dfrac{\text{LT Liab}}{\text{S}=\text{U}}\right]_t = \underset{(1.65)}{.4853} - \underset{(-1.67)}{3.0049\,(\text{G}\dot{\text{D}}\text{P})_t} - \underset{(-2.51)}{3.1480\,(\text{GDP}-\text{I})_t}$

$S = .176 \qquad \bar{\text{R}}^2 = .225 \qquad \text{DW} = 2.28 \qquad \text{AR(1)} = .824$

Norway: Nonfinancial Corporations
1973-91

R35. $\Delta\left[\dfrac{\text{LT Liab}}{\text{A}}\right]_t = \underset{(.21)}{.0203} - \underset{(-2.59)}{.6028\,(\text{G}\dot{\text{D}}\text{P})_t} - \underset{(-5.81)}{.6118\,(\text{GDP}-\text{I})_t}$

$S = .033 \qquad \bar{\text{R}}^2 = .092 \qquad \text{DW} = 1.89 \qquad \text{AR(1)} = .381 \qquad \text{AR(2)} = .523$

United Kingdom: Nonfinancial Corporations
1977-90

R36. $\left[\dfrac{\text{LT Liab}}{\text{S}=\text{U}}\right]_t = \underset{(5.26)}{.2084} - \underset{(-2.60)}{.9302\,(\dot{\text{I}}\text{P})_t} + \underset{(1.93)}{.7065\,(\text{P}\dot{\text{P}}\text{I})} - \underset{(-3.67)}{2229.379}\left[\dfrac{\text{SP}_{t-1}}{(\text{Div}+\text{RE})_t}\right]$

$S = .038 \qquad \bar{\text{R}}^2 = .518 \qquad \text{DW} = 1.99$

United States: Nonfinancial Corporations
1966-92

R37. $\left[\dfrac{\text{LT Liab}}{\text{S}=\text{U}}\right]_t = \underset{(7.68)}{.2291} - \underset{(-1.23)}{.3193\,(\dot{\text{I}}\text{P})_t} - \underset{(-.54)}{.2255\,(\text{P}\dot{\text{P}}\text{I})_t}$

$S = .061 \qquad \bar{\text{R}}^2 = .090 \qquad \text{DW} = 1.62 \qquad \text{AR(1)} = .414$

1967-92

R38. $\Delta\left[\dfrac{\text{LT Liab}}{\text{A}}\right]_t = \underset{(3.43)}{.0150} - \underset{(-2.44)}{.0549\,(\dot{\text{I}}\text{P})_t} - \underset{(-3.35)}{.1349\,(\text{P}\dot{\text{P}}\text{I})} - \underset{(-7.27)}{.0449\,(\text{DV})_t^{81}}$

$S = .006 \qquad \bar{\text{R}}^2 = .858 \qquad \text{DW} = 2.03 \qquad \text{AR(1)} = .641$

United States: Manufacturing Corporations
1968-92

R39. $\Delta\left[\dfrac{\text{LT Debt}}{\text{A}}\right]_t = \underset{(3.44)}{.0075} - \underset{(-4.24)}{.0942\,(\dot{\text{I}}\text{P})_t} - \underset{(-2.66)}{.0622\,(\text{P}\dot{\text{P}}\text{I})_t}$

$S = .005 \qquad \bar{\text{R}}^2 = .526 \qquad \text{DW} = 1.81 \qquad \text{AR(1)} = .508 \qquad \text{AR(2)} = -.433$

Table 3 (continued)

$\underline{S}$	=	Standard error of estimate adjusted for degrees of freedom.
$\overline{R}^2$	=	Coefficient of determination adjusted for degrees of freedom.
DW	=	Durbin-Watson statistic.
AR(1)	=	First-order autocorrelation coefficient used in the Cochrane-Orcutt correction for autocorrelation in the residuals.
AR(2)	=	Second-order autocorrelation coefficient used in the Cochrane-Orcutt correction for autocorrelation in the residuals.

The t-scores in the parentheses beneath the estimated coefficients are computed using White's Heteroskedastic-consistent procedure for calculating standard errors.

Turning next to the inflation rate variable, 16 of the 17 estimated coefficients in Table 3 are negative as predicted by the theory. The one exception occurs for the U.K. in R36 where the estimated coefficient on (PPI) is positive and statistically significant. This result is not consistent with the predictions of the theory. Of the 16 estimated coefficients that are negative, 12 are statistically significant at the five percent level on a one-tail test. Italy (in R30 and R31) is the only country where the negative estimated coefficient on the inflation rate variable (GDP-I) is not statistically significant for either the sources and uses of funds or the balance sheet measures of long-term financial leverage. For Japan (in R32) and the nonfinancial corporate sector of the United States (in R37), the estimated coefficients on the two inflation rate variables in the sources and uses of funds regressions were not statistically significant. However, when the more narrow measure of financial leverage (i.e., LT Bonds/S=U), is used as the dependent variable for U.S. nonfinancial enterprises, the regression R37i in endnote 15 indicates that the estimated coefficient on (PPI) is negative and statistically significant.

In summarizing the regression results for all nine countries in Table 3, it appears that Canada, Finland, France, Germany, Japan, and the United States provide the most support for the financing prediction of the risk and return sharing theory. In these countries most of the evidence indicates that marginal adjustments to long-term financial leverage move countercyclical to output growth rates and inflation rates. Speculative operating strategies that produce cyclical expansions in economic activity are accompanied by a conservative financial policy that reduces long-term financial leverage. Alternatively, conservative operating strategies that produce recessions are accompanied by speculative financing decisions that increase financial leverage. The countercyclical pattern of long-term financial leverage seems to be an established stylized fact of business cycles in these countries. On the other hand, the statistical support for this prediction from the theory is mixed in Italy, Norway, and the U.K. In the case of Italy (i.e., R30 and R31) long-term financial leverage was found to be countercyclical to output growth, but essentially independent of inflation rates in both the sources and uses of funds and balance sheet regressions. For Norway the estimated coefficient on output growth in the sources and uses of funds regression (i.e., R34) is positive, but not statistically significant by conventional standards. Moreover, the common balance sheet specification of long-term financial leverage used in R35 - i.e., Δ(LT Liab/A) - produced a coefficient of determination of less than 10 percent.[16] Finally, long-term financial leverage in the U.K. was observed in R36 to be negatively related (and statistically significant) to output growth as predicted by the theory, but also positively related (and statistically significant) to inflation rates. This result is not predicted by the theory nor observed in other countries in the OECD sample.

4.4 Dividend Policy and the Business Cycle in Nine OECD Countries

Up to this point the financing implications of the risk and return sharing theory of the business cycle have been empirically tested by relating changes in long-term financial leverage to pricing and production variables that were assumed to reflect changes in the operating strategies of nonfinancial enterprises in nine OECD countries. Pricing and output decisions that lead to business cycle expansions were viewed as speculative, while those leading to recession were viewed as safe and conservative. The theory then went on to argue that speculative (or safe) product market strategies that cause business cycle expansions (or recessions) would be matched with safe (or speculative) financing decisions that reduce (or increase) long-term financial leverage. Table 3 and endnotes 15 and 16 provide a great deal of empirical support for that prediction from the theory.

Another way to empirically test the financing implications of the risk and return sharing theory is to relate the dividend payout rate to these representative measures of a change in operating strategy. The dividend payout rate is defined to be the ratio of cash dividends paid to shareholders to the sum of dividends and retained earnings net of depreciation, or Div/(Div + RE).[17] This means that one minus the dividend payout rate—i.e., RE/(Div + RE)—is a measure of the earnings retention rate. According to the theory of Section II, managers that coalesce the welfare of bondholders and stockholders over the business cycle choose high earnings retention rates during periods of cyclical expansion when they are in the process of implementing risky operating strategies. Similarly, they choose high dividend payout rates during periods of recession when they are implementing relatively safe and conservative operating strategies. This suggests that the dividend payout rate should follow a countercyclical path just like long-term financial leverage.

Table 4

Dividend Payout Decisions and Economic Activity in Nine OECD Countries

Canada: Nonfinancial Corporations

NA

Finland: Nonfinancial Corporations

1968-91

R40. $\left[\dfrac{\text{Div}}{\text{Div}+\text{RE}}\right]_t = \underset{(8.39)}{.0922} - \underset{(-4.54)}{.3507}(\text{GDP})_t - \underset{(-3.84)}{.2761}(\text{GDP–I})_t + \underset{(3.92)}{.0200}(\text{SP})_t$

$S = .015 \quad \bar{R}^2 = .685 \quad DW = 1.77 \quad AR(1) = .313$

France: Industrial Enterprise

1970-92

R41. $\left[\dfrac{\text{Div}}{\text{Div}+\text{RE}}\right]_t = \underset{(8.95)}{.3319} - \underset{(-5.89)}{.7115}(\text{IP})_t - \underset{(-4.26)}{.9626}(\text{CPI})_t - \underset{(-2.42)}{.0404}(\text{SP})_t$

$S = .024 \quad \bar{R}^2 = .563 \quad DW = 2.04$

Table 4 (continued)

Germany: Nonfinancial Enterprises

NA

Italy: Nonfinancial Corporations

NA

Japan: Manufacturing Industries

1973-29

R42. $\Delta \left[\dfrac{\text{Div}}{\text{Div} + \text{RE}} \right]_t = \underset{(4.62)}{.0694} - \underset{(-9.10)}{1.7684}(\text{IP})_t - \underset{(.91)}{.1165}(\text{WPI})_t$

$S = .056 \qquad \bar{R}^2 = .779 \qquad DW = 1.90$

Norway: Nonfinancial Corporations

1969-91

R43. $\left[\dfrac{\text{Div}}{\text{Div} + \text{RE}} \right]_t = \underset{(16.28)}{.2294} - \underset{(-1.31)}{.2911}(\text{GDP})_t - \underset{(-2.80)}{.4374}(\text{GDP-I})_t - \underset{(-2.81)}{14.3317} \left[\dfrac{\text{SP}_{t-1}}{(\text{Div})_t} \right]$

$S = .026 \qquad \bar{R}^2 = .737 \qquad DW = 1.89 \qquad AR(1) = .350$

United Kingdom: Nonfinancial Corporations

1977-90

R44. $\left[\dfrac{\text{Div}}{\text{Div} + \text{RE}} \right]_t = \underset{(11.17)}{.5649} - \underset{(-2.37)}{1.3562}(\text{IP})_t - \underset{(-2.72)}{1.5472}(\text{PPI})_t + \underset{(2.50)}{1263.110}\Delta \left[\dfrac{\text{SP}_{t-1}}{(\text{Div} + \text{RE})_t} \right]$

$S = .059 \qquad \bar{R}^2 = .395 \qquad DW = 1.79$

United States: Nonfinancial Corporations

1965-92

R45. $\left[\dfrac{\text{Div}}{\text{Div} + \text{RE}} \right]_t = \underset{(19.54)}{.5312} - \underset{(-2.88)}{1.0589}(\text{IP})_t + \underset{(.50)}{.2084}(\text{PPI})_t - \underset{(-1.40)}{.1441}\Delta(\text{SP})_t$

$S = .072 \qquad \bar{R}^2 = .422 \qquad DW = 1.98$

United States: Manufacturing

1966-92

R46. $\Delta \left[\dfrac{\text{Div}}{\text{Div} + \text{RE} + \text{Deprec}} \right]_t = \underset{(1.48)}{.0039} - \underset{(-5.80)}{.1981}\Delta(\text{IP})_t - \underset{(-2.98)}{.2213}\Delta(\text{PPI})_t + \underset{(14.61)}{2.1910}\Delta \left[\dfrac{\text{SP}_{t-1}}{(\text{Div} + \text{RE})_t} \right]$

$S = .014 \qquad \bar{R}^2 = .788 \qquad DW = 2.06$

Table 4 presents a regression test of this hypothesis. In the table regression estimates of parameter values on output growth and inflation rates are presented for countries that have income statement data allowing the construction of the dividend payout rate variable. (In this connection the OECD does not report income statements for nonfinancial enterprises in Canada, Germany, and Italy; hence there will be no test of this financing prediction for these countries.) The regression specification takes the following form.

$$\text{(Dividend Payout Rate)} = \begin{array}{l} \text{Constant} \\ + c_1 \text{ (Output Growth)} + c_2 \text{ (Inflation Rate)} \\ + c_3 \text{ (Equity Variables)} + \text{Random Disturbances} \end{array} \tag{13}$$

The prediction from the theory is that c_1 and c_2 are negative just as the estimated coefficients on these explanatory variables were in the financial leverage regressions in Table 3. Once again, equity variables are included in the regressions when they improve the overall statistical results.

The regressions in Table 4 indicate that there is strong support for the dividend payout prediction of the theory in Finland, France, the U.K., and the manufacturing sector in the United States. In these countries the estimated coefficients c_1 and c_2 are both negative and statistically significant by conventional standards. In periods of economic expansion when firms in these countries are implementing speculative operating strategies in the product market, they are also implementing safe and conservative financing decisions. The conservative financing decision now takes the form of a reduction in the dividend payout rate which means firms finance the expansion with internally generated equity. Operating decisions leading to a recession would be associated with high dividend payout rates as equity investors allow their call option on the firm to partially expire in these countries. For Finland, France, and the manufacturing sector in the United States the results in Table 4 confirm those in Table 3. This was not the case for the U.K. In Table 3 the change in long-term financial leverage was positively related to the U.K. inflation rate, $(P\dot{P}I)$, whereas in Table 4 the dividend payout rate was negatively related to this inflation rate. The hypothesis that firms adjust their financial strategy to offset changes in their operating risk receives more support in the U.K. when the dividend payout rate is the financial choice variable compared to changes in long-term financial leverage.

The evidence supporting the prediction that dividend payout rates in a debt and equity economy are countercyclical to output growth and inflation rates is somewhat weaker in Japan, Norway, and the nonfinancial enterprise sector in the United States. For example, in Norway the dividend payout rate in R43 is negatively related to output growth and inflation rates, but only the coefficient on the inflation rate is statistically significant by conventional standards. This same result was observed in Table 3 when adjustments to long-term financial leverage represented the financial choice variable. Japan and the U.S. nonfinancial enterprises experienced similar departures from the empirical predictions of the theory. In both cases the estimated coefficient on the output growth variable $(I\dot{P})$ was negative and statistically significant. This result is consistent with the empirical implications of the theory. However, for both countries the estimated coefficient on the inflation rate variable is positive, although in neither case is it statistically significant.[18] This was also the result in Table 3 (i.e., R32 and R37) when the measure of long-term financial leverage was taken from the sources and uses of funds statements for both countries. The pricing decisions of firms in Japan and the U.S. are not statistically significant predictors of the dividend payout rate or the sources and uses of funds measure of financial leverage. For these measures of a financial strategy the countercyclical relationship is primarily with output growth rates.

5. Summary and Conclusions

In this paper and earlier work, we have presented a model describing how the financial side interacts with and coordinates the real side of a debt and equity economy, and in the process shapes the business cycle paths of output growth, inflation rates, the risk structure of corporate investments, financial leverage, and dividend payout rates. The way this model works is that external shocks initiate business cycles by changing the planned savings and required rate of return of equity investors. The resulting change in share prices then sends a signal to the managers of firms to change the risk of their operating strategies so that they conform to the shock dependent risk aversion of their shareholders. A rational bond contract protecting creditors then requires these managers to change the risk of their financial strategies in a way that offsets the change in the risk of their operating strategies. The end result is that bondholders and stockholders equitably share the risk and return resulting from the business decisions put in place by firms over the business cycle. This would seem to be the only way a rational partnership economy with debt and equity sharing rules based on differences in risk aversion could carry out business activity.

Several empirical predictions follow from this model of the business cycle. The first prediction is that changes in share prices precede changes in the risk structure of the assets of firms. The second prediction is that financial leverage and dividend payout rates are countercyclical; rising in recessions when firms implement safe and conservative operating strategies of reducing output prices, production, and risky investments, and falling in expansions when they implement speculative operating strategies. In parts B-D of Section IV these predictions from the model were empirically tested using financial statement data for nine OECD countries. Rather than review the country specific results again, we summarize this work by posing the following general questions: Taking everything into consideration, for what countries does the risk and return sharing theory qualitatively account for the predicted co-movements among the operating decisions variables and the financing decision variables used in this study, and for what countries should we begin to look elsewhere? Looking at all of the results together (i.e., Tables 1-4 and endnotes 10, 12, 15, 16, and 18) it appears that Canada, Finland, France, Japan, and the United States are at one end of the spectrum. There is fairly strong statistical support (in terms of the predicted signs and statistical significance of estimated parameters) for most of the predictions of this theory in these countries using the common set of proxies chosen to represent the changes in operating strategies and financing strategies of their nonfinancial enterprises. There is also considerable support (although not as much) for the theory as a whole in Germany, Italy, and Norway using the same criteria. The least support for the empirical predictions of this model was observed for nonfinancial enterprises in the united Kingdom, although 14 years of data might be too small a sample from which to draw any conclusions. But even in the case of the U.K. there are important pieces of evidence supporting the theory. In this connection it was observed in R45 of Table 4 that dividend payout rates in the U.K. followed the countercyclical path predicted by the risk and return sharing theory.

In closing, it has sometimes been suggested that finance is merely about pieces of paper, and pieces of paper do not matter very much when it comes to describing something real like the business cycle. A different view is presented here. This paper and our previous work represent attempts to elevate the status of the financial aspects of business cycles. In this connection our research has uncovered some heretofore unknown financing relationships that seem to qualify as "financial facts" of post World War II business cycles. Moreover, these financial relationships exist in the data in spite of the seemingly great differences in corporate governance structures, tax regimes, business-government relationships, and structures of financial intermediation in the sample countries. Institutional differences may be important for some things, but they do not seem to be of over-riding importance when it comes to accounting for the financial facts of business cycles. The uncovering and interpreting of these financial relationships promises to be an interesting area for future research.

Acknowledgement

I want to thank Rona Velte for preparing this manuscript for publication, and John and Katherine Krainer for help in gathering the data

References

Bernanke, Ben and Mark Gertler. 1989. "Agency costs, Net Worth, and Business Fluctuations." American Economic Review 79: 14-31.

Krainer, Robert. 1985. The Financial System and the coordination of Economic Activity. New York: Praeger Publishers.

Krainer, Robert 1992. Finance in a Theory of the Business cycle. Oxford: Blackwell.

Mayer, Colin. 1990. "Financial Systems, corporate Finance, and Economic Development," in Asymmetric Information, Corporate Finance and Investment, edited by R. G. Hubbard. Chicago: The University of Chicago Press, 307-332.Miller, Merton. 1988. "The Modigliani-Miller Propositions After Thirty Years." Journal of Economic Perspectives 2: 99-120.

Endnotes

[1] Bernanke and Gertler (1985) have developed an interesting alternative theory (based on agency costs) to the one presented below. They suggest that: 1) debt financing by firms is negatively related to agency costs; 2) agency costs are negatively related to net worth; 3) the net worth of firms is positively related to economic activity; which means 4) that debt financing by firms is positively related to economic activity. For example, in periods of recession profits and net worth tend to be low. When this happens, the agency cost of debt tends to be high because stockholders have more of an incentive to urge firms to pursue speculative operating strategies since their stake in the firm tends to be low. In other words, firms like football teams are more likely to gamble in terms of their operating strategy when they are behind (as they are) in a recession. Bondholders of course realize this and will be more reluctant to lend to the firm during recessions. As a

result, firms tend to issue bonds during periods of economic expansion when profits and net worth are high and agency costs low since stockholders are less likely to urge managers to pursue speculative operating strategies. The theory presented below will imply a very different cyclical pattern of financing than the one in Bernanke and Gertler.

An interesting empirical study somewhat related to the empirical work presented in Section IV is in Mayer (1990). Mayer analyzes a data set that is similar to the one we use, but from a very different perspective. The question he addresses is how, on average, do the nonfinancial enterprises of eight OECD countries finance their tangible capital. His main finding is that earnings retention is the most important source of funds used to finance tangible capital accumulation. Security issues on the capital market play a relatively minor role except in the case of the United States. The largest suppliers of external funds are financial intermediaries, and on the basis of this he suggests that in terms of economic development, an efficient banking system may be more important than an efficient bond market.

[2]   To prove this all that is needed is to show that the slope of (8) is larger than the slope of (5), or:

i.
$$\frac{R}{R(s)} - \frac{1}{\frac{R}{R(b)} + \left[\frac{R - R(b)}{R(b)}\right]\frac{K(b)}{K(s)}} > 0$$

Rearranging (i) we get:

ii.
$$\frac{R^2 \cdot K(s) + R^2 \cdot K(b) - R \cdot R(b) \cdot K(b) - R(s) \cdot R(b) \cdot K(s)}{R(s)\{R \cdot K(s) + K(b)\{R - R(b)\}\}} > 0$$

Since $\{R - R(b)\} > 0$ by (1), the denominator is positive which means that all that must be done is sign the numerator. The numerator of (ii) can be written as:

a.
$$\frac{[\bar{X}(b) + \bar{X}(s)]^2}{[K(b) + K(s)]^2} \cdot [(b) + K(s)] - \frac{[\bar{X}(b) + \bar{X}(s)]}{[K(b) + K(s)]} \cdot \bar{X}(b) - \frac{X(b)}{K(b)} \cdot X(s)$$

since

$$R = \frac{\bar{X}(b) + \bar{X}(s)}{K(b) + K(s)}$$

$$R(b) . K(b) = \bar{X}(b)$$

$$R(s) . K(s) = \bar{X}(s)$$

Squaring the first term, multiplying the first and second term by K(b), multiplying the third term by [K(b) + K(s)], putting the rearranged expression over the common denominator of [K(b) + K(s)]K(b), and simplifying transforms (a) to

b.
$$\frac{\bar{X}(s)K(s)[R(s)-R(b)]}{K(b)+K(s)}$$

This expression is positive since [R(s) - R(b)] is positive by (1). Since the numerator and denominator of (ii) are both positive (i) is positive which means the e'e' schedule in Figure 1 must intersect the dd schedule from below at point z.

3 An alternative interpretation of the risk and return sharing theory is to assume that the economy is comprised of two distinct sets of firms: 1) small firms pursuing risky operating strategies (e.g., introducing new products and adapting new technologies) financed with equity and bank loans; and 2) large firms pursuing conservative operating strategies financed with equity and long-term bonds. In this interpretation a positive external shock that reduces the risk premium required by investors results in small firms obtaining a relatively large amount of equity and bank loan financing thereby enabling these firms to implement their relatively risky operating strategies. The growth of these small firms implementing risky operating strategies results in the expansion phase of the business cycle. Since small firms are growing relative to large firms, long-term bond financing declines relative to equity and bank loan financing. Negative external shocks that raise the risk premium required by investors has the opposite effect. In this case large firms implementing conservative operating strategies continue their slow but steady growth while small firms find it harder to obtain equity and bank loan finance. The end result is that the proportion of real output produced by small firms declines and the economy moves into the recession phase of the business cycle. Since large firms partly financed with long-term bonds produce a larger share of the output in recessions, long-term bond financing grows relative to equity and bank loan financing. In this interpretation of the theory the cyclical variation in operating and financing strategies is the result of the relative growth of small and large firms, whereas in the interpretation in the body of the paper a single representative firm cyclically varies its financing to match the cyclical variation in its operating strategies. In both interpretations society's savings are channeled into investment with the appropriate type of securities depending on the risk of the operating strategies implemented by firms.

4 Business cycles in the risk and return sharing theory are the result of a risky arbitrage process between the capital market and the product market of an economy. For example, when the economy is located on (or above) the dd schedule and below (or on) the equilibrium ee schedule (i.e., ee in Figure 3), the market value of companies exceeds book value. This is the capital market signal for existing firms to expand, and new firms to be created. The expansion of the old firms and the creations of new firms results in a general economic up turn. On the other hand, when the economy is located on (or below) the dd schedule and above (or on) the equilibrium ee schedule, the market value of companies is less than the book value. The signal from the capital market is for firms to sell part or all of their resources back to the product market, and use the proceeds to buy back their securities in the capital market. This selling of resources back to the product market represents the recession phase of the business cycle.

5 What is emphasized in the risk and return sharing theory of the business cycle presented in this paper and our previous work is the link between the risk aversion

of investors, the operating strategies of firms, and the business cycle. An outside shock changes the risk aversion of investors, which is then reflected in a change in share prices, which then provides a signal for firm managers to change the operating strategy of firms, which in turn results in a cyclical expansion or contraction in general economic activity.

6   The one exception is the nonfinancial corporate sector in the United States where total assets (including inventories and net fixed tangible assets) are valued at reproduction cost. For that reason Tables 1-4 presented below will also include regression tests of the three empirical predictions from the risk and return sharing theory using historical cost financial statement data for the U.S. manufacturing sector. For a description of this data see endnote 7 below. The purpose of including the U.S. manufacturing sector is to see whether historical cost and reproduction cost measures of operating strategy and financing strategy produce different results in the empirical tests of the theory.

7   The historical cost balance sheets are found in the *Quarterly Financial Reports for Manufacturing, Mining, and Trade Corporation, U.S. Bureau of the Census,* U.S. Government Printing Office, Washington, D.C. The reproduction cost balance sheets were constructed from data provided to the author by John Musgrave of the Bureau of Economic Analysis, U.S. Department of Commerce. What we did to create the reproduction cost based balance sheets was to take the cash, short-term securities, and accounts receivable from the historical cost balance sheets for the "all manufacturing sector" that is published in the *Quarterly Financial Reports* and add them to the stock of inventories, the net stock of equipment, and the net stock of structures valued at current (or reproduction) costs from the Musgrave data for the "all manufacturing sector." The sum of these six asset categories was taken to be our measure of the current cost of assets in the manufacturing sector.

It should be noted that the nonfinancial enterprises for which the OECD provides financial statements is a much broader sector than the manufacturing sector we are now about to analyze.

8   See Miller (1988) for an analysis of how the 1986 Tax Reform Act altered the financing decisions of firms. The dummy variable takes on the value of one for the years 1985 and 1986, and zero elsewhere. The same procedure was used in Krainer (1992, chapter 4).

9   The balance sheet measures of inventory accumulation and long-term financial leverage for the OECD sample of countries will be slightly different than the measures used in Table 1 and Krainer (1992, chapter 4). In Tables 2 and 3, inventory accumulation and long-term financial leverage are measured by $\Delta(\text{Inv}/A)$ and $\Delta(\text{LT Liab}/A)$, rather than $(\Delta\text{Inv}/\Delta A)$ and $(\Delta\text{LT Liab}/\Delta A)$ as was the case in our previous work with U.S. firms. The reason for this is that ΔA is negative in 1987 for Germany, and very small for Italy (in 1982-83) and Japan (in 1982) creating outliers that heavily influence the regression results.

10 When the lagged value of U.S. real share prices, $(\text{SP})_{t-1}^{U.S}$, is substituted for Canadian share prices in R5 and R6, the results improve dramatically as the following indicates.

Canada

1969-92

R5i $\left[\dfrac{Inv}{S=U}\right]_t = \underset{(-2.07)}{-.1465} + \underset{(2.80)}{1.1576(\dot{IP})_t} + \underset{(2.23)}{.4257(\dot{WPI})_t} + \underset{(2.07)}{.0887(SP)_{t-1}^{U.S.}}$

$S = .056 \qquad \bar{R}^2 = .576 \qquad DW = 1.72$

1972-92

R6i $\Delta\left[\dfrac{Inv}{A}\right]_t = \underset{(-2.30)}{-.0102} + \underset{(2.90)}{.0527(\dot{IP})_t} + \underset{(3.02)}{.0471(\dot{WPI})_t} + \underset{(1.56)}{.0048(SP)_{t-1}^{U.S.}}$

$S = .006 \qquad \bar{R}^2 = .263 \qquad DW = 2.14$

The estimated coefficients on (WPI) are now larger in R5i and R6i, and their t-scores indicate that they are statistically significant. In addition, the estimated coefficient on $(SP)_{t-1}^{U.S.}$ is statistically significant in R5i. The high standard error of estimate and low coefficient of determination in R6 of the table and R6i above is the result of one large residual in 1979. Inserting a dummy variable, $(DV)^{79}$, that takes on the value of unity in 1979 and zero everywhere else considerably improves the statistical significance of the regression as the following indicates.

Canada

1972-92

R6ii $\Delta\left[\dfrac{Inv}{A}\right]_t = \underset{(-2.85)}{-.0118} + \underset{(3.27)}{.0531(\dot{IP})_t} + \underset{(2.34)}{.0430(\dot{WPI})_t} + \underset{(1.91)}{.0056(SP)_{t-1}^{U.S.}} + \underset{(25.18)}{.0194(DV)_t^{79}}$

$S = .003 \qquad \bar{R}^2 = .746 \qquad DW = 1.93$

In R5i and R6ii all of the slope coefficients are positive and statistically significant by conventional standards, thus supporting the theory for Canada.

Similarly, in the case of Finland in R8 there was one very large residual in 1984. Inserting the dummy variable, $(DV)^{84}$, that takes on the value of unity in 1984 and zero elsewhere increases the statistical significance of this regression.

Finland

1969-91

R8i $\Delta\left[\dfrac{Inv}{A}\right]_t = \underset{(-3.32)}{-.0309} + \underset{(2.26)}{.3448(G\dot{D}P)_t} + \underset{(1.96)}{.1887(GDP-I)_t} + \underset{(1.85)}{7.0076\Delta}\left[\dfrac{SP_{t-1}}{(Div)_t}\right] + \underset{(22.19)}{.0546(DV)_t^{84}}$

$S = .013 \qquad \bar{R}^2 = .572 \qquad DW = 1.97 \qquad AR(1) = .417$

In this regression the estimated coefficient on the price-earnings ratio is now statistically significant at the five percent level on a one-tail test.

[11] The financial statement data for U.S. nonfinancial enterprises was obtained from the 1981 and 1993 issues of the OECD publication entitled Non-Financial Enterprises

Financial Statements. The 1981 issue of this publication provided the data for the period 1965-80. The 1993 issue provided the data for 1981-92. The sample of companies in the second period was somewhat larger than the first period. This did not pose a problem for the sources and uses of funds measure of inventory accumulation. However, in the balance sheet regression of inventory accumulation there was one very large residual for the year 1981 which was the beginning year for the second sample. To accommodate this change in sample size between the two periods, a dummy variable (DV)[81]—that took on the value of one in 1981 and zero elsewhere—was used in all the balance sheet regressions. The regression results without this dummy variable are:

United States, Nonfinancial Enterprises

1967-92

$$R21i \quad \Delta\left[\frac{Inv}{A}\right]_t = \underset{(-1.79)}{-.0034} + \underset{(1.06)}{.0282\,(\dot{IP})_t} + \underset{(.70)}{.0377\,(\dot{PPI})_t} + \underset{(2.61)}{.3709\,\Delta}\left[\frac{SP_{t-1}}{(Div + RE)_t}\right]$$

$$S = .009 \qquad \bar{R}^2 = .083 \qquad DW = 1.91 \qquad AR(1) = .277$$

The estimated coefficients on output growth (IP) and inflation (PPI) while positive are not statistically significant. The same procedure of including (DV)81 was also used in the balance sheet financial leverage regression presented in Table 3.

[12] Unfortunately the data for Italy comes from two different samples (1968-83 and 1982-90) that differed somewhat substantially in terms of size. For example, in the overlap year of 1982 the total sources and uses of funds for companies in the earlier sample is only 13,332 billions of lira while for the later sample it is 40,716 billions of lira. In the case of the balance sheet, total assets for the earlier sample were 101,179 billions of lira in 1982, and 314,859 billions in the later sample. The regressions for Italy reported in Tables 2 and 3 use the data from the 1968-81 sample and then add on the 1982-92 data from the 1982-92 sample. Since the decision variables of interest in this study are ratios—i.e., Inv/S=U and (Inv/A)—the problems of linking the data from the two samples is somewhat (but not completely) mitigated. We also experimented with both slope and intercept dummy variables, including them in the regressions when they were statistically significant and excluding them when they were insignificant. In this connection including the dummy variable (DV)[82-92], that takes on the value of unity for the years 1982-92 and zero elsewhere, improved the results in the balance sheet regression R14 listed in Table 2. The results for this regression are:

Italy

1969-92

$$R14i \quad \Delta\left[\frac{Inv}{A}\right]_t = \underset{(-2.94)}{-.0542} + \underset{(2.75)}{.3007\,(GDP)_t} + \underset{(2.28)}{.1885\,(GDP-I)_t} + \underset{(2.54)}{.0086\,(SP)_{t-1}} + \underset{(2.36)}{.0191\,(DV)_t^{82-92}}$$

$$S = .012 \qquad \bar{R}^2 = .347 \qquad DW = 2.08$$

In this regression all of the estimated slope coefficients are positive and statistically significant.

Finally, a dummy variable was also included in R12 for Germany (indicated by DV[87]) that took on the value of one for the year 1987 and zero elsewhere. The reason for this was that the OECD reported that German accounting practices were changed in 1987 to make them conform to European Community accounting practices. The effect of this accounting change was to make the balance sheet measures of inventory investment and financial leverage—Δ(Inv/A) and Δ(LT Liab/A)—outliers for the year 1987 compared to other years in the sample.

[13] Unfortunately, the sources and uses of funds statements for Germany combined both short-term and long-term debt into a single debt measure so that it was impossible to obtain a measure of long-term financial leverage for this body of data. For that reason, all measures of long-term financial leverage were taken from the balance sheets.

[14] Capital market variables that improved the overall statistical significance of the country regressions were the following.

1. Canada: The change in real share prices $\Delta(SP)_t$; and the change in U.S. real share prices $\Delta(SP)_t^{U.S.}$.

2. Finland: The price-earnings ratio in Finland measured as the ratio of lagged real share prices to current dividends, or $SP_{t-1}/(Div)_t$.

3. France: Real share prices $(SP)_t$; and the price earnings ratio measured as the ratio of lagged real share prices to current dividends, or $SP_{t-1}/(Div)_t$.

4. Germany: Lagged real share prices to annual surplus, or $SP_{t-1}/(Profit)_t$.

5. Italy: The change in lagged real share prices, or $\Delta(SP)_{t-1}$.

6. Japan: The price-earnings ratio measured as the ratio of lagged real share prices to current dividends, or $SP_{t-1}/(Div)_t$.

7. U.K.: The price-earnings ratio measured as the ratio of lagged real share prices to the sum of current dividends and retained earnings, or $SP_{t-1}/(Div + RE)_t$.

Only for Norway and the United States did these particular capital market variables not improve the overall statistical results of the regressions. For this reason, capital market variables were not included in the financial leverage regressions in these two countries.

[15] A more favorable result is obtained when only marketable corporate bonds are in the numerator of the leverage measure in R37. In other words, defining financial leverage as the ratio of new issues of marketable corporate bonds to total sources and uses of funds, (LT Bonds/S=U), yields the following parameter estimates for $(\dot{IP})$ and $(\dot{PPI})$.

United States, Nonfinancial Enterprises

1967-92

$$R37i \quad \left[\frac{LT\ Bonds}{S=U}\right]_t = \underset{(10.81)}{.1705} - \underset{(-4.29)}{.5700}(\dot{IP})_t - \underset{(-3.52)}{.5888}(\dot{PPI})_t$$

$S = .028 \qquad \bar{R}^2 = .566 \qquad DW = 1.80 \qquad AR(1) = .516 \qquad AR(2) = -.252$

In this regression the estimated coefficients on output growth and inflation rates are negative and statistically significant by conventional standards of significance.

[16] Using a more narrow definition of financial leverage and the specification in R3 and R4 in Table 1 produces a result that is more consistent with the prediction of the risk and return sharing theory. The more narrow definition of financial leverage has long-term marketable bonds in the numerator rather than long-term total liabilities. The specification change is to use the ratio of differences rather than the difference in ratios as the measure of adjustments in long-term financial leverage. Rerunning R35 with these changes and including the change in real share values as an additional explanatory variable produces the following results.

Norway

1972-91

$$\text{R35i} \quad \left[\frac{\Delta \text{ LT Bonds}}{\Delta A} \right]_t = \underset{(5.86)}{.3673} - \underset{(-3.69)}{3.0057\,(\dot{\text{GDP}})_t} - \underset{(-4.51)}{2.2401\,(\text{GDP}-I)_t} - \underset{(-2.85)}{.3197\Delta(\text{SP})_t}$$

$$S = .111 \qquad \bar{R}^2 = .507 \qquad DW = 2.10 \qquad AR(1) = -.311$$

The parameter estimates on both output growth (GDP) and the inflation rate (GDP-I) are both negative and statistically significant. These results are consistent with the theory.

[17] The dividend payout rate for the U.S. manufacturing sector is computed somewhat differently than the dividend payout rate for the other countries (including U.S. nonfinancial enterprises) in this OECD sample. The reason is that retained earnings in the manufacturing sector was — $37.9 billions for the year 1992 resulting in a very small denominator, (Div + RE), and a very large payout rate, Div/(Div + RE) for that one year. To reduce the impact of the very large payout rate for that year, depreciation charges were added to the denominator of the dividend variable so that the dividend payout rate for this sector is Div/(Div + RE + Deprec).

[18] Adding depreciation charges and direct taxes to the denominator of the dividend payout variable (i.e., Profit = Div + RE + Deprec + Tax) improves the result. In this connection define (Div/Profit) = Div/(Div + Re + Deprec + Tax) to be the dividend payout rate variable. The parameter estimates on (IP) and (PPI) then become:

United States, Nonfinancial Enterprises

1967-92

$$\text{R45i} \quad \left[\frac{\text{Div}}{\text{Profit}} \right]_t = \underset{(40.10)}{.1606} - \underset{(-3.79)}{.1005\,(\dot{\text{IP}})_t} - \underset{(-3.41)}{.1542\,(\dot{\text{PPI}})_t} + \underset{(6.02)}{.4277\Delta} \left[\frac{\text{SP}_{t-1}}{(\text{Div} + \text{RE})_t} \right]$$

$$S = .012 \qquad \bar{R}^2 = .399 \qquad DW = 1.86 \qquad AR(1) = .365$$

As can be seen the estimated parameters on (IP) and (PPI) are now both negative and statistically significant as predicted by the theory.

Appendix On Data Sources

I Table 1

1. $\left[\dfrac{\Delta \mathrm{Inv}}{\Delta A} \right]^{HC} =$ The change in inventories (valued at historical cost) divided by the change in total assets (valued at historical cost). **Source:** Various issues of Quarterly Financial Reports for Manufacturing, Mining, and Trade Corporations, U.S. Bureau of the Census, U.S. Government Printing Office, Washington, D.C.

2. $\left[\dfrac{\Delta \mathrm{Inv}}{\Delta A} \right]^{RC} =$ The change in inventories (valued at reproduction cost) divided by the change in total assets (valued at reproduction cost). **Source:** Data provided to the author by Mr.John Musgrave of the Bureau of Economic Analysis, U.S. Department of Commerce.

3. $\left[\dfrac{\Delta \mathrm{LT\ Debt}}{\Delta A} \right]^{HC} =$ The change in other long-term loans divided by the change in total assets (valued at historical cost). **Source:** Same as I-1 above.

4. $\left[\dfrac{\Delta \mathrm{LT\ Debt}}{\Delta A} \right]^{RC} =$ The change in other long-term loans divided by the change in total assets (valued at reproduction cost). **Source:** Same as 1-2 above.

5. $\dot{\mathrm{IP}}$ = The percentage rate of change in the industrial production index (1985=100). **Source:** The International Financial Statistics Yearbook 1991, International Monetary Fund, Washington, D.C.

6. $\dot{\mathrm{PPI}}$ = The percentage rate of change in the producer price index (1985=100). **Source:** Same as 1-5 above.

7. SP = The real value of share prices. This variable is the share price index (1985=100) deflated by the consumer price index (1985=100). **Source:** Same as 1-5 above.

8. $(\mathrm{DV})^{85\text{-}86}$ = A dummy variable that takes on the value of unity in 1985-86, and zero elsewhere in the United States.

II. Tables 2-4

1. $\left[\dfrac{\mathrm{Inv}}{S=U} \right]$ = Inventory investment as a use of funds divided by the total sources and uses of funds for the sample countries. **Source:** Various issues of the OECD Financial Statistics, Part 3, Non-Financial Enterprises Financial Statements, Paris.

2. $\Delta \left[\dfrac{\mathrm{Inv}}{A} \right]$ = The change in the ratio of inventories to total assets from the balance sheets for the sample country. **Source:** Same as 11-1 above.

3. $\dot{\mathrm{IP}}$ = Same as 1-5 above for the sample country.

4. $\dot{\mathrm{GDP}}$ = The percentage rate of change in real GDP for the sample country. Source: Same as 1-5 above.

5. WPI   = The percentage rate of change in the wholesale price index (1985=100) for the sample country. **Source:** Same as I-5 above.

6. CPI   = The percentage rate of change in the consumer price index (1985=100) for the sample country. **Source:** Same as 1-5 above.

7. GDP-I   = The percentage rate of change in the GDP deflator index (1985=100) for the sample country. **Source:** Same as 1-5 above.

8. PPI   = Same as 1-6 above for the sample country.

9. SP   = Real share prices. **Source:** Same as 1-7 above for the sample country.

10. Δ(SP)   = The change in real share prices. **Source:** Same as 1-7 above for the sample country.

11. $\left[\dfrac{SP_{t-1}}{(Div)_t}\right]$ = The price to permanent earnings ratio where permanent earnings are measured with cash dividends to shareholders. **Source:** Same as 1-7 and ll- I above for the sample country.

12. $\left[\dfrac{SP_{t-1}}{(Profit)_t}\right]$ = The price to reported stockholders profit ratio. Source: Same as 1-7 and ll- I above for the sample country.

13. $\left[\dfrac{SP_{t-1}}{(Div+RE)_t}\right]$ = The price to earnings ratio where earnings are measured as the sum of dividends and retained earnings net of depreciation. **Source:** Same as I-7 and II-1 above for the sample countries.

14. $\left[\dfrac{LT\ Liab}{S=U}\right]$ = Long-term liabilities as a source of funds divided by the total sources and uses of funds. **Source:** Same as II-1 for the sample country.

15. $\Delta\left[\dfrac{LT\ Liab}{A}\right]$ = The change in ratio of long-term liabilities to total assets. Source: Same as II-1 above for sample country.

16. $\left[\dfrac{Div}{Div+RE}\right]$ = The dividend payout rate of cash dividends divided by the sum of cash dividends and retained earnings net of depreciation after taxes. **Source:** Same as II-1 above for the sample country.

17. $\left[\dfrac{Div}{Div+RE+Deprec}\right]$ = The dividend payout rate of cash dividends divided by the sum of cash dividends, retained earnings net of depreciation, and depreciation. **Source:** Same as II-1 above for the sample countries.

18. $(DV)^{87}$ = Dummy variable that takes on the value of one in 1987 and zero elsewhere in Germany.

19. $(DV)^{81}$ = Dummy variable that takes on the value of one in 1981 and zero elsewhere in the United States.

20. $(DV)^{79}$ = Dummy variable that takes on the value of one in 1979 and zero elsewhere in Canada.

21. $(DV)^{84}$ = Dummy variable that takes on the value of one in 1984 and zero elsewhere in Finland.

22. $(DV)^{82-92}$ = Dummy variable that takes on the value of one in 1982-92 and zero elsewhere in Italy.

Corporate Leverage and the Business Cycle in Industrialized Countries

Rama Seth
Federal Reserve Bank of New York

Abstract

The paper examines the relationship between capital structure and the bankruptcy risk arising from macroeconomic rather than firm specific activities. It shows that in the U.S. firms in cyclical industries have been increasing their leverage at a more rapid pace than firms in non-cyclical industries. As a result, firms with high interest burdens have become more concentrated in cyclical industries. Japanese firms have decreased their leverage roughly uniformly across sectors. Non-cyclical Canadian and German firms, by contrast, have decreased more rapidly than cyclical firms.

1. Introduction

It is a well established fact that the United States is the only major industrialized country in which firms have experienced increases in both leverage and interest burden over the 1980s.[1] For firms deciding whether or not to increase leverage, the interaction between ownership structure and business cycles cannot be ignored. Researchers have argued, for example, that they do not find the increase in corporate leveraging in the United States disturbing, because those sectors with highly leveraged firms have been noncyclical. Does this then imply that leveraging up by firms in the United States is not a cause for concern? Furthermore, has deleveraging by firms in the rest of the industrialized world rendered firms more resilient? The answer depends not only on the degree of leverage of firms in cyclical sectors but also on the change in leverage of cyclical firms.

This paper is concerned with the relationship between capital structures and bankruptcy risks, rather than with the theory of capital structure.[2] Moreover, the bankruptcy risks are only related to the macroeconomic activity and not to the firms' characteristics. A substantial body of literature exits on the relationship between ownership structure and the business cycle. For example Gertler and Hubbard (1993)[3] have argued that low-leveraged firms have a lower probability of financial distress during recession. Jefferson (1994) contends that there is a feedback between nominal debt commitments and macroeconomic performance.[4] Sharpe (1993) finds that low-leveraged firms are less sensitive to demand-induced fluctuations.[5] Using macroeconomic variables as instruments for demand, Sharpe (1991) also finds that high leverage makes employment significantly more sensitive to demand-induced fluctuations in sales.[6]

Our study introduces a different slant on the relationship between corporate ownership and cyclical fluctuations than those mentioned above. Our premise is that high leverage in sectors that are more cyclical pose greater problems for macroeconomic stability. We do not test this premise but instead pose a the positive question: Are highly leveraged firms indeed concentrated in the more cyclical sectors of the economy?

Previous studies have analyzed the distribution of corporate debt across sectors, but only in the United States. This article examines six major industrialized countries, including the United States. Earlier studies of the United States concluded that, to the extent that a pattern is discernible, highly indebted firms are concentrated in sectors that have been "the bedrock of economic stability in this country."[7] Although this finding is valid, a potentially destabilizing influence arises because the firms that have been increasing their leverage most rapidly have been concentrated in cyclical sectors. Studies that examined a slice of the highly leveraged activity also concluded that the United States has experienced a case of "Debt Without Disaster." This follows from the finding that "most highly leveraged corporate takeover activity is skewed toward industries that have been relatively unaffected by general economic downturns over the last forty years."[8] Whereas this may also be true, highly leveraged corporate takeover activity forms only a part of all the highly leveraged activity in the United States.

Previous work, including studies that examined the differential increase in leverage, have only grouped firms into two types of sectors: cyclical and noncyclical.[9] The cut-off point in such a grouping is arbitrary, and moving the point would change the composition of the two groups.[10] Moreover, dividing the entire economy into two sectors —stable and unstable — obscures shifting patterns within these two broad categories. This study circumvents the problem of a bipartite ad hoc grouping by estimating sector-specific cyclicality coefficients.

Many of the previous studies also suffer from the problem created by using industry-level data. These data, available from the Department of Commerce, do not represent a consistent group of firms across years. This inconsistency makes the interpretation of the data difficult, because the composition of the industry itself is likely to change over the years. By using firm-specific data, this study is able to examine a consistent sample of firms across time.

Firm-specific data reveal that the patterns of corporate leveraging in at least some of the countries bear watching. In the United States, firms in cyclical industries have been increasing their leverage at a more rapid pace than firms in noncyclical industries. As a result, firms with high interest burdens have become more concentrated in cyclical industries. This could be worrisome especially if firms in cyclical sectors continue to have a stronger growth in leverage than those in noncyclical sectors. In other industrialized countries, the decrease in leverage has made some economies more resilient than others. Japanese firms have decreased their leverage roughly uniformly across sectors. By contrast, noncyclical Canadian and German firms have decreased their debt more rapidly than cyclical firms. This pattern of deleveraging has made their economies less resilient than would appear at first sight.

2. Leverage and Cyclicality: Why High Leverage is a Problem

The potential magnitude of the problems created by highly leveraged firms depends on how closely their performance is tied to business cycles.[11] If highly levered firms are also cyclical (that is, if firms' ability to repay varies positively with the level of economic activity), a slowdown in economic activity would adversely affect these firms' output. The stronger the economic downturn, the greater the decline in output for these firms. Moreover, the more leveraged the firms, the faster they may reach the point where they are unable to meet their fixed income obligations.

Firms faced with diminishing cash flows could respond in one of two ways. On the one hand, they could continue to service their debt at the expense of cutting investment outlays or laying off workers.[12] Such expenditure reduction would directly feed the incipient recession. On the other hand, they could respond by restructuring their debt obligations or by declaring bankruptcy. Either response could cause a credit squeeze as financial institutions become illiquid and/or bondholders face a decrease in wealth. Healthy corporations would thus be deprived of credit, a fact which could intensify recessionary pressures on the economy.

Corporations' high debt may make the bankruptcy route less likely, intensifying the adverse effects of macroeconomic shocks. Jensen (1987) has argued that a fall in the asset value of a firm resulting in insolvency might require creditors to liquidate a previously low-leveraged firm. This liquidation results because its going concern value at insolvency, when the firm's debt-asset ratio exceeds one, is not much different from its liquidation or salvage value.[13] Creditors may be persuaded, however, to restructure the fixed income obligations of a highly leveraged firm whose asset value at the point of insolvency is sufficiently large. In any event, if the economy was tipping towards a recession, creditors would still have to contend with large amounts of debt restructuring if highly leveraged firms are concentrated in cyclical industries.

Some evidence does suggest that highly leveraged firms in the United States would be exposed to bankruptcy risk in the event of a recession.[14] A deterioration in the debt-asset ratios and interest burdens of firms is evident when simulating the effects of recessions such as those of 1973-74 and 1981-82. Moreover, U.S. firms appear to recession be more vulnerable to in recent years because of their capital structure. When the simulations are performed using the 1988 capital structure of corporations as the base, the deterioration in leverage ratios and interest burden is more striking than when the 1986 capital structures are used as the base. These results suggest that the changing capital structure of firms has made them even more vulnerable to a recession in recent years.

3. Methodology

The analysis consists of three parts. First, we divided the economy into ten relatively homogenous sectors and estimated the cyclicality of each of the sectors. Second, we measured the degree of leverage and interest burden, both level and growth, of firms in each of the sectors. Finally, we computed the co-movement in leverage and cyclicality and interest burden and cyclicality. A positive correlation between the degree of leverage (interest burden) and cyclicality implies that firms with high leverage (interest burden) are also concentrated in cyclical sectors. A negative correlation implies the reverse, that is, firms with high leverage (interest burden) are concentrated in sectors that are relatively noncyclical.   Changing patterns in leverage (interest burden) are revealed by the correlation between the *growth* in leverage (interest burden) and cyclicality.   Again, a positive correlation implies that firms that are increasing their leverage (interest burden) most rapidly are concentrated in cyclical sectors.

Our study is a first attempt to assess the relationship between leverage and cyclicality. It computes a correlation coefficient between a debt measure and a proxy for cyclical fluctuations in output.   A natural extension would be to use other measures that account for time, firm and country effects to more fully gauge this relationship.

4. Measures of Leverage and Cyclicality

Leverage is measured as the ratio of the book value of debt to assets in a sample of firms, for which data are available, in each sector in each country.   Although market values of debt would have been preferable, data limitations constrain us to book-value measures.   The high cross-sectional correlation between the book and market value of debt found by Bowman (1980) is reassuring.[15]   An extension of the current work, however, could use alternative definitions of leverage.

One alternative measure that we computed is the interest burden.   To measure the interest burden, we calculated the ratio of the interest payment to cash flows.   The interest burden is a good measure of sectoral vulnerability because if cash flows cannot cover interest payments a restructuring may be required before the point of insolvency.

A sector is cyclical if its performance is in tandem with the economy as a whole. Performance indicators include output, earnings and equity, and asset returns.[16]   We define seven measures of cyclicality, two of which are based on output/income (for the United States only), three on earnings, one on equity returns, and one on asset returns.   Each measure is the regression coefficient relating an indicator of sectoral performance to a corresponding indicator of economy-wide performance (in the case of earnings, equity, and asset returns, we proxy economy-wide performance by the performance of firms in our sample.)   The resulting regression coefficient measures the sectoral sensitivity to economy-wide activity.   The greater the sensitivity, the more cyclical the sector.   We classify a sector as cyclical when the sectoral regression coefficient is equal to or greater than the corresponding coefficient, (the cut-off point) calculated for all sectors taken together.[17]

To appropriately ascertain sectoral vulnerability to macroeconomic shocks, a measure of cyclicality should not be sample- or leverage-dependent.   The measure satisfying both these conditions is the sectoral sensitivity to output derived by regressing the sectoral change in output on the percentage change in private sector GNP.   This measure is free from sampling bias because it relies on data for the whole economy rather than on our sample of firms.   The sectoral sensitivity to output is also independent of firms' leverage because sectoral output is used to construct it.   This measure, however, is not computable in a comparable way across countries.   We therefore estimate several measures of cyclicality for the United States and choose the one for that correlates the most with the income sensitivity to output.   Because the correlation is highest for the coefficient derived from the regression relating the ratio of firm earnings to assets to the percentage change in GNP, we choose the earnings sensitivity to output as our preferred measure of cyclicality for all countries (see Table 1). Notably the balance-sheet data better reflect sectoral vulnerability than do stock market returns.

In the chosen measure, economy-wide performance is proxied by the performance of all firms in our sample rather than by analyzing accounting data and macroeconomic data. We therefore conveniently circumvent the problem dissimilar bases: data for accounting is prepared annually while data for macroeconomic conditions is prepared more frequently.

Table 1

Correlation Between the Sectoral Sensitivity to Output and the Other Cyclicality Measures (United States)

	Sectoral Sensitivity of Equity Returns to:		Sectoral Sensitivity of Earnings to:		
	Stock Market Returns[1]	Asset Returns[2]	Full Sample Earnings/Assets[3]	GNP[4]	GNP[5]
Compustat Data	0.08	0.32	0.70	0.79	0.85
Global Vantage Data	0.09	-0.02	0.71	0.53	0.79

[1] Stock Market Beta
[2] Beta derived from regressing sectoral asset returns on market asset returns
[3] Ratio of earnings to assets averaged across firms in each sector regressed on the ratio of earnings to assets across all firms
[4] Percentage change in earnings regressed on the percentage change in GNP
[5] Ratio of sectoral earnings to assets regressed on the percentage change in GNP

4.1 Data Description

The empirical analysis is based on a sample of financial and nonfinancial firms in six countries for which data are available from Global Vantage, (including for the United States) from Compustat (for the United States only).[18] We use Compustat primarily for the empirical work done on the United States, because it offers data for a larger sample of firms and for a longer period of time.[19] Although Compustat data are available as far back as 1969, we chose 1977 as the beginning of our cycle because going back further restricted our sample size. Moreover, the period 1977-1988 encompasses two business cycles.

Firms are grouped together under a ten-industry classification scheme. An industry classification suggested by a two-digit Standard Industrial Classification code is not possible given the relatively small sample of foreign firms for which we have relevant data. Our industry classification groups together industries that have a similar cycle, either because firms in these industries produce similar end-products or because they are vertically linked.[20]

The classification we have used suffers from problems caused by aggregation. In particular, companies are likely to be diversified and to operate in various industries. We assume that the SIC classification captures the essence of the firms' activities, and we introduce another layer of aggregation based on the similarity of industries. Although this additional layer is somewhat ad hoc, our analysis shows that our results do not depend on choice of sectoral aggregation.

It should be noted that the present study is not concerned with why the debt levels of firms in certain industries are the way they are; only with whether or not high debt firms are also in the more cyclical industries. The inclusion of financial firms is therefore justified, even though it has been found that the level of debt of these firms is a function of their particular country's regulation.[21] For the same reason, we have not attempted to include a variable capturing the cross-country differences in the regulation of financial institutions, or any other variable that may explain cross-country differences.

Of course cross-country differences in institutions, culture, and behavior are important. The absence of a fire wall between commerce and banking in Germany and Japan, for example, may result in firms having a higher leverage ratio than those in the United States, where such a wall exists. The paper, however, is not concerned with the general debt level in any particular country. Only with whether the debt of firms in that country is relatively more so in cyclical industries or not. As mentioned earlier, it is concerned only with whether the debt of firms in that country is relatively more so in cyclical industries or not. One caveat is that the debt levels of financial companies have been shown to be unrelated to their bankruptcy risk.[22] The results should therefore be interpreted with caution.

5. Empirical Results

Our results indicate that the changing nature of corporate leverage could potentially create problems for the U.S. economy. Moreover, the decrease in corporate debt in most other countries has not made firms uniformly more resilient to adverse economic shocks. In Charts 1 and 2 we group countries in four quadrants.

5.1 United States

Our results, which confirm most previous studies, show that cyclical industries in the United States historically have had a concentration of low-leveraged firms.[23] Firms in more cyclical industries, however, have increased their leverage the most rapidly. The average annual growth between 1977 and 1988 of sectoral debt-to-asset ratios averaged across the cyclical group is significantly higher than the growth averaged over the noncyclical group (Table 2). This conclusion contradicts previous studies that only look at the manufacturing sector, and exclude agriculture and mining and services.[24] When we exclude these sectors from our study, the difference in average growth rates of debt-asset ratios, between the cyclical and noncyclical group, is no longer significant. As a result of the differential rate of *increase* in leverage, firms that have had the most rapid increase in interest burden, have also been concentrated in the more cyclical industries. Our results do not appear to depend on our choice of sectoral aggregation.   The earnings sensitivity of firms in the 95th percentile of the leverage distribution (using debt-to-asset ratios) was less than the average level, 0.5, of all firms taken together until 1983 but rapidly increased thereafter. Moreover, the earnings sensitivity of firms in the uppermost tail of the leverage distribution increased even more rapidly than that of firms in the upper half of the distribution (see Table 3). Because the earnings sensitivity of high leverage firms, in the 95th and the 50th percentile have on average been close to zero looking at these figures would have been misleading.

Table 2

Average Annual Growth in Sectoral Debt-to Asset Ratios in the United States (Time Period 1978-88)

	Number of Companies	Average Growth in Debt-to Asset Ratios
Cyclical Sectors	861	2.2
Primary Metals and Transportation	108	3.7
Construction	71	3.0
Printing and Paper	78	2.0
Mining and Other	69	1.9
Other Durable Manufacturing	393	1.7
Petrochemical Manufacturing	142	0.8
Noncyclical Sectors	729	1.0
Other Nondurable Manufacturing	115	2.3
Services Except Finance	341	1.0
Banking, Insurance, Finance	92	0.6
Utilities	181	0.1

* Average of growth in debt-to-asset ratios for cyclical industries is significantly higher than the average for noncyclical industries at the 10 percent level of significance.

Table 3

Earnings Sensitivity to Output by Percentile Distribution of Leverage in Various Years

YEAR	95th	50th	Full Sample
1978	-0.40	-0.55	0.47
1979	-1.76	-0.49	0.47
1980	-1.03	0.41	0.47
1981	-0.24	-0.03	0.47
1982	-0.92	0.67	0.47
1983	0.10	0.86	0.47
1984	0.96	0.13	0.47
1985	0.80	0.99	0.47
1986	1.75	0.37	0.47
1987	1.75	1.11	0.47
1988	2.15	1.26	0.47
AVERAGE	0.02	0.23	0.47

* Because the last column includes all companies, the sample remains the same each year; hence, Beta is the same each year. The debt-to asset ratio is calculated for each company for each year and averaged across years for the bottom row. Companies are ranked by their debt-to-asset ratio each year, and grouped into percentiles. The earnings sensitivity to output is calculated.

This evidence appears to be contrary to that presented in some previous studies that focus on highly leveraged takeover activity. These studies, referred to earlier, conclude that most leveraged buy-outs (LBOs) occurred in noncyclical industries; as a result, highly leveraged activity may not be damaging to corporate America after all. We have three counter points to this argument. First, LBOs represent a relatively small proportion of the many types of highly leveraged activity in corporate restructurings.[25] Our study includes all highly leveraged activity except that involving firms going private, as in LBOs. For example, our sample includes the 1988 $2.7 billion stock repurchases by United Airlines, which formed 70 percent of the market capitalization. This data would not have been included in a sample including only takeover activity.

Second, results obtained by examining LBO activity alone are suspect. One study examining the relationship between increasing leverage and LBO activity in a sample of U.S. manufacturing industries found none.[26] The absence of a positive relationship between an increase in corporate leveraging and LBO activity shows that results obtained from examining LBOs are not necessarily representative of highly leveraged transactions.

Finally, previous studies have estimated that up to two-fifths of takeover activity has been related to firms in cyclically sensitive sectors.[27] Although this figure represents less than half of all mergers and acquisitions and LBOs, it shows that a fair amount of highly leveraged takeover activity is in fact taking place in the more vulnerable sectors.

5.2 Other Countries

Firms in most other industrialized countries decreased their leverage between 1982 and 1988. An exception in Australia, where firms increased their leverage during this period, but they also had a healthy increase in their cash flows. Growth in cash flows actually surpassed growth in interest obligations, resulting in a decline in the interest burden of Australian firms in our sample. It is hard to reconcile firms' lower interest burden with corporate distress that was evident in Australia in the late 1980s. The relatively small number of firms, (72 for Australia as compared with nearly, 1,600 for the United States), may form a sample that does not fully represent the corporate sector. There is no evidence, however, of a correlation between the earnings sensitivity to output and the average *level* or the *growth* in leverage of firms in Australia. The absence of a positive correlation suggests that the increase in leverage may potentially be less destabilizing than if leverage had increased uniformly in all sectors.

In Japan, the decrease in corporate leverage appears to have had more of a stabilizing influence than in Germany, Canada, or the United Kingdom. In Japan, corporate leverage seems to have declined uniformly across industries. In Germany and Canada, however, firms in the more cyclical industries decreased their leverage more slowly than did other firms. Firms in cyclical industries in the United Kingdom have had, on average, high *levels* of debt. Even though U.K. firms in cyclical industries decreased their leverage rapidly, their interest burden did not decline as rapidly as that of firms in the less cyclical industries.

The slower decline in the leverage of cyclical firms in Germany and in Canada meant that the most cyclical of German and Canadian firms also had the slowest decline in their interest burden. On the one hand, this may be of some concern to Germany, a country that has also had the highest concentration of firms in cyclical industries (see Table 4). On the other hand, institutional arrangements in Germany may make corporate bankruptcies less likely. It is difficult to conclude which of the two opposing factors is the stronger one at this time.

Table 4

Distribution of Firms Across Industry Groups in Major Industrialised Countries, 1988 (Percent)

SECTOR/COUNTRY	AUS	CAN	GER	JAP	UK	USA
Mining and Other	36	22	1	NA	3	4
Construction	14	5	15	8	12	4
Petrochemical Manufacturing	5	5	15	14	8	9
Printing and Paper	5	9	1	2	4	5
Other Nondurable Manuf.	5	7	9	7	15	7
Primary Metals and Transp.	5	11	12	11	6	7
Other Durable Manufacturing	9	10	25	37	18	25
Utilities	9	6	12	1	0	11
Banking, Insurance, Finance	NA	1	NA	NA	NA	6
Services Except Finance	14	25	11	21	33	21
% of Firms in Cyclical Industries	32	27	63	50	31	54

Sources: Compustat, Global Vantage

Chart 1

Relationship between firms' leverage and the earnings sensitivity to output in selected industrialized countries

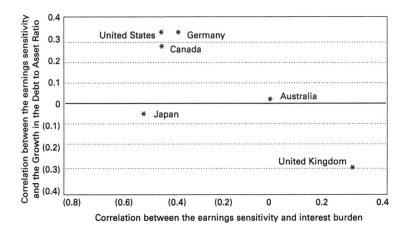

Source: Global Vantage. Compustat (for the United States).
Note: Figures are averages for the period 1982-88. Except for the United States in which the period is 1977-88. Non-financial firms only.

Chart 2

Relationship between firms' interest burden and the earnings sensitivity to output in selected industrialized countries

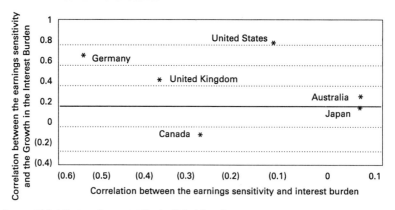

Source: Global Vantage. Compustat (for the United States).
Note: Figures are averages for the period 1982-88. Except for the United States in which the period is 1977-88. Non-financial firms only.

6. Conclusions

Our results indicate that, the recent increase in corporate leverage in the United States may be more disconcerting than previous work has led us to believe. Second, the increase in leverage in Australia may not be as destabilizing as it appears to be at first glance. Finally, in terms of reducing financial fragility, the decrease in leverage has benefited some countries more than others; in particular, Japan has benefited more than Germany, Canada or the United Kingdom.

The stronger the barriers to foreign financial institutions in any economy, the greater its vulnerability to a domestic credit squeeze. By contrast, the stronger the interpenetration of the banking system, the easier it is to compensate declines in domestic liquidity by capital inflows. It follows that the destabilizing influence of an increase in leverage in cyclical industries could be mitigated by a breakdown of national financial barriers. The beneficial effects of foreign investment, however, would be reduced in the event of a global credit squeeze. Only if the rest of the world was facing more stringent credit conditions than the domestic economy, however, would the deleterious effects swamp the beneficial effects of greater penetration by foreign financial institutions.

Acknowledgement

The views expressed are those of the author and do not necessarily reflect those of the Federal Reserve Bank of New York or the Federal Reserve System. I am grateful to an anonymous referee for comments on an earlier draft, and to Tara Hunter for typing assistance.

Endnotes

[1] See for example, Eli M. Remolona, "Understanding International Differences in Leverage Trends," Federal Reserve Bank of New York Quarterly Review, Spring 1990, pp. 31-42.

[2] For an extensive review of this literature see Milton Harris and Arthur Raviv. 1991. "The Theory of Capital Structure," Journal of Finance 46.

[3] Mark Gertler and Glenn Hubbard. 1993. "Corporate Financial Policy, Taxation, and Macroeconomic Risk, Journal of Commerce 24.

[4] Philip Jefferson. 1994. "Nominal Debt, Default Costs, and Output". Journal of Macroeconomics 16.

[5] Steven Sharpe. 1993. "Financial Market Imperfections, Firm Leverage and the Cyclicality of Employment, Board of Governors of the Federal Reserve System Finance and Economics Discussion Series, 93-10.

[6] Steven A. Sharpe, "Debt and Employment Volatility over the Business Cycle," Board of Governors of the Federal Reserve System Finance and Economics Discussion Series, 172, October 1991, p.36.

[7] Stephen S. Roach. 1988. "Living With Corporate Debt." Economic Perspectives, Morgan Stanley (November). See also Ben S. Bernanke, John Y Campbell, and Toni M. Whited. 1990. "U.S. Corporate Leverage: Developments in 1987 and 1988." Brookings Papers on Economic Activity 1.

[8] Robert M. Giordano. 1988-1989. "Debt Without Disaster." Financial Market Perspectives, Goldman Sachs, (December/January). See also Claudio V. Borio. 1990. "Banks' Involvement in Highly Leveraged Transactions," BIS memorandum. (July).

[9] See for example, Stephen S. Roach. 1990. "Defusing the Debt Bomb." Special Economic Study, Morgan Stanley (October 15).

[10] For an illustration, see William Lee. 1990. "Corporate Leverage and Consequences of Macroeconomic Instability." Studies on Financial Changes and the Transmission of Monetary Policy," Federal Reserve Bank of New York (May).

[11] By virtue of higher leverage, the corporate sector may be exposed to risks other than those caused by the concentration of highly leveraged firms in cyclical industries. See William Lee, "Corporate Leverage." (Footnote 12).

[12] See for example, Richard Cantor.1990. Studies on Financial Changes and the Transmission of Monetary Policy," Federal Reserve Bank of New York, (May).

[13] Michael C. Jensen, "Eclipse of the Public Corporation", Harvard Business Review, September-October 1989, Number 5.

[14] Ben S. Bernanke and John Y. Campbell "Is There a Corporate Debt Crisis," Brookings Papers on Economic Activity, 1:1988.

[15] Bowman. 1980. "The Importance of a Market Value Measurement of Debt in Assessing Leverage," Journal of Accounting Research 18 (Spring): 242-54.

[16] The measure based on equity returns is leverage dependent, whereas the measure based on asset returns is independent of leverage. For a proof, and the computation of the asset measure, see Rama Seth. 1990. "Leverage and Cyclicality." Working papers in Applied Economic Theory, Federal Reserve Bank of San Francisco, No. 90-01, (April).

[17] The cut-off point for cyclicality as measured by output is then necessarily equal to one. The cut-off points for cyclicality as measured by earnings and equity returns, however, are sample dependent. It should be noted that the exact cut-off point that determines which sectors are cyclical is to some extent arbitrary. As we explain later, however, the choice of cut-off point is not central to the analysis.

[18] Global Vantage, Standard and Poor's international version of Compustat, provides data on publicly traded companies in several countries. It makes some attempt to report variables on the same accounting basis as that of Compustat. We have made no attempt to further correct for cross-country differences.

[19] The aggregate figures for the United States reveal qualitively similar trends, whether we use data from Global Vantage or that from Compustat.

[20] Our grouping, NSIC, is as follows:

NSIC GROUP	COMPONENT SIC's
1 Agriculture, Forestry, Fishing, Mining	1-2, 7-9, 10-14
2 Construction and Construction Materials	15-17, 24-25, 32
3 Chemicals and Chemical Products	28-30
4 Paper and Printing	26-27
5 Nondurable Manufacturing	20-23, 31
6 Primary Metals and Transportation Equipment	33, 37
7 Fabricated Metals, Machinery, and Misc.	34-36, 38-39
8 Utilities	49
9 Financial Industries	60-67
10 Services	40-48, 50-59, 70-89

[21] See Andrew Chen and Sumon Mazumdar. "Impact of Regulatory Interactions on Bank Capital Structure." 1994. Journal of Financial Services Research 8:283-300. The authors have argued that regulatory interactions impact upon bank leverage and risk taking decisions, and this impact is nonlinear and non-uniform.

[22] Eugene Fama and Kenneth French. 1992. "The Cross-Section of Expected Stock Returns." Journal of Finance, 47:427-65.

[23] One recent study, Bernanke et al, 1990, found that there was no particular concentration of highly levered firms in cyclical or in non-cyclical industries. This conclusion differs from ours, and is probably due to the different measure of cyclicality used. They regressed growth in real earnings on growth in real GNP to obtain the cyclicality coefficient. Table 1 in this study suggests that their measure of cyclicality may be inferior to one obtained by regressing the growth in earnings to assets on the growth in GNP.

[24] See Roach, "Corporate Debt," p.#5, and Giordano, "Without Disaster," p.#12.

[25] According to Giordano, 1988/1989, LBOs represented only 20 percent of "all restructurings involving the substitution of debt for equity."

[26] Margaret M. Blair and Robert E. Litan. 1989. "Explaining Corporate Leverage and LBO Activity in the 1980s," Brookings Papers.

[27] Giordano, "Without Disaster," pp. 10-11. See also Statement by Alan Greenspan, Chairman of the Board of Governors of the Federal Reserve System, before the Senate Finance Committee, January

Institutional and Investment Performance Attributes of American Depository Receipts

Sudhir Nanda
Pennsylvania State University, Harrisburg

James E. Owers

and

Chenyang Feng
Georgia State University

Abstract

American Depository Receipts (ADRs) are a form of financial instrument with a long history of use in international finance. ADRs have unique attributes from the perspectives of both issuers and investors. While they have existed for much of the twentieth century, only recently have they come to play a major role. Despite this major role, there has been relatively little examination of ADRs from a research perspective.

This paper identifies the significant institutional features of ADRs and outlines their historical development and recent rapid growth. It then empirically examines their post-listing investment performance. It transpires that ADR research involves the dimensions of international financial investments and markets, initial public offerings, and changes in the market ADRs are traded. The investment performance and financial market micro structure attributes of ADRs are consistent with the hypothesis that international financial markets are materially segmented. The institutional attributes of ADRs are interesting from a variety of perspectives, including how they might affect investment performance. Differences in types of ADRs are found to be associated with variation in performance. For example, there are material differences in the investment performance of ADRs based on the domicile of the firm issuing the underlying securities. Whether the home country economy is developed or developing affects after-market investment performance. The significance of the developed/developing nature of the home country economy is different for ADRs traded on the Exchanges versus NASDAQ.

1. Introduction

ADRs are created when the securities of a foreign firm trade in U.S. financial markets using market mechanisms very similar to domestic securities. All transactions are in dollars, and investors have no need to purchase foreign currency or work with off-shore trading procedures. These trading features do not mean that the risks associated with changes in foreign currency value are not an important factor in ADR returns, as so dramatically illustrated in December 1994 in the case of Mexican ADRs. ADRs are a specific form of Global Depository Receipts (GDRs). The key attributes of Depository Receipts are that they are negotiable certificates representing ownership in foreign-domiciled companies which have the effect of facilitating cross-border investment with low transactions costs and generating a larger potential set of investors in the firm's securities.

The institutional features of ADRs have many variations, and reflect the evolution of ADRs as a major financial instrument. The significance of this background is great, because it has influenced the detailed features of ADRs and the pattern on their usage. Institutional variations also have the potential to impact the investment performance of ADRs. Given the relative lack of research papers integrating these dimensions, both the institutional context for, and the investment performance of ADRs are considered in this paper.

This is reflected in the organization of the paper. The next section outlines the institutional features of ADRs. Section 3 traces the development of ADRs, noting their origin in the early years of the twentieth century and their recently increasing role. Literature relevant to this study is reviewed in section 4. The empirical dimensions are covered in section 5, which is followed by the results. The conclusion and summary synthesize the contribution of the paper.

2. The Institutional Context of ADRs

The historical background of ADRs is interesting in that it relates to major geopolitical developments during the 20th century. Many of the essential features of ADRs were found in instruments developed by Dutch financiers in response to conditions of World War I. The various challenges of British property rights interpretations and physical hazards of transporting stock certificates to the U.S. during the conflict led to arrangements whereby instruments would be issued in New York backed by Trust interests in Europe, particularly Holland. Although not referred to as ADRs, an examination of the instruments developed during this time indicates that ADR-type securities existed during the first World War. This occurred as one of several developments widely interpreted to have helped establish New York City as a major international financial center.

The first instruments formally termed "American Depository Receipts" were issued in 1926. Despite this early development of ADRs, it is quite recently that they came to play a major role in International Finance. Their respective appeal to both investors and issuers is clear. The investor can acquire a direct interest in a foreign firm without dealing in a foreign currency or addressing trading customs outside the U.S. The details associated with offshore settlement procedures, unfamiliar market processes and custody services, limited information, variable tax provisions,

and foreign investment restrictions are substantially avoided when using
ADRs/GDRs as cross-border investment vehicles.   ADRs are negotiable and
generally liquid.[1] All transactions are in U.S. dollars, and dividends are paid in
dollars through a depository after being converted at a favorable wholesale rate.
ADRs thus provide investors with an expanded investment opportunity set, and tend
to minimize both direct and indirect costs of investing directly in foreign securities.

The foreign issuing firm gains access to the U.S. financial markets, providing
investors the opportunity to make dollar-denominated investments in their securities.
In addition to enlarging the market for firm's securities, there can be operating
benefits resulting from wider awareness of the firm via its ADRs. In addition to raising
additional capital, ADRs have recently been used in some acquisitions, where a
foreign firm offers its ADRs as consideration when making an offer to purchase a
target company in the U.S.

ADRs have a relatively simple overall institutional structure. In the creation of an
ADR, there are "trustees" in both the home country and the U.S. The home country
trustee acquires the securities on which the ADR is based, holds them in trust, and
the U.S. correspondent institution (typically one of: The Bank of New York, Citicorp,
and Morgan Guaranty Bank) issues the ADR backed by the in-trust securities.[2] Thus
the firm which originally issues the securities need not necessarily be a formal party
to the arrangements, and this is related to the sponsored/unsponsored categories
discussed below. The instruments can be equity or debt, and the debt has several
variations in type. This paper focuses on equity ADRs, which are the predominant
form and have the potential to support powerful empirical tests.

Unsponsored ADRs are issued by depositories without a formal agreement with the
company.[3] In contrast, issuers of sponsored ADRs have a formal arrangement with the
foreign company, which takes the form of a Depository Agreement or service contract.
Sponsored ADRs are predominant, and come in three types.[4] *Sponsored Level-I
Depository Receipts* are the simplest type. They trade in the OTC market but the company
is not required to meet full SEC disclosure requirements, or U.S. Generally Accepted
Accounting Principles (GAAP) standards. Sponsored Level-I depository receipts are the
most rapidly growing category, and are the "vast majority" of approximately 1,450 ADRs
trading in the U.S. as of December, 1995. The Level-I ADRs may represent 5-15% of the
firm's shareholder base.[5] Level-I ADRs are not "Listed ADRs."

When the foreign firm wants to have a listed ADR on a U.S. market or use the ADRs
as an instrument for raising capital, then *Level-II or Level-III Depository Receipts* are
required. There are varying SEC registration and reporting requirements, and GAAP
standards must be met. For example, firms with Level II or III ADRs must file a Form
20-F, providing reports meeting U.S. GAAP disclosure requirements or their domestic
statements with a reconciliation to GAAP. In addition, listing requirements must be
met. We note that the NASDAQ/OTC market encompasses a range of categories.
Securities trading in the National Market System (NMS) segment of NASDAQ must
meet more stringent requirements than those trading on the Pink Sheets.

Private Placement Depository Receipts can take place as 144A programs. These are
offered to approximately 4,500 Qualified Institutional Buyers (QIBs), and provide the
opportunity to raise capital with no SEC registration. A secondary market is
maintained among QIBs to provide liquidity. 144A programs can and frequently do
precede public offerings of ADRs.

3. The Development and Scope of ADRs

The historical role of ADRs is surprisingly extensive; the first ADR was issued by Selfridges Ltd., a British corporation in 1926. However, the significance of ADRs has been concentrated in a shorter time frame. The overall historical and geopolitical context for the development of ADR-like instruments during World War I was noted above. Given the long time frame over which ADRs have been employed, it is reasonable to address the issue of why they have received relatively little attention in the research literature. A factor in answering that question is the pattern of usage during the 70 years since their introduction.

The early years of development of ADR-type securities occurred as the U.S. was changing from being primarily a debtor nation to a creditor nation.[6] While there were major domestic investment opportunities in newly emergent industries such as automobiles and radio, the newly attained creditor status of the U.S. was associated with increased investment in foreign firms.[7] There were many different perspectives on ADRs when they became formalized during 1926 and 1927, much of which is documented mainly in *The New York Times*. Additionally, there were cross-border rivalries and different opinions which led to a generally slow start for ADRs.

The protectionist notions which became prominent during the depression are well summarized by Kindleberger (1978): "When every country turned to protect its national private interest, the world public interest went down the drain, and with it the private interests of all." (page 290). The implications for the slow rate of development of ADRs during the 1930s are clear.

Not surprisingly, during World War II there was little expansion in the use of ADRs. However, in the 1950s there was a reduction of inhibitions to cross-border securities trading, and Japanese ADRs emerged, with five being listed by 1952. This was followed by an increase in interest by European firms, and the mid 1950s saw important increases in the use of ADRs. The number of foreign firms with ADRs increased from 30 in 1955 to 80 by mid-1956. Although by 1959 there were three major New York depositories (Morgan Guaranty Co., Irving Trust, and Chemical Corn Exchange Bank), debates continued over such issues as differential information disclosure, and whether issues were sponsored. At the time, most were unsponsored.

By 1961, 150 firms from 17 countries had issued ADRs. Reflecting their gradual "acceptance," Japan had by then reduced restrictions on the issuance of ADRs. Few ADRs traded on the NYSE[8], with differential disclosure continuing to restrict foreign firms. The frictions of international finance were prominent when, on July 18, 1963, an Interest Equalization Tax (IET) was imposed on U.S. investors to address an outflow of American capital. This 15% tax on the purchase of new ADRs greatly reduced the interest of American investors. Dual markets for "before" and "after" IET ADRs emerged, with sellers of the former having to provide an affidavit of such status. The combined uncertainty regarding the passage of this proposal (which was complicated by the assassination of President Kennedy) and SEC regulations regarding registration of foreign securities and filing requirements, greatly inhibited the development of ADRs.

Table 1

Panel A. Recent development of ADR Programs upto December 31, 1993. Data includes all listed and non-listed ADRs.

	Total Number of ADRs	Number of Listed ADRs
1986	700	116
1987	754	139
1988	782	150
1989	804	170
1990	836	176
1991	886	186
1992	924	215
1993	996	256

Panel B. Domicile of firms whose securities underlie ADRs (as of Dec. 31, 1993).

United Kingdom	21.1%
Australia	17.5
Japan	14.8
South Africa	8.6
Hong Kong	5.1
Mexico	4.7
France	2.7
Netherlands	2.6
Germany	2.5
Italy	2.4
Malaysia	1.6
Other	16.4
Total	100%

Source: The Depositary Receipt Directory, The Bank of New York.

These factors indicate that a history of the development of ADRs is a somewhat intriguing chronicle of examples of the impediments to market integration and international financial investment. In this general context, growth of the ADR market was slow, and by 1968 there were approximately 200 ADRs, the vast majority trading OTC. The most common domiciles of issuers were Britain (80), South Africa (30), and the former West Germany (20).

It was not until the elimination of the of the IET in 1974 that ADRs experienced material growth, but still the issue of accounting disclosure and filing with the SEC remained. Some firms refused to comply, but they still continued to trade on the Pink Sheets. By 1978, there were 390 ADRs, most traded OTC and were unsponsored. By then, Japan-domiciled firms led in terms of number of ADRs (105), followed by South Africa (92) and the United Kingdom (89).

During the 1980s there was a regulatory easing and an increased interest in foreign securities by U.S. investors, resulting in a dramatic increase in ADRs. This is associated with the surge in international portfolio investment by U.S. investors using 401(k) and other plans. As of December 1995, there were 1,450 ADRs from over 40 countries, and annual trading volume in ADRs was in the order of $300 billion. Reflecting the increasing (relative as well as absolute) significance of ADRs, in 1994 Telefonos de Mexico was the highest volume security traded on the NYSE.

Panel A of Table 1 reports the total number of ADR programs in the U.S., along with the number of listed ADR programs. Listing requires that U.S. GAAP standards be met, and this translates into Level-II and Level-III sponsored Depository Receipts. Table 1, Panel B indicates the percentage of Depository Receipt programs by domicile of issuer. These data calibrate the rapid growth in ADRs in recent years, and establish the empirical analysis of the investment performance of ADRs as a significant topic to research. In 1994, 73% of the 289 new ADR programs established (public and private sponsored) were from emerging markets. This level was less than 20% in 1990. Since 1990, there has been increased participation in this market by South American and Asian firms. There has been a similar spurt in Global Depository Receipt issuance by firms from emerging markets.

4. Literature Review

ADRs have a multi-dimensional context in the finance literature. They involve elements of international market segmentation, IPOs, the impact of exchange listing and change of listing status, for example from NASDAQ to Exchange Listed (NYSE and AMEX). While our empirical tests concentrate on the post-listing investment performance of ADRs, this literature review is somewhat wider in scope in order to indicate the number of dimensions to ADRs.

Jayaraman et al. (1993) examine the impact of the listing in the U.S. of ADRs on the risk and return of the underlying stock in the *home-country* market. Examining a sample of 95 listings during 1983-1988, they find a positive association between the listing of ADRs and the return on the securities trading in their home-country markets. There is a positive abnormal return in the home market of 0.47% on the listing day. This result is significant only for the subsample of 44 Japanese firms. In contrast to the sample used in the empirical analysis of the present paper, their sample consisted predominantly of firms from developed countries. Jayaraman et al. interpret the positive reaction to emanate from the benefits of accessing additional capital markets with potentially lower capital costs. They did not find negative post-listing performance as was observed by Sanger and McConnell (1986) for firms that change their listing from OTC to the NYSE. If international financial markets are integrated across countries, listing on a foreign market would not be expected to have a significant price impact. However, a significant return may arise if markets are even partially segmented.

Other studies on international markets find results that are different from Jayaraman et al. Howe and Kelm (1987) find insignificant returns on the listing day and in the post-listing period, along with significant negative pre-listing returns. Alexander et al. (1988) examine a sample of 34 non-U.S. domiciled firms that listed on a U.S. exchange. They find significant positive cumulative returns until three months prior to listing, insignificant abnormal returns at listing, and significant negative abnormal returns in the 36-month post listing interval. Their sample of firms had a negative abnormal return of -9.30% in the two month period after listing. A larger post-listing decline is observed for non-Canadian firms, suggesting that these markets were previously more severely segmented from the U.S. An implication of their study is that international listings increase integration of capital markets.

Lau et al. (1994) examine a much larger sample of U.S. firms listing on ten different international stock exchanges. They observe positive abnormal returns in the U.S. markets around the time that the firm's application for listing is accepted, suggesting the existence of information effects. Negative abnormal returns (-0.36%) are observed on the first trading day, and significant negative returns are observed in the 125 day post-listing period for listings on the Tokyo and Basel exchanges.

Some of these studies have also examined the impact on volatility in the home market. Jayaraman et al. find a significant increase of 56% in volatility in the home market after the ADR becomes listed in the U.S. The ADR trading is associated with a permanent increase in the volatility of the returns on the underlying security. They ascribe this to the activities of informed traders who take advantage of additional information being revealed as a result of differential disclosure requirements, and increased trading time. Lau et al. find that volatility is not affected by cross listing, suggesting that abnormal returns are not caused by changes in systematic risk.

Our analysis of the listing and trading practices of ADRs reveals that the market-change literature is relevant to an examination of ADRs. Many new listings of ADRs on the NYSE, AMEX and National Market System (NMS) component of the NASDAQ market are in fact changes in the market on which ADRs are traded. The institutional context of ADRs means that for many years, they traded primarily in the NASDAQ market, typically on the Pink Sheets. Many have subsequently transferred to the NMS or become exchange listed. Thus, the market-change literature is also part of the context for this paper, and it provided significant methodological insights. Kadlec and McConnell (1994) examine the impact of listing on the NYSE by OTC stocks. Their results indicate a positive abnormal return of 5 to 6 percent at announcement of the upcoming listing. Listing is also associated with an increase in registered institutional holdings, and a reduction in the bid-ask spread. They conclude that investor recognition and increase in liquidity are the source of value increase. These insights are applicable to ADRs as they expand the markets in which the firm's shares are traded.

The return performance of ADRs will be influenced by details of their nature. For example, for some NYSE/AMEX/NASDAQ ADRs, the first day of trading represents its world-wide IPO, whereas for others this is an additional listing on another international market, or even a change from the pink sheets within the set of U.S. markets. A number of studies have documented the large positive abnormal returns on the first day of trading for IPOs. Ritter's papers ([1987], [1991]) on IPOs provide results documenting this outcome. The results suggest that underwriters offer these securities at a discount to the value set in the post-listing aftermarket.

Aggarwal and Rivoli (1990) examine the long-run performance of IPOs. They observe an abnormal return of -13.73% from the close of trading on the first day to 250 days after the IPO. Ritter (1991) found that IPOs underperform industry and size-matched control groups by 29% over a three year period. Similar results have been observed in Germany (Uhlir [1989]), Brazil, Mexico and Chile (Aggarwal et al. [1993]), and the U.K. (Levis [1993]).

The listing of ADRs has some similarity to the experience of IPOs in that a new security is trading. However, the ADR and IPO experiences are somewhat different if the security underlying the ADR has previously traded in its home market, and thus there are market measures of intrinsic value, converted at the spot exchange rate. Nevertheless, theoretical and practical motivations for ADRs (such as international capital market segmentation) means that the ADRs may not necessarily trade at pure arbitrage values, at least immediately. Kato et al. (1991) and Marr et al. (1991) examine issues related to market integration and the potential for arbitrage.

Jegadeesh et al. (1993) is also contextual for this paper as there are apparent patterns of post-issue strategies by ADRs issuers. While it appears to remain a topic for systematic study, examination of the process associated with ADRs indicates that the "road show" relating to the promotion of a particular ADR frequently follows the initiation of trading.[9]

This review of the literature related to ADRs indicates the considerable range of issues associated with these instruments. And clearly this review is not exhaustive[10]. In combination with the institutional variation in ADRs, it is apparent that these instruments have the potential to generate many additional research questions and associated hypotheses. In this paper we empirically address questions relating to the immediate post-listing performance of ADRs. The next section describes the empirical methods, and this is followed by the presentation of evidence relating to the research questions of the paper.

5. Data, Sample and Methodology

5.1 Data and Sample

This study examines equity ADRs which began trading on major U.S. markets since 1962, a data-source determined starting point. The Center for Research in Security Prices (CRSP) returns files are available for Exchange-Listed firms since 1962, and for NASDAQ firms since 1972. The sample covers the period 19631992. Three U.S. banks provide the majority of the supply of ADRs into U.S. markets. The empirical examination of the risk/return performance of ADRs focuses on listed ADRs (i.e. Sponsored Levels-II and III) traded on major U.S. markets - the New York and American Stock Exchanges (NYSE and AMEX), and the NASDAQ market.[11] The initial sample of newly-listed ADRs was identified from the CRSP tapes. This was checked for availability of other data requirements necessary to apply the empirical methodology and address the identified research questions.

Much of the data for the analysis came from the CRSP data tapes. The returns data from the CRSP tapes dictate an after-market analysis. The CRSP tapes do not contain issue prices and returns for the first day of trading when the ADR issuance is accompanied by a stock offering.[12] Additional data was accumulated from two primary resources: Library research (a major source was the *Investment Dealers' Digest, with Moodys' International Manuals* being used to confirm information); and industry sources. ADRs were excluded if they started trading prior to the day preceding the first return date on the CRSP tapes. Some others were excluded due to confounding events.[13] ADRs on preferred stock or those representing multiple classes of stock were also excluded.

Table 2 provides descriptive information regarding our empirical sample of 143 ADRs. Reflecting the universe of ADRs, the largest number of programs in our empirical sample comes from the United Kingdom. The number of newly-listed ADRs varies widely from year to year. The beginning of the NASDAQ sample in 1973 reflects CRSP data availability for these firms beginning in 1972. The 143 ADRs in our sample which became listed during the period 1963-1992 (and met our sample criteria) are 66.5% of the 215 listed ADRs trading at the end of 1992 (Table 1, Panel A).

Table 2

Panel A. Distribution of the sample of 143 ADRs by the domicile of the underlying firms and by exchanges.

Domicile of Underlying Stocks	Number of ADRs on NASDAQ	Number of ADRs on NYSE/AMEX
Australia	13	7
France	5	—
Italy	—	4
Ireland	3	2
Israel	2	—
Japan	10	9
Mexico	—	5
Netherlands	4	—
Norway	2	2
South Africa	6	—
Spain	—	4
Sweden	4	—
United Kingdom	20	28
Others*	6	7
Total	75	68

* include Bermuda, Chile, Denmark, Finland, France, Hong Kong, Netherlands, New Zealand, and Portugal.

Panel B. Distribution of ADRs on NYSE/AMEX and NASDAQ, by year of listing.

Year of Listing	Number of ADRs on NASDAQ	Number of ADRs listed on NYSE/AMEX
1964	-	1
1970	-	2
1971	-	1
1972	-	5
1973	2	0
1974	2	0
1975	1	1
1976	1	5
1977	6	0
1978	1	0
1980	1	0
1981	9	1
1982	5	0
1983	9	2
1984	5	2
1986	5	6
1987	10	9
1988	3	7
1989	4	6
1990	4	7
1991	0	7
1992	7	6
Total	75	68

5.2 Empirical Methods

The methodology for the empirical analysis in the paper is a combination of event-study techniques as adapted for market listing change papers and newly listed return measures (essentially the Initial Public Offering [IPO] techniques).

The event methodology consists of the established event-analysis techniques (as in Dodd and Warner (1983) and Hite and Owers (1983)) with the adaptations to accommodate the newly listed status of ADRs analyzed. In examining the investment performance of ADRs, for each ADR j, the market model is used to calculate an abnormal return (AR) for event day t as follows:

$$AR_{jt} = R_{jt} - (\alpha_j + \beta_j R_{mt}) \tag{1}$$

where R_{jt} is the rate of return on security j for event day t, and R_{mt} is the rate of return on the CRSP value-weighted index on event day t. The coefficients α_j and β_j are the ordinary least squares estimates of the intercept and slope, respectively, of the market model regression, which is run over an estimation period from t = +51 to t = +200, relative to the initial return date (referred to as event date t = +1). In addition to the market model, analysis was undertaken with mean-deviation benchmarks, as examined by Brown and Warner (1985). The results are very robust with respect to methodology. The various methodologies produced inconsequentially different findings.

6. Empirical Analysis: Motivation and Findings

This section reports the findings regarding the overall research question of how ADRs perform in the after-market, and motivates and addresses other research issues.

6.1 Overall ADR Post-Listing Performance

The first question is how well ADRs perform in the post-listing period. This serves as an indication of the return experience of investors who purchase the newly traded security at a price available to all, and thus does not assume purchase at the issue price.[14] Based on the findings in previous studies of cross-listings and IPOs, the post-listing investment performance of ADRs is a matter for empirical investigation.

We posit the following research question to begin our investigation of the post-listing performance of ADRs: Newly listed ADRs will provide zero abnormal returns to investors in the immediate after-market.

Table 3 reports the findings related to this question. There are positive abnormal returns over the initial 50-day trading interval, and any subintervals including day +50. For example, the abnormal return during the intervals (+20, +50) and (+30, +50) are significant at the 1% level. However, it is important to note that there are no significant positive returns if the interval of analysis is restricted to any initial trading period up to 30 days. This is evident from the AR results in Panel A and the CARs and interval test-statistics presented in Panel B. The CAR for all 143 ADRs is 0.88% at day +30, rising to 2.89% at day +50.[15] This results in significant positive abnormal returns to investors who acquire the portfolio of ADRs at the end of the first day of trading (or thereafter) and hold it to day +50.

Table 3

Panel A. Daily average market model adjusted percentage abnormal returns (ARs) and cumulative sum of the daily average abnormal returns (CARs) from the first day of CRSP returns through trading day 50, for 143 ADRs meeting data criteria during the period 1963 - 1992.

Day	AR	CAR	Test-statistic for individual day AR
+1	0.44	0.44	1.15
+2	0.02	0.46	-0.44
+3	-0.38	0.08	-2.11
+4	0.24	0.32	1.49
+5	-0.35	-0.03	-1.44
+6	0.33	0.30	1.36
+7	0.13	0.43	0.23
+8	-0.03	0.40	-0.50
+9	0.41	0.81	1.19
+10	-0.19	0.62	-1.59

Panel B. Mean cumulative abnormal returns (CARs) in percent for specified intervals and test-statistic for the identified interval.

Days in interval	CAR	Test-statistic
+1 to +5	-0.03	-0.61
+1 to +10	0.62	-0.24
+1 to +20	1.12	0.59
+1 to +30	0.88	0.88
+1 to +40	2.52	1.94
+1 to +50	2.90	2.28
+10 to +50	2.08	2.38
+20 to +50	2.26	2.90
+30 to +50	1.19	2.82

In contrast to the profile of findings from previous IPO studies, we do not find overall evidence that ADRs experience losses in the immediate after-market. However, given the variation within the overall sample of ADRs, we now investigate whether this result holds for partitions of the sample.

6.2 Exchange-Listed versus NASDAQ ADRs

There are substantial differences between the firms whose ADRs trade on the exchanges and those trading in the NASDAQ market. These reflect different market-listing criteria and disclosure requirements. The association between a firm's characteristics and the market on which its securities trade is similar for both ADRs and domestic securities. Generally those trading on the Exchanges (NYSE and AMEX) are larger and there is differential/more information available regarding them.

These differences have the potential to lead to different investment performance between Exchange-Listed and NASDAQ ADRs. The market-change literature has identified factors such as liquidity variations and investor recognition as having potential impact. Additionally, there are variations in institutional and trading practices which potentially lead to different investment performance. For instance, there are differences in regulations in "shorting" the security, especially in the interval just after trading begins.

This raises the research question: Will the different institutional and informational contexts have implications for the post-listing investment performance of Exchange-Listed versus NASDAQ ADRs?

Tables 4 and 5 provide evidence that the overall answer is yes - there are differences. Table 4 documents evidence of positive abnormal return performance for NASDAQ ADRs over the first 20 days of trading. The CAR at day +20 is 3.05%, and at day +50 is 3.49%. There is significant abnormal return accumulation up to day +20, but little thereafter.

Table 4

Panel A. Daily average market model adjusted percentage abnormal returns (ARs) and cumulative sum of the daily average abnormal returns (CARs) from the first day of CRSP returns through trading day 50, for 75 ADRs trading on NASDAQ meeting data criteria during the period 1963 - 1992.

Day	AR	CAR	Test-statistic for individual day AR
+1	0.78	0.78	2.04
+2	0.27	1.05	0.67
+3	-0.17	0.88	-0.75
+4	0.46	1.34	2.64
+5	-0.43	0.91	-1.30
+6	0.40	1.31	1.28
+7	0.02	1.33	-0.49
+8	0.06	1.40	-0.21
+9	0.38	1.77	0.76
+10	-0.06	1.71	-0.55

Panel B. Mean cumulative abnormal return (CAR) in percent for specified intervals relative to first trading day and test-statistic for the identified interval.

Days in interval	CAR	Test-statistic
+1 to +5	0.91	1.48
+1 to +10	1.71	1.28
+1 to +20	3.05	2.23
+1 to +30	2.33	1.66
+1 to +40	4.99	2.66
+1 to +50	3.49	1.89
+10 to +50	1.17	1.36
+20 to +50	1.12	0.96
+30 to +50	0.62	0.63

In contrast, as reported in Table 5, with the exception of intervals including days +40 to +50, the Exchange-Listed ADRs exhibit primarily negative abnormal returns, albeit not with high levels of significance. The Exchange-Listed ADRs experience a CAR over (+1, +20) of -1.01% (test-statistic = -1.49), in contrast to the significant positive CAR over the same interval for NASDAQ ADRs (+3.05%, test-statistic 2.23).

A profile of the findings for Exchange-Listed versus NASDAQ traded ADRs indicates that they are quite different. For NASDAQ ADRs, there is a significant 0.78% (test-statistic = 2.04) abnormal return on day 1. These ADRs experience generally positive abnormal returns from day +1 to day +40 (CAR = 4.99%). There is a decline from 4.99% CAR at Day +40 to 3.49% at day +50. In contrast, the Exchange-Listed ADRs experience some losses in the first week of trading (CAR of -1.07%, test-statistic = -2.43). They have no positive abnormal return accumulation up to day +40, and then gain 2.43% CAR over (+40, +50).

Table 5

Panel A. Daily average market model adjusted percentage abnormal returns (ARs) and cumulative sum of the daily average abnormal returns (CARs) from the first day of CRSP returns through trading day 50, for 68 Exchange-Listed ADRs meeting data criteria during the period 1963 - 1992.

Day	AR	CAR	Test-statistic for individual day AR
+1	0.06	0.06	-0.47
+2	-0.26	-0.19	-1.34
+3	-0.61	-0.80	-2.27
+4	-0.01	-0.81	-0.61
+5	-0.27	-1.07	-0.74
+6	0.24	-0.83	0.63
+7	0.24	-0.58	0.86
+8	-0.13	-0.71	-0.50
+9	0.45	-0.26	0.93
+10	-0.32	-0.58	-1.66

Panel B. Mean cumulative abnormal return (CAR) in percent for specified intervals and test-statistic for the identified interval.

Days in interval	CAR	Test-statistic
+1 to +5	-1.07	-2.43
+1 to +10	-0.58	-1.64
+1 to +20	-1.01	-1.49
+1 to +30	-0.74	-0.73
+1 to +40	-0.20	0.02
+1 to +50	2.23	1.33
+10 to +50	2.49	2.02
+20 to +50	3.50	3.20
+30 to +50	3.35	3.42

6.3 Domicile of Firm: Developed or Developing Economy

There are several reasons why the investment performance of ADRs from developed and developing countries might differ. We have noted that the degree of market segmentation and different information availability regarding the underlying firm may have an impact on the investment performance of ADRs. There are additional institutional factors which might lead ADRs from developed and developing countries to have different attributes. For example, individuals and institutions may prefer to hold ADRs of firms in developing countries (rather than direct ownership of the foreign-listed shares) because of lower transactions costs, higher liquidity, the avoidance of restrictions on foreign ownership, security custodial issues, and potential tax considerations. But counteracting factors might emanate from lower quality information being available regarding firms in developing countries.

Table 6

Panel A. Daily average market model adjusted percentage abnormal returns (ARs) and cumulative sum of the daily average abnormal returns (CARs) from the first day of CRSP returns through trading day 50, for 75 ADRs trading NASDAQ meeting data criteria during the period 1963 - 1992, and partitioned into securities issued by firms domiciled in developed (n = 59) versus developing (n = 16) economies.

Day	Developed		Developing	
	AR	CAR	AR	CAR
+1	0.93	0.93	0.21	0.21
+2	0.71	1.63	-1.33	-1.11
+3	0.14	1.77	-1.30	-2.41
+4	0.89	2.67	-1.16	-3.57
+5	-0.25	2.42	-1.10	-4.67
+6	0.60	3.02	-0.32	-4.99
+7	0.08	3.10	-0.17	-5.16
+8	0.09	3.19	-0.06	-5.22
+9	0.68	3.87	-0.74	-5.96
+10	0.07	3.95	-0.58	-6.54

Panel B. Mean cumulative abnormal return (CAR) in percent for specified intervals and test-statistic for the identified interval.

Days in interval	Developed		Developing	
	CAR	Test-statistic	CAR	Test-statistic
+1 to +5	2.42	3.06	-4.67	-2.68
+1 to +10	3.95	2.87	-6.54	-2.74
+1 to +20	5.72	3.60	-6.83	-2.08
+1 to +30	4.94	2.65	-7.26	-1.48
+1 to +40	8.84	4.05	-9.24	-2.07
+1 to +50	6.89	2.81	-9.56	-1.30
+10 to +50	3.01	1.66	-3.09	-0.24
+20 to +50	2.30	1.21	-3.19	-0.25
+30 to +50	1.30	0.85	-1.91	-0.27

What impact will these considerations have on the post-listing investment performance of ADRs? We approach that empirical question as follows: In the context of the variation in disclosure, institutional issues associated with ADRs and the differential requirements for ADRs traded on exchanges versus non-exchange markets, the domicile of the issuing firm (developed or developing economy) will impact the return performance of newly traded ADRs.

In addition, the size correlations associated with those ADR programs which are Exchange-Listed (NYSE/AMEX) versus those which trade in the NASDAQ market have the potential to imply that the developed/developing performance will vary from Exchange-Listed to NASDAQ ADRs.

Tables 6 and 7 present notable findings relative to these questions. Table 6 reports a dramatic difference in return performance for NASDAQ traded ADRs according to whether they originate from developed or developing economies. Both individual day test statistics (Table 6, Panel A) and interval statistics (Table 6, Panel B) are significantly positive for developed-economy ADRs and significantly negative for developing-economy ADRs. The CARs at day +50 differ by 15.95%. Thus the overall results for NASDAQ firms reported in Table 4 are a weighted average of two quite different subsamples, ADRs from developed and developing economies.

Table 7

Panel A. Daily average market model adjusted percentage abnormal returns (ARs) and cumulative sum of the daily average abnormal returns (CARs) from the first day of CRSP returns through trading day 50, for 68 Exchange Listed ADRs meeting data criteria during the period 1963 - 1992, and partitioned into securities issued by firms domiciled in developed (n=52) versus developing (n=16) economies.

Day	Developed		Developing	
	AR	CAR	AR	CAR
+1	0.03	0.03	0.19	0.19
+2	-0.10	-0.07	-0.76	-0.57
+3	-0.46	-0.53	-1.09	-1.66
+4	0.13	-0.40	-0.48	-2.13
+5	-0.17	-0.57	-0.56	-2.70
+6	-0.02	-0.59	1.09	-1.60
+7	0.42	-0.17	-0.32	-1.92
+8	0.17	0.00	-1.11	-3.03
+9	0.45	0.45	0.45	-2.58
+10	-0.16	0.30	-0.86	-3.44

Panel B. Mean cumulative abnormal return (CAR) in percent for specified intervals and test-statistic for the identified interval.

Days in interval	Developed		Developing	
	CAR	Test-statistic	CAR	Test-statistic
+1 to +5	-0.57	-1.02	-2.70	-3.17
+1 to +10	0.29	-0.36	-3.44	-2.73
+1 to +20	-0.20	-0.58	-3.65	-2.02
+1 to +30	-0.33	-0.18	-2.07	-1.17
+1 to +40	0.02	0.47	-0.94	-0.80
+1 to +50	2.57	1.44	1.14	0.14
+10 to +50	2.12	1.60	3.72	1.27
+20 to +50	2.99	2.63	5.17	1.84
+30 to +50	3.20	2.83	3.85	1.94

In a notable reflection of the manifestation of differential disclosure and other requirements, the findings for Exchange-Listed ADRs reported in Table 7, Panels A and B, show relatively little difference between developed and developing-economy originated ADRs. There is evidence of negative performance for developing economy ADRs over the first 20 days of trading, and no significant abnormal returns (positive or negative) for developed economy ADRs until day +40.

We can conclude that there are significant differences in post-listing investment performance between developed-economy ADRs and developing-economy ADRs, with the former performing better than the latter. Furthermore, this propensity is greatly magnified for NASDAQ ADRs in contrast to Exchange-Listed ADRs.

7. Summary and Conclusions

As described in the institutional sections of the paper, American Depository Receipts (ADRs) are a form of financial instrument with a long history of use in International Finance. However, only recently have they come to receive much research attention. There is considerable institutional variation, and the historical development of ADRs generates an interesting chronicle of the development of the global financial system. The combination of their institutional features and the market mechanisms by which they are traded make ADRs quite unique financial instruments.

These attributes motivated an analysis of their investment performance, and material differences are found between various categories of ADRs. Overall, ADRs provide positive abnormal returns over the initial 50 trading days. Further analysis showed marked differences between the investment performance of OTC traded ADRs versus exchange listed ADRs. These contrasts were stark when the developed/developing nature of the issuing firm's home-country economy was used as a subsample partition. ADRs from developing economies have notably negative investment performance, and developed economy ADRs provide positive abnormal returns, particularly when traded OTC. These findings are noteworthy, and motivate further research of the investment performance of ADRs.

Acknowledgement

This paper has benefited from input from colleagues at our respective institutions, and comments from participants at sessions at the 1995 Annual Meetings of the Global Finance Association and the Financial Management Association. We thank Mario Levis and the anonymous reviewer for many helpful suggestions and Ufuk Ince for excellent research assistance. The second author gratefully acknowledges support from the Georgia State University College of Business Administration Research Program Council.

References

Aggarwal, R. and P. Rivoli, 1990, Fads in the initial public offering market, Financial Review, 19(4), p. 45-57.

Aggarwal, R., R. Leal and F. Hernandez, 1993, The aftermarket performance of initial public offerings in Latin America, Financial Management, 22(1), p. 42-53.

Alexander, G., C. Eun and S. Janakiramanan, 1988, International listings and stock returns: some empirical evidence, Journal of Financial and Quantitative Analysis, 23(2), p. 135-51.

Brown, S. and J. Warner, 1985, Using daily stock returns: the case of event studies, Journal of Financial Economics, 14, p. 331.

Dodd, P. And J. Warner, 1983, On corporate governance: a study of proxy contests, Journal of Financial Economics, 11, p. 401-38.

Doukas J. and K. Yung, 1992, ADRs, Investors' information and initial public equity offerings (IPO) Underpricing, Journal of International Securities Markets, 7, p. 341-8.

Harr, J., K. Dandapani and S. Harr, 1990, The American depository receipt (ADR): A creative financial tool for multinational companies, Global Finance Journal, 1(2), p. 163-71.

Hite, G.L. and J.E. Owers, 1983, Security price reactions around corporate spin-off announcements, Journal of Financial Economics, 12(4), p. 409-36.

Howe, J. and K. Kelm, 1987, The stock price effects of overseas listings, Financial Management, 16(3), p. 51-6.

Hubbard, D., 1992, An accounting study of American depository receipts, (unpublished dissertation, Virginia Polytechnic Institute and State University).

Jegadeesh, N., M. Weinstein and I. Welch, 1993, An empirical investigation of IPO returns and subsequent equity offerings, Journal of Financial Economics, 34(2), p. 153-75.

Jayaraman, N., K. Shastri and K. Tandon, 1993, The impact of international cross listings on risk and return: the evidence from American depository receipts, Journal of Banking and Finance, 17, p. 91103.

Kadlec, G. and J. McConnell, 1994, The effect of market segmentation and illiquidity on asset prices: evidence from exchange listings, Journal of Finance, 49, p. 611-36.

Kato, K., S. Linn and J. Schallheim, 1991, Are there arbitrage opportunities in the market for American depository Receipts?, Journal of International Markets, Institutions & Money, 1(1), p. 73-85.

Kindleberger, C.P., 1978, The world in depression (Basic Books, New York).

Lau, S., J. Diltz and V. Apilado, 1994, Valuation effects ofInternational stock exchange listings, journal of banking and finance, 18, p. 743-55.

Levis, M., 1993, The long-run performance of initial public offerings: the U.K. experience 1980-1988, Financial Management, 22(1), p. 28-41.

Marr, M. Wayne, J. Trimble and R. Varma, 1991, On the integration of international capital markets: evidence from euroequity offerings, financial management, 20(4), p. 11-21.

McConnell, J. and G. Sanger, 1984, A trading strategy for new listings on the NYSE, Financial Analysts' Journal, 40(1), p. 34-48.

McConnell, J. and G. Sanger, 1986, Stock exchange listings, firm value and market efficiency: the impact of NASDAQ, Journal of Financial and Quantitative Analysis, 21(1), p. 1-25.

McConnell, J. and G. Sanger, 1987, The puzzle in post-listing common stock returns, Journal of Finance, 42(1), p. 119-40.

Officer, D. and R. Hoffmeister, 1987, American depository receipts: a substitute for the real rhing?, Journal of Portfolio Management, 13(2), p. 61-5.

Perotti, E. and S. Guney, 1993, The structure of privatization plans, financial management, 22, p. 84-98.

Ritter, J., 1987, The costs of going public, Journal of Financial Economics, 19(2), p. 269-82.

Ritter, J., 1991, The long run performance of initial public offerings, Journal of Finance, 46, p. 328.

Uhlir, H., 1989, Going public in F.R.G., in a reappraisal of the efficiency of the financial markets, (Springer Verlag, New York).

Webb, S., D. Officer and B. Boyd, 1995, An examination of international equity markets using ADRs, Journal of Business, Finance and Accounting, 22(3), p. 415-30.

Endnotes

1 The precise nature of an ADR's liquidity is influenced by the particular market on which it trades, and the liquidity of the underlying security.

2 ADRs frequently represent an ownership interest equivalent to five or ten (respectively) shares in the underlying foreign firm, but the number varies widely.

3 According to the Bank of New York, unsponsored ADRs are "becoming obsolete." There is clearly an unstructured dimension to unsponsored ADRs. There are reported anecdotes from the past of more than one unsponsored ADR being established over the common underlying security. In some cases the number of shares represented by different unsponsored ADRs were not the same, providing the clear potential for confusion.

4 The classification of ADR "levels" is a market convention and it does not have any legal standing.

5 We are grateful to The Bank of New York for providing us with this, and other, information regarding ADRs.

6 In terms of the Net International Investment Position, the U.S. has been a debtor nation prior to World War I, and again since 1985.

7 While the origination of ADRs followed the U.S. having recently attained creditor status, we do not suggest a strong line of causation. This is not consistent with the surge in interest and volume in ADRs in the post 1985 interval, when the U.S. has again become a debtor nation. The complexities of capital flows and relative sizes of pools of investible funds mean that the Net Investment Position of he U.S. is only one factor in the role of ADRs.

8 It appears as if there were only 2 at this time.

9 Based on inspection of a number of ADR issues, it appears that the post-issue timing of the "road-show," earnings announcements and patterns of price changes may be fruitful areas for systematic research.

10 Other papers addressing ADRs or ADR-related issues include Officer and Hoffmeister (1987), Haar et al. (1990), Doukas and Yung (1992), and Webb et al. (1995).

11 Most listed ADRs trading in the NASDAQ market trade in the National Market System (NMS) segment of that market.

12 Obtaining issue prices represents a data collection task outside the scope of this study. As in the case of IPO studies, following research using returns for the first day of trading will add substantially to knowledge regarding ADRs.

13 One ADR where the returns series indicated more than a 200% abnormal return on one day during the first week of trading was also excluded.

14 If ADRs are mostly underpriced, then it can be expected that, as with IPOs, typical issues are not readily available to many investors at the issue price. That is the issue referred to in the endnote 12, and one which remains for research examination.

15 This indicates the potential benefit of systematically investigating the post-listing strategies noted previously.

Determinants of Cross-Border Listings
The Dutch Evidence

Ali Fatemi
Kansas State University

and

Alireza Tourani Rad
University of Limburg

Abstract

In this study we compare the various characteristics and the financial performance of two sets of Dutch firms: those listed on the Amsterdam Stock Exchange (ASE) and at least one other exchange outside of the Netherlands and a comparable group listed only on the ASE. Comparing the two sets of firms with respect to their leverage, liquidity, profitability and market value ratios we find the two groups significantly different from one another. Cross-border listed firms are more liquid and produce a better return on their assets despite their lower profit margin on sales. They also generate a higher return on their shareholders' equity and have higher market values than firms listed only on the national exchange. We also observe that cross-border listed firms exhibit less stock price volatility than the otherwise comparable group of nationally-listed firms. The paper also addresses the question of managerial motivations for cross-border listing decisions. Results, based on a survey of chief financial executives of a sample of internationally-listed Dutch firms, indicate that financial, organizational and investor-relations reasons are the most frequently cited reasons for cross-border listings.

1. Introduction

The increasing integration of financial markets across international boundaries has been the subject of extensive research in recent years. Contributing to this integration process have been (1) individual and institutional investors flocking to the offshore markets in an effort to identify investments which offer superior returns for the risks involved and (2) an increasing number of firms cross-listing their shares on foreign stock exchanges in an attempt to expand their sources of equity capital and to, ultimately, reduce their cost of capital. The potential benefits resulting from such cross-listings have been discussed by Stapleton and Subrahmanyam (1977) and Alexander et.al. (1987), among others. The empirical evidence regarding the benefits has, however, been inconclusive. Alexander et.al (1988) studied a sample of 34 firms from seven countries[1] which undertook to dually list their shares in the U.S. (NYSE, AMEX, or NASDAQ) between 1969 and 1982. Consistent with the predictions of a model of segmented capital markets, they observed a significant decline in the expected return on the common stock of all but the Canadian firm. Their results, however, are perplexing and contradictory in nature, in that no corresponding significant increase in the stock prices of these firms was observed. Further, their results run counter to those reported by Howe and Kelm (1987), who examined the effect on the stock prices of U.S. firms which undertook to list their stocks on the Basel, Frankfurt and Paris stock exchanges. They observed (1) that overseas listings result in significant wealth losses for the U.S. shareholders, (2) that most of the wealth losses occur during the pre-listing period and (3) that the post-listing period is not consistently associated with negative abnormal returns. More recently, Lee (1991) investigated the impact of foreign listing for a sample of U.S. firms that listed their shares on the London or Toronto stock exchanges. His results indicate that overseas listings do not bring about any significant or permanent change in the U.S. shareholders' wealth. In summary, the evidence with regard to the wealth effects of cross-border listings remains largely ambiguous.

The effect of cross-border listings on the volatility of the firm's shares also remains, fairly inconclusive. Makhija and Nachtmann (1989) report an increase in the daily variance of returns for a sample of NYSE firms subsequent to their listing on the Tokyo Stock Exchange. On the other hand, Howe and Madura (1990), studying a sample of U.S. companies cross-listed on the German, French, Japanese and Swiss stock markets, conclude that international listings do not appear to cause significant shifts in risk, regardless of the risk measure examined. Barclay et.al. (1990) examining a sample of 16 U.S. Stocks cross-listed on the Tokyo Stock Exchange, also find no significant changes in the variance of returns. In a more recent study, Howe et.al. (1993) used a sample of 40 U.S. firms with exchange-listed option that listed their stocks abroad. Utilizing implied volatility measure of risk, they found a significant increase in the anticipated volatility following the international listing.

Accordingly, it may follow that the most reliable generalization one can make about the effects of cross-border listings is that such effects are time-and-state-dependent. The question remains, however, as to what motivates a firm to initiate and carry out the process of a cross-border listing.

This study is designed to answer this question. It investigates the determinants of cross-border listing. The approach taken here is different than that taken in the extant research which has dealt with this questions and it is along the line of study by Mitto (1992). It utilizes the direct survey method, as opposed to the statistical inference method used by other studies such as Sudagaran (1988). The latter compares the characteristics of 223 cross-listed firms to those of 258 firms not listed abroad to determine which, if any of these characteristics, are instrumental to the cross-listing decision. He finds a positive correlation between the likelihood of overseas listing and the relative size of a firm in its domestic capital market, the proportion of its revenues generated in foreign countries (indicating a firm's dependence on foreign consumer and product markets), the percentage of the firm's long-lived assets that are invested abroad, and the relative number of employees in foreign subsidiaries. Overall, it appears that the absolute size of firms, their main line of business and their nationality influence the decision to list on foreign stock exchanges. While highly instructive, Sudagaran's conclusions are subject to the limitations which his aggregation of data, for firms located in 10 different countries, does impose. More specifically, the ability to draw inference may be severely handicapped due to the fact that the institutional aspects and the micro-structures of national markets are far from homogeneous. Indeed, previous research on the influence of stock markets on corporate performance indicates that considerable differences exist among the structures of the national markets which make up the European capital markets. For example, in comparing the German and the U.K. firms, Mayer and Alexander (1991) observe that there are far fewer quoted companies in Germany. This difference may be due to the German banks' practice of providing more debt finance to the medium-sized firms which, in turn, limits the need for these firms to go public. Small and medium-sized firms in the U.K., on the other hand, may involuntarily be driven to the stock market due to an absence of alternative institutional arrangements. The extension of this argument would, then, suggest that the institutional factors, under which a firm operates, would influence its decision to list abroad as well. Accordingly, a country-by-country analysis may result in a better understanding of the issues involved in international listings. Mitto (1992) also argues that a single country study controls for many factors that may vary across countries. His study provides insights into managerial perceptions of costs and benefits of foreign listing through a survey of Canadian firms that have listed their stocks on the US and the UK markets. Mitto finds that access to foreign capital markets and increased marketability of stock are considered to be the major benefits. We follow a country-by-country approach in this paper, within which we evaluate the determinants of international listings for the Dutch firms.

2. The Institutional Aspects of the Dutch Markets

At the end of 1993 there were 560 firms listed on the Amsterdam Stock Exchange (ASE), the only stock exchange in the Netherlands, with a total market value of a little under Dfl. 500,000 million and a total turnover of Dfl. 250,000 million. Of the 560 listed firms, 488 were domestic and of these 239 were not investment trusts.

The ASE is divided into three kinds of markets: the Official Market (OM); the first-tier market for the listing of large and foreign companies; the Parallel Market (PM); the second-tier market for smaller firms; the unofficial market, a market for unofficially quoted firms. The PM in the Netherlands, like its counterparts in other European countries, was to act as an organized equity market for small and medium-sized companies with growth opportunities. Generally speaking, its listing requirements were less stringent than those for the OM. This helped small and young firms to raise equity capital. In its early years the PM was quite successful and there were more new listings on the PM than on the OM. But the board of the ASE decided that as of November 1993 the PM should merge with the OM.

A distinctive feature of the Dutch economy is the lack of a market for corporate control. All the listed Dutch firms have adopted one or more defense measures to protect themselves from the threat of hostile takeovers. There has never been a successful hostile takeover in the Netherlands. There has been relatively very few mergers of listed companies and all of them were realized in a friendly manner.

The structure of capital market in the Netherlands is rather unique. A few large multinational companies with worldwide operations, such as Shell, Philips, Unilever, DSM, and AKZO, dominate this market. Royal Dutch alone represents more than 30% of the market capitalization and about 14% of the turnover. The five largest firms are responsible for 60% of the total market capitalization and 33% of the turnover.

Although the importance of their role in the overall economy and the capital markets of the Netherlands has diminished over the years, these firms still have a formidable presence in the Dutch markets.[2] At the same time, the Dutch market can also be characterized by the presence of a large number of small-sized companies and a relative absence of medium-sized firms.[3] These smaller firms, like their much larger counterparts, are heavily involved in international activities. Faced with a small domestic market, many firms in the Netherlands have found their survival dependent on success in the foreign markets.[4] Given this unique distribution of company size and the strong international orientation, the Dutch market is an ideal market for exploring the possible differences which may exist with respect to the characteristics which differentiate firms listed only on a national exchange from those listed on an international exchange as well.

3. Factors Motivating Firms to List Abroad

The principal question this study was designed to answer was one of determining what factor(s) contribute to a decision by a Dutch firm to have its shares listed on a foreign stock exchange. To this end, we conducted a survey of 40 Dutch firms with their shares listed on the Amsterdam Stock Exchange and on at least one exchange outside of the Netherlands. The process consisted of an initial mailing of a questionnaire and a follow-up telephone interview to clarify vague responses and/or fill in any missing information. The overall useable response rate was 80%. The financial officers of these firms were asked to indicate their motives for the international listing decision, and to elaborate on their choice for the specific country and the corresponding stock exchange. These rationales are classified into the following categories, and are summarized in Table 1.[5]

3.1 Financial Factors

Overall, 43% of the respondents indicated that financial considerations are the most important factors for listing the firm's shares on a foreign exchange. The motive most frequently cited, among these, relates to a desire by the firm to increase the potential investor base. Cross-border listings provide the firm the opportunity to widen its ownership base, which at the limit, can dampen the volatility of the firm's stock price. This can be accomplished when the firm's equity is traded in a thin local market and it chooses to cross-list its shares on a highly liquid (and deep) exchange elsewhere.[6] Additionally, even when the liquidity difference between the foreign and the home exchange is not significant, the expansion of the information set available to the investors can bring about a reduction in volatility. This is driven mainly by a foreign exchange's requirement that the listing firm adapt to the exchange country's national reporting requirements. Finally, consider a scenario under which the international legal and/or institutional factors affect the investment environment in a manner which creates a de-facto segmentation of the markets. Within such a framework, cross-listings would expand the investor base regardless of the preceding liquidity and information arguments. This expansion can lead to a reduction in volatility; an outcome which our sample firms may be seeking. Given that within an agency-theoretic framework a reduction in volatility (systematic or total) is a managerial objective, it is not surprising that the expansion of investor base is the leading motivation for cross-listing decisions.

Insofar as what prompts the firm to choose one particular location/exchange for the cross-listing of its shares, the cost factor (broadly defined) stands out as the leading element. Respondents attached a significant weight to the initial cost of listing, the annual listing fees and the costs of conforming to the exchange's reporting and disclosure requirements. This is not surprising in the light of the fact that the summation of these costs can become material enough to offset the incremental benefits. Consider, for example, the decision by a Dutch firm to cross-list its shares on either the Luxembourg or the Paris exchange. Listing fees on Luxembourg are minimal and the firm can submit its prospectus in the Dutch language. Paris, on the other hand, is known for its high listing and registration fees and all filings have to be done in the French language. Consider, as another example, the choice for a Dutch firm within the U.S. markets: listing on the NYSE or obtaining the right to have its shares traded on the NASDAQ system. The stringent reporting and listing requirements of the NYSE was the stated reason for some of the respondents' choice of the NASDAQ. Philips N.V., on the other hand, had found it beneficial to move its ADRs from NASDAQ to NYSE in order to appeal to those institutional investors which limit their holdings to shares listed on the NYSE.

3.2 Organizational Factors

"Listing our stock in the U.S. was an inevitable action after U.S. sales had amounted to a third of our total sales." Interchanging various locations for the "U.S.", and other fractions for the "one third" fraction in this statement would replicate a set of explanations offered by 20% of the respondents. To these firms, cross-boarder listings are the logical consequence of increased sales activity in a geographical area. As might be expected, these firms are industrial, service or retail businesses. Financial institutions, by contrast, stated that following their customers necessitated their decision to list their shares abroad. This represented 3% of all responses. Finally, a few firms (1.5% of the respondents) indicated that a potential to establish a market for the firm's products motivated their cross-listing. Overall, organizational factors motivated about a quarter of the respondents to cross-list their shares.

3.3 Public Relations and Marketing Factors

Marketing and public relations factors were the chief reasons for 26.5% of the respondents to list their shares on an international exchange. Among these, 19% of the responding firms listed their shares on a foreign exchange in order to increase corporate visibility and to enhance corporate image. Most respondents referred to these outcomes as measures designed to enhance the firm's marketing efforts by broadening product identification in the foreign country. The public relations aspect, i.e., an improved name recognition which exposure in the national financial community brings about, took a distant second position of importance in this category.

Our results also indicate that improved credibility and prestige may play a critical role in the choice of the foreign exchange. This is based on a frequent explanation offered by firms choosing to switch from NASDAQ to NYSE. These firms indicated that they regarded an NYSE listing a more prestigious prize than trading on the NASDAQ, and that switching to the NYSE expressed the firm's intention to upgrade its position in the U.S.

3.4 Other Motives

Many countries impose local ownership requirements on firms operating in their country. Usually, such requirements can be circumvented through joint ventures. However, joint ventures also have the disadvantage of positioning the firm in situations that it might be forced to share its know-how with the local partners. This can be avoided if a listing of the shares on an exchange in the host country would provide a means through which the local ownership requirement is met.

Cross-listings may also generate political support for the listing firm and can be used to reduce the political risk. In our survey, a mere 1.5% of respondents ranked this factor as a major motive to list abroad.

In many countries, firms have established employee stock ownership plans (ESOP's) as a way of motivating their working force. The idea behind these plans is that employees with ownership interests in the firm will perform better than employees without such interests. At the same time, the increased internationalization of the production, sales and service processes has necessitated a greater dependence on foreign labor. Accordingly, firms have found themselves needing to pay more attention to labor relations in foreign affiliates. The incentive effects of stock option and stock purchase plans are likely to be enhanced if the employees have the opportunity to trade their shares on a local exchange. In our sample, about 3% of the respondents considered the perspective of an increased employee motivation as a reason to list abroad.

Table 1 provides a summary of our respondents' overall ranking of the different motives for international listings and the factors that influence their choice of the foreign exchange. The most important factors for the Dutch firms surveyed are: financial, marketing and organizational, in that order.

Table 1

Motives for International Listings and Factors Influencing the Choice of the Exchange

Financial Factors		
increased investor base, dispersion of share ownership	27.5%	
cost of listings, accounting principles	12.5%	
attracting capital	3.0%	
		43.0 %
Organizational Factors		
increased sales activities	20.0%	
follow customers	3.0%	
market potential	1.5%	
		24.5%
Investor Relations, Marketing		
increased corporate image, recognition	19.0%	
publicity	4.5%	
prestige	3.0%	
		26.5%
Political Factors		
entrance to national markets	1.5%	
		1.5%
Employee Motivation		
increased employee interest	3.0%	
		3.0%
Others	1.5%	
		1.5%
TOTAL		100%

Note: Response rates are standardised to add up to 100%.

4. Characteristics of Firms Listing Abroad

While the preceding results shed light on what motivates a firm to list its shares abroad, they are of little help in understanding the differences which may exist between a firm choosing to cross-list its shares abroad and a firm choosing to remain only a nationally listed one. To explore these differences, we compare the financial characteristics of a group of internationally listed firms to those of a group of firms listed only on the Amsterdam Stock Exchange. The criteria for the inclusion of the internationally listed firms in this sample were that (1) their financial data (required for this analysis) could be obtained from either their annual reports or from the Dutch financial newspaper (Het Financieele Dagblad) for the 1989-1992 period and that (2) data on their stock prices for the 1/1/1989 to 12/31/1992 period would be available on Datastream. To avoid the potential problems which the inclusion of financial institutions and firms in the insurance and real estate industries may bring about, these firms were excluded from the sample, leaving us with a total of 21 internationally listed firms.

To compare the characteristics of internationally listed firms with those of the nationally listed firms, we restricted the sample of the latter to firms in the same lines of business as the former. From this tentative comparison group, we then retained only those firms nearest in size to their internationally listed counterparts.[7]

The two groups of firms were compared on the basis of their average performance over the 1989-1992 period with respect to: two measures of financial leverage (debt ratio and interest coverage), two measures of liquidity (current and quick ratios), three measures of profitability (sales profitability, return on assets and return on equity), the dividend payout ratio, two market value ratios (the dividend yield and the market to book ratio), total assets and the stock price variability (measured by the standard deviation of the stock price over the four-year period covered). The results are reported in Table 2.

Table 2

Charateristics Comparisons of the Internationally-Listed and Nationally-Listed Firms

Basis of Comparison	International		National Only		t-statistic 0:
	Mean	Std. Error	Mean	Std. Error	Int'l = Nat'l
Debt ratio	0.71	(0.01)	0.69	(0.02)	0.62
Interest coverage ratio	8.34	(1.54)	9.02	(1.60)	-0.19
Current ratio	1.40	(0.04)	1.27	(0.05)	2.39*
Quick ratio	0.91	(0.03)	0.95	(0.04)	-0.97
Sales profitability	9.01	(0.65)	15.49	(4.58)	-1.81†
Return on assets	12.8	(0.78)	10.38	(0.63)	2.56*
Return on equity	21.69	(1.78)	16.96	(1.77)	1.96†
Payout ratio	32.47	(2.03)	32.46	(3.16)	0.26
Dividend yield	2.67	(0.29)	7.76	(2.97)	-2.09*
Market to book ratio	2.50	(0.29)	2.02	(0.20)	1.45
Total assets	37937.29	(11167.82)	959.16	(95.87)	2.75*
Stock price variability	61.4		421.7		-7.24*

* Significant at the 5% level
† Significant at the 10% level

The results indicate that compared to those listed only on the ASE, firms which have their shares cross-listed on an international exchange are significantly more liquid, as judged by their current ratios. Further, these firms have a significantly lower profit margin ratio. However, due to their better asset utilization their return on assets is significantly higher than their peers. They, consequently, produce a higher return on their shareholders' equity. Further, despite the fact that their payout ratio is not any different, their marginally higher market to book ratio puts their dividend yield at a significantly lower level. As expected, these firms are siginificantly and substantially larger as well.

Finally, the results indicate that the volatility of the share prices of these firms is significantly lower than those listed only on ASE. This lends support to the hypothesis that cross-listings are motivated by a desire to circumvent the barriers present in mildly segmented capital markets.

5. Summary and Conclusions

We compared various characteristics and the financial performance of two sets of Dutch firms: those listed on the Amsterdam Stock Exchange (ASE) and at least one other exchange outside of the Netherlands and a comparable group listed only on the ASE. Comparing the two sets of firms with respect to their leverage, liquidity, profitability and market value ratios we find the two groups significantly different from one another. Cross-border listed firms are more liquid and produce a better return on their assets despite their lower profit margin on sales. They also generate a higher return on their shareholders' equity and have higher market values than firms listed only on the national exchange. We also observe that cross-border listed firms exhibit less stock price volatility than the otherwise comparable group of nationally-listed firms.

The question of managerial motivations for cross-border listing decisions was also studied. Results, based on a survey of chief financial executives of a sample of internationally-listed Dutch firms, indicate that financial, organizational and investor-relations reasons are the most frequently cited reasons for cross-border listings.

Acknowledgement

The authors would like to thank the participants at the second annual Global Finance Conference, San Diego, USA and an anonymous referee for their comments and suggestions.

References

Alexander, G.J., C.S. Eun and S. Janakiramanan, 1987, Asset pricing and dual listing on foreign capital markets: a note, Journal of Finance, pp. 151-158.

Alexander, G.J., C.S. Eun and S. Janakiramanan, 1988, International listings and stock returns: some empirical evidence, Journal of Financial and Quantitative Analysis, June, pp. 135-151.

Barclay, M., R. Litzenberger and J. Warner, 1990, Private information, trading volume, and stock return variances, Review of Financial Studies, pp. 233-254.

Foerster, S. and A. Karolyi (1993) International listings of stocks: the case of Canada and the U.S., Journal of International Business Studies, pp. 763-784.

Howe, J. and K. Kelm, 1987, The stock price impacts of overseas listings, Financial Management, pp. 51-56.

Howe, J. and J. Madura, 1990, The impact of international listings on risk: implications for capital market integration, Journal of Banking and Finance, pp. 1133-1142.

Howe, J., J. Madura and A. Tucker, 1993 International listings and risk, Journal of International Money and Finance, pp. 99-110.

Lee, I., 1991, The impact of overseas listings on shareholder wealth: the case of the London and Toronto stock exchange, Journal of Business Finance & Accounting, pp. 583-592.

Makhija, A. K. and R. Nachtmann, 1989, Variance effects of cross-listings of NYSE stocks in Tokyo, working paper Katz Graduate School of Business, University of Pittsburgh.

Mayer, C. and I. Alexander, 1991, Stock markets and corporate performance: a comparison of quoted and unquoted firms, Centre for Economic Policy Research Discussion Paper, No. 571.

McConnell, J.J. and G.C. Sanger, 1984, New listings on the NYSE, Financial Analysts Journal, pp. 34-38.

Mitto, R.S., 1992, Managerial perceptions of the net benefits of foreign listing: Canadian evidence, Journal of International Financial Management and Accounting, pp. 40-62.

Saudagaran, S.M., 1988, An empirical study of selected factors influencing the decision to list on foreign stock exchanges, Journal of International Business Studies, pp. 101-127.

Stapleton, R. and M. Subrehmanyam (1977) Market imperfections, capital market equilibrium and corporation finance, Journal of Finance, pp. 307-319.

Endnotes

[1] The composition of sample firms consisted of: 13 Canadian, 10 Japanese, seven Australian, two South African and one each Dutch and British.

[2] Consider, for example, the fact that 55 percent of all employment opportunities in the Netherlands are supplied by firms listed on the Amsterdam Stock Exchange.

[3] The few medium-sized firms that operate in this market tend to be smaller than their counterparts in neighboring countries, such as Belgium and Germany.

[4] Exports, for examples, amount to 60 percent of national income and the percentage of firms with more than 100 employees involved in exporting is nearly 50 percent.

[5] It must be noted that although the rationales are classified in five different categories, this does not imply that the motives are completely independent. On the contrary, when a firm applies for a listing there are usually several motives which induce such an action.

[6] Novo Industri's listing of its shares on the NYSE is a classical example of this.

[7] Two definitions of size were used: (1) the market value of common shares outstanding and (2) total assets. The results reported in Table 2 pertain to the total assets definition of size. Identical results, not reported here, were obtained with the alternate definition.

Alternative International Equity Offering Methods and their Impact on Liquidity

Alexander Arauner
and
Mario Levis

City University Business School

Abstract

This paper examines the effects of a public US listing of non-US companies on the liquidity of the underlying shares. Our sample consists of 231 international equity offerings from 33 countries; 86 companies conducted a public offering on NYSE or NASDAQ, and 145 companies raised capital in the private placement market. We find that the decision between a public offering or a private placement under Rule 144A has an impact on the cost of capital of a firm. Our cost-benefit analysis shows that the benefits of a public offering outweigh the cost advantage of private placements. We provide empirical evidence that the interaction between the domestic and the foreign stock market leads to lower bid-ask spreads for internationally listed firms.

1. Introduction

In recent years international equity markets have experienced substantial growth in cross-border equity trading and global issuance of equities. Issuing activity has involved companies from more than 40 different countries world-wide. The need to raise equity capital at competitive rates has contributed to the development of international equity offerings of non-US companies with a significant US tranche. The main vehicle for foreign companies to access the US market is ADRs (American Depositary Receipts) which can be publicly listed or traded over-the-counter. The total capital raised via ADRs has constantly grown from US$ 2.6 billion in 1990 to US$ 14 billion in 1994 with an increasing trend towards a full listing on NYSE or NASDAQ.

Although ADRs have developed into an important instrument to raise capital internationally, existing research remains limited. Previous research has mainly looked at the efficiency of the ADR market (e.g. Kato, Linn, Schallheim (1991), Officer and Hoffmeister (1987), and Rosenthal (1983)), the impact of the ADR on the underlying stock (Jayaraman, Shastri, and Tandon (1993) and Lau and Diltz (1994)), and the integration effects of international equity offerings (Doukas and Yung (1992) and Marr, Trimble, and Varma (1991)).

Freedman's (1991) model shows that an international cross-listing changes the market-microstructure of a stock. Her results suggest an increase in the total trading volume, an increase in the depth[1] of the market, and in the informativeness[2] of prices of the dually listed security. Empirical research, such as Damodaran, Liu, and Harlow (1993), Foerster and Karolyi (1993), and Noronha, Sarin, and Saudagaran (1995) also find some evidence for an increase in the liquidity of stocks that became internationally listed. Foerster and Karolyi's (1993) results show that Canadian companies listing on an US exchange experience an increase in their trading volume in the post-listing period. Noronha, Sarin, and Saudagaran (1995) find an increase in the depth and the trading volume from the pre- to the post-listing period for a sample of internationally listed US companies but no change in bid-ask spreads. Domowitz, Glen, and Madhavan (1994) examine the impact of Mexican companies' ADR programmes on the market quality of their primary Mexican stock market. Their results show a decrease in bid-ask spreads but a lower depth in the post-listing period which indicates there may have been a trade-off between bid-ask spreads and depth.

Foreign issuers can use two alternative methods to raise equity capital in the US market. The decision between a public offering and a private placement under Rule 144A bears important policy implications since it affects the investor base, liquidity, and disclosure requirements of the company. Such changes may have a direct effect on the value of the firm and its cost of capital. Merton (1987) and Amihud and Mendelson (1986) modify the original CAPM framework and provide evidence that additional factors influence expected returns. The latter, for example, show that firms with a higher liquidity have lower expected returns.

Differences in liquidity across financial assets can arise because of differences in the market-microstructure in which securities are traded. Previous studies[3] show that the bid-ask spread of a company is related to the number of shareholders holding the asset which reflects the public availability of information about the asset. This forms the link between Merton's (1987) model, in which expected returns increase with systematic risk, firm specific risk, and relative market value and decrease with the relative size of the firm's investor base[4] (or as characterised by Merton "the degree of investor recognition"), and Amihud and Mendelson's (1989) spread effect.

The purpose of this paper is to provide further empirical evidence of the impact of international listings on liquidity, and hence on the cost of capital. It is implicitly assumed that the decision to raise equity capital in the US market is motivated by a desire to lower financing costs. This paper conducts an evaluation of private placements and public offerings in a cost-benefit framework and an analysis of the trade-offs involved. Our results show that public offerings have, on average, higher total direct costs than private placements. But these higher costs are traded off by a higher liquidity and a larger potential shareholder base for internationally listed firms.

Our sample consists of 231 international equity offerings (over a 10-year period from 1984 to 1994) from 33 countries. Therefore, it offers an unique opportunity to test the liquidity implications of international cross-listing on a major US stock exchange

(NYSE and NASDAQ) compared to a private placement in the US market. Our spread estimates show that internationally listed firms have lower bid-ask spreads for each size-based portfolio. Further analysis provides evidence that internationally listed firms have lower bid-ask spreads after controlling for other factors. Our results also show that the volume traded on the foreign stock exchange influences the bid-ask spreads on the domestic stock exchange. Based on Amihud and Mendelson (1988) we quantify the liquidity benefit of an international listing. For our average sample firm we calculate the present value of the saving in trading costs showing that the present value of saving outweighs the average total direct costs of a public offering. Our results show that the decision to conduct a public offering instead of a private placement in the US market reduces the cost of capital by 11 basis points.

Previous research analysing domestic exchange listings and international cross-listings only examines changes in the liquidity from the pre-listing period to the post-listing period. Our approach to assess the liquidity impact of international listings is different from previous research. We choose a three-year data period (from January 1992 to December 1994) for all international equity offerings to calculate bid-ask spreads based on the method of George, Kaul, and Nimalendran (1991).

The remainder of the paper is organised as follows. Section 2 outlines the institutional characteristics discussing the factors that influence the benefits and the costs of raising equity capital for public offerings and private placements. Section 3 discusses the results of previous studies that examined differences in liquidity across various financial assets. Section 4 describes the sample and the methodology. This section is split into three parts explaining the sample selection procedure, the data period, and the estimation of bid-ask spreads. Our empirical findings are presented in Section 5. Part 1 of this section explains the estimation of the autocorrelation coefficient which is used to estimate bid-ask spreads. Part 2 provides evidence of differences in bid-ask spreads for listed and internationally unlisted firms. Part 3 examines the factors influencing bid-ask spreads. Part 4 evaluates the trade-off between the costs and benefits associated with each offering method. Section 6 concludes the article.

2. Institutional Aspects

Foreign issuers seeking to raise equity capital in the US market have a choice between a public offering or a private placement. The two methods differ markedly, since the costs and benefits of each method are influenced by the regulatory framework governing the issuance of equity by non-US registered companies.

Although precise estimates of the cost of raising equity depend on company specific factors we provide some comparative figures for the gross underwriting spread and other direct expenses which make up the two components of the total direct cost of raising capital[5]. Other direct expenses include registration fees and printing, legal, and auditing costs and can be anywhere between US$500,000 to US$1 million for a public offering, because the registration process with the SEC involves high legal and accounting costs (Velli, 1994). Listing on the NYSE involves an initial fee of US$ 100,000 and an annual fee based on the number of shares listed. But the maximum annual fee to be paid by a company is limited to US$ 500,000. The cost for a private placement under Rule 144A is lower and runs between US$ 250,000 to US$ 500,000 for accounting and legal fees. In order to obtain some comparative estimates for gross underwriting spreads, we carried out some limited investigations using data of 37 public offerings and 20 private placements. Our results indicate that the gross underwriting spread for private placements is 4.10% while the equivalent average spread for public offerings is 4.62%.

An additional factor to be considered in the choice of the method for an international offering is the time required to conduct a public offering or a private placement. This time constraint can become a very important cost factor if the market conditions for issuing equity deteriorate, possibly leading to higher indirect costs of raising capital. The time required differs markedly between the methods: it takes between 6 to 8 months to conduct a public offerings but only 2 months to conduct a private placement.

The issuing firm must also consider the possible trade-off between the costs and the benefits of a public offering. Public offerings involve higher initial costs because the SEC does not recognise a company's compliance with the regulations of its domestic stock exchange[6]. The main difference between a public offering and a private placement under Rule 144A is the requirement for foreign issuers to provide a quantitative reconciliation[7] of their financial statements according to US Generally Accepted Accounting Principles (GAAP). This so called "full disclosure" approach often forces foreign companies to disclose more comprehensive information than required under their home country regulations. But the SEC believes that high standards of transparency in financial reporting enhance market efficiency because a listing offers trade reporting and facilitates a comparison of companies across countries (Breeden, 1994). Therefore, monitoring and transaction costs for investors may be lower since a listed company is treated under US law as any other US company and trading takes place on an organised stock exchange which provides more active trading and superior trade reporting.

Although, by introducing Rule 144A in 1990, the SEC relaxed its regulations for issuance and trading of non-registered foreign securities private placements still face some major drawbacks. Rule 144A only allows the sale of privately placed securities to investors other than QIBs (Qualified Institutional Buyers)[8], thus limiting the potential shareholder base. Liquidity in the secondary market is very low because those foreign issues trade on the over-the-counter (OTC) Electronic Bulletin Board market which has no volume reporting or real-time-quotes. All these differences should be reflected in the bid-ask spreads.

3. Cross-Sectional Variation in Liquidity

In the literature liquidity has generally been proxied by three different measures: (1) bid-ask spreads, (2) volume, and (3) depth. In the following section we only discuss the factors influencing bid-ask spreads and volume. Previous research has shown that bid-ask spreads are related to a number of other variables including the price level, trading volume, and volatility. Benston and Hagerman (1974), Stoll (1978), and Barclay and Smith (1988) provide evidence that price level, return volatility, and volume explain a significant fraction of the cross-sectional variation in bid-ask spreads. Jegadeesh and Subrahmanyam (1993) confirm these findings by examining the change in bid-ask spreads of the underlying shares after the introduction of the S&P 500 index futures contract, and control for price, return volatility, and volume. It is usually argued that a higher volume should result in lower spreads because it offers market makers greater flexibility to offset inventory imbalances. Larger volatility should lead to higher spreads because it implies higher inventory risk. The inverse relationship between price level and spreads is due to a lower fixed-cost component. For a given number of shares per trade, fixed costs can be spread across more dollars in high priced stocks.

The model of Chowdry and Nanda (1991) predicts that multimarket trading affects the liquidity of an asset. In order to test implications for the bid-ask spread of internationally listed stocks, we need to include a fourth explanatory variable, which models potential competition of the additional trading location. Neal (1987) develops a model of bid-ask spreads based on the theory of contestable markets to examine the effect of multiple-listed options on spreads. This model relates the bid-ask spread to trading volume, price, volatility, and competition and predicts lower spreads for a market with potential competition. The competition variable is constructed as a multiple listing dummy variable which is zero if the option is listed on a single exchange and one for multiple-listed options. Their results show that multiple-listed options have lower bid-ask spreads than options which are listed on a single exchange.

Freedman's (1991) model for international cross-listings predicts that an additional trading location leads to an increase in the total trading volume (foreign + domestic volume). This suggests that volume traded on the foreign stock exchange should have a positive influence on the domestic trading volume. Domestic trading volume and foreign trading volume could also be influenced by arbitrage opportunities between the foreign stock exchange and the domestic stock exchange. These arbitrage opportunities could arise from currency fluctuations leading to differences in the price of the US dollar denominated ADR and the underlying security traded in the respective domestic currency. Kim, Mathur, and Szakmary (1995), for example, provide some evidence to suggest that changes in the exchange rate have become more important as a pricing factor for ADRs in recent years. The relatively high volatility in the currency market in recent years could have opened up more arbitrage opportunities leading to a higher trading volume.

4. Sample and Methodology

4.1 Sample selection

To identify international equity offerings from non-US companies which included a US tranche, we search two data sources: a) the ADR data base of The Bank of New York, and b) Omnibase, a data base for international securities issues from Security Data Company (SDC). We obtain an initial sample of 465 international companies that made an international equity offering between 1984 and 1994. In a next step we split our preliminary sample of international equity offerings into two subsamples:

1.) Internationally listed firms;
2.) Internationally unlisted firms.

To be included in the sample of internationally listed firms, a company had to be listed on the NYSE or the NASDAQ by December 1994. Information concerning a firm's listing status and their date of listing is obtained from the NYSE and NASDAQ. We obtain an initial sample of 187 internationally listed firms (115 NYSE and 72 NASDAQ listings) and 278 internationally unlisted firms. We require for all international equity offerings that at least 50 historical daily closing prices are available on Datastream and that trading volume is not zero for two consecutive weeks which are part of the sample period[9]. These criteria eliminate 54 internationally listed companies[10] and 133 not internationally listed firms from our sample. This high rate of exclusion for not internationally listed firms is mainly due to non-availability of daily stock price data of companies from emerging markets (e.g. 23 Chinese companies, 28 Indian companies, 19 Indonesian companies, 16 Israeli companies, and 10 Hungarian companies). This leaves us with a final sample of 145 internationally unlisted companies.

Our preliminary sample of 133 internationally listed firms (84 NYSE and 49 NASDAQ listings) is reduced further because we only consider international cross-listings. This particular criterion, which requires an internationally listed firm to be also listed in its country of origin (or as referred to in the following on its "domestic stock exchange"), eliminates 47 companies (18 on the NYSE and 29 on NASDAQ). Thus, our final sample includes a total of 86 internationally listed firms.

Table 1 shows the distribution of our final sample of 231 companies that issued equity internationally between 1984 and 1994 by country of origin. The wide geographic distribution across 33 countries has been driven by two main factors. The first factor is privatisations that have taken place all over the world from the mid-80's onwards. The second wave of international offerings has been fuelled by companies from emerging markets which have been assisted by international institutions, such as the IFC (International Finance Corporation) for example, to tap international markets. The subsample of internationally listed companies comprises 66 listed on the NYSE and 20 listed on NASDAQ. This subsample is compared to our subsample of internationally unlisted equity offerings which consists of 145 companies.

Table 1

Distribution of sample firms that issued equity internationally between 1984 - 1994 by country of origin and offering size of US tranche: Internationally listed vs. internationally unlisted companies

The sample consists of 231 international equity offerings from 33 countries world-wide. All 231 international equity offerings are from non-US companies but included a US tranche. All firms are listed on their domestic stock exchange. 86 companies from 21 different countries are listed on a US stock exchange whereby 20 companies are listed on NASDAQ and 66 on NYSE. The sample of internationally unlisted firms consists of 145 companies from 28 different countries. The last row of the table reports the average size of the US tranche in US$ million.

Table 1 (continued)

Country of origin	Internationally listed firms			Internationally unlisted firms	Total sample
	All listings	NYSE	NASDAQ		
Argentina	4	3	1	5	9
Australia	2	1	1	5	7
Austria				1	1
Belgium				2	2
Brazil	1	1			1
Canada	7	3	4	7	14
Chile	8	8		2	10
Columbia	1	1			1
Denmark	3	3		1	4
Finland	2	1	1	7	9
France	5	4	1	13	18
Germany	1	1		4	5
Greece				2	2
Hong Kong	1	1		6	7
Indonesia				7	7
Ireland	2	1	1		2
Italy	2	2		4	6
Japan	4	4			4
Korea	2	2		7	9
Mexico	8	8		5	13
Netherlands				2	2
New Zealand	1	1			1
Norway	3	2	1	7	10
Philippines				7	7
Singapore				3	3
Spain	6	6		5	11
Sweden	3		3	11	14
Switzerland				2	2
Taiwan				7	7
Thailand				7	7
Turkey				1	1
UK	20	13	7	14	34
Venezuela				1	1
Total	86	66	20	145	231
Average offering size (in US$ m)					
Mean	230.12	280.54	58.69	106.40	143.10
Median	114.05	157.25	50.75	48.80	65.12

Table 1 also reports the average offering size of the US tranche which is US$ 143.10 million for the total sample. But the offering size of internationally listed companies is larger (US$ 230.12 million), on average, than of private placements (US$ 106.10 million). The larger offering size of public offerings is due to the offering size of NYSE-listed companies (US$ 280.54 million) compared to NASDAQ-listings (US$ 58.69 million).

4.2 Data period

For all international equity offerings, our data covers the period between January 1992 and December 1994. The choice of our data period to calculate spreads and their related variables is influenced by two considerations. Firstly, our aim is to provide recent evidence of how the choice of the offering method influences the liquidity of the stock in its domestic market. Our two subsamples differ in that 40 percent of the internationally listed firms were listed before 1991 but none of the internationally unlisted equity offerings in our sample took place before mid-1990[11]. Hence, we believe that an alternative approach investigating bid-ask spreads for a subsequent period (e.g. 1 or 2 years) after the respective listing or offering date could bias the results. This is due to the fact that many markets have improved their trading systems since the beginning of the 90s, and thus possibly increased the liquidity of their market. But Barry and Brown (1984) find an association between the period of listing and security returns. Since the period of listing could also influence bid-ask spreads, we test the robustness of our results taking account of the period of listing. However, we find that the differences in the period since listing or since offering equity (for internationally unlisted firms) between our two samples do not bias our results[12]. Secondly, this approach enables us to include international initial public offerings (IPOs)[13] in our sample for which no pre-listing period data is available.

All our calculations for companies listing (listed sample) or offering equity (internationally unlisted sample) before the beginning of our data period (January 1992) are based on 3-years data. Due to our approach to use only post-listing data, as explained above, the calculations for companies that were listed between 1992 and 1994 are based on data from their listing date onwards through to the end of 1994. This exclusion of pre-listing period data ensures that we do not bias our results if an international cross-listing changes the market-microstructure of a stock as suggested by Freedman (1991). The calculations for internationally unlisted companies that raised equity between 1992 and 1994 are based on the same principles as applied to internationally listed companies. Hence, we only use data from their offering date onwards through to the end of 1994 (the post-offering period) because an international equity offering, although unlisted, is expected to have an effect on the microstructure of a stock.

The data on prices and microstructure-related variables used in this study were collected from Datastream. Our data consists of daily observations on stock prices, which are used to calculate bid-ask spreads, and weekly observations on domestic trading volume, foreign trading volume, variance of returns, and closing prices. Domestic trading volume is calculated from the weekly closing price times the weekly number of shares traded, and then converted into US dollar at the corresponding weekly exchange rate. Foreign trading volume is calculated by multiplying the number of foreign shares traded and the weekly price (in US$). Weekly closing prices are converted into US dollar at the corresponding exchange rate. In order to avoid the problem of a positive spurious correlation between the spread and volatility, as pointed out by Neal (1987), we use variances calculated from weekly returns. Data on the amount of equity issued in the foreign market and the gross-underwriting spread were obtained from the ADR data base of The Bank of New York.

4.3 Estimation of bid-ask spreads

Two alternative trading systems[14] can be distinguished, as described by Pagano and Roell (1991): Whereas in an auction market (or often referred to as order-driven system) all outstanding orders are transacted at a single price via a centralised mechanism, in a dealership market (or referred to as quote-driven market) they are placed with individual dealers, who execute them at pre-set prices[15]. Since our sample[16] includes a large number of stocks which are traded under an auction market system in their domestic market, and therefore quoted bid-ask spreads cannot be observed, we need to employ a method estimating bid-ask spreads from transaction returns.

Roll (1984) derives a simple measure of the spread which is based on two main assumptions: (i) that markets are informationally efficient; (ii) that the probability distribution of observed price changes is stationary. Roll (1984) also assumes for simplicity that all transactions are with the market maker and that the spread is held constant over time. The intuition behind Roll's spread measure is that price changes will only occur if unanticipated information is received by market participants. If no new information arrives it is reasonable to assume that successive transactions are equally likely to be purchases or sales as traders arrive randomly on both sides of the market. However, if the last transaction is at the bid (ask) price, the next price change cannot be negative (positive) because there is no new information. Therefore, the observed price changes are no longer independent and the effective individual spread s_i can be inferred from the first-order serial covariance of price changes

$$S_i = 200 * \sqrt{-Cov(R_{iTt}, R_{iTt-1})} \tag{1}$$

where R_{iTt} is the difference in daily log prices $\ln(P_t/P_{t-1})$.

Previous papers, however, have argued that Roll's estimator provides downward biased spread estimates because it only measures the order processing costs. Order processing costs reflect the market makers' compensation for handling the transaction. Glosten (1987) and Stoll (1989) show that adverse selection and/or inventory costs are two potential sources of a downward bias in Roll's spread estimates. Adverse selection costs arise from the presence of asymmetric information between the market maker and his counterparties. Inventory holding costs are due to the risk of price fluctuations faced by the market maker if he holds a high level of inventory.

George, Kaul, and Nimalendran (1991) show that time variation in expected returns may lead to an additional downward bias in spread estimates and propose two alternative estimators. Their estimators are based on the findings of Conrad and Kaul (1988, 1989) who show that expected returns of portfolios of stocks vary through time and are positively autocorrelated. Moreover, Conrad, Kaul, and Nimalendran (1991) find that individual security returns contain a positively expected return component, although they are negatively autocorrelated. This positive autocovariance will lead to a downward bias in the spread estimates. In order to take account of time variation in expected returns, George, Kaul, and Nimalendran (1991) propose the following estimator

$$S_i = 200 * \sqrt{-Cov(E_{iTi}, E_{iTt-1})} \qquad (2)$$

where E_t is the (time varying) expected return. Kofman and Moser (1995) use this estimator which employs a model for the conditional expectation of E_t. Based on the evidence in Conrad and Kaul (1988) they impose a first order autoregressive process to estimate the expected return from the transaction price series

$$E_t = R_t - \rho * R_{t-1} \qquad (3)$$

where ρ is the first-order autocorrelation coefficient. In order to estimate the autocorrelation coefficient, we employ a similar technique as Kofman and Moser (1995)[17]. All the spread estimates are calculated using the autocorrelation coefficient obtained from our preliminary analysis.

5. Empirical Results

5.1 Estimation of autocorrelation coefficient

To adjust for the bias in Roll's estimator, requires an estimate of the autocorrelation coefficient. We construct an equally-weighted "market portfolio" to calculate daily portfolio returns from bid quotes for the 1990 to 1994 period. According to George, Kaul, and Nimalendran (1991) returns based on bid-to-bid prices reflect the effects of time varying expected returns. Our "market portfolio" is comprised of 100 randomly selected UK companies, drawn from the FTSE-350 list, because bid quotes are only available for UK companies. These "market portfolio" returns are used to estimate the first-order autocorrelation coefficient. Our results show that the assumption of an AR(1) process for expected returns appears to describe the behaviour of portfolio returns very well. We obtain an estimate of the autocorrelation coefficient of 0.28[18] and assume that this is the same for all the stocks in our sample. Hence, all our spread estimates are calculated using an autocorrelation coefficient equally to 0.28.

5.2 Relation of bid-ask spreads and market value

Table 2 reports average daily estimates of the bid-ask spread for listed companies and unlisted companies. Each spread estimate is calculated for individual firms during the observation period and then averaged across firms. Since spreads are negatively related to firm size, we split each subsample into four portfolios based on market value. This enables us to verify the validity of our spread estimates and to compare our resulting estimates across different size classes. The average estimates are all positive and range between 1.36 percent for portfolio 1 (largest) of the listed firms and 2.77 percent for portfolio 4 (smallest) of the internationally unlisted firms. The fact that we obtain positive average estimates[19], even for the largest firms (portfolio 1), indicates that our adjustment for positive autocorrelation in portfolio returns reduces the downward bias in spread estimates substantially.

Table 2
Spread estimates of internationally listed vs. internationally unlisted equity offerings

The Table below shows the average spread estimates of the sample of internationally listed firms and the sample of internationally unlisted firms. Each sample is split into four portfolios based on market value. The test-statistics (t-statistic) are performed as a paired t-test of the difference in the estimates for each group. The spread estimates are calculated using a variant of the GKN-estimator which adjusts for autocorrelation in portfolio returns. A percentage spread is calculated as

$$S_i = 200 * \sqrt{-Cov(E_{iTi}, E_{iTt-1})}$$

where E_t is the (time varying) expected return.

Portfolio	Internationally listed companies			Internationally unlisted companies			t-statistic
	Sample size	Average market value (in US$ million)	Bid-ask spread	Sample size	Average market value (in US$ million)	Bid-ask spread	
1 (largest)	21	17151.28	1.36	37	16640.09	1.77	-3.06
2	22	4956.17	1.46	36	1962.96	1.62	-0.98
3	22	1484.58	1.62	36	644.28	1.96	-1.64
4 (smallest)	21	376.98	2.22	36	219.92	2.77	-1.97
All firms	86	5927.79	1.65	145	4927.56	2.02	-2.35

Our results show that listed companies have significantly lower bid-ask spreads (1.65 percent) than unlisted companies (2.03 percent). This is verified by performing a paired t-test of the difference in the two estimates. A t-value of -2.35 indicates that the spread estimates for listed companies are significantly lower than for unlisted equity offerings. Table 2 also shows that this finding is robust when we split each subsample into four equal size-based portfolios[20] and compare the means of the corresponding portfolios (see column 4 for internationally listed companies and column 7 for unlisted companies). In addition Table 2 confirms the negative relationship between size and bid-ask spreads, as found by previous studies, showing that bid-ask spreads increase from portfolio 1 to 4 for listed companies (1.36 percent vs. 2.22 percent) as well as for internationally unlisted firms (1.77 percent vs. 2.77 percent).

To further examine the relationship between firm size and bid-ask spread and the influence of a listing on the liquidity of international equity offerings, we regress the estimated bid-ask spread of each company (SPREAD$_i$) on the log of size (as measured by the market value) of each individual company (LNSIZE$_i$), and on a listing dummy variable (DLIST$_i$) which is assigned a value of one in the case of an internationally listed company and a value of zero for not internationally listed equity offerings. The t-statistics are adjusted for heteroskedasticity of the residuals by White's consistent covariance estimator.

Our regression results in Table 3 corroborate our previous findings. The coefficient for LNSIZE$_i$ is negative (-0.2045) and highly significant (t = -5.01) confirming the strong negative relationship between firm size and bid-ask spread found in previous studies. The coefficient for (DLIST$_i$) is negative (-0.2358) and significant (t = -2.07) indicating that listed firms have lower bid-ask spreads than unlisted companies after controlling for firm size.

Table 3

Impact of international listing on liquidity of international equity offerings

The Table below gives the OLS estimates of the following equation:

$$SPREAD_i = B_0 + B_1\ LNSIZE_i + B_2\ DLIST_i$$

The dependent variable is the individual spread estimate (SPREAD$_i$). The independent variables are: LNSIZE$_i$, the natural logarithm of the market value; DLIST$_i$, a dummy variable which is 1 if a company is internationally listed and 0 otherwise. t-statistics for OLS regressions are adjusted for heteroscedasticity of the residuals by White's consistent covariance estimator.

Variable	Estimated Coefficient	t-statistic
Intercept	3.4704	11.38
LNSIZE$_i$	-0.2045	-5.01
DLIST$_i$	-0.2358	-2.07
Adjusted-R^2	0.19	

5.3 Factors influencing bid-ask spreads

Table 4 presents summary statistics[21] of the variables which are assumed to influence bid-ask spreads. Whereas the price level and variance do not differ substantially between listed and unlisted companies, the former group has on average a much higher trading volume. Although the difference between the mean and the median values for the weekly trading volume on the domestic stock exchange suggest the presence of positive skewness, the differences between the two groups remain sizeable. Moreover, internationally listed stocks are traded in substantial amounts on the foreign stock exchange. The weekly average volume traded on the foreign stock exchange is US$ 31.18 million compared to US$ 91.58 million on the domestic stock exchange, and therefore reaches about 33 percent of the domestic volume. These results, the substantially higher domestic trading volume and the additional high foreign volume for internationally listed firms, are consistent with Freedman's (1991) model which predicts an increase in total trading volume (foreign + domestic volume) for internationally listed stocks. The increase in total trading could also be due to arbitrage opportunities between the domestic and foreign stock exchange. Kim, Mathur, and Szakmary (1995) find that changes in the exchange rate have become more important as a pricing factor for ADRs in recent years.

Table 4

Sample statistics. Bid-ask spread, weekly closing price (in US$), and weekly return variance. Market value, domestic trading volume, and foreign trading volume (all in US$ million)

The Table below shows summary statistics of all our sample firms for which data on trading volume (domestic and/or foreign trading volume) are available. Bid-ask spreads are reported in percent. Market value, domestic trading volume, and foreign trading volume are reported in US$ million. Weekly closing prices are reported in US$. Weekly return variances are reported in percent. The test statistics (t-statistic) are reported for a standard t-test for equality in means for the internationally listed sample and the internationally unlisted sample.

Variables	Combined sample	Internationally listed sample	Internationally unlisted sample	t-statistic
Sample size	202	66	136	
Bid-ask spread				
Mean	1.89	1.60	2.03	-3.60
Median	1.73	1.46	1.94	
Market value (in US$ m)				
Mean	5713.39	6755.19	5207.82	0.90
Median	1678.65	3309.73	1367.95	
Weekly closing price (in US$)				
Mean	64.10	56.83	67.63	-0.27
Median	9.49	10.30	8.98	
Weekly return variance				
Mean	0.002660	0.002575	0.002702	-0.32
Median	0.001947	0.001841	0.002026	
Weekly trading volume (in US$ m) on domestic stock exchange				
Mean	58.37	91.58	42.25	1.60
Median	14.05	29.05	12.68	
Average weekly trading volume (in US$ m) on foreign stock exchange				
Mean		31.18		
Median		9.82		

To examine the impact of foreign trading volume on bid-ask spreads, we have to control for a number of factors that are assumed to influence bid-ask spreads. We use a similar specification to Neal (1987), which relates the bid-ask spread to trading volume, price level, volatility, and competition. Our competition variable, however, is constructed as an interactive listing dummy which consists of a dummy variable ($DLIST_i$) for internationally listed companies multiplied by their trading volume on the foreign stock exchange ($LNFVOL_i$). This results to the following regression:

$$SPREAD_i = B_0 + B_1 LNVAR_i + B_2 LNVOL_i + B_3 LNPRICE_i + B_4 LNFVOL_i * DLIST_i \quad (4)$$

where:

$SPREAD_i$ is the estimated bid-ask spread for each company;

$LNVAR_i$ is the natural logarithm of the weekly return variance;

$LNVOL_i$ is the natural logarithm of the weekly trading volume on the respective domestic stock exchange;

$LNPRICE_i$ is the natural logarithm of the weekly closing price;

$LNFVOL_i$ is the natural logarithm of the weekly trading volume on the foreign stock exchange (NYSE or NASDAQ);

$DLIST_i$ is a listing dummy which is assigned a value of 1 for listed and a value of 0 for internationally unlisted companies.

Table 5 shows the estimated coefficients of our regression model. The signs of the coefficients for variance ($LNVAR_i$), volume ($LNVOL_i$), and price ($LNPRICE_i$) are consistent with previous studies. Variance ($LNVAR_i$) has a very strong positive relationship with bid-ask spreads (t = 7.89). The high level of significance of the coefficient of the variance ($LNVAR_i$) is consistent with the findings of Jegadeesh and Subrahmanyam (1993)22. Trading volume on the domestic stock exchange ($LNVOL_i$) has a negative effect on bid-ask spreads (t = -1.77). The price level ($LNPRICE_i$) also has a negative effect on bid-ask spreads, as predicted by theory but the t-statistics (t = -0.62) indicate that the price level does not have the same strong influence on bid-ask spreads as found in previous papers. This is probably due to very large differences in the average price level across countries irrespective of their liquidity characteristics23. The coefficient for the interactive listing dummy ($DLIST_i$ * $LNFVOL_i$) is negative and significant (t = -2.20). The negative sign is consistent with our expectation suggesting that an increased volume on the foreign stock exchange for internationally listed stocks lowers bid-ask spreads on the domestic stock exchange. The trading on the foreign stock exchange represents potential competition to market makers on the domestic stock exchange leading to an improvement in the liquidity of internationally listed stocks.

Table 5

Effect of international listing on liquidity of international equity offerings adjusted for price, volume and variance

The Table below gives the OLS estimates of the following equation:

$$SPREAD_i = B_0 + B_1 LNVAR_i + B_2 LNVOL_i + B_3 LNPRICE_i + B_4 LNFVOL_i * DLIST_i$$
(column 2)

$$SPREAD_i = B_0 + B_1 LNVAR_i + B_2 LNVOL_i + B_3 LNPRICE_i + B_4 LNFVOL_i * DLIST_i + B_5 DPERL_i$$
(column 3)

The dependent variable is the individual spread estimate ($SPREAD_i$). The independent variables are: $LNVAR_i$, the natural logarithm of the weekly return variance; $LNVOL_i$, the natural logarithm of the weekly trading volume on the domestic stock exchange; $LNPRICE_i$, the natural logarithm of the weekly closing price; $LNFVOL_i$, the natural logarithm of the weekly trading volume on the foreign stock exchange (NYSE or NASDAQ); $DLIST_i$, a listing dummy which is 1 for internationally listed and 0 for internationally unlisted companies; $DPERL_i$ is a dummy variable for the period of listing which is 1 for companies offering equity before 1991 and 0 for companies offering equity after 1991. Column 2 shows the results for our total sample. Column 3 tests the robustness of our results for the period after 1991. The t-statistics for each coefficient are in brackets. t-statistics for OLS regressions are adjusted for heteroscedasticity of the residuals by White's consistent covariance estimator.

Independent variable	Estimated coefficient	Estimated coefficient
Intercept	6.9724	7.0440
	(12.00)	(11.92)
LNPRICE	-0.0176	-0.0144
	(-0.62)	(-0.50)
LNVAR	0.7839	0.7956
	(7.89)	(7.88)
LNVOL	-0.0617	-0.0678
	(-1.77)	(-1.89)
LNFVOL* DLIST	-0.0675	-0.0768
	(-2.20)	(-2.34)
DPERL		0.1362
		(1.44)
Adjusted R^2	0.44	0.44

To take account of a potential bias imposed by the differences in the period of listing (see 4.2 Data period), we perform an additional test. We include a period of listing dummy variable ($DPERL_i$) into regression (4) which is 1 for companies listing before 1991 and 0 for companies listing after 1991.

$$SPREAD_i = B_0 + B_1 \, LNVAR_i + B_2 \, LNVOL_i + B_3 \, LNPRICE_i +$$
$$B_4 \, LNFVOL_i * DLIST_i + B_5 \, DPERL_i \tag{5}$$

Table 5, column 3 shows that the listing dummy variable for the period of listing ($DPERL_i$) is not significant (t = 1.44) at the five-percent level. The estimated coefficients for the other variables are virtually the same as for regression (4) showing that our results are not biased by comparing samples of different life cycles as international companies.

5.4 Cost-benefit analysis of different offering methods

In this section we present a quantitative evaluation of the costs and benefits of a public offering and a private placement based on the methodology of Amihud and Mendelson (1986). Using the size-adjusted difference in bid-ask spreads of 0.24% (see Table 3) the weekly saving in transaction costs for trading the average weekly volume of US$ 58.37 million (see Table 4) would amount to US$ 140,112 (0.24% x US$ 58.37 million). The present value of this weekly saving, assuming a 10% discount rate (or a weekly rate of 0.1923%), is equal to a perpetuity

$$US\$ \ 140,112 \ / \ 0.001923 = US\$ \ 72.86m.$$

The costs for a NYSE-listed firm consist of the gross-underwriting spread, the other total expenses, the initial listing fee on the NYSE, and the annual fees for a NYSE-listing. Taking the average gross-underwriting spread for a public offering of 4.62%, which we estimated, the commission paid to the investment bank amounts to US$ 6.61 million assuming an average offering size of US$ 143.10 million (see Table 1). The other direct expenses are US$ 1 million and the initial listing fee is US$ 100,000. Discounting the annual fee of US$ 500,000 for a NYSE-listing at 10% provides us with a present value of US$ 5 million. Hence, the total costs are:

$$US\$ \ 6.61m + US\$ \ 1m + US\$ \ 0.1m + US\$ \ 5m = US\$ \ 12.71m.$$

Subtracting the total costs from the total benefits provides a net present value of US$ 60.15 million for a public offering. We proceed in calculating the reduction in the cost of capital. Amihud and Mendelson (1986) calculate the reduction in the cost of capital by the following equation:

$$NPV = (E/R) * (\Delta R/R) \tag{6}$$

where NPV is the net present value of the public offering, (E/R) the present value of the firm's cash flow without the liquidity-enhancing project (or simply the market value of the firm), and $\Delta R = R - R_1$ the change in the cost of capital. We assume, as above, that R, the old discount rate, is 10%. Hence, the reduction in the cost of capital for our average sample firm which has a market value of US$ 5713.39 million (see Table 4) is equal to

$$(US\$ 60.15m * 10\%)/ US\$ 5713.39m = 0.11\% \text{ (or 11 basis points)}.$$

The reduction in the cost of capital, however, could be even bigger if we included the trading volume on the foreign stock exchange into our calculations.

6. Conclusion

Using a sample of 231 international equity offerings from 1984-1994, this study documents that internationally listed firms have a liquidity advantage over firms that choose a private placement in the US instead of a full listing on NASDAQ or NYSE. Results indicate that companies which choose to comply with the stringent registration requirements of the SEC, and thus incur the substantial costs associated with this procedure, are "rewarded" by having lower bid-ask spreads. This result holds when comparing bid-ask spreads corrected for size effects. The lower bid-ask spread is explained by a larger potential shareholder base and by the permission to be traded on a recognised stock exchange. Trading on a regulated marketplace provides timely trade reporting and increases market efficiency. We show that the benefits generated by lower bid-ask spreads for internationally listed firms outweigh the higher costs of a public offering leading to a 0.11% reduction in the cost of capital. This study also contributes to the microstructure literature as it shows that bid-ask spreads of internationally listed stocks are influenced by the competition of an additional trading location. Consistent with previous theoretical implications, we provide evidence that internationally listed firms have a higher trading volume. This could be due to increased arbitrage between the underlying stock and the ADR, caused by currency fluctuations. In order to shed further light on the interaction of currency fluctuations, underlying stock prices, ADR prices, and trading volume effects, a time-series analysis examining the effect of changes in the exchange rate on trading volume and prices would be required.

Acknowledgement

We would like to thank Gordon Gemmill, Mezianne Lasfer, and Dylan Thomas for helpful suggestions. The comments of Marcus Gerbich, Ane Tamayo, and Ayo Salami and seminar participants at City University Business School are greatly appreciated. We are also grateful to The Bank of New York and Citibank for providing some of the data. All remaining errors are our responsibility.

References

Amihud, Y. and H. Mendelson, 1986, Asset pricing and the bid-ask spread, Journal of Financial Economics 17, 223-239.

Amihud, Y. and H. Mendelson, 1987, Trading mechanisms and stock returns: An empirical investigation, Journal of Finance 42, 533-553.

Amihud, Y. and H. Mendelson, 1988, Liquidity and asset prices: Financial management implications, Financial Management 17, 5-15.

Amihud, Y. and H. Mendelson, 1989, The effects of beta, bid-ask spread, residual risk, and size on stock returns, Journal of Finance 44, 479-486.

Bagehot, W., 1971, The only game in town, Financial Analysts Journal 22, 12-14.

Barclay, M. and C. Smith, 1988, Corporate payout policy: Cash dividends versus open-market repurchases, Journal of Financial Economics 22, 61-82.

Barry C. and S. Brown, 1984, Differential information and the small firm effect, Journal of Financial Economics 13, 283-294.

Benston, G. and R. Hagerman, 1974, Determinants of bid-ask spreads in the over-the-counter market, Journal of Financial Economics 1, 353-364.

Breeden, R., 1994, Foreign companies and US securities markets in a time of economic transformation, Fordham International Law Journal 17, 77-96.

Chowdhry, B. and V. Nanda, 1991, Multimarket trading and market liquidity, Review of Financial Studies 4, 483-512.

Conrad, J. and G. Kaul, 1988, Time variation in expected returns, Journal of Business 61, 409-425.

Conrad, J. and G. Kaul, 1989, Mean reversion in short-horizon expected returns, Review of Financial Studies 2, 225-240.

Conrad, J., G. Kaul and M. Nimalendran, 1991, Components of short-horizon individual security returns, Journal of Financial Economics 29, 365-384.

Conroy R., R. Harris and B. Benet, 1990, The effects of stock splits on bid-ask spreads, Journal of Finance 45, 1285-1295.

Copeland, T. and D. Galai, 1983, Information effects on the bid-ask spread, Journal of Finance 25, 1457-1469.

Damodaran, A., C. Liu and W. Van Harlow, 1993, The effects of international dual listings on stock price behaviour, Unpublished manuscript (Stern Business School).

Domowitz, I., J. Glen and A. Madhavan, 1994, International cross-listing, market quality, and ownership rights: An analysis of the Mexican stock market, Unpublished manuscript (Northwestern University).

Doukas, J. and K. Yung, 1992, ADRs, investors' information and initial public equity offerings (IPO) underpricing, Journal of International Securities Markets 7, 341-348.

Euromoney, 1994, The US welcomes the alien invasion, April, 61-63.

Foerster, S. and G. Karolyi, 1993, International listings of stocks: The case of Canada and the US, Journal of International Business Studies, Fourth Quarter, 763-783.

Freedman, R., 1991, A theory of the impact of international cross-listing, Working Paper, University of British Columbia.

George, T., G. Kaul and M. Nimalendran, 1991, Estimation of bid-ask spreads and its components: A new approach, Review of Financial Studies 4, 623-656.

Glosten, L., 1987, Components of the bid-ask spread and statistical properties of transaction prices, Journal of Finance 42, 1293-1308.

Harris, T., 1993, Understanding German financial statements: Lessons from Daimler-Benz's listing, Salomon Brothers, United States Equity Research Accounting, 7 October.

Jayaraman, N., K. Shastri and K. Tandon, 1993, The impact of international cross listings on risk and return: The evidence from American Depositary Receipts, Journal of Banking and Finance 17, 91-103.

Jegadeesh, N. and A. Subrahmanyam, 1993, Liquidity effects of the introduction of the S&P 500 index futures contract on the underlying stock, Journal of Business 66, 171-187.

Kato, K., S. Linn and J. Schallheim, 1991, Are there arbitrage opportunities in the market for American Depositary Receipts?, Journal of International Financial Markets, Institutions and Money 1, 73-89.

Keim, D., 1983, Size-related anomalies and stock return seasonality: Further empirical evidence, Journal of Financial Economics 12, 13-32.

Kim M., I. Mathur and A. Szakmary, 1995, Price transmission dynamics between ADRs and their underlying foreign securities, Unpublished manuscript (Southern Illinois University).

Kofman P. and J. Moser, 1995, Spreads, information flows and transparency across trading systems, Working Paper Series, Federal Reserve Bank of Chicago, February.

Kyle, A., 1985, Continuous Auctions and Insider Trading, Econometrica 53, 1315-1335.

Lau, S. and J. Diltz, 1994, Stock returns and the transfer of information between the New York and Tokyo stock exchanges, Journal of International Money and Finance 13, 211-222.

Lee, I., S. Lochhead, J. Ritter and Q. Zhao, 1995, The costs of raising capital, Unpublished manuscript (University of Illinois).

Marr, W., J. Trimble and R. Varma, 1991, On the integration of international capital markets: Evidence from Euroequity offerings, Financial Management 20, 11-21.

Merton, R., 1987, Presidential address: A simple model of capital market equilibrium with incomplete information, Journal of Finance 42, 333-350.

Neal, R., 1987, Potential competition and actual competition in equity options, Journal of Finance 42, 511-531.

Noronha, G., A. Sarin and S. Saudagaran, 1995, Testing for liquidity effects of international dual listings using intraday data, Journal of Banking and Finance, forthcoming.

Officer, D. and J. Hoffmeister, 1987, ADRs: A substitute for the real thing?, Journal of Portfolio Management 13, 61-65.

Pagano, M. and A. Roell, 1991, Auction and dealership markets: What is the difference?, Discussion Paper No. 125, Financial Markets Group, London School of Economics.

Poon, S. and S. Taylor, 1992, Stock returns and volatility: An empirical study of the U.K. stock market, Journal of Banking and Finance 16, 37-59.

Reinganum, M., 1981, A misspecification of capital asset pricing: Empirical anomalies based on earnings yields and market values, Journal of Financial Economics 9, 19-46.

Roll, R., 1984, A simple implicit measure of the effective bid-ask spread in an efficient market, Journal of Finance 39, 1127-1139.

Rosenthal, L., 1983, An empirical test of the efficiency of the ADR market, Journal of Banking and Finance 7, 17-29.

Stoll, H.,1978, The pricing of dealer services: An empirical study of NASDAQ stocks, Journal of Finance 33, 1152-1173.

Stoll, H., 1989, Inferring the components of the bid-ask spread: Theory and empirical tests, Journal of Finance 44, 115-134.

Velli, J., 1994, American Depositary Receipts: An overview, Fordham International Law Journal 17, 38-57.

Endnotes

1 Kyle (1985) defines depth as the size of an order flow innovation that is required to change prices a given amount. In other words, in a highly liquid market almost any amount of stock could be bought or sold immediately without moving the current market price.

2 The informativeness of prices measures to what extent the price at which market makers are willing to trade a certain quantity, that is necessary to clear the market, reveal the value of the asset.

3 Bagehot (1971) and Copeland and Galai (1983).

4 The relative size of a firm's investor base can be expressed by dividing the effective number of shareholders of a firm by the aggregate number of investors in the market as a whole.

5 For more details concerning the components of the costs of raising capital see Lee, Lochhead, Ritter, and Zhao (1995) who examine this issue for US corporations raising capital in the domestic markets.

6 This approach towards regulating foreign securities is in contrast to the principle of mutual recognition, pursued by the London Stock Exchange, which acknowledges the validity of other countries' laws, regulations, and standards as long as certain minimum standards are met.

7 This requires that for each income statement net income and shareholders' equity must be reconciled to US GAAP and each material variation must be shown as a separate reconciling item. A good example is provided by Harris (1993) who discusses the implications of a full reconciliation to US GAAP for US investors based on a case study of Daimler Benz.

8 QIBs are defined as investors acting on their own account and having assets invested in securities of more than US$ 100 million.

9 Since we calculate spreads from transaction prices, this selection criterion is necessary to avoid obtaining downward biased spread estimates which are caused by "zero" transaction returns due to non trading.

10 The elimination of 54 companies appears to be a very high percentage of the total population. However, this can be explained by the fact that ca. 25 companies obtained a listing on the NYSE only in the last quarter of 1994 and could, therefore, not be considered.

11 This is mainly a reflection of the introduction of Rule 144A in 1990 as described in the institutional aspects.

12 See Table 5 for more details.

13 Approximately, 25 companies of our NYSE-listed companies and 80 of our internationally unlisted offerings are IPOs.

14 However, there are a number of hybrid market structures because some markets run different systems depending on the trading activity of a particular stock or the time of the day.

15 Market makers quote bid and ask prices at which they are willing to buy and sell shares up to a specified size.

16 Approximately 70% of our sample firms are traded in auction markets or a hybrid version of an auction market. Only UK companies (ca. 14% of our sample firms) and Chilean companies (ca. 4% of our sample firms) are traded in a "pure" dealership market. For further details, see Euromoney (1994).

17 They use LIFFE (London International Financial Futures Exchange) data, for which bid/ask quotes are available, to make inferences for the DTB (Deutsche Terminboerse) where only transaction data is available.

18 This result is consistent with previous studies examining portfolio return autocorrelations across different international markets. Reinganum (1981) finds daily autocorrelations in the magnitude of 0.37 for the highest market value portfolio of US stocks and Keim (1983) reports 0.35. Poon and Taylor (1992) find similar results for the Financial Times All Share Index (0.19).

19 Roll (1984) finds that about 50 percent of his individual firm spread estimates are negative. In order to test for the robustness of our estimates, we estimate spreads using arbitrary values for the autocorrelation coefficient (between 0 and 0.28). Although the magnitude of the individual estimates declines, the difference between internationally listed and unlisted estimates remains the same.

20 Using a different procedure to size-match the portfolios does not alter the magnitude in the differences between listed and unlisted companies for each portfolio.

[21] The summary statistics only comprise companies for which volume data is available. This eliminates 20 companies in the internationally listed sample for which no foreign and/or domestic volume is available, and 9 companies in the internationally unlisted sample for which no domestic volume is available.

[22] With respect to Amihud and Mendelson (1987) who point out that the return variance is itself a function of the bid-ask spread and thus a biased estimator of the "true" variance we calculate return variances from weekly returns. Conroy, Harris, and Benet (1990) note that using weekly instead of daily returns diminishes the role of spreads because bid-ask spreads become less influential as the length of the holding period increases.

[23] In our sample German and Swiss stocks have very high price levels (500-4000 US$) and Hong Kong, Singaporian, and Chilean stocks have price levels below one US$.

Shipping Initial Public Offerings: A Cross-Country Analysis

Costas Th. Grammenos
and
Stelios N. Marcoulis
City University Business School

Abstract

Examination of 31 shipping initial public offerings (IPOs) that appeared in seven different countries during the period 1983 to 1995 reveals that the number and size of shipping companies entering the equity capital markets has increased over time. Furthermore, the majority of these companies are new companies created by older companies or resulting from the merger of older companies. Average direct costs of these shipping initial public offerings were found to contain a relatively high fixed cost component. Shipping IPOs show statistically significant low mean initial day returns with the exception of limited life shipping funds which show negative mean initial day returns. Initial day returns were found to be, in contrast to other studies, positively related to the pre-ipo debt levels of the company. Furthermore when excluding the shipping funds from our sample, initial day returns were also found to be positively related to the proportion of equity offered by the company.

1. Introduction

Over the years, the traditional main sources of capital for the shipping industry have been, apart from the owners funds and retained earnings, banks, specialised financial institutions and shipyards with the equity capital markets playing a minor role. This was due to a number of factors such as the reluctance of the owners of the shipping companies to dilute control and disclose information, and the unattractiveness of the shipping industry to institutional and private investors due to its inability to provide stable income streams.

The severe crisis of the shipping industry in the first half of the eighties resulted in the erosion of the capital base of many shipping companies and in a substantial decline in the role of banks as providers of finance for the shipping industry. More than ever, shipping companies, their financiers and other related parties realised the need for a sound capital base. This recognition, coupled firstly with the substantial amounts required [Grammenos[1] (1989), Peters[2] (1993)] to replace the ageing wet and dry fleets worldwide and secondly the internationalisation of world equity markets, has created a better environment for the utilisation of equity markets as an available source of shipping finance. Such a development, however, is contingent on the need for structural and cultural reorganisation of the shipping companies to satisfy capital markets' requirements and investors' expectations.

The aim of this paper is to investigate for the first time major characteristics and issues regarding shipping companies that go public to raise equity either to fund their growth or for other purposes. Our evidence suggests that the number and size of shipping companies raising public capital have increased over time and that the majority of shipping companies entering the capital markets are new companies being created from old ones or resulting from merger activities. The shipping companies in our sample are becoming bigger over time, reorganising themselves, and at an increasing rate satisfying their capital needs through the capital markets. Moreover, our study shows that shipping companies with high pre-ipo gearing levels experience more underpricing of their share issues than the ones with low pre-ipo gearing levels. Therefore, in the context of reorganisation, shipping companies may have to lower their gearing levels before entering the capital markets to minimise potential underpricing.

We use a unique dataset of shipping IPOs of 31 shipping companies which obtained public listings on the stock exchanges of the following seven countries: Hong-Kong, Singapore, the US, Norway, Sweden, Greece and Luxembourg during the period 1983 to 1995. These companies are presented in appendix 1 along with their year of initial public offering, and are categorised by country in which their offerings appeared. The sample is relatively small due to the fact that we focus strictly on companies whose prime business is in the operation of vessels (we exclude shipyards). However, it represents the overwhelming majority of shipping IPOs issued in these countries over this period. Data regarding the initial public offering were derived from the individual offer prospectuses of each company. Price data for all issues were collected principally from DataStream.

Prospectuses for the 31 IPOs in our sample come from seven countries and as a result some of the Swedish and Norwegian prospectuses had to be translated into English. More importantly, the information content of each prospectus varied considerably across countries. For example, prospectuses for the US, Hong-Kong and Singapore, and Greece tended to be more detailed than some of the Norwegian, Swedish and Luxembourg ones. Furthermore, the IPO prospectuses for small companies and companies which have been listed for a long time in these three countries, tend to include less information than the bigger and more recent ones, for example in the cases of Argonaut and Concordia, two early issues in Sweden the direct costs are not stated in the prospectuses while a similar phenomenon is observed in the case of Larvik, a small Norwegian IPO.

The paper is organised as follows. Section 2 presents the sample characteristics of the 31 shipping companies in our sample entering the IPO market and initial discussion. Section 3 gives evidence regarding the average initial day returns of shipping IPOs. Section 4 presents cross -sectional underpricing tests. Section 5 gives evidence regarding the direct costs of shipping IPOs. Finally, concluding remarks appear in section 6.

2. Sample Characteristics and Initial Discussion:

Table 1 presents evidence on the average gross proceeds and the average size of the companies according to the stated primary purpose of issue. It should be noted that all monetary amounts in table 1 are in 1995 US dollars. This required the conversion of individual home currencies to US dollars at the rate prevailing at the time of flotation. These figures were then adjusted for inflation using the US consumer price index. The prospectuses do not always specify a single use for the acquired equity funds. In such cases we classify an IPO according to the primary purpose of the issue that is to say the one stated in the prospectus for which the majority of the funds raised will be spent.

Table 1

Average Gross Proceeds and Company Size of the companies in our sample according to the Primary Reason for Going Public

Purpose of Issue	No.of Offers (%)	Average Gross Proceeds	Average Size of Company
Vessel Acquisition	19(63%)	$58,949,220	$152,634,410
Asset Play	7(24%)	$61,199,180	$71,891,235
Debt Repayment	3(13%)	$61,726,890	$203,139,845
Trading Activities	1 (3%)	$48,103,845	$152,634,410

Note: One offering in the US did not state the reason for going public and is not included in the above table.

Table 1 shows that 19 out of 30 (63%) shipping companies enter the IPO markets for vessel acquisition purposes. Vessel acquisitions are primarily realised by the shipping companies as part of their investment policy, either on an offensive or a defensive basis. Either way, they improve their competitive edge by expanding into new or existing markets or by replacing vessels that are older and possibly not desirable to be chartered by first class charterers or uneconomic to operate. The second largest group, 7 out of 30 (23%) shipping companies (shipping funds), enter for speculative asset play reasons.

These seven companies (there were also three aborted ones) appeared in the US (six) and Luxembourg (one) during the period 1987-89 and were established by their promoters as limited life shipping funds, that is to say their life was more or less predetermined to last between five and seven years. The goals for their establishment were to buy second hand vessels when the market is down, trade the vessels until there is a significant improvement in the resale market, then sell the vessels at a profit and liquidate the company distributing its net assets to its shareholders. Apart from the available funds to be generated by the eventual sale of the vessels, it was also the companies' intentions to pay dividends from the available cash flow generated from operations.

These funds are in most cases regarded as vehicles that allow their promoters to provide managerial services without taking serious investment positions. Reasons for this type of activity included the erosion of the equity base of the shipping companies during the crisis of the eighties and the resulting reduction in the number of financial institutions willing to provide funds for the shipping industry. Furthermore, external factors persuaded promoters and potential investors that the timing was right for investing in the shipping industry: improving shipping markets as manifested by increased scrapping followed by rising demand, rationalisation of the shipbuilding industry along with the fading out of governmental shipbuilding subsidies.

Three out of thirty (10%), entered the IPO market for debt repayment purposes, while only one company, Jinhui Shipping and Ttransportation, has obtained a public listing to raise capital to expand its trading activities. Finally, we found that out of the fifteen companies which stated a secondary purpose in their prospectus eleven (73%) were for working capital requirements.

Table 1 suggests that there is a remarkable similarity in the size of the issue across the four categories, ranging from $48,103,845 to $61,726,890. It also indicates that the companies entering the IPO markets for debt repayment appear to be on average bigger than those entering the IPO markets for vessel acquisitions. It can also be seen that the shipping funds entering the IPO market for speculative asset play are on average much smaller than any of the other three categories.

Table 2 partitions our sample of shipping IPOs as per purpose of issue per country. It can be seen that six out of seven asset plays appear in the US and came to the market between 1987 and 1989 during the "boom" of the shipping funds placements. Asset play seems to be the dominant purpose for issuing in the United States with vessel acquisitions and debt repayments ranking well below it. This is not the case elsewhere however; in the countries of the Far East, Sweden and Greece vessel acquisitions are the only reasons leading shipping companies to enter the IPO market. In Norway the story is almost similar with just under 80% of the issues being for vessel acquisitions purposes.

Table 2

Primary Reasons for Going Public per Country:

Country	Purpose of Issue			
	Vessel Acquisitions	Asset Play	Debt Repayment	Trading Activities
Hong Kong, Singapore	3	0	0	0
US	2	6	2	0
Sweden	4	0	0	0
Norway	8	0	1	1
Greece	3	0	0	0
Luxembourg	0	1	0	0

Note: One offering in the US did not state the reason for going public and is not included in the above table.

Figure 1 presents a general tendency of the number of shipping IPOs to increase over time. It furthermore illustrates that the majority of shipping IPOs are clustered in two distinct time periods. The first during the period 1988-89 (30%) and the second during the period 1993-94 (42%). The rise of shipping IPOs during 1988-89 can be partly explained by the shipping funds, and by other companies, mainly tanker operators who considered the market conditions and prospects to be favourable for them to enter the market.

The second boom of shipping IPOs during 1993-94 is associated with three main developments. First, the majority (54%) of companies entering the IPO market at this time were tanker operators whose primary aim was vessel acquisitions. Tanker companies entered the market at that time with expectations that the tanker market was going to improve substantially primarily due to increased scrapping and slow replacement through newbuildings therefore reduced supply and also robust demand.

Second, the activities of 15% of the companies entering the IPO market during this time period are in the developing economies of China and the Pacific Rim. They therefore raised capital for expansionary purposes during this period based on the assumption of stable high rates of growth in these economies.

Figure 1

Volume of shipping IPOs over Time

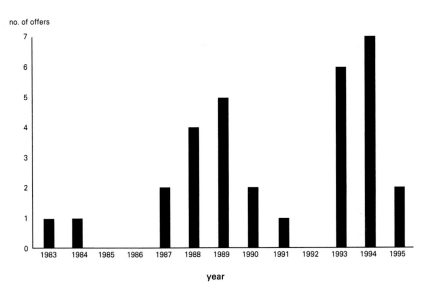

Third, another 15% of the companies tapping the capital markets during 1993-94 are Greek coastal companies. Their entry to the Athens Stock Exchange at this particular period is at least partly due to the change of the regulatory environment of the Athens Stock Exchange. Initially, law 959/1979 was prohibiting the listing of shipping companies on the Exchange but a modification introduced by law 1982/1990 set the initial framework within which domestic coastal shipping companies could list. The result of that was seen in 1994 when two coastal shipping companies Strintzis and Dane were introduced on the Athens Stock Exchange.

Table 3 provides details on the size, proportion of equity offered, age of the company and fleet, and gearing of the companies in our sample of shipping IPOs.

Table 3

Descriptive Statistics of major characteristics of the Shipping IPOs in our sample

	All	Hong-Kong and Singapore	US	Sweden	Norway	Greece	Luxembourg
Mean Size of Company	$137,074,345	$223,360,630	$142,786,230	$117,180,035	$137,079,835	$52,887,460	$127,578,900
Median Size	$91,551,460	$276,074,600	$67,549,590	$114,031,570	$158,349,085	$33,245,820	
Proportion of equity offered	52%	29%	73%	42%	48%	25%	47%
Standard Deviation	30%	7%	35%	7%	23%	3%	
Mean Age of Company at the time of going public	5.00	7.00	2.91	0.00	5.11	13.33	0.00
Standard Deviation	7.93	7.16	4.80	0.00	9.13	10.60	
Mean Age of the fleet at the time of going public	12.00	10.26	11.83	7.83	11.43	25.00	4.67
Standard Deviation	5.50	2.70	3.04	3.52	3.40	0.75	
Mean Gearing of company at the time of going public	1.45	0.70	2.50	0.53	2.07	0.41	0.00
Standard Deviation	1.82	0.50	1.81	0.35	2.50	0.10	

1. All monetary amounts have been converted to 1995 US dollars.
2. The above figures have been calculated on many instances from reduced samples due to data unavailability.

The average size[3] of all shipping companies going public is $137,074,345 with the companies from the Far East exhibiting the highest average size ($223,360,630) and Greek companies exhibiting the lowest average size ($52,887,460). The size of the companies in the US and Norway is close to the all country average while the average size of the companies in Sweden lies slightly below the average. Greek companies have the smallest size because they are all passenger carrier companies which are usually smaller than their cargo carrier counterparts. The size of the company listed in Luxembourg, Anangel, is slightly below the average standing at $127,578,900.

The average size of shipping companies going public, as can be seen in figure 2, exhibits an increasing trend over the period analysed; in 1983 the average size was approximately $65 million, in 1993 it was approximately $150 million and by 1995 it is approximately $285 million. This trend may suggest that in order to raise equity on the capital markets shipping companies are becoming bigger to satisfy both market and investor requirements .

Figure 2

Average size of shipping companies entering the IPO markets over time

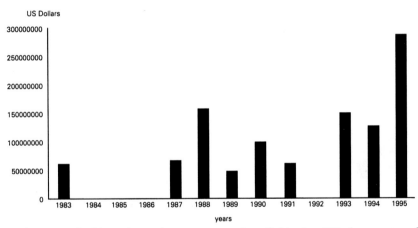

The last part of table 3 shows the average gearing of shipping IPOs by country of origin. The average gearing[4] of companies coming to the market is 1.45[5] but this figure exhibits considerable variation across countries. It is quite high in the US and Norway standing at 2.50 and 2.07 respectively whereas it is much lower in the Far East, Sweden and Greece standing at 0.7, 0.53 and 0.41 respectively. Here it should be noted that the average gearing of US companies may not be a very representative figure because the six US listed funds entered the market as new companies free of debt. Out of the remaining five companies, two enter the IPO market with debt repayment as their primary purpose. Average gearing also exhibits considerable variation within some countries as is indicated by its standard deviation. In Norway it is higher than the mean, standing at 2.5 and in the US it is also very high at 1.81. In Hong-Kong and Singapore and Sweden it is lower standing at 0.5 and 0.35 respectively whereas in Greece it is a very low 0.10.

Figure 3

Debt to equity ratios of shipping IPOs at the time of entering the market

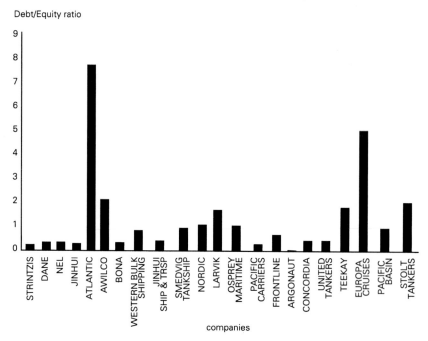

Gearing during the seventies and eighties had been quite high for a large number of shipping companies when debt/equity ratios of 3 were not unusual. This proved to be quite painful during the crisis period of the mid-seventies and the first part of the eighties, and in a number of cases catastrophical; particularly for companies which did not generate stable income through medium or long - term time - charters and/or contracts of affreightment but operated in the spot market [Grammenos (1981)]. Since then shipping companies have had a more conservative approach towards gearing levels with debt to equity levels above 2 being less normal. This is confirmed in figure 3 which presents the debt to equity ratios for a reduced sample of 22 shipping companies[6] based on their last available quarterly or annual reports before they enter the capital markets. The two companies with very high debt to equity ratios, Atlantic and Europa Cruises, alongside Teekay which also has a high debt to equity ratio (1.75), enter the capital markets with the primary purpose of reducing their debt levels. This trend of shipping companies reducing their debt levels, alongside financial institutions becoming more stringent in their lending policies[7], could also improve the industry's attractiveness in investor's perception. Since shipping investors tend to correlate high levels of debt with high risk of making capital losses, decreasing debt levels of publicly quoted shipping companies may help to change this perception.

Another characteristic of shipping IPOs which also varies considerably across countries is the mean proportion of equity offered. The Stockholm and Athens Stock

Exchanges require at least 25% of the shares in the company to be owned by the general public. In Hong-Kong and Singapore, listing requirements specify either the minimum of 25% of total capital, or not less than HK$50,000,000 and $1,500,000 (whichever is greater) must be in public hands (in the case of Singapore in the hands of not less than 500 shareholders). Regarding the US, stock exchange requirements vary according to which stock exchange the company seeks listing, in the case of the NYSE there must be at least 1,100,000 publicly held shares outstanding, in the case of the AMEX there must be at least 500,000 publicly held shares outstanding, and in the case of the NASDAQ there must be at least 100,000 publicly held shares outstanding. Finally, in Norway the Oslo Stock Exchange requires that for a company to obtain a public listing there must be at least 500 shareholders.

As can be seen in table 3 the proportion of equity offered by the IPOs analysed fluctuates between 73% in the US to 29% in the Far East and 25% in Greece. It should be noted however that while the 6 US speculative limited life funds gave out 98% of their equity the average proportion of equity offered by the other 5 US companies is only 43%. Broadly similar percentages of equity were offered by Swedish (42%) and Norwegian (48%) companies.

We also examined the behaviour of the proportion of equity offered across the size of the companies in our sample. Our findings indicate that bigger companies offer relatively less of their equity, the correlation coefficient between size and proportion of equity offered being -0.38 (statistically significant at the 5% level of significance).

A further characteristic of the shipping IPOs which should be mentioned in this context is the average age of the company's fleet. Greek companies seem to be the outlier here with an average age of 25 years, 13 years older than the all country average. This is due to the fact that all the Greek companies in our sample operate coastal vessels which often have a higher economic life than other bulk carrier or container vessels. Excluding Greece it can be seen that the US and Norway have the highest average age, 11.83 years and 11.43 respectively. However, it should be stated here that the US average age is driven upward by the shipping funds which in order to satisfy the aims mentioned in section 2.1, acquired older vessels with an average age of 13.74 years. The average age of the remaining US listed shipping companies is 9 years. The countries from the Far East have a lower average age than the all country average, standing at 10.26 years whereas Sweden has a much lower than average mean age, 7.12 years. The Swedish companies are in their majority tanker operators. The Luxembourg quoted company has an average age of 4.67 years.

Companies in our sample have been classified according to their primary activities (70% or more) as dry bulk operators, tanker operators, passenger carrier operators and diversified operators. The average age of vessels for each category is 10.75, 10.28, 23.33 and 8.86 years respectively. Apart from the passenger carriers, these figures compare favorably with the corresponding world average figures as at 1st January 1995 which are: 13.1 years [Fearnleys (1995)] for the world tanker fleet with an assumed average economic life of at least 20 years; 13 years [Fearnleys (1995)] for the world dry bulk fleet with an assumed average economic life of at least 25 years; and 18.4 years [ISL Statistics (1995)] for the passenger fleet with an assumed average economic life of more than 25 years.

Figure 4

Company groupings at the time of going public (w.r.t to time of incorporation)

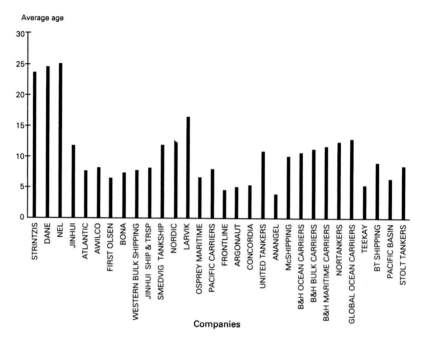

Figure 4 presents the average age of the companies' fleets at the time the companies enter the capital markets. Excluding the Greek coastal companies, it can be seen that the majority of the companies in our sample have vessels whose age on average, as already mentioned in the preceding paragraph, is less than 15 years. The importance of age is threefold: First, it affects the income of a shipping company; second, it affects its operating costs; and third it influences the perception of the company in the eyes of charterers and investors. The age profile of a company's fleet has direct and profound financial implications.

New vessels are more expensive; yet it is not clear whether they are favored by the existence of a two-tier market; in which new modern vessels will command a monetary premium over old vessels. In the case of tankers, Tamvakis (1995) does not find enough evidence to support a two tier market hypothesis. Given that, it is possible that in a good market both old and new vessels earn roughly the same freight. This would imply that in a good market, older vessels may earn more profits, while, provided they were bought when the market was "low", they may survive a bad market less painfully than new vessels, since new ones would have the additional burden of high capital outlay and debt repayment.

However, operating older ships may entail relatively higher running costs, e.g. fuel, insurance costs, manning requirements and maintenance.[8] Furthermore, factors such as the US Oil Pollution Act of 1990[9] and often the reluctance of major oil companies and other first class charterers to employ older vessels, may result in the creation of a two-tier market, not in terms of monetary premiums but in terms of preference for employment. This, in our opinion, is an area in which fruitful research may be conducted.

In addition to the above, investors' perceptions must be considered in this discussion. On the one hand, investors with a long-term investment horizon may consider a shipping company investing in new modern vessels, a better investment; while on the other hand, speculative investors may consider a shipping company investing in older vessels with a view to sell them when the market conditions are favourable, a more appropriate investment.

We also examined the average age of companies fleets at the time of entering the IPO market and found that it is increasing over time. This, coupled with our earlier findings that bigger shipping companies increasingly tap the IPO markets over time along with the fact that 63% of the issuing companies clearly state that the primary purpose of their issue is for vessel acquisition purposes suggests that these shipping companies are looking to the IPO market for their fleet replacement/expansion requirements.

Figure 5

Company groupings at the time of going public (w.r.t to time of incorporation)

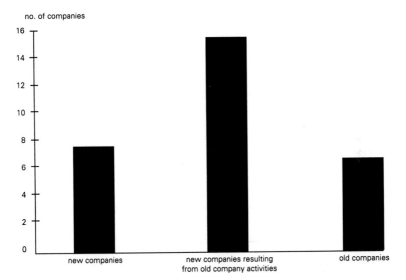

no. of companies

Finally, another characteristic which we examined is the age of the shipping company at the time of going public. The average age of our sample of companies going public is 5 years. However, there are wide fluctuations both across and within countries. In Greece the average age is 13.33 years whereas in Sweden it is zero[10], and Hong-Kong, Singapore, the US, and Norway exhibiting average age figures in the range of 2.9 to 7 years. The company in Luxembourg, like those in Sweden, is new. Furthermore, the standard deviation (7.93 years) of the average age of the shipping companies in our sample suggests wide fluctuations across companies; These are due to the fact that each company in our sample belongs to one of three very different groups regarding its incorporation as an entity: companies with a continuing history of over five years; completely new companies; and finally new companies which were created by old companies or are the result - in a few cases - of mergers between old companies, the latter appearing in Norway.

The frequencies of the above three groups presented in figure 5 suggest that the majority of the companies in our sample (52%) are new companies created by old companies or resulting from mergers between old companies. These companies seem to be the result of the structural and cultural reorganisation needed by the shipping industry contingent upon it successfully raising equity on the capital markets. Completely new companies and companies with a continuing history of five years or more represent 26% and 22% of the sample respectively.

3. Initial Price Reactions of Shipping IPOs

3.1 Underpricing of Initial Public Offerings

It is a well documented phenomenon that investors, on average, earn large initial returns on initial public offerings (IPOs) of equity securities in many countries. An interesting review and analysis of papers covering the international insights of underpricing in 25 countries, both in terms of magnitude and persistence, is provided by Loughran, Ritter and Rydqvist (1994). They find that short-run underpricing appears in all 25 countries they analysed. It is interesting to note the significant initial returns for countries included in our sample. Based on the papers of McGuiness (1992) and Koh and Walter (1989) Loughran, Ritter and Rydqvist (1994) report mean initial day returns of 17.6% for Hong-Kong and 27% for Singapore. Combining the samples of Ridder (1986) and Rydqvist (1993) they report average initial day returns of 39% for Sweden. Finally based on the recent study of Ibbotson, Sindelar and Ritter (1994) they report average initial day returns for the US of 15.3%. With reference to Greece, Kazantzis and Thomas (1995) report average initial day returns of 51%. Expected returns of these magnitudes over so many countries, in such a short period, seems to contradict market efficiency. Several theoretical models, an overview of which is beyond the scope of this paper[11], have attempted to explain why this phenomenon occurs.

Our study contributes to existing empirical literature on initial public offerings by providing new evidence using initial public offerings of shipping companies across countries. Previous empirical studies have not focused on shipping IPOs. Shipping IPOs are rather different than IPOs of ordinary industrial companies. Their market value is very often closely associated to the underlying value of their physical assets, i.e their vessels. As such, shipping IPOs are probably closer to IPOs of closed end funds and property companies. In both of these type of companies underpricing has been found to be either non-existent or considerably lower than that found for industrial companies. For example Peavy III (1990) and Weiss (1989) do not find any evidence of underpricing in the IPOs of closed end funds while Wang and Chang (1992) do not find any evidence of underpricing in property IPOs.

3.2 Shipping IPOs Initial Returns - Descriptive Statistics and Discussion

The descriptive statistics in Table 4 show that the mean first - day return for all shipping IPOs in our sample is 5.32%. This mean first - day return is statistically significant at the 5% level of significance. However, doubts regarding the consistency of this underpricing are caused by the median first - day return of all shipping IPOs which is 1.27%, substantially lower than the mean first - day return. It is also worth noting that the percentage of IPOs exhibiting negative first - day returns is quite high, standing at 39%. The percentage of IPOs with zero first day returns is 10% with the remaining 51% being underpriced.

Table 4

Descriptive Statistics of Initial Returns of Shipping IPOs

	All	Hong-Kong and Singapore	US	Sweden	Norway	Greece	Luxem-bourg
Mean returns[1] (%)	5.32	4.35	2.64	22.81	2.35	4.1	-2.00
Standard deviation (%)	16.813	1.7	9.87	40.71	8.55	16.73	0.00
t-statistic[2]	1.93						
Median returns (%)	1.268	4.71	0.00	5.00	1.43	8.000	
Percentage with negative returns	39%	0%	45%	50%	33%	33%	100%
No. of observations	31	3	11	4	9	3	1

1. The sample mean first-day return is defined as the arithmetic average of the percentage changes in price from the offering date to the close of the first day of trading for each issue.
2. t - statistics are not reported for each country due to the small amount of observations per country.

A closer look at the cross - country differences among mean first - day returns reveals that apart from the case of Sweden the fluctuations were not large. In Sweden the mean first - day return is 22.81% whereas in the other Scandinavian country of our sample, Norway, it is a negligible 2.35%. However, Sweden contains one company, Frontline, which may be considered to be an outlier in our sample exhibiting underpricing of 83.33%. The median first - day return of IPOs in these countries are much closer than their mean values and are 5% for Sweden and 1.43% for Norway. This indicates that there are wide fluctuations in cross-sectional initial day returns in these countries (especially in Sweden).

These wide fluctuations are better observed when the standard deviation of the first - day returns are considered, it is 40.71% for Sweden and 8.55% for Norway. The figure for Sweden is more than twice the all country average while the figure for Norway is half the all country average. Finally, the percentage of negative mean initial - day returns are 50% for Sweden and 33% for Norway, quite high in both cases.

In the US the mean first - day return is 2.64% with a standard deviation of 9.87%. The two countries of the Far East also exhibit a low level of mean first - day return, 4.35% but standard deviations are also low at 1.7%. Furthermore, the median first - day return (4.71%) is in contrast to all other countries, almost identical to the mean first - day return. Finally, the percentage of negative mean first - day returns is lowest in these shipping IPOs, standing at 0%. In Greece[12], the mean first - day return is equal to 4.1% with the standard deviation being 16.73% while the median first - day return is 8% with the percentage of negative initial - day returns standing at 33%. Anangel, the Luxembourg quoted company appears to be slightly overpriced with average initial returns being -2%.

Overall, the average underpricing of shipping companies in each country is lower than those documented in the literature for each country. It seems that due to the cyclical nature of the shipping industry, shipping companies enter the IPO market either when the shipping market prospers or when the expectations for the performance of the shipping markets are high, as was shown in section 2. Furthermore, it also seems that relatively less information asymmetry exists in the shipping industry IPOs due to the existence of an international vessel sale and purchase market. As a result the assets of the shipping companies (the vessels) have a relatively readily observable and available market price. This is in line with the theoretical models of Baron (1982) and Rock (1986) who argue that underpricing results from different kinds of information asymmetry. Baron contends that underpricing is due to the fact investment bankers are better informed about capital markets than are issuers, while Rock argues that underpricing is caused by information assymetry between different classes of investors.

It could be argued that shipping funds established in the US and Luxembourg during 1987-89 exhibit similar characteristics to closed end funds. Peavy (1990) finds evidence that closed end funds in the US during the period 1986 to 1987 were on average overpriced. He argues that since IPOs of closed end funds exhibit little asymmetry of information this evidence is in line with the theoretical models of Baron (1982) and Rock (1986). Levis and Thomas (1995) studied a sample of 105 closed end funds in the UK during the period 1984 to 1992 and found evidence of underpricing whose magnitude however is low (1.91%). Furthermore, they concluded that since this underpicing represents a premium of more than 5% over underlying net asset value alternative interpretations cannot be ruled out.

Our sub-sample of seven limited life shipping funds exhibits an average first day return of 2.51%. In line with the findings presented above our sub-sample exhibits little (although more than the closed end funds) information asymmetry since the net asset value is reported in the prospectus either in the form of the funds to be raised and/or in the form of the assets (vessels) to be purchased. Therefore the overpricing exhibited by the shipping funds could be the resultant of two main forces, little information asymmetry and external factors, such as improving shipping markets, which persuaded shipowners and investors that the timing was right for investing in the shipping industry.

Having established the overpricing of the shipping funds we also calculated the average initial day return for our sample of shipping IPOs excluding the seven limited life shipping funds. Average initial day returns increase from 5.32% to 7.59% which is significant at the 5% level.

4. Underpricing Tests

To examine determinants of first day returns panel A of table 5 presents the results of univariate regressions for the whole sample of 31 shipping IPOs. As can be seen, only one factor, gearing, appears to be statistically significant in explaining cross-sectional differences in underpricng. It seems that shipping companies with higher levels of debt experience undepricing of a larger magnitude than those with a lower level of debt.

Table 5

Underpricing Tests

PANEL A : Univariate Regressions for the whole sample		
Variable	Coefficient	t-statistic
Gross Proceeds of the Issue	-0.0004	-0.02
Size of the Company	-0.0564	0.22
Proportion of Equity Offered	-0.0100	-0.40
Gearing	0.0443	2.80**
Age of the Company	0.0134	1.05
Age of the fleet	-0.0731	-0.86

PANEL B: Univariate Regressions excluding the shipping funds from the sample		
Variable	Coefficient	t-statistic
Gross Proceeds of the Issue	0.0616	0.24
Size of the Company	-0.0752	-0.29
Proportion of Equity Offered	0.0705	2.08*
Gearing	0.0272	3.00**
Age of the Company	-0.0012	-0.07
Age of the fleet	-0.0819	-0.82

PANEL C: Multivariate Regression excluding the shipping funds from the sample		
Variable	Coefficient	t-statistic
Proportion of Equity offered	0.0569	1.12
Gearing	0.2278	2.61**

Notes:
* implies significance at the 5% level.
** implies significance at the 1% level.

This finding is in contrast to a study on the informational role of debt in the pricing of initial public offerings by Hegde and Miller (1995) who hypothesize that the expected value/risk of a company going public are increasing/decreasing functions of the company's pre-IPO debt ratio therefore suggesting that the degree of underpricing should be a decreasing function of a company's pre-IPO debt ratio. Using a large sample of US IPOs they find empirical evidence to substantiate their hypothesis.

We believe that our results are different to those of Hegde and Miller (1995) due to the reasons mentioned when discussing gearing in the sample characteristics and initial discussion section. These reasons are firstly the potential catastrophical consequences of high debt in periods of market downturns when the income may decrease or even cease altogether if it is not secured by solid long-term time charters or contracts of affreightment; and secondly the negative investor perception towards shipping companies with high debt levels. Such reasoning may, in contrast to Hegde and Miller (1995), mean that high/low gearing levels reduce/increase the value and increase/decrease the risk of the shipping company therefore explaining the positive relationship between underpricing and gearing.

Panel B of table 5 presents the results of the same univariate regressions but for a reduced sample of 24 shipping IPOs; the shipping funds are excluded. Results regarding gearing remain unchanged but it is interesting to note that the proportion of equity offered is also significant in explaining cross-sectional underpricing differences. It appears that companies that offer more equity to the public exhibit higher underpricing than those which offer less equity to the public.

This last finding is in line with Leland and Pyle (1977), Downes and Heinkel (1982) and Grinblatt and Hwang (1989) who argue that the amount of equity retained by owners signals their private valuation. In their models, risk-averse owners achieve a higher expected utility level by holding a diversified portfolio, rather than by having a large part of their wealth as a stake in their own firm. Owners, however, can be assumed to have private information about the true value of their companies. Therefore, owners of high-value companies will be willing to forego more of the benefits of diversification in order to avoid selling undervalued stock. Investors will realize these incentives and therefore will be willing to pay more for stock in firms where the owners are retaining a large holding.

Using the reduced sample set we then ran a multivariate regression with gearing and proportion of equity offered as the explanatory variables to determine which has the most explanatory power over cross-sectional underpricing. Results of this multivariate regression are presented in panel C of table 5 and indicate that gearing is statistically significant while the proportion of equity offered is not in a multivariate setting.

The remaining variables, namely gross proceeds of the issue, size of the company, age of the company and age of the fleet did not seem to explain cross-sectional differences in underpricing across companies for either data sets.

5. Direct Costs of Shipping IPOs

The major direct costs incurred by shipping companies wishing to go public are underwriting commissions, issuing house and broker fees, legal fees, accountant fees and printing and advertising costs. Usually the company's direct costs of issue including underwriting commissions are disclosed in the prospectus. Table 6 presents summary statistics of the direct costs of our sample of shipping IPOs.

Direct costs are defined as the difference between net and gross proceeds of the issue reported in the prospectus.[13] The average direct costs for a reduced sample of twenty seven[14] shipping IPOs is 7.89% of the amount raised, or $3,621,730 in monetary terms. The standard deviation of this percentage cost is 3.88% thus emphasizing the relatively high amount of fixed cost included in the direct cost. Total mean gross proceeds are $61,052,570.

Within our sample, Hong-Kong and Singapore, exhibit the second highest mean gross proceeds ($65,752,400), higher than the all country average. Average direct costs are 8.88% or $3,815,930 in monetary terms, with a standard deviation of 5.72%. This standard deviation is the highest in our sample and indicates that fixed costs are the lowest in these initial public offerings.

In the United States average direct costs are the highest, $4,299,900 in monetary terms or 10.43% of the amount raised. The percentage we obtain is similar to that documented in a recent study by Lee, Lochhead, Ritter, and Zhao (1995) who find average direct costs of raising capital in the US to be 11%. The standard deviation of the direct costs for the US companies in our sample is 4.32% thus implying a relatively high fixed cost component. The mean gross proceeds of the US shipping IPOs amount to $64,291,320 and are slightly higher than the all country average.

Table 6

Descriptive Statistics of the Average Direct Costs of Shipping IPOs

	All	Hong-Kong and Singapore	US	Sweden	Norway	Greece	Luxembourg
Mean of costs/gross proceeds	7.89%	8.88%	10.43%	7.35%	5.49%	6.50%	4.00%
Standard deviation of percentage cost	3.88%	5.72%	4.32%	2.11%	1.45%	1.50%	
Mean cost	$3,621,730	$3,815,930	$4,489,270	$2,119,815	$4,066,310	$756,600	$2,406,205
Median cost	$3,667,310	$2,259,510	$3,954,170	$2,119,815	$3,879,025	$658,420	
Mean gross proceeds	$61,052,570	$65,752,400	$64,291,320	$56,321,875	$74,717,335	$12,570,465	$60,155,170
Median gross proceeds	$57,828,730	$74,709,665	$59,784,120	$56,321,875	$71,504,630	$8,619,260	
Number of IPOs	27	3	10	2	8	3	1

Notes:
1. All monetary amounts have been converted to 1995 US dollars.
2. Gross proceeds have been calculated before the exercising of any over allotment options.

Norwegian shipping IPOs' direct costs are less than the all country IPOs average. They are 5.49% of the amount raised, or $4,066,310. Their standard deviation (1.45%) is alongside that of Greece, the lowest in our sample, thus indicating a high fixed cost component. Mean gross proceeds in Norway are the highest, standing at $74,717,335.

In Sweden, average direct costs, at 7.35% of the amount raised or $2,118,815, are slightly less than the all country average. They also exhibit relatively low standard deviation (2.11%) thus suggesting that the fixed cost component is quite high. Their mean gross proceeds ($56,321,875) rank higher only to Greece and are marginally lower than the all country average.

Finally, in Greece average direct costs are 6.50% of the total amount raised or $756,600. The standard deviation of these costs is the second lowest in our sample (1.50%), much lower than the all country average thus once again providing evidence of a large fixed cost component. Mean gross proceeds in Greek shipping IPOs are by far the smallest, standing at an average of $12,570,465. The figures for Greece are smaller due to the fact that our sample consisted only of passenger - carrying companies which in general are smaller than their cargo - carrying counterparts.

An issue which arises in the context of the average direct costs of shipping IPOs is that of the possibility of economies of scale. Gerbich, Levis and Rowland (1995) in a study of property initial public offerings find that small property IPOs cost on average 13.9% of the gross proceeds whereas large property IPOs cost on average 7% of the gross proceeds. Lee, Lochhead, Ritter, and Zhao (1995) in their study on the costs of raising capital in the US find evidence of substantial economies of scale. To examine this issue in the context of shipping IPOs we ranked our sample according to gross proceeds and then divided it into two groups. The first group contained those IPOs which raised under $60,000,000 (approximately the mean gross proceeds of our sample) whereas the second group contained those which raised over $60,000,000. The mean direct cost of group 1 was estimated to be 8.70% while the corresponding figure for group 2 was 7.00%. Therefore, although not substantial, there appears to be some economies of scale in the direct costs of the IPOs in our sample.

6. Conclusions

This paper offers the first analysis of shipping IPOs across country groups. We have identified a number of characteristics quite unique to this industrial sector and some key differences associated with the individual countries in our sample.

Shipping companies raise capital in the IPO markets primarily for vessel acquisitions while other reasons include asset play and debt repayment. The number of shipping IPOs shows an increasing trend over time. This shows that the role of the equity capital markets in the financing of the shipping industry is gaining prominence from the perspective of the shipowner.

Companies listing in Hong-Kong and Singapore tend to exhibit the highest average size with companies listing in Greece exhibiting the lowest. The average size of US, Norwegian, and Swedish companies is close to the all country average. Furthermore, the size of shipping companies entering the IPO markets tends to increase over time. This coupled with the above finding of the number of IPOs increasing over time means that shipping companies are reorganising themselves towards becoming bigger in order to raise equity on the international capital markets.

Average Gearing is found to be 1.45 which may be considered high taking into account the cyclical nature of the shipping industry. Gearing also exhibits considerable variation across and within countries. It is highest in the US and Norway, and low in the other countries.

Regarding the proportion of equity offered, the shipping IPOs fell into three characteristic groupings. The shipping funds in the US offer on average 98% of their equity, Hong-Kong and Greek companies offered 29% and 25% respectively while in Sweden, Norway and the remainder of the US, companies offered between 42% - 48%. Furthermore, we find a trend of less equity being offered over time and also a trend of less equity being offered by bigger companies; while the highly geared companies tend to offer higher proportions of equity to the public.

Regarding the average age of the shipping company fleets we found that, excluding the coastal companies of Greece, it ranges between 4.67 and 11.83 years. We also found that the average age of the fleets of the companies in our sample is increasing over time. This confirms our earlier finding that the primary reason for which shipping companies tend to increasingly use the IPO markets over time is to replace and/or expand their fleets.

The stock exchange seems to primarily attract new companies which were created by older companies or resulting from the merger of older companies. In the introduction to this paper we mention that if shipping companies are going to tap the capital markets they need to reorganise themselves both structurally and culturally. These companies may be the result of such reorganisation. However, the stock exchange seems to also attract completely new companies as well as companies with a continuing history of over five years.

Results regarding the average initial day returns of the shipping IPOs in our sample are found to be consistent with the bulk of the existing empirical evidence. In our sample underpricing is of small magnitude (5.32%) on average but it is statistically significant. The seven shipping funds are on average overpriced. The small underpricing of the whole sample and the overpricing of the shipping funds could be attributed to industry specific characteristics; and to less asymmetry of information than a typical IPO.

Underpricing tests revealed that gearing is positively related to underpricing and was the only factor found to have explanatory power over cross-sectional underpricing of the whole sample. Gearing, coupled with the proportion of equity offered were found to be significant and positively related to cross-sectional underpricing for a reduced sample which excluded the seven shipping funds. Our findings on the proportion of equity offered are consistent with other empirical evidence while our finding regarding gearing are not.

We also examined average direct costs of going public for a reduced sample of 27 shipping companies. These costs were found to be just under 8% of the amount raised. The standard deviation of these direct costs is 3.88% and is interpreted as evidence of a relatively high fixed cost component in average direct costs. The highest average direct costs were found to be in the US, the figure of over 10% being in line with recent empirical evidence. The lowest were found to be in Norway, standing at 5.5%.

Acknowledgement

This paper benefited greatly from remarks and suggestions from M. Levis of City University Business School.

Appendix

Shipping IPOs in our sample partitioned by Country

Company	Year of Offer
Hong-Kong and Singapore	
Pacific Carriers	1990
Jinhui	1991
Osprey Maritime	1994
US	
B & H Bulk Carriers	1987
B&H Ocean Carriers	1988
Global Ocean Carriers	1988
Stolt Tankers	1988
MC Shipping	1989
B&H Maritime Carriers	1989
Nortankers	1989
Europa Cruises	1989
BT Shipping	1989
Pacific Basin	1994
Teekay	1995
Sweden	
Argonaut	1983
Concordia	1984
Frontline	1988
United Tankers	1990
Norway	
Awilco	1993
First Olsen	1993
Bona	1993
Western Bulk Shipping	1993
Smedvig Tankship	1993
Nordic	1993
Atlentic	1994
Jinhui Shipping and Transportation	1994
Larvik	1994
Greece	
Strintzis	1994
Dane	1994
NEL	1995
Luxembourg	
Anangel American	1987

References

Baron D.; A model of the demand for investment bank advising and distribution services for new issues; Journal of Finance; 1982, Vol.37, pp.955-976.

Downes D. and Heinkel R.; Signaling and the valuation of unseasoned new issues; Journal of Finance; 1982; Vol.37, pp.1-10.

Fearnleys World Bulk Fleet; Published by Fearnresearch Oslo; January 1995

Gerbich M., Levis M. and Rowland V.P.; Property initial public offerings; Journal of Property Finance; Vol.6, 1, 1995, pp.38-54.

Grammenos C.Th.; The need for sound credit analysis and profitability in bank shipping finance; Paper presented at the general meeting of the Baltic and International Maritime Council; 28 May - 1 June 1995.

Grammenos C.Th.; New and old considerations in international banking for ship finance; Unpublished paper presented at Harvard Business School, 9-12-81.

Grammenos C.Th.; Lloyds List, 7-12-1989.

Grinblatt M. and Hwang C.; Signaling and the pricing of new issues; Journal of Finance; 1989, Vol.44, pp.393-420.

Hegde S., and Miller R.; The informational role of debt and the pricing of initial public offerings; Working paper; November 1995.

Ibbotson R., and Ritter J.; Chapter of initial public offerings; North Holland Handbooks for Operations Research and Management Science; North Holland, Amsterdam, 1992.

Ibbotson R., Sindelar J, and Ritter J.; Initial Public Offerings; Journal of Applied Corporate Finance; 1994, Vol.7, pp.6-14.

Institute of Shipping Economics and Logistics (ISL) Statistics; Yearbook 1995.

Kazantzis and Thomas; Institutional constraints and the IPO puzzle: Evidence from a European emerging market; Paper in this volume.

Koh F. and Walter T.; A direct test of Rock's model of the pricing of unseasoned issues; Journal of Financial Economics; 1989, Vol.23, pp.251-272.

Lee I., Lochhead S., Ritter J., Zhao Q.; The costs of raising capital; Working Paper, 1995.

Leland H. and Pyle D.; Informational asymmetries, financial structure and financial intermediation; Journal of Finance; 1991, Vol.46, pp.75-109.

Levis M. and Thomas D.; Investment trust IPOs: Issuing behaviour and price performance Evidence from the London Stock Exchange; Journal of Banking and Finance; Vol.19, 1995, pp.1437-1458.

Levis M.; The long run performance of initial public offerings: the UK experience 1980-1988; Financial Management; Spring, 1993, pp.28-41.

Loughran T., Ritter J. and Rydqvist K.; Initial public offerings: international insights; Pacific Basin Finance Journal; Vol.2, 1994, pp.164-199.

McGuiness P.; An examination of the underpricing of initial public offerings in Hong-Kong, 1980-90; Journal of Business Finance and Accounting; 1992, Vol.19, pp165-186.

Peavy J. III; Returns on initial public offerings of closed end funds; The Review of Financial Studies; Vol.3, 4, 1990, pp.695-708.

Peters Hans J.; The international ocean transport industry in crisis - Assessing the reasons and outlook; Policy Research Paper No.1128; The World Bank, Washington DC, April, 1993.

Ridder A.; Access to the stock market - an empirical study of the efficiency of the British and the Swedish primary markets; 1986, Caslon Press, Stockholm.

Ritter J.; The hot issue market of 1980; Journal of Business; Vol.57, 2, 1984, pp.215-240.

Rock K.; Why new issues are underpriced?; Journal of financial economics; 1986; Vol.15, pp.187-212.

Rydqvist K.; Compensation, participation, restrictions, and the underpricing of initial public offerings: Evidence from Sweden; Unpublished working paper; 1993, Stockholm School of Economics.

Tamvakis M.N.; An investigation into the existence of a two-tier spot freight market for crude oil carriers; Journal of Maritime Policy and Management; 1994,Vol.22, 1, pp.81-90.

Wang K. Chan S. and Gau G.; Initial Public Offerings of equity securities - Anomalous evidence using REITs; Journal of Financial Economics; 1992, Vol.21, pp.381-410.

Weiss K.; The post offering price performance of closed end funds; Financial Management; 1989, Vol.18, pp.57-67.

Endnotes

[1] According to 1988 estimates, approximately US$200 billion will be needed in the nineties for world fleet replacement.

[2] That amount rose according to 1993 estimates to US$400 billion.

[3] Calculated as the number of post IPO shares times the offer price.

[4] Calculated as the ratio of long-term debt over shareholders equity.

[5] Our sample includes two companies, Atlantic Containers and Europa cruises whose debt to equity ratios are 8 and 5 respectively. Excluding these two companies the average gearing ratio drops to 0.95 which is very close to the median gearing of the whole sample (0.90).

[6] The remaining 9 were formed at the same time as they entered the capital markets therefore were debt free.

[7] However, in 1995 increased competition among international financial institutions in attracting desirable clientele, has led to an increase in financial leverage of shipping companies sometimes accompanied by relaxation in the required securities Grammenos (1995).

[8] It should be noted that two sister vessels may be in a materially different operating state if the one is well maintained and the other is not.

[9] OPA 90 is designed to protect US waters from oil pollution; it requires vessels to have double hulls therefore increasing newbuilding costs; it also imposes unlimited liability for damage resulting from oil spills therefore increasing insurance costs. Furthermore, OPA 90 provides for the gradual phasing out of older single hull vessels.

[10] However, it should be noted that although as a separate entity they appear to be completely new at the time of going public, all four Swedish companies were created by old companies.

[11] For a thorough discussion of theoretical models of IPOs underpricing see Ibbotson and Ritter (1994).

[12] Following a decision of the Board of Directors of the Athens Stock Exchange on 4/12/1992 regarding investor protection, a daily barrier of plus/minus 8%, or plus/minus 4% in the price fluctuation of a listed security can be imposed depending on its marketability. The president of the Athens Stock Exchange can circumvent this barrier under specific circumstances.

[13] The overallotment option is not taken into account in these calculations.

[14] The remaining four do not give information regarding direct costs in their IPO prospectuses.